# HANNIBAL

# HANNIBAL
## A HELLENISTIC LIFE

## EVE MACDONALD

YALE UNIVERSITY PRESS
NEW HAVEN AND LONDON

For information about this and other Yale University Press publications, please contact:

U.S. Office: sales.press@yale.edu   www.yalebooks.com
Europe Office: sales@yaleup.co.uk   www.yalebooks.co.uk

Typeset in Adobe Garamond Pro by IDSUK (DataConnection) Ltd
Printed in Great Britain by Gomer Press Ltd, Llandysul, Ceredigion, Wales

Library of Congress Cataloging-in-Publication Data

MacDonald, Eve.
   Hannibal : a Hellenistic life/Eve MacDonald.
    pages cm
   Includes bibliographical references and index.
   ISBN 978-0-300-15204-3 (cloth : alkaline paper)
   1. Hannibal, 247 B.C.–182 B.C.   2. Hannibal, 247 B.C.–182 B.C.—Influence.
   3. Hannibal, 247 B.C.–182 B.C.—Military leadership.   4. Generals—Tunisia—
   Carthage (Extinct city)—Biography.   5. Punic War, 2nd, 218–201 B.C.   6. Rome—
   History—Republic, 265-30 B.C.   7. Carthage (Extinct city)—History.   I. Title.
   DG249.M33 2015
   937'.04092—dc23
   [B]

                                                                2014035399

A catalogue record for this book is available from the British Library.

10 9 8 7 6 5 4 3 2 1

To my aunt, Elizabeth (Betty) MacDonald (1930–2011),
for her inspiration and encouragement

# Contents

*List of Illustrations*                                               ix

*Acknowledgements*                                                    xi

*Family Tree*                                                         xiii


Introduction: No Ordinary Enemy                                      1

1    Hannibal and Carthage                                           7

2    The Great Man in the Hellenistic World:

     From Alexander to Hamilcar                                      24

3    His Father's Son                                                43

4    Barcid Iberia from Gades to Saguntum                            61

5    Legend: Hannibal into Italy                                     82

6    Hannibal the Conqueror: From the Trebia

     to Trasimeno                                                    100

7    The Apogee: Cannae and the War in Italy                         119

8    After Cannae                                                    139

9    Hannibal's Dilemma, 212–209                                     160

10   Over the Alps, Again                                            180

11    Hannibal Returns                          198

12    Hannibal into Exile                        218

      Epilogue: Hannibal's Afterlife            227


      *Notes*                                   *239*

      *Bibliography*                            *298*

      *Index*                                   *316*

# ILLUSTRATIONS

## Plates

1. Bronze gilt cuirass from Ksour es-Saf, Tunisia, *c.* third century BCE. ©
   Tunis, Musée National du Bardo.
2. View from Eryx towards Drepanum (Trapani) and the Aegates Islands.
   Author's photograph.
3. *The Oath of Hannibal* by Benjamin West, 1770. Royal Collection Trust ©
   Her Majesty Queen Elizabeth II 2014.
4. *The Oath of Hannibal*, eighteenth-century cartoon. Courtesy of the
   Trustees of the British Museum.
5. Punic di-shekel showing Melqart (possibly Hamilcar) with club on
   obverse and an elephant and rider on reverse, dated *c.* 237–209 BCE.
   Courtesy of the Trustees of the British Museum.
6. *Hannibal Crossing the Alps* by Heinrich Leutemann, 1866, etching, hand
   coloured. Held in the public domain at Yale University Art Gallery.
7. *Hannibal with the head of Hasdrubal*, Giambattista Tiepolo, 1725–1730.
   © Kunsthistorisches Museum, Vienna.
8. Hannibal's monument in Turkey, commissioned by Atatürk. Author's
   photograph.
9. Bust of Hannibal (?) from Capua. Courtesy of the Mary Evans Picture
   Library.

## Maps

1.   The central Mediterranean: Carthage, Rome and Sicily
2.   The western Mediterranean
3.   Carthage and environs

All maps drawn by Stephen Copp.

# ACKNOWLEDGEMENTS

THERE ARE SO VERY many people who have been incredibly helpful in the process of writing this book. First on that list are my very patient editors at Yale University Press, Heather McCallum and Rachael Lonsdale. I also valued the comments of the anonymous readers who provided a great deal of clarity, useful observations and encouragement, as well as pointing out many errors, problems and omissions. Any left are mine alone. My good friends and colleagues Sandra Bingham and Stephen Copp have helped in the creation of this story in so many ways, including very practical ones. My students at the University of Reading who took the 'Carthage' module and had many ideas, thoughts and comments that helped to focus my thinking on the topic of Hannibal in the final stages of the book. There are also many other good friends, family (often both) and colleagues who have always been willing to encourage and listen when I am sure there were better things to consider than Hannibal – again many thanks. The greatest thanks of all must go to my husband, Keith Tracey, whose patience, editorial skills and even more patience helped to make this a much better work.

# Family Tree

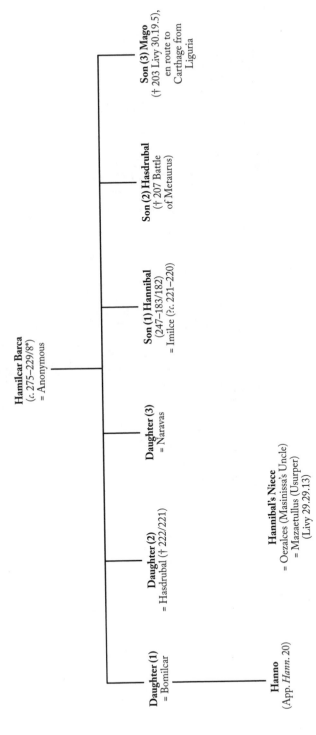

**Hamilcar Barca**
(*c.* 275–229/8*)
= Anonymous

**Daughter (1)**
= Bomilcar

**Hanno**
(App. *Hann.* 20)

**Daughter (2)**
= Hasdrubal († 222/221)

**Hannibal's Niece**
= Oezalces (Masinissa's Uncle)
= Mazaetullus (Usurper)
(Livy 29.29.13)

**Daughter (3)**
= Naravas

**Son (1) Hannibal**
(247–183/182)
= Imilce (?c. 221–220)

**Son (2) Hasdrubal**
(† 207 Battle
of Metaurus)

**Son (3) Mago**
(† 203 Livy 30.19.5),
en route to
Carthage from
Liguria

NOTE  We know of at least six children born to Hamilcar Barca. The first three were girls and these anonymous daughters were married to form political and military alliances. His sons, 'the lion cubs' reared to destroy Rome (Valerius Maximus 9.3.2 claims four sons), fought together in the Second Punic War, as did his grandson Hanno (who commanded the left wing of cavalry at Cannae according to Appian, *Hann.* 20).  Except for Hannibal's, the ages are largely hypothetical. Cornelius Nepos tells us that Hamilcar was 'very young' when he took command in Sicily. However, by that time he was already the father of four children so he could not have been that young – the estimate used here places him in his late twenties at the time of Hannibal's birth in 247 (Lancel, 1999, 9).  Hannibal's niece was married to Masinissa's uncle; she was the daughter of one of his sisters, but which one is unclear.  For the family history see Hoyos, 2005, 21–23.

* All dates in BCE.

**Map 1** The central Mediterranean: Carthage, Rome and Sicily

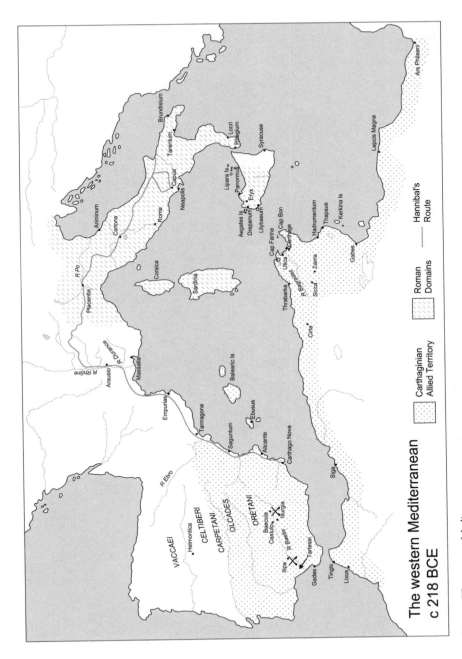

The western Mediterranean
c 218 BCE

Carthaginian
Allied Territory

Roman
Domains

Hannibal's
Route

Map 2 The western Mediterranean

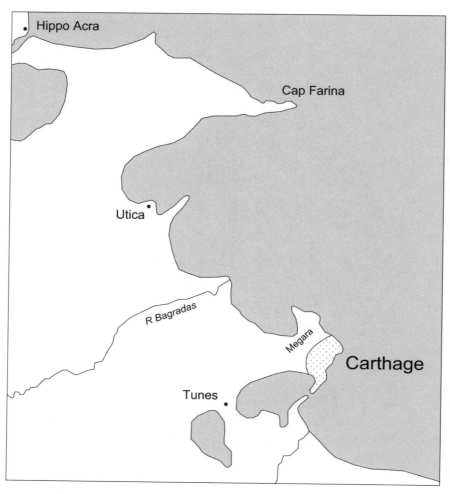

**Map 3** Carthage and environs

# INTRODUCTION
## NO ORDINARY ENEMY

W HEN DUSK FELL on a hot, windy day in the summer of 216 BCE on the plains of Apulia near the town of Cannae, as many as 45,000 Roman soldiers lay slain.[1] The following morning a ghostly landscape appeared with the dawn. A mist had settled on the heaps of bodies during the cooling temperatures of the night and some of the wounded, not yet corpses, staggered up out the grey light only to be finished off by the enemy (Livy 22.51.6–7).[2] On this field at Cannae lay many of the governing elite of the city of Rome, one standing consul, ex-consuls, praetors and other magistrates killed in the battle. Cannae was the scene of one of the most devastating military defeats ever inflicted on a Roman army and the architect of that defeat was a thirty-one-year-old Carthaginian commander named Hannibal Barca. Hannibal's victory had brought the Roman Republic to the brink of oblivion.

As a result of Cannae and his other victories, Hannibal is often referred to as the one great enemy in the epic story of the rise of Rome. To the Roman historian Livy he was almost superhuman, 'possessed of enormous daring in facing dangers and enormous resourcefulness when in the midst of those dangers. He could be physically exhausted or mentally cowed by no hardship . . . On horse or foot he was by far the best soldier, the first to enter battle, he was the last to leave once battle was joined' (21.4.5–8). Hannibal was brave, inexhaustible and virtually impossible to defeat. When Pliny the Elder singled him out as 'no ordinary enemy', he had become the standard against which all other enemies of Rome were measured (NH 7.29). Hannibal's reputation, even among those who fought against him, was as the most brilliant and determined military commander of his generation.

From the precipice of Cannae the Romans fought back. In a long war, which encompassed the whole of the western Mediterranean, they went on to defeat Hannibal (218–202 BCE). In the Roman and many modern views the battle against Hannibal was the turning point in the history of Rome's power.[3] Once the Romans had defeated Hannibal, no one stood between them and complete dominance of the Mediterranean; no other enemy would challenge Roman hegemony like Hannibal. The war with Hannibal defined Roman *imperium* and articulated all the future battles that Rome would fight in its progress to empire. Just over fifty years after the Hannibalic War the Romans went on completely to destroy Hannibal's city, Carthage (146 BCE). From that time they took sole ownership of the man, his identity and reputation, and they alone were able to construct his legend.

The great Roman orator Cicero asked, 'who of the Carthaginians was superior to Hannibal in wisdom and valour, and actual achievements?' He was the man in Cicero's estimation 'who had single-handedly fought for so many years for empire and for glory with such numbers of our generals. His own fellow citizens banished him from the city; but we see that he, though our enemy, is celebrated in the writings and memory of our citizens' (*Pro Sestio* 68.142). Roman ownership of Hannibal's story was further compounded when, a century after the destruction of Carthage, Julius Caesar camped near the ruins of the city during the civil wars and dreamt of a 'whole army weeping' (Appian, *Lib.* 136). Out of that dream came a new Roman colony, called *Colonia Iulia Concordia Karthago*, established by Caesar's heir Octavian Augustus.[4] The new Carthage sat directly on the ruins of the old, the Romans built over the heart of the Carthaginian town, the Byrsa hill, and any remaining vestiges of Hannibal's city were destroyed. From that moment onwards the Romans were fully in possession of the story of both Hannibal and Carthage. 'Here I begin the war by which the fame of the *Aeneadae* was raised to heaven and proud Carthage submitted to the rule of Italy' wrote Silius Italicus in his first-century CE narrative poem the *Punica* (1.1–3).[5] The Roman writers and historians constructed the legend of the Great War fought by the implacable enemy general and the Carthaginian culture that produced him. ·

Hannibal's biography must begin from this point, for the Hannibal we know has been adapted to the narrative of Rome's rise to greatness. If we can be certain about anything at all to do with Hannibal, it is what he meant to the Romans and those who fought against him. The Greek historian Polybius is the most reliable of all the ancient sources on Hannibal. He was closely connected to the story and may have actually witnessed the destruction of Carthage in 146 BCE. A Greek brought to Rome as a captive in the second century, Polybius wrote a history of the Romans to explain to his fellow Greeks how these upstarts had come to control so much of the world in such a short time (1.3.3–6).[6] Polybius was a young man when Hannibal died in *c.* 183 BCE, perhaps seventeen years old. Hannibal's exploits were both celebrated and reviled in the popular history of the day and Polybius' youth would have been steeped in these stories. For Polybius and the historians who followed him such as the Roman Livy, the life of Hannibal embodied Rome's struggle with Carthage and played an essential and epic part in that story.

The Romans also provided an assessment of Hannibal's less attractive attributes and Livy's portrait recalls that 'the man's great virtues were matched by his enormous vices: pitiless cruelty, a treachery worse than Punic, no regard for truth, and no integrity, no fear of the gods or respect for an oath, and no scruples' (21.4.9–10).[7] The Roman sources gave this brave and fierce enemy the more commonly acknowledged attributes of a stereotypical Carthaginian: a Punic deceit and treachery.

By the third/second century the Romans referred to Hannibal and the Carthaginians as Punic.[8] Punic was the name given to the cultural stereotype articulated by the Roman authors. It was the name used by Carthaginian enemies and is the modern term for the wars between Rome and Carthage, and for the Carthaginian language and culture.[9] Punic is an ethnic term whilst Carthaginian reflects the political entity and is the name given to the conquered by the conquerors. It is almost certainly not a term Hannibal would have used to refer to himself. In Livy's description one of Hannibal's greatest flaws was this, 'a treachery more than Punic' (*perfidia plus quam Punica*, Livy 21.4.9). Livy's audience would instinctively have understood what was meant by this Punic duplicity or treachery. In the decades following Livy, Valerius Maximus would write that 'Punic craftiness (was) notorious throughout the terrestrial globe' (7.4.4).

This notorious stereotype of the Carthaginians may have developed as a direct result of Hannibal's invasion of Italy. Hannibal is by far the most discussed aspect of Carthaginian culture in the ancient sources and the eternal question remains: did the man create the stereotype or did the stereotype create the man? As his notoriety and fame grew in Italy during the period of the war it is possible that Roman anti-Hannibalic propaganda began to take hold and remained firmly in place after his final defeat.[10] In the Roman mind the Carthaginians were forever afterwards judged by their encounters with Hannibal. The Punic label stuck and is now the conventional term used when referring to the culture associated with Hannibal, Carthage and his world.[11]

These two sides of Hannibal – the brave general and the untrustworthy Punic – were not necessarily contradictory to the Romans. In the Roman history of Rome, Hannibal could be both the most worthy of opponents whose eventual defeat made Rome great, and the most dishonest and stereotypical of Punic villains whose own actions justified the destruction of Carthage and its people. Modern historians are left with this dichotomy. The Romans admired and feared Hannibal in equal measure. Some Romans believed that Hannibal's treacherous actions typified the Carthaginian people and had brought destruction down upon the city.[12] In short, the story was constructed to imply that the Carthaginians got what was coming to them.

The works of the historians of the Hannibalic War who contradicted the purely Roman view of Hannibal and Carthage have not survived. We know they existed and that Polybius and others consulted a much wider range of sources on the period than we have access to today. There were important Greek historians who took a pro-Carthaginian stance. We know specifically of one named Sosylus, a Spartan, who travelled in Hannibal's camp and wrote a history of the Punic Wars from this insider's perspective.[13] Another historian named Silenus from Kale Acte in Sicily also travelled with Hannibal and wrote a history of his life (Cornelius Nepos, *Hann.* 13.3).[14] Cicero referred to Silenus as 'a painstaking student of Hannibal's career' but only fragments of his history survive (*De div.* 1.49). The views on Hannibal that might contradict the orthodox interpretation of events have largely been lost. We are left with the overwhelming story of Roman power. History is truly written by the victors and their written perspective of the Carthaginians and the life of Hannibal is all that remains. What survives provides us with an image of Hannibal that is reflected through a Roman eye.

When Hannibal first came to the attention of the Romans and thus entered history he was campaigning in the Iberian peninsula (modern Spain and Portugal) in 221–219 BCE. There he chose the path that would eventually make him Rome's 'greatest enemy'.[15] Ever since then, the epic nature of his battles with Rome and journey to Italy that took him over the Alps with his army and elephants has astounded commentators and the public. The ancient and the modern worlds have been fascinated by his daring and audacity. The stunning military victories that followed on from his journey over the Alps cemented his legend. The next decades of his life were spent wandering Italy and the Mediterranean fighting the Romans. He became a symbol of opposition to Rome's growing power and this led to his celebrated reputation as a strategic genius and a heroic fighter.

To understand Hannibal and the path he followed it is vital to look at the history, the legend and the culture that produced him. That the real Hannibal was an extraordinary individual is not in question but so much of his life has become legendary that the context for his achievements needs to be rooted in his time and place. The third-century Mediterranean was culturally dominated by the Hellenistic kingdoms created in the aftermath of the conquests of Alexander the Great (356–323 BCE). It was a period of growth and expansive warfare across the Mediterranean. Hannibal's Carthage was located at the centre of the sea, occupying a prime position on the North African coast and deeply influenced by the social and political changes under way. The third century also witnessed the rising power of another central Mediterranean city, Rome. These two powerful city-states would begin the century as allies on the fringes of Hellenistic power and end it as bitter enemies deeply involved in the struggles of the Hellenistic kings. Thus the challenge Hannibal presented to Rome and the brilliance of his military victories took place against the backdrop of Hellenistic warfare and legendary military achievements. This Hellenistic world provided the contextualization for Hannibal, both in his own and in his enemy's eyes.

Equally important for our understanding of Hannibal is the unique heritage and the role that Carthage played in Roman history and memory. The destruction of Carthage has made Hannibal one of the best known yet least understood of all the great figures of antiquity.[16] Hannibal left us no surviving memoirs and his culture was completely destroyed, yet interest in his life has been sustained through the millennia. There are multitudes of fictional and historical accounts of Hannibal's story that stretch back through the centuries, in many languages. Historians have analysed his life, incredible military achievements and legacy.[17] Portraits of Hannibal always reflect the way in which contemporary cultures have engaged with the history of Rome and the questions people ask of the past. Interest in Hannibal continues to this day and he plays an enduring role in modern culture. Today, it is useful to reconsider how the memory of great wars echo through history as interpretations of events shift and change. In this story of Hannibal I have tried to consider the life and great events of his time while also reflecting on how and why we continue to look back at him with fascination from the twenty-first century.

This book is the story of one man's epic struggle with the nascent power of Rome. It is the story of an empire built and another destroyed. There are high adventures, daring deeds and legendary battles that still resound today. It is also the story of Carthage itself, of the lost city and culture that are central to any portrait of Hannibal. For it is Carthaginian culture that shaped both Hannibal and the way he was represented in our sources. Carthage was one of

the great cities of antiquity and in the third century its influence stretched
across North Africa and through the islands of the central Mediterranean
(Map 2). Founded by Phoenicians early in the first millennium BCE, Carthage
was a city that flourished at the centre of a network of trade routes that criss-
crossed the Mediterranean.[18] The culture of the city was based in the traditions of the eastern Mediterranean region of the Levant but Carthage had
grown to be a multicultural metropolis with an expansive outlook by the time
of Hannibal's birth in the mid-third century BCE. It was a city closely connected
to the wider Mediterranean but at the same time inherently foreign to the
Greek and Roman authors of its history.[19] The narrative of the life and death
of Hannibal has come down to us filtered through a Roman lens but was
deeply rooted in Carthaginian culture and traditions. It is therefore essential
to begin this story of Hannibal by looking at what we know about the legends
and history of the Punic city of Carthage.

# CHAPTER 1

# HANNIBAL AND CARTHAGE

A Tyrian colony; the people made
Stout for war, and studious of their trade:
Carthage the name; belov'd by Juno more
Than her own Argos, or the Samian shore.
Here stood her chariot; here, if Heav'n were kind,
The seat of awful empire she design'd.
**(Virgil, *Aeneid* 1.21–26[1])**

THE FORTUNES OF THE great ancient city of Carthage and the story of Hannibal are woven together in history and myth. Hannibal was Carthage's most famous son and his name in the Punic language means 'he who finds favour with Ba'al'.[2] Ba'al was the chief god in the Carthaginian pantheon and Carthage was the most prosperous city and cultural centre of the Punic world. Hannibal's Carthage was a long-established city on the African shore of the central Mediterranean with a reputation for great wealth and beauty.[3] By the time of Hannibal's birth in 247 BCE the city had existed for almost six centuries. The rich cultural heritage and origins of Carthage shaped Hannibal's early life and were fundamental to his education and the creation of his identity.

Legend has it that Hannibal's family traced their roots back to the very foundation of the city when Phoenicians from Tyre established a colony on the spot early in the first millennium BCE (Silius Italicus, 1.70–77). 'In this period, 65 years before the founding of Rome, Carthage was established by the Tyrian Elissa, by some authors called Dido' claimed the Roman historian Velleius Paterculus (1.6.4). The 'nobly born' Hannibal is the only other Carthaginian whose renown is as great as that of Dido, refugee from the city of Tyre, legendary queen and founder of the city.

The story of Hannibal's Carthage begins with these Phoenicians, who came from the port cities of the Levant such as Sidon, Tyre and Byblos (modern Lebanon) in the early Iron Age. At the beginning of the first millennium BCE the Phoenicians spread out across the Mediterranean and their ships, especially those from Tyre, explored widely for natural resources to be traded in the urbanized world of the Near East.[4] Phoenician ships plied their trade on the shores of the Mediterranean as they picked up valuable materials and dropped off objects and spread ideas. The ancient Greeks adopted their alphabet, and the stories and myths of the Near East moved across the Mediterranean with their ships.[5]

Hannibal's city Carthage was one of a number founded early in the first millennium by intrepid Phoenician seafarers exploring westwards.[6] We learn about the nature of early Phoenician expansion from passing references in the ancient literary record. The sophisticated urban centres of the ancient Levant were key to the trading wealth of the Phoenicians and passages in the Hebrew Bible describe what drove the trade. The Book of Ezekiel (27:12) claims that 'Tarshish was thy merchant by reason of the multitude of all kind of riches; with silver, iron, tin and lead, they traded in the fairs'. This was a time when silver, iron, tin and lead were a source of great wealth and these most valuable commodities were to be found in the western and central Mediterranean regions of Iberia (tin, silver) and Etruria (iron ore, copper). Tarshish refers to Tartessos, the Greek word for the mineral-rich region of Iberia beyond the Pillars of Herakles along the Guadalquivir river (the Baetis in antiquity) just north-west of the Phoenician colony of Gadir (ancient Gades/modern Cadiz, Map 2).[7] Many centuries later, during the Hannibalic War, this area witnessed some of the most intense fighting as the Carthaginians and Romans sought to control the still important natural resources.

The early Phoenicians established a network of trading posts at strategic points that criss-crossed the Mediterranean Sea to capitalize on this market. Communities existed in western Iberia, the Balearic Islands, Sardinia, Elba, Malta, Sicily and along the coast of North Africa as far as the Atlantic. With settlements extending over such a large area there must have been large-scale exploitation of mineral wealth. There is little doubt that the Phoenicians 'prospered greatly' from their expeditions and they are frequently described as 'wealthy' by ancient authors.[8] The connection with trade, commerce and wealth was a distinctive part of the Phoenician/Carthaginian heritage and identity ascribed to them by the Greeks and the Romans.

The first Phoenician city at Carthage dates from *c.* 814 BCE and the first people to settle there came from Tyre.[9] The earliest archaeological evidence for settlement at the site, while still being uncovered, agrees with the late ninth-century date. Certainly by the eighth and early seventh centuries the Carthaginians were trading with the wider Mediterranean and had developed extensive local agricultural output and relatively high levels of industrialization. Carthage flourished in its earliest stages, leading some to believe that it was intended to be a city on a grand scale from the very beginning.[10]

According to the legend of the foundation of Carthage a Tyrian princess named Elishat established the city. The Phoenician Elishat, transcribed as Elissa by the Greeks, became Dido in Latin: Dido is thought to be a kind of surname for Elissa, meaning 'the wanderer'. Dido and her brother Pygmalion were the children of Mettenos, a ninth-century BCE king of Tyre who died young, leaving no adult heir. The princess Dido, elder of the two, married the high priest of the god Melqart who ruled Tyre as regent/king. At some point Pygmalion claimed the throne as the legitimate male heir and killed Dido's husband. Pygmalion's reign lasted from *c.* 831–785 BCE and split the nobility of Tyre. The faction that supported Dido fled the city with a fleet, taking with them sacred objects from the Temple of Melqart.

One version of the myth tells us that the queen 'embarked for Africa with her property and a number of men who desired to escape from the tyranny of Pygmalion and arrived at that part of Africa where Carthage now stands' (Appian, *Lib.* 1).[11] Even in the surviving accounts of the earliest legends there may be echoes of Hannibal. As Dido and the refugees made for Africa where the Phoenician colony of Utica had already been established, the local inhabitants (known as Libyans in the ancient sources) resisted a new Tyrian settlement. Dido then tricked the Libyans into giving up their territory, and in one story she negotiated with a local chieftain to buy 'as much land as could be encompassed by an ox-hide'. Then, by cutting the hide round and round into a very, very long thin strip she was able to acquire the area that became the citadel of Carthage, known as the Byrsa hill (Appian, *Lib.* 1; Justin 18.5.9). Dido's marking out of the heart of the city of Carthage becomes a clever ruse used to outwit the local chieftains. Such duplicity and trickiness come to characterize all Carthaginians, and Hannibal especially, who excel in the 'art of turning negotiations to their own advantage'.[12]

The Tyrians called their city Qart Hadasht, which means the 'new city' and implied a New Tyre.[13] The best-known episode of the foundation myth weaves

the story of Dido with the Trojan Aeneas and the foundation of Rome. Aeneas'
flight from burning Troy brings him to Carthage where the charms of the
lovely Dido distract him from his greater mission – to go to Italy and help
found the Roman people. After a tryst, Aeneas reluctantly leaves his new
love and duty bound continues on his journey and destiny to Italy. In his wake
he leaves a heartbroken and humiliated Dido, who is driven to commit
suicide. Virgil's enduring version of the myth famously articulates the
curse that the rejected Dido, on her deathbed, hurled at the descendants of
Aeneas. This curse, in the Roman imagination, gave rise to their great
enemy Hannibal:

> These are my prayers, and this my dying will;
> And you, my Tyrians, every curse fulfill [sic].
> Perpetual hate, and mortal wars proclaim
> Against the prince, the people and the name;
> . . . .
> Rise some avenger of our Libyan blood
> With fire and sword pursue the perjured brood.
> Our arms, our seas, our shores, opposed to theirs
> And the same hate descend on all our heirs.
> **Aeneid 4. 894–904**

This legend came to define Carthage for the modern world. John Dryden's
stunning translation of the *Aeneid* in 1697 brought Carthage and her myth into
the popular imagination in the English language.[14] From around the same
period numerous plays and operas focused on the tragic story of the exotic queen
who, her virtue corrupted by the Trojan prince, ended her life by her own hand.
From Christopher Marlowe's *Dido, Queen of Carthage,* to Purcell's *Dido and
Aeneas* and the nineteenth-century opera *Les Troyens* by Berlioz the story was
kept alive throughout the early modern period.[15] The timeless popularity of the
epic of Virgil means that Dido was and is one of the most celebrated
Carthaginians, outshone only by Hannibal himself.

In antiquity, it was not until the third century and Hannibal's war with
Rome that the legend of the Phoenician Queen Dido was linked with that of
her lover the Trojan Aeneas. This version is thought to have been devised in
the Greco-Roman tradition as an explanation for the wars between Rome and
Carthage. It was a means of tying together the origins of the Romans, Greeks
and Carthaginians of the western Mediterranean into the same epic tradition
of the Trojan War.[16] Almost two centuries later when the poet Virgil wrote the

most enduring version of the tale, the emperor Augustus was building a new Roman town on top of Hannibal's destroyed city (late first century).[17]

Of all the many colonies of Phoenician origin in the Mediterranean we have a foundation myth only for Carthage. The story may well be a creation of classical authors who sought to place Carthage into the pattern of Greco-Roman foundation traditions. Or the legend of Dido may hide the core of a history that helps to explain why Tyrian Carthage rose to prominence among the western Phoenician cities.[18]

From the ninth-century foundation, Carthage grew and gradually became one of the most important and prosperous cities in the western Mediterranean and the most powerful city in the Punic world.[19] Carthage drew a population of Libyans from the surrounding area, people from nearby Utica and further immigrants from Tyre and other cities of the Levant. Its very origins were multicultural. With the foundation of a colony sent out from the city to the island of Ebusus (Ibiza) in 654 BCE the transition from a colonial foundation into a power in its own right had begun (Diodorus Siculus 5.16).[20] The historical development of Carthage from an autonomous political entity in the seventh century to the conflicts with Rome in the third century was fluid. The increasingly crowded western Mediterranean saw more immigration from the east with many new colonies set up by Greeks from Asia Minor and Greece proper from the eighth to sixth centuries. These settlements encroached on both the Carthaginians and their allies, the Etruscans, whose spheres of influence lay in the central/western Mediterranean.

The traditions and culture of Carthage evolved gradually from the Tyrian foundation, and over the sixth to fifth centuries BCE we see the beginning of conflict between competing interests in the region.[21] The Carthaginians built their state and its maritime foundation looking outwards to the sea with the merchant and military fleets integral to its development. We see Carthaginians, often in alliance with their close trading partners the Etruscans, battling against the increasing presence of Greek colonies and their expanding interests. A pivotal moment was the naval battle of Alalia (Aleria) which took place off the east coast of Corsica in c. 530 BCE. The conflict saw a Carthaginian fleet allied with Etruscan forces engage a navy of Ionian Greeks (Phocaeans) who had been committing acts of piracy out of their base at Alalia.[22] The base on Corsica may have been an extension of the Phocaean settlement of Massalia (Marseilles) at the mouth of the Rhône. Although there was no clear victor, the naval engagement at Alalia put an end to Greek expansion into the western Mediterranean (Herodotus 1.165–166).[23] Hannibal may have learned about this battle as the moment when Carthage decided to take a stand over its role in the central Mediterranean.

The tripartite balance between the Etruscans, the Greeks and the Carthaginians shifted with the rise of Rome, which in 509 BCE established itself as a republic. The first treaty between Carthage and Rome dates to this period and sets out the spheres of influence around each city at the time (Polyb. 3.22–23).[24] The treaty reflects the more powerful status of Carthage in the early relationship between the two states. Etruscan power waned in the face of Roman conquests and in the fifth century Carthage became involved in a series of conflicts with the Greeks for territorial hegemony on the island of Sicily.[25] What began with Carthage being drawn into battles in defence of their allies in western Sicily, the Elymians and old Phoenician colonies on the coast, led to a more direct Carthaginian influence on the island by the fourth century. In the frequent battles between the tyrants of Greek city-states on Sicily, the Carthaginians were often supplying commanders and troops to their allies. The use of force to protect the interests of one's alliances was standard for inter-state relations at the time.[26] Carthaginian fortunes fluctuated and following a great defeat of an army of allies under a general named Hamilcar at Himera in *c.* 480 BCE there ensued a period when the Carthaginians remained outside Sicilian affairs for decades.[27]

The focus of our surviving history is almost exclusively on conquest, and details of the more prosaic aspects of life at Carthage are sporadic. The close link between Sicily and Carthage is confirmed repeatedly by our historical sources and by the fourth/third century there was an established Carthaginian territory in the west of the island. The volume of trade across the Mediterranean increased over this period with western Sicily and Carthage very much at the centre.[28] When Diodorus Siculus (13.81.4–5) describes the heavy investment in olive oil production by the elites of the city of Acragas (Agrigentum, modern Agrigento) on the south coast of Sicily, he also tells us that there was a single market for this oil, and that was Carthage (Map 1).[29]

Carthage developed allied coastal settlements east and west along the Mediterranean. Some were colonies and others were allied communities used like stepping-stones along the shore, providing a safe haven for merchant ships. In return, the Carthaginian navy supplied protection for these cities. The description of a journey along the coast of North Africa from a type of ancient sailor's handbook claimed that Carthage controlled an area from Lepcis Magna (in modern Libya) to the far west and the Atlantic Ocean.[30] This probably means that along this vast stretch of coast were cities with their own institutions and governments that were allied to Carthage.[31] By Hannibal's time, a Carthaginian cultural empire of sorts may have existed alongside one of shared military and economic interests.[32]

Throughout its long history the people of Carthage continued to maintain a deep connection with their mother city Tyre. At various points, Carthage seems to have absorbed populations from Tyre (and other cities in the Levant) coinciding with periods of political strife and external pressures in the east.[33] The Carthaginians continued to pay a regular tribute to the great temple of the god Melqart at Tyre. The very popular Carthaginian name Hamilcar, in fact the name of Hannibal's father, means 'servant of Melqart' in Punic. The importance of Melqart, known as 'Lord of the City' at Carthage, dated back to the very foundation. The relics from Melqart's temple at Tyre brought to Carthage by Dido were connected to the most sacred aspects of the city. As late as the second century Polybius writes of a Carthaginian ship at the mouth of the Tiber in Italy: 'such ships were specially selected at Carthage for the conveyance of the traditional offering of first-fruits to their gods that the Carthaginians send to Tyre' (Polyb. 31.12.11–12). Diodorus adds to this by telling us that it was Carthaginian custom 'to send to the god a tenth of all that was paid into the public revenue' (20.14.1–3).[34] With a tithe of the public purse at Carthage going to Tyre the connection between the cities must have been strong. Some elite Carthaginian families may even have used the title 'sons of Tyre', which could be a conscious appropriation of these important origins. For the Carthaginian elite, including Hannibal and his family, Tyre and their connection to this heritage was, throughout the history of the city, always present.[35]

Carthage was a diverse, multicultural port city with a close link to the Near East. The city's prosperity was renowned across the Mediterranean, and Carthaginian ships travelled far and wide. Evidence from the Carthaginian sailor's coastal guide of an explorer named Hanno claims that his voyage reached well beyond the Mediterranean – down the western coast of Africa to the Niger delta.[36] This expansive trading network can be perceived in the diversity of cultural artefacts that passed through the ports of the city. From the very earliest foundation wine and oils, pottery and jewellery were imported from across the seas.[37] Egyptian cultural artefacts such as scarab rings and faience votives mix in the tombs of the Carthaginians with Corinthian and Athenian pottery and typically Phoenician artefacts like the delicately decorated ostrich eggs used as vessels.[38] Over time influences ebbed and flowed along with the styles of art and commemoration. From the diversity and mixture of artefacts found in Punic-era tombs at Carthage a picture of the heterogeneous nature of Carthaginian culture appears.[39] The sophisticated ideas of the wider Mediterranean world permeated the culture of Carthage reflecting an outward-looking view and a great diversity in its population.

The Roman sources of later years reveal a deep prejudice against cultures that lived by the sea. The Romans tied the nature of the Carthaginians as merchant traders to cultural stereotypes that rested on the notion that living in a city by the sea led to immoderate behaviour. Through the words of a Roman envoy, the historian Appian puts the entire blame for the woes of the Carthaginians, the wars in Sicily and the loss of Sardinia on the lure of the sea and profit (*Lib.* 86). Cicero claimed that the Romans were justly concerned that the Carthaginians were imposing themselves on their territory and acted in self-defence against an inherently aggressive power. The aggression of Carthage, as embodied in the actions of Hannibal, derived in the Roman mind from its maritime location.[40] The belief that the sea was a negative factor in the character of a people was embraced. Cicero goes on to state that 'the Carthaginians were given to fraud and lying, not so much by race as by nature of their position'. He claimed that 'owing to their harbours, which brought them into communication with merchants and strangers speaking many different languages, they were inspired by the love of gain with the love of cheating' (*De agr.* 2.95). Cicero notes that the Romans liked to view the multicultural and multilingual Carthaginians as inherently dangerous and threatening. The Roman expression of the negative aspects of Hannibal's character was deeply rooted in the suspicions around his culture of origin.

In reality the Carthaginians were of course no more aggressive or threatening than the Romans but the origin of wealth in the two states was very different. The Romans were traditionally an agrarian society. Even though Carthage had extended its influence far into the surrounding territory and developed intensive agricultural production from early in its history, the merchant stereotype of its Phoenician origin persisted. By the time of Hannibal the elite families of Carthage were large landowners with estates in the wealthy agricultural areas that surrounded the city and spread into the countryside of North Africa.[41] Hannibal's family estates seem to have been centred on land holdings in the eastern coastal areas of Carthaginian territory, near the city of Hadrumentum (modern Sousse, Map 2).

The reality of life for the people of Carthage is not always in keeping with the portrait of the Carthaginians painted by their enemies. Much of the problem lies in the image created by the Romans. Hannibal was born into a world where fiercely contested warfare dominated the relationship between Carthage and Rome. There would have been a natural intensity to the depiction of the other side and although we only have the Roman view of the Carthaginians, similar attributes must have been applied to the Romans by their enemies. Broadly speaking, the Carthaginians are portrayed negatively in both Greek and Roman literary descriptions, although not exclusively so.[42] Although the different cultures coexisted quite peacefully over a long period in the western Mediterranean, war and its propaganda often overwhelm more subtle relationships. The characterization of Carthaginian culture that permeates the later Roman tradition is largely adverse. 'Such was Punic bravery, equipped with tricks and treacheries and deceit,' commented Valerius Maximus on Hannibal's victory at Cannae where the Romans 'were deceived rather than vanquished' (7.4, ext.2).[43] Punic treachery and Phoenician covetousness, deceit and deception were the dark arts of the enemy embodied by Hannibal and the Carthaginians according to the pro-Roman sources.[44]

The earliest portrayal of a Carthaginian in Latin literature is found in the works of the playwright Plautus, who wrote Latin comedy for the Romans in the late third/early second centuries. 'By god – his aspect indeed is Punic' (*Poen.* 975–977), Plautus would write at the end (or just after) the Second Punic War, a time when Hannibal was fresh in the minds of the Romans and very much still alive. The play, called the *Peonulus*, or 'little Punic', is based on a no longer extant Greek comedy called the *Karchedonias,* 'the Carthaginian'. Plautus' play has often been used to argue just how familiar the Romans were with the Carthaginians. Punic jokes, like those about the French or Germans in the UK, thread through the play, the Romans and Italians laughing at the cultural curiosities and national stereotypes of the main character, a Punic merchant. The *Poenulus* provides some remarkable and quirky insights into the accepted cultural characterizations of the Carthaginians just at the end of the Hannibalic War.[45]

The cast of characters includes Hanno, a devout and reasonably sympathetic Carthaginian merchant, travelling in search of his daughters who have been stolen from Carthage. The play humorously reflects the reality of life for the many tens of thousands who were captured and enslaved in these years of warfare. The Carthaginian characters wear culturally specific clothing, a Punic dress, and one actor asks, 'who is this man with the long tunic as if an innkeeper's slave?' (*Poen.* 975–977).[46] In Plautus, the 'Punic tunic' was an unmanly piece of clothing and the slur of unmanliness is repeated by Polybius when he records that the Carthaginians wore undergarments beneath their tunics.[47] Equally, to the Roman eye, both Hanno and his slaves would have been viewed as foreign because they had pierced ears and wore earrings (978–981).[48] Insults hurled at Hanno by the other characters in the play make reference to Sardinian fleeces, salt fish and garlic. The audience would have seen these as goods traditionally carried by Carthaginian merchants. Cargos of elephants and wild beasts used in processions, games and triumphs all evoke Carthaginian life as well.[49] We know that in a triumphal procession during the First Punic War more than a hundred elephants were paraded through Rome (Pliny, *NH* 7.139, 8.16–17, Livy, *Per.* 19). Thus the link between Carthage and elephants may have been a well-established trope even before Hannibal's great exploits. Plautus also implies that Carthaginian ships did not carry pork, and Polybius' omission of pigs from the wildlife of North Africa may confirm that the Carthaginians did not eat pork and that pigs did not factor in their sacrifices either, implying similar dietary traditions to Jewish or Islamic custom (Polyb. 12.3.1–4).[50]

Plautus' Carthaginian trader '. . . knows all languages; but though knowing he fakes that he doesn't know. He's thoroughly Punic' (*Poen.* 112–113). The image of the cunning multilingual merchant is reinforced when Virgil writes of the 'double tongued people of Tyre' (*Aen.* 1.661).[51] Speaking many languages made one suspect, and the characterization of Hanno as a trickster is a classic ethnic stereotype. It also allows Plautus to showcase the Punic language in the play. Punic, as written by Plautus, sounds like gibberish, and is thought to be an imitation of how the language sounded to Latin ears.[52] Poking fun at the sound of other peoples' language, at their culturally specific attire, food traditions and customs is a familiar practice in the modern world. Plautus plays with his Punic language and makes fun of words that sound like words in Latin but have different meanings (*Poen.* 1014).

Many aspects of Hanno in the play may well be caricatures of Hannibal himself and the audience would have understood who was being referred to directly.[53] Plautus' play makes clear the level of familiarity that Romans and Italians had with Carthaginians and Hannibal specifically.[54] Although Hanno goes about his business 'craftily and cunningly' (*Poen.* 111), he also shows many traits that the Romans would have considered virtuous and natural. Plautus portrays Hanno as deeply religious and devout; the portrait is not wholly negative and there are elements of sympathy. So, the characterization of the Carthaginians in Roman and Greek culture was far from monolithic or simplistically negative.[55] Hannibal's Punic culture was different, yet at the same time very familiar to contemporary Romans. The propaganda of the later Roman historians certainly masks a more nuanced and deeply held understanding between the two cultures.[56]

We learn from Plautus that the Carthaginian men of Hannibal's time were culturally different from their Greek and Roman counterparts. Their style of dress was different, they pierced their ears, were often multilingual and did not eat pork. Earlier ancient writers such as Herodotus (fifth century BCE) note that, traditionally, Phoenician men were circumcised but those who had close contact with the Greeks adapted to local custom and did not circumcise their children. Whether the Carthaginians continued the ritual of circumcision is unknown but if they did, it would have further contributed to the Roman and Greek view of Carthaginian 'otherness' (Herodotus 2.104.3–4; Aristophanes, *Birds* 227–228). Although it is difficult to tie the cultural traditions identified with Carthaginians to Hannibal specifically, they would, no doubt, have influenced the portrait of him that has been passed down to us.

The physical city of Carthage in Hannibal's time was 'surrounded with harbours and fortified with walls, it appeared to project out of Africa' much like a ship anchored off the coast (Cicero, *De agr.* 2.87).[57] The city sat out on a peninsula and travellers who approached Carthage from the sea would have seen the urban landscape rising up behind massive sea walls. A monumental sea gate, facing east, comprised of two arches flanked by two towers would have been the visitor's first impressive glimpse into the city.[58] Behind the sea walls the grand acropolis rose at the centre of the city. This was the Byrsa hill, crowned by a temple built to the Phoenician–Punic god Eshmun. The temple was most likely to have been in a Near Eastern style, which means it would have been surrounded by walls that enclosed the precinct of the god. Within the walled precinct would have been a flat-roofed temple.[59] Eshmun was an important deity in the civic culture at Carthage. It was under the protection of Eshmun that the Carthaginians placed their law-making and governance. This is emphasized by the meeting of the Senate in the precinct of the god.[60]

Up the sides of the Byrsa hill there was multi-storey housing with narrow stepped streets. The buildings were multiple family dwellings six storeys high with a shared central courtyard: the central zone of the city was densely populated.[61] The more substantial urban homes of the elites such as Hannibal's family were situated slightly away from the main hub of the town, perhaps nearer to the sea or up on the hills that rise north of the Byrsa. These hills provide extensive views across the gulf and a cooling breeze in the hot months of the summer.[62]

At the base of the Byrsa hill was the large open space of the main market area (the agora/forum). This was the central public square, and it contained another important city temple, dedicated perhaps to the god Reshep who was at the time equated with the Greco-Roman Apollo.[63] Inside the richly adorned temple was a statue of the god in a shrine of beaten gold weighing 1,000 talents (1 talent = 26kg) (Appian, *Lib.* 127). The busy market area was also the place where the sitting magistrates dispensed justice and performed the daily tasks of urban governance (Livy 34.61.15). Next door to the market, farther to the south, were the impressive ports of the city. From the later phases of

Punic Carthage the city had two magnificent harbours in this location, the remains of which can still be seen today.[64] An ancient account of the ports reveals their monumental construction; at capacity they would have been bustling with activity. They had a common entrance from the sea *c.* 24 metres wide, which could be closed with iron chains. 'The first port was for merchant vessels, and here were collected all kinds of ship's tackle. Within the second port, the military harbour, was an island and great quays were set at intervals round both the harbour and the islands' (Appian, *Lib.* 96). The military harbour was full of ship sheds, had capacity for 220 vessels and, resting on top of them, magazines for their tackle and furniture. The façade was elegantly decorated and in front of each dock stood two Ionic columns giving the appearance of a continuous portico to the harbour and the island.[65]

The prominence of the ports reflects the city's location on the northern tip of Africa jutting out into the sea-lanes on a narrow peninsula. Carthage was connected to the land by a narrow stretch with a great defensive wall built across it to defend from inland incursions.[66] This massive triple wall stood *c.* 14 metres high. It protected the land-side of the city, and along its length at intervals of every 60 metres were four-storey towers. The walls were used for housing the armed forces and supplies for the military at Carthage. By the latter part of the city's existence this included room for 300 elephants, stables for 4,000 horses and barracks for 20,000 soldiers (Appian, *Lib.* 95).[67]

Carthage was as renowned for its government as for its physical beauty. The Greek mathematician and geographer Eratosthenes, a contemporary of Hannibal, wrote that 'not only are many of the Greeks bad, but many of the barbarians are refined . . . Romans and Carthaginians, who carry on their governments so admirably' (Strabo 1.4.9). Aristotle wrote about the government of Carthage in his *Politics*, a work that looks at the nature of government and the forms available in the fourth century BCE. He included Carthage as the only non-Greek system of government worthy of analysis. Aristotle came to the conclusion that 'the government of the Carthaginians is oligarchical, but they successfully escape the evils of oligarchy by enriching one portion of the people after another by sending them to their colonies. This is their panacea and the means by which they give stability to the state' (*Politics* 2.8.9).[68]

Hannibal's family, the Barcids, were connected to the governmental elite of Carthage both in a political and military sense and he was brought up to function at the highest level of the city's administration. By the time of their ascendancy, in the third century, the government of Carthage was a factional oligarchy where elite families vied for power and influence. A family like

Hannibal's, whose influence endured over a long period, was sustained by close family ties, alliances formed through marriage and client–patron relations. Polybius tells us that the power of the oligarchical government at Carthage, by the beginning of the Second Punic War, had moved towards an excess of democratic behaviour with 'the people' given too much say (6.51.3–8).[69] Polybius was no great admirer of democracy and he implies that Hannibal and those who held sway at Carthage in his time sustained their political support through the popular assembly.[70] This was the body of male citizens of Carthage who formed the lowest rung of the governmental hierarchy.[71]

The Barcid family belonged to an established group of elite citizens from whom the governing magistrates at Carthage were chosen. The Punic name meant 'the great ones' ('drm) and it functioned as a senate. In Aristotle's description of the Carthaginian government he referred to the Senate at Carthage as a 'council of elders' (gerousia) and remarked that the Carthaginians believed that 'the rulers should be chosen not only for their merit but also for their wealth'. The decisions of day-to-day government at Carthage were made by magistrates, called sufetes, who were chosen annually from the three hundred or so members of the Senate. The sufetes embodied the ruling power of the Carthaginian Republic; the equivalent Roman term was praetors in Livy (33.46.3–4).[72] Within the broad range of the Senate were other groups who held influence at Carthage. There was an inner group of elites within the wider membership of the ruling Senate. We learn, again from Aristotle, that this 'council of one hundred and four' was chosen 'according to merit' and that another smaller group of thirty senators was considered to be a type of supreme 'council of elders'.[73]

The poorly understood system at Carthage can perhaps be clarified by looking at the much better understood Roman political and military structures. The highly competitive nature of the senatorial elite families at Rome and the outlet this gave individuals to engage in military action and achieve a great reputation, accrue massive wealth and political clout, drove the almost continual engagement in war and conquest during the Roman Republic. It seems very likely that elite Carthaginian males (as well as the population as a whole) also were engaged in and profited from the exploits of the Carthaginian navy, especially in the period after c. 400 BCE when Carthage appears to have become more 'imperial' in its outlook.[74] Individual families and their supporters seem to have held sway for periods of time, with military success underlying political power in the assembly.[75] A warlike aristocracy was a common link between Rome and Carthage. Hannibal's family was among those who led the direction of policy at Carthage through the latter half of the third century.[76]

Hannibal and his two younger brothers were raised for command and to 'fight Rome' (Valerius Maximus 9.3.2). Hannibal would inherit a position in the Carthaginian hierarchy as a military commander from his father via his brother-in-law.[77] In Rome military command was usually acquired through familial connections and generals were chosen from ex-consuls and praetors, the civic rule entwined with military power. At Carthage the generals seem to have held military positions before civic magistracies. It is difficult to tell if Hannibal's career path was exceptional or the norm.[78] The power of commanders in the field and the degree of their political autonomy have been much discussed in relation to Hannibal, his father and brothers and other Punic generals in Iberia in the period of the Hannibalic War.[79] The Carthaginian military commanders during the Punic Wars appear to have operated with a wide range of autonomous power and decision-making authority. Policy seems to have been driven from the field as much as from the Senate at Carthage.[80] This was not dissimilar to the process of Roman decision-making in the field, which has been described as 'ad hoc' and driven by the decisions of individual military commanders.[81] In the ancient world the farther a general was from home, the more autonomy he had. The autonomy of the Carthaginian general was balanced by a very harsh system of punishment for those considered not to have succeeded. A military commander who was deemed to have failed could expect to face a trial and prosecution on return to Carthage. Indeed, on more than one occasion during the First Punic War the punishment of choice for a failed commander was crucifixion.[82] The great advantages and opportunities that the elite Carthaginian men acquired with command came with equally great consequences if they were seen to fail.

We know little about the creation or enforcement of laws at Carthage as the evidence is scant. One fascinating fragment comes from Plato, who discusses the Carthaginians' strict laws concerning the drinking of alcohol. Plato mentions that at Carthage drinking alcohol was banned for a 'soldier on the march', who should confine himself for the whole of that time to water. The ban on alcohol extended to slaves in the city and magistrates during their year of office, and to pilots (in the busy ports) and judges while on duty. Carthaginian lawmakers did not believe anyone should taste wine at all during the daytime, except for reasons of bodily training or health; or at night, 'be he man or woman—when proposing to procreate children' (Laws 647a–b). This intriguingly modern view on alcohol consumption suggests a highly regulated society. Wine in the ancient world was often used to cut water to make it safer to drink and perhaps one assumption we can make, based on the Carthaginian ban on wine-drinking during the day, is that their water supply was relatively safe and clean.

Carthage had developed into a monumental and multicultural city by the third century. It was reputed to be well governed and had a large and diverse urban population, rich industrial production, agricultural wealth and a maritime culture that stretched across the Mediterranean. Carthage is frequently described as 'beautiful' and 'wealthy'.[83] These claims are repeated so often as to be suspect, for whenever 'the prosperity of the Carthaginians, abounded in wealth of every kind' (Diodorus Sic. 20.3.3) or 'Carthage, reckoned to be the wealthiest city in the world' (Polyb. 18.35.9) is mentioned by the later sources, it is always in connection with an invasion of their territory.[84] Even if the ancient sources tend to overstate the prosperity of Carthage, we do know it was a thriving and crowded city that had a well-constructed urban centre with a high standard of living.[85] Carthage was also a city of libraries as the Roman natural historian Pliny tells us (*NH* 18.22–3) consisting of scrolls of papyri in the Egyptian tradition. The only known Carthaginian text that survived its demise is a famous agricultural treatise written by an agronomist named Mago that was much read and translated by the Romans and Greeks.[86]

With so much of the public city of Punic Carthage destroyed in 146 BCE and again when the Roman city was constructed on the ruins, elements of guesswork and intuition are inevitable in any description of the physical landscape and its population. Our understanding of the institutions and culture of the city comes through a distorting lens from the Greek and Latin writers. It was in the realms of religion and culture that Carthage and, by extension, Hannibal were perceived as most foreign in the contemporary Greek and Roman sources.[87] The Carthaginians worshipped a pantheon of gods centred on Ba'al Hammon, a multifaceted deity with eastern roots reflecting the Phoenician heritage of Carthage and the female deity Tanit.[88] The god Melqart played a particularly important role in the imagery and self-representation of Hannibal and his family. Melqart was also a heroic god of the western Mediterranean linked to Herakles and connected to great adventures and military prowess. He was a patron god both of the city of Carthage and of the adventures of Hannibal.[89]

The most renowned and controversial site of religious significance at Carthage is the Tophet, also referred to as the Sanctuary of Tanit, which was located behind the commercial ports near the sea.[90] Here worship took the form of the dedication of cremated remains of very young children and small animals (sometimes mixed), interred and then marked by stelae and stone naiskoi (a dedicatory monument in the shape of a small temple) in the open air. The rituals at the Tophet were intimately connected to the worship of Ba'al Hammon and his consort the goddess Tanit (sometimes called Tinnit on inscriptions). This open-air sanctuary (or temple) contains some of the oldest remains recorded from the very first occupation of the city.[91] The ritual significance of the Tophet at Carthage and the importance of the site to the population of the city are clearly emphasized by the continual use of the site over the centuries.

There are a myriad of different types of offering and thousands of stelae that record dedications made to Ba'al Hammon and Tanit in fulfilment of a vow by the population at Carthage and also from farther afield.[92] From the first foundation through to the destruction of the city and beyond, the sanctuary was used and reused, cleared and reconstructed, and it evolved as part of the intrinsic identity of Carthage. The act of sacrifice by fire played an important symbolic part in the foundation myth of Carthage when Dido threw herself on a pyre. Fire was key to the worship of Melqart whose annual ritual of death and rebirth involved fire and also appears in other early stories of the history of the city.[93] The religious significance of the site is clear but what actually happened there is still very much debated. Whether the remains at the Tophet are the result of infant sacrifice, as our ancient sources attest, or the dedication of infants and neonates who had died of natural causes, is not universally agreed. The debate that started with the discovery of the site in the 1920s continues to this day. There is little doubt that at a site of such complexity no one simple ritual took place over the centuries. The urns contain many different types of offering and at least some of these seem to be the remains of sacrificed children.[94]

By the third century many other cults from outside these traditions were also found at Carthage. The influence of the Hellenistic world and culture of the Greeks spread across the Mediterranean, both artistically and linguistically, to Carthage. Educated Carthaginians were taught in the traditions of the Near East but also learned Greek as Hannibal did.[95] Through long-standing Carthaginian involvement in Sicily, Hellenization became more visibly apparent over the course of the fourth and third centuries. The cult of Demeter and Persephone, the important Sicilian version of the Greek cult, arrived in the early fourth century from Sicily.[96] There is evidence of the influence of Hellenistic artistic styles prevalent during the third century as well. A stunning decorated cuirass perhaps from a tomb of a commander in the Carthaginian army of Hannibal's generation embodies the reflection of styles and influences from the wider Mediterranean in its Ionic columns, rosette decoration and classically styled face (Plate 1).[97]

The city and culture of the Carthaginians were sophisticated and, like the character of Hanno in the *Poenulus,* operated across a multicultural Mediterranean in many guises. Carthage was a city open to foreign cultural and religious influences. The arrival of new ideas and trends in its ports was a regular occurrence. At the same time the Tophet reveals a culture of deeply held beliefs linked to the very foundation of the city. The continuing connection to Tyre shows that Carthaginians retained aspects of the traditions of their Near Eastern heritage. This proud city at the centre of the Mediterranean, truly a crossroads absorbing cultures from north, south, east and west, created Hannibal. By Hannibal's time there would not have been one identity that defined a Carthaginian, but many that reflected the complexity of the city's origins and history.[98]

Hannibal would have been fiercely aware of his noble heritage and the long history of Carthage and its legends. The unique blend of influences on and wider Mediterranean outlook of the city of Carthage helps us to see Hannibal more clearly. Carthage, its legends and rich culture infuse our understanding of Hannibal even though preconceived stereotypes of the Roman conquerors are deeply embedded in our information. Hannibal, however, was much more than just a Carthaginian. He lived most of his life away from Carthage and was a creation of the wider Mediterranean culture of the Hellenistic period in the east and the west. This was a world that embraced the role of the heroic general and the brave deeds of risk-taking adventurers. Hannibal was both 'the most famous Carthaginian of them all' and a man whose individual brilliance and reputation outshone his culture and community in the eyes of his conquerors.[99]

# CHAPTER 2

# THE GREAT MAN IN THE HELLENISTIC WORLD
## FROM ALEXANDER TO HAMILCAR

... from this point onwards history becomes an organic whole: the affairs of Italy and of Africa are connected with those of Asia and Greece. **(Polybius 1.3.4)**

THE HELLENISTIC AGE REFERS to the period in the Mediterranean from the death of Alexander in 323 BCE to the defeat of the last Hellenistic monarch, Cleopatra, at the battle of Actium in 31 BCE. Hannibal grew up and was educated in the second half of the third century, less than a hundred years after Alexander's death. This proved to be a defining era for Carthaginian, Greek and Roman history.[1] The picture we have of Hannibal's life and death is infused with the complexities of the wider Hellenistic Mediterranean.[2] Ideas of power and empire in the Mediterranean had been permanently transformed by the time Alexander died. Appian describes how writing his history of the period led him 'from Carthage to Spain, from Spain to Sicily or to Macedonia, or to join some embassy to foreign countries, or some alliance formed with them; thence back to Carthage or Sicily, like a wanderer' (*Preface* 12). By the third century the Mediterranean world was more closely interlinked than ever before. The city-states of the eastern Mediterranean that had existed before Alexander on the fringes of Persian power, each with more or less regional influence, imploded and populations moved around. Big powers and large kingdoms of all kinds (from monarchies to republics) looked to increase their wealth and hegemonic control. The powerful city-states in the central Mediterranean, such as Carthage, Rome and Syracuse, once outside the sphere of influence of the Hellenistic kingdoms, were pulled farther into the fray.[3] The period has been described as 'Mediterranean Anarchy' which sums up the environment in which Hannibal, the most successful general of his generation, would flourish.[4]

Hannibal's style of military leadership developed in the wake of the legend of Alexander the Great and his conquests. Alexander's exploits created a new paradigm for boundless military conquest, and Hannibal would have grown up listening to stories about the legendary leader who had conquered kingdoms beyond the known world. The harsher reality of Alexander's exploits would have been keenly felt at Carthage when Tyre was sacked in 333 BCE. Around this time the Carthaginian government sent an envoy named Hamilcar Rhodanus to meet Alexander.[5] In one version of the story Hamilcar gained access to the king by stealth, ingratiating himself with his entourage whilst pretending to seek refuge with the Macedonians. Hamilcar then sent reports back to Carthage about Alexander's plans using hidden texts, written on wood tablets and then covered with wax (Justin 21.6.1–7). He seems to have been a spy embedded in Alexander's army. On Hamilcar's return to Carthage after Alexander's death, he was executed 'on the grounds that he had tried to sell the city to the [Macedonian] king' (21.6.7).

The foundation of Alexandria, Alexander's new city in Egypt, must have caused the Carthaginians some concern over competition for trade routes and encroachment on territory allied to Carthage in North Africa. It was even rumoured that Alexander intended to make Carthage his next great conquest, but any plan was cut short by his premature death (Diodorus Sic. 18.4.4; Justin 21.6.1–7). These stories and legends of the siege of Tyre and Alexander's plans would have been carried to Carthage with an influx of Tyrian refugees who must have arrived in the aftermath of the destruction of their city.[6]

Alexander's death in 323 BCE left a vacuum and the cities and states of the eastern Mediterranean were swept up in the scramble that followed. The generals who succeeded Alexander (the so-called 'Successors') vied to inherit the mantle of power left by his untimely death at the age of thirty-three. Out of Alexander's empire the Successors shaped large kingdoms through a process of almost constant warfare. An uneasy balance of power existed between these kingdoms of Ptolemaic Egypt, Seleucid Asia and Antigonid Macedonia. As conflict flared around disputed territories, demonstrations of military might became an essential part of the political process. One of the important symbolic notions of the Hellenistic period was conquest – the spear-won land – and the rulers of these kingdoms established their legitimacy through military victory.[7]

The first leader of the 'Hellenistic mould' to make a direct impact on Carthage was the Syracusan tyrant Agathocles (c. 360–289/288 BCE). Agathocles had seized control in Syracuse (c. 317 BCE) and set out to conquer and consolidate power in Sicily. This brought him into conflict with Carthaginian allies in the west of Sicily. After suffering a serious defeat at the hands of the Carthaginians, Syracuse was essentially under siege by 310 BCE. Agathocles' response was to raise a mercenary army and launch a surprise attack on the city of Carthage. It was a bold attempt to alleviate the siege at home. Agathocles' forces landed not far from Carthage across the gulf on Cap Bon (Map 1). Leaving his fate to fortune Agathocles burned his ships and set off to plunder the countryside. There in the agricultural heartland of Carthage he encountered a landscape '. . . full of gardens, of orchards watered by streams. The country houses followed one on the other, built with luxury . . . everywhere a picture of wealth in the estates of the Punic aristocracy' (Diodorus Sic. 20.8.3–4).[8] The Carthaginians, whose army was distracted by the siege in Sicily, were completely unprepared and pulled together a haphazard force to meet the invader (Diodorus Sic. 20.11). The subsequent defeat inflicted by Agathocles on Carthage was catastrophic and led to chaos in Carthaginian territory and revolt among Carthage's allies in Africa.[9]

The Carthaginians struggled to deal with the expedition of Agathocles and a succession of fiercely fought battles challenged their position in Africa for the first time on land. An attempted alliance between the armies of Agathocles and the Ptolemaic king of Cyrene, Ophellas, might have ended in total disaster for Carthage. However, some kind of inexplicable treachery, nowhere well explained, led Agathocles to attack and kill his erstwhile ally Ophellas and incorporate his soldiers into his own army.[10] Carthage remained isolated and increasingly cut off from her traditional allies in Africa. The Syracusan forces took the allied cities of Utica and Hippo Acra to the north of Carthage and the Libyan allies flocked to the side of the Hellenistic hegemon Agathocles. In 307 BCE, after four event-filled years with Carthage still standing despite all the odds, Agathocles returned to Sicily to try to retain his power there. He left his army and his sons in Africa to their fate. The Carthaginians eventually won back all the territory they had lost but Agathocles' bold adventure had exposed to the wider world their vulnerability to invasion (Diodorus Sic. 20.5–69; Justin 22–23).[11]

The expedition of Agathocles illustrates exactly how the knock-on effect of the expansionist tendencies of the Hellenistic Age impacted the central and western Mediterranean.[12] Conquest became the norm for kings and tyrants like Agathocles and the generals of the Carthaginian Republic who fought against him. Individual military commanders expanded their horizons for conquest beyond the traditional zones of conflict. Agathocles' invasion of Africa shifted the rules of engagement within which Carthage and Syracuse had been battling for almost two centuries. It was no longer just about conflict in Sicily and defending allies against incursions from one or the other side. Larger, more geographically expansive power was being sought and the threat of an invasion of Africa would become Carthage's greatest vulnerability.

In the heyday of the Hellenistic kings an era of the heroic commander feted by writers and the public for his individual military exploits developed. These celebrated generals represented the model of power and 'heroic leadership' which Alexander had embodied. As subsequent leaders employed the image of Alexander to claim their legitimacy, the symbolism of power and conquest which he had typified spread across the Mediterranean, from the Successor kings to the city-states of the west.[13] The powerful republics of Carthage and Rome were equally influenced by stories of these magnificent feats of military glory. The tales of the great generals inspired by divine patronage were the stuff of legend. Hannibal would have studied their battles, learned their techniques and been schooled in the strategies of war as befitted the son of one of Carthage's great generals.[14]

The third century was a period of economic growth and increased trade around the Mediterranean. It was also a time of increasing prosperity at Carthage. The city was ideally situated in the middle of the Mediterranean to capitalize on the trade from an ever-widening world.[15] As great wealth and royal rivalries drove the successors of Alexander to further competitive warfare they began what must have been one of the world's first arms races, as bigger and better warships, catapults, siege engines and weaponry were commissioned.[16] One of the earliest and most celebrated of the Hellenistic kings to explore the potential of advanced weaponry was the Macedonian Demetrius known as *Poliorcetes* (Besieger of Cities). Plutarch, the first-century CE compiler of great Greek and Roman lives, wrote that 'Demetrius was skilled in directing catapults and battering rams to crush city walls'. Demetrius' tortoise-like armoured battering rams were 180 feet long and manned by 1,000 men. His giant catapults hurled 180-pound stone balls a quarter of a mile and his most fearsome device was an enormous wheeled fortified tower called *Helepolis* (the Taker of Cities). This tower was 50 feet square at its base, more than 100 feet tall and was armed with its own banks of catapults and sling throwers.[17] Reports from Agathocles' assault on Utica describe a siege engine with prisoners from the city dangling from the machine as it was moved into position to attack – thus presenting a quandary for the defenders inside the walls, forced to shoot their own citizens to defend themselves against the machine (Diodorus Sic. 20.54.3–7).

Nowhere was the innovation more apparent than in the investment and development of warships. Control of the sea brought control of the lucrative trade across the Mediterranean. Shipwreck evidence from around the Mediterranean reveals a jump in the number of ships frequenting the shores. This augmented connectivity resulted in more trade and greater wealth. Corresponding to this growth was an enormous increase in the number and size of warships. In the Classical period, the standard oared ship was the trireme, a ship that had three levels of oars with a single oarsman pulling each oar.[18] The trireme was the main warship until the arrival of the four (*quadrireme*) in the fourth century, which Aristotle (via Pliny) tells us was a Carthaginian innovation (*NH* 7.207–8). A four was a different concept, with two banks of oars and two men to each oar. Then came fives and sixes (*quinqueremes* and *hexiremes*).[19] Exactly how the fives functioned is still debated, however they seem to have had either two or three banks of oars with five oarsmen on each side.[20] The more imposing fives and sixes originally functioned as the flagships of the naval commanders but by the mid-third century Polybius implies that the five had become the standard warship in the Carthaginian navy (1.20.9–16). Innovations in the technique of naval warfare developed out of the main maritime battles, and especially significant in the ancient sources were the sea battles fought by Carthage and Rome in the First Punic War.[21]

The Carthaginians had inherited the traditions of a sophisticated maritime culture from the Phoenicians and by the third century the city was renowned as a naval power. The naval prowess of Carthage was something that had developed organically. Her influence rested on the sea, and ships were the means by which Carthage communicated and connected with her allied cities. Much of the wealth of the state seems to have derived from maritime commerce with the control of the ports and the duties charged for access. Consequently Carthage attained the reputation for naval prowess over her rivals, being 'superior at sea both in efficiency and equipment, because seamanship has long been their national craft' (Polyb. 6.52.1–2). The self-perception of the Carthaginians was also connected to the sea and the citizens of Carthage both commanded and manned her navy. As it was the principal means of power at Carthage there was an important focus on the skills involved in all aspects of the navy, from command to construction. From the production of ships to the workings of the ports to the seamanship of the sailors, the navy touched all strata of the population at Carthage.[22] Evidence suggests there was a standing navy at Carthage but in times of need there are indications that this was supplemented by privately funded naval enterprises. It seems that individual citizens built, equipped and manned ships for specific missions. For example, in 250 BCE a Carthaginian admiral named Hannibal the Rhodian and his excellent crew were able to evade the Roman blockade of Lilybaeum in Sicily. We are told that the Rhodian had fitted out the ships himself (Polyb. 1.46.4–13). There may have been an incentives culture associated with success in naval warfare at Carthage, which gave further impetus to the individual in command.[23]

The Carthaginian reputation as a naval power was severely threatened over the course of the middle third century. Carthage had previously confronted few rivals who could equal her control of the sea in the western Mediterranean. The advent of new Hellenistic hegemons and Roman expansion challenged the status quo at Carthage. This is also the critical period that links Hannibal's story and that of the Hellenistic world through the advent of Pyrrhus, king of the Greek Adriatic state of Epirus (319–272 BCE).

As a quintessential Hellenistic leader, Pyrrhus was a dynamic military commander whose political intentions were expansive and ambitious, driven by the conquest of neighbouring kingdoms. He was well connected in dynastic terms being brother-in-law to Demetrius Poliorcetes through his first wife Antigone (the stepdaughter of the Egyptian ruler Ptolemy I) and subsequently marrying Lanassa, the daughter of the Syracusan tyrant Agathocles. By invading Italy early in the second quarter of the third century Pyrrhus brought the Hellenistic world fully into the politics of the western Mediterranean.[24]

Hannibal was an admirer of the Epirot general. He was raised on Pyrrhus' battles, adventures and approach to the Romans.[25] In 281 BCE Pyrrhus' invasion of southern Italy at the behest of the city of Tarentum (modern Taranto) brought about a paradigm shift in the relations between the Greeks in the west, the Carthaginians and the Romans. For the first time, a Hellenistic king and army engaged the Romans on the Italian mainland and the affairs of Italy and Sicily became entwined with those of the Hellenistic world. The army led by Pyrrhus included twenty battle elephants called 'the strange monsters of the Macedonians' (Justin 18.1). This would be the Romans' and Carthaginians' first military encounter with 'the civilized core of the Mediterranean world'.[26]

Roman expansion into the south of Italy had precipitated the invasion of Pyrrhus. Successive wars had led to the conquest of the central Italic Samnite peoples and to Rome's control over the key trade and transport routes through the Apennines. The final Roman victory over the Samnites (290 BCE) removed the buffer zone between Rome and the Greek cities of the south of Italy (known as Magna Graecia). The wealthy Greek cities of Magna Graecia had become increasingly nervous of Rome's growing influence in Italy during the fourth and early third centuries. Since c. 350 BCE the powerful city of Tarentum, in origin a Spartan colony, had employed Greek generals to fight wars against its neighbours. Pyrrhus was the last in a list which also included his uncle Alexander of Epirus († c. 330 BCE).[27]

Pyrrhus crossed from Epirus to Italy in 281 BCE and narrowly won two hard-fought battles against Roman forces, the first at Heraclea in 280 BCE and the second at Ausculum in 279 BCE (Map 1). In both battles Pyrrhus was victorious but sustained such heavy losses that the Romans had effectively chastened the Hellenistic king.[28] 'The triumph . . . was not bloodless; for Pyrrhus himself was severely wounded and a great number of his soldiers killed; and he had more glory from his victory than pleasure' (Justin 18.1). These battles gave rise to the phrase 'Pyrrhic victory', with Pyrrhus reported to have commented 'if I win one more battle with the Romans, I shall not have left a single soldier of those who crossed over with me' (Diodorus Sic. 22.6.2).

Carthage's long-standing involvement in western Sicily was focused on the allied port cities at the west of the island, Panormus (Palermo), Drepanum (Trapani) and Lilybaeum (Marsala).[29] In the summer of 278 BCE a Carthaginian army was laying siege to Syracuse. The Syracusans leapt at the opportunity to invite Pyrrhus and his army to Sicily to fight against their old enemies and relieve the siege.[30] In exchange for help Pyrrhus was offered control of the Sicilian cities of Agrigentum, Leontinoi and Syracuse, and his marriage to Lanassa tied him to the leadership of the city. The Hellenistic hero sailed boldly into Syracuse, relieving the city and catching the Carthaginian fleet off guard. Pyrrhus became, for a short while, a king of Syracuse and Epirus and set about expanding his hegemony on the island.[31] The Carthaginians fared much less well against Pyrrhus' battle-hardened forces than they did against the Romans. They suffered a series of heavy defeats over the three years Pyrrhus operated in Sicily (from the autumn of 278 BCE to the spring of 275 BCE).[32] When Pyrrhus stormed Eryx, the fortified stronghold of the Carthaginians in western Sicily, Carthage's influence was restricted to their well-protected port of Lilybaeum. Lilybaeum held out and the Carthaginian navy managed to sustain their outpost on the island against the onslaught.[33] Now the fractured political situation in Sicily caught up with Pyrrhus, who was faced 'on all sides with disaffection and insurrections against his authority' (Plutarch, Pyrrh. 23). The Romans had rebounded with a vengeance in Italy and Pyrrhus' allies there were calling for his return. This allowed him an almost honourable withdrawal from Sicily, which he left in turmoil, 'like a storm tossed ship' (Plutarch, *Pyrrh*. 24). Pyrrhus was chased across the Straits of Messina, losing ships to the Carthaginians as he withdrew from the island.

Pyrrhus' invasion had threatened both Roman and Carthaginian power and regional interests. The two powers turned to each other at this moment and agreed to cooperate against their mutual enemy. Polybius writes that 'a further and final treaty with Carthage was made by the Romans at the time of Pyrrhus' invasion' (279/278 BCE). In the treaty the Carthaginians agreed to aid the Romans by providing 'the ships for transport and hostilities, but each country shall provide the pay for its own men . . .'. An important stipulation in the treaty was that 'the Carthaginians, if necessary, shall come to the help of the Romans by sea too, but no one shall compel the crews to land against their will' (Polyb. 3.25.1–5). There had been a long history of treaty and cooperation between the Romans and Carthaginians dating back to the sixth century that carefully laid out the spheres of interest of the two states. This treaty added the condition that the two cities must provide military help to each other against Pyrrhus.[34] It also makes clear that the naval might of Carthage was of great interest to the Romans, indicating their superiority of resource in this area.

Once Pyrrhus had withdrawn, the Carthaginians in Sicily and the Romans in southern Italy surged forward (Polyb. 1.6.8).[35] The Roman historian Dio believed it was not until the moment of Pyrrhus' withdrawal from the field that Carthage and Rome became wary of each other's growing influence (Cassius Dio 11.1–4). The good relations maintained between Rome and Carthage ended here and it was in Sicily that the post-Pyrrhic surges led to the first hostile contact. It was the beginning of what we call the First Punic War (264–241 BCE).[36] Pyrrhus himself is reported to have seen the potential when he commented, 'what a battlefield we are leaving to the Carthaginians and the Romans' (Plutarch, *Pyrrh*. 23).[37]

No event had more of an impact on Hannibal, from his earliest childhood to his formative years, than the First Punic War.[38] In essence Carthage and Rome were fighting for control over the island that lay between their spheres of influence, Sicily (Map 1).[39] It was an epic war, lasting twenty-three years and resulting in a reordering of geopolitical power in the central Mediterranean.[40] It is unlikely that either Carthage or Rome had intended to embark upon such a war in 264 BCE. As in more modern 'great' wars, the combatants could not have anticipated such a massive strategic and military conflict, much less one that lasted over two decades and cost the lives of hundreds of thousands of combatants and civilians.[41]

In Polybius' narrative of the First Punic War, Carthage and Rome were two equal powers in dispute over the 'empire of the world' (Polyb. 1.3.7).[42] The events that drew the two sides into actual war were more prosaic and revolved around the city of Messana (Messina) and a group of mercenary soldiers called the Mamertines. These were the men of Mamers, who was the Oscan god of war (equivalent to Roman Mars).[43] The Mamertines had been one of many factions active in Sicily in the period of Pyrrhus's invasion and had originally served under Agathocles († 289/288 BCE). When Agathocles died the mercenaries seized control of Messana, an important city guarding the narrow body of water between Sicily and Italy. At the narrowest point the Straits of Messina are less than four kilometres wide and the city sits just twelve kilometres across the water from the mainland Italian city of Rhegium (Reggio Calabria) (Map 1). The Romans had seized Rhegium (c. 270 BCE) and ousted another group of mercenary soldiers from that stronghold.[44]

After Pyrrhus, Hiero II (271–216 BCE) came to rule at Syracuse and attempted to oust the Mamertines from Messana. As early as 269 BCE, the Mamertines were soundly defeated by Syracuse in battle and their leaders captured.[45] In light of this disaster 'some of them appealed to the Carthaginians, proposing to put themselves and the citadel into their hands, while another party sent a delegation to Rome' (Polyb. 1.10.1–3). Carthaginian forces were then invited to occupy the citadel at Messana with troops from their base nearby on the island of Lipari. When Roman troops arrived on the scene the Mamertines turned on the Carthaginians and dislodged them from the citadel.[46] As loyalties shifted, the Mamertines invited the Romans to enter the city and the Carthaginians turned to an alliance with their old foes, the Syracusans.

The situation was fluid and our ancient sources seem to have condensed the events of a number of years into a much shorter time.[47] Polybius, who wrote about a hundred years after the event, was so unsure of his sources that he accused them of falsehoods and manipulation of the evidence (1.15.6–12). We do know that these first actions of the war left the Romans in possession of Messana and the Carthaginian commander crucified for abandoning his post.[48] Crossing from Italy to support the Mamertines was a radical leap for the Romans and may have gone beyond the terms of existing treaties that clearly stated Sicily was within the Carthaginian sphere of influence.[49] Even the pro-Roman Polybius notes that 'it was all too clear that to give the help required [to the Mamertines] would be thoroughly inconsistent' (1.10.3–5).[50] The Romans seemed swayed more by the potential threat posed by the Carthaginians ensconced at Messana than by any hypocrisy in their own foreign policy. The Roman support of the Mamertines represented a significant moment in the rise of Roman imperial aspirations, since for the first time they engaged in warfare off the Italian mainland. 'I shall take as the starting point of this book the first occasion on which the Romans crossed the sea from Italy' (Polyb. 1.5.1).

For the Carthaginians this was clearly an aggressive act by the Romans. Carthage, in coming to the aid of the Mamertines, was acting as it had done for the previous centuries, reacting to requests for military aid from allies in Sicily. From a Carthaginian perspective, Roman actions towards Messana could only have been seen as an attempt to take Sicily. Roman tradition would contend that the Sicilian conquest was an unintended consequence of the long struggle that resulted from their coming to the aid of the Mamertines.[51] Can we believe that the Roman politicians did not realize that crossing into Sicily to aid the mercenaries would mean they had stepped beyond their traditional realm of influence and into that of the two most powerful cities in the region, Syracuse and Carthage? On the other hand, one of our later Roman sources claims that Carthaginian ships had appeared off Tarentum when Rome was laying siege to it (c. 272 BCE), and that constituted the initial break of the treaty of non-interference they had signed (Cassius Dio, frag. 43).[52] The Romans claimed that initial Carthaginian aggression meant they had to act in Messana or their own spheres would have been challenged by Carthage. Rome acted in the way it did because of the potential threat from Carthage. It seems that both sides, in the spirit of the Hellenistic age, were very willing to engage beyond their traditional domains and the lasting result would bring Rome directly into conflict with Carthage. Decades of warfare were to follow.[53]

The Romans had proven to be equal (almost) to Pyrrhus on land but up to the point when they entered the battle for Sicily they did not have a navy to speak of. As Polybius tells us, they had 'not only no decked ships but no warships at all' and at the start of the war over Sicily 'they borrowed pente-conters [fifty-oared boats] and triremes from their allies . . . and ferried their troops across [the Straits] to Messina' (Polyb. 1.20.13–16).[54] However, Polybius stands accused of underestimating Roman naval experience for rhetorical purposes and 'the idea of the Romans as beginners is in total contradiction with everything we know about Roman maritime interests during the centuries before the war'.[55]

The Romans went on to build a new fleet based on a Carthaginian quin-quereme prototype, which was considered the best ship constructed at the time. The design for the new Roman navy was taken from a Carthaginian ship captured off the Campanian coast early in the war. These ships were mass-produced on an industrial scale, with Rome acquiring forested lands in Italy to access the materials needed (Polyb. 1.20.7–16).[56] The result was that two great fleets would face each other in the First Punic War, called by Polybius the greatest naval war ever fought. 'Those who marvel at the great sea battles and great fleets of an Antigonus, a Ptolemy or a Demetrius would . . . on inquiring into the history of this war, be astonished at the huge scale of the operations involved,' exclaimed Polybius (1.63.7).

This long war played out in phases over the twenty-three years both 'at sea and on land'.[57] There were periods of intense fighting as the focus of the battle shifted clockwise around Sicily and then moved to North Africa. The momentum of the war swung back and forth between the two sides, with each suffering disaster and victory in turn. Cities were besieged and enormous sea battles took place in the waters around the island. In the second year of the war (263/262 BCE), the Senate at Rome decided to send both their consular armies to Sicily, a force of about 40,000 soldiers, illustrating Rome's intentions towards Sicily and the intensity of the war's first phase.[58] When the Roman army arrived in Sicily 'most of the cities rose against the Carthaginians and Syracusans, and came over to the Romans' (Polyb. 1.16.1–3).[59]

After an initial victory the Roman consul Valerius Maximus Messalla laid siege to Syracuse. The Syracusan king Hiero quickly realized that, considering the size of the army he was confronted with, 'the Romans' prospects were far brighter than those of the Carthaginians' and pursued a policy of peace (Polyb. 1.16.4–5). The Romans came to generous terms with Syracuse and from that point had a base from which to operate in Sicily. The Romans moved on from Syracuse to lay siege to the most important city on the south coast of Sicily, Agrigentum (Greek Acragas). They intended to collect food supplies for their own troops and disrupt the supply chain of the Carthaginian forces.[60]

The Carthaginians saw Agrigentum as a strategic base from which to defend the south-west corner of Sicily and they had held it for the previous decade (Map 1).[61] The Carthaginian garrison in the city was now vastly overwhelmed as they faced a combined threat of the Roman consular armies allied with Syracuse. They sent news to Carthage and requested reinforcements. At Carthage a new army was raised made up of 'Ligurians, Celts, and still more Iberians'. This force was sent to Sicily in the hope of defending Agrigentum from the impending Roman attack (Polyb. 1.17.4–5).[62]

The land army of Carthage has always been perceived as its weak point, judged so because it traditionally relied on mercenaries for its overseas fighting forces. 'They had always been in the habit of employing hired soldiers,' notes Polybius (1.71.1–2). The Carthaginians are believed to have used mercenary soldiers to fight foreign wars, whilst citizen-levied troops were used for fighting at home and in their navy. It was certainly not as unambiguous in reality but the ancient writers make much of the difference between the Roman citizen army and the hired troops of the Carthaginians. The make-up of the Carthaginian army was in no way unusual for the time and would have been like that of many Hellenistic armies of the day. In the third century soldiering was a profession and men were recruited and paid to go where the fighting was.[63] The fact that the Carthaginians were known to offer a high rate of pay for their military service meant that they had little trouble raising new forces to fight in Sicily (Diodorus Sic. 16.81.4).[64]

Up to 50,000 people were trapped within the walls of Agrigentum when the Roman troops set up a blockade. There was nothing to eat as the Romans disrupted the harvest and not long into the siege the people were 'pressed by famine' (Polyb. 1.18.7). When the newly raised Carthaginian army arrived it encircled the Roman troops, laying siege to the besiegers. Desperation inside the city eventually pushed the Carthaginian commander Hanno to engage the Romans in an attempt to relieve the population. In a closely fought pitched battle the Romans were victorious on the day. After a five-month siege the Carthaginian commander inside the city took the chance to evacuate his army, saving his soldiers from defeat and capture but leaving the population defenceless.[65]

The Romans, then, 'finding nobody to oppose them burst into the city and plundered it, enslaving great numbers of the inhabitants and taking huge quantities of booty of every description' (Polyb. 1.19.15). So great was the destruction that some claimed the Romans enslaved the whole population (Diodorus Sic. 23.9.1). 'When the news of what had occurred at Agrigentum reached the Roman Senate, in their joy and elation they no longer confined themselves to their original designs' (Polyb. 1.20.1–3). After the sack of the beautiful and richly adorned city the attitude of Rome towards Sicily changed. The Roman commanders shipped their victory loot back to Rome and the statues and gold of the treasury of Agrigentum were displayed to the Roman people in a grand triumph. Polybius asserts that the wealth that flowed to Rome from Agrigentum shifted Roman intentions and that what had started as a war for Messana turned into a 'war for Sicily'.[66]

After the siege and sack of Agrigentum the first of many sea battles took place (in *c.* 260 BCE) off the promontory of Mylae (Milazzo) that juts out from northern Sicily towards the Carthaginian base of Lipara on the Aeolian Islands (Map 1). For the previous four years the Carthaginians had been harassing the Romans and raiding Italy, using their maritime superiority to disrupt Roman transports (Polyb. 1.20.1–9). The Romans addressed the issue by building a navy to match their enemy's, 'a hundred quinqueremes and twenty triremes', with the larger ships based on a Carthaginian model (1.20.15) but with the benefit of an impressive-looking innovation. This was the *corvus* (or *corax*, Latin for crow), known otherwise as a boarding bridge. The *corvus* was a device fitted to the prow of a Roman warship that allowed the ship's crew to grapple and then board an enemy vessel with greater flexibility. Third-century naval battle tactics relied on ramming, a strategy that meant that the Carthaginian fleet, with its superior skill and manoeuvrability, had the advantage. Carthaginian sailors were able to outrun and outmanoeuvre almost any ship but with the *corvus* the Romans could disrupt the seamanship of their enemies and fight land skirmishes at sea.[67]

A Carthaginian navy put to sea from its base at Lipari with 130 ships while the Roman navy had 100 quinqueremes and 20 triremes at their disposal.[68] The Carthaginians sailed out with some confidence, their admiral in a 'seven-banked galley that formerly belonged to King Pyrrhus' (Polyb. 1.20.9 and 1.23.3–4). The ships of the Carthaginian navy were fast and light, easily manoeuvrable and their seamen the best in the Mediterranean. Carthaginian sailors were, according to the sources, unaware of the new Roman adaptation and, as soon as any ships collided, the *corvus* grappled onto the Carthaginian vessel and held fast, allowing Roman troops to board the enemy ship quickly and efficiently. The Romans attacked the Carthaginian sailors 'hand to hand on deck, some of the Carthaginians were cut down and others surrendered from dismay at what was happening, the battle having become just like a fight on land'. The quick seamanship and superior abilities of the Carthaginian sailors were useless when confronted with Roman legions boarding over the bridge (Polyb. 1.23.3–10).

Some thirty Carthaginian ships (including the admiral's prized Hellenistic galley) with all their crews (except the admiral himself, who escaped on the ship's tender) were captured.[69] A further fifty Carthaginian ships (with estimates of 300 rowers on a quinquereme) were sunk completely. The efficiency of the Roman victory has raised some question about Polybius' argument that the Romans were 'sea novices'. There was obviously enough experience in the Roman command to manoeuvre ships and exploit to the full their new boarding bridge tactics.[70] After Mylae, Carthaginian naval superiority seemed an illusion, and further losses followed off Sardinia. The war continued with skirmishes back and forth (Polyb. 1.24.8–13, 25.1–4). The Carthaginian defeats in the naval conflict are astounding when one considers that Carthage was the sea power and Rome the land power. The relative strengths and weaknesses of the two sides may well be exaggerated for narrative effect in our sources, but the reversals suffered by Carthage speak of complacency in their leadership and a lack of ability to adapt their strategy. They were left vulnerable and in disarray.[71]

The Romans, feeling confident and aggressive, reasoned that by taking the war to Carthage itself they could best capitalize on their successes. If they blockaded Carthage in Africa then Sicily would surely fall quickly. The Roman army massed on the south coast of Sicily and prepared to sail across. The Carthaginians were determined to prevent this invasion at all costs, remembering the lessons learned from Agathocles decades previously. The result was the massive naval battle at Ecnomus in the summer of 256 BCE, four years after Mylae. The battle saw the full complement of both forces ranged against each other off the southern coast of Sicily, just east of Agrigentum (Map 1).

Polybius records that the Carthaginians set out with a fleet of 350 decked ships and the Romans with around 320, plus ships carrying horses and supplies for the planned invasion (Polyb. 1.25.7–9). These numbers have been revised downwards by modern scholars to 230 ships for the Romans and perhaps 200 for the Carthaginians but there is no solid factual basis for this assessment. Ancient estimates put Roman forces at 140,000 men and the Carthaginians close to 150,000 (1.26.7–9). Even Polybius seems surprised by the numbers and notes that 'these figures are bound to strike not only an eye-witness but even the reader with amazement at the vast scale of the encounter and the enormous outlay and resources of the opposing states'.[72] Allowing for the exaggerations and scaled down to the modern estimates, there were still as many as 250,000 oarsmen and marines involved, which makes it, quite likely, the largest sea battle ever fought.[73]

A Carthaginian fleet had sailed across from Carthage to Lilybaeum and rounded the coast anticlockwise to their base at Heraclea Minoa (Map 1). They were positioned to block the Roman crossing. As the Roman fleet left port it was under the command of both the consuls, Marcus Atilius Regulus and Lucius Manlius Vulso, sailing side by side in flagship *hexiremes* (sixes) at the head of the convoy of ships. They were making for Cap Bon, the northernmost tip of Africa. The Carthaginians lined up with Sicily on their left and 'extending their right wing to the open sea . . . with all their ships facing the Romans' (Polyb. 1.27.3). Their tactics were intended to break through the Roman lines. This was a method they often used, sailing into the enemy ships, disrupting their formation and with their superior seamanship, outmanoeuvring them.[74] Once they had broken up the Roman line, the Carthaginians felt they had a better chance of avoiding the *corvus* by engaging the Roman ships in separate battles, giving themselves more space to operate. The Carthaginians initially succeeded in splitting up the Roman line, 'thus the whole conflict consisted of three parts and three sea-battles were going on at a wide distance from each other' (Polyb. 1.28.3). The battle was closely fought but resulted in a narrow Roman victory, with the capture of sixty-four Carthaginian ships. In addition the Carthaginians lost more than thirty ships and the Romans twenty-four.[75]

At Carthage the city walls were draped in black cloth, presenting to the world their deep mourning and the human price of this naval disaster.[76] The cost was enormous both in terms of casualties from the loss, captured ships and also the financial outlay for supplies, weapons and vessels. The demographic loss to the city and citizenship alone must have numbered tens of thousands. The Carthaginians might well have sued for peace after the succession of defeats they had suffered and some of our sources suggest they did send envoys to Rome at this time. The main history for the events however, that of Polybius, makes no mention of any peace overtures.[77]

Thus the Carthaginians did not capitulate in the face of the defeat at Ecnomus and more soldiers were recruited, more ships built. A mission to recruit troops from Greece was dispatched from Carthage. The city was seeking manpower and military advisors to help turn the tide of the war. The tenacity of the Carthaginians, especially when confronted by an invading force, provides some insight into the general characteristics of their leaders, who displayed traits usually reserved for the Romans. Protecting Carthage was of paramount importance. The use of citizens in battles for the protection of the city reflects this as well.

Carthage readied herself for the inevitable after the defeat at Ecnomus. The invasion of Agathocles had certainly not been forgotten and the Carthaginians prepared for the onslaught of another army. The two Roman consuls had regrouped their armies and then 'put to sea and continued their advance towards Africa' (Polyb. 1.29.1). The Roman force touched land at Cap Bon just as Agathocles had done over fifty years earlier and perhaps the Syracusans were there to advise their Roman allies.[78] Cap Bon is the nearest point to Sicily and the invading force proceeded south along the coast. The Romans set up base at the city of Clupea (*Aspis* in Polyb. 1.29.5–6, modern Kelibia), which has one of the few natural ports on the east side of the promontory (Map 1). We do not hear of any attempt at defending the Carthaginian countryside as the Romans plundered the 'handsome and luxuriously furnished houses'. Properties were 'ransacked, livestock confiscated and thousands captured by the Roman forces who were unchallenged'.[79] After receiving orders from Rome one consul Regulus remained on African soil while the other, Manlius Vulso, returned with the fleet to Rome carrying the plunder and prisoners they had captured (Polybius lists 20,000 slaves). Regulus was left with forty ships, 15,000 foot soldiers and 500 cavalry (Polyb.1.29.9).[80]

The material impact of the invasion is visible at the archaeological site of Kerkouane, situated between the tip of Cap Bon and Clupea. Kerkouane (its ancient name unknown) was a small Punic coastal town that produced a purple-coloured dye much coveted in the ancient world. The town is one of the few purely Punic occupation sites to have been excavated and it gives an insight into the high standard of urban living in a small town that lived off agriculture and fishing. The archaeological record shows us that Kerkouane had only just recovered from Agathocles' invasion at the end of the fourth century when the Romans under Regulus arrived. The evidence provides a more human aspect to the extensive wars between Carthage and Rome. The small population of Kerkouane lived in a well-constructed cohesive urban centre in small very well-built houses, some of which were decorated with mosaic floors and had internal plumbing and small bathtubs. The sheer number of well-constructed bathrooms in the town has led some scholars to hypothesize that a kind of ritual bathing was an important part of daily life in Punic Kerkouane. It is thought that the invasion of Regulus led to the abandonment of the town. The population was perhaps among the twenty thousand captives taken back to Rome and anyone who remained must have moved away from the exposed location on the sea. It is a beautiful site today that provides a glimpse of the destruction of the countryside during this devastating invasion.[81]

Regulus began his land campaign in the spring of 255 BCE. He moved west towards Carthage, which lay on the other side of the gulf. At the town of Adyn (perhaps the site of Uthina – just south of Tunis) he met his first Carthaginian opposition led by two generals, Bostar and Hasdrubal. The seasoned Roman commander quickly took the initiative and attacked the Carthaginian positions. Regulus was victorious and moved his forces north through the hills to take the town of Tunes (modern Tunis), which sits eighteen kilometres south of Carthage between the city and its agricultural heartland (Polyb. 1.30.4–15) (maps 1 and 3).[82]

Faced with a confident Roman army, a devastated countryside and defections of the Libyan and Numidian allies to their enemy, the Carthaginians were under a great deal of pressure. After a succession of defeats the previously hinted at peace treaty may have seemed an unpalatable necessity. A group of men from the Senate entered into negotiations with Regulus but failed to come to an agreement. Polybius claims that Regulus had insisted on such harsh demands that the Carthaginian senators were deeply offended and rejected them out of hand (1.31.7–8).

Just at this dark hour for Carthage an expedition returned from Greece with new recruits and an experienced Spartan commander named Xanthippus among them. Xanthippus was given 'authority to conduct operations as he himself thought most advantageous' by the Carthaginian Senate (Polyb. 1.33.5). The Spartan general reorganized Punic battle lines employing the elephants to maximum advantage. With his revamped Carthaginian army, Xanthippus engaged Regulus' forces on open ground. The battle ended in a complete Roman defeat.

The Spartan Xanthippus had saved the city of Carthage, and Hannibal may have studied this famous victory in his youth. It is also possible that Hannibal's father Hamilcar had fought under the Spartan general.[83] This victory was a dramatic turnaround for the Carthaginians, who now held the Roman consul captive.[84] An unexpected Carthaginian victory had again shifted the momentum of the war and it was the turn of the Romans to suffer a series of disasters.[85] Rome, upon receiving the news of Regulus' capture, prepared another fleet to 'rescue their surviving troops' in Africa who had fled back to Clupea (Polyb. 1.36.5). After picking up the survivors these ships were caught in a terrible storm while sailing along the south coast of Sicily towards Syracuse. The loss in terms of lives and ships was enormous and after the storm only eighty of over 350 Roman ships remained intact. This account of the Roman disaster would put the numbers of men lost at almost a hundred thousand and whilst these may be inflated numbers the losses were surely in the tens of thousands. Some scholars believe that the Roman innovation of the *corvus* made their ships significantly less stable in open seas and may have exacerbated the calamity.[86]

The crisis in Africa averted, the Spartan Xanthippus departed from Carthage, surely much wealthier for his endeavours. The focus of the war returned to Sicily but there the momentum again shifted back to the Romans, who rebounded from their defeat with amazing alacrity (so quickly it is 'not easy to believe', comments Polybius in 1.38.6). The fortunes of the Carthaginians fluctuated. When they lost Panormus in 254 BCE it was a significant blow. The city's deep natural harbour set on the mountainous north-west corner of Sicily had been a Phoenician/Carthaginian allied port for many centuries.[87] The Carthaginians still held the west coast ports of Drepanum and Lilybaeum but they had failed to capitalize on Roman setbacks and political infighting during this period of the war.

After the fall of Panormus magistrates at Carthage reportedly sent the captured consul Regulus to Rome 'clad as a prisoner in Punic garments'. The legend of Regulus permeates the Roman epic history of the Punic Wars and the story goes that Carthage hoped to negotiate a peace treaty or perhaps a prisoner exchange by sending the ex-consul. However, when Regulus appeared before the Senate he described a desperate financial situation at Carthage and urged the Romans never to accept a peace but to fight on until Carthage was destroyed. After this mission Regulus honoured his vow to return voluntarily to Carthage and there he was executed (or died in captivity).

There are a number of elaborate variations of the death of Regulus but the fact that Polybius makes no mention of them leads to the suspicion that they were invented by later Romans hoping to use the story to emphasize the valour of the consul in the face of perceived Carthaginian cruelty. The earliest surviving version comes in a poem by Horace (first century BCE), who imagines Regulus' last days in Rome before returning to captivity and death:

[T]o strengthen the Senate's wavering purpose,
by making of himself an example no
other man had made, and hurrying,
amid sorrowing friends, to glorious exile.

Yet he knew what the barbarian torturer
was preparing for him. Yet he pushed aside
the kinsmen who blocked his path,
and the people who delayed his going
(*Odes* 3.5)

Later Roman authors embellish the tale further, revelling in the idea of the barbarity of the Carthaginians. The legends describe how the Carthaginians put Regulus to death in a series of particularly gruesome ways. In one version his captors enclosed Regulus in a box with iron spikes and left him to die in a standing position. Even if the torture is entirely made up by Roman sources with the intention of juxtaposing the cruelty of the Carthaginians with the manly courage of the Romans, it makes for one of the lasting images of the First Punic War.[88]

The authenticity of the reports on the death of Regulus is brought further into question by a story that only appears in one later source, Diodorus Siculus. Diodorus claims that Regulus' widow was accused of the torture and murder of two Carthaginian prisoners of war in retaliation for her husband's death. So serious was the accusation that the family of Regulus was almost prosecuted in the Roman courts (24.12). Modern scholars have often wondered if the story of Regulus' torture was made up after the fact in order to rationalize the actions of his widow.

With the rejection of their peace offer, Carthage was facing further defeat and their territory had been reduced to the western edge of Sicily, again. Rome was in control of the rest of the island but the Romans in turn suffered a dramatic naval defeat in a battle off Drepanum in 249 BCE. In 247 BCE Hannibal's father Hamilcar stepped into command of the Carthaginian land forces on Sicily. The tide had been relentless and the one remaining Carthaginian base in Sicily was under a Roman blockade. Hamilcar would need to make an immediate impact if the paradigm was to shift away from the continuous defeats suffered by the Carthaginians so far. Hannibal was born that same year, when the long and bloody war was already seventeen years old. The rise of his father to military command in this epic struggle against the Romans, both practically and psychologically, would shape Hannibal's subsequent life and choices.

CHAPTER 3

# HIS FATHER'S SON

I contrasted this situation, which did not please me, with another, more in harmony with my sentiments – the scene in which Hannibal's father, Hamilcar Barcas, made his son swear before the household altar to take vengeance on the Romans. Ever since then Hannibal has had a place in my phantasies. (**Freud, *Interpretation of Dreams*, 196**)

SIGMUND FREUD IMAGINES HANNIBAL'S relationship with his father Hamilcar in his *Interpretation of Dreams*. Freud tells us that when he was at school the history of Rome and Carthage engaged him and, like many others who saw themselves as outsiders in society, he related more to the Carthaginians than the Romans.[1] Freud identified with Hannibal and dreamt of a father like Hamilcar to stand up for him against bullies. In the mid-nineteenth century the Impressionist artist Cézanne imagined in a poem how the young Hannibal would cower before his powerful father. These two paragons of modernity, Freud and Cézanne, both connected personally to Hannibal's story although they interpreted the relationship with his father differently. Both men underscore the enormous influence that Hamilcar had on Hannibal's life and the choices he made. Many historians, ancient and modern, have attributed Hannibal's actions and his war against Rome to Hamilcar's unfulfilled wishes and see in the son the dreams of the father.[2] Whilst it is questionable whether we can attribute Hannibal's actions directly to Hamilcar, his father's life and reputation are crucial for any understanding of the choices Hannibal made.

Hannibal's father was a 'young man' when he took up command in Sicily, which places him in his late twenties or early thirties.[3] This may have been the typical age in the military career of a Carthaginian to take up command of an army. Hamilcar was married at the time with three daughters and a son just born. As an elite Carthaginian general from an aristocratic family he would have identified himself with the origins of his great city. The rise to prominence for a family in Carthage may have involved being able to link back to the very roots of the city's foundation, imagined or real. A strong sense of family identity may be read in the claim that the noble 'Hamilcar, sprung from the Tyrian house of ancient Barcas' (Silius Italicus 70–77). The surname Barca meant 'lightning' or 'thunderbolt' and the link back to Tyre could be Silius Italicus' imaginative creation of a genealogy that traced the Barcids back to Dido herself. It is equally possible that the claim originated in the Barcid family's own propaganda. Connecting your family back to the original founders established a close link to Tyre and would have been a prestigious association for a family at Carthage. Thus if Hamilcar was a 'son of Tyre' the Barcid family could link their heritage to the followers of the legendary queen Dido. Little else is known about the family history other than the father and the sons and anything beyond that lies in the poetic licence of later Romans.[4]

Hamilcar was acclaimed as a brilliant and unorthodox military commander during the First Punic War. His leadership during the war and in the subsequent years both at Carthage and in Iberia was celebrated and propelled him yet further forward among the Carthaginian ruling elite. His fame spread across the wider Mediterranean. The Roman biographer Cornelius Nepos would write that 'Hamilcar and Hannibal are generally admitted to have surpassed all men of African birth in greatness of soul and sagacity' (de Regibus 5).

In 247 BCE the arrival of Hamilcar in Sicily seems to have altered the situation in the last phase of the war.[5] 'Hamilcar's campaign in Sicily against the Romans might be compared to a boxing match in which two champions, both in perfect training and both distinguished for their courage, meet to fight for a prize' (Polyb. 1.57.1). The young Hamilcar took up command in Sicily and brought innovative thinking to the Carthaginian strategy in the war. He certainly represented a new generation which had come of age during the war with Rome. After seventeen years of fighting, the young men of the Carthaginian elite had witnessed the failure of their traditional military establishment to meet the challenge presented by Rome.[6] Hamilcar set out to change the pattern of the war that, up until this point, had been entirely dictated by the Romans. He harassed and disrupted the Roman occupation of the western part of Sicily by raiding along the Italian coast and generally making the Romans less comfortable in their fight. He did not engage the Roman standing army itself but strategically attacked Roman patrols. The intent was to make the Roman hold on the west of Sicily as unstable and expensive as possible and to restore Carthaginian morale.[7]

Hamilcar's attempt to take the initiative away from the Romans and carry the fight into Italy reflects an important shift in the Carthaginian view of the war. Hitherto Carthage had fought a defensive war by trying to hold on to territory as it was pulled away piece by piece. There had, until then, been at least two efforts by Carthage to make peace with the Romans but nothing had come of them. Hamilcar's initial manoeuvres included raiding the southern Italian coastal area of Bruttium and the region of Locri (Polyb. 1.56.2–11). He continued to attack Italy and to unsettle the newly allied Roman territory in the south of the peninsula. In this way he hoped to relieve some of the pressure on Sicily by turning Roman attention back towards their Italian allies who were suffering under the attacks. It is clear that Hannibal built on this idea in his execution of the subsequent war in Italy decades later.

In Sicily Hamilcar moved to occupy the high ground at the north-west tip of the island, 'the so-called place at Heirkte' (Polyb. 1.56.3). From there he waged a guerrilla war until a key outpost overlooking the port of Panormus and part of the city of Eryx (modern Erice) were recaptured (Map 1). The strategic site of Eryx sits on the highest point in north-west Sicily and had been sacred to the goddess Astarte from the very earliest period of Phoenician settlement. The precinct of the goddess commanded views to the west and north on the western coast of Sicily and directly overlooked the key port of Drepanum (Trapani) (Polyb. 1.55.7–10). Hamilcar seized back the town of Eryx but the Romans managed to hold on to the precinct of the goddess above them. He had cut off the Roman supplies and communication lines but was also in a precarious position himself (Polyb. 1.58.2–3). A kind of stalemate ensued as both sides battled for control of the divine favour and the strategic advantage offered by this holy site (Plate 2 shows the commanding view over the west coast of Sicily from Eryx).[8]

Hamilcar's small victories and his success in clawing back territory in the west of the island had a positive psychological effect that must have restored some Carthaginian pride after a decade of humiliating defeats. Every family in Carthage would have been touched by the loss of its citizens, many thousands of whom had died or been captured and sold into slavery. All strata of the population at Carthage were committed to a war which took a deep economic and psychological toll on them. Hamilcar gained great acclaim from his command in this phase of the war. From this his popularity and influence grew at home.

These small victories could not erase the reality facing Carthage: that they were struggling to hold on to what little territory they had left in Sicily. They had wrested some control back from the Romans but the overall impression is that, despite Hamilcar's efforts on land, Carthage had reverted to a broadly defensive strategy in the last six years of the war. A disjointed approach by the navy and the army may lie at the root of the problem. There seems to have been unwillingness to form a cohesive plan, perhaps a result of infighting among the elite families in charge of the different branches of the military. Carthaginian prosperity had been built upon its fleets and the ability to control ports in the central Mediterranean. The concept of losing Sicily may once have been unthinkable to the Carthaginians but they had under-estimated the resolve of the enemy they were fighting. Although Hamilcar remained undefeated in his six years in Sicily, the Carthaginians' ability to continue to fight and to maintain the supply of their forces seems to have been coming to an end.[9]

For at least a decade the resources of the Carthaginians and the Romans had been stretched to their very limits by this debilitating war. 'Both the Romans and Carthaginians were destitute of money,' wrote Appian in about the year 252 BCE and yet the war continued for another decade (Sic. 5.1). The Carthaginians were so short of cash that they had tried and failed to borrow 2,000 talents from Ptolemy II of Egypt (1 talent = 26kg). Polybius claims that both sides' strength was paralysed and resources exhausted 'by protracted taxa-tion and expense' (1.58.9). The Roman state had turned to private finance to raise funds for the construction of a new fleet during the final phase of the war. The two sides faced not only financial depletion but also near collapse of their reserves of manpower.

The dire financial situation may be visible in the coinage minted during this period at Carthage, with its debased silver content.[10] From the Roman writer Suetonius comes an anecdote about a famous Roman woman named Claudia who came from a patrician family. As she was travelling on a litter through Rome, held up by throngs of the poor and homeless blocking her route, she remarked that it was too bad that her brother (Publius Claudius Pulcher, defeated off Drepanum in 249 BCE) could not lose another fleet so that the riff-raff would be cleared from the streets of the city (Tib. 2.3). After their defeat in the sea battle at Drepanum the Romans had been forced to draft in slaves and the urban poor to man ships near the end of the war. We have to imagine that Carthage had done the same.[11]

The end of the drawn out war came abruptly in early March 241 BCE when a Carthaginian relief fleet raised to supply the garrison at Eryx met a newly raised Roman fleet north of Levanzo, one of the Aegates Islands that lie off the west coast of Sicily (see Map 1 and Plate 2). The Carthaginian ships were laden with provisions when the Roman ships engaged them as they rounded the north tip of the island.[12] The Carthaginians ships, made less manoeuvrable by the weight of the supplies they carried, were crewed by new recruits and untrained marines (Polyb.1.61.4). They had also been taken by surprise by the appearance of this new Roman fleet. Roman maritime efforts had been severely restricted after the loss off Drepanum eight years previously. Since then the Carthaginians may have been lulled into the belief that they had, at least, won the sea war. Polybius wrote that they 'never expected the Romans to dispute the sea with them again' (1.61.5). But when, once more, the Romans did return to the sea with another fleet they surprised the Carthaginians and swiftly won the day. With 'fifty Carthaginian ships sunk and seventy captured with all their crews', the total number of prisoners may have been 10,000 (1.61.6). The surviving Carthaginian ships, aided by a favouring wind, fled back to Carthage.[13] Although this was not as dramatic a victory for the Romans as previous battles, it was the final straw for Carthage and for the garrison on the mountain at Eryx. The Roman consul sailed on to Lilybaeum. When news of the defeat reached Carthage, the walls of the city would once again have been draped in black. Hamilcar was given 'full powers to deal with the situation' and sued for a settlement (Polyb. 1.62.3).[14]

The negotiated peace that officially ended what we call the First Punic War was named after the victorious Roman consul Lutatius. The terms of the Peace of Lutatius were punitive for Carthage. After so much loss on both sides the Romans were driven to punish the Carthaginians financially, if only to repay the loans made by their own wealthy citizens. The treaty read:

> there shall be friendship between the Carthaginians and the Romans on the following terms . . . The Carthaginians shall evacuate the whole of Sicily and the islands between Italy and Africa [i.e. the Aeolian Islands, Pantelleria and Lampedusa]; they shall not make war upon Hiero, nor bear arms against the Syracusans nor their allies. The Carthaginians shall give up to the Romans all prisoners without ransom. The Carthaginians shall pay the Romans 2200 Euboean talents of silver over a period of twenty years. (**Polyb. 3.27.1–6**)

Defeat in the First Punic War severely restricted Carthaginian power and influence. The city of Carthage was cowed but Hamilcar Barca had remained undefeated in the field. The withdrawal from the long held and much coveted ports of Sicily began. It was a disaster for Carthage, the ports were now lost, the state was bankrupt and the people exhausted. The Carthaginians accepted the Roman terms and faced the humiliation of the peace. Sicily (except the territory controlled by Syracuse) became Rome's first overseas province and a stepping-stone on her way to empire.[15] Polybius' account of the First Punic War does not portray the outcome as inevitable and insists that the battles were closely fought and the naval capacity of the two powers equally matched. In Polybius' view the war could have gone either way but the Romans had the deeper resources and won with a bit of luck and smarter naval tactics. Hamilcar would return home and rise to the pinnacle of military power, setting in motion events that led to another epic struggle with Rome.[16]

The lessons learned by Carthage from their defeat in the First Punic War were absorbed by the generation who would fight the next war. Hannibal was just six years old, beginning his education and starting to formulate a concept of the city around him and of his place in that city.[17] The traditions of schooling in Carthaginian culture are unknown but we can assume that as a favoured son of an illustrious family Hannibal had an elite upbringing and was taught at home by tutors. Studies would have included military command and Greek, the language of learning in the Hellenistic Mediterranean. The impact of the loss of Sicily on Hannibal's generation of Carthaginians, brought up to be proud of their heritage and noble past, must have been profound. The war with Rome cast a long shadow over boys his age, used to regaling each other with tales of great victories and adventurous generals they had learned about. The realities of the enormous loss of life in the naval battles would have created a cohort of heroes and a deep-rooted enmity in those who lived through the events. The generation of Carthaginians who grew up in this period blamed the Romans for the First Punic War but it is equally clear that the majority of Carthaginian commanders (with the notable exceptions of Hamilcar and Xanthippus the Spartan) had not been up to the task.

These years of Hannibal's early childhood were lived during a harrowing time for the city of Carthage. For, adding to the misery of the Carthaginians, the peace with Rome brought no respite from war. Following the end of the First Punic War the next three years saw Carthage consumed with 'so serious a civil war . . . that the city was never in so great a danger except when it was destroyed' (Cornelius Nepos, *Ham.* 2.1).[18] At the conclusion of the peace in 241 BCE Hamilcar had transferred his soldiers from the mountaintop stronghold at Eryx to the port of Lilybaeum. There he resigned his command and sailed back to Carthage leaving Gisgo, the commander at Lilybaeum, the task of disbanding the army and sending the troops home (Polyb. 1.66.1). The next danger arose from within the ranks of the Carthaginian army and among its mercenary soldiers.[19]

At Lilybaeum Gisgo was left with much to do. Carthaginian power in the west of Sicily was at an end and the loss must have been intensely felt by the Punic population of the city. Families connected to both Sicily and Carthage for centuries must have been forced to give up their land, houses and identity. There would have been refugees from a population that had been under a blockade for much of the previous decade. Many may have tried to cross from Lilybaeum to Carthage, seeking a new life in the city. There is silence in the ancient sources about the non-military population but we can imagine the scenes at the port of Lilybaeum that summer.

The military population are better documented. The troops of the Carthaginians were both recruited from allied territories and hired as paid soldiers from regions unconnected to Carthage. There were Numidian horsemen who made up the cavalry and Libyan foot soldiers from neighbouring kingdoms in Africa. Others troops came from allied territories further afield such as the slingers from the Balearic Islands.[20] Additionally there were soldiers who had no connection to Carthaginian allied territory and were hired from regions renowned for producing soldiers: the Greek east, the northern Italian peninsula, or Lusitania (part of modern Portugal). Polybius specifically notes 'Iberians, some Celts, some Ligurians and some from the Balearic Islands' (1.67.7) among the mercenaries at Carthage.

Having fought and lost an exhausting and expensive war, Carthage was faced with the reality of having a large force of unpaid defeated soldiers waiting in Lilybaeum under Gisgo's command. We have already seen that the Carthaginians had a reputation for offering a high rate of pay to their mercenaries (Diodorus Sic. 16.81.4). Soldiers would have expected prompt payment in full so Hamilcar's lieutenant Gisgo planned a staggered withdrawal. The transportation of all the soldiers to Carthage together did not seem a sensible solution thus he sent them in detachments so that they could be paid and dispatched to their own lands, group by group, before discontent led to trouble (Polyb.1.66.4).[21]

As is often the case, civilian leaders at home do not share the perspective of military commanders in the field, and Carthage was no exception.[22] The Carthaginian state was in financial disarray and despite Gisgo's careful plan, the civilian leaders hoped to negotiate with the soldiers once they were

gathered together. Gisgo's advice was ignored and shiploads of mercenaries
arrived in the city. It was summer and a backlog of unpaid, discontented
soldiers clogged the streets day and night. The situation grew more unruly as
the soldiers 'committed frequent offences' and were in a 'licentious spirit'
(Polyb. 1.66.6). Gisgo's strategy of orderly demobilization was foiled.

The nineteenth-century author Gustave Flaubert picked up on Polybius'
description of these mercenary troops when he wrote his flamboyant depiction of the Carthaginian military after the First Punic War in his celebrated
novel *Salammbô* (published in 1862). 'Men of all nations were there,' Flaubert
imagined:

> Ligurians, Lusitanians, Balearians, Africans, and fugitives from Rome.
> Beside the heavy Dorian dialect were audible the resonant Celtic syllables
> rattling like chariots of war, while Ionian terminations conflicted with
> consonants of the desert as harsh as the jackal's cry. The Greek might be
> recognised by his slender figure, the Egyptian by his elevated shoulders,
> the Cantabrian by his broad calves. There were Carians proudly nodding
> their helmet plumes, Cappadocian archers displaying large flowers painted
> on their bodies with the juice of herbs, and a few Lydians in women's
> robes, dining in slippers and earrings. Others were ostentatiously daubed
> with vermilion, and resembled coral statues.[23]

Flaubert's account is purely fictional and deeply orientalist but captures an
essence of the vibrant and multicultural fighting force that gathered at
Carthage that summer of 241 BCE.

The soldiers remained unpaid and naturally suspected that Carthage was
trying to avoid paying them altogether. The situation was explosive. The
Carthaginian government persuaded the commanding officers of the various
mercenary detachments to withdraw from the city, reasoning that they would
be better supplied in the countryside. The fact that the soldiers were willing to
leave suggests that rebellion was not yet on their minds. From Carthage the
mercenaries were sent to the Libyphoenician town of Sicca, which lay 170
kilometres to the southwest (see Map 1). There they awaited their final
payment. Libyphoenician refers to the culture that developed in the Libyan-
populated regions that were controlled by Carthage and indicates a heterogeneous mix of the indigenous and Carthaginian populations (Pliny, *NH* 5.24).
The chosen destination probably reflects the fact that a majority of the mercenary soldiers were Libyphoenician or Numidian. Each man was provided with
a gold stater to cover expenses for the journey. The coin, perhaps the equiva-

lent of a Greek stater, was probably worth about four days' wages for a mercenary soldier.[24] The removal of the soldiers with what Polybius refers to as their
'baggage', the wives and children and hangers-on, must have been a relief to
the citizens of Carthage but enormously disruptive to the inhabitants of the
countryside as the soldiers made their way to Sicca (1.66.6–9).[25]

Once at Sicca the soldiers remained idle, with nothing to do but keep
drinking, ponder the amount of back pay owed and the promises made by
their generals. They were now in a hinterland that had suffered harsh treatment by Carthage during the war. The twenty-three-year conflict had brought
high levels of taxation and conscription to this important agricultural region.
The combination of a discontented local population and unpaid soldiers led
to rapidly growing fury. When Hanno, the Carthaginian commander in
Africa, arrived at Sicca he was met with a clamour of new demands. Carthage
could barely afford what was already due. The soldiers sensed they were not
going to be paid and the generals who had made promises to them in the field
were nowhere to be seen.[26]

In this atmosphere, rumour and disaffection grew to such an extent
that 20,000 soldiers left Sicca and marched back to Carthage, camping
18 kilometres south-west of the city at the town of Tunes (modern Tunis)
(Polyb. 1.67.13). At Tunes, the very large contingent of Libyans, along with an
assortment of rebellious soldiers of many different ethnicities – Iberians, Celts
and Ligurians and 'a mixture' of Greeks – could count on local support (Polyb.
1.67.10–11).[27] Negotiators from the Carthaginian Senate met the rebels at their
camp and crumbled before their demands. They acquiesced to all requests, even
as these became larger and more exorbitant by the day. The Carthaginians were
outnumbered, without resources and intimidated by the increasingly hostile
mercenaries.

Hamilcar Barca, the general who had commanded these men in Sicily, had
yet to be involved in the crisis (Polyb. 1.68.1–9). This raises the question of his
whereabouts. The ancient sources do not convincingly explain Hamilcar's
movements after he left Sicily. As he sailed from the island at the end of the war
he disappears from our view. Polybius argues that because he had promised the
mutinous soldiers so much in Sicily and since none of those promises had been
met, he was not a popular choice to placate them (1.68.12). There may be
some truth in this but as Hamilcar was the most respected general among the
troops, we might equally expect him to have been called upon at this moment.
The historian Appian mentions that Hamilcar was involved in a prosecution
for his actions in the running of the war in Sicily. Legal proceedings against
him at home may therefore have been the reason for his abrupt departure from

the field in Sicily. This may also explain why he was not given command at the beginning of the subsequent insurgency (Appian, *Ib.* 4).[28]

The Carthaginian practice of holding military commanders to strict account through trial was widely known. 'In their wars they advance their leading men to commands, taking it for granted that these should be the first to brave the danger for the whole state; but when they gain peace, they plague these same men with suits, bring false charges against them through envy, and load them down with penalties . . .' (Diodorus Sic. 20.10.2–5).[29] Although we know little about internal Punic politics and it is difficult to ascertain the motivation of the main players, there are strong indications of a real divide at this point between the government at Carthage and the generals returning from Sicily. It is highly likely that Hamilcar was defending himself against a prosecution in the courts at the beginning of the mercenary rebellion.

Eventually Gisgo, the commander from Lilybaeum, was called up to meet the rebels. On the mercenary side two leaders had emerged: Spendius, who was an ex-Roman slave from Campania, and a Libyan named Mathos. Both men were powerful voices with personal reasons for rebellion, and neither would have been inclined to come to a settlement with the Carthaginians. Spendius, as an ex-Roman slave and deserter from the Roman army, was intent on avoiding repatriation to Rome under the terms of the treaty of Lutatius. Mathos represented local discontent at the harsh conditions that had been imposed by Carthage on the Libyan homeland during war with Rome. Along with the other Libyans fighting in the rebellion, his became the voice of local independence against Carthaginian hegemony.

Gisgo's attempt at arbitration was rejected and in the ensuing turmoil he was seized and held in chains. This marks the beginning of 'open war' between the mercenary troops and the city of Carthage (Polyb. 1.70.6). A critical blow to Carthage came when the Libyan contingent sent envoys to the Libyphoenician towns across Carthaginian territory urging their cooperation in rebellion. This was the land whence they derived their taxation income, surplus food supplies and their soldiers.[30] The mercenary rebellion became an all-out revolt in the heartland of Carthage and meant that the city was 'deprived of all these resources at one blow' (Polyb 1.71.2). Carthage was now fighting a civil war.

Thus began what is often called the 'Truceless War', a term found in Polybius and elsewhere used with the sense of 'relentless'. Both concepts characterize the lawless brutality of what was to unfold in Africa (1.65.6).[31] Polybius reasons that many of the Libyan allies joined the rebels because of Carthage's system of government and taxation (1.72.1–6). The war against the

Romans over Sicily had been an extraordinary drain on the wealth and productivity of both Carthage and the towns of their African territories. Twenty-three years of naval and land warfare, and the invasion of African territory by the Romans, took their toll on the prosperity of Carthage's agricultural production and allied territories of their heartland. The taxation burden had fallen heavily on the Libyans and Libyphoenicians, whose crops were confiscated and taxation doubled with harsh penalties for those who resisted. The general Hanno had enforced the policy of heavy taxation and subjugation in Africa while Hamilcar operated in Sicily. The consequence of Hanno's policies was that the Libyan population 'required no incitement to revolt' (Polyb. 1.72.4).[32]

The Libyan leader Mathos had 70,000 troops with him and began the war with a multi-pronged attack in the spring of 240 BCE.[33] Carthaginian-allied cities to the north, Utica and Hippo Acra (modern Bizerte), were laid under siege while the main rebel camp at Tunes cut Carthage off from the rest of the countryside by blocking access to the peninsula (see Map 3). The Carthaginians were trapped behind their walls with very few supporters able or willing to supply help for the city. The rebels were seasoned soldiers 'schooled in the daring tactics of the Barcids' and Hanno, sent out to relieve the siege, was no match for them (Polyb. 1.74.9).

When Hanno's preliminary headway against the rebels quickly gave way to disaster, a change of leadership was called for. Polybius' criticism of Hanno is harsh: 'he had no idea how to avail himself of opportunities and generally showed an entire lack of experience and energy'. Hanno is described as 'heedless and lacking judgement' and without any creativity he was limited to charging the enemy camp with 'his strong force of elephants'. More criticism focused on his lack of ability to capitalize on any success. When Hanno proved incapable of dealing with the rebel army, Hamilcar Barca was brought back to a position of command (1.74.2–4).

The demolition of Hanno's reputation should be read with caution as it reflects Polybius' extremely pro-Barcid bias in this section of his narrative.[34] Nonetheless, the result of Hanno's failure to tackle the rebel army was that Hamilcar, once again, became the saviour of the Carthaginian military effort. Hamilcar did not replace Hanno but joined him in command with a newly recruited army. Reports of this force depict a motley crew. Hamilcar was given 'seventy elephants, all the additional mercenaries they had been able to collect and the deserters from the enemy, besides their citizen forces, horse and foot, so that in all he had about 10,000 men' (Polyb. 1.75.2–3). He immediately lured the mercenary army into an ambush and his quick success 'restored some confidence and courage' among the Carthaginians (1.76.1–9, 11). The mercenaries, however, did not retreat and proceeded to encircle Hamilcar's army while he was encamped on a plateau (Polyb. 1.77.6–7).

The timely arrival in Hamilcar's camp of the Numidian prince Naravas of the Massyli changed the momentum and proved a key event in the campaign. The Massyli, the Masaesyli and the Mauri were the distinct Numidian peoples who occupied the area of North Africa westward from Carthaginian territory to the Atlantic in the third century.[35] The family of Naravas had traditionally allied with Carthage and he was particularly interested in 'the friendship of Barcas'.[36] Polybius emphasizes that Naravas wanted to serve under Hamilcar personally (1.78.1–9). Hamilcar certainly welcomed the 2,000 highly skilled cavalry into his army at that critical moment. Naravas' allegiance was so significant that Hamilcar promised his daughter in marriage to the prince if he remained loyal to Carthage. All of Hannibal's sisters were married off in order to secure key political alliances and their links give us some insight into the importance of the Numidian alliance that Naravas offered. Hamilcar personally was able to command such allegiance among local leaders and their troops. His reputation and prestige maintained this alliance that would play a key role in his military conquests and in Hannibal's later successes.[37]

Naravas and his cavalry made an immediate impact on the war. In their first battle they played an essential part in the victory that saw 10,000 enemy troops killed.[38] With cavalry, elephants and foot soldiers, the Carthaginian military redeemed themselves under Hamilcar's command. They regained authority in the region and the loyalty of some of the Numidian and Libyan troops. Captives were treated leniently. They were offered a place in Hamilcar's army or freedom (with an oath not to take up arms against Carthage). This intelligent policy aimed at undermining the rebels' support would turn out to be the beginning of the long fight for the restitution of Carthaginian power in their Libyan heartland (Polyb.1.78.9–15).

The Libyan rebel army, however, was not easily defeated, being determined, powerful and well organized. Polybius dismisses them as brigands and uncivilized barbarians fighting to overthrow the 'civilized' forces of Carthage. The idea of Libyan independence was embraced broadly across the territory and it was not the first time that the local population had risen up to support an army hostile to Carthage. When Agathocles invaded Africa in *c.* 310 BCE he counted on the support of 'the Libyan allies of the Carthaginians, who had for a long time resented their exactions'. Agathocles had correctly predicted they 'would grasp any opportunity for revolt' (Diodorus Sic. 20.3.3).

The political overtones of Libyan independence during the insurgency of 241–237 BCE were clearly expressed in the coinage minted by the mercenary troops. The rebels produced coinage in the name of an independent Libya. Whilst these coins were re-struck on Carthaginian issues and stylistically based on Carthaginian prototypes, some of them convey a strong political message of independence in their imagery and legends. Particularly noteworthy are the silver shekel and half-shekel that bear the symbol of the lion and the legend LIBYA, in a Greek script. Perhaps we can view these coins used to pay the rebel soldiers as a call to arms for the local population. The production of Libyan coinage can be seen to demonstrate an interest in political legitimacy and local identity as an alternative to Carthaginian hegemony.[39]

The flame of rebellion spread to the Carthaginian settlements on the island of Sardinia.[40] At some point in 240/239 BCE and 'in emulation' of the revolt of Mathos and Spendius, one insurgency led to another (Polyb. 1.79.1).[41] The garrisons on Sardinia had surely gone unpaid, given the situation at Carthage. Another commander named Hanno was sent with a newly raised army to re-garrison the island but on arrival these new troops promptly joined the rebels. The rebellious Sardinian troops crucified Hanno and set about torturing and murdering all the Carthaginians on the island (Polyb. 1.79.4). Carthage was powerless to respond; already engaged in a fierce fight for Africa, Sardinia was a battle too far.

The Mercenary War started in 241 BCE and lasted until the end of 238 BCE but the duration of its separate phases is not clear.[42] Despite the detailed narrative preserved in Polybius, the chronology is difficult to pin down. It is clear that an extremely violent conflict developed, with escalating atrocities committed on both sides. Polybius describes a scene where Autaritus, a Gaulish leader, addressed an assembly of troops and argued for the execution of all their prisoners (Polyb. 1.80.6). The intention was to push the soldiers beyond any kind of possible reconciliation with the Carthaginian authorities. The leaders wanted to make sure there would be no surrender and 'they set themselves to devise some infamous crime which would make the hatred of the troops for Carthage more savage' (Polyb. 1.79.8). The decision was not unanimous and certain insurgents spoke against the executions but in the end they were carried out. The rebels set upon their captives, including the general Gisgo. First they cut off their hands then their 'other extremities too and after this mutilation and breaking their legs' finally threw the captives, still alive, into a ditch (Polyb. 1.80.13).[43]

The rebels swore an oath committing them to torture and kill every Carthaginian they came across and to cut the hands off every ally of Carthage. Seven hundred hostages were executed. The rebel commanders must have known they would receive no clemency from Carthage after these acts and that the war would not be settled by negotiation. The extreme treatment of their prisoners may have been designed to deter the rebel soldiers from deserting to Carthage now that Hamilcar, popular and charismatic, was in charge and had the upper hand.[44] Hamilcar responded in kind to the violent treatment of prisoners: shifting from his initial policy of leniency towards his captives, he began retaliatory executions. Those prisoners he had taken in the field and those brought to him as captives were 'put to the sword . . . or thrown to the elephants' (Polyb. 1.82.2). There would be no mercy on either side.

Hamilcar and Hanno who had been commanding two separate armies came together to avenge Gisgo and the other victims of the executions (1.81.1–2). Polybius makes much of the two generals joining forces, uniting their armies and then quarrelling 'so seriously that the Carthaginians ordered one of the two to leave his post' (1.82.3–6). The choice of which commander they preferred was left with the troops. When the preference of the soldiers was Hamilcar, Hanno retired from the battleground but not from the political landscape. He would remain an implacable enemy of the Barcid clan through the next decades of their supremacy.[45] The citizens of Carthage sent out another general to work under Hamilcar, who now commanded one unified army (Polyb. 1.82.12).

This disagreement in the field would have serious repercussions for Hannibal in future years. The figures of Hamilcar and Hanno may well have represented two sides in an internal political struggle at Carthage.[46] Both Polybius and Livy mention divisions between political factions at Carthage throughout the history of the Punic Wars but little specific detail is given. The theory of factions based on populist versus traditionalist elements in the Carthaginian government has developed in modern scholarship based on the ancient writers, but equally these factions may simply represent different extended familial groups vying for power. The long-standing animosity between the Barcids and the faction led by Hanno would result in a disjointed policy that was to have a direct impact on Hannibal's ability to sustain his efforts in the subsequent war.

As the fighting continued, both good and bad 'fortune' plagued the Carthaginians. A storm destroyed a supply fleet coming to Carthage's aid from allied cities along the coastal stretch south and east of Carthage (Polyb. 1.82.6 – called the *Emporia*: see Map 2).[47] Then another blow fell when Hippo Acra and Utica defected to the enemy. These cities had been the only centres to remain loyal to Carthage in their northern coastal region. After long being under pressure from the rebels, the citizens slaughtered their garrison of soldiers and threw the bodies from the city walls. Mathos and Spendius, the leaders of the rebellion, emboldened by the events at Utica, moved on to lay siege to Carthage.

Just how close Carthage came to defeat is perhaps best seen in the reactions of Carthage's enemies, Syracuse and Rome. Cut off by land from all its resources, supplies had to arrive by sea. Carthage was forced to 'resort to an appeal to the states in alliance . . .' (Polyb. 1.83.1). It is telling that in this moment of need Syracuse came to the aid of Carthage but Rome's reaction was more ambiguous. The Syracusan king Hiero was most helpful and 'prompt in meeting requests'. Polybius reasoned that it was very much in his own interest to do so, for Hiero understood that the demise of Carthage would only favour Roman hegemony and Syracuse would be the loser if Rome were to become supreme (1.83.3–5).

The Roman reaction to the plight of Carthage is more equivocal. When the Carthaginians 'captured at sea, traders coming from Italy to Libya with supplies for the enemy' it implies that Rome was providing for the rebels (Polyb. 1.83.7). Up to 500 prisoners were taken to Carthage and in the negotiations that followed the Romans agreed to return to Carthage all the remaining captives from the Sicilian war, numbering some 2,743, according to the Roman tradition.[48] After this, Rome's merchant ships began to supply Carthage in accordance with the treaty that ended the First Punic War. It is clear that Rome's first instinct was to help the rebellious mercenaries, an action that betrays Roman intentions towards Carthage. Despite the terms of the treaty they would take any opportunity to damage their enemy.

By 238 BCE the war seemed to be drawing to a close but hostilities rumbled on. Hamilcar had besieged the besiegers, trapping them between Carthage and his army (Polyb. 1.84.1). The fighting continued, with the Libyan soldiers shadowing Hamilcar's army, not engaging in battle but laying ambushes and traps by anticipating the movement of his troops. This was a tactic the Roman general Fabius Maximus Cunctator (the delayer) would use against Hannibal in the Second Punic War. Polybius' hero Hamilcar was able to overcome these tactics by cutting off and isolating groups of the Libyans. When he finally confronted Spendius and his army, they were trapped and 'did not dare risk a battle nor were they able to escape' (1.84.11). Hamilcar surrounded and then starved the rebels. The gruesome violence of the war continued with the Libyans forced to cannibalize their captives and their slaves before finally giving themselves up to the enemy. Yet this capitulation did not end the war.

The Libyan leaders including Spendius, the Gaul Autaritus and eight others surrendered to Hamilcar 'to discuss terms . . . near the place called the Saw' (Polyb.1.85.7).[49] Modern historians have identified the location as near

Zaghouan, about 40 kilometres south of Tunis and 20 kilometres west of modern Hammamet (perhaps at Djebel Djedidi) near a ridge of hills called Djebel es Serra. The agreement was that the Carthaginians could choose any ten of the rebels as prisoners and the rest of their army would go free. Hamilcar then chose the ten envoys he was negotiating with as his prisoners. To the soldiers in the camp it seemed as if their own leaders had betrayed them by coming to terms with Hamilcar. As news of the deal reached the soldiers they refused to accept the conditions, fearing a trap. They once more took up their arms. Hamilcar surrounded and destroyed them.[50]

With Mathos' army still at Tunes the war was not quite over. Hamilcar first secured the countryside then re-established control over lost regions and finally laid siege to the remaining rebel forces. The city of Tunes was surrounded, with Hamilcar to the south and a general named Hannibal to the north, the side that faced Carthage. The ten Libyan leaders whom Hamilcar had taken prisoner at the 'Saw' were crucified just outside the walls of the town. Despite these public executions Mathos was not persuaded to surrender, surely seeing his own fate below him along the city walls. In desperation he turned and attacked Hannibal's army to the north. Mathos managed to capture the commander Hannibal and drive the Carthaginians out of their own camp. In revenge Mathos then took his newly captured prisoners to the location of his comrades' execution. He removed Spendius from his cross and there crucified the Carthaginian commander Hannibal in retaliation (Polyb. 1.86.4–6).[51]

The rebellion continued through the year 238 BCE. A complete mobilization occurred at Carthage with all citizens of military age conscripted into the fight and the previously dismissed commander Hanno returned to the field. When the army of Carthage was finally victorious the entire force of rebel Libyans had either been killed in battle or re-engaged as allies. It had been an exhausting struggle, but Hamilcar is given credit both for the victory and for expanding Carthaginian territory in Africa in the aftermath. He 'extended the Carthaginian frontiers, and brought about such a state of peace all over Africa as to make it seem that there had been no war there for many years' (Cornelius Nepos, *Ham.* 2.5). The scars left on the countryside and at Carthage must have run deep but history has preserved the reputation of Hamilcar and not the suffering of the Libyans. Thus Carthage moved from the brink of disaster to a position of strength in Africa over the 'three years and four months' of the rebellion (Polyb. 1.88.7).[52]

The relief of final victory must have been immense for the Carthaginians but there was a bitter note at the very end of the war. Just as Carthage was preparing to finish off the rebellion by reinstating its military presence in Sardinia, the Romans seized the island. At first Rome had refused to get involved in the rebellion in Sardinia as it was legally recognized as Carthaginian territory. Subsequently, the Romans changed their policy and at the end of the Mercenary War (238/237 BCE) accepted an invitation from the rebels on the island. Carthage voiced objections to the Romans, stating that its sovereignty over Sardinia had been agreed in the Peace of Lutatius. The Romans decided to challenge Carthage on this matter and, as Livy says, 'the Romans tricked the Carthaginians into the loss of Sardinia' (21.1.5).[53]

Rome used the pretext of Carthaginian preparations against Sardinia to declare war, claiming falsely that Carthage was gathering an army together to attack Rome and not to reclaim Sardinia. The Carthaginians were deeply embittered by this betrayal but were not yet able to embark on another war with Rome. They were left with no choice but to yield to the new demands. The Romans must have anticipated this and Sardinia was ceded to them. Carthage even agreed to pay an additional indemnity of 1,200 talents to Rome to avoid a conflict.[54]

The Romans justified their actions by arguing that Sardinia lay in close proximity to the Italian coast, which meant that the island could be used as a launching pad for any future attack on Rome. It seems that in the Roman view the hostilities between the two states were far from over. To the Carthaginians the Roman seizure of Sardinia was a great betrayal, a humiliation and a cynical move at a time of great hardship. Even Polybius' assessment is critical of the Romans at this juncture. He claims the taking of Sardinia as one of the chief causes of the Second Punic War and referred to it as 'theft' (Polyb. 3.30.4).

The descriptive account of the Mercenary War in Polybius is unprecedented in its detail of violence, torture and barbarity. It was a war that 'far excelled all wars we know of in cruelty and defiance of principle'. The last scene of the war was 'a triumphal procession of young men leading Mathos through the town and inflicting all kinds of torture on him' (Polyb. 1.88.6–7). The cruelty of the Carthaginians and the Libyans emphasizes the bloody and uncivilized aspects of the conflict. Hamilcar is the main protagonist in a story with many antagonists – the Libyan rebels, the hostile Carthaginian opposition and the Romans. This tale above all paints a picture of the Libyan and mercenary soldiers as dangerous, lawless, extremely cruel and violent. They are portrayed as barbarians wanting to overthrow a civilized power. Any legitimate concerns that the Libyans had against Carthaginian hegemony in Africa are swept away by Polybius in the narrative of Hamilcar's supremacy.[55]

The story of the Mercenary War is more than just a tale by Polybius to warn his readers about mercenary soldiers. It portrays the rise of Hamilcar and the powerful impact that Carthage's neighbours would have on its history. The crucial mistakes that Carthage made during the years of this civil war are laid bare (1.88.8–12). Polybius' historical interest in cause and effect has given us a close view of an ancient civil conflict and important insights into Carthaginian struggles against the Libyan uprising.[56] The tales of the war illuminate the proximity of Carthage and her neighbours. From the time of the foundation of Carthage, the Tyrians had intermarried with the indigenous peoples of North Africa.[57] Hamilcar learned key lessons about sustaining an army of loyal Libyan, Libyphoenician and Numidian troops. For the Barcid family military success would be connected to personal alliances with the neighbouring peoples in North Africa.[58] The period of Hamilcar's rise to power sees a corresponding rise of important political and military figures in the Numidian kingdoms.[59]

The events of these years shaped Hannibal's approach to military conquest, cooperation and alliance. With violence and the threat of destruction close at hand, equally dangerous had been the treachery of the Romans. Hannibal learned the lessons of these crucial events; especially the importance of the personal loyalties of soldiers, of never trusting the Romans, the fickle nature of the politics of the Carthaginian Republic, and how politicians could betray a general in the field.[60] Once the dust had settled at Carthage the loss of Sardinia sent the Carthaginians in search of further territory in the Mediterranean. Hamilcar, hero of Carthage, subdued great swathes of land in Africa before he went off to Iberia and took his young son Hannibal with him (Polyb. 2.1.5). From there arose the next conflict with Rome.

# CHAPTER 4

# BARCID IBERIA FROM GADES
# TO SAGUNTUM

My father Hamilcar, when I was a small boy not more than nine years old, just as he was setting out from Carthage to Spain as commander-in-chief, offered up victims to Jupiter, Greatest and Best of gods. (**Cornelius Nepos,** *Hannibal* **2.3–4)**[1]

I N THE SUMMER OF 237 BCE Hannibal left Carthage with his father. He was nine years old and would not return to the city until 202 BCE as a forty-five-year-old man.[2] Hamilcar's departure to Iberia (modern Spain and Portugal) was celebrated with rituals and offerings to the gods. After the disasters of the previous decades, the renewal of prosperity at Carthage relied on the acquisition of new territory, new ports, and Hamilcar sought divine backing for his expedition. Among the citizens of Carthage there may have been a renewed sense of continuity and stability as people looked to the future. Hannibal recalled the sombre moment when his father stood and offered a sacrifice to the god Ba'al before he set off on this new endeavour. 'Hamilcar poured a libation to the gods and performed all the customary rites' and then, since 'the omens were favourable', he beckoned to his nine-year-old son Hannibal to approach. The scene was set in front of an altar covered with the bloodied remains of the sacrifice, which in the Punic tradition meant the head of a cow.[3] Hamilcar turned to his eldest son and asked if he wanted to join him on the expedition. The boy Hannibal 'accepted with delight' and at that moment Hamilcar took him 'by the hand, led him up to the altar and bade him to lay his hand upon the sacrificial victim'. In front of the gods Hannibal had to swear an oath 'never to be a friend of the Romans' (Polyb. 3.11.5–7).[4] For Livy the story of the Second Punic War began here at the moment of departure, with the oath of enmity that Hannibal swore against Rome (21.1.4–5). In reality the nine-year-old Hannibal was more likely to have been enthralled by the idea of accompanying his father than bothered about an oath. Hamilcar, celebrated as the saviour of Carthage, was taking his son on a great adventure.

The account of the oath at the beginning of the Iberian campaigns is one of the most repeated from Hannibal's life.[5] It is also one of the few anecdotes that may have come from the mouth of Hannibal himself. The oath captures the Roman view of the motivation for Hannibal's invasion of Italy. Early modern European art embraced the scene and there are many interpretations, especially from the seventeenth and eighteenth centuries that depict the innocent young boy, overshadowed by the altar and bloody sacrifice, towered over by his father and also the figure of a great deity. The use of the oath story was commonplace enough to extend to political satire in late eighteenth-century Britain, with the imagery being evoked to portray the Duke of Bedford as a contemporary Hannibal (Figs 3 and 4).

In the eyes of the Romans, the hostility of Hamilcar was passed on to his son and this drove Hannibal's actions. The Roman writers of the Empire looking back on the history of the Punic Wars would make this hostility profound and personal.[6] Valerius Maximus, who wrote during the reign of the emperor Tiberius, related a story of Hamilcar who, watching his three sons playing together, declared 'these are the lion cubs I am rearing for the destruction of Rome' (9.3. ext.2). We are also told that from his earliest boyhood, 'he [Hannibal] had been trained to fight against the Romans' (Zonaras 8.21). This reflects how Roman imperial memory looked back to the time of Rome's rise to power, when the city flourished on the traditional values of the Republic.[7] For the Romans, the more profound the hatred felt by the Carthaginians – and by Hamilcar and Hannibal personally – the greater was Rome's triumph. It also made it easier for them to justify the eventual destruction of Carthage and her culture. Thus the emphasis on the hatred of Hamilcar and Hannibal became a literary construct. There is little reason to doubt that the Barcids and many other Carthaginians were suspicious of Rome; however, we should not see this as the driving force behind their subsequent conquests.[8]

When the correct religious observances had been carried out and fruitful omens observed Hamilcar left Carthage. It was the summer of 237 BCE. He had with him an army recruited for conquest and his mission was that of 'subjugating Iberia to the Carthaginians' (Polyb. 2.1.5–7).[9] It is difficult to define Hamilcar's exact role as the Carthaginian context in itself is unclear, but he has been compared to a Roman proconsul given an army to command and land to conquer.[10] The Iberian peninsula was to be his challenge and Hamilcar's mandate was the acquisition of territory for Carthage's benefit. Six years later (in 231 BCE), when he met a Roman delegation sent out to investigate Carthaginian power in Iberia, Hamilcar explained to the Romans why Carthage had been forced into the region: they had gone to acquire new territory to pay off their war debt (Cassius Dio, frag. 48). The debt, he might have added, which the Romans had unjustly increased after they had seized Sardinia.[11]

Following his success against the mercenaries Hamilcar had emerged as a dominant figure at Carthage and his supporters must have controlled the council and the people's assembly. How much opposition existed to Hamilcar and his son's subsequent policies is a matter of some debate.[12] Resistance to Hamilcar's Iberian expedition from within the Carthaginian elite is articulated through Hanno, the general outshone by Hamilcar in the Mercenary War. Hanno's was the voice of opposition to the Barcid policies and he led an anti-Barcid faction through the whole period of their dominance. In 238/237 BCE Hanno argued for a policy that would see Carthage consolidate its African power base in the aftermath of the mercenary rebellion.[13]

The Carthaginian conquest of Iberia and the creation of this new province set in motion a chain of events that culminated in the start of the Second Punic War and Hannibal's invasion of Italy. In the twenty years between the two Punic Wars Carthaginian influence in the far west of the Mediterranean grew while Roman interests expanded into their neighbouring territories. Both states were expansive in their outlook and involved in increasing their wealth and influence at the expense of their neighbours. The geopolitical implications for those caught in the middle meant that their option was either to choose sides or play one power off against the other. The events during these decades would draw Rome and Carthage again into another war that would engulf the whole of the western Mediterranean.[14]

The expedition set out from Carthage and crossed to Iberia at the Pillars of Herakles, the closest point between Africa and Europe. They landed at the ancient city of Gades (Gadir/Cadiz) on the Atlantic coast.[15] Gades, in the literary tradition, was the oldest Phoenician settlement in the western Mediterranean and situated on a series of islands in the estuary of the river Guadelete (Map 2).[16] Long a prosperous city, it shared a language and culture of origin with Carthage and it is thought that the two centres had been closely allied before Hamilcar's arrival in the 230s.[17] Gades was a pilgrimage city in the ancient world and intimately connected with the worship of the Phoenician god Melqart, whose great sanctuary and temple occupied one of the islands in the estuary and drew worshippers from across the Mediterranean. Early in the colonization of the western Mediterranean the Phoenician/Punic god Melqart was syncretized with the Greek Herakles and the annual spring festival of renewal at the temple at Gades was frequented by many cultures. As an adult, Hannibal considered this Melqart/Herakles his personal patron god, the all-conquering hero of the western Mediterranean. The worship of Melqart was also an important link between Gades, Tyre and Carthage. It is not unreasonable to assume that Hamilcar would have called upon the deity when he arrived at Gades for support in his upcoming campaign. A 'son of Tyre' bringing the power of Carthage to Iberia would have expected to make a pilgrimage to Melqart's temple, just as his own son would do almost two decades later before his march into Italy.[18]

Gades was the closest port to the mineral-rich region known in the Hebrew Bible as Tarshish, in Greek as Tartessos and occupied by the Turdetani people. The motivation for the expedition to this region of Iberia is easily understood, given the fiscal difficulties at Carthage after the wars.[19] Control over the area, inland from Gades, was a driving force behind the Barcid campaigns in Iberia and, similarly, the later Roman conquest. In the third century southern Iberia was a mix of old Phoenician (and some Greek) coastal colonial settlements with Iberian and Celtiberian (name for the mixed zone between Celtic and Iberian) peoples living in inland urban settlements. The main regions that attracted the Carthaginian conquest were the Atlantic corner of Gades, inland along the river Baetis (Guadalquivir) and to the east along the coast through modern Andalucía into the region of modern Valencia (see Map 2). The area held great potential for the exploitation of its natural resources and agricultural land, whilst the people were not politically unified but divided into a myriad of kingdoms. Carthage had long employed Iberian soldiers in its armies and there may well have been personal connections between the Barcid leadership and certain peoples in the region.[20]

The situation on the ground made for fertile conquest and Hamilcar set about winning an empire using Gades as his base. Cornelius Nepos summed up Hamilcar's tenure: 'after crossing the sea and coming into Spain, [he] did great deeds through the favour of fortune. He subdued mighty and warlike nations and enriched all Africa with horses, arms, men and money' (*Ham.* 4.1). Hamilcar made a great name for himself in Iberia, conquering the warlike Iberians and carving a power base out of the southern hinterland of the peninsula. His original army may have numbered 20,000 but with conquest came further recruits so that a decade later the Carthaginian army in Iberia had more than doubled in size to 56,000.[21]

From 237 BCE to 229 BCE Hannibal grew from a boy to a young man while Hamilcar constructed a Carthaginian empire in Iberia. He came of age at his father's side studying and learning, along with his two younger brothers Hasdrubal and Mago. The three boys were nurtured under the tutelage of Hamilcar and his lieutenants, absorbing the arts of war from a young age (Zonaras 8.21).[22] Brought up in camp, the boys would have learned to ride and fight on horseback, and taken lessons in military strategy and command. Tutors were employed to teach them more traditional skills and we know that a Spartan named Sosylus was later named as one of Hannibal's teachers of Greek (Cornelius Nepos, *Hann.* 13.3). Sosylus, as Hannibal's tutor in political affairs, leadership and language, also influenced how he was portrayed by posterity.[23] As conquest turned to consolidation, Hamilcar's reputation and support at Carthage rose along with his successes in the field. The expectations placed on his sons, especially the eldest, Hannibal, must have increased with each success. Hamilcar brought his sons up to rule his newly acquired territory and to conquer.

Hamilcar's approach to military conquest was straightforward. Towns and cities could choose to submit to the power of the Barcid general and be treated with relative clemency but if they decided to oppose then the consequences were harsh. In one passage Diodorus (25.10.1–3) claims that Hamilcar made war on various Iberian and Celtic tribes (including Tartessi) and destroyed their whole army, then '. . . he took over and enrolled the three thousand survivors in his own army'. Diodorus goes on to relate the story of Indortes, who raised an army to resist Hamilcar and was tortured and crucified. Hamilcar then released Indortes' army and incorporated many of the soldiers into his own force. He used the policy of the carrot and the stick.[24] This process was repeated over and over until there was a significant territorial base for the Carthaginians. Control over this territory relied very much on the personal prestige of Hamilcar Barca.

Hamilcar's route to a Carthaginian province in Iberia went from establishing control to consolidation of the territory gained. Thus 'after bringing many cities throughout Iberia under his dominion, he founded an important city . . . named Acra Leuka' (Diodorus Sic. 25.10.3). This model of conquest followed the example set by Hellenistic monarchs whose acquisition of territory was accompanied by the foundation of new cities.[25] Akra Leuka, which means the White Fort or the White Cape in Greek, is often identified as the modern city of Alicante because of the specific geography of the coast. There is almost no material evidence for the city and Diodorus is the only source to mention the foundation. Many arguments against its location at Alicante are convincing, especially that no Punic remains have been uncovered at the ancient site there. The sparse evidence leaves the location and even existence of Hamilcar's city open to question and exemplifies the problems with our sources for this period.[26]

The Romans kept a wary eye on expanding Carthaginian territorial hegemony to their west. They were surely informed of events by their close allies the Massalians (from Marseilles) whose view from the mouth of the Rhône was geographically closer to the action in Iberia. The Massalians may have been nervous about Carthaginian control expanding in their direction but during the period of Hamilcar's conquests, the Romans were busy consolidating their power base elsewhere. Rome was committed to an attempt to control Illyrian piracy (c. 230/229 BCE) across the Adriatic Sea from Italy and to dealing with the Gauls in the north of the Italian peninsula (the Po valley) (Polyb. 2.2.1–4). It is in this context that the late Roman historian Cassius Dio (frag. 48) mentions Roman envoys sent to Hamilcar in 231 BCE. The veracity of the event is questioned because Dio is the only source to make reference to it. However, the brief account maintains that the Romans sent a delegation to 'investigate' Hamilcar. This official Roman visit to the Carthaginians in Iberia preceded an invasion of Illyria with 'both consuls involved, a land army and an armada of 200 ships' (Polyb. 2.11.1).[27] The intention of the Roman delegation to Hamilcar may have been to secure all other frontiers before committing Rome to a large military excursion. Even more relevant may be that the final instalment of war indemnity from Carthage, the end of the ten-year period after the First Punic War, would have coincided with the visit of Roman envoys to Hamilcar.[28]

The delegation took the form of an official embassy. When the two sides met, Hamilcar told the Romans that their 'theft' of Sardinia (in 238 BCE) and imposition of increased payments on Carthage had left him with no other choice but extension into other spheres. If a true representation of the event, this illustrates the Roman perception of Carthaginian Iberia as a potential threat a decade before Hannibal. The meeting implies that tensions between the two states simmered beneath the surface during the inter-war period. Hamilcar's powerful position at Carthage may also have raised Roman interest in meeting the man. His growing influence became more apparent when a rebellion broke out in North Africa among the Numidians. Hamilcar sent Hasdrubal, his son-in-law, to deal with the revolt. Policy at Carthage was being influenced both in terms of financial and military support by Barcid Iberia.[29]

Some two years after the supposed embassy, in the winter of 229–228 BCE, Hamilcar was killed. Many ancient authors record what Livy refers to as

Hamilcar's 'timely death' (21.1.1) and there are different versions of the events. Diodorus' romantic explanation is often cited: he tells us that Hamilcar, laying siege to a city called Helice, fell victim to trickery by a local king who had at first pretended to be friendly and then launched an attack.[30] The heroic Hamilcar, with his army routed, and in order to save his two elder sons (Hannibal and Hasdrubal), single-handedly diverted the hostile troops from his army and plunged into a deep river on horseback. 'He perished in the flood under his steed' but his sons were saved (25.10.4). Polybius only tells us he died 'bravely in a battle against one of the most warlike and powerful tribes' (2.1.8), whilst Cornelius Nepos says that 'he fell in battle fighting against the Vettones', a tribe located in the vicinity of modern Toledo (*Ham.* 4.2).[31]

Hamilcar had been a 'young man' (Cornelius Nepos, *Ham.* 1.1) when he took up his command in Sicily in the First Punic War (247 BCE) and at his death he could have been anywhere between his mid-forties to mid-fifties.[32] He is described as 'the general who must be acknowledged as the greatest on either side, both in daring and in genius . . .' and even in defeat Hamilcar was the undisputed star of the First Punic War (Polyb. 1.64.6). A Punic di-shekel minted with silver from the Iberian mines conquered by Hamilcar shows a stern, bearded face, with sharp features and a heavy brow (Plate 5).[33] The figure is certainly meant to represent the Carthaginian god Melqart in the guise of Herakles but this bearded portrait of a mature version of the god may also show attributes similar to those of Hamilcar. Whilst this is a precarious assumption, there is every reason to believe that his sons wanted him to be remembered as the embodiment of the legendary hero.

Hamilcar was one of the most dynamic characters and successful military commanders of the mid-third century. In the life of his eldest son, Hamilcar was a towering influence and heroic figure. Hannibal would have learned at his side, fighting with him, watching and understanding the politics and strategic approach as he set out to subdue Iberia. It was truly an apprenticeship in the realities of the life that Hannibal and his younger brothers, Hasdrubal and Mago, were brought up to live. This would have been especially poignant to the two elders boys when their heroic father was killed before their eyes on campaign.[34]

After Hamilcar's death, the assembly at Carthage 'handed over command of the army to Hasdrubal his son-in-law and chief naval officer (*trierarch*)' (Polyb. 2.1.9). Hasdrubal, known as 'the fair', was a man who evoked a great deal of hostile comment from many of our ancient sources without any substantial detail provided. The connection between Hamilcar and Hasdrubal went back at least as far as 241 BCE. Appian's chronologically confused account of the events at the end of the First Punic War tells us that Hamilcar 'was brought to trial . . . by his enemies for the handling of events in the war', and he was able to avoid punishment because he 'secured the favour of the chief men of the state'. Among the chief men of the state who backed Hamilcar was Hasdrubal, 'who had married Barca's daughter' (Appian, *Ib.* 4).[35] Hamilcar had three daughters that we know of and the girls, whose names are not known, were all married to form strategic alliances (see Family Tree). Hamilcar had linked himself through the marriage of his daughters with leading Carthaginian politicians and to Prince Naravas who belonged to powerful Numidian royalty.[36] Hasdrubal, his successor, was both an important political ally and a member of the Barcid family through marriage. He was a natural successor to Hamilcar in Iberia. Hannibal, at only eighteen years old, was considered too young to succeed his father.

The Roman historians have left us with an interesting but opaque view of Hasdrubal's character. He seems to have been a kind of fixer and is accused of purchasing much of his political power at Carthage through bribes and influence in the popular assembly (Cornelius Nepos, *Ham.* 3.3). Politically he relied on the support of the assembly at Carthage, and Livy claims that Hasdrubal was made leader in Iberia against 'the wishes of the Carthaginian establishment' (21.2.4). Livy then goes even further and undermines Hasdrubal's character by suggesting that he and Hamilcar had more than just a familial relationship. 'Hasdrubal had initially attracted Hamilcar's interest, *they say*, by his youthful good looks,' claims Livy with heavy innuendo. The implication that Hasdrubal was a passive recipient of Hamilcar's attentions was intended to undermine his masculinity and therefore his character and integrity.[37] We do know that Hasdrubal had been back and forth between Carthage and Iberia during Hamilcar's tenure and was his trusted lieutenant and son-in-law. He had been sent by Hamilcar to put down a rebellion in Numidia with troops from Iberia and his role was perhaps as the face of Barcid political power in Carthage itself (Diodorus Sic. 25.10.3). This political role and his willingness to force pro-Barcid decisions through the assembly at Carthage might explain his negative reputation in the sources.

At eighteen, Hannibal now took on a more active role as lieutenant to Hasdrubal, commanding a unit of cavalry. When he first appears in Livy he is a brave captain serving as an apprentice to his brother-in-law. 'The older soldiers thought that a young Hamilcar had been brought back to them; they saw that same dynamism in his expression, the same forcefulness in his eyes, the same facial expression and features . . .' In Livy's picture Hannibal recalled his father and stirred the loyalty of his soldiers. Livy continues, 'there was no one whom Hasdrubal preferred to put in command when a gallant or enterprising feat was called for, while there was no other officer under whom the rank and file had more confidence and enterprise' (Livy 21.4.2–5).

Hannibal was leading forays for his brother-in-law deep into the territory of the Celtiberians. Despite being the son of the great Hamilcar he behaved just like one of the soldiers and this engendered deep loyalty among those who fought with him. 'Only the time which he had left from discharging his duties was given to sleep, and it was not brought on by a soft bed or silence – many often observed him lying on the ground, amidst the sentry-posts and pickets, wrapped in a soldier's cloak.' Enormously skilled and brave, whether 'on horse or foot he was by far the best soldier; the first to enter battle, he was the last to leave once battle was joined' (Livy 21.4.2–10). Apart from Livy's description of the enthusiastic campaigner, there is little specific information about this important time in Hannibal's life. We know that it was a significant period for the Carthaginians in Iberia. It is entertaining to imagine the young, dynamic Hannibal, now the head of his family upon the death of his father, riding into battle and in turn teaching his younger brothers the arts of war.

The Iberians under Carthaginian rule gave Hasdrubal the title of 'general with unlimited power' after he married the daughter of an Iberian prince (Diodorus Sic. 25.12). Hasdrubal was, of course, already married to Hannibal's sister but we have no knowledge of her whereabouts or even if she was still alive.[38] He had inherited a great deal of autonomous power in Iberia and used this to consolidate the Carthaginian position. But Polybius, quoting the Roman senator and contemporary of Hannibal, Fabius Pictor, describes Hasdrubal as a megalomaniac intent on overthrowing the government at Carthage. 'Fabius tells us how, having acquired a great dominion in Iberia, Hasdrubal arrived in Africa and attempted to abolish the constitution of Carthage and change the form of government to monarchy.' Carthage's leading statesmen rebuffed Hasdrubal's challenge thus he returned and 'governed Iberia as he chose, without paying any attention to the Carthaginian Senate' (Polyb. 3.8. 1–5). Even if we dismiss the allegations of autocratic rule and take into account Fabius Pictor's hostility to the Barcids, the criticisms of Hasdrubal shine a dim light on underlying political conflict and friction at Carthage about the succession to power in Iberia after Hamilcar's death.[39]

Hasdrubal acted immediately to bring revenge down upon those responsible for Hamilcar's death with an army of 50,000, 6,000 cavalry and 200 elephants. As a result the Orissi (Oretani) tribe and 'their twelve cities . . . fell into his hands' (Diodorus Sic. 25.12). Overall Hasdrubal's policies continued the consolidation of territorial gain and expansion in Iberia through a mix of military intervention and soft power. He used his marriage to the daughter of an Iberian chieftain to seal an alliance and build his support (Diodorus Sic. 25.12).[40] In this same period Hannibal may also have been betrothed and subsequently married to an Iberian princess named Imilce. She was the daughter of a powerful chieftain from the strategic city of Castulo, capital of the Oretani people.[41] Castulo sat on the banks of the Guadalimar river, a tributary of the important (Baetis) Guadalquivir that formed a key artery in Carthaginian territory with links to the resource-rich mines of the region (Map 2). The marriage of Hannibal was used to bind the loyalty of the people of Castulo. The personal bonds between the extended Barcid family and the Iberian people are illustrative of their power base. Personal loyalty was key to the allies in Iberia and family ties sealed the links with Carthage.[42]

One of the enduring contributions of the Barcid dynasty to modern Spain is the city of New Carthage (Cartagena) on the south-eastern coast in the region of Murcia. Diodorus wrote that Hasdrubal 'thereupon founded a city on the sea coast and called it Carthago Nova' (25.12).[43] New Carthage was established at some point between 229 BCE and 228 BCE (even as late as 225 BCE – the sources do not agree) as the capital of Carthaginian Iberia on the location of a pre-existing Iberian town. New Carthage was a showcase city, known for its excellent location and easy sail across the Mediterranean to Carthage. The harbours at New Carthage are still some of the best ports in the western Mediterranean, with two deep natural harbours surrounded by imposing hills. The modern Cartagena now hosts the Spanish navy and has been one of the most important naval ports in Spain since the sixteenth century CE.

When Polybius visited New Carthage in the mid-second century BCE he described its terrain less than a century after its foundation.[44] The impression is of an imposing city lying '. . . halfway down the coast of Iberia in a gulf that faces south-west and is about twenty stades long (c. 3.6km) and ten stades (c. 1.8km) broad at the entrance'. The essence of the gulf remains the same today and the topography provided a safe and protected harbour. 'At its mouth lies an island which leaves only a narrow passage on either side, and this breaks the waves of the sea, the whole gulf is perfectly calm.' The city stood 'in the innermost nook of the gulf on a hill in the form of a peninsula' (Polyb. 10.10.1–5). The hills behind protected the city from the land and the deep harbours protected it from the sea.

Parts of the impressive Carthaginian defensive wall at New Carthage have been excavated and these give an idea of the grand size of the city at its very conception. The fortification that surrounded the land-side of the city is made up of two parallel walls with space in between and is built of large sandstone blocks. The walls stand up to three metres high in places today and are estimated to have been ten metres tall when first constructed. If the walls of New Carthage can be used as evidence for the rest of the city, it was built to the most advanced concepts in defensive architecture of the third century.[45] The city was the capital of the Carthaginian Empire in Iberia until its fall (Polyb. 3.15.3). Hannibal was based here from its foundation through to his departure for Italy and it was the perfect capital of the Barcid province. It was in a 'favourable position for action in Iberia' and located for easy access to North Africa as well as being close to the rivers that linked up with the mining towns of the region (Polyb. 2.13.1–2). The location connected the newly acquired Iberian territories to the city of Carthage.

The construction of this new, prestigious city under Hasdrubal enhanced Barcid power in Iberia and at Carthage. The city was a statement of Carthaginian authority and prosperity. New Carthage included a temple to the god Eshmun on its most prominent hill, and in its topography the city mirrored the landscape of Carthage itself where Eshmun was worshipped on the Byrsa hill.[46] On the second-largest hill sat a 'magnificent' building called the palace of Hasdrubal (10.10.9–10). These two important buildings dominated the cityscape. How large the urban population was in the Carthaginian period is open to question. New Carthage must have been a substantial centre for the Iberian peninsula and possibly comparable to Massalia further up the coast.[47]

The newly established harbour city was built to be 'the chief ornament' of Carthaginian and Barcid power in Iberia (Polyb. 3.15.3).[48] As the Carthaginian leader in Iberia Hasdrubal had a dual role: that of local hegemon and autocrat among the Iberians at the same time as representative of Carthage. These two roles could coexist. It was in his role as representative of Carthage that Hasdrubal received a delegation from the Roman Senate in the year 226 BCE. The meeting occurred during the late summer or perhaps autumn and resulted in a new formal agreement between the two sides that is referred to as the Ebro Treaty. The terms stated that the Carthaginians agreed not to venture north of the Ebro river in arms (Polyb. 2.13.7) (Map 2). The Roman motivation behind the treaty was clearly to contain Carthaginian power inside the Iberian peninsula during a period when Rome was involved in the conquest and settlement of northern Italy and faced a threat from the Gauls beyond the Alps. This implies that the Romans (or their allies from Massalia along the coast) continued to worry about growing Carthaginian influence much farther to the north than the area they controlled in Iberia at the time. The Romans 'for the present . . . did not venture to impose orders on Carthage or to go to war with her, because the threat of a Celtic invasion was hanging over them . . .' reasoned Polybius (2.13.3–5). Polybius suggests that Rome intended to go to war with Carthage sooner or later but it was in the Roman interest to seek an agreement with Carthaginian Iberia during these years.[49]

More difficult to ascertain is the Carthaginian motivation for signing the Ebro agreement. Polybius chose to leave out the Carthaginian incentives for signing such a document and many questions remain. Can we assume that when the 'Carthaginians engaged not to cross the Ebro in arms' (Polyb. 2.13.7) they acknowledged the Ebro as a natural border for their power in the Iberian peninsula? Or did they, like the Romans, consider the treaty a holding measure, while they consolidated their hegemonic control over the Iberian peninsula? Did the Carthaginians in turn impose terms upon the Romans? Perhaps they legitimately expected the Romans not to interfere in their territory south of the Ebro. The Carthaginians seemed to take the treaty of 226 BCE as a Roman acknowledgement of their hegemony south of the river and equally seemed to acknowledge Roman (or Roman allied) influence north of it. It seems possible that Hasdrubal was willing to accept that Carthaginian power need not extend further than the Ebro and pursue a policy of shared division of territory between the two states. What is difficult to discern is how much of Polybius' account is contrived to suit the Roman justification for the start of the subsequent war. For the Ebro agreement rests at the heart of future Roman accusations against Carthage for breaking the treaty. The two sides may have had very similar reasons for concluding the treaty but ensuing events mean that the details have been argued over for centuries.[50]

In 222/221 BCE, four years after the Ebro agreement, Hasdrubal was assassinated by a disgruntled Iberian ally. 'To succeed him the Carthaginians appointed Hannibal as supreme commander in Iberia; they chose him, notwithstanding his youth, because he had already shown that he combined a daring spirit with a quick and fertile brain' (Polyb. 2.36.3). The mantle of Carthaginian power in Iberia thus passed to twenty-five-year-old Hannibal, son of Hamilcar. He was first chosen as leader by the Carthaginian troops in Iberia, then the Senate and the people at Carthage 'unanimously confirmed the soldiers' choice' and ratified the appointment (Polyb. 3.13.3–5). At twenty-five he was a young man but his appointment was the army's sentimental choice. He had certainly been fully prepared for the challenges that faced him. Hannibal had been brought up to command, to lead the Carthaginian army and to rule after his father and brother-in-law. The seven years of Hasdrubal's leadership had continued Hannibal's role as the apprentice to power.[51]

Hannibal was ready to take on full control of Carthaginian political and military power in Iberia. When Hannibal succeeded Hasdrubal in 221 BCE he immediately began to campaign, just as his father and brother-in-law had done before him. The soldiers had unanimously chosen Hannibal as their commander and he set out to subdue the important Olcades tribe (Map 2). Camped in front of their most important city Althaea with his army, Hannibal 'terrified' the inhabitants after a series of attacks and rather quickly captured the town. The result was that the remaining towns of that tribal group were 'overawed and submitted to the Carthaginians' without any further resistance. Hannibal pressed farther and deeper into the Iberian peninsula that season with great success. He imposed 'a tribute upon the towns and taking possession of a large sum of money, he withdrew into winter quarters at New Carthage' (Polyb. 3.13.4–7).

A key to Hannibal's success as a general lay in the loyalty of his troops, whom he treated with 'great generosity, distributing a bounty to them at once and promising further payments later'. Hannibal was able to engender 'great goodwill . . . and inspired high hopes for the future' through these means (Polyb. 3.13.8). The ability to nurture and sustain the loyalty and belief of his soldiers was integral to Hannibal's military achievements. The allegiance of his soldiers created an aura of invincibility that accompanied Hannibal: his forces believed and trusted in him, and he rewarded them for this trust and devotion. Hannibal was a natural risk-taker and in order to succeed in his plans he needed an army that would follow him anywhere and believe in his ability to pull off what seemed impossible. He reached his triumphs by being bold, taking the initiative, outwitting his opponents and gambling on his own skills. The ability to inspire deep loyalty in his soldiers gave him the greatest possible chance of success.

Hannibal spent the winter of 221/220 BCE in New Carthage perhaps in the company of his wife Imilce. The couple represented a crucial alliance at the core of Carthaginian power in Iberia, the Barcid family and local royalty. Hannibal may have been married for a few years by this point as the alliance with Imilce's home Castulo had been in place since early in Hasdrubal's tenure (Livy 21.11.13 and 24.41.7). It is even possible that the couple had children by 220 although there is only one, not very credible, mention of 'a first-born and only son' in the Roman sources (Silius Italicus 4.770–790).[52] The winter in the city would have seen a court of sorts develop around Hannibal and his wife. The young Carthaginian colleagues of Hannibal and commanders from allied Iberian troops spent their time preparing for the next campaigning season. Hannibal would have received envoys from

Carthage, spies and ambassadors as well as dispensing justice in the Carthaginian territory.

The spring of 220 BCE brought new campaigns as Hannibal again 'took the offensive', this time against the Vaccaei tribe (Polyb. 3.14.1). Hannibal captured the important town of Hermandica that lies deep inland in the region of modern Salamanca.[53] These quick successes were an early indication of the military genius of Hannibal, whose reputation as a commander strengthened with each encounter. The legend that grew up around Hannibal was founded in these early years of conquest and campaigning against the fierce Iberian warriors.[54] His ability as a soldier and reputation as a leader and commander made him virtually unassailable for more than a decade.

An incident during the campaign of 220 BCE perfectly illustrates Hannibal's genius and adaptability. On his way back to New Carthage at the end of the campaigning season, he found himself vastly outnumbered and surprised by an army of the Carpetani tribe (a mountain tribe from north of the Tagus river). Hannibal quickly reacted and immediately retreated to the far side of the Tagus, pursued by the Carpetani. He used the water as a buffer and positioned his forty elephants to challenge the enemy as they crossed. Polybius describes how 'the barbarians tried to force a crossing at various points, [and] the greater number of them were killed as they left the water by the elephants'.[55] On the far bank of the river the remainder of the enemy army could only watch as Hannibal then 'moved over to the offensive, crossed the river, attacked the barbarians and put to flight a force of more than one hundred thousand' (Polyb. 3.14.2–10).[56]

After a year in command Hannibal had moved farther into the Iberian interior than his father or brother-in-law and conquered new territory. The power of the Carthaginians had proven impossible to resist and 'none of the other tribes south of the Ebro [river] ventured lightly to face them, with the exception of the people of Saguntum' (Polyb. 3.14.9). Saguntum was an important town dramatically located on a high ridge near the sea 250 kilometres north of New Carthage and 135 kilometres south of the Ebro (Map 2). It would be events around this city in the first years of Hannibal's command that provoked Carthage and Rome again into war.[57]

The first recorded moment when Hannibal encountered his future adversaries was in late 220.[58] He returned to New Carthage after his highly successful season of campaign and found an embassy waiting for him from Rome made up of high-level delegates from the Senate. The city would have been busy with the return of its dynamic commander and his victorious troops. The bustling ports and multicultural population surely impressed the Roman legates. They were also perhaps concerned at the confidence they met in the town. Hannibal granted an audience to the Romans. These important men of the Senate were used to carrying a great deal of authority and expected to be treated with respect. The Romans included the ex-consul P. Valerius Flaccus and ex-praetor Q. Baebius Tamphilus.[59] The meeting between the young confident Hannibal, just back from campaign, and the mature, experienced Roman senators did not go smoothly. The ambassadors reproached Hannibal for involving himself in the internal affairs of Saguntum. Their mission was 'to issue a formal caution to Hannibal to leave the people of Saguntum in peace as allies of the Roman people' (Livy 21.6.3–6). Hannibal dismissed the embassy with some scorn. He called them hypocrites and accused them in turn of meddling in internal Saguntine politics. He claimed that Roman involvement had resulted in the death of leading pro-Carthaginian citizens in Saguntum.[60] History has judged Hannibal's behaviour as rash, hot-headed and full of the impetuousness of youth. Polybius believed that he could still have negotiated with the Roman envoys at this moment but failed (or chose not) to take the opportunity.[61] Hannibal defended his actions as being based on 'an old principle of Carthage never to neglect the cause of the victims of injustice'. The Romans warned Hannibal again not to interfere with Saguntum and then sailed to Carthage to convey the same message. Hannibal also sent to Carthage, 'asking for instructions' and reporting that the Romans were interfering with Carthaginian allies in the region (Polyb. 3.15.8).[62] Polybius claims that from this moment on the Romans believed that war was inevitable and that they would fight the Carthaginians in the Iberian peninsula.[63]

The argument between the two sides rests on the existence of a formal Romano-Saguntine *amicitia* (friendship). The Romans alleged that Hannibal had interfered with their ally, the Saguntines, and therefore the Carthaginians were the aggressors. The Carthaginian argument rested on the fact that Saguntum lay well south of the Ebro river and was thus not protected in the treaty with Rome. Carthage claimed that Saguntum had acted aggressively towards Carthaginian allies, both within the city and among neighbouring tribes. The details of the Ebro agreement reached in 226 BCE are key to these arguments. As far as we know there was no mention of the city of Saguntum in the Ebro treaty but in the period between 226 BCE and 219 BCE there seems to have been a relationship formed between Rome and the city, even though it lay within the agreed sphere of Carthaginian influence. A plausible scenario is that the Saguntines were wary of growing Carthaginian influence and reached out to the Romans as a counterbalance, or perhaps reached out to the

Roman allies, the Massalians. The question as to when the Romans and the Saguntines formed their alliance is at the heart of the issue. Polybius' statement that it was 'an acknowledged fact that the Saguntines placed themselves in Rome's protecting grasp a good many years before the time of Hannibal' does little to resolve the issue (3.30.1).[64]

The events leading up to the conflict saw the Saguntines and a neighbouring tribe allied to Carthage involved in an incident (in *c.* 220 BCE or earlier).[65] There is no information on the nature of the disagreement but as Carthaginian hegemony in Iberia expanded, the local cities and states would naturally have become polarized. Some of the Saguntines, feeling the threat of the growing Carthaginian involvement in their immediate vicinity, may have applied to the Romans for support. The Roman alliance with Saguntum perhaps dated from no later than *c.* 223 BCE.[66] There were Saguntines who saw Rome as a counterbalance to the growing power of Carthage but within the city there were also pro-Carthaginian factions. At some point (anywhere between 223 BCE and 220 BCE) the Romans became involved in an internal dispute and some of the leading men at Saguntum, apparently members of the pro-Carthaginian group, were put to death. So there were two events – one internal and one involving a neighbouring tribe – that interconnected and brought Hannibal face to face with Rome. Settling a regional dispute by calling in larger powers was not an unusual event in the third century but the details are obscured by other narrative agenda in our sources.[67]

Hannibal wintered in New Carthage and moved to lay siege to Saguntum in the spring of 219 BCE (Polyb. 3.17.9; Livy 21.15.3). Set high up on a ridge surrounded by a fertile plain, Saguntum was well fortified and supplied to resist an army. So secure was its position that the only other successful siege of Saguntum in its entire history took place during the Peninsular War in 1811 when an army of Napoleon Bonaparte captured the town. Hannibal's siege lasted about eight months. It was a long and arduous assault on a town built to repel such an attack. At the walls of Saguntum Hannibal learned harsh lessons about being tied up in a long siege and he would later avoid doing the same thing in Italy. Although the exact dates are unclear, the campaign may have begun any time between late March and early May so the siege may have lasted until some time in December/January 219/218 BCE.[68]

Curiously, the Romans did nothing to help their allies throughout the whole period of the siege. This may be indicative of some indecision or disagreement at Rome as to the course of action needed. In January 219 BCE the Romans chose their consuls for the year, and they took up office in March. It may be that the debate on the course of Roman policy and the indecision were caused by the ambiguous relationship between Saguntum and Rome and whether interference was truly justified based on a pre-existing alliance or not.[69] A more circumspect view of these events sees the Romans as having provoked Hannibal into war using Saguntum as the bait.

Hannibal's approach to Saguntum was consistent with the methods used by Hamilcar and Hasdrubal, and by most generals operating in the Mediterranean in the third century. When a treaty or alliance was possible, clemency was in order. A city that resisted could expect harsh treatment if it fell and the Saguntines put up a fierce resistance. Livy's version of events is detailed, although the siege of Saguntum receives the most elaborate treatment in Silius Italicus' epic poem the *Punica*.[70] Hannibal looms large as 'his war-trumpets sounded first before the gates of dismayed Saguntum, and he chose this war in his eagerness for a greater war to come', wrote the poet (*Pun.* 1.271–272).

The Carthaginians made a three-pronged attack on the city and applied the most advanced siegecraft, with catapults, ballistas, platforms and assault towers. The Saguntines were determined in defence and used a weapon of their own that caused havoc among the Carthaginian troops. Livy calls it a *phalarica*, a kind of flaming iron javelin, its head wrapped with 'tow and smeared with pitch. The head was three feet long, and so able to pass through a man's body as well as his shield' (Livy 21.8.10–12). The *phalarica* was effective even if it did not penetrate the body and only stuck to the shield, as the 'flames made the soldier drop the shield in alarm and expose himself' to more conventional weapons.

The Saguntines were forced back to their citadel when their city walls were undermined by the Carthaginians' determined assault. Hannibal, as was usual for him, engaged in the fighting from the very beginning and at one point, 'approaching the wall with insufficient caution, collapsed with a serious spear-wound to the front of his thigh' (Livy 21.7.10). The wound was bad enough for him to retreat temporarily from the field of battle to recover but throughout most of the siege he was 'on hand in person to give encouragement' and promise great spoils of victory when the town was taken (Livy 21.11.3–5).

Hannibal left the siege only one other time. He had to march off with part of his army to deal with an uprising among the Oretani and Carpetani in the area of the city of Castulo. The fact that his wife Imilce originated from this region made him want to deal with it personally (Livy 21.11.13 and 24.41.7). In his absence he left his lieutenant Maharbal son of Himilco, who carried on the attack and fought with equal vigour.[71] In the end though, late in 219 BCE, after eight long months Saguntum could hold out no longer. With no help from Rome or other allies, the city fell and was sacked. The population was dispersed, slaughtered or sold into slavery.

> Brave infant of Saguntum, cleare
> Thy coming forth in that great yeare,
> When the Prodigious Hannibal did crowne
> His rage, with razing your immortall Towne.
> **(Ben Jonson** *c.* **1572–1637)** [72]

The sack of the city of Saguntum became an event of mythic proportions that resonated through Roman history. Seen as parallel to the sack of Troy in Roman epic it has been graphically portrayed in Livy's history and beyond as a great Carthaginian outrage. For Livy it was the reason why the war against Hannibal had to be fought.[73] The telling of the sack of Saguntum begins an epic tale of war that placed the deeds of the Romans among those of the heroes of the ancient Greeks. The story echoed down the ages so that in seventeenth-century England Ben Jonson's poem captured the Roman perspective of a 'Prodigious Hannibal' whose 'rage' drove the Carthaginians to sack Saguntum and to provoke war with Rome. Jonson leaves no doubt whom posterity thought responsible and who was on the side of 'right'.[74]

There are practical questions to be raised over the lack of Roman support for Saguntum. If it was such a great outrage, why did Rome not come to the aid of its ally? Livy's confused chronology has been blamed on the fact that he (or his sources) tried to cover up Roman indecision and compress the events of 220–219 BCE. In fact Livy admits that the chronology does not make sense and that he was having trouble piecing it together himself (21.15.3–6). In 219 BCE the Romans were distracted in Illyria where Demetrius of Pharos, once an ally, had made a pact against Rome with the new king of Macedon, Philip V. In late spring 219 BCE we know that the Romans sent their consul Lucius Aemilius Paullus to Illyria with 'a force' (Polyb. 3.16.7). Perhaps Hannibal took his chance against Saguntum while the Romans were looking east (Polyb. 3.16.5–7).[75] Polybius also expresses his frustration with the sources, calling them 'the common gossip of a barber's shop' (2.20.5), especially Sosylus and another named Chaereas, otherwise unknown, who claimed that the Romans had dithered over the situation at Saguntum.[76] The lack of clarity in our sources should make the tale as it stands suspect. There seems little doubt that events have been adapted to fit a particular narrative and to place the blame on Hannibal's shoulders.

When the news of the sack of Saguntum finally reached Rome, probably in February/March 218 BCE, the Roman Senate debated their next course of action. The record indicates that even though 'the Punics were their enemy of old . . .' the path to war was not unanimous (Livy 21.16.5). Some in the Senate wanted an aggressive reaction, like L. Cornelius Lentulus who demanded immediate war. Lentulus, 'in his address declared that they must not delay but must vote for war against the Carthaginians and must divide the consuls and armies, sending one force to Iberia and the other to Africa' (Zonaras 8.22.2–3). Others in the Senate were less eager to leap into a war. A faction of doves was led by Q. Fabius Maximus who 'replied that it was not so absolutely necessary to vote for war, but that they ought first to send an embassy, and then if the Carthaginians persuaded them that they were guilty of no wrong, the Romans should remain quiet, but if they were proved to be in the wrong, the Romans should wage war against them in order, he added, that we may cast the responsibility for war against them' (Zonaras 8.22.2–3).[77] The Romans were eager to cast the blame entirely on Hannibal and willing to absolve Carthage of responsibility for the hostilities. Fabius Maximus' intentions were to release the Romans from any charge of culpability in declaring war. Such is the confusion around the reasons for the start of the war that Polybius denies that there was any debate about the declaration of war at all and insists that 'an embassy was immediately dispatched to Carthage' (3.20.1–7).[78]

In the Carthaginian Senate during this same period debate must have raged as well but the details are even less clear than at Rome. It is certain that the Carthaginian elites were, like the Romans, divided over the issue of another war. Some of the Roman and Carthaginian leaders may even have joined together in their efforts to avert war.[79] Hanno, the old enemy of the Barcids, led the criticism in the Senate at Carthage when Livy tells us (with the clarity of hindsight) that he warned of the destruction that another war with Rome would bring. Hanno ties the fate of Saguntum in a narrative circle to the eventual fate of Carthage (Livy 21.10.4–13).[80] The majority in the Carthaginian Senate, however, were firmly behind Hannibal and deeply suspicious of the Romans, who had been consistently unwilling to back down from any opportunity to undermine Carthage. The huge successes of the Barcid leaders meant it was virtually impossible for the Carthaginians to turn their back on their own commander at this moment. Therefore, both Carthage and Rome were firmly committed to their unassailable right to continued conquest and expansion. Neither side could or would retreat from the conflict.

The remit of the Roman embassy sent to Carthage in 218 BCE seems to have been to force Carthage into declaring war. This was a very senior embassy of five men which included the two outgoing consuls. The meeting took place in the Senate at Carthage and focused on the technical aspects of the treaties between the two cities and their claim and counterclaim about who had broken the terms of which agreement.[81] Each side blamed the other. The Romans certainly saw Iberia as a rich prize to be won from Carthage.[82] The Roman embassy issued an ultimatum demanding that Hannibal and his advisors be handed over to Rome. They must have known that handing over Hannibal would be equivalent to handing over Iberia and it was an impossible demand. The territory Hannibal controlled across the Mediterranean was larger than Carthage's own African territory.[83] The Romans made it impossible for the Carthaginians to avoid war. In the Carthaginian Senate there was a dramatic scene as the senior member of the Roman embassy, wrapped in his toga, spoke. He declared that 'he held both war and peace for them' and he would let fall from his toga whichever of the two they chose. The Carthaginian *sufet* (chief magistrate) answered defiantly that the ambassador should let fall whichever result the Romans wanted. The Roman envoy chose war and many of the Carthaginian senators cried out at once 'and we accept it' (Polyb. 3.33.1–4). The result of this encounter was that in 218 BCE Carthage was again at war with Rome. The sack of Saguntum gave the Romans the perfect opportunity to fight a war they were already preparing for. What they had never envisioned, however, was that this war would be fought in Italy and would challenge their power at its very roots.

Polybius and Livy both argue unequivocally that Hannibal's immediate plan, as soon as he came to power, was to make war against Rome and that everything he did was contrived to bring about that end. He was 'a young man with a burning desire for power and seeing only one way to it' in Livy (21.10.4). Polybius believed the Carthaginians to be at fault, and Hannibal especially, so that 'everything that befell both peoples, the Roman and the Carthaginian, originated from one effective cause – one man and one mind – by which I mean Hannibal' (9.22.1). For Livy, 'from the day Hannibal was declared commander it was as if Italy had been decreed his area of responsibility and war with Rome his assignment' (21.5.1). And elsewhere Polybius states: 'as soon as he took up his command it became clear . . . that his purpose was to declare war on Rome . . .' (2.36.3–4).

So the sources we have are explicit, yet it is worth considering whether this carefully constructed argument of pro-Roman authors is consistent with what we know. The whole responsibility for the Second Punic War has been placed squarely on Hannibal's shoulders. After the fighting both the Carthaginians and the Romans unreservedly blamed Hannibal. It suited both sides to find a scapegoat. Following Livy, later historians portrayed the war as a personal battle between the Barcid family and the Romans. In other passages, however, Polybius is more circumspect in assessing the role of the Romans in the lead-up to war. He reflects on Rome's duplicity over Sardinia and mentions the increased indemnity imposed on the Carthaginians at the end of the Mercenary War as disingenuous. Polybius concludes, however, that the 'hatred of Hamilcar' was passed on to his sons and became the catalyst for war. Polybius differentiated between the beginning of the Second Punic War and the causes. He discussed the siege of Saguntum and Hannibal's subsequent crossing of the Ebro in these terms: 'I should agree in stating that these were the beginnings of the war, but I can by no means allow that they were its causes' (3.6.3). The cause was not the same as the action that started the conflict. In Polybius' assessment the larger geopolitical considerations needed to be taken into account.[84]

Hannibal's actions after coming to command the Carthaginian forces were a continuation of the policies of Hamilcar and Hasdrubal before him. Was there a premeditated plan, as Polybius suggests when he claims that Hannibal was following his father's advice or did Hannibal react to the events that unfolded on the ground (3.14.10)? Livy states that 'had he [Hamilcar] lived longer the Carthaginians would clearly have launched under Hamilcar the invasion that they actually launched under the command of Hannibal' (21.2.1). In Livy's view the consolidation of Carthaginian control over much of the Iberian peninsula was only a precursor to a grand invasion of Italy.[85] The Romans had spent the years since the First Punic War expanding their influence and power to the north and east. Resurgent Carthaginian power in Iberia now caught the attention of Rome. Foreign policy at both Carthage and Rome was expansive and 'ad hoc'.[86] There was little chance that another war could have been avoided unless one or the other state capitulated completely. We can never know the full story but a healthy scepticism over the Roman version of the origins of the war makes sense. The story has been adapted to fit the final outcome and the two sides were equally willing to engage in another war. One aspect is clear: in 218 BCE there does not seem to have been any real chance of a peaceful settlement. The fall back position for settling disputes in the third century was war.[87]

# CHAPTER 5

# LEGEND
## HANNIBAL INTO ITALY

he who should strike the enemy, shall be a Carthaginian in my eyes, whoever he shall be. Wherever he hails from . . . (**Hannibal in Ennius, *Ann.* 234–235**)

HANNIBAL'S LEGEND WAS SHAPED in Iberia where the destruction of Saguntum brought him face to face with the power of Rome. Silius Italicus' *Punica* captures the romantic sense of the dynamic young leader: 'the Carthaginians looked on and the Asturians trembled for fear, when he [Hannibal] rode his startled horse through bolts hurled by Jupiter' (1.252–255). The myth of Hannibal grew out of these early campaigns. His philosophy of leadership gained him great loyalty from his troops, whilst his victories among the Iberians and the sack of Saguntum made him famous. By 218 BCE, as Hannibal prepared to leave Carthaginian Iberia and fight the Romans, he was backed by an army that would follow him anywhere and the reputation of being able to outmanoeuvre the gods themselves.

As the later Roman historian Dio commented, Hannibal believed it 'better to be the first to act than the first to suffer' (Cassius Dio 13.54.5). War was now inevitable, and Rome was preparing to send its armies to Iberia and to Africa. Hannibal made his own plans, backed by Carthage and almost certainly informed of the Roman preparations. Instead of waiting for a Roman attack he planned to take the fight to the Romans in Italy. Hannibal's strategy relied on the receipt of accurate information and in these months there would have been a constant flow of people travelling from Rome through Sicily, to Carthage and

Iberia.[1] There were merchant ships that plied the seaways of the Mediterranean and linked the cities with their trade. Merchants in the ancient world were often accused of spying and, indeed, were often used as spies.[2] Later in the story, Livy mentions the presence of Carthaginian agents in Rome, and we assume that Hannibal was kept abreast of Roman plans throughout much of the war (22.33.1). His network of informants and spies was extensive and he may well have employed specific groups of his followers as intelligence-gatherers. Evidence from later Roman armies notes the existence of detachments of soldiers whose specific purpose was to gather intelligence; the Latin term was *speculatores*.[3] Hannibal may even have had agents embedded in the Roman armies among the auxiliary troops. These may have been men who posed as deserters and were in reality acting as spies. One of Hannibal's great skills, his ability consistently to surprise his enemy, is perhaps illustrative of the scope of his intelligence network, certainly at the beginning of the war.[4]

After the fall of Saguntum Hannibal acted to secure Iberia and Carthage against the inevitable Roman attack. He also sent out envoys to test the opinion of the tribes on the land route to Italy. Hannibal had to understand how his army would be received along the path he planned to take if he was to seize the initiative from Rome. He may also have encouraged his envoys to stir up trouble among the restive Gauls of the north of Italy. The land route to Italy was his only real option since the Romans controlled the key ports and islands between Iberia and Italy, including the Ligurian coast and southern Gaul (see Map 2). A Carthaginian fleet had not matched the Romans for decades and with the loss of Carthage's ports on Sicily, Sardinia and Corsica, the sea options were severely limited.[5] Clearly Hannibal had little choice but to fight this war on land and would need the support of allies all along the road.

At New Carthage in the winter of 218 BCE preparations were made. The spoils from the sack of Saguntum were divided among the victors, including a portion delivered to Carthage. Then Hannibal sent his troops to winter quarters or (for the Iberians) homewards for rest. Hasdrubal Barca, Hannibal's younger brother, was deputized and 'instructed . . . how to manage the government of Iberia and prepare to resist the Romans if he [Hannibal] himself happened to be absent'. Soldiers were sent from Iberia to Africa (13,850 infantry, 1,200 cavalry and 870 Balearic slingers) and from Africa to Iberia, 'binding . . . the two provinces to reciprocal loyalty' (Polyb. 3. 33.5–6).

Hasdrubal's forces were made up of a fleet consisting of fifty quinqueremes, two quadriremes and five triremes (thirty-two of the fives and all the threes 'fully manned'). Plus a further '2550 cavalry made up of Libyphoenicians, Libyans and Numidians and an infantry of 11,850 Libyans, 300 Ligurians and

500 Balearians as well as twenty-one elephants' (Polyb. 3.33.5–16). In case his readers wondered about the accuracy of these very specific details, Polybius claims his source is impeccable. 'I found on the Lacinian promontory a bronze tablet on which Hannibal had made out these lists himself during the time he was in Italy' (3.33.17–18). The inscription, which no longer survives, was a kind of *res gestae* written down by the great man himself and then set up on a column for posterity.[6] The details of the numbers of soldiers and type of troops that he left for his brother provide a glimpse of Hannibal's meticulous nature and his careful and structured planning. The march into Italy was a bold and risky strategy and his plans had to be perfect.

Early in 218 BCE, before any official declaration of war but knowing what was coming, the opposing sides made their preparations.[7] The Roman Senate set out to raise two consular armies with the intention of sending one to Iberia and one to Africa (Polyb. 3.40.2; Livy 21.17 1–9). 'They [the Romans] never thought that the war would take place in Italy' and were preparing to fight in Iberia with Saguntum as their base (Polyb. 3.15.13). One consul, Publius Cornelius Scipio, was given Iberia as his 'province'; the other, Tiberius Sempronius Longus, Sicily and Africa.[8] The Romans sent out a strong signal of purpose with the number of soldiers they raised to fight. That year they levied six legions (4,000 infantry in each) making up troops totalling 64,000 infantry (24,000 Roman and 40,000 from allies) and 6,200 cavalry (1,800 Roman and 4,400 from allies) and launched a fleet of 220 quinqueremes (Livy 21.17.1–9). The size of the Roman force tells us that Rome believed it was going to war with Carthage intending to capture her territory, and to win quickly.

The Romans planned a two-pronged attack. The largest portion of the fleet (160 quinqueremes) and two legions with allied troops were given to Sempronius, who went to Sicily and prepared to attack Carthage. Publius Scipio was 'bound for Iberia with sixty ships' (Polyb. 3.41.2) and two legions and allied troops. The remaining two legions were under the command of the praetor Lucius Manlius Vulso, who would head to northern Italy to continue to pacify the Gauls of the Po valley, for 'at the same time as they were engaged in enrolling the legions . . . [the Romans] were also pursuing a scheme . . . for establishing two colonies in Cisalpine Gaul' (Polyb. 3.40.3–8). News of Hannibal's plans may have stirred up local anti-Roman feeling in Gaul, just as he had hoped it would. The Gallic tribe of the Boii had risen in revolt, 'encouraged by the messages they had received telling them that the Carthaginians were close at hand'. Despite this trouble, the level of confidence among the Romans was high. They had raised a huge army and were well prepared, no doubt expecting a relatively straightforward victory and an extension of their territory.

At New Carthage the scouts sent to reconnoitre the route to Italy returned to Hannibal with a positive response from the 'Celtic chiefs both on this side of the Alps and in the mountains themselves' (Polyb. 3.34.3–6). He was no doubt kept informed of the Roman plans through the winter, and early spring of 218 BCE began with a recall of troops from their winter quarters. Hannibal was 'in high spirits' as he rallied his soldiers and citizens for war with Rome.[9] The essence of Hannibal's brilliance lies in how he changed the paradigm of the war before it had even begun.

The army Hannibal took with him on his adventure into Italy was made up of 'Africans, Spaniards, Ligurians, Celts, Phoenicians, Italians and Greeks' (Polyb. 11.19.4).[10] It was not simply a matter of a hired army but there was certainly a mix of different forces and types of soldiers, some under their own command and others under the control of Carthaginian commanders. The army was a multicultural and varied force, with individual units wearing their own traditional uniforms of battle, heterogeneously attired and perhaps to outsiders looking uncoordinated. Hannibal's troops were not merely mercenary soldiers but 'a paid professional force' organized into units who were committed and loyal to their leader. If we believe an offhand comment by Cicero, 'Hannibal . . . thought that in his army there ought to be no rivalry of birth, but only of merit . . .' (*Verr.* 2.5.31), there was an egalitarian approach to his military command, which valued talent (and commitment) rather than just status. Many of the troops in Hannibal's army were levied from territories now subject to Carthaginian rule and this connected them to Carthaginian power, although military obligation did not necessarily form part of their subject agreements.[11] The lack of citizen involvement in the army, the antithesis of the Roman system, is often cited as a reason for the ultimate lack of success of the Carthaginians. This is a highly Romano-centric viewpoint and most soldiers, citizen or not, were inspired by and loyal to their commander. A leader of Hannibal's stature and ability was able to combine the disparate parts of his army into a successful and unified machine.[12]

Under Hannibal's leadership this army was considered equal to the Romans and the most effective force of the age.[13] In Livy's portrait Hannibal was 'possessed of enormous daring in facing dangers, and enormous resourcefulness when in the midst of those dangers. He could be physically exhausted or mentally cowed by no hardship. He had the ability to withstand heat and cold alike; his eating and drinking depended on the requirements of nature, not pleasure' (Livy 21.4.5–8). Livy described Hannibal as a tough soldier who lived by example and never revelled in the luxuries of command.[14]

Ancient descriptions of Alexander the Great also emphasized his ability to endure physical toil and go without food and drink (Arrian, *Anabasis* 7.28, Plutarch, *Alex.* 4.4).[15] The characterization of Hannibal's abstinence and concern for his soldiers and allies may be more than a literary conceit in Livy. This could very well reflect more formal aspects of Hannibal's approach to command. The attributes Livy recorded may have been part of a philosophy of leadership that Hannibal consciously adopted, based on the role model of Pyrrhus and, of course, Alexander. We know that in the fourth-century treatises on the ideal form of command, such as that of Xenophon, preached abstinence and sobriety in a leader.[16] This type of manual must have informed Hannibal's education in military leadership and in the actions of great generals. Hannibal certainly cultivated this style of leadership; he was a soldier's man and a student of great military commanders.[17]

Like a virtuoso chess player Hannibal moved the diverse groups in his army in a coherent strategy. Each cohort had a different role to play in the field. Cavalry were essential in the battles that Hannibal would fight and it was the Numidians who made the difference.[18] The other troops that originated from across North Africa included Libyans, Libyphoenicians, Gaetulians and Moors. The Celts and Iberians in Hannibal's army were renowned for their skill in war – they were 'chieftain societies' and thus their allegiance and motivations were driven by patronage and connection to an individual leader.[19] As far as we can tell these disparate groups seem to have maintained their own command structures and adhered to their own formations. Each of the ethnic groups in the army wore their own battle attire, so to an observer Hannibal's forces would have looked like a patchwork of distinctive clothing and colour.

The chain of command and the top tier of organization of Hannibal's forces are deduced mainly from comments in our sources about individual commanders whom Hannibal relied upon. We cannot therefore fully identify the overall structure of the army but can see that he had a group of highly talented, loyal and expert commanders upon whom he could rely to carry out his orders and take the initiative when needed. Most of all his two brothers were a key part of the wider military machine that Hannibal created. Hasdrubal was left in Iberia as Carthaginian commander and Mago would accompany Hannibal on his march across the Alps.[20]

The road to war would lead Hannibal along the coast of the Iberian peninsula, across the Pyrenees into southern Gaul and over the Alps into Italy. This route was known in antiquity as the 'road of Herakles', based on the myths and legends of Herakles in his tenth labour. To accomplish this labour the hero was sent from Greece to collect the Cattle of Geryon that grazed on Erytheia, an island at the western edge of the world (Hesiod, *Theogony* 980). This mythical island sat on the spot where Europe and Africa met. The island of Erytheia was linked by ancient sources to the city of Gades (Pliny, *NH* 4.36).[21] In antiquity, the island now known as St Peter (Santi Petri), at the southern extent of the archipelago, housed a temple renowned across the Mediterranean, dedicated to the Phoenician god Melqart whom the Greeks and Romans equated with the hero Herakles.[22] Before he departed on his journey into Italy, Hannibal first made a pilgrimage to the temple of the god.

Livy claims that 'after a review of all his auxiliary troops, Hannibal set off for Gades. There he discharged his vows to Hercules, and bound himself with further vows for the continued success of his venture' (Livy 21.21.9). This means that Hannibal went to the temple of Melqart and there pledged to the god the spoils from the siege of Saguntum and sought his continued support.[23] In offerings made in worship the Carthaginians often included the phrase, 'because he heard his voice' when a prayer was fulfilled.[24] Having made gifts to the god, Hannibal must have felt favoured by divine sanction. Every spring (February/March) the ritual of the rebirth of Melqart was celebrated at Gades and it may have been this ceremony that Hannibal attended (Silius Italicus 3.1–31).[25] The Barcid family believed in the Phoenician god Melqart as their patron and protector. Hannibal would have been conscious that the journey he planned to undertake, by land to Italy, would emulate that of Melqart's Greek counterpart, Herakles.

Popular legends described Herakles as 'the greatest commander of his age' (Dionysius, *Rom. Ant.* 1.41). In the myth Herakles voyaged at the head of a great army into Italy and when his way was blocked 'a great a battle was fought' (Dionysius, *Rom. Ant.*1.41). The story articulates how the Greek hero was woven into the traditions of the western Mediterranean at the time of the early expansion of both Phoenicians and Greeks. By the third century versions of Herakles' tales were popular across the region of the Celts, the Celtiberians, the Gauls and into Italy. The legends served to connect the colonial settlements of the western Mediterranean and the indigenous peoples with the heartland of Greek/Phoenician mythology and religion. The myth was known to all along the route. Thus Hannibal, just as Alexander had gone to the oracle at Siwa for divine sanction, visited the temple sacred to Melqart/Herakles in Gades.[26] From there he would follow the path of Herakles and cross the Alps with an army.[27]

Hannibal made this pilgrimage in part to seal the link between his upcoming endeavour and those adventures of Melqart/Herakles. He was aware of his reputation and at one level deliberately engaged in something called 'myth management' or, in today's world, public relations.[28] Herakles of legend was the great commander, the superhuman hero and, in the western Mediterranean, a saviour.[29] His adventures involved freeing towns and cities from monsters, villains and tyranny. Many cities and towns in the western Mediterranean, including Rome, claimed a link with Herakles. Hannibal, or those who wrote his history, sought to link the legend of the Greek Herakles and the worship of Melqart to Hannibal's reputation as a leader. This multi-valent approach became an essential part of the ideology of Hannibal through which he could claim divine support for his war.[30] More than ever before, Hannibal would need divine favour and this journey, if successful, would place his deeds among the ranks of the immortals and make him 'the first after Hercules' (Appian, *Syr.* 10).[31]

Hannibal returned to New Carthage with the blessing of the god and set out along the coast with '90,000 infantry, 12,000 cavalry and thirty-seven elephants' (Polyb. 3.35.1).[32] The army departed from New Carthage towards the end of May (or early June) and marched through Carthaginian territory towards the river Ebro, beyond which lay the unknown.[33] As Hannibal's journey continued, its significance grew until it attained a quasi-mythological status. This may indicate that the origin of the tales associated with the journey came from people close to the commander and implies that a pro-Carthaginian source we no longer have access to may have been the first to capture the heroic nature of the adventure.

Livy repeats a story of a dream that Hannibal had as his army approached the Ebro river near the town of Onussa.[34] 'Hannibal saw in a dream a young man of godlike appearance who claimed he had been sent by Jupiter to guide Hannibal to Italy.' In his dream the guide told Hannibal to follow and not take his eyes off him at any point.

> At first, they say, Hannibal was frightened, and he followed without letting his gaze wander around, or back, at any stage; but then, with the curiosity of a human being, he began to wonder what it could be that he was forbidden to look back at. He could not help looking, and saw behind him a snake of an amazing size sliding along, and causing massive destruction to trees and bushes, a deafening thunderstorm following in its wake. Hannibal asked the young man what the monstrous apparition was and what the portent meant. He was informed that it was the destruction of Italy, and that he should simply proceed on his journey, asking no further questions and leaving destiny shrouded in darkness. **(Livy 21.22)**

The story of this dream fascinated many ancient sources and equally engages modern historians of Hannibal.[35] The tradition of a dream before battle can be traced back to the Persian king Cyrus and would continue through antiquity beyond the moment when the Roman emperor Constantine adopted Christian symbols after a dream he had before the battle of the Milvian Bridge in 312 CE. The oldest extant version of Hannibal's dream is found in Cicero, who claimed that his source was Coelius Antipater, who we know had access to the Greek historian Silenus' work.[36] The meaning of the dream has been open to interpretation since Cicero's time. Hannibal's guide in the dream, an escort granted to him by the gods for his passage through Gaul and over the Alps, imparted divine sanction to his mission. Herakles, who is a likely candidate, was never identified as such in the Roman versions of the tale. Nonetheless we can imagine that it would have been made explicit in a pro-Carthaginian version by the original author.[37] The story of the dream gives us a further glimpse into the epic construction of the legend of Hannibal and how he claimed ownership of the myth.

In a very practical way the divine sanction implied in the dream would act as a unifying symbol for an army.[38] The reporting of dreams and the dreams of a commander were key to morale. The culturally diverse members of Hannibal's fighting force could connect to the Heraklean-inspired epic journey that they were about to undertake. The dream was a vehicle for the general to be seen as guided by the divine, and rumours of it would have spread among Hannibal's troops, encouraging them to believe even further in their leader's mission. A multicultural Hellenistic army needed the unifying force of a leader who was divinely sanctioned. The dream and the connection to the gods would also work on the minds of the Roman allies. Winning over the Iberians, the Celts, the Ligurians, the Greeks, the Samnites and Lucanians along the road was key to Hannibal's strategy for success – all those diverse peoples and cultures that lay on the route to conquest.[39]

In the Hellenistic period armies were often personal and soldiers felt a direct and immediate loyalty to their commander. Hannibal had, in this group who set off with him from Iberia, the quintessential Hellenistic army loyal to him and dependent on his skills. Beyond just being paid to fight, the soldiers who would do battle under Hannibal's command had a vested interest in the success of their general. They had to believe in the legend of their commander and his divine protection, for the mythic nature of their journey must have played a part in their commitment and identity.[40]

Inspired by his dream, Hannibal led his army across the Ebro in three divisions, stepping into a new world (Livy 21.23.1). The ethnic make-up north of the river was not dissimilar to that in the south. Colonial foundations (mostly Greek) dominated the coastal regions and diverse Iberian and Celtic tribes occupied the inland areas. The Pyrenees, which divided Gaul from Iberia, formed Hannibal's first barrier as he cut inland to avoid the Roman-allied Greek cities along the coast. The region between the Ebro and the Pyrenees was taken with some effort; heavy fighting ensued, with 'many severe engagements and with great loss' (Polyb. 3.35.3–4). Once the region was subdued, Hannibal left his commander Hanno in charge, with 10,000 foot soldiers and 1,000 cavalry. He sent an equal number of troops home as a goodwill gesture, to ensure loyalty behind him in Iberia and as a fallback, 'if he ever had to call on them for reinforcements' (Polyb. 3.35.6).

A different version of these events in the early part of the march in Livy describes how '3,000 of the Carpetani abandoned the march . . . and Hannibal sent home more than 7,000 men whose hearts he had felt were not in the campaign, and he pretended that the Carpetani too, had been discharged by him' (21.23.4–6). In Polybius and Livy the numbers are the same – 10,000 troops left the march – and Hannibal's goodwill towards his soldiers is evident in either scenario; what is fundamentally different is Livy's portrayal of the soldiers deserting, whilst Polybius represents Hannibal as choosing to leave troops behind.

This disparity in the sources may reflect a change in Hannibal's plans once the Ebro was crossed. If he had set out from New Carthage with the possibility of both Roman consular armies coming towards him and then had learned that only one was heading his way, Hannibal could rely on a smaller force. With the supply and maintenance of his army on the road a constant concern it was prudent to slim down his numbers and make his force more mobile, easier to manage and sustain.[41] He also left a considerable amount of 'the heavy baggage' with Hanno, lightening the load of his soldiers and making his army more agile (Polyb. 3.76.5).

Thus Hannibal and a force now made up of '50,000 foot and 9,000 horse' ascended the Pyrenees and moved on across Gaul to encounter the next barrier on the route, the Rhône (Map 2).[42] Moving quickly, Hannibal marched towards the Rhône, avoiding Roman-allied Massalia/Marseilles. Modern estimates put his army's progress at about 15 kilometres a day.[43] The Roman consul Publius Scipio made his way towards Hannibal and sailed along the Ligurian coast with his two legions. He had been waylaid by a rebellion of the Celts in northern Italy and when he disembarked his troops near Massalia it was perhaps already early/mid-September (Polyb. 3.40.3–14). The last news he had of Hannibal was that 'he . . . was . . . crossing the Pyrenees . . . but because of the difficulty of the terrain on his route and the number of Celtic tribes lying between the Pyrenees and the Rhône, Publius Scipio felt sure that the Carthaginians were still many miles away' (Polyb. 3.41.6).

Hannibal had however 'continued his march, keeping the Sardinian Sea on his right, and suddenly appeared with his army at the crossing of the Rhône' well ahead of the estimates made by the Romans for his progress (Polyb. 3.41.7). The consul was surprised that Hannibal and his army could have marched so quickly and sent out cavalry to reconnoitre the Carthaginian position and to confirm their whereabouts. The Roman army at Massalia decided that they would try to engage the Carthaginians in battle here in Gaul. Thus Publius Scipio 'stayed behind . . . to discuss with the military tribunes what was the best ground on which to give battle to the enemy' (Polyb. 3.41.8–9).

Hannibal, on the western bank of the Rhône, had no intention of waiting for the Roman army that was 'four days' march' away at the sea and began to prepare his crossing. Polybius' detail here is again specific and fascinating. He describes the scene as Hannibal made preparations to take his army of 50,000 infantry plus cavalry and elephants across the river. 'He used every resource to make friends with the natives living by the bank, and bought up all their canoes and boats, of which there was a large number, since many of the inhabitants of the Rhône valley are engaged in sea-borne trade' (Polyb. 3.42.1–4).

It took two days to build, borrow and buy enough craft and in that time 'a large force of barbarians had gathered on the opposite bank to prevent the Carthaginians from crossing'. With the preparations continuing beside the river, part of the army (mostly Spaniards in Livy 21.27.2) were sent by night north under the command of Hanno (called the son of Bomilcar the *sufet*) in order to cross the river and circle back on the enemy waiting on the east bank of the Rhône. On the fifth day after arriving at the river, with the forces under Hanno now in place and ready to attack (signalled by a column of smoke in Polyb. 3.43.6), the crossing began. These manoeuvres again highlight Hannibal's use of advanced communication techniques, with smoke signals and scouting key to preparing for the movement of his forces.[44]

Hannibal himself was in the front of the boats that raced each other across the river. The men 'cheered and shouted as they tried to outstrip one another and strained against the current . . . The Carthaginians following the progress of the boats with loud cheers . . . while the barbarians [Celts] yelled their war cries'. Just at this moment the advance troops of Hanno set upon the Celts and their camp. The Carthaginians took them 'completely by surprise' and caused the enemy troops to fall into disarray. At the same time Hannibal 'formed up his first division as it landed and at once engaged'. With the crossing won, the rest of the army was transported across and camped on the east bank of the river that night. Only the elephants and their minders still remained on the west bank of the Rhône.

The Carthaginian elephants had been an integral part of the army for almost forty years but had probably not been engaged in an adventure of this nature before.[45] The elephant became synonymous with the ruling Barcid family and was an important part of their self-definition (see Plate 5). Certainly the effort Hannibal employed in bringing them along on the march gives us an idea of how important he considered them.[46] The general consensus is that the Carthaginian elephants sitting on the banks of the Rhône were mainly African forest elephants, a species related to the African savannah elephant but slightly smaller. Ancient armies never used the sub-Saharan African savannah elephant, most familiar to a modern audience.[47] The African forest elephants no longer inhabit North Africa but in the Carthaginian period were fairly common.[48] The Indian species of elephant may also have made an appearance in the Hannibalic War – but the evidence is questionable.[49] Whichever species was waiting on the banks of the river, the Carthaginians had long experience of their behaviour and reactions, and would have known how to make the most of their impact and also what they might do in water.

It was the next day when Hannibal learned of the presence of the Roman consul and his army at Massalia. He sent a body of 500 Numidian cavalry to observe their movements. That same morning Celtic chieftains from across the mountains in Italy were presented formally to his troops. One named specifically as Magilus and others spoke to the army, assuring them of the support waiting on the other side of the Alps. Hannibal's words to his assembled troops on that day beside the river Rhône may come from the imagination of Polybius but are worth considering. The biggest psychological challenge, the physical strain and dangers, lay ahead. The risks they were going to take, the journey they would embark on, had to be worth it. Hannibal urged his troops to 'take heart' from their crossing and 'from the news of their allies . . . and have confidence in himself . . . and show courage worthy of their own record' (Polyb. 3.44.1–13).

The elephant crossing was still to come, and when that very afternoon the Numidian cavalry returned, 'in headlong flight' it became even more urgent not to delay (Polyb. 3.45.1). The Numidians had not gone far when Publius Scipio's detachment of Roman cavalry arrived and the two sides engaged, with 'courage and fury'. The Romans lost 140 in the engagement but pursued the Numidians, who had lost more than 200, right up to the camp and took a good look around. They then turned and galloped back to the coast to inform the Roman command (Polyb. 3.45.1–3). At this moment Hannibal made a strategic decision that reflects his determination to fight the war in Italy. He could have stopped and engaged the Roman army at the Rhône but he decided to continue his march. Although Livy claims that Hannibal weighed up his options before deciding to march on, Polybius does not even entertain the question (Livy 21.29.6–7).

The next morning at dawn Hannibal dispatched all of his cavalry towards the sea to act as cover. He knew that the Roman army would be marching north as soon as their horsemen reached the commander. Hannibal moved the 'infantry out of camp and set them on the march [north] while he himself waited for the elephants and the men who had been left to cross the river' (Polyb. 3.45.5–6). Again this emphasizes the value that Hannibal placed on the elephants, especially if we factor in the elaborate scheme devised to get them across the river and the effort involved. Elephants can swim but according to our sources Hannibal did not consider the option. Even though in the late summer/early autumn the river would have been at its lowest, perhaps the elephant riders judged the current was still too strong.[50]

The scene at the banks of the Rhône on the day of the elephant crossing must have been discussed by the locals for generations to come and only added to the legend of Hannibal (Polyb. 3.46.1–12; Livy 21.28.5–12). The Carthaginians had constructed a type of pontoon made of strong rafts lashed together. This was brought right up onto the bank of the river. Earth was used to cover the rafts so that the elephants would not notice as they began to walk on to them. The elephant walkway projected 65 metres into the river, with two very large solidly built detachable rafts at the far end attached to boats. With two female elephants in front, the 'Indian mahouts' led them out on to the pier and down to the last detachable rafts. These were cut free once the elephants were on board and the rafts began to move off into the river towed by the boats. The elephants panicked: some jumped into the water and walked on the riverbed using their trunks for air, others froze and stayed on the rafts. Many of the elephants' minders were drowned or swept downstream but in the end all thirty-seven elephants made it across.[51]

Once across, the elephants formed a 'rearguard together with the cavalry' and the last of the Carthaginian troops marched north up the banks of the Rhône (Polyb. 3.47.1). The Roman consul and army 'arrived at the place where Carthaginians had crossed the Rhône three days after they had resumed their march' (3.49.1). Again the speed at which Hannibal moved his army across difficult territory 'astonished' Publius Scipio, who 'had felt certain that they would never venture to advance into Italy by this route . . .' (3.49.2).[52] The Roman consul turned his army around, marched back to Marseilles and began to embark his forces. Once on the coast Publius Scipio made one of the best decisions, from the Roman perspective, in the early part of the war. The consul sent his army, under the command of his brother Gn. Cornelius Scipio, onwards to the Iberian peninsula while he returned to Italy to raise more troops. He planned to march north to meet the Carthaginians as they descended from the mountains. Sending his army on meant that the Romans were able to occupy the Carthaginians in Iberia and keep them from providing reinforcements or supplies to Hannibal for a number of years.[53]

There is a long, historic debate over where exactly Hannibal crossed the Rhône. The location of the crossing is important because it helps to identify the route taken by the Carthaginian army through the Alps. Polybius (3.42.1) recorded that Hannibal crossed the river a four days' march from the sea in the territory of a tribe that Livy named as the Volcae (21.26.6–7). The delta of the Rhône river has built up considerably since the third century and on the basis of a 15 kilometre per day march, some calculations place the crossing north of the confluence of the Durance river whilst others put the crossing south of the Durance (Polyb. 3.50.1). If Hannibal had been consciously following what was known in antiquity as the 'road of Herakles' then his route should have taken his army up the Durance valley and across the Alps into Italy. This course through the most southern of the Alpine passes became impossible for Hannibal with a Roman army so close at hand. Therefore the Carthaginian army had to turn north and Hannibal was forced to change his plans and seek another way through the mountains (Polyb. 3.47.1; Livy 21.31.1–4). He believed it essential to set the agenda himself and not allow the Romans to choose the place of their first meeting in battle.[54]

In 1891 Theodore Ayrault Dodge published one of the great military histories of Hannibal. By the time Dodge wrote his history, over a hundred and twenty years ago, there were already three hundred and fifty published works on Hannibal's crossing of the Alps. Just over fifty years ago the book *Trunk Road for Hannibal* described a British Alpine expedition that attempted to take an elephant named Jumbo over the Col du Clapier to prove the feasibility of that particular route.[55] The interest continues and there have been many other re-creations and re-enactments by those attempting to experience the journey, including a recent television programme following three brothers on bicycles.[56]

Part of our modern and ongoing fascination with Hannibal's journey rests in the disagreement over which route he took, with opinion balanced between the Col du Clapier and Col de la Traversette.[57] After he crossed the Rhône, our ancient sources agree that Hannibal turned north, 'marching steadily from the crossing-place for four days and reached a place called the Island . . . deriving its name from its situation; for the Rhône and the Isère running along each side of it meet at its point' (Polyb. 3.49.5; Livy 21.31.4).[58] After this four-day march, Livy and Polybius go their separate ways and it becomes very difficult to follow one or the other through to Italy without having to make major (and unrealistic) adjustments to their descriptions.[59] Polybius is usually considered the more reliable source because he claimed to have spoken to people who made the march, so we shall follow his information as far as that will take us.[60]

At a place called the 'island' Hannibal intervened in a clash between two brothers 'disputing the crown' in the region of the Allobroges. The victorious brother was grateful and Hannibal 'derived great assistance' from the king, who replenished supplies, rearmed his soldiers and provided the whole army with 'warm clothing and foot-wear' for their trek across the mountains (Polyb. 3.49.8–12). It was by now late September or possibly even early October and although the weather was still warm, it would soon be winter in the mountains. The newly allied chieftain supplied Hannibal with a much-appreciated rearguard as they started to climb the mountains into the territory of the hostile tribes (again the Allobroges but a less friendly group of the larger tribe).[61]

After a 140-kilometre (800 *stades*) march that took ten days along the bank of the river the army 'began the ascent of the Alps' and their local escorts returned to their homes (Polyb. 3.50.1). The hostile chieftains, up until this point, had left the Carthaginians alone, fearing the cavalry and their well-armed escort. Now that the climb had begun the cavalry would be less effective and the Carthaginian troops more vulnerable. Hostile tribesmen occupied strategic positions along the route by day. Polybius implies that had Hannibal proceeded he would have been ambushed and his army destroyed. In camp that night Hannibal set his men to take positions up above the local tribesmen along the pass and thus he managed to out-ambush the ambush. When the Carthaginian army began to move out, the locals attacked. The footing was slippery, uneven and the baggage-carriers and horses were easy targets, which caused mayhem along the narrow path they followed. Hannibal and his men counter-attacked and they 'inflicted enormous losses on the Allobroges' although his own troops also suffered greatly (Polyb. 3.51.1–13).

Hannibal's army endured another ambush and the loss of more 'men, pack-animals and horses' as the army trudged upwards through the narrow passes of the mountains. The hostile resistance eventually gave way to sporadic attacks by small groups, who harassed the column 'either from the rear or from the front and carried off some of the pack-animals'. The enemy 'never dared to approach' the elephants and after 'an ascent of nine days Hannibal reached the summit'. Once there, he gave the army two days' rest (Polyb. 3.53.4–10).

'The Alps stand to the whole of Italy like a citadel to a city,' comments Polybius (3.54.2) and at the top of the pass Hannibal is said to have gathered his men and looked down to the valley of the Po river. Italy lay before them and the exhausted and wounded men stared out across the valley while Hannibal reportedly rallied them with stories of their many allies who waited below and the great spoils to be won. Polybius' version of the crossing is thought to derive from one of his sources, either the pro-Hannibalic Sosylus or Silenus or the Roman Fabius Pictor. The difficulty is that there is no pass through the Alps where you can stand at the summit and look out over the Po valley and Italy. Thus one of the sources made this story up, or perhaps imagined what it should have been like at that moment on the summit of Europe, looking down to Italy. If the Roman Fabius Pictor was Polybius' source, the view as described from the top of the Alps might actually be the view at the northern edge of the Apennines looking towards the Alps and the Po from the south, which would be a uniquely Roman view. From the Apennines you can see the whole of the Po and the Alps very much as described by Polybius – like a citadel.[62]

'As it was now close on the setting of the Pleiades, snow had already gathered on the summit.' The constellation Pleiades sets towards the horizon in late October so Hannibal and his army had reached the summit of the pass just before then.[63] The army did not rest long at the top of a pass that was over 2,000 metres in altitude and freezing in the late October/early November snow.[64] The descent proved almost as treacherous as the ascent and although no enemy soldiers harassed the army on the way down, the footing was deadly. With a new snowfall lying on the hardened snow of the previous year and on a narrow, steep track, 'both men and beasts could not tell on what they were treading . . . all who stepped wide of the path or stumbled were dashed down the precipice'. It was slow going but then 'they reached a place where it was impossible for either the elephants or the pack-animals to pass owing to the extreme narrowness of the path' and landslides had carried away the face of the mountain in places (Polyb. 3.54.1–7, 3.55.1).

The Carthaginian army was caught: they could not turn back – yet going forward would be too treacherous. Hannibal camped the army on this exposed ridge and 'sweeping it clear of snow set the soldiers to work to build up the path along the cliff' to make it passable for the animals (Polyb. 3.55.6). This was an enormous task for an exhausted force but there was little choice – die on the mountain or move forward. Livy provides intriguing detail on how the Carthaginian army forged the path:

> they felled some massive trees . . . stripped the branches and made a huge pile of logs. This they set on fire . . . and as the rocks became hot they made them disintegrate by pouring vinegar on them. After scorching the cliff-face with fires in this way, they opened it up with picks and softened the gradient with short zigzag paths so that even the elephants, not just the pack animals, could be brought down (21.37.2–4).[65]

The construction of a route out of the mountains took four days, during which the pack animals almost starved to death (Livy 21.37.4; Polyb. 3.54.7–8). When they finally reached pastureland the army rested and allowed the animals to graze. It took them another three days before they were ready to make the last push towards the plains (Livy 21.37.6; Polyb. 3.56.1).

The whole journey from New Carthage to the Po valley had taken five months and the army that had survived the trek was a shadow of that which had departed from Iberia.[66] Hannibal's forces now numbered 20,000 infantry and 6,000 cavalry, according to his own account (Polyb. 3.56.4). He had lost '36,000 men and a huge number of horses and other beasts after crossing the Rhône' (Livy 21.38.5).[67] He had, as Napoleon Bonaparte would note two millennia later, 'sacrificed the half of his army for the mere acquisition of his field of battle, the mere right of fighting'.[68] By crossing the Alps and bringing the fight into Italy, Hannibal had taken the initiative away from Rome. Although it is impossible to know what his expectations might have been, Hannibal may have judged the sacrifice of half an army to be worth that.

The greatest achievement of Hannibal's long march to Italy was the paradigm shift that it created in the war. The Carthaginians had never attempted to invade Italy before and had surrendered the initiative in the First Punic War. By invading Italy Hannibal had seized the momentum and put the Romans on the back foot where they would remain for another five years. Most importantly, the Roman fleet assembled in Sicily and poised to invade Carthage was recalled to northern Italy. The Romans were forced by Hannibal's actions to move away from their plans of invasion and adopt a defensive strategy.

The symbolic aspects of Hannibal's journey began to take hold and as news of his approach reached the Roman population it must have seemed like the coming of a supernatural force. Invasion of Italy was an extremely rare occurrence in the whole history of Rome, and one that would not be achieved again for another six hundred years.[69] The legend of the Alps was so significant that the rationalist Polybius, feeling he had to play down Hannibal's achievements, criticized 'some . . . writers' for trying to impress their readers with the supernatural abilities of Hannibal. Polybius claimed these authors built up the story to such a degree 'that unless some god or hero had met Hannibal and showed him the way, his whole army would have gone astray and perished utterly . . .' (3.47.6–9). Polybius felt the need of the rational historian to diminish the claims of divine backing for Hannibal's achievements, thus proving that the crossing of the Alps had quickly become legendary.[70]

    The reality of the group that came down from the mountains was quite different. The men 'had suffered terribly from the toil of the ascent and descent of the passes and the roughness of the road . . . they were also in wretched condition owing to the scarcity of provisions and neglect of their persons' (Polyb. 3.60.3). It is hard to imagine that this army would be able to take on and fight Roman legions. In the territory of an allied tribe, the Insubres, Hannibal 'made every provision for carefully attending to the men and the horses likewise until they were restored in body and spirit' (3.60.7–8).[71] To restore to fighting fitness a demoralized and dejected force of men who had witnessed the loss of half their colleagues seems an extraordinary challenge. That this army would go on to fight and win two battles in the month that followed is quite astonishing. It may well be therefore that the losses and the hardships of the long journey have been exaggerated in our sources for dramatic impact.[72]

> Renouncing all communication with his country, he marched through hostile or unknown nations, which he was obliged to attack or subdue; he crossed the Pyrenees and the Alps, which were presumed to be impassable, and descended upon Italy, sacrificing the half of his army for the mere acquisition of his field of battle, the mere right of fighting. (**Napoleon Bonaparte on Hannibal**)[73]

This most symbolic aspect of Hannibal's life, the crossing of the Alps with a fully equipped army and elephants, is a feat of daring and genius still admired today. The exploit leaves even a modern audience questioning the sanity of taking tens of thousands of soldiers plus horses and elephants across the mountains. When Napoleon campaigned against the Austrians in the north of

Italy in the late eighteenth century he too crossed the Alps with a fully equipped army, an act that modern historians still consider with awe: 'A move so incredible that it had no modern precedent; a startled world was inevitably put in mind of the one ancient soldier who had done it: Hannibal.'[74] Napoleon himself, a student of ancient history and of great military leaders, later discussed Hannibal in his own correspondence and claimed that 'Hannibal forced the Alps . . . but we have turned their flank!' Napoleon offered more insights on Hannibal's actions and motivations from exile on St Helena at the end of his life. 'Hannibal is, perhaps, the most surprising character of any, from the intrepidity, confidence, and grandeur evinced in all his enterprises. At the age of twenty-six, he conceived what is scarcely conceivable, and executed what must have been looked upon as impossible.'[75]

Napoleon's comments on Hannibal's motives provide us with the unique view of one military genius on another, separated by two millennia. Napoleon the strategist reflected on the Carthaginian military genius and in the same passage pondered the degree that luck and pure bloody-mindedness must have played in Hannibal's career:

> Will anyone believe that he owed his career and so many great deeds to the fickleness of chance and the favours of fortune? Certainly he must have been possessed of a spirit of the strongest kind, and have had an extremely high opinion of his knowledge of war, this man who, when hailed by his young conqueror, would not hesitate, although he had just been defeated, to rank himself immediately behind Alexander and Pyrrhus, who were, according to him, the two best generals ever.[76]

The impact of the Alps throughout the ages has placed Hannibal's crossing in the realm of myth and heroes (Plate 6). He is compared to Jason and the Argonauts, to Aeneas, and ranked alongside Achilles.[77] This most heroic deed played a key role in the psychological impact Hannibal had on the Romans and the people of Italy once he arrived. By taking his army across the Alps and into Italy Hannibal reinforced his reputation for divinely inspired leadership. The Alps were high, mighty, freezing and dangerous. Crossing them was an epic feat of heroes.

# CHAPTER 6

# HANNIBAL THE CONQUEROR FROM THE TREBIA TO TRASIMENO

By Thrasimene's lake, in the defiles
Fatal to Roman rashness, more at home;
For there the Carthaginian's warlike wiles
Come back before me, as his skill beguiles
**(Lord Byron, *Childe Harold's Pilgrimage* Canto 4, LXII)**[1]

Hannibal arrived in Italy and brought war to Rome. His strategy was to disrupt the Roman offensive against Africa and Iberia and to shift the focus on to Italy and Rome's allies. Hannibal's appearance in Italy forced the Romans on to the defensive. They do not seem to have entertained the idea of an invasion of Italy before it happened. 'In Rome itself,' Polybius writes '. . . news came that Hannibal was in Italy with his army and already laying siege to some cities. Something that seemed altogether astounding to them' (3.61.7–9). The Romans felt confident that their consul would intercept Hannibal in Gaul and deal with his army before the Alps were crossed. They were caught off guard, had underestimated their enemy and been slow in their communications.[2] Yet still at Rome they must have been upbeat about their prospects. Hannibal's successes so far had been against fierce yet divided Iberian and Celtic tribes. Taking on the disciplined might of the Roman legions would be a completely different proposition.

On Hannibal's appearance in the late autumn of 218 BCE, the consul Tiberius Sempronius Longus was recalled from Sicily where he had been planning to invade Africa. The Carthaginians had been skirmishing with the

Romans at sea, hoping to reclaim the port of Lilybaeum and disrupt their plans (Polyb. 3.61.9–10; Livy 21.49–51).[3] A comprehensive and coordinated strategy between Hannibal and Carthage seems more apparent at this point than at any other in the war. The withdrawal of the consular army from Sicily alleviated the direct threat to Carthage, a critical objective for Hannibal. Previous invasions of North Africa, by Regulus and Agathocles, had wrought havoc and would have created difficulties for Hannibal in Italy. By grasping the initiative he achieved his aim: the war would be fought in Italy and Roman plans had been disrupted.

Hannibal's prospects for success lay in disabling the complex Roman system of power in the Italian peninsula. His ability to prise the allied cities away from Rome and isolate the Romans in Italy would be the key to future triumph. Much of Italy had been tied to Rome since the early third century through a structure of legal alliance, colonial foundation and citizenship grants.[4] From the north of Italy and the Celtic tribes of Cisalpine Gaul to the Greek cities of the south and the central Italian Lucanian and Samnite peoples, the allies were vital. They supplied the Roman army with the auxiliary troops who made up a large proportion of the fighting force. Hannibal's intention was, where possible, to destablize the existing alliance system. Considering the size of his army at this moment he clearly needed soldiers and supplies quickly. To achieve this he had to appeal to a wide range of peoples and cultures and be seen as a realistic threat to the formidable Roman power base. By causing 'great alarm' in Rome with his appearance in the north of Italy and achieving the impossible by crossing the Alps, Hannibal spread confusion and discord among the Romans and their allies.[5]

The first action in Italy was to attack the main town of the Taurini tribe (possibly modern Turin), who were the enemies of the Carthaginian allies, the Insubres (Polyb. 3.60.8). A sense of Hannibal's method can be discerned from the early encounters with the northern Italians. An approach was made to 'solicit their friendship and alliance' but when this was rejected, Hannibal laid siege and took the town in three days. 'He put to the sword all those who resisted him' and, as a result, the 'neighbouring tribes of barbarians . . . imme-diately flocked to him' (Polyb. 3.60.8–9). This had been standard Barcid procedure in Iberia and worked effectively among the Celtic tribes in the north of the Italian peninsula. Now was not the moment for Hannibal to show clemency, positioned as he was between the towering Alps and a newly arrived Roman army that had moved into the region. He had no choice but to push forward and could not leave hostile forces in his rear. The Romans, by crossing over the Po river, had placed themselves between Hannibal and the wide-ranging Celtic armies that might otherwise have come to join him. It was now in Hannibal's interest to quickly gain the upper hand and free those would-be allies from their Roman obligations. Polybius claimed that this was the determining factor in Hannibal's decision to 'advance and attempt some action to encourage those who were ready to share in his enterprise' (3.60.13). He needed a quick win and could not afford to wait until the spring. This would have given the Romans a chance to shore up their defences and tie their allies closer to them.

The first engagement between a Roman army and Hannibal's forces in Italy took place near to the Ticinus, a tributary that feeds the Po from the north (see Map 1).[6] Livy provides a sense of the rumour and tales of power that heralded Hannibal's arrival in Italy by reporting the words of the Roman consul Publius Scipio just before the two sides met. 'I want to see if this Hannibal really is, as he himself claims, on a par with Hercules on his travels, or rather has been left by his father as a mere tribute – and tax-payer, indeed a slave of the Roman people' (Livy 21.41.7). The fighting words of Publius Scipio and dismissal of Hannibal's reputation, although possibly an invention of Livy, reveal the power of the legend. Hannibal's status had grown with each achievement, first in Iberia with his rapid expansion of territory, then at Saguntum, and finally with the audacity of his march into Italy. The speech also makes reference to Hannibal's claim to his patron and protector, Melqart/Herakles. The Roman army that awaited Hannibal in the north of the Italian peninsula and even the consul Publius Scipio, for all the bravado, were 'amazed at his . . . audacity and daring' (Polyb. 3.61.6).[7]

Publius Scipio's route to meet Hannibal in the north of Italy had been an arduous one. The Roman consul was forced to react to Hannibal; to change his plans and deal with the unpredictable movements of the Carthaginian. It was late September when he left his brother Gnaeus with his army at the mouth of the Rhône. He took a small contingent of troops with him and retreated to Italy. On arrival at Pisa he then marched through Etruria and met up with the two legions under the command of the praetor Lucius Manlius Vulso. These legions had been levied and stationed in northern Italy to contend with the hostile Boii tribe of Celts. It was with this army that Scipio hastened to the Po valley to await the enemy.[8]

In heavy fog on a late autumn morning Hannibal advanced from the west along the Po and Scipio came from the east – both armies on the north side.[9] The two forces marched for a day before they were almost on top of each other. 'The next morning the two generals led out all their cavalry' and as they 'drew near . . . quickly formed themselves into battle order'. The atmosphere was tense and both sides were eager to engage. At first the balance between the cavalry charges was maintained but Hannibal's Numidian cavalry 'outflanked the Romans and fell upon them from the rear'. The end result of the skirmish was that the Romans 'broke and fled . . . and only a few remained with the consul' (Polyb. 3.65.1–7). Publius Scipio was wounded and in one version of the story he is saved from certain death by his son (of the same name: the future Roman hero Scipio).[10] A less gallant version of the story has the consul saved by a Ligurian slave (Livy 21.46.9–10). Either way, Publius Scipio managed to lead his soldiers in retreat 'to a place of safety' back across the river to the Roman colony of Placentia (Piacenza) (Livy, 21.46.1–10; Polyb. 3.66.2).

Hannibal, with his first victory in hand, pursued the Romans. The significance of this win should not be underestimated for as he moved across the countryside he acquired allies and much-needed supplies. Supporters flocked to his side as the Celtic tribes in the valley 'declared their backing for the Carthaginians . . . sending contingents to serve' (Polyb. 3.66.6–7). The lure of the famous Carthaginian leader and anti-Roman sentiment were strong. The first skirmish had been enough to convince some of the wavering Celts that the 'prospects of the Carthaginians were now decidedly brighter' (Polyb. 3.67.1–4).

Hannibal was moving through unfamiliar territory and had to rely on the knowledge of his local supporters. He followed Scipio to Placentia and crossed the Po with his army after a two-day march. The Carthaginians built a bridge of boats to cross the river. Livy mentions how the elephants were used to break the current while the river was forded, which is an intriguing idea, although he dismisses it as 'unlikely' (Polyb. 3.66.6; Livy 21.47.5–6). Hannibal 'drew up his army in full view of the enemy' and presented the Romans with the opportunity to do battle. The Romans did not take up this invitation to fight. The consul was seriously wounded and they were wary of any engagement. That night the Celtic auxiliary troops in the Roman army staged a rebellion and attacked the Romans from within their camp; 'they killed and wounded many men', spreading terror by cutting off the heads of the slain. With this dramatic gesture the Celts in the Roman camp went over to Hannibal. Their desertion was another blow to the Romans. Publius Scipio, wounded and now abandoned by his allies, would not be drawn out. He wisely realized it would be a disaster to engage with the Carthaginian army at that moment (Polyb. 3.66.10–67.3). Hannibal now held the upper hand.

The harsh reality faced by the Roman legions was that, with their allies in rebellion, they could no longer remain safely ensconced at Placentia.[11] Publius

Scipio also grasped that after Ticinus the open country 'between the Po and the Alps was not a suitable battleground for the Romans given the superiority of the Carthaginian cavalry' (Livy 21.47.1).[12] As a result the consul moved his army that same night, just before dawn and 'marched towards the river Trebia and the hills in its neighbourhood' (Polyb. 3.67.9). Hannibal sent his Numidian cavalry in pursuit and the main army followed. In the hills to the east of the Trebia the Romans set up a camp fortified with 'a trench and palisade'. There, they awaited the arrival of reinforcements in the form of the other consular army from the south (Polyb. 3.68.1–6).

The legions of Sempronius made their way across the whole of the Italian peninsula from Sicily to join up with Publius Scipio's army. They had been preparing to invade Africa and now faced a completely different challenge. It was a long and rugged journey and differing versions of how the army travelled north have survived (Polyb. 3.68.14; Livy 21.49–51). Livy portrays the consul and legions sailing up the Adriatic coast and assembling at the port city of Ariminum (modern Rimini) (Map 1).[13] According to Polybius, however, the soldiers were administered an oath by the consul in which they agreed to rendezvous on a certain day at Ariminum, thus alleviating the need to feed the whole mass of troops en route by not having them march together. In this version, the soldiers arrived by foot overland and Sempronius himself marched through Rome with at least some of his army, to the cheers of the people.[14]

Hannibal would have expected the Romans to provide reinforcements with Publius Scipio wounded and confined to camp. In the meantime he had complete control of the plains of northern Italy. The Carthaginians set up camp about 40 stades (approx. 7 kilometres) away from the Romans across the Trebia on the west side of the river (Polyb. 3.68.7). More cities, towns and tribes flocked to Hannibal's side. The commander of the garrison at Clastidium (modern Casteggio), about 50 kilometres west of Placentia, switched sides and gave the town up to Hannibal. The Romans had used Clastidium as their storehouse for grain and supplies, thus the defection was a much-appreciated boost for the Carthaginians (Polyb. 3.69.1; Livy 21.48.9). Hannibal spared the lives of the Roman garrison in the town and conferred honours on the man who had aided him. He approached the betrayal of the garrison with clemency in order to encourage others who might be willing to follow suit. This war for Italy would be won by the allies, and Hannibal was keenly aware how much he needed to manage the locals as well as win military engagements. Clearly the preparation in advance of the invasion had been extensive. There was a kind of domino effect brought about by Hannibal's presence which, combined with the weakened Roman reputation, succeeded in bolstering the Carthaginian cause.

The arrival of the new legions boosted the Roman morale, and the next skirmish between the two sides saw the Romans get the better of the Carthaginians (Polyb. 3.69.10–14). This encouraged the consul Sempronius, who was eager 'to bring on a decisive battle as soon as possible' while his colleague Publius Scipio held the opposite view (Polyb. 3.70.1–4). Hannibal too felt that a battle was essential. His new Celtic allies were fickle and the best way to make use of their 'enthusiasm' was to take on this newly raised Roman army that was untried in battle (3.70.9–11). Sempronius Longus was 'urged on by his own ambition' according to Polybius, whose hostility towards the man shines through his history.

The Roman system created a situation in which a consul's military glory was limited to his sphere of influence and year in office. New consuls would take up office in March. Thus an early spring battle would not have suited Sempronius' ambitions as he might not have been in control of the legions a few months later. Hannibal had no time limit on his generalship and there would be no Carthaginian commanders sent to relieve him. Polybius' narrative is decidedly pro-Scipionic and portrays Sempronius' desire to fight while his colleague was injured as a means of ensuring he claimed the glory for any victory that ensued.[15] Hannibal was happy to let the rivalries in the competitive Roman system play out to his advantage. His meticulous planning meant that the crucial aspect of the situation would be controlling the place and time of battle.

It was around the winter solstice on a cold and snowy day that Hannibal 'mustered his Numidian horsemen, all men capable of great endurance' and ordered them to ride up to the enemy's camp and draw out the Romans (Polyb. 3.71–74; Livy, 21.54–56).[16] For 'his hope was to get the enemy to fight him before they had breakfasted or made any preparations' (Polyb. 3.71.10). Again the element of surprise was vital and Hannibal's troops were well fed and had 'anointed themselves around their fires'. This meant they had coated their skin in oil to protect them from the freezing water of the river they had to cross. In the Roman camp Sempronius' confidence from his previous encounter was high and when he saw Hannibal's troops he ordered his own to pursue. The day was exceedingly cold '. . . while the [Roman] men and horses nearly all left the camp without having their morning meal . . . and had to cross the Trebia, the water was breast high' (Polyb. 3.72.1–4).

Breakfast, not something that we find discussed often in the ancient sources, seems to have played a key role in the battle of Trebia. Twice in the lead-up to the battle the point is made that the Carthaginian side had eaten breakfast and the Romans had not. Polybius mentions breakfast in just one other part of the narrative.[17] The story underlines the fact that Hannibal took great care of his troops, and this care meant that his troops trusted him. The emphasis on breakfast illustrates Hannibal's skills as a leader and therefore the most likely origin for this information is a pro-Carthaginian source. As Trebia was the only battle fought in winter conditions in the war it may be that the importance of breakfast related to traditions of winter fighting that were commonly employed. It was rare for fighting to take place at that time of year and up until the Romans gained an overseas empire fighting had traditionally been seasonal.

When Hannibal saw that the Romans had crossed the river he drew up his infantry while a covering force of pikemen and slingers stepped forward. In his army, in addition to 20,000 infantry made up of Iberians, Celts and Africans, were 10,000 cavalry, including his Celtic allies. The cavalry were stationed on the wings, with the elephants in front. Sempronius recalled his cavalry and drew up his infantry in 'the usual Roman order'. The consul's forces numbered 16,000 Roman and 20,000 allied infantry with 4,000 cavalry (Polyb. 3.72.11–13; Livy 21.55.4 – their numbers differ slightly). Thus the Romans outnumbered Hannibal's infantry but had significantly less cavalry.[18]

Not only had Hannibal chosen the field and manner of the battle but he had also added an element of surprise. Before dawn that morning he had sent out his brother Mago, 'still quite young, but full of martial enthusiasm' (Polyb. 3.71.5) and a hand-picked force of 2,000 cavalry to position themselves in the water-courses that threaded their way through the plains. Thus concealed, they waited. The two lines engaged fiercely in the battle. Once the fighting had begun, Mago and his cavalry charged the Roman centre 'from the rear, upon which the whole Roman army was thrown into the utmost confusion and distress'. The conditions for the Romans were awful – freezing and wet. They were overwhelmed by the more 'numerous cavalry and hindered by the river and the force and heaviness of the rain . . .' Whilst the Roman soldiers in the van had managed to break through the centre of the Carthaginian line, they were harried on all sides. It is fascinating to note how this development would play into the strategy Hannibal famously employed in a later battle. His first set piece with the Romans had been an immense learning experience. In the end, those Romans who still could retreated to Placentia and 'of the remainder the greater part were killed near the river by the elephants and cavalry' (Polyb. 3.73.1–74.8).

At Trebia Hannibal exhibited his tactical skill and brilliance. He lured the Romans into battle on his terms, understood the mind of his enemy and had prepared his men for the conditions they had fought in. By following these tenets of military leadership he made himself the master of northern Italy.[19] The Carthaginians had lost mainly Celts in the battle. Most of the African and Spanish contingents survived, but even greater losses came after the battle because of the cold, harsh conditions: many men and all the elephants except one perished (Polyb. 3.74.8–11). The psychological impact of the victory, despite the subsequent losses, was crucial as it built on the legend and added to the supernatural reputation of Hannibal. 'Such was the panic brought to Rome by this debacle,' says Livy 'that people believed the enemy would immediately march on the city' (21.57.1).

Hannibal was now in his winter quarters and had much to consider. These important early encounters had worked in his favour. The combined components of surprise, the weather and his aura intimidated the enemy and encouraged the local population, who were far from settled in their Roman alliance. His troops were fiercely loyal and trusted their leader. The next move, however, would be more complicated. Hannibal had to consider how to keep his allies on side and how to lure the Romans further into his strategic web.

That winter he kept his Roman citizen prisoners of war just barely alive but the Roman-allied prisoners were shown 'the greatest kindness'. He made common cause with them and 'called a meeting where he told the allied soldiers that he had not come to make war on them but on the Romans for their sakes'. He advised the allies that 'if they were wise they should embrace his friendship, for he had come first of all to re-establish the liberty of the people of Italy'. His motive, he claimed, was to help the 'allies recover the cities and territories that the Romans had taken from them' (Polyb. 3.77.3–7). And with these words Hannibal dismissed the allied troops to their homes without ransom. His intention was to win both the military and the political war by making the allies believe that he offered a better option than the Romans. It was a strategy that proved effective over the next few years but would be extremely difficult to sustain in the longer term.[20]

There is an intriguing story of Hannibal in the winter of 218/217 BCE, perhaps repeated by the Romans to show how little trust he could place in his Celtic allies. At winter quarters Hannibal was rumoured to have employed a typical 'Punic deception', going about camp in disguise. Fearing assassination by his Celtic allies he had wigs made in a number of different styles and colours that kept everyone guessing, 'even those who knew him well' (Polyb. 3.78.1–4). Livy offers a plausible explanation for the heightened level of Celtic hostility during the winter of 218/217 BCE. For it was 'their own lands [that] were the seat of war and they were burdened with the winter quarters of both armies' (Livy 22.1.1–4). According to Livy the Celtic leaders attempted many plots but Hannibal kept them guessing by changing his appearance and even speaking in different languages.[21]

The Roman narrative frequently repeats tales of Hannibal's trickery and deception, and equally stories of the untrustworthiness of the Celts as allies, which makes this anecdote difficult to decipher. The tales of disguise may have been repeated to persuade the Romans that the Celts who had abandoned them were worthless allies and even Hannibal could not trust them. But there are also echoes of myth and legend in the story. If Hannibal could move about his camp unrecognized and could change his appearance, he was much like the gods in the ancient stories who could disappear and reappear at will, as Poseidon had, visiting the camp of the Greek soldiers at Troy in Homer's *Iliad*.[22] A closer truth may lie in how vulnerable the Carthaginian leader was in these first months to the whims of the Celtic allies upon whom he depended to supplement troops, supplies and food. Surely the Romans, who were not totally friendless in northern Italy, had let it be known that to capture or kill Hannibal would be a well-rewarded act.

Back in Rome Sempronius had made his way to the city to oversee the consular elections for the following year. The consul designates, Gnaeus Servilius and Gaius Flaminius, busied themselves 'mustering the allies and enrolling their own legions, sending depots of supplies to Ariminum and Etruria which they meant to be their bases in the campaign' (Polyb. 3.75.5). There was no peace for the Roman army in winter quarters, according to Livy, who claimed that Hannibal's cavalry roamed far and wide cutting off Roman supplies 'from every quarter, with the exception of those things shipped up the Po' (21.57.5).

The defeat at Trebia turned Roman minds towards religion. They felt abandoned by the gods, and details of prodigies and omens are recorded in Livy's account of that winter. These things happen, Livy says, when bad news 'has turned people's minds to superstition' (21.62.1–2). The defeat in the north weighed heavily on the population at Rome and some of these omens included glowing ship-like figures in the sky, the Temple of Hope being struck by lightning, a crow that settled on the couch of the goddess Juno at Lanuvium, and in Picenum stones that had fallen as a rain shower. This last omen caused 'a nine-day sacrifice to be prescribed . . . and the city was ritually purified and full-grown sacrificial animals were killed for the gods'. There was a general supplication to the gods as the Roman people tried to win them over to their cause against Hannibal. Public prayers were offered, among other places at the temple of Hercules (the Latin for Herakles), who was specifically named.

This illustrates the impact Hannibal's propaganda had on the people and the priests at Rome.[23] In the Roman mind, Hannibal's personal invocation of Herakles' divine support made it essential for the Romans to work even harder to win him back to their side. Livy maintains that for the Romans 'the making of these vows and expiations, as prescribed by the Sibylline Books, went far to alleviate men's anxiety concerning their relations with the gods' (21.62.11).

With the arrival of spring Hannibal made preparations to move and he departed for the south once the passes through the moutains were clear.[24] He may have left his winter quarters as late as May.[25] The route Hannibal took across the Apennines was the least expected and the one most likely to take the Roman consul by surprise. As Polybius explains, 'Hannibal was always inclined by temperament to favour the unexpected solution' (3.78.6).[26] The Carthaginian army crossed over the mountains and passed through a mud-filled swampy marshland, believed to be the flooded Arno river valley (Livy 22.2.1–3.1; Polyb. 3.79.1–11). Hannibal would have been certain to avoid areas where the Romans were stationed, including Ariminum, Arretium and Luca (see Map 1).[27]

In the marshes of Etruria the Carthaginian general and his troops were bogged down by extremely wet ground, and experienced a four-day march of great hardship. The African and Spanish troops, who had crossed the Alps with Hannibal, managed better than the Celtic allies whose enthusiasm for the adventure waned as they trudged through sodden ground. The army marched across the wet terrain in a line with 'the Africans, the Iberians and all the best fighting troops in the forward part of his column and interspersed [with] the baggage train among them . . . the Celts were stationed behind the troops, and the cavalry brought up the rear of the army, the command of the rearguard being entrusted to his brother Mago' (Polyb. 3.79.1–4). This order was to ensure that the Celts would not turn back, tired of suffering through mud and water.

Hannibal himself rode the last surviving elephant on the march south. He must have cut quite a figure in the Etrurian spring, leading his multicultural multilingual army on an elephant. But the trek proved harsh for Hannibal too and he suffered an eye infection. The infection went untreated and was exacerbated by 'sleep deprivation, the damp nights and the swampy atmosphere' (Livy 22.2.10–11). As a result he lost the sight of one eye and suffered intensely from the pain but he could not stop and get treatment (Polyb. 3.79.12). The hardship of the march and the loss of an eye have only added to Hannibal's legend, and both were perhaps emphasized for the benefit of the myth.[28] A one-eyed Hannibal fits well into the tradition of great warriors of the ancient world: 'let us further add, that the most warlike commanders, and most remarkable for exploits of skilful stratagem, have had but one eye; as Philip, Antigonus, Hannibal, and Sertorius . . .' (Plutarch, *Sert.* 1.4).[29]

The Roman consuls of 217 BCE mobilized their troops and allies and even received help in the form of a contingent of Cretans and light infantry from King Hiero II of Syracuse (Polyb. 3.74.7).[30] The Romans had an extremely large force active in the field by the spring of 217 BCE, reflecting the immense resources they could draw upon. There were two legions and allied units in Iberia under Gn. Scipio and directly after Trebia they had sent legions to Sicily and Sardinia to defend the islands. Garrisons were posted to cities in the south, places like Tarentum, whose loyalty was far from assured (Polyb. 3.75.4). The new consul Servilius took up the troops of Publius Scipio, supplemented by new recruits. He established a base at Ariminum while Flaminius had Sempronius' legions and went to Etruria (Livy 21.63.15).[31] The Roman legions were positioned to guard the two main routes south that Hannibal might take.[32] Flaminius pitched his camp near Arretium (modern Arezzo) close to the road that passed through Etruria and Umbria south to Rome.

As Hannibal approached the Roman base through the Arno valley he pitched camp near Faesulae (modern Fiesole about five kilometres north-east of Florence) which lies 60 kilometres from Arretium. The Carthaginian army rested after their long muddy march, which Polybius claimed took them four days and three nights across sodden ground. Hannibal sent out his scouts to reconnoitre the Roman positions. Although we cannot be sure of the numbers, estimates for Hannibal's troops range from forty to fifty thousand soldiers by this point.[33] This was double the number he had arrived in Italy with.

Hannibal's scouts returned with some encouraging information about the Roman consul camped at Arretium. They told Hannibal about Flaminius who was an experienced commander and had fought in Cisalpine Gaul in the 220s. Some of Hannibal's new allies, having recently deserted from the Roman army, certainly had experience of Flaminius and had been able to provide some insight into his character. He was by reputation bullish and confident about his own abilities, and would be eager to take on the challenge represented by Hannibal. To Polybius, Flaminius was 'a thorough mob-courtier and demagogue with no talent for the practical conduct of war and exceedingly self-confident' (3.80.3).

Livy's account is even more damning. He accuses Flaminius of scorning the auspices by refusing to perform the rituals associated with becoming consul when he took up office. Flaminius had gone straight to meet his army and had assumed the consulship there, which meant that from 15 March he had been with his army in the north of Italy. Urgency rather than disrespect for the gods may have led Flaminius north before the official ceremony in Rome but the omens Livy goes on to describe were 'frightful': a calf he was sacrificing 'charged from the hands of the celebrants, spattering the bystanders with blood' (21.63.5–14). The Roman sources, with clear hindsight, lay the blame for the upcoming defeat entirely at the feet of Flaminius and historical tradition is extremely hostile towards him. Posterity remembers Flaminius with the damning judgement of Polybius: 'cowardice and stupidity are vices which, disgraceful as they are in private . . . are, when found in a general, the greatest of public calamities' (3.81.7).

It was June before Hannibal and his troops were encamped at Faesulae and had recovered from their march.[34] The Carthaginian army left its base and moved south towards the Roman camp through the valley of the Arno and in passing taunted Flaminius by 'invading the country in front of him' (Polyb. 3.81.1–2). 'All these factors led Hannibal to conclude that Flaminius would give the Carthaginian army plenty of opportunities to attack him' (3.80.5). Hannibal was determined to provoke the Roman consul by tempting him with his army, flaunting it in front of his eyes. 'He appreciated and anticipated Flaminius' actions, his plan achieved the results he intended' (3.81.12).

The advancing Carthaginians continued south through the lush Val di Chiana. Hannibal may have intended Flaminius to think that they were heading towards Rome in order to get him to follow. Then Hannibal veered to the east, 'keeping the city of Cortona and its hills on his left and Lake Trasimene on his right' (Polyb. 3.82.9).[35] As they marched the Carthaginian army burned crops and devastated the countryside, always with the object of luring the enemy into action. It may well be that when Flaminius was drawn out of his camp in pursuit of Hannibal he had originally planned to follow until the Carthaginian army was trapped between the two Roman armies, fully expecting Servilius' legions to descend from the north (3.86.1–3).[36] He could not have intended to engage in battle with only the two legions and allied troops he had under him, which probably numbered 25,000 in total. Hannibal's army was, if we are to believe the numbers, almost twice as large. Speculation aside, we can never know exactly what Flaminius was thinking when he followed Hannibal along the north shore of Lake Trasimeno.

On 20 June Hannibal led his army through a narrow pass between the lake and the hills to the north. This defile opens up into a small plain surrounded by hills and sealed by the lake. Flaminius camped on the lake shore close by 'at a very late hour' that same night (Polyb. 3.83.7). Hannibal knew that the Roman army was close behind and set a trap. Whether this had always been his intention or was a last-minute improvisation due to the proximity of Flaminius we do not know. Polybius tells us that all Hannibal's preparations were made during the night: 'coasting the lake and passing through the defile', Hannibal occupied the hill in front and there placed his Spanish and African forces. Polybius' very specific description puts Hannibal's 'Balearic slingers and pikemen round to the front by a detour and stationed them in an extended line under the hills to the right of the defile, and similarly taking his cavalry and Celts . . . he placed them in a continuous line under these hills' (3.83.1– 4).[37] At dawn the next day Flaminius led his two legions into the gap. He did not, it seems, send scouts ahead to reconnoitre or he might have realized what lay in store (Livy 22.4.4). Perhaps the idea that Hannibal had concealed a 50,000-strong force in the defile in the mist seemed almost beyond credibility (Map 1).[38]

Still today, a visit to Trasimeno on an early summer morning sees the mist sitting low on the lake, hiding the hills that surround it (Polyb. 3.84.1). As the Roman legions filed into the ambush the visibility was poor. Hannibal 'led his vanguard along the lake' to meet the advancing Romans and gave the signal when he was just in touch with their head. Then the Carthaginian army 'swooped down, each [soldier] taking the shortest route to the enemy . . . the Romans felt they were surrounded before they could actually see it' (Livy 22.5.5–7). The Roman commanders struggled to form their troops into battle lines and 'fighting broke out at the front and on the flanks before the line could be drawn up'. With the enemy soldiers and commanders now in total disarray, the Carthaginian troops attacked at will. Livy's graphic description gives a sense of the mayhem: 'in such dense fog, ears were more useful than eyes. It was to sound that they turned their faces and eyes, to sounds of wounds being dealt, of blows falling on bodies and armour, and of the mingled cries of confusion and panic' (22.5.3–4).[39]

The ambush had worked – and worked magnificently. Even Hannibal must have been surprised by how successful his strategy had been. They had not only killed the consul Flaminius but also roughly 15,000 of his men, with a large proportion of the survivors taken prisoner. The Carthaginians had lost between 1,500 and 2,500 soldiers, many of them Celts. Livy tries to portray a terrible situation slightly more positively by adding that many more died of their wounds (numbers in Polyb. 3.85.5; Livy 22.7.3).

Once more Hannibal was gracious in victory to the Italian allies, whom he set free after the battle, repeating that 'he had not come to fight with the

Italians but with the Romans for the freedom of Italy'. The captured Roman soldiers were so numerous that he had to 'distribute them among his troops to keep guard over'. He buried his dead, paying honours to those of the 'highest rank among the fallen' (Polyb. 3.85.3–5) and 'also made every effort to seek out Flaminius' body for burial but he failed to find it' (Livy 22.7.5). It has been suggested that one of the Celtic warriors had cut Flaminius' head off as a trophy.[40] The Carthaginian forces combed the battlefield collecting the armour and weaponry of the fallen soldiers. This Roman armour was eventually distributed to Hannibal's Libyan infantry, whose equipment was apparently inferior to that of the Roman infantry – especially the shields. At Cannae the following year, Livy would note that 'one might have taken the Africans to be a Roman battle line, for they were armed with captured weapons . . . most taken at Trasimeno' (Livy 22.46.4).[41]

A few days after the slaughter at Trasimeno Hannibal, always well informed, heard that the remaining consul Servilius was close at hand. He sent his chief cavalry commander Maharbal out to meet any advanced guard. Servilius had set out for the south as soon as he had news that Hannibal was in Etruria. His advance group of cavalry was sent on under the leadership of the praetor Gaius Centenius (Polyb. 3.86.3). Maharbal's Numidians (and pikemen) encountered 4,000 Roman cavalry somewhere in Umbria and killed about half the force, capturing the rest (Livy 22.8.1). The victory was complete and without cavalry Servilius could advance no further on Hannibal.

Hannibal now had to make his next move and choose the direction of his march. He left Etruria, dismissing 'the idea of approaching Rome for the present', and moved southwards through Umbria. He then crossed over to the Adriatic via Picenum (modern Le Marche).[42] It took him ten days. 'At this time he sent messengers to Carthage by sea with news of what had happened, this being the first time he had come in touch with the sea since he invaded' (Polyb. 3.86.8–9). The ability to communicate more straightforwardly with Carthage meant that for the first time in eighteen months Hannibal had direct contact with his home city. Carthage's response to the victory at Trasimeno is under-reported but we can assume that 'the news was received with great rejoicing by the Carthaginians', as Polybius claims. There were vows to send more aid to their young general in the field and promises to step up the Carthaginian side of the operations. Carthage would 'give every possible support to the conduct of the war both in Italy and in Iberia' (Polyb. 3.87.5).[43]

Hannibal was now in contact with Carthage but a clear and detailed account of the specific measures he took after Trasimeno eludes us. A

Carthaginian fleet captured Roman 'transport vessels carrying supplies from Ostia to the army in Iberia' in the summer of 217 BCE (Livy 22.11.6). The appearance of a Carthaginian fleet off the Etruscan port of Cosa might suggest that the old Carthage–Etruscan alliance had been revived. Hannibal would have found support for his invasion in the region and perhaps he originally intended to link up with the fleet in Etruria before an attack on Rome.[44] Polybius suggests that there had been a pre-arranged meeting for Carthaginian ships off Etruria but that they were forced to depart quickly once a much larger Roman fleet approached (3.96.7–9). Plans for resupply and a link with the Carthaginian navy may well have been part of Hannibal's original overall strategy but our sources do not reveal enough detail to allow for a coherent reconstruction. A coordinated land and sea operation makes sense in this context but the superiority of the Roman fleet, and the lack of a friendly port from which the Carthaginians could operate, made this policy less effective than it might have been. It would keep Hannibal distant from Carthage.[45]

The lack of tangible support from Carthage meant that Hannibal had to supply his army by taking what he needed from the countryside. Loot was in no short supply and there was 'so large an amount of booty that his army could not drive or carry it all' (Polyb. 3.86.10). Food supplies, shelter and the continued upkeep of his forces were his main concerns and this created its own set of problems. Winning the Italian allies over would have been much easier without having to pillage their crops to supply his army. As he moved east the army camped near the Adriatic. Livy claims that Hannibal spent time restoring his tired and battle-worn troops, and 'paid great attention to the health of his men as well as his horses by proper treatment' (3.87.1). The state of his troops must have been a cause for concern. His horses had mange and his men had spent over fourteen months either on the march or in battle. 'By bathing the horses in old wine' he was able to cure their mange. This was perhaps an old Carthaginian veterinary trick not known elsewhere. The rich and fertile lands of Picenum made certain the men were well fed (Polyb. 3.88.2).[46]

Hannibal's strategy relied critically on local recruitment: he was able both to pick up soldiers along the way and to attract deserters from the Roman alliance. After each victory many more joined the cause of the Carthaginian commander. It was also essential for Hannibal to acquire the support of the Italian cities, the crucial allies of the Romans, for without urban support his campaign would be unsustainable.[47] A considerable number of the different ethnic and language groups that populated the Italian peninsula had been battling the Romans for centuries and many were happy to take up Hannibal's fight. There is a fascinating inscription of an Etruscan man named Felsnas who lived to be 106 years old and claimed in his epitaph to 'have fought with Hannibal's men' at Capua. Felsnas was one of a multitude who joined Hannibal. What is remarkable, considering his long life, was that this was presumably what he was best remembered for: the glory acquired by fighting 'with Hannibal's men'.[48]

As so much of the story of Hannibal comes to us through Roman eyes, we can see how deeply Hannibal's myths had infiltrated the city in Rome's response to the calamitous defeat at Trasimeno. The reaction at Rome was dramatic and the Romans did not 'bear the reverse with moderation and dignity' (Polyb. 3.85.9). When news of the cavalry defeat followed three days later, more desperation took hold. One consul was dead, an army had been annihilated and few families in Rome would have been untouched by the loss (Livy 22.7.6–14).[49] The Roman political system allowed for the appointment of a dictator – who would have absolute power in civil and military affairs in times of crisis. However, the appointment of a military dictator had 'been neither needed nor employed for a long time'. Normally a dictator would be chosen by the consuls but Flaminius was dead and Servilius cut off from Rome by Hannibal's armies, so 'the people took the hitherto unprecedented step of appointing a dictator themselves' (Polyb. 3.86.7; Livy 22.8.5–7).

The threat of Hannibal resulted in the dictatorship of Quintus Fabius Maximus. He was chosen by the *comitia centuriata* (the people's assembly) and had held the dictatorship in a civil capacity once before, and twice been consul. Marcus Minucius was chosen as his second in command, designated Master of the Horse (*magister equitum*), and was 'his successor when the dictator is otherwise occupied' (Polyb. 3.87.9). The unusual nature of this dictatorship is suggestive of rivalries between families at Rome in face of the threat of Hannibal. Fabius Maximus as dictator would normally choose his own Master of the Horse but the election of Minucius, who was a political opponent of the dictator, indicates some wrangling among different factions in this time of crisis.[50]

At Rome the religious response to the crisis was of equal significance to the political. So much so that Fabius Maximus 'on the day of his entry into office convened the Senate opening the session with matters of religion . . .' The consul Gaius Flaminius was condemned more for his 'disregard for ritual and auspices than his recklessness and incompetence' (Livy 22.9.7). The Romans declared that the cause of the defeat was the anger of the gods, who needed appeasement, and Fabius Maximus and the Senate made the decision to 'consult the Sibylline Books' so that the gods' wishes could be understood

(Livy 22.9.8).[51] Following the orders of the sacred books, games were vowed to Jupiter, two new cults would be introduced to Rome and temples established for their worship.[52]

One of the new temples promised at Rome was intended to directly counter the threat of Hannibal. It was to be dedicated to Venus Erycina, the goddess whose cult centre was in north-west Sicily on Mount Eryx (Livy 22.9.7). Venus Erycina was a Latinized name for the goddess worshipped by the Carthaginians as Astarte, who was syncretized to Aphrodite by the Greeks and Venus by the Romans. Her cult centre in Sicily may, in origin, have been connected to Melqart and had played a strategic part in the First Punic War.[53] In the final phase of the First Punic War the Romans had held firm to her sanctuary in the face of fierce opposition by Hamilcar Barca. The establishment of a cult to the goddess in Rome can be seen as a means of appropriating the power of Astarte/Aphrodite/Venus for use against the Carthaginians. The Romans were attempting, symbolically, to take her away from her long-standing connection to Carthage and thus to Hannibal. Greek mythical traditions in Sicily, where support for the Carthaginians remained strong, also tied the foundation of the cult to Aeneas, the Trojan founder of Rome. Thus the links of the Romans to the Greek traditions, so important among the allies in southern Italy and Sicily, were being emphasized.[54] Hannibal had understood from the beginning that the politics of religion and myth would loom large in the struggle for Italy and now the Romans were fighting back.

Underlying Fabius Maximus' reaction to the defeat at Trasimeno was the belief of the Roman people that they had been abandoned by the gods.[55] Hannibal's propaganda had worked on the minds of the Romans and they feared the gods must be on his side after his miraculous feats and now his great victory. Hannibal claimed to have Herakles on his side and to be supported by divine favour. So Fabius Maximus took practical steps to challenge this supremacy. Fabius' own family history also plays a large part in the decision to adopt the particular cult of Venus Erycina. This cult connected Fabius' dictatorship with the wars of his grandfather against the Samnites (in 295 BCE) when another temple to Venus (*Venus Obsequens*) had been vowed during his consulship.[56] Together with an effort to assuage public fear, this was an attempt by Fabius Maximus to mark a new beginning in Rome's war with Hannibal by connecting his dictatorship to the victories of his illustrious ancestors, thus emphasizing how power politics played out by rival families underlay much of the decision-making at Rome in this period.[57]

The cult of Mens, vowed at the same time as that of Venus Erycina, had a more prosaic intent. Mens was a goddess of 'good sense' and perhaps embodied what the dictator Fabius Maximus would bring to his government. Mens was the opposite to what Flaminius had shown at Trasimeno. This balance reflects Roman culture in the third century, when influences from abroad and more traditional beliefs mixed in the city. The exotic cult of Venus Erycina both suggested the acquisition of the Carthaginian goddess and tied the Romans to an epic Greek past. Mens was a cult steeped in the traditions of Roman and Latin culture, very earthy and central Italic, based on the values of indigenous Rome.[58] The battle for divine support had many implications for the politics of Italy in the third century; Hannibal had understood from the outset that it was a fight that would have to be won to ensure victory.

For Hannibal the years 218–217 BCE brought brilliant victories and mythic challenges. Our sources have a single focus of the war in Italy during this period, beguiled by Hannibal's charismatic leadership and military achievements. The war had, however, quickly spread to much of the western Mediterranean and was being pursued in other theatres, engulfing Iberia and Sardinia as well as Sicily in these years.[59] Hasdrubal Barca, Hannibal's younger brother, had been left to continue the consolidation and defence of Carthaginian Iberia. When Gn. Scipio (consul himself in 222/221 BCE), the older brother of Cornelius Scipio, had taken over the legions and fleet from his brother (the bulk of two legions and allies, roughly 25,000 men) at the mouth of the Rhône he had gone straight to Emporium (modern Ampurias). Emporium was a colony founded by Rome's main allies in the region, the Massalians (Polyb. 3.76.1). By the time he arrived there in the autumn of 218 BCE it was already close to the end of the fighting season (Polyb. 3.49.4; Livy 21.32.3).[60]

Hanno, the Carthaginian commander Hannibal had left in charge of the territory beyond the Ebro, responded with force to the Roman invasion and set out to engage them at a city called Cissa.[61] The battle that followed was a disaster for the Carthaginians. Hanno and one of the key Iberian allied leaders Andobales, called 'despot of all central Iberia', were both captured. Gn. Scipio won the battle and took possession of 'valuable booty', all the heavy baggage that Hannibal had left behind when he had set out for Italy (Polyb. 3.76.6–7; Livy 21.60.7). This was a region that Hannibal had subdued on his march through to Italy but it had quickly been secured by the Romans.[62] The Romans aimed to stop Hasdrubal from linking up with his brother via the overland route into Italy. They attempted to restrict the Carthaginians to their power base in Iberia, while prising their allies away from them.[63]

When news of this defeat reached Hasdrubal he immediately set out from the south and crossed the Ebro. There he found Gn. Scipio's Roman fleet unprotected. The men of the fleet were both 'off their guard and unduly confident'. Hasdrubal attacked and killed a 'large number of them'. The rest had to take refuge on their ships. Hasdrubal then retreated south of the Ebro where he fortified and garrisoned the cities 'and passed the winter in New Carthage'. Gn. Scipio returned to his fleet and punished the crews for what had happened. He 'inflicted the customary penalty', which is likely to have been execution by beating for desertion (or exile, if one survived the thrashing) and then retreated to his winter quarters at Tarraco (Polyb. 3.76.12).[64]

The year 217 did not go as well for Hasdrubal Barca as it had for his brother in Italy. In the spring Hasdrubal launched both naval and land attacks on the Romans north of the Ebro. Hasdrubal's fleet met the Roman forces, who were supported by the Massalians. He was defeated at the mouth of the Ebro, with the loss of twenty-five ships (Polyb. 3.95.1–6; Livy 22.19.1–12).[65] The Romans pressed on deep into Carthaginian territory past the Ebro and their ships raided the countryside even to the south of New Carthage and the island of Ebusus (Ibiza). The Balearic Islands, whose highly specialized slingers played such an important role in Hannibal's light infantry, sent envoys to Rome seeking to make peace.[66]

The Romans encouraged, bought and supported any disturbance to Carthaginian power among their allies and a Celtiberian rebellion ensued. In many ways this was the reverse of what was happening in Italy and made it impossible for Hasdrubal Barca to fulfil his promise to support his brother there. The successes of Gn. Scipio at the Ebro and the consequences seem to have encouraged the Roman Senate to send reinforcements. A newly raised fleet of twenty ships arrived under the command of Publius Scipio some time later in 217 BCE (Polyb. 3.97.2). Publius Scipio had been named proconsul and 'from this time the two Scipio brothers carried on the war in Iberia' (Appian, *Ib*. 15).[67] The sustained Roman pressure in the Iberian peninsula was meant to ensure that they were not fighting all three Barcid brothers in Italy and it would be years, rather than months, before Hasdrubal could even attempt to join up with Hannibal.[68]

# CHAPTER 7

# THE APOGEE
## CANNAE AND THE WAR IN ITALY

And he sang . . . of the victorious delays of Fabius, of the ill-starred fight
of Cannae; and the gods that turned to answer pious prayers . . .
**(Propertius 3.3. 9–10)**

HANNIBAL AND HIS ARMY moved freely in the period immediately after
Trasimeno. There were no Roman forces to oppose him as he restored
his troops and gathered supplies. He received envoys from cities around Italy.
Some came to him to test the waters, others just to meet the man, give advice
and understand his plans (Livy 22.13.2–3).[1] Italy was allied Roman territory
but many alliances had been imposed by force rather than choice. There was
no shortage of hostility to Rome and many may have hoped to use Hannibal
as an antidote to Roman hegemony. Hannibal would have welcomed all
who sought alliance but with a large force to feed he could not stay in one
place for too long. After resting by the Adriatic the Carthaginian army moved
south into the region of Apulia. Hannibal went to the south because he believed the Roman alliance was most vulnerable there and his tactics might
be most successfully employed. By moving south, staying to the east of the
Apennines, Hannibal also avoided territory directly controlled by the Romans.
The army plundered as they went, attacking the Roman colony of Luceria and
the countryside around it, moving into the fertile agricultural region of the
modern Gargano, near the town of Arpi (Polyb. 3.88.2–6) (see Map 1).

Unchallenged, Hannibal attacked Roman allies and colonies and appeared
to have complete control of the countryside. He may have hoped to provoke

the Romans into another battle that would help to seal his success. When he received reports that the newly appointed dictator Fabius Maximus was nearby with an army, Hannibal prepared to engage. Moving towards Fabius, he 'led his forces out and drew them up in order of battle at a short distance from the Roman camp but after waiting some time and as nobody came out to meet him he retired again to his own camp' (Polyb. 3.89.1).[2]

As dictator, Fabius Maximus took control of four legions and set out with a clear strategy to take on Hannibal. He had no intention of engaging the Carthaginian army directly in battle but planned to shadow them. Fabius Maximus became famous for this policy of non-engagement and is known to posterity by the epithet *Cunctator*, the delayer. 'Risk averse' might be the better description of Fabius, who understood the dangers of a set-piece battle against Hannibal's highly effective, disciplined fighting force and superior cavalry. Fabius was 'a man of admirable judgement and great natural gifts', in the eyes of Polybius (3.87.6). Considering that most of his troops were no match for the battle-hardened Carthaginian army at that moment his options were limited. The Romans had other strengths and 'these advantages . . . lay in an inexhaustible supply of provisions and men' (Polyb. 3.89.9). Two millennia later when Napoleon invaded Russia in 1812 the great Russian general Kutuzov employed similar tactics to defeat a superior fighting force, relying on an almost limitless supply of men and provisions and a better knowledge of the countryside.[3]

The two strategists, Hannibal the risk-taker and Fabius Maximus the risk-averse, attempted to outmanoeuvre each other. Fabius endeavoured 'to move parallel to the enemy, always occupying in advance the positions which his knowledge of the country told him were the most advantageous' (Polyb. 3.90.1). The Roman intention was to harass Hannibal at close quarters, to skirmish with the men sent out to forage but not to fall into a trap or be provoked into battle. This strategy allowed the Romans to bide their time and gave their soldiers experience against the Carthaginian army. Hannibal sensed how dangerous this might be to his army and 'felt immediate apprehension about the dictator's wariness' (Livy, 22.12.5–6). His soldiers would have been frustrated and isolated as Fabius' tactics constrained Hannibal's ability to reach out to allies in Italy. The number of soldiers in the Carthaginian army was limited and he was far from home. They were vulnerable and would be defeated by increments if this situation continued. As Polybius noted, 'Fabius was determined not to expose himself to any risk or to venture on a battle but to make the safety of the army under his command his first and chief aim' (3.89.2). Up until now Hannibal had controlled all his engagements with

Roman commanders, whose confidence and aggression had led them to engage. Fabius was different.

Through the late summer and into the autumn of 217 BCE Hannibal plundered and provoked while Fabius delayed and contained. Livy records Fabius' scorched-earth policy. He issued 'an edict for all people whose towns and settlements lacked fortifications to move to places of safety, and for all those in the area along the route Hannibal was likely to take to leave their farms . . . to burn their buildings and destroy their crops . . . so as to leave the enemy no supplies of any kind' (22.11.4). The tactics had an impact and there are reports of severe supply shortages for Hannibal later in 217/216 BCE (22.32.3). However, since Polybius has the Carthaginians 'in possession of a huge amount of booty' by the end of the campaigning season of 217 it becomes difficult to judge the real effectiveness of the policy (3.92.9).[4]

Hannibal's reaction to Fabius' tactics was to lead his army west into the mountains of the Samnites and across into Campania to the fertile lands of what was called in Latin the *ager Falernus*. 'The plain around Capua is the most celebrated in all Italy, both for its fertility and beauty,' exclaims Polybius (3.91.2). The area is notable because it was officially Roman territory (ceded by Capua in 340 BCE) and the Campanians had been granted a limited form of Roman citizenship in the fourth century.[5] The population was a heterogeneous mix of Greek, Oscan speaking (the Italic peoples of the region) and Roman colonists with a strong independent streak. The area contained key towns such as Capua, 'once the wealthiest of cities', and also ports along the coast like Cumae, Neapolis (Naples) and Nuceria (Polyb. 3.91.6). Hannibal reasoned that his presence there would 'either . . . compel the enemy to fight or make it plain to everybody that he was winning and that the Romans were abandoning the country to him' (Polyb. 3.90.11).[6]

Once in Campania, Hannibal found himself in what Polybius describes as 'a kind of theatre' with the sea to the west and high mountains on the south and east. The circle of mountains, 'through which there are only three passes from the interior, all of them narrow and difficult', provided the seats of the theatre, although the region is more accessible than Polybius makes out (3.91.8–10).[7] Fabius Maximus maintained his strategy despite agitation among some of the Roman generals, and especially from his Master of the Horse, Minucius, who could not bear to stand by and watch Hannibal move about with impunity. In the Livian tradition, the Roman second in command rails against the policy of containment: 'have we come here as spectators' to watch 'the sight of our allies being butchered and their property burned?' (22.14.3). The Roman forces were positioned in the hills above the Campanian plain, moving in tandem with the Carthaginians and guarding the passes through the mountains while watching the roads north to Rome.[8] Minucius made fun of 'Fabius's tactics where, as he put it, the dictator took great trouble to provide the army with splendid seats to witness the spectacle of Italy being laid waste' (Plutarch, *Fab.* 5.5).

Hannibal's motivation to remain in the south through this summer is addressed by Polybius: 'he hoped [this policy] would cause alarm among the cities and persuade them to throw off their allegiance to Rome' (3.90.10–13). As Fabius Maximus watched Hannibal's army from the hills, 'a farm that belonged to the dictator had been pointed out to the Carthaginians by some deserters'. Hannibal ordered the whole area to be razed to the ground except this farm. He wanted to 'create the impression that some secret pact had been made and this was Fabius's payment for it' (Livy 22.23.4–5). The policy was designed to increase Roman hostility to their dictator's delaying tactics. Hannibal hoped to make it both more difficult for Fabius Maximus to maintain his distance and to turn people against the Romans.[9] Up until this point, however sympathetic some of the allies might have been to Hannibal's cause, none had been persuaded to change sides, with most in the region waiting to see what the next phase in the war would entail.[10]

As autumn arrived, Hannibal turned back to Apulia. He had been about a month in Campania, 'having done his best to provoke the Romans'. He found himself still without any significant defections to his side and an urgent need for safe winter quarters for his men and baggage. Hannibal 'wanted to secure . . . a place suitable for his winter quarters, so that his army should not only fare sumptuously for the present but continue to have abundance of provisions' (Polyb. 3.92.8–9). The Roman dictator had also made the same calculations and positioned his army to try and block Hannibal's retreat into Apulia. For Fabius 'was sure that Hannibal would go back by the same passes he had used to enter Falernian territory' (Livy 22.15.3).[11]

Turning back towards Apulia meant crossing the Apennines, a significant barrier – especially as Hannibal knew the Romans occupied the high ground and blocked the passes that led through the mountains. To the Romans this must have seemed the moment when Fabius Maximus' summer-long policy of attrition would finally pay off.[12] Four thousand Roman troops had been positioned in the narrowest part of the pass, probably the valley of Callicula, north of Cales.[13] Fabius waited 'with the greater part of his army encamped on a hill in front of the pass'. When the Carthaginians arrived and made their camp, Fabius 'thought he would be able to carry away their booty . . . and possibly even to put an end to the whole campaign' (Polyb. 3.93.1). It is revealing of how wary the Romans were of Hannibal that they did not attack him here when they occupied the high ground and had him trapped.

Hannibal assessed his situation and devised a plan to meet the challenge. He seemed to be cut off 'and it did not escape his notice that his own strategy was being turned against him' (Livy 22.16.4–5). He ordered one of his key lieutenants Hasdrubal, titled the 'officer in charge of services', to collect and bundle as much dry wood as could be found.[14] Next he gathered together two thousand of the strongest oxen they had in the 'captured stock' (Polyb. 3.93.4). Then they took dry bundles of wood mixed 'together with bunches of twigs and dry vine-shoots and attached them to the horns of the oxen' (Livy 22.16.5–8). The plan was for the light infantry (pikemen) to drive the oxen by night with their horns aflame towards a 'saddle' that lay between the Romans guarding the narrow pass and the Carthaginian camp. Hannibal sought to create a diversion for his army to use as cover as they moved by night through the narrowest part of the pass and into the Apennines. He ordered his men to 'get their supper and retire to rest early', taking care as always that they were at their best for the next challenge (Polyb. 3.93.6).

'When the third watch of the night [c. 03h00] was over . . . he now bade them light all the bundles and drive the oxen up to the ridge.' As soon as the Roman soldiers guarding the pass 'saw the lights advancing up the slope', they thought that Hannibal was moving his army in that direction. Drawn by the lights they 'left the narrow part of the pass and advanced to the hill to meet the enemy'. The Roman soldiers were confused when they reached the oxen. Their fear was that something 'much more formidable' than the reality awaited them (Polyb. 3.93.7–3.94.2). Hannibal's supernatural reputation must have helped this ruse succeed. The Roman troops were obviously in awe of his abilities, and in the dark especially wary about what magical plan might unfold at his bidding. When the Romans had moved away from the narrow pass, Hannibal made for the gap 'with his heavy-armed troops in front, next to them his cavalry, next the captured cattle, and finally the Spaniards and Celts' (Polyb. 3.93.10). In this way Hannibal brought his whole army and all his treasury safely through the narrow gorge and evaded the Romans.

There are records of a remarkably similar use of oxen with their horns aflame by the famous general Tian Dan in China some fifty years before Hannibal's ruse. It would indicate how widely informed Hannibal was and how closely connected the world had become if he had known of this subterfuge beforehand.[15] We have no way of knowing the origins of the idea with any certainty so it seems likely to be an extraordinary coincidence. The plan was successful and the dawn found the Roman forces on the ridge of a saddle facing the Carthaginian light infantry among the oxen. Hannibal sent some of his Spanish troops back and they attacked the Romans, killed about a thousand and brought their own light infantry down through the pass safely (Polyb. 3.94.6).[16] Once again, superior skill, imagination and intelligence had left the Romans in disarray.

The ever-cautious Fabius had 'heard the commotion, but thought it was a trap and was reluctant to fight any battle, especially in the dark' (Livy 22.18.1). Thus a rather dejected Roman army followed Hannibal back through Samnium and into Apulia. The search for winter quarters led Hannibal to the countryside around Luceria and up to the town of Geronium, where there was 'plenty of corn' (Polyb. 3.100.1–2). He had generally spread 'terror' around the countryside during the campaigning season so when he sent a message to the citizens of Geronium 'asking for their alliance and offering pledges' they ignored the request (Polyb. 3.100.3). Hannibal then took the city by siege and the inhabitants were 'put to the sword' (Polyb. 3.100.4). In contrast, Livy claims that the city was already abandoned when Hannibal decided to settle there for the winter and he used the abandoned buildings as grain stores (22.18.7).[17]

Back in Rome the political fallout from Hannibal's miraculous escape played out and 'Fabius' delaying tactics were now discredited in Rome as well as in the camp' (Livy 22.15.1). Fabius Maximus was a soldier of great experience but his tactics provoked strong opposition within his own army and from the Roman population. 'The soldiers mocked Fabius and contemptuously called him Hannibal's *paedagogus,*' wrote his biographer Plutarch (*Fab.* 5.4). This was considered a demeaning term and is difficult to translate into English. The *paedagogus* was a slave employed to accompany boys to school, carry their books, and was in essence a private tutor. Hannibal's miraculous escape from Campania, when it looked as if he was trapped, 'brought down more abuse and contempt upon Fabius than anything that had come before' (*Fab.* 7.2). Fabius Maximus was recalled to Rome around the time that Hannibal was searching for winter quarters. Livy tells us that the visit was for religious purposes but there is speculation that he was recalled to answer questions from the Senate about his increasingly unpopular strategy. While Fabius was away in Rome, Minucius took command of the legions. Before he left for Rome, Fabius had advised his second in command to keep to the strategy of shadowing Hannibal but Minucius was 'entirely wrapped up in the project of risking a great battle' (Polyb. 3.94.10).[18]

The Carthaginian forces at Geronium were busy gathering enough supplies to see them through the winter. Hannibal's main concern was keeping his men, livestock and horses fit and well, as 'his cavalry was the arm on which he relied above all others' (Polyb. 3.101.11). Food supply was a significant concern and he needed fodder and pastureland to keep his considerable number of livestock healthy. This left him vulnerable to attack. The priority given to provisioning meant that Hannibal dispatched a large proportion of the army out to forage, leaving a skeleton crew to defend their quarters. Minucius watched from nearby as the men went about collecting grain and stores. Hannibal occupied a forward position, fortifying a camp in front of Geronium, and stationed some of his light infantry on a hill between himself and the Romans to supply cover to the foragers. Minucius sensed that the Carthaginians were vulnerable and led out his own light-armed troops in an attack on the hill. The Romans took the position and Hannibal and his men were forced to withdraw (Polyb. 3.101.4–7).

The skirmish laid bare Hannibal's main weakness: that his men had to forage and his animals needed food. This diminished his manpower both for fighting and protecting his camp. Minucius' aggressive tactics bore fruit on a day when 'a great number of the enemy were dispersed over the country . . . he drew up his legionaries in front of the Carthaginian camp . . . and sent his cavalry and light-armed troops out to attack the foragers, with orders to take no prisoners'. Hannibal was caught without the manpower to march out and meet the Roman legions or protect the men who were foraging. Minucius had Hannibal cornered and managed to kill 'many' of his soldiers. It was the arrival of Hannibal's lieutenant Hasdrubal with 4,000 cavalry that finally caused the Romans to withdraw. The Carthaginians had to abandon their forward position and retreat into Geronium. From then on they foraged much more cautiously (Polyb. 3.102.1–11). In the whole period Hannibal spent in Italy, this was one of the few times he allowed the opposition to dictate the terms of engagement. His preoccupation with gathering supplies meant he had not been prepared for a battle.[19]

Minucius' success against Hannibal was blown all out of proportion in Rome. The events were reported 'in terms that exaggerated the true facts and so delighted the people' since any good news was welcome (Polyb. 3.103.1).[20] Different factions in Rome were struggling for control over the direction of the war and one of the tribunes (Metilius) 'mounted the rostrum and delivered a rabble-rousing speech in which he glorified Minucius' (Plutarch, *Fab.* 8.3–4). Pressure on the politicians must have been intense as the result was an unprecedented shift in policy that gave Minucius equal status to Fabius Maximus. The Romans seized upon any reason to feel better about the war, thus 'all found fault with Fabius while Minucius' reputation rose so much'.

Consequently 'two Dictators were actually appointed for the same field of action' at Rome. Once Fabius was back in the field, he and Minucius decided to split the army into two forces and they camped about 12 stades (c. 2 kilometres) apart (Polyb. 3.103.6–8).[21] This division among the Romans reflected the more usual routine of the two consuls' alternating command. It also played into Hannibal's hands, for a divided and distrustful enemy gave him the advantage.

While the Romans divided their army, 'nothing taking place amongst the enemy escaped the notice of Hannibal, for he had ample intelligence from deserters, as well as information from spies' (Livy 22.28.1; Polyb. 3.104.1). Hannibal focused on provoking Minucius whom he understood to be overconfident, aggressive and just the sort of opponent he would choose to lure into a battle. Taking the initiative, Hannibal decided to occupy a small hill between his camp and that of Minucius, which 'offered a strong position'. The hill was treeless but with hollows and bumps that provided an ideal location to conceal troops and draw Minucius into an ambush. Hannibal 'sent out into the night bodies of troops' to occupy strategic positions unseen and at dawn he moved with his light-armed infantry on to the hill. Minucius reacted as Hannibal expected. He dispatched his light infantry and cavalry and then set out at the head of his legions (Polyb. 3.104.1–7). The first wave of Roman light infantry was pushed backwards and fell on the legions behind throwing them into confusion. At this moment, the ambush was unveiled and Minucius found himself surrounded. From afar, Fabius Maximus watched the action unfold. He drew up his legions and came to the rescue, providing cover for Minucius' retreat. Hannibal pursued, but abandoned the chase with the arrival of Fabius' disciplined troops and the battle was brought to a close. The Romans had suffered heavy losses and Minucius had been taught a lesson (Polyb. 3.105.1–10).

Much of the narrative of the autumn of 217 BCE is told by the Roman historians with hindsight, to justify Fabius Maximus' policies. 'And to those in Rome it became indisputably clear how widely the foresight, good sense and calm calculation of a general differ from the recklessness and bravado of a mere soldier' is Polybius' scathing assessment of Minucius and the populist politics that supported him (3.105.9). The wisdom of Fabius Maximus and the foolishness of Minucius are probably exaggerated for the purpose of narrative in Polybius, Livy and Plutarch. The two men and their different strategies reflect the extremes of the Roman political reaction to Hannibal. The political infighting at Rome was the result of Hannibal's skilled tactics and creative abilities. He was playing the Romans like pieces in a board game. The assessment of posterity is that Fabius Maximus, by delaying a full engagement with Hannibal in the crucial autumn of 217 BCE, may have saved the Romans from total defeat. The poet Ennius in the second century would write, 'one man alone, by his delaying, restored our state' (*Ann.* 363).[22]

December 217 BCE saw the term of office for the dictators come to a close (the appointment had been for six months) and new consular elections were held in January 216 BCE. Rome's constitutional state was hardly typical at the end of that year. There were two dictators and one surviving consul (Servilius) in the field. The newly elected magistrates came to power in March, and in the intervening period, Servilius and Marcus Atilius Regulus (elected to replace the dead Flaminius) were granted proconsular authority. They took control of the Roman forces in the field in Italy (Livy 22.25.1–19).[23]

Political and constitutional discord broke out at Rome during this period. A full account can be found in Livy, although he tends to simplify the arguments, presenting a straightforward battle between traditional factions of patricians and plebians in the Roman Senate, and portrays anyone who opposed Fabius' tactics as a dangerous populist.[24] Underlying these structural arguments were real disagreements between powerful individuals over the strategy to be adopted in the upcoming campaigning season. The resulting convoluted process of the election of the consuls for 216 BCE reflects these disagreements and the unusual constitutional situation (Livy 22.32–33).[25]

Beyond the wrangling of the political elite at Rome there was a deep sense of anxiety among the population that exposes Hannibal's infiltration of the popular imagination. Livy records the arrest of a Carthaginian spy at Rome, who was released after his hands were cut off, and the crucifixion of twenty-five slaves in the Campus Martius for conspiracy (22.33.1). Bad omens persisted, as well as more 'showers of stones', 'blood had flowed profusely from statues amongst the Sabines, and also amid the waters at Caere . . . and a number of people had been fatally struck by lightning' (Livy 22.36.7–9). These details in Livy give a sense of the atmosphere of paranoia in the city with political intrigue and turmoil among a population suspicious of each other and insecure about the future. Most of all the Roman people worried deeply that the gods had turned their backs on Rome.[26]

Hannibal had other things on his mind throughout the winter and early spring of 216 BCE but his intelligence network would have kept him apprised of the situation at Rome. Meanwhile his army, the size of a small city, would have been organized and run like an urban community. For five months in camp this meant constant activity, with combat training continuing and economic activity growing up around this soldiers' city. In the archaeological

record little evidence can be tied to these brief months but examples of
Carthaginian coins minted 'in camp' for payment of troops have survived
from other regions in Italy.[27] Hannibal's army would have had legions of
followers, referred to as baggage by Polybius, including women, children,
opportunists, deserters and slaves. Also by this point, along with the rest
would be merchants, suppliers and blacksmiths aware of the demands to
supply an army on the move. Taking all this together, we may assume that
Hannibal's managerial skills must have been formidable.[28]

And 'all through the winter and spring the two armies remained encamped
opposite each other' (Polyb. 3.107.1). Hannibal could only move his forces
out of camp once 'the season was advanced enough for them to get supplies
from the year's crops' (3.107.2). In Apulia crops are harvested in late May or
early June.[29] The newly elected Roman consuls Lucius Aemilius Paullus and
Gaius Terentius Varro took up office in March but did not join the armies in
the field until June/July. From March through to June they would have
been recruiting soldiers for their new legions and calling up allies to supply
auxiliary troops. The consuls were experienced men of the Republic although
perhaps not the most battle-hardened. Aemilius Paullus, a few years previously as consul in 219 BCE, had 'conducted the Illyrian war with courage'
(Polyb. 3.107.8). Varro was the first man in his family to become a senator
(a *novus homo*). Livy's derisive comment that 'his father had been a butcher
who had kept his own stall' belies the fact that Varro had followed a traditional senatorial career leading to the top position in the Republic (Livy
22.25.18–19).[30] How much experience of military command Varro had
before the consulship of 216 BCE is somewhat more debatable.[31]

Hannibal is certain to have scouted the entire countryside over the winter
and made himself familiar with the lie of the land and the key strategic locations. His next move would be calculated to force the hand of the Romans. So
when the Carthaginian army moved 96 kilometres south and east from their
winter quarters, they arrived at the small walled town of Cannae near the
banks of the river Aufidis (Map 1).[32] Previously the Romans had held Cannae
as a grain store for their supplies coming from Canusium. Hannibal seized
Cannae for its strategically placed citadel that afforded a commanding position over the countryside. From Cannae he could disrupt the Roman supply
lines (Polyb. 3.107.5). It was a tactically inspired move that cut the Romans
off from their stores and made it difficult if not impossible for them to avoid
engaging. Taking Cannae ensured that the Romans were provoked into battle,
and the landscape around the town was ideally suited to make the most of
Hannibal's cavalry (Polyb. 3.107.5–7).[33]

At Cannae Hannibal waited for the Romans to respond. They had shadowed him from winter quarters and camped in the vicinity.[34] Up to this point the two proconsuls, Servilius and Regulus, had been 'expressly ordered not to risk a general engagement but to skirmish, so as to train the men and give them confidence' (Polyb. 3.106.4). Once Hannibal had taken Cannae, the Senate decided to engage in battle and the new consuls arrived on the scene with their freshly recruited legions. The total troop numbers for the two sides are notoriously difficult to assess. Polybius (3.114.5) and Livy (22.46.4) both believe that Hannibal had 40,000 infantry and 10,000 cavalry. This nice round number of 50,000 leads to some suspicion over its accuracy but without alternative figures the number must be accepted.[35]

Estimates of the Roman troop numbers vary widely but all our sources agree they were high. Polybius claims that 'they decided to bring eight legions into the field, a thing which had never been done before by the Romans' (3.107.9). The intention was to overwhelm Hannibal with sheer numbers. Even in Livy's time there was uncertainty and, whilst he notes the 'discrepancies in the sources regarding number and kind of troops involved', he records eight legions, but with 'increased numbers in terms of infantry and cavalry', providing an estimate of 87,200 including allied troops (22.36.1–2).[36] The full complement of Roman troops could well have been over 80,000 but it is unlikely that all were available to fight Hannibal at Cannae, and most recent assessments have put the number at about 70,000 infantry and 6,000 cavalry.[37] Estimates for the total number of Carthaginians in the field on the day of Cannae rest at about 42,000, with around 8,000 left to garrison their camp.[38] We cannot know the precise numbers, but if we bear in mind the Roman intent to end the war with this battle, they may have outnumbered Hannibal's troops by close to 2:1 (Polyb. 3.109.4).

In late July 216 BCE Hannibal would have seen this massive Roman army come into view and watched from Cannae as they set up a camp about 2.5 kilometres away.[39] There would have been no mistaking the approach of the Romans in the dry summer heat of Apulia. An army of 80,000 would have raised a dust cloud visible for tens of kilometres. By the summer the hills and fields were bare, the crops harvested and the landscape of wide rolling plains would have provided good visibility in all directions.[40] Hannibal may have been surprised by the size of the force ranged against him or perhaps excited by the challenge presented to him. His thoughts in the lead-up to battle are not recorded but for a risk-taker like Hannibal this was the ultimate gamble. The course to victory required very careful strategic thinking and deployment, with no detail left to chance.

Under the Roman system, when both consular armies were in the field, 'each consul took command of the army on alternate days' (Plutarch, *Fab.* 15.1). The problems inherent in this system in terms of continuity, strategy and coherence are obvious; nonetheless, it was the means by which the Romans dealt with the rivalry between the two most important men in the Republic when they were in the field. So on the day Aemilius Paullus took command, 'seeing that the district round [their camp] was flat and treeless, [he] was opposed to attacking the enemy there as they were superior in cavalry'. We also learn that Terentius Varro 'was of the contrary opinion' (Polyb. 3.110.2).[41]

Hannibal was well placed to exploit strategic dissent in the Roman camp as he watched and waited. The following day, with Varro in command, the Romans 'broke camp and advanced with the intent of approaching the enemy'. While the Romans were still marching Hannibal met them with his light infantry and cavalry, a skirmish broke out and only 'nightfall . . . made them draw off from each other, the attack of the Carthaginians not having had the success they hoped' (Polyb. 3.110.4–8). This engagement boosted Roman confidence, and perhaps Hannibal intended that it do so. Aemilius Paullus, in charge the next day, ordered the Romans to construct two camps, one on either side of the Aufidus river. This was to be the place of battle.

Hannibal readied his men for imminent confrontation. He spoke to his troops and encouraged them by evoking their bravery and depth of experience, and their trust in him. He wanted the men to be thankful, for although greatly outnumbered, 'to fight here where the advantages are manifestly ours' was considered something to be grateful for (Polyb. 3.111.4). The soldiers' belief in their commander was paramount. A much later ancient military strategist wrote that Hannibal was successful in encouraging his men in battle because he had convinced them that those 'who died courageously in war returned to life after a short period' (Polyaenus, *Strat.* 6.38.2). A belief in the immortality of the brave soldier would have been useful and necessary when facing an opponent whose numbers were double your own.[42]

Hannibal then moved his troops out into the plain and set up a camp near the Romans across the river from the town of Cannae (Polyb. 3.111.11).[43] The following day he drew his troops up along the river with the 'evident intention of giving battle'; however, Aemilius Paullus was 'not pleased with the ground . . . and kept quiet'. Perhaps Paullus wanted to deny Hannibal the initiative and the right to choose the precise time and place of battle.[44] Polybius, the best source for Cannae, portrays the tension and disagreement between the Roman consuls to the benefit of Aemilius Paullus. We have to keep in mind that Polybius wrote his history under the patronage of a grandson of Aemilius Paullus, and as such the portrayal of Varro's aggression and Paullus' reticence may be greatly overstated to exonerate Paullus from blame for the disaster that was to follow.[45] It is even possible that the record of command has been adjusted to absolve Aemilius Paullus of responsibility.[46]

The atmosphere was tense, full of 'prolonged suspense' and the men were jittery. Hannibal sent some cavalry out to 'intercept the water-bearers' from the smaller of the two Roman camps, a further provocation of the Roman soldiers who showed 'great eagerness for battle' (Polyb. 3.112.1–5). At last, at dawn on the next day, the two sides lined up to face each other in the field. The temperature was hot and a wind blew from the south. We are told that Varro was in command and moved his forces out of both Roman camps. He crossed the river with his troops from the larger camp and at once put them in battle order with the whole army facing south. 'He stationed the Roman [citizen] cavalry close to the river on the right and the foot next to them in the same line . . . the allied horse he drew up on the left wing and in front of the whole force at some distance he placed his light-armed troops' (Polyb. 3.113.3–5). The Roman infantry units (maniples) were placed closer together than was customary, deepening the centre. This may have been a result of the large number of soldiers in the field rather than for any specific tactical reason.[47]

This battle would be Hannibal's greatest gamble yet and he sent his skirmishers, 'slingers and pikemen, over the river and stationed them in front and leading the rest of his forces out of camp he crossed the stream in two places and drew them up opposite the enemy'. Hannibal set his army out after Varro and was able to adapt his forces to the enemy's formation. On the left wing of his line 'he placed his Iberian and Celtic horse facing the Roman cavalry' and then his heavily armed Africans. 'Next came the Iberian and Celtic infantry, and after them the other half of the Africans, and on his right wing, his Numidian horse' (Polyb. 3.113.6–7). Hannibal had drawn his whole army up in a line with the centre positioned slightly forward and tapering back on either side to form a kind of 'crescent shape'. Polybius expressly states that Hannibal's 'objective was to employ the Africans as a reserve force and to begin the action with the Iberians and Celts' who formed a thin forward line at the top of the curve (3.113.9). The Celts and the Iberians are described as especially terrifying in the battle line, the bare torsos of the Celts and gleaming white tunics with purple fringes of the Iberians magnifying their 'large physiques' (Livy 22.46.5–6).

On the field that day was the cream of the Carthaginian and Roman military command. The 'Roman right wing was under the command of Aemilius

Paullus, the left under that of Terentius Varro, and the centre under the consuls of the previous year, Atilius [Regulus] and Servilius'. On the Carthaginian side 'Hasdrubal commanded the left, Hanno the right [Livy 22.46.7 claims it was Maharbal on the right] whilst Hannibal himself with his brother Mago held the centre' (Polyb. 3.114.6–8).[48]

Hannibal's forces were significantly outnumbered, especially in foot soldiers, and once the infantry lines engaged the Roman forces began to push the Celtic and Iberian troops back. This was Hannibal's plan: to use the weakness in the centre of his line that he had already noted at the battle of Trebia to draw the Romans into the middle. Once the superior Roman centre had pushed forward he would let the heavier infantry and cavalry on the flanks surround them. Despite Hannibal's previous victories, the Roman forces must have had some confidence in their vastly superior numbers and been eager to push forward. As the Roman troops pressed further into the Carthaginian centre, the heavily armed Libyan units, using Roman weapons from Trasimeno, turned inwards and attacked the Romans from the sides. Meanwhile, the Carthaginian cavalry under Hasdrubal had beaten the Roman citizen cavalry and were able to come around behind the Roman infantry and attack the Roman allied cavalry on the other flank. Under pressure from the front and back, the Roman allied cavalry fled the field. The result was that the Roman infantry was completely encircled by the Carthaginians. They were cut down and destroyed (Polyb. 3.115–116).[49]

Livy sums up as follows: 'so went the battle of Cannae . . . the fleeing consul [Varro] had with him barely fifty men and almost the entire army shared the fate of the other consul who died there' (22.50.1–3). The actual number of Romans killed or captured on the field of Cannae is unclear. Polybius and Livy supply different details about the death toll. 'Roman casualties are reported to have been 45,500 infantry and 2,700 cavalry, with the number of citizens and allies roughly the same.' Livy continues to list the illustrious dead, who included the consul Lucius Aemilius Paullus as well as 'both quaestors of the consuls . . . as well as twenty-nine military tribunes, some of whom were former consuls, praetors and aediles'. These included the consul Servilius of the previous year, the Master of the Horse Minucius and 'eighty senators or men who had held offices that qualified them for selection for the Senate'. The surviving consul Varro escaped with the men mentioned above to nearby Venusia. The number of captured soldiers was 3,000 infantry and 1,500 cavalry (Livy 22.49.15–18).

Polybius' account of the Roman losses differs from Livy's; he claims that 'seventy escaped to Venusia with Terentius [Varro] and about 300 of the allied horse reached different cities ... Of the infantry about 10,000 were captured fighting but not in the actual battle, while perhaps 3,000 escaped from the field to neighbouring towns ... all the rest, numbering about 70,000, died bravely' (3.117.3). Polybius' total number of casualties is inconsistent with his total number of Roman troops at the battle and has been shown to contain errors, thus Livy's numbers are generally preferred.[50] The exact figures for Roman dead at Cannae can never be precisely known but surely numbered many tens of thousands. The impact of the defeat was devastating – the almost total obliteration of an army of eight legions.

Hannibal's great victory had also come at a heavy price for his army. The total dead numbered close to 8,000 and, Livy added, they were Hannibal's 'finest soldiers' (22.52.6). The majority of the casualties were the Celts, according to estimates in Polybius, who calculated the number of dead at 5,700 from Hannibal's army (3.117.6). For Hannibal, although his casualties were relatively few in number, they formed a significant percentage of his troops and he could ill afford to lose so many men. The loss of even the lower number of fighting men, considering that replacements were limited, may have restricted his options for future operations.[51]

At dawn the next day 'the Carthaginians proceeded to gather the spoils and inspect the slaughter, which was a shocking sight' even to the victors (Livy 22.51.5–9). The style of warfare – close-fought combat and cavalry attacks with swords and spears – left injuries that could take some time to cause death. The Carthaginians had been outnumbered and had set out to disable as many of the Romans as possible as quickly as they could. Livy records the gory details of severed thighs and knee-tendons, with half-dead men rising up from the carnage still alive to be cut down again, others begging to be put out of their misery. The bodies were sorted and 'Hannibal had his men gathered for burial ... and some sources have it that the Roman consul was also sought out and accorded burial'. There was an enormous amount of loot: 'apart from the horses, prisoners, and whatever silver there was ... everything else was parcelled out as plunder for the army' (Livy 22.51.5–52.4).

With this inspired victory, Hannibal cemented his reputation as one of the great military commanders of all time. His was a dazzling combination of personal charisma and man management together with strategic and military brilliance. The army that he had gathered to fight at Cannae was an exceptional force devoted to their brilliant commander. All aspects of the battle have been celebrated: the strategy, the precision of execution and the brilliance of Hannibal's lieutenants in carrying the action through to completion. The victory at Cannae has always been viewed as a 'masterpiece' and studied since antiquity by military strategists.[52]

In the immediate aftermath of battle, Maharbal, one of Hannibal's lieutenants, pressed his commander to march on Rome. 'Follow behind me. I shall go ahead with the cavalry – so the Romans will know of our arrival before they are aware of our coming!' he urged.[53] But Hannibal did not see the point of marching to Rome at that very moment. The enthusiastic Maharbal then uttered one of the most famous lines of the war, 'You know how to win a battle, Hannibal, but you do not know how to use the victory!' (Livy 22.51.2–4). Was Hannibal right to refuse or did Maharbal have a point?[54] In hindsight, perhaps Maharbal was correct but with Rome 400 kilometres away, it would have required an exhausted army to march for almost three weeks. An advance on Rome would have been followed by a long siege of a well-fortified city.

In reality Hannibal may have assumed that marching on Rome was an unnecessary option. By the conventions of third-century warfare a defeat of the magnitude of Cannae demanded that the losing side sue for peace, terms be agreed and the victors impose their conditions on the defeated. The decisions Hannibal made after his great victory at Cannae suggest that he believed the Romans would sue for peace, although Carthaginian experience in the First Punic War might have told him otherwise.[55] Yet the scale of the defeat Rome had suffered was unprecedented. Warfare in the Hellenistic period seldom aimed at the total destruction of a whole state or city. The later Roman destruction of Carthage in 146 BCE is a notable exception to the general rule. An army victorious in war would have managed to seize a city or two, destroy fields and crops, win a few set battles and perhaps a decisive one, so exhausting the enemy that they capitulated. Subsequently the victorious side would expect to receive an advantageous peace.[56]

The question of Hannibal's reaction to his victory at Cannae has been debated for millennia. The Roman satirist Juvenal (second century CE) parodied the debate when he described the poor students of rhetoric endlessly discussing whether 'to march from Cannae to Rome' (Satires 7.160–4). Hannibal's immediate reaction to victory at Cannae was to send envoys to Rome to negotiate a peace. He gathered all the prisoners together and as usual 'separated them into groups . . . and had kind words for the allies, whom he once again released without ransom'. Then he brought the Roman prisoners together and addressed them, something he had not done before. He told them that 'his war with the Romans was not a fight to the death but a struggle for honour and power . . . As his ancestors had capitulated before the valour of Rome, so his goal now was to see others in turn capitulating before his success and valour' (Livy 22.58.2–3). The prisoners were then granted the opportunity to ransom themselves and it was decided that ten spokesmen would be chosen by them to go to the Senate in Rome. These ten were allowed to depart, leaving only their word that they would return. Along with the prisoners Hannibal sent a Carthaginian nobleman named Carthalo whose role was to offer terms, 'if the Romans inclined towards a peace' (Livy 22.58.7).

Meanwhile in Rome a state of panic took hold. The praetors summoned the Senate while 'ears were ringing with the noisy lamentations of women'. Inside the city, laws were made to forbid women from appearing in public and restrictions were placed on family mourning. Guards were situated at the gates of the city to stop people from fleeing (Livy 22.55.1–8; Plutarch, *Fab.* 18.1). The true magnitude of the defeat was known when a letter arrived from Canusium where the surviving consul Terentius Varro was holed up with about ten thousand men. The impact on the city is evident from the reaction of the people and the government. The annual rites of the goddess Ceres (the Greek Demeter) were cancelled. Traditionally, married women carried out the worship of the goddess of grain and fertility, and a woman in mourning was prohibited from participating in the rites. In Rome after Cannae there 'was no married woman left untouched by bereavement' so the festival of this important goddess could not be celebrated (Livy 22.56.4–5).[57] The death toll at Cannae reached every family in Rome.

Livy provides graphic details of the omens and prodigies in the city, where an atmosphere of hysteria reigned. Especially troubling was 'the conviction that year of two Vestals, Opimia and Floronia, on charges of sexual misconduct'. If Vestal Virgins, keepers of the sacred hearth of the city, allowed the fire in the temple's hearth to be extinguished or lost their virginity, the city was thought to be in peril. One of the Vestals was buried alive and the other committed suicide. The man guilty of misconduct with one of the women was flogged until 'he expired under the lash' (22.57.2–3). The Senate sent Fabius Pictor (the same author used as a source by Polybius and Livy) to Delphi in 216 BCE to seek advice from the Oracle of Apollo and the Sibylline Books were consulted on how to appease the gods (Livy 22.57.5).[58]

The cure prescribed by the Sibylline Books shocked even Livy, as it included what he called 'outlandish sacrifices'. The sacrifice demanded by the sacred books involved 'a Gallic man and woman and a Greek man and woman being buried alive in the Forum Boarium (the cattle market), in a spot enclosed with stones which had already been the scene of this very un-Roman practice of human sacrifice', Livy tells us (22.57.6). This particular custom of human sacrifice, of Gauls and Greeks, is recorded on two other occasions in the

Republic (in 228 BCE and 114/113 BCE) and was eventually banned by a senatorial decree in 97 BCE (Pliny, *NH* 30.12).[59] The meaning behind the sacrifice remains an enigma. One argument assumes that in this ritual the Gauls and the Greeks were chosen to represent the future enemy and to ward off the possibility of losses in battle.[60] Livy suggests rather obliquely that the sacrifice signified a 'renewal of the war effort' and secured future victory by appeasement of the gods.[61]

The Roman Senate appointed Marcus Junius as dictator and Tiberius Sempronius Gracchus as his Master of the Horse. They held a 'troop levy' and conscripted boys from the age of seventeen, and some who must have been even younger, for Livy tells us they were still wearing the toga *praetexta* (worn by boys under sixteen). The manpower shortage even led to the buying and arming, 'at state expense, of eight thousand sturdy young men from the slave population' (Livy 22.57.11). The practice of conscripting slaves into the army had, on occasion, been employed before this but it was rare in the third century.[62] The Romans formed four new legions and one thousand cavalry with these new conscripts (roughly eighteen thousand men).[63]

Carthalo, Hannibal's envoy, was turned away by the Romans and returned to Apulia to describe the reaction in the city. A lictor (who symbolized the power of the consul) had met Carthalo on the road and informed him, in the name of the dictator, that he must leave Roman territory by nightfall (Livy 22.58.9). The Roman citizen prisoners proceeded on after Carthalo turned back. The ten men addressed the Senate and, after lengthy and heated debate, it was decided emphatically 'that the prisoners were not to be ransomed'. Nor would any private citizens be allowed to pay for the release of their sons, husbands and brothers (Livy 22.59–61.10; Polyb. 6.58.8). The 'no peace, no ransom' reaction from Rome was an integral part of the Roman narrative of their own exceptional nature.[64] The prisoners therefore returned to Hannibal empty handed.

In the months after Cannae, after consolidating his victory and accepting the allegiance of some of the Apulian cities, Hannibal sent his brother Mago to Carthage with news of his great triumph. The nature of our sources means that we rarely view the events of Hannibal's life from anything other than a Roman perspective. A brief mention in Livy or Polybius of the reaction to events at Carthage is all that has come down to us of the Carthaginian perspective on the war. The voyage to Carthage was dangerous, with the Roman navy patrolling the coasts and as yet no friendly ports open to the Carthaginians between Italy and North Africa.[65] A ship from Carthage must have picked Mago up in one of the cities on the southern tip of Italy where he had gone to enlist 'the Bruttian and [other] communities that were abandoning their allegiance to Rome' (Livy 23.11.7).[66]

For the first time in many years a member of the Barcid family returned to Carthage and was granted an audience in front of the Senate. And what news he brought. Mago related the marvellous exploits of his older brother. He told them that 'Hannibal had met six commanders on the battlefield, four of them consuls and the two others a dictator and Master of Horse and with them six consular armies'. Mago inventoried the numbers killed (in all the battles so far) as 'upwards of 200,000' and the more than '50,000' prisoners taken. The people of southern Italy who had come over to Hannibal after Cannae were listed too: 'the Bruttii, the Apulians, and a number of the Samnites and Lucanians had defected to the Carthaginians, and Capua had surrendered to Hannibal – Capua, the capital not just of Campania but now, after the drubbing the Romans had received . . . of Italy too'. Surely, Mago concluded, 'for these victories, so great and numerous the immortal gods should truly be thanked' (Livy 23.11.7–12).

Then Mago, with great dramatic flourish, 'ordered gold rings to be poured out at the entrance to the senate house'. These rings, taken from the fingers of dead Roman knights (*equites*), created a 'mound . . . so great that, according to some sources, they amounted to more than three measures (*modios* – Latin term used to measure dry goods)', although Livy goes on to note that he thought this an exaggeration (23.12.1–2). Mago's display was indeed dramatic and the majority of the Senate of Carthage was 'overjoyed' with the news. The purpose of Mago's visit was to press home Hannibal's need for more support from Carthage. 'The campaign was being fought a long way from home . . . and grain and cash were being used up in large quantities,' he insisted. The realities of Hannibal's struggle were here laid bare for the leading men of Carthage and they were told that to win he needed more resources. If the Carthaginians wanted to help Hannibal, Mago urged, the Senate needed to 'send reinforcements, and . . . grain, and money, for their pay, to the soldiers who had served the Carthaginian people so well' (Livy 23.12.3–4).

The only resistance, according to Livy, came from Hanno, veteran of the Mercenary War and long-time enemy of the Barcid family in the Senate. His was the sole voice of dissent and caution, we are told; refusing to be drawn into the elation of victory, he asked sceptically if 'the Romans had [yet] sent Hannibal ambassadors to sue for peace?' (23.13.1). Despite Hanno's reservations, Carthaginian 'hearts filled with joy' and thus by 'a huge majority . . . a senatorial decree was passed that authorized sending 4,000 Numidians [cavalry] and forty elephants, and . . . talents of silver' (exact amount not clear). Mago and an unnamed Carthaginian general (called a *dictator* in Livy) were dispatched to Iberia to raise 20,000 infantry and 4,000 cavalry 'as reinforcements for the armies' (Livy 23.13.7–8).[67] Could the young Mago Barca ever have imagined when he left his brother on this mission, first to Carthage and then to Iberia, that he would never see him again?[68]

CHAPTER 8

# AFTER CANNAE

The victor is not victorious if the vanquished does not consider himself so.
**(Ennius, *Ann.* frag. 31.493)**

I N THE LATE SUMMER of 216 BCE Hannibal had little time to enjoy the
fruits of his victory after the destruction of the Roman armies at Cannae.
He was in his element on the battlefield in the role of master strategist directing
the different pieces of his army. In Polybius' mind Hannibal's genius rested in
his personal command over a heterogeneous force of 'men who had nothing
naturally in common' but whom he kept at a high functioning level.[1] He is
compared to a good ship's captain steering his vessel, keeping everyone in
harmony (Polyb. 11.19.3). Hannibal, in fact, used the diversity of his army to
exploit the consistency of the Roman legions, employing elements of surprise
and unorthodox tactics to keep his enemy off balance.[2]

The brilliance of the victory at Cannae faded quickly for Hannibal as he
faced the daunting task of trying to defeat the Romans off the battlefield as
well. More than ever his depleted forces needed allies, bases and support from
the cities and states of southern Italy. The past year had seen Hannibal
directing his army across Apulia, Samnium and into Campania but until
Cannae he had not acquired any significant supporters in the region. If he was
to win the war, it was crucial that he consolidate his victories and build a
power base in the south of Italy. His strategy for ultimate victory was to detach
allied territories from Rome. If he was successful, the Romans would eventually be unable to retain their authority throughout the peninsula. The political

battleground after Cannae lay between Hannibal's pledge to free the southern Italians from Roman hegemony and Rome's notion of an 'Italia' to unify their allies.[3] A sense of Rome's tactics in the face of Hannibal's victories echoes in the anti-Hannibalic propaganda of the time. In a speech at Venusia after Cannae the surviving Roman consul Varro accentuated 'this . . . Carthaginian enemy, not even native to Africa, [who] brings from the farthest limits of the earth – soldiers who have no knowledge of human law and civilization . . .'. These words were designed to emphasize the foreign (and thus barbaric) nature of the Carthaginian Hannibal and his multi-ethnic army. Varro went on to ask the southern Italians whether they wanted 'to have laws imposed from Africa and Carthage, to permit Italy to be a Numidian and Moorish province?' (Livy 23.5.11–12). The speech may be a purely Livian invention but it no doubt reflects the Romans' appeal to their allies and their counter-propaganda against Hannibal. Hannibal might claim that he brought freedom but the Romans would argue that he was bringing a foreign kind of non-Italic freedom.[4]

Just after Cannae the Romans appeared, by any contemporary standard, to have lost the war. By the time Mago stood in front of the Senate at Carthage he could list the peoples and cities that had come over to the Carthaginian side in the months after the battle (Livy 22.61.11–13, 23.11.11).[5] The situation, however, was much more nuanced than Livy's portrayal suggests, and far from every city in the regions listed (Bruttium, Apulia, Campania) switched allegiance to Hannibal. Livy overstates the Roman losses and the reality is that Rome still held substantial territory, influence and power in the south of Italy. What rings true in Livy is that up until Cannae, 'the loyalty of the allies had remained unshaken, but now it began to waver, and the sole reason for that was surely the loss of faith in the empire' (22.61.10). There had been a significant shift of loyalty away from Rome to Hannibal but there were still many bases from which the Romans could carry on the fight.

Ultimately cities switched sides or remained loyal to Rome depending on local conditions.[6] Southern Italy was made up of city-states that had been, until Cannae, under the umbrella of Roman control with each place linked directly to Rome through alliances and treaty obligations. These links had been pieced together slowly over the course of the Roman conquests in the fourth and early third centuries. This long process, including wars against the Etruscans, three Romano-Samnite wars and the invasion of Pyrrhus, had created a patchwork system of allies. The ruling elite of each city negotiated alliances based on power and patronage. To succeed with his plan, Hannibal would have to convince these elite families that he could provide an advantage over the Romans. The competitive nature of the urban elites within each town meant that when one elite family supported the Romans there was another disgruntled family waiting to seize its opportunity. Hannibal's approach had to address these specific circumstances. This was a complicated and difficult undertaking and although Hannibal did gain new allies, many cities remained loyal to Rome.

Some similarity existed in each case that a city joined with Hannibal. If Hannibal approached a city he first made contact within the ruling elite. There is always mention of factionalism among the ruling families when a city went over to the Carthaginians.[7] Livy gives the example of Statius Trebius, a local elite from Compsa (23.1.1–3). Compsa was a strategically placed Samnite city on the frontier between Samnium, Lucania and Apulia, at the headwaters of the river Aufidus (Map 1). The Trebius family were the political opponents of a rival clan allied to the Romans. Hannibal's approach would entail making contact with Trebius and negotiating with his group so that they in turn could influence the city's population into switching allegiance.[8] The intervention of one elite family in the town on behalf of Hannibal proved enough at Compsa.

Hannibal's policy of leniency towards the Italian allies captured in his previous victories had been designed to influence opinion in the cities. Even before Cannae, a group of Capuan *equites* (knights) who had fought for the Romans at Trasimeno convinced Hannibal that Capua would be willing to revolt (Livy 22.13.2–3). At Nola in Campania we hear of Lucius Bantius, who had been found 'half-dead in a heap of corpses' on the field at Cannae. Hannibal had admired his bravery and treated him kindly in the aftermath. As a result Bantius was inclined to 'put Nola under the authority and control of the Carthaginians'; however, the Roman consul Marcellus convinced him otherwise with praise of his military ability and gifts, including a 'superb horse and 500 denarii' (silver coins) (Livy 23.15.7–15). The battle for the hearts and minds of the Italian allies of the south was thus won or lost one city at a time.

Hannibal had first moved to secure support in the Apulian and Samnite territories and in Bruttium in the south. When Arpi, the most important town in Apulia, came over to Carthage other towns in the region followed soon after (Polyb. 3.118.3; Livy 22.61.10–12).[9] Hannibal then moved on to Campania and advanced first towards the port of Neapolis (Naples). Access to a port on Italy's west coast would provide Hannibal with relatively straight-forward access to Carthage and Iberia for supply and reinforcements.[10] The paradox for Hannibal was that the more allies he gained, the further stretched his army became and the more pressing his need for reinforcements from Carthage. Neapolis, however, held firm and Hannibal chose not to try to take the city by siege (Livy 23.1.5–10). Over the course of 216–214 BCE Hannibal would attempt, repeatedly, to take Neapolis but it stayed loyal to Rome. In addition, having learned the hard way from his experience at Saguntum, he knew that a long siege would only tie up a substantial part of his army and expose his other allies to Roman attacks.[11]

After sounding out Neapolis, Hannibal turned towards nearby Capua. Although not a port, Capua was the largest city in Campania, 'long basking in prosperity and the favour of fortune' (Livy 23.2.1) and had been an ally of the Romans from the fourth century. In origin Capua was Etruscan but since the fifth century it had been a Samnite city; the people spoke Oscan and had been heavily influenced by coastal Greek colonial foundations.[12] Capua reflected the multi-layered cultural mix of the cities of Campania in the third century. With an independent Senate and citizen council, the population of Capua possessed a form of limited Roman citizenship (*civitas sine suffragio*). This did not give Capuans the right to vote or stand for office in Rome but gave the people some legal protection under Roman law. The requirements of their limited citizenship also included direct taxation, obligatory military service and tribute.[13] In origin this status may have held some advantages but by the latter part of the third century it was largely seen as a burden, a form of 'taxation without representation'.[14]

Capua was a strategic centre for the control of southern Italy. When Hannibal crossed into Campania after Cannae a delegation of Capuans made contact. This same group had just been to see the Roman consul Varro at Venusia hoping to use the situation to negotiate. They had rejected Varro's reasoning and now turned to Hannibal to make an alliance (Livy 23.7.1). In Livy's view the Capuans were imperialist in their outlook and intended to 'make a treaty now with Hannibal on their terms and once he had finished off the war and retired in triumph to Africa, the Campanians would be left with sway over Italy' (23.6.1). A man named Pacuvius Calavius, leader of the pro-Carthaginian party in the city, led the approach on behalf of Capua (Livy 23.8.2).

Although the Capuans did not make contact with Hannibal until he had entered Campania, they had been leaning towards the Carthaginian cause since the victory at Trasimeno. Defection to Hannibal gave the Capuan government a powerful negotiating position and the terms agreed stated that 'no Carthaginian general or magistrate had authority over a Capuan citizen, nor was a Capuan citizen obliged to perform any military or other service against his will' (23.7.1). Capua, as Livy reports, viewed its allegiance with Hannibal as a means of increasing its hegemony in Campania. In practical terms, Hannibal received very little from the arrangement while the Capuans were given authority without any obligations to Carthage. The enforced military service which the Romans had imposed was obviously a bone of contention among the Capuans and they were seeking to govern their affairs independently.[15]

Despite the unfavourable terms for Carthage, it is hard to overstate the symbolic importance of the defection of Capua and what it meant to Hannibal at that moment. It was a great political blow to the Romans, who had already suffered the celebrated battlefield defeats. The betrayal felt at Rome permeates Livy's account as he heaps abuse on the population of Capua and calls them 'arrogant and untrustworthy' (23.5.1). It was even more deeply felt since many of the leading citizens were connected by links of patronage and marriage to Roman senatorial families. That the Romans were so astonished by Capua's defection seems surprising, given that over the previous century the city had sided against the Romans on more than one occasion. Capua had never been the most restful of allies to Rome.[16]

The close link between Rome and Capua was exemplified by the three hundred Capuan *equites* serving with Roman forces in Sicily. These soldiers became a focus for negotiations between Hannibal and the city. The settlement meant that Hannibal handed over three hundred of his prisoners to Capua, allowing them to make an exchange with the Romans for their sons.[17] The Capuan soldiers serving in Sicily eventually chose not to return to their city and the Romans offered them citizenship in exchange for their loyalty. The result was to split families in Capua into pro- and anti-Hannibal factions, ultimately undermining the Carthaginian success in the city. Tensions between the two sides were high and we learn that any Roman citizens left in Capua were rounded up and locked in the baths, where they asphyxiated in the heat (Livy 23.7.2–3).[18]

In late September 216 BCE, with the negotiations completed, Hannibal sent a message to the praetor of the town saying that 'he would be in Capua the following day'.[19] The advent of the legendary Carthaginian general meant that the 'whole population' turned out to see him 'with enthusiasm'. Arriving in the city in triumph to cheering crowds must have been extremely satisfying for Hannibal, who had been fighting in Italy for two years with no opportunity to celebrate his own triumphs. As crowds lined the streets 'eager to catch a glimpse of the general now famous for so many victories', did Hannibal believe he was finally seeing the fruits of his hard work? The 'entire community was agog at the prospect of welcoming and setting eyes on the Carthaginian!'[20] These events reflect the heroic status that Hannibal carried with him after his great victories. Livy tells us that Hannibal spent the day touring the city and on the following one made an address in the Senate of Capua. 'He [Hannibal] thanked the Campanians for preferring friendship with him to an alliance with Rome and amongst the extravagant promises was a commitment that Capua would shortly be the capital of all Italy . . .' (Livy 23.7–10.10).

Hannibal slept that same night at the home of two of the elite Capuan citizens who had been instrumental in turning the city. He was entertained in the evening with an extravagant banquet that began before sunset, at which his hosts and Pacuvius Calavius along with a famous Capuan soldier were invited to dine with the general and his entourage. Not everyone in Capua was excited to see Hannibal, and Livy claims that the son of Pacuvius Calavius, who attended the dinner with his father, had boldly planned to assassinate Hannibal whilst he feasted. The father was able to talk the son out of the murder in the end but the story reflects the real and constant danger Hannibal would have lived with in Italy. With loyalties split, the Romans must have encouraged any and every opportunity to rid themselves of their charismatic enemy (Livy 23.8.1–10.10).[21]

In the autumn of 216 BCE Hannibal's army was spread thinly across southern Italy. A garrison was left in Capua to secure the city and protect it from Roman reprisals. Two other armies were operating in Apulia and in Bruttium. More than ever Hannibal must have hoped for reinforcements from Carthage. He no doubt expected his brother Mago to return to Italy with new troops by the following spring at the latest. Hannibal needed to capture a port city to disembark these expected reinforcements and with the campaigning season still open he pushed on. After Capua he played 'cat and mouse' with the Romans. His first target was again Neapolis, where he 'alternated promises and threats', perhaps mistakenly assuming that after Capua's change of allegiance Neapolis might be more pliable, but to no avail (Livy 23.14.5). Then Hannibal changed course towards Nola, one of the southernmost cities on the Campanian plain, whose territory bordered Neapolis to the east, on the opposite side of Mount Vesuvius from the sea. Although not a port, Nola was an Oscan-speaking city with links and a long history of allegiance to Neapolis and also to Cumae, another key centre further north (see Map 1).[22] As Hannibal approached Nola, the governing body of the city sent word to the Roman praetor Marcus Claudius Marcellus who was nearby at Casilinum (Livy 23.14.10). Marcellus was a veteran of the Gallic wars of

1. Bronze gilt cuirass from Ksour es-Saf, Tunisia, *c.* third century BCE. This beautifully decorated cuirass was found in a tomb in the coastal region of Carthaginian territory, south of Hadrumentum. Hellenistic in style it may have been made in Italy and could have belonged to a soldier of Hannibal's generation.

2. The view from Eryx (modern Erice) looking west towards Drepanum (Trapani) and the Aegates Islands. The hill top position of Eryx commands the west and north-west coast of Sicily.

3. *The Oath of Hannibal* by Benjamin West, 1770. The scene of the oath is here imagined in the eighteenth century with romance and exoticism. The focus of the painting is the sacrificial bull and hesitancy of the young boy while the shadowy figure of a romanized Ba'al lurks above.

4. *The Oath of Hannibal*, eighteenth-century cartoon. 'The Bedfordshire Hannibal' illustrates just how familiar the story of Hannibal's oath was in the eighteenth century when contemporary politicians could be lampooned in the popular media with scenes from the general's life.

5. Punic di-shekel showing Melqart (possibly Hamilcar) and elephant (*c.* 237–209 BCE). The figure of Melqart is depicted with the Heraklean attribute of a club on the obverse and an elephant and rider on the reverse. The coin was minted in Iberia and is perhaps the most renowned of all the images associated with the Barcid family and their conquests.

6. *Hannibal Crossing the Alps* by Heinrich Leutemann, 1866. This hand-coloured etching captures the nineteenth-century fascination with the life of the Carthaginian general and the drama of the Alps crossing.

7. Painting by Giambattista Tiepolo, 1725–1730. This early eighteenth-century painting illustrates the moment when Hannibal recognizes his brother Hasdrubal's head after it was catapulted into his camp following the defeat at the battle of the Metaurus (in 207 BCE).

8. Hannibal's head as portrayed on a monument in Gebze near Istanbul, twentieth century. The monument was commissioned by Atatürk and built after his death. Gebze is thought to be a possible location of ancient Libyssa, where Hannibal died.

9. Hannibal(?) marble bust from Capua. The best-known image of Hannibal may not actually be Hannibal. The portrait was found in or near Capua and is clearly that of a helmeted military figure wearing the cloak (*paludamentum*) of a Roman commander.

the 220s and an experienced commander. His army approached Nola carefully, taking a route through the mountains perhaps in order to avoid meeting Hannibal. When the Romans arrived, Hannibal and his forces left Nolan territory, advancing to blockade Nuceria, taking and sacking the city (Livy 23.15.2–6).

Hannibal then returned to his camp outside Nola. The city's loyalty hung in the balance. Marcellus' army held the town and the two sides skirmished in the space between the city walls and the Carthaginian camp (Livy 16.16.2–5). The very presence of Hannibal unsettled the city and although the population was still tenuously loyal to Rome, Marcellus decided he had to 'risk a battle' before the town switched sides. Hannibal drew his forces up in formation outside the city wall and presented his army for an encounter. Marcellus left Hannibal waiting outside the city walls. Just as Hannibal stood down and sent some of his forces back to his camp, assuming there would be no contact, Marcellus unleashed his troops from within the walls. In the resulting melee, the Carthaginians suffered significant losses (how many we cannot know, as even Livy doubts his own numbers: perhaps some 2,800 Punic soldiers compared to 500 Roman, 23.16.15). The Roman sources stress the importance of the victory as the first good news since the war began. Marcellus was the first Roman general to engage with Hannibal after Cannae and gained a remarkable reputation from his successes.

After Hannibal retreated he moved on to lay siege to Casilinum, which he would take the following spring. Marcellus laid down the law in Nola, determined to make an example of the Nolans and to frighten them into submission. Key members of the population, who had been agitating for Carthaginian allegiance, were declared traitors. Marcellus had seventy men beheaded and their estates made 'common property of the Roman people' (Livy 23.17.2–4). Thus the people of Campania found themselves caught between two powers and were forced to walk a fine line.[23] Nola would continue to be a target for Hannibal and over the next three years he would try again and again to take the city.[24]

After the encounter with Marcellus, Hannibal settled in around Capua for the winter of 216 BCE. Capua was renowned for its perfumes and scented oils imported from the East. Its reputation, in the stern Roman mind, was one of exuberant decadence. The land here was rich and fertile and the ports on the coast nearby allowed the Capuans to import luxuries of all sorts. Livy implies that the whole Carthaginian army was quartered inside Capua that winter and the warmth and hedonism of the town corrupted Hannibal's stern and battle-hardened soldiers.[25] In the Roman imagination the corrupting luxury of Capua took 'men whom the most intense misery had failed to break' and ruined them with 'excessive comfort and unlimited pleasure . . .'. 'Sleep, drink, dinner-parties, whores, baths and inactivity that, from habit, became sweeter every day – all this sapped their physical and moral strength' (Livy 23.18.10–13). The legend as told claims that once the Carthaginian soldiers slept in soft beds and in the arms of softer women they were no longer capable of the valour and the morality of good soldiers. In the Roman mind these men, including the invincible Hannibal himself, lost their edge among the soft scents and warm baths of the city. The reality of that winter must have been significantly less luxurious for the majority of troops. Winter quarters for most of the army was more likely to have been their camp on Monte Tifata, the mountain that sits behind Capua. Certainly the higher-ranked soldiers stayed in the city and still more of the army would have been billeted in other cities now allied to Carthage (Livy 23.18.10–16).[26]

During the winter of 216/215 BCE Hannibal must have been pondering his next move. His biggest obstacle was that he did not have the manpower to sustain drawn-out political wrangling with each city he approached. Moreover, the specific terms under which he assembled his new allies seemed to have been based on the Carthaginian model. This meant that new allies were not necessarily obliged to provide troops to Hannibal to join the military struggle against Rome. Some of the new allies certainly did supply troops, however, especially in defence of their own territories (see Livy 24.15.7 on the Bruttians and Lucanians among Hanno's army). In this way Hannibal set himself apart from the Romans, whose alliances were almost always associated with some kind of mandatory military service. Importantly, by doing so, Hannibal undermined his own chances of success.

For Hannibal and his army, the transfer of allegiance away from Rome reduced the pool of recruits available to the Romans. From 216 BCE onwards Hannibal had towns to operate from and could rely on steady supplies. Along with the new allies, he also acquired the responsibility of protecting these cities from Roman retribution. It was essential that there were tangible rewards for the elites who had delivered their cities to Hannibal. We shall see that when these were not forthcoming the alliances began to crumble.

Whilst inter-elite rivalry won allies for Hannibal, inter-urban rivalries in the south worked against him. Hannibal's overall strategy had been successful in Iberia, in the north of Italy and in much of Apulia, but the sophisticated urban centres in the wealthy region of Campania were not so easily swayed. Capua was an important ally for Hannibal but its defection actually favoured the Romans because of the inter-urban rivalries in Campania. The prospect of Capua achieving pre-eminent status in the region with dominance over neighbouring cities was enough to convince other Campanian towns to remain loyal to Rome. Indeed, by granting Capua its desired pre-eminence Hannibal worked against his own freedom agenda.[27] In the same way, the Romans played on the strong rivalries between the cities of Campania (i.e. Capua, Neapolis, Nola, Cumae) and used the mutual hostility to retain their remaining allies.[28]

The piecemeal nature of Hannibal's alliances made a coherent defensive strategy difficult to implement. For the first time since leaving the Iberian peninsula Hannibal had to defend territory, which meant he had to divide his army into units commanded by lieutenants.[29] The resources available to protect the new allies were limited and the longer the war dragged on, the more stretched these resources became. In the ensuing years the Romans ground down Hannibal's gains and won back the pieces of Italy that had been lost, one by one. Yet the fact that, despite their massive manpower advantage, the Roman armies never massed again to meet Hannibal in a fixed battle in Italy reveals just how close Hannibal came to victory. They adopted the strategy that Fabius Maximus had advocated before Cannae and made use of their numerical superiority. They divided their forces and harried the Carthaginians from all directions, skirmishing to train their newly recruited troops but not engaging unless they had full advantage. Nevertheless, it took them almost a decade to regain control of southern Italy – which illustrates the astonishing tactical and military skill that Hannibal displayed. To carry on military operations, often successfully, without reinforcements against so many Roman legions was a staggering achievement.

Campania was one of the key theatres of the war. The Romans were determined not to lose any more territory and garrisoned key towns in the region. Over the years 215–205 BCE the Romans were usually able to commit four to six, but sometimes seven, two-legion armies in Campania alone.[30] In the crucial year of 212 BCE, the Romans raised twenty-five legions in all theatres, the largest number in the war (Livy 24.11.1–2; Polyb. 2.24.1–16).[31] This is a huge number of active soldiers, amounting to well over 200,000 men. If we consider that two centuries later when Rome controlled much of the Mediterranean their armed forces totalled twenty-eight legions under the emperor Augustus, it seems even more impressive.[32] Much of the detail and emphasis on Roman manpower comes from Polybius, and one of the themes of his work lies in convincing his audience that the Romans were dominant just because of these population resources: 'how great was the power which Hannibal later ventured to attack' (2.24.1). In every scenario suggested, Hannibal was vastly outnumbered and almost inevitably the brilliant victories of 217–216 BCE turned into a stalemate and the erosion of his capabilities. A war of attrition was always going to favour the Romans.[33]

Through the winter of 216/215 BCE Rome was again fraught with political turmoil. Its fate in the balance, Rome turned to its veterans. Plutarch describes them as those who 'in their youth campaigned against the Carthaginians over Sicily: in their prime they fought the Gauls for the defence of Italy itself and as veterans they found themselves matched once more against the Carthaginians' (*Marc.* 1). The consuls elected for 215 BCE at Rome were Tiberius Sempronius Gracchus and Lucius Postumius Albinus. Albinus was killed fighting the Boii Gauls near modern Modena in the Po valley before he could even take up his post in March 215. A replacement consul was elected and it was the tough old soldier M. Claudius Marcellus, veteran of many battles, who had just successfully defended Nola in the autumn. As the election result was announced, a clap of thunder was heard. To the superstitious Romans this annulled the result and 'Marcellus withdrew from office' (Livy 23.31.13). The position of consul was then open for Fabius Maximus, who held the title for the third time (Livy 23.31.14).[34] Marcellus was riding a wave of popularity for his spirited defence of Nola in the previous months and took up the command of his army in the south as *propraetor* (Livy 23.39.8). The other consul, Gracchus, was given the army of the newly raised slave volunteers and freedmen along with 25,000 allied troops. Gracchus would command these forces in Campania and Apulia for the following three years, first as consul and then with pro-consular *imperium* (Livy 23.32.1).

The family and associates of the Fabii clan, headed by the venerable Fabius Maximus, held at least one of the two consulships for the subsequent three years. The Fabii were scions of the conservative patrician families at Rome. Their domination of consular elections over the next few years raises questions about the manipulation of the electoral process. It is possible that Fabius Maximus, as head of the college of priests, had declared Marcellus' election invalid and engineered the annulment but then promised him the position the next year. Fabius Maximus would be elected to his fourth consulship in 214 BCE, with Marcellus as his colleague, and his son would be consul in 213 BCE. The Roman leadership during this period focused on continuity and control over the fighting rather than on the tradition of alternating yearly magistracies. There were exceptional appointments that allowed for successive consulships and our sources allude to conflict between the great families of the Republic over the distribution of the magistracies, although irregularities are explained as being necessitated by war.[35]

Hannibal's strategy to cut Rome off from as many allies as possible was also directed towards inflicting serious damage on the finances of the city. It was both manpower and wealth that drove the Romans' ability to rearm and repopulate their legions. In the spring of 215 BCE the Roman state faced a serious financial crisis and money and supplies were requested from all the theatres of war (Livy 23.21.1). Titus Otacilius, commander in Sicily, wrote that 'his soldiers and crews were not being paid or receiving their grain rations on time and there were no resources to make this possible'.[36] Otacilius turned to the Syracusan king Hiero for a loan of silver and grain. He received both rations and pay for his forces in Sicily. Money earmarked to repay Hiero then had to be diverted to the fleet on the east coast of Italy (23.38.12). Extreme financial distress saw the doubling of the tax paid by Roman citizens (the *tributum*) and the debasement of the coinage: there is evidence of a reduction in the standard weight of the bronze coinage (in 215 BCE).[37] The extreme measures taken by Rome to increase revenue and manpower included the lowering of the wealth qualification needed for a citizen to be recruited into the army, and the recruitment of slaves and the urban poor to replace them in the fleet. New sailors were provided and paid for by individual citizens as a kind of tax based on income.[38] The Roman state existed on various forms of credit, including contributions by wealthy individuals that went to support orphans and widows, and some members of the army went voluntarily unpaid.[39] The death toll and state of continual warfare had stretched the capacity of the Roman state to breaking point in these three years when the Romans were operating on a vast scale in many theatres.

Over half a century earlier Pyrrhus had compared the Roman people to the Lernaean Hydra, a multi-headed mythical beast whose ability to regrow a head each time one was cut off meant it was almost impossible to defeat (Plutarch, *Pyrrh.* 19).[40] Hannibal, said to have been a keen student of Pyrrhus, must have understood this comparison more profoundly each year that he passed in Italy.[41] Despite inflicting crushing defeats on the Romans and causing massive upheaval at Rome and throughout Italy, Hannibal could not get the Romans to agree to negotiate peace. In fact, even when the Romans were facing both manpower and financial crises they never failed to turn out substantial armies in Italy and in other theatres of the war. Hannibal's forces probably numbered their highest in 215 BCE when he may have been able to field four armies; but regularly only three were in operation.[42] The only mention of reinforcements for Hannibal from outside Italy comes in 215 BCE when recruits along with elephants from Carthage were landed at a port in Bruttium (Livy 23.43.5–6). Estimates put the number of Hannibal's main army at 40,000 plus a division in Bruttium. The Roman forces active in Italy may, on an annual basis, have been double that number plus allied divisions.[43]

The disparity in the number of troops available between Hannibal and the Romans only magnifies how important it was for his forces to be resupplied and for his support base to be broadened. The opportunity for alliances outside Italy came to Hannibal in the period after Cannae. His victory had resounded around the Mediterranean, and Hellenistic monarchs in the east and in Sicily reached out to him in friendship. As early as 217 BCE, when Philip V of Macedon heard of the Roman defeat at Trasimeno, the exiled Illyrian ruler Demetrius of Pharos immediately began agitating for Philip to expand his horizons (Polyb. 5.101–2).[44] As the news of Cannae spread to the courts of the Hellenistic monarchs, Philip's own ambitions may have increased as Hannibal's status rose and a Roman defeat looked imminent (Livy 23.33.1–4). The Hellenistic world loved a charismatic and daring military commander and Hannibal's bold victories had placed him in hallowed company (Livy 35.14.5–12; Plutarch, *Pyrrh.* 8.2).[45]

The ambitious young king Philip may have then taken the first step and made contact with the Carthaginians (Livy 23.33.4). Hannibal, in need of allies both inside and outside Italy, would have welcomed and perhaps been flattered by the approach from a king whose direct line reached back to Alexander the Great. The realpolitik behind Philip's actions lay with the on-going Roman involvement in Illyria that conflicted with Macedonian inter-ests along the Adriatic coast. The Illyrian king Demetrius had joined Philip's court as a refugee from Roman conflict in Illyria in 219 BCE and his presence at the Macedonian court turned Philip's focus to the Adriatic Sea and Roman affairs.[46] The Macedonian kings took a dim view of Roman interference in Illyria, a region they considered to be under their hegemony (see Map 1).[47] The Roman-imposed client ruler in Illyria had become a bone of contention with Philip. In 217 BCE the Romans had requested that Philip deliver up Demetrius of Pharos but he had refused (Livy 22.33.3–5). The Macedonian king then built a fleet to support his increasing interests in the Adriatic, perhaps with the intention of placing Demetrius back in control as a client king by ousting the pro-Roman leader.[48]

In the summer of 215 BCE direct negotiations between Philip and Hannibal took place when the king sent an Athenian envoy named Xenophanes on a mission to Italy (Livy 23.33–34; Polyb. 7.9). The Macedonian ship had managed to avoid the Roman-controlled ports of Brundisium and Tarentum by landing in the Hannibal-friendly region of Bruttium near Locri and the Temple of Juno Lacinia (Livy 23.34.2). Xenophanes brought an offer of friendship and alliance from the Macedonian king to Hannibal. No doubt Hannibal welcomed him warmly. The alliance was concluded between the two parties and formalized by an oath that is described as a 'sworn treaty of friendship' (Polyb. 7.9.1). Xenophanes left Hannibal to return to Philip accompanied by Carthaginian representatives named as Gisgo, Bostar and Mago.

As the Macedonian ship set off from the south coast it was noticed by a Roman fleet under the command of Publius Valerius Flaccus, who was patrolling the waters along the coast of Bruttium perhaps from the Roman base at Rhegium. Flaccus sent ships from the fleet to intercept the vessel. When the Roman marines boarded the ship they found a collection of Carthaginians and Macedonians on board and were understandably wary. Livy describes how 'the Carthaginian dress and appearance raised suspicions . . . and when they were interrogated their accent gave them away' (23.34.5–6). Searching further, the Roman soldiers discovered the document meant for King Philip sent directly from Hannibal.[49]

As a treaty the document is a general declaration of 'friendship and goodwill' with a pledge of mutual support against Rome and an agreement to restore Philip's ally Demetrius in Illyria to the territory that had been conquered by the Romans. The treaty also gives a clear idea of Hannibal's strategic aims. It presumes that Hannibal has been victorious in Italy and that the power of the Romans is reduced, so that 'when the gods have granted us victory in the war against the Romans and their allies, if the Romans shall request the Carthaginians to make terms of peace, we . . . shall include you too' (Polyb. 7.9.12–13). Hannibal assumed in the treaty that he would be able to limit the power of the Romans to interfere in Carthaginian affairs. Philip aimed to keep the Romans out of his sphere of influence and future Macedonian–Carthaginian allied projects were discussed.[50]

A close study of the text of Polybius' document has shown that the original language was Punic and that it had been translated into Greek. The treaty's wording reflects the essential Punic/Phoenician nature of the document '. . . in the presence of the gods who fight on our side, and of the sun, the moon and the earth; in the presence of rivers, harbours and waters . . . in the presence of all the gods who rule Carthage; in the presence of all the gods who rule Macedon and the rest of Greece' (Polyb. 7.9). The act of invoking lakes and streams and also the gods of other states and nations was formulaic in Near Eastern treaties and indicates a mode of treaty-making alien to Greek or Roman traditions.[51] This document shows us that, in international relations, Hannibal and the Carthaginians used legal traditions rooted in their Phoenician heritage.

The document was Hannibal's personal oath of friendship to Philip.[52] Whilst Hannibal's oath played an important part in the agreement so too did the state of Carthage. The wording of the text implies that the oath was made on behalf of Carthage: 'this is a sworn treaty between Hannibal the general, Mago, Myrcan, Barmocar, such other members of the Carthaginian Senate as were present with him' (Polyb. 7.9.1).[53] Technically, the treaty was the kind of agreement issued by a Carthaginian general in the field when treating with another individual.[54] Philip, as an important king of a major power in the Hellenistic world, would have expected a more formal treaty to follow on from these negotiations. On other occasions Hannibal referred the final negotiation of his treaties with foreign cities, for example with Tarentum and Syracuse, to the Carthaginian Senate for ratification. Perhaps the presence of Carthaginian senators in Hannibal's camp made such further referral unnecessary.[55]

The new alliance between Hannibal and Philip had the desired effect on the Romans, who worried that 'they could see on the horizon a war of massive proportions with Macedon, at a time when they could barely cope with the Punic War' (Livy 23.38.5). Rome immediately went on the offensive and engaged the Macedonian navy in Illyria where they easily dominated. Roman naval supremacy during the whole Hannibalic War played a crucial, yet unsung, part in the ultimate victory. Carthaginian ships were continually bettered by the Roman navy in battles off the coasts of Sardinia, Iberia and eventually Sicily.[56] Through their naval superiority the Romans were able to contain any real advantage that Hannibal's alliance with Philip might offer.[57]

Hannibal's victories unsettled Roman alliances in all regions. Directly after Cannae powerful leaders reached out to him in Italy and across the Adriatic. As hostilities spilled over from Italy into the neighbouring states it would only be a matter of time before the epicentre of the First Punic War, Sicily, was drawn into the struggle. Livy comments that 'one might well have thought that the theatre of war had shifted from Italy, so focused on Sicily were the two peoples' (24.36.4). Indeed, the story of Syracuse, the wealthiest and most powerful city in Sicily, would play an epic part in the outcome of the war.[58]

When Hannibal first invaded Italy, Syracuse was still ruled by the nonagenarian king Hiero II whose long reign had begun early in the First Punic War. By shifting allegiance from Carthage to Rome in the 260s, Hiero had navigated the first war with much of his territory intact. This had revitalized the city's fortunes and Hiero's long allegiance to the Romans defined his rule.[59] In the inter-war years Syracuse was a loyal ally of Rome but functioned independently as a regional power. After Cannae, the extent of Hannibal's military victory unsettled the population of Syracuse and exposed a latent hostility to the Roman alliance among the younger generation. During his long rule, Hiero had kept order in the city but now, in his nineties, his influence waned. In the aftermath of Hannibal's victories, Hiero's son, heir and co-regent Gelo declared his allegiance to the Carthaginians, setting off a period of dynastic strife and rebellion.[60] Then Gelo died suddenly in mysterious circumstances, 'so timely a death as to taint even the father with suspicion', and not long afterwards Hiero too passed away after a fifty-four-year reign (Livy 23.30.11–12). The deaths left Syracuse with a power vacuum (Polyb. 7.8.4).

Hannibal kept abreast of developments at Syracuse using spies, agents and envoys. The stage was set for Carthaginian and Roman allied factions within the city to struggle over the succession. 'Hiero's death changed the whole situation,' claimed Livy, and rule passed to Hiero's fifteen-year-old grandson Hieronymus. When he assumed the throne at Syracuse real power lay in the hands of Hieronymus' uncles, Adranodorus and Zoippus (husbands of Hiero's daughters) who had been appointed as guardians to the young king, along with thirteen Syracusan noblemen (Livy 24.4.1–4). The struggle for power at Syracuse initiated a period of violence, intrigue and assassination at the court of the old king. There was turmoil and conspiracy as agents of both Rome and Hannibal vied for influence with various factions.[61] In the aftermath of Hiero's death, a plot on the life of the young heir was exposed, implicating one of his guardians, the pro-Roman Thraso (falsely accused, according to Livy 24.4.5–5.14).

Hieronymus was then persuaded to send envoys to Hannibal in Italy to broach the idea of cooperation with the Carthaginians (Polyb.7.2.2). Hannibal surely received the embassy with enthusiasm and sent one of his lieutenants (the commander of the triremes, also named Hannibal) and two special envoys to negotiate with the new king. The envoys were Hippocrates and Epicydes, brothers of mixed Carthaginian–Syracusan origin who served in Hannibal's army.[62] The scope of Hannibal's control over the events in the war outside Italy has often been debated but there seems little doubt that he was directing Carthaginian policy in Sicily from his base in Italy.

Whilst Hannibal negotiated a new alliance with Syracuse, the Roman commander in Sicily, Appius Claudius Pulcher, sent representatives to Hieronymus to 'renew the treaty made with his ancestors'. The Roman delegation was given an audience with the king. Hannibal's envoys were present at the meeting, which was both a hostile and profoundly insulting gesture to the Romans. The boy king, whose head had naturally been turned by the tales of Hannibal's great victories and charismatic leadership, even taunted the

Roman envoys in front of the Carthaginians. Hieronymus told the Romans he 'sympathized with them for having been wiped out by the Carthaginians in battles in Italy' (Polyb. 7.3.2–4).[63] The Roman envoys reacted in protest and warned the young king not to accept the words of their enemies or violate the existing treaty made with his grandfather.

The governing council at Syracuse was split on how to act but under the influence of Adranodorus (the king's uncle) and his supporters the decision was taken to go to war against Rome (Polyb. 7.3–5). After discussions with Hieronymus, the Carthaginian delegation continued on to Carthage followed by a Syracusan mission sent 'to establish a treaty of the terms negotiated with Hannibal' (Livy 24.6.7).[64] Hieronymus was a teenage boy and at the mercy of his divided advisors. It is not surprising that he turned out to be a most unstable ally and whilst one group of envoys negotiated a treaty at Carthage, he decided to change the terms of that agreement. The first agreement envisioned Carthage as supplying land and sea forces against the Romans in Sicily, and once the Romans were expelled the two powers would split Sicily in two, with the river Himera as the border (Map 1). Another set of advisors saw the opportunity to extend Syracusan hegemony beyond their traditional realm. They coaxed the young king with talk of his noble lineage (he was related to King Pyrrhus through his mother) and the further potential for Syracusan greatness (Polyb.7.4.1–2; Livy 24.6.7).

Hieronymus sent another group of negotiators to Carthage with new conditions that claimed the whole of Sicily as his by right. Syracuse offered to assist Carthage in Italy as long as Carthage helped the king recover the island for his own rule (Polyb. 7.4.2). This vision saw a future where neither Rome nor Carthage had an interest in Sicily. The Carthaginians, although they 'perceived the full extent of the young man's instability and unbalanced condition', needed Syracuse and access to the ports in Sicily for their own interests. Thus they seemed willing to agree to the concept of a Sicily fully dominated by Syracuse if it meant the demise of Roman power on the island (Polyb. 7.4.7–8; Livy 24.6.8).

When Hannibal was informed of the new terms of the treaty he cannot have been pleased, but the new alliance was hugely significant for his efforts in Italy. He could have asked for no more substantial an ally than Syracuse and no more of a distraction for the Romans than Sicily in rebellion. If the Carthaginians could once more access Sicilian ports, then Hannibal would more easily receive his supplies. Perhaps he was also willing to concede future power to a young, unstable boy king whose prospects were far from settled.

In 214 BCE as Syracuse prepared for war Hieronymus, who had now reigned for thirteen months, travelled with an army to the nearby town of Leontinoi. There his short rule came to an end when he was assassinated in an ambush (Polyb. 7.7.3). It is entirely possible that Roman agents were to blame for the assassination. The Romans had the most to gain from the king's death but there were many elements at play in the struggle for Syracuse. In addition to the agents of Rome and Carthage vying for influence with the different factions in the city, there was an important anti-monarchist group among the population. The boy king had proven to be impetuous and irrational and any number of factions may have been responsible for his downfall. In the chaotic aftermath of the assassination, Adranodorus tried to seize power, but he too was killed. There followed the brutal slaughter of every man, woman and child related to the royal family of Hiero (Livy 24.25–26). When a new government took power, steps were taken towards re-establishing a Roman alliance and contact made with Appius Claudius Pulcher, based with his fleet at Lilybaeum. As these negotiations continued, Hippocrates and Epicydes, Hannibal's envoys who had been elected magistrates in Syracuse, seized power and established control in the city. They were certainly acting on behalf of the pro-Hannibalic faction at Syracuse and most likely under Hannibal's direct orders (Livy 24.27.1, 30.2–32.9; Polyb. 8.3.1).[65]

As the control of Syracuse lay in the balance a Carthaginian army with naval support supplemented the Syracusan forces defending the city. Meanwhile another Carthaginian army under the commander Himilco landed in Sicily at Heraclea and recaptured the city of Agrigentum for the Carthaginians, almost fifty years after it had fallen in the First Punic War. Himilco's aim was the encouragement of a wider rebellion among the cities on the island. The Romans simultaneously built up their military presence in Sicily. Their talismanic general Marcellus joined Appius Claudius Pulcher, perhaps as early as the autumn of 214 BCE, and assumed overall command of the military expedition in Sicily.[66] Roman forces included the fleet stationed at Lilybaeum with over 100 vessels and a land army of three legions (reinforced to a total of 130 ships and four legions by 213 BCE).[67] In the spring of 213 BCE the two Roman commanders made a joint land and sea attack on Syracuse.

The struggle for Sicily would be crucial if the Carthaginians were to aid Hannibal in the war in Italy. Syracuse was one of the largest cities in the Mediterranean with a major urban centre and large ports. It was well defended both by nature and construction. The Roman geographer Strabo, writing two centuries later, called Syracuse a *pentapolis* – a city made up of five towns. The centre of the city was the island of Ortygia that sat between the two harbours and was the focus of civic life, with the neighbourhoods of Achradina, Tycha and Neapolis spread out on the mainland.[68] The circuit walls of Syracuse enclosed the island of Ortygia and the suburbs on the mainland. They ran for 17 kilometres and included a vast area to the north of the city, the plateau known as Epipolae.[69]

The Romans launched a two-pronged attack on the city of Syracuse with the land force assaulting the wall at the Hexapylon gate and the navy focusing on Achradina. Marcellus' attack fleet included 60 quinqueremes equipped with the most up-to-date weaponry and even a floating siege engine that Polybius calls a 'sambukas' (8.4.3).[70] The confident Marcellus had assumed that once he sailed up to the walls of the city with his impressive fleet, 'his personal prestige would combine to overawe the Syracusans'. It turns out that behind the walls of Syracuse was an even more impressive weapon and Marcellus had not taken into account the power of the famous scientist and engineer Archimedes (Plutarch, *Marc.* 14).[71] In the initial stages of the attack the sophisticated Roman machines of war were rendered 'insignificant not only in the philosopher's [Archimedes'] estimation but also by comparison with those which he had constructed himself' (*Marc.* 14).

Archimedes was a native of Syracuse whose father had been an astronomer and mathematician and was possibly related to the old king Hiero.[72] After studying in Alexandria in the mid-third century, Archimedes had returned home to Syracuse during the long period of Hiero's rule. The old king had built Syracuse into a Hellenistic centre that fostered an environment of learning and scientific experimentation. Archimedes lived and studied under this patronage. Part of his work was directed at developing the urban defences and fortifications of the city. These had originally been constructed in the fifth century but the advent of sophisticated siege weaponry in the Hellenistic period meant that the walls and forts had been upgraded during Hiero's rule, and Archimedes is credited with this work (Diodorus Sic. 14.18.4–8).[73] Elaborate land defences and sea walls protected Syracuse. It would not fall easily, and when the initial Roman attack on the city was repulsed, all credit for this lay with Archimedes.[74]

By every account Archimedes' counter-siege engines were miraculous and he embodied the innovative approach to war in the spirit of the Hellenistic age. His machines included 'catapults, beams that dropped heavy rocks, grappling irons and small catapults called *scorpians*'. With these machines the Syracusan defenders sank Roman ships, knocked out their lines of infantry and caused general mayhem among their troops. So efficient was the defence mounted by the Syracusans using the weaponry of Archimedes that 'the Romans began to believe they were fighting against a supernatural enemy' (Plutarch, *Marc.* 15.1–17.4).

The evidence for this wondrous defence of Syracuse under Archimedes' direction comes purely from anecdotes in later sources, the earliest being Polybius and frequent mentions can be found in Cicero. Plutarch's *Life of Marcellus* contains a long digression on Archimedes defence of the city. Unfortunately, hard facts about the life and death of Archimedes are difficult to come by, perhaps because Archimedes, much like Hannibal, became so famous in the ancient world after his death. His name came to embody ancient science and innovation; he was one of the world's first celebrated scientists, much like a Hellenistic Einstein. Even today with his 'Eureka' moment in the bath, Archimedes is a household name and a symbol of genius in the ancient world.

The stories of the great siege and counter-siege of Syracuse developed in Roman tradition and gave birth to the Archimedes legend.[75] 'So long as he was present they did not dare even to attempt an attack by any method which made it possible for Archimedes to oppose them' (Polyb. 8.7.9). In many ways Archimedes became to science what Hannibal became to military genius in the Roman imagination: both of them men of enormous achievement who challenged the might of Rome. The 'machines of Archimedes' were so successful in defending Syracuse that they forced the Romans to stand back from their assault. The Romans decided the best course of action was to stay well clear of the city walls and set up a blockade to starve Syracuse into submission by cutting off both land and sea routes (Livy 24.34.16).[76]

The Carthaginian army under Himilco then approached Syracuse (from his base at Agrigentum) with the intention of relieving the city. He realized 'that his enemy, well fortified and numerically strong, was safely ensconced around Syracuse' so he decided to move out into Sicily and encourage other cities to join the Carthaginian cause. Hannibal must have closely followed the events in Sicily and been instructing representatives, supporters and agents to ensure that there was upheaval in all the major centres on the island. At this moment Morgantina (a city approx. 100 km north-west from Syrcause) betrayed its Roman garrison and went over to Carthage (Livy 24.36.9–10). With the island itself now in the balance, Marcellus left Syracuse under blockade and moved with part of his army to prevent more defections from cities in Sicily.[77]

The war for Syracuse turned into a brutal struggle for the cities of the interior of Sicily. Morgantina's defection 'gave encouragement to other city-states, and Roman garrisons now began to be expelled from the citadels, or crushed after being treacherously betrayed'. Details of events at the strategically crucial inland town of Henna (modern Enna) describe the gruesome slaughter of 'an unarmed crowd' trapped and massacred in the theatre by the Roman garrison (who were themselves threatened with massacre). This fuelled the rebellion of more cities, as 'even those who had been vacillating earlier now went over to the Carthaginians' (Livy 24.37–39).[78] At Henna, Marcellus had employed the same deterrent he had employed previously in Campania, at Nola. He thought it would ensure the loyalty of other Sicilian towns but in this he seems to have been mistaken.

The winter of 213/212 BCE saw Marcellus back at Syracuse camped near the northern entrance to Syracuse, called the Hexapylon gate. Carthaginian attempts to lift the siege and break the blockade continued. Some supplies did reach the city but there was essentially a stalemate. The first success for the Romans came in the early spring when a deserter from the city reported that 'copious quantities of wine' were being consumed inside the town during a festival celebrating the worship of Artemis (Livy 25.23–24). The witness reported that drinking was excessive because, due to the blockade, there was little else for the population to consume except wine. Marcellus took advantage of the distraction to seize the area of Epipolae, the plateau overlooking Syracuse to the north. He set his men to scale the walls by night while the population was distracted at the festival. Marcellus followed and looking down to Syracuse from his perspective high on the plateau he saw 'probably at the time the world's most beautiful city stretched out before his eyes' (Livy 25.24.11).[79] The fall of cities like Syracuse often provoked a poetic reaction from Hellenistic and Roman generals, and the Roman historians writing their history. Marcellus was reminded 'of the Athenian fleets that had been sunk there, of the two mighty armies that had been destroyed along with their leaders and of all the critical wars fought with the Carthaginians' (Livy 25.24.12–13).[80] Marcellus wept, they say, both at the beauty and also at the glory of the city he was about to sack.[81]

Yet events did not proceed quite as quickly or as smoothly as Marcellus had envisioned. As his troops advanced towards Achradina they encountered fierce resistance and had to pull back. Confusion reigned in the city, with the Romans in control of a significant part of the suburban area of Neapolis and Tycha and the Syracusans under Epicydes holding the centre of the city and the island of Ortygia. Bomilcar, the Carthaginian admiral at Syracuse took advantage of this (and a rough sea) to break the Roman blockade and with thirty-five ships made for Carthage. He reported the events at Syracuse to the

Carthaginians and then, within a few days, returned to Syracuse with a fleet of 100 ships and provisions (Livy 25.25.11–13).[82]

The Carthaginians attempted to break the siege by throwing everything they could into the endeavour. Another Carthaginian fleet arrived and landed on the shore between the city and the Roman camp. These events are reported in a paragraph or two in Livy but took place over months and resulted in a stalemate of sorts with the territory of Syracuse held piecemeal by both sides. In the autumn of 212 a plague ravaged the city after the long, hot summer months. It affected both armies but seems to have had a greater impact on the Carthaginians.[83] Only when the plague finally killed both the Carthaginian general Himilco and the Syracusan/Carthaginian leader Hippocrates did the Romans take all of Syracuse under their control.

The population, already decimated by the plague, was not spared and the Romans killed whomever they found and looted everything. In the ovation celebrated in Rome, Marcellus paraded 'most of the statues and other offerings which the Syracusans had dedicated to the gods, including their finest works of art; for he intended that these should not only decorate his triumph but also adorn the capital' (Plutarch, *Marc.* 21).[84] Marcellus' sack of Syracuse was a seminal event for the Romans when they looked back on their history. Syracuse was a sophisticated Hellenistic city adorned with statuary, paintings and temple offerings and votives. The Romans were awed by the wealth; there was 'as much booty as there would scarcely have been had Carthage been captured then' (Livy 25.31.11; see also Plutarch, *Marc.* 19.3, Polyb. 9.10.1–13). The ancient sources itemize the loot and speak of quantities of bronze, melted down and used in buildings, of silver and tapestries (Pliny, *NH* 14.13). Livy records that 'along with a model of Syracuse after its capture, catapults, ballistae, and a whole panoply of war engines were carried in the procession . . . there were heads of silver and bronze artefacts, furniture, precious clothing, and many famous statues, Syracuse having been one of the Greek cities most richly endowed in such things' (26.21.6–9). These accounts of the wealth won and the great glory achieved at Syracuse illustrate the way in which the war with Hannibal was woven into the fabric of Roman society, both in a physical sense and through the legends of the fall of great cities.

# CHAPTER 9

# HANNIBAL'S DILEMMA, 212–209

Hannibal was not as determined to defend Capua as the Romans were to tighten their blockade. (**Livy 26.12.1**)

HANNIBAL MUST HAVE DESPAIRED at the loss of Syracuse in 212 BCE, an event that would turn out to be a pivotal moment in the war. If Carthage could have held the city and again acquired the wealth of Sicily along with it, an overall victory might have been possible. The fight for Sicily was not over yet and the Carthaginians did not give up altogether. They still held Agrigentum and continued with a significant investment in men and resources there. It was a base from which to operate across the island. Hannibal sent a Libyphoenician cavalry commander named Muttines to Agrigentum to direct the opposition to Rome. Muttines made a reputation for himself as a brilliant soldier, schooled by Hannibal in tactics. In Sicily he worked hard to 'keep the Carthaginian allies loyal by bringing them timely assistance' when the Romans threatened (Livy 25.40.5). Despite a valiant effort by Muttines it would only be a matter of time before the whole island was controlled by Rome.[1]

For the Romans, the sack of Syracuse was a turning point and marked the beginning of almost a century of the looting of cities across the Hellenistic world. The art and treasures of the ancient world would find their way to the city of Rome where they were used as trophies of war – in some cases even fixed to the doors of houses, to adorn public spaces and private homes (Livy 38.43.9–10).[2] In the rhetoric of the Romans looking back on their history, these trophies would effect a change in the traditional character of the Romans. The loot of the conquered would irrevocably influence life at Rome. Later Romans would criticize this wave of luxury that flooded into the city and some claimed this splendour caused a breakdown in the moral fibre of the Romans. The 'Greek' luxury was seen to have eroded the core values of the Roman Republic, the very values that had been so important in defeating Hannibal.[3]

According to Cicero, the only object from Syracuse that Marcellus is reported to have kept for himself was 'a globe of the heavens made by the great Archimedes' (*De Rep.* 1.21). But Archimedes himself did not survive the sack of the city; he fell victim to the enthusiastic looting that stripped Syracuse of all her wealth. 'While many foul instances of anger, many of greed were being carried out', the fate of Archimedes, the chief defender of the city and greatest thinker of the age, was sealed by a Roman soldier (Livy 25.31.9). Not knowing who he was, a soldier came across an old man intently drawing diagrams in the earth. Archimedes, the distracted genius, was too absorbed by his geometry to respond to the soldier's questions and was killed despite Marcellus' orders that he be spared (Valerius Maximus 9; Cicero, *De finibus* 5.50).[4]

Marcellus' looting of Syracuse provoked a fair amount of contemporary criticism and later Roman commentators used the event to rationalize the subsequent decline of the Roman Republic. But this criticism may conceal a more concrete reason for the censure. Underlying Marcellus' success was great public acclaim for his victory and this would have intensified the sharp personal rivalries at Rome. Marcellus' willingness to engage with Hannibal and fight for glory won him much 'popular support' at Rome, which must have rankled with the Fabian supporters whose cautious approach had been official policy for almost half a decade. Marcellus may therefore have been denied an official triumph for his victory at Syracuse by rivals in the Senate at Rome opposed to his growing reputation, and was granted only an official 'ovation' instead.[5]

Hannibal's attention was now stretched thinly across the south of Italy. Without reinforcements he did not have the ability to protect his allies and expand his territory. Wherever Hannibal went one or two Roman armies tracked him. The other Roman armies would then focus their forces on where he was not. So when Hannibal went into Campania the Romans would move towards the cities of Apulia and Magna Graecia.[6] In this way Hannibal's territorial gains and alliances were slowly but surely stripped away by superior Roman manpower.

But all was not lost and in 212 BCE, even before Syracuse had fallen, Hannibal turned his focus to another important Greek city in Italy, the Spartan colony of

Tarentum (Taras, modern Taranto) (Polyb. 8.24–34; Livy. 25.7.–11, 13.1).[7] Hannibal would have known that the Tarentine–Roman alliance was an uneasy one for it was the Tarentines who had called on Pyrrhus for help against Roman incursions in southern Italy earlier in the century. After the Pyrrhic War Tarentum fell to Rome (c. 270) and perforce became an ally. Given this recent history it was perhaps surprising to Hannibal that the ruling citizens of Tarentum had not immediately moved to his side in the aftermath of Cannae. In fact, Polybius expected Tarentum to abandon Rome and claimed erroneously that the city was among those that switched sides directly after Cannae.[8]

However, Tarentum is exemplary of the difficult situation in which the cities of southern Italy found themselves. Many factors, including economic ties, may have preserved Tarentine loyalty to Rome but the Romans did not take any chances. The city sat on the Via Appia between the eastern port of Brundisium and Venusia (modern Venosa), both key Latin colonies that had been established earlier in the third century (see Map 1).[9] The Romans, eager to protect their colonies and transport links early in the war, had moved quickly to secure the area and occupied the town with a garrison: this made a quick transfer of allegiance to Hannibal difficult for the population.[10] The city elites were divided between pro- and anti-Roman factions but most importantly, at some point early in the war, members of the leading families had been taken as hostages to Rome. The Romans kept hostages from many cities of the south and this seems to have preserved an uncomfortable loyalty of the chief towns of Magna Graecia, and Tarentum especially.[11]

Two years after Cannae, in 214 BCE, while Hannibal was in Campania near Lake Avernus he received a delegation made up of five men of the Tarentine elite. They told Hannibal that most of the younger men of the city would choose an alliance with him (Livy 24.13.1–2). It is revealing of Hannibal's personal appeal that from across Italy people flocked to his side, especially younger men of fighting age.[12] These young men of the city had fought with the Romans against Hannibal, and had, like the other allies, been released and treated with the 'usual courtesy that the Carthaginian had accorded all the allies of Rome' (Livy 24.13.1–2). It may have been in response to this delegation and show of interest from the young men that Hannibal turned his mind to the port of Tarentum. Livy claims he was 'overtaken by a keen desire to take possession of this rich and famous city' (24.13.5). For Hannibal, Tarentum was especially appealing for its access to the east and his new ally, the Macedonian king across the Adriatic.[13] As Hannibal continued to be stifled in Campania, trying and failing to take Neapolis and Nola anew, he had looked elsewhere for a port.[14]

In the autumn of 214 BCE, at the same time as Marcellus went to Sicily, Hannibal marched an army up to the walls of Tarentum. He did not lay waste the countryside around the city, as he hoped for a peaceful surrender. There was no reaction and the city did not open its gates to the Carthaginian, its Roman garrison still firmly in control. Hannibal withdrew his army and spent another winter in Apulia. This year he chose the town of Salapia for quarters and from there built up his troop base. Reports of Hannibal's liaison with a local woman that winter were still discussed centuries later, and Pliny records that the town was 'famous as the place of Hannibal's amour with a courtesan' (*NH* 3.103). The echoes of Hannibal's time in Italy resound in this story, which illustrates that it was the most exciting thing to have happened in Salapia for centuries.[15] The liaison was perhaps somewhat more than a brief encounter for it to be remembered and identified so clearly with Hannibal. It could not have been his only encounter with a courtesan in his years in Italy. In fact Appian records a variation of the story that saw 'Hannibal move his army to Lucania and into winter quarters, and here this fierce warrior gave himself up to unaccustomed luxury and the delights of love' (*Hann.* 43).[16]

The campaigning season of 213 BCE started disastrously when news arrived that Arpi, the very first of the towns to ally with Hannibal after Cannae, had fallen to an army led by Q. Fabius Maximus junior, the dictator's son (Livy 24.46.1–7). The summer saw Hannibal in the southern regions of Apulia known as the Salentine peninsula, the heel of the boot of Italy. Here Hannibal had close access to Tarentum and was also in a region where he could look east towards his allies in Macedon if any reinforcements were to be forthcoming.[17] He spent that season gathering support and subduing cities in the Salentine peninsula, essentially providing an environment in which Tarentum could throw off its Roman garrison. In the winter of 213–212 BCE, Hannibal set up his camp three days' march from Tarentum in Apulia.[18] He now seems to have set his sights on taking the city, perhaps to provide an option beyond Campania and looking outwards for support from his allies across the Adriatic.

Hannibal must have received news of events at Rome that would be instrumental in a shift in the relationship with Tarentum. The captives from the cities of the region held at Rome had attempted an escape. These men were captured on the way south and brought back to the city. There, in front of the assembly, they were sentenced as traitors. Their punishment began with a flogging and they were then thrown to their deaths from the Tarpeian Rock on the south-east slope of the Capitoline Hill (Livy 25.7.10–14). These young men were the sons of the Tarentine and southern Italian elites and their execution generated a great deal of 'ill-feeling in the two most famous Greek city-states in Italy' (Livy 25.8.1–2 referring to Tarentum and Thurii). The deaths of the hostages moreover removed any Roman hold over Tarentum.

The events around Tarentum and the cities of Magna Graecia are characteristic of the shifts of momentum in these years. Just when things looked impossible for Hannibal, the execution of the Tarentine prisoners led some of the Greek cities to change sides and he found himself with new allies and options.[19] That winter Hannibal was ready nearby as a group of thirteen young men from Tarentum conspired to overthrow the garrison. By night the young Tarentines left the city and sought out Hannibal in his camp. With the Roman garrison stationed at Tarentum precautions had to be taken to conceal any nocturnal forays and the men posed as hunters. Hannibal received them graciously and granted them an audience. Together they sketched out a plan to take the city and agreed to meet again. When the two sides met anew, Hannibal promised that the Carthaginians would 'neither exact tribute nor impose any other burdens on the people of Tarentum' (Polyb. 8.25.2).[20] From then on the conspirators regularly met Hannibal by night and the ground was prepared for a surprise attack on Tarentum.

The day chosen for the attack, early in 212 BCE, was during a festival when it was known that the Roman commander at Tarentum would be attending. By this time the guards at the city gates were well used to the leading conspirator, whose name was Philemenus, leaving the city to hunt or forage, and did not suspect anything on the day. The plan to take the city needed careful execution. Hannibal emphasized to his commanders that they must 'carry out his orders to the letter' (Polyb. 8.26.9). The elaborate plot involved a party of Numidians foraging in the countryside to distract Roman attention while Hannibal and 10,000 hand-picked troops marched towards the city led by the hunter Philemenus and a decoy wild boar (Polyb. 8.26; Livy 25.9–12).

Hannibal approached the city from the east and advanced towards the Teminid gate. He had chosen to enter the city here because, unusually for an ancient city, Tarentum had an area within the city walls that was used as a cemetery just inside the eastern quarter (Polyb. 8.28.6–7).[21] Lighting signal fires from within and without the city, the attackers converged in silence and took the guards completely by surprise. The Roman commander, Gaius Livius, had been sleeping off a day of revelry. When he was woken by the chaos and noise of the attack he made for the port, where he jumped into a boat and proceeded to the citadel of the city, which guarded the deep southern port at the end of a promontory. There was intense street-to-street fighting and in the end the Roman garrison was confined to the citadel. The attack was successful but only partially and left the urban centre open to surprise attacks and reprisals. It also meant that it was impossible to leave Tarentum unguarded. Without the manpower to mount a siege on the citadel Hannibal set about trying to starve the garrison out through a blockade.

Hannibal must have frequently requested support from Carthage for backup from the sea. Tarentum could not be held without help from the navy and the Tarentines needed extra manpower to counter the Roman naval supremacy. When the Carthaginian admiral Bomilcar was forced to flee Syracusan waters near the end of the siege there he chose to sail on to Tarentum (Livy 25.27.12). Without support from the sea Hannibal could not control access to the citadel at Tarentum and the Romans would be free to supply their garrison. There are few recorded instances of coordinated Carthaginian movement by sea and land over the course of Hannibal's years in Italy. While there must have been frequent attempts to link up and communicate, there is a frustrating gap in our knowledge of the relationship in these years between Carthage and Hannibal.

Hannibal returned to his camp outside the city and left the Tarentines and a garrison of soldiers to blockade the Romans holed up in the citadel. It was an incomplete conquest but the fall of Tarentum was enough to disturb the whole region. Soon after, the cities of Metapontum and then Thurii and Heraclea followed the Tarentines in declaring allegiance to Hannibal. Hannibal found himself with new allies in the deep south of Italy willing to join the Carthaginians against Rome (Appian, *Hann.* 6.35). There is little doubt that almost the whole area was turned by the change of Tarentine allegiance, reflecting its regional influence and the importance of the alliance for Hannibal.[22] In Magna Graecia, apart from the garrison at Tarentum, by the summer of 212 BCE only the city of Rhegium remained under Roman control (Map 1).

In the meantime Hannibal's extended absence from Campania had left the city of Capua at risk and the Roman consuls of 212 BCE had taken the opportunity to tighten the knot around the city with a total blockade.[23] Capua was already suffering crippling food shortages, being cut off from its fields, and the Roman consuls intended to starve the city into capitulation (Livy 25.13.1). Inside the city the Capuans loyal to Hannibal and a garrison of Carthaginian troops were left to provide resistance against Rome. Hannibal received a desperate message from Capua requesting food and relief from the siege. He sent his commander Hanno from Bruttium into Campania with orders to bring provisions to the town. Hanno and his army were near the strategic town of Beneventum collecting grain and supplies when the consul Fulvius

Flaccus approached with his army. The Romans attacked and took the Carthaginian camp while Hanno was absent. Livy reports losses of over 6,000 men with 7,000 taken prisoner.[24] Hanno had to race back to Bruttium with the remainder of his army, abandoning the starving Capuans to their own devices (Livy 25.13.3–14.14).

Once again messengers from Capua were sent out to Hannibal: they reported that the consuls were at Beneventum and implored him not to leave 'the people abandoned and undefended' (Livy 25.15.1–2).[25] The Roman consuls had seized the opportunity created by Hanno's defeat to attack Capua with six legions. They sent for the proconsul Tiberius Gracchus, who was nearby with his army in Lucania to protect Beneventum (which lay on a key route through the Apennines from Apulia into Campania). Suddenly, just as Gracchus made his way towards Beneventum, he was killed. Events leading to the death of the illustrious proconsul are so confused that even Livy laments 'the uncertainty surrounding where and how such a famous and distinguished man met his end' (Livy 25.16–17). Gracchus was either betrayed by the Lucanians in his command to the Carthaginian general Mago (known as 'the Samnite') and ambushed, or, in a far less gallant version, he was surprised while bathing. Legend has it that the body of Tiberius Sempronius Gracchus was brought to Hannibal. Hannibal buried his enemy, with whom he had battled numerous times over the years, with full military honours.[26] When Gracchus died, his army, made up of slaves conscripted after Cannae, 'deserted its standards', the troops' loyalty being more to the commander than the cause (Livy 25.20.1).

Hannibal, as he finally approached Capua, was faced with a serious dilemma. The citadel at Tarentum was still in Roman hands and the city of Capua was now almost completely cut off. As the crow flies, the cities lie some 300 kilometres apart and Hannibal could not be in both places at once. So much of the war relied on his personal command that he found himself stretched across the south of Italy. Politically he had little choice but to try to help his allies at Capua. He must have understood that Rome intended to make an example of the Capuans to lay bare Hannibal's inability to protect those who became his allies.[27] His only real hope of relieving the city was to attempt to draw the consuls into a battle and defeat them. The Romans, however, were much less likely to stand and fight on Hannibal's terms than they had been four years earlier.

Hannibal knew that the Romans found their blockade of Capua more difficult to maintain if he was nearby. When he attempted to approach the city, he was quickly lured away by the consuls, Appius Claudius and Flaccus.

They marched off in different directions to draw Hannibal away and then circled back to Capua.[28] Hannibal chose not to follow and instead went into Apulia where his remaining allied towns were under pressure from the praetor C. Fulvius Flaccus (the brother of the sitting consul). Fulvius and his army, in Livy's estimation, had become over-confident; following recent successes in Apulia, they were 'so laden down with booty that they had become neglectful and apathetic' (25.20.6–7). Still well informed, Hannibal probably received news of Fulvius' attitude and may have turned away from Capua when offered a chance to draw him into battle. The Carthaginian forces approached the army of Fulvius and Hannibal chose the ground for the encounter near the town of Herdonea. In a set-piece he destroyed the Roman army and took their camp. Only 2,000 of the 18,000 men survived (25.21.1–10). Livy writes with dismay of how, after so many defeats, a Roman commander could still walk casually and unprepared into a battle with Hannibal. This, the so-called First Battle of Herdonea, was Hannibal's largest battlefield victory since Cannae. These events, combined with the death of the proconsul Gracchus, illustrate just how far Hannibal was from being defeated. He remained a formidable force and most of the Roman commanders were wary of approaching.[29]

The victory at Herdonea must have buoyed the Carthaginians and their allies but in the meantime the Romans had completed their heavy fortification of the area around Capua. As Syracuse fell to Marcellus near the end of 212 BCE, the barrier around Capua tightened, with more troops becoming available to seal off the city (Livy 25.23.1).[30] Capua was encircled by a ditch and rampart. Roman supplies came from their grain stores and supply post at Casilinum and two other camps nearby. The city was completely blockaded and made a new series of pleas to Hannibal for help.

By 211 we find Hannibal impotent in the face of the Roman blockade and increasingly desperate. Hannibal returned to Campania and set up a camp on Monte Tifata but faced an implacable barrier between his forces and his allies inside the town: 'he could not force his way into Capua nor could he lure the Romans out of their camp' (Polyb. 9.3.4–5). The Romans were especially determined to make an example of Capua, whose defection to Hannibal they viewed as a profound betrayal. They dedicated nearly half of the legions stationed in Italy to the siege and despite a few brave coordinated attempts with the Capuans, Hannibal could not crack their defences.

The situation exemplified Hannibal's continuing predicament in Italy; he was essentially stuck. He could ill afford to lose Capua but neither could he let himself be trapped in Campania where the Roman forces were massed. The scorched-earth policy meant Hannibal could not sustain his army for long in the region anyway.[31] To alleviate the siege of Capua and distract the Romans from their task, Hannibal hatched a dramatic and somewhat reckless plan. Before he executed it he paid a Numidian soldier to take a letter to the Capuans explaining his actions. In the letter Hannibal implored the people in Capua not to lose heart and tried to reassure them that he was not deserting the field, but trying to relieve their suffering (Livy 26.7.6–8; Polyb. 9.5.1–6). His idea was to attempt to draw the Roman armies away from Campania and thus ease the pressure on the city. The strategy was always going to be risky. The Romans had become far less gullible and less likely to be drawn into Hannibal's stratagems in the years after Cannae. Nonetheless, Hannibal must have felt it was worth an attempt so he gathered up his army and turned north, marching the 195 kilometres from Capua to the gates of Rome (Livy 26.7–26.11; Polyb. 9.4–9.7).

Two different scenarios are reported: Polybius' account puts Hannibal outside the walls of Rome unannounced but, according to Livy, the consul Flaccus had already sent a dispatch to Rome alerting the Senate (Livy 26.8.1; Polyb. 9.6.1–5).[32] In the Senate, Hannibal's long-time opponent Fabius Maximus argued that this was a ruse to raise the siege of Capua (Livy 26.8.3). In the city, however, sheer panic spread through the people when the messenger arrived with the news of Hannibal's approach. 'The women's lamentations [were] heard coming from private homes: all over the city married ladies poured into the streets, and ran around the shrines of the gods. They swept the altars with their dishevelled hair; they fell to their knees with hands held palm-up to heaven and the gods, and they begged the gods to rescue the city . . .' (Livy 26.9.6–8). The senators may have become wiser to the reality of the threat represented by Hannibal but he retained the power to spread deep alarm among the population at Rome.

Hannibal first camped about twelve kilometres from the city.[33] Rome was not undefended: the proconsul Fulvius Flaccus marched there with his army and entered the city while Polybius claims there was also a newly raised legion inside the walls at the time (9.6.6).[34] Hannibal then moved closer to Rome, to the river Anio about five kilometres away. He settled his army there and with a contingent of two thousand cavalry approached the walls of Rome 'as far as the temple of Hercules, near the Porta Collina'. At the temple of Hercules Hannibal paid homage to his protector, the god he claimed as his own, flaunting the relationship in front of the Romans.[35]

One can imagine the sight of Hannibal 'brazenly and nonchalantly' riding up to the walls of Rome, inspecting them and the layout of the city (Livy 26.10.3). People in their thousands must have taken the chance to view the great enemy in the flesh. The Romans were perhaps not so impressed when they finally saw that Hannibal, no monster, was just a man like any other. A story in Livy claimed that the land Hannibal was camped on outside Rome came up for sale and was sold 'with no diminution in the price'. The sale struck Hannibal as 'so outrageously presumptuous that he immediately summoned the auctioneer and ordered the bankers' shops around the Forum to be put up for sale' (26.11.7).

The proconsul Flaccus eventually sent out a cavalry contingent to drive Hannibal back to his camp but the moment is etched in history – the Carthaginian at the gates of Rome (Livy 26.10.4). Outside Rome the two sides skirmished but reports provide conflicting scenarios. Livy claimed that bad weather (twice) caused a battle to be broken up, and that Hannibal then retreated from the city. He made a fast march down to the south of Italy and the proconsul Flaccus returned to the siege of Capua. Polybius' account records that the newly raised legions in the city drew up outside the walls and 'thus checked Hannibal's attack'. The countryside was plundered and Hannibal withdrew, because, Polybius argued, he thought sufficient time had passed for the siege of Capua to have been lifted enough for him to have achieved his purpose (9.6–7). Hannibal was harried on the retreat and when he heard that the siege of Capua continued, he marched straight to the tip of Italy and appeared there 'so unexpectedly' that he almost managed to take the Roman-allied city of Rhegium by surprise (Livy 26.12.2; Polyb. 9.7.10).

Knowing Hannibal's interest in the art of surprise it may be, as Livy claims, that the whole exercise had been a spontaneous act and that the 'urge took him' (26.7.2). It is possible that the march on Rome was a more thoughtful exercise and it is tempting to consider the wider picture. If Hannibal was aware of simultaneous pressure being exerted by his brothers on the Romans in Iberia that year (see pp. 170–174 below) he may have been encouraged to try to force the Romans' hand. The march could have been part of a wider Carthaginian strategy. Perhaps Hannibal believed that if he could conjure up some element of surprise and appear before the walls of Rome, he might cause such dismay and alarm as to 'gain some advantage' (Polyb. 9.4.7).

The reality of his extraordinary march from Capua to Rome and then down the whole of southern Italy to Rhegium also reveals his sense of futility as the Romans blocked each move. Hannibal had taken a last gamble and hoped that his march to Rome would relieve his allies trapped in Capua, but that gamble failed. The people inside Capua inevitably felt betrayed: Hannibal had not returned, nor had he been able to lift the siege. The commanders of the Carthaginian garrison inside the city, Bostar and Hanno, wrote an angry letter to their general. They accused Hannibal of turning his back on his allies and leaving them to 'all manner of torture'. The letter continued, calling the Romans 'far more dedicated an enemy than the Carthaginian was a friend'. The Carthaginian commanders attempted to sneak the missive out of the city with some Numidians posing as deserters.[36] The men managed to get out of the city into the Roman camp but when one was recognized by a Capuan woman in the camp (she had been his mistress) the letter was confiscated. These men and other Numidian deserters in the Roman camp were rounded up and returned to Capua. They had been flogged and had their hands cut off (Livy 26.12.10–19).

Livy claims that 'the sight of such savage punishment broke the Capuans' spirit' (26.13.1), especially since these were not strangers, but men who had been living among them during the siege. The citizens began to debate surrendering to Rome. The Senate of Capua decided to send a delegation to the Romans to negotiate the surrender. The decision was not universal, and twenty-seven of the Capuan senators withdrew to the house of Vibius Virrius who had been a leading supporter of Hannibal's cause. There they feasted and drank wine, then took poison and 'breathed their last before the gates were opened to the enemy'.

The surrender of the city resulted in the execution of seventy of the surviving senators; 300 Campanian nobles were imprisoned in Rome; the population was dispersed and the rest of the citizens sold into slavery. The city remained populated by its non-citizens, while its wealthy agricultural lands and civic buildings became the property of the Roman people. The riches of Capua became the wealth of Rome. Not surprisingly, there was no sign of clemency and the Romans were resolute in imposing their absolute power on their rebellious former ally (Livy 26.16.6–11, 13). Moreover, now freed from their battles in Campania and around Capua, the Romans could redirect more resources to operations in other theatres of the war, and especially in Iberia where their forces were under immense pressure from Hannibal's brothers.[37]

Hannibal's war with Rome continued in Italy during these crucial years but the perspective from Carthage was, of necessity, focused more on the battle for Iberia. The Carthaginians do not seem to have been interested in taking over Italy and Hannibal was there to defeat Rome, not conquer the peninsula in the name of Carthage. In Iberia the situation was profoundly different and in many respects more vital to the final outcome of the war than were events in Italy.[38] There were long-standing cultural and economic associations with parts of southern Iberia that connected the city of Carthage to the region. We have seen how Carthage directly controlled territory in the

Iberian peninsula for over two decades prior to Hannibal's invasion of Italy. For centuries before, the region had been a source of key resources for Carthage in the form of precious metals and soldiers. Carthaginian territory in Iberia would have been populated by many citizens of Carthage who lived and flourished in newly established cities on the peninsula. The longer the Carthaginians could hold their territory in the Iberian peninsula, the more difficult it would be for Rome to defeat them.

Hannibal's two brothers Hasdrubal and Mago, commanding the Carthaginian forces in Iberia, had been engaged in an intense struggle whilst Hannibal remained in Italy. The conflict fought by the Barcid brothers, whom their father Hamilcar had referred to as 'lion's cubs', was chiefly with two Roman brothers, Gnaeus and Publius Scipio, known by the epithet 'thunderbolts' of Rome (Valerius Maximus 9.3. ext.2; Silius Italicus 7.106; Cicero, *Pro Balb*. 34). The epic battles that ensued sapped a great deal of Carthage's resources and reduced the supply of troops and reinforcements that were available for Hannibal in Italy.

As early as 216 BCE, before Cannae, Hasdrubal Barca had been ordered to march to Italy to support his brother and open a new front in the war (Livy 23.27.12).[39] The battle plan that Hannibal had constructed from early on in the war may have relied on this. Hasdrubal's departure was delayed by an uprising of his Iberian allies (perhaps the Turdetani), which had led to severe fighting in the spring of that year (Livy 23. 26–7).[40] Another Carthaginian general, named Himilco, arrived in Iberia with infantry and cavalry and helped to put down the rebellion. When rumours swirled that Hasdrubal had been ordered to march to Italy even greater turmoil ensued among the allies. The impression gained from Livy is that the Iberian soldiers were unwilling to follow another Carthaginian into Italy. Hasdrubal's army marching north met the Romans at the Ebro river in the autumn of 216 BCE, perhaps a month or two after Cannae. The Scipio brothers chose their ground south of the Ebro, meaning to stop Hasdrubal and his army crossing the river. When the two sides clashed, a weakness in Hasdrubal's battle line caused the middle to give way. The Iberian troops had failed to hold the centre. In Livy's estimation the Iberians preferred to be defeated at home than risk the route across the Alps (23.29.6–13).

Hasdrubal Barca escaped the field but lost much of his army and with it a great deal of Carthaginian prestige in Iberia. In the aftermath of Hannibal's victories in Italy, while the Romans counted the devastating losses at Cannae, the Carthaginians found themselves in a more precarious position in Iberia than they had previously imagined possible. In the late summer of 216 BCE we have seen that Mago Barca journeyed to Carthage with news of Cannae and a mission to muster reinforcements and supplies for his brother in Italy. Just as he was about to return to Italy, accompanied by a force of 12,000 infantry, 1,500 cavalry and twenty elephants, plus a treasury of 1,000 silver talents and an 'escort of sixty warships', news arrived from Iberia of his brother's military disaster and the defection of Iberian allies to the Romans (Livy 23.32.5–6).[41] The Carthaginians quickly changed plans and sent Mago to Iberia.[42]

Closely tied to Carthaginian efforts in Iberia were events in Africa. A complicated diplomatic endeavour unfolded as both sides courted the rulers of the Numidian kingdoms that bordered Carthaginian territory. Carthage worked to keep, and Rome vied to win over, these important allies. Thus when Syphax, the king of the Masaesyli, received a toga *praetexta* and an ivory curule chair from Roman envoys as gifts to consolidate their alliance, the significance of his status was confirmed. Similar gifts had been given to Ptolemy of Egypt, putting the Numidian king on a par with the powerful Hellenistic ruler as a Roman ally (Livy 27.4.8).[43] Syphax was thus flattered and coaxed by the Romans into an agreement. He first ordered his troops serving with the Carthaginian armies in Iberia to desert and then staged a rebellion at home between 214 BCE and 213 BCE (Livy 24.48–49). Syphax's cooperation with the Romans further diminished Carthaginian efforts to reinforce the Barcid brothers. In the same period, Livy makes reference to many Roman victories in Iberia.[44] Carthage had to withdraw a significant army to fight against the Numidian king in Africa, leaving Hasdrubal and Mago Barca without the manpower needed to defend themselves against the Roman armies.[45]

The narrative during these years details significant Carthaginian losses but raises many questions about the location and even the realities of the defeats. Livy stands accused of exaggerating his accounts and conflating different events.[46] There is no doubt that there was fierce fighting in Iberia and Africa in this period but the specific details prove elusive and the situation was fluid.[47] Substantial Roman pressure continued through 212–211 BCE, although the degree to which Rome had the advantage in Iberia seems over-played by the sources. As Livy tells it, the two Roman commanders 'joined forces after leaving their winter quarters' in a concerted effort to 'bring the war in Iberia to an end' (Livy 25.32.1–2).[48] By 211 a force of about 20,000 Celtiberian troops supported the Roman armies in Iberia.[49]

There were three Carthaginian commanders now active in opposition to the Romans. Hannibal's brothers Hasdrubal and Mago each led an army, and another Hasdrubal, known as the son of Gisgo, led a third. Hasdrubal Gisgo and Mago had combined their armies whilst Hasdrubal Barca was stationed near a city called Amtorgis in the region of the upper Baetis river (Livy

25.32.9).[50] Early in the year both the Carthaginian and Roman armies would have followed the events in Italy and Sicily. Hannibal was under deep strain with the fall of Syracuse and the city of Capua was under a tight blockade. The Roman commanders decided to split their army in two in order to tackle the divided Carthaginian forces. The armies of Hasdrubal Barca and the other Carthaginian commanders significantly outnumbered the Romans. They may have positioned themselves so as further to drive apart their enemy and capitalize on the numerical advantage.[51]

The combined armies of Mago Barca and Hasdrubal Gisgo set out to take on Publius Scipio, whose army was made up of about two-thirds of the combined Roman and allied troops. Hasdrubal Barca was left to encounter the other Scipio, whose force was a combination of the remaining Roman army and Celtiberian allies. Fighting in the company of Mago Barca was 'a new enemy. This was the young Masinissa . . . an ally of the Carthaginians' (Livy 25.34.1–5).[52] The prince Masinissa was from the Massyli kingdom. The Massyli were an important Numidian people bordering the territory of Carthage whose alliance had been sought once Syphax had gone over to the Romans. Masinissa was the son of King Gaia whose realm sat between Carthage and Syphax. The prince had been brought up and educated at Carthage and was related to the Barcid clan through marriage; his aunt was Hannibal's niece.[53] Close in age to Mago Barca, at twenty-seven years old Masinissa had already shown great qualities of leadership, strength and promise (Livy 24.48.13–49.6).[54] The young Numidian prince had gone to Iberia at the head of a powerful contingent of cavalry to confront and harass the Romans. His surprise attacks spread confusion among the Roman troops and panic in the camps.

When Publius Scipio learned that one of the Celtiberian princes allied to Carthage, Indibilis, was advancing with 7,000 new troops he moved to cut them off before the two forces could meet up and overwhelm him (Livy 25.34.6–8). The Roman proconsul set out by night to engage the Celtiberians in battle but was then attacked from behind by Masinissa's Numidian cavalry, who had followed them. The final blow came when the full Carthaginian army approached from behind. Thus Publius Scipio was completely surrounded and he and most of his army were lost.

Hasdrubal Barca may have been operating somewhere in the region of Castulo against Gn. Scipio at this point. After the demise of Publius Scipio, the surviving Roman army was extremely vulnerable. It included most of the Celtiberian allies who would by now have been aware of their numerical shortcomings and the defeat of the other Roman army. Hasdrubal Barca was able to encourage an internal rebellion in the Roman force and soon the Iberians abandoned Gn. Scipio. Hasdrubal pursued the Roman army as they marched north in retreat. The Numidian cavalry in Hasdrubal's army harassed Gnaeus' retreating soldiers. The victorious generals who had just defeated the other Roman army then reached Hasdrubal Barca (about four weeks had passed, according to Livy) and were able to completely surround the Romans. The last stand of Gnaeus Scipio took place on a bare hillock. He died fighting bravely as he urged his men on: but only a few survived (Livy 25.36.13).

The story as told by Livy jumps about and it is widely accepted that there is a flaw in his chronology of the deaths of the Scipio brothers and the destruction of their armies in Iberia. Livy places these events a full year earlier than seems likely. The revised date for the death of the Scipios must be 211, so we can assume that it occurred around the time that Hannibal marched on Rome.[55] It is tempting to consider whether Hannibal was aware of his brother's victories before he decided to march on the city. As well as trying to alleviate the siege of Capua, by appearing in front of the city gates Hannibal may have hoped to capitalize on the news from Iberia. Our chronology of the events, however, does not allow for any certainty. The Carthaginian victories in Iberia, although they may have revived Hannibal's aspirations for a peace deal, had come too late to aid Capua.

The war in the Iberian peninsula had been an enormous struggle, essentially led by two families of talented military commanders battling for the loyalty of the Iberians and control of the resources. The Scipios and the Barcids had fought each other for eight years, engaging, stealing allies, attacking cities and trying to create the advantage. The number of recorded victories for both sides suggests an overall stalemate, with military successes seeming to provide no apparent strategic advantage. It was a shifting and complex situation but the objective of the elder Scipio brothers had been to destabilize the Carthaginian alliances in Iberia and to occupy Hannibal's brothers, preventing any attempt to unify the armies of Carthage in Italy. In this they had succeeded.

Later in 211 the Romans dispatched Caius Claudius Nero with reinforcements of 12,000 infantry and 1,100 cavalry.[56] It was also decided that a commander with proconsular power was needed and that the 'people should hold an election to create a proconsul for Iberia' (Livy 26.18.1–11). Livy maintains that in Rome no one was very eager to take up the position of commander in Iberia and when the people 'turned towards the magistrates and scrutinized the faces of the leading citizens' they all looked at each other and shrugged (26.18.6). In this hesitancy can we read reluctance among the

Roman elite to take up the role? Perhaps the elite of Rome were disinclined to leave the focus of the fight in Italy, where, after years of hardship, they were just beginning to enjoy the glory and wealth from the sack of major centres like Syracuse and the recapture of Capua. By comparison, the war in Iberia had not yielded any rewards and was fraught with unstable allies and swiftly changing momentum. The indecision and reluctance in the Roman Senate may conceal a broader debate between those who were willing to give Iberia up and focus on Italy to bring about a swift end to the war and those with a more expansive outlook.[57]

At this moment of uncertainty, so the story goes, the younger Publius Cornelius Scipio (son of the consul of the same name) 'suddenly . . . declared his candidacy and stood on higher ground so he could be seen' (Livy 26.18.4–11). Scipio the younger was then unanimously elected by the people and given a proconsular imperium as a private citizen, even though he had not yet held a senior magistracy in the Senate and was legally too young to hold the position.[58] Yet he was 'the son of Publius Cornelius who had fallen in Iberia' and was now, with the death of his father and uncle, the head of a very powerful family (Livy 26.18.4–11).[59] The underlying steps that led to the unprecedented election of Scipio to the position of proconsul remain obscure. The most convincing argument links the fight in Iberia directly to the family of Scipio. For eight years the loyalty of key Iberian allies had been to the elder Scipio brothers personally and it would be essential for the proconsul in Iberia to build upon what remained of this loyalty.[60] Taking the risk of appointing a young and relatively untried commander was a noteworthy shift from the conventional Roman approach.[61] For Scipio personally there was the added element of ambition and desire to avenge the deaths of his father and uncle.[62]

In many ways it was Hannibal who created Scipio, a young man whose formative years were shaped by the struggle of the Second Punic War. Scipio and his generation had no experience other than that of the talented Carthaginian general as a foe. Scipio learned tactics and strategy from the master. In 218 BCE, as a seventeen-year old, Scipio had bravely saved his wounded father's life at the battle of Ticinus and almost two years later he is noted as being among the survivors of Cannae.[63] After Cannae, Scipio commanded a group of young Roman elites who took an oath 'never to betray the republic', neatly matching Hannibal's oath never to befriend the Romans (Livy 22.53.10–13).[64] He was not yet twenty. In 213 BCE he was elected to the office of curule aedile, although below the minimum age for the position. In Rome, with the loss of so many adult men in the battles with Hannibal, extraordinary measures such as the speedy advancement of precocious military talent were permitted.[65]

The legend of Hannibal also helped to create the legend of Scipio. The Roman sources construct the narrative of Scipio's life as the divinely inspired antidote to Hannibal's great victories. He rose to prominence as the prodigal son sent to avenge his father and uncle. At last, in Roman eyes, they had a hero whose reputation outshone (or at least equalled) that of Hannibal. The legend of Scipio has passed down from Polybius, through Livy and into the Middle Ages and the early modern world. By the time of Milton's *Paradise Lost*, Scipio was imagined among the semi-divine: 'He with Olympias, this with her who bore Scipio, the height of Rome.'[66] In the Roman view Scipio would become the greatest military hero of the Republic and was venerated as a legend.

In Rome stories of Scipio's divine parentage circulated: 'perhaps deliberately put about, perhaps spontaneous', they were intended to bring back 'into currency the rumour that earlier circulated about Alexander the Great', that his real father was Zeus, in the form of a snake that had often been spotted in his mother's bedroom (Livy 26.19.5–9).[67] The Romans learned from Hannibal to engage in myth management and Scipio embodied all the virtues of the perfect Roman leader. As an equal to Hannibal, Scipio became 'the most famous man of all time'. The ever-pragmatic Polybius lamented these exaggerations, claiming that 'mankind can hardly avoid being led astray and forming a false opinion on these matters, since the description provided by those who have written about him departs so widely from the truth' (10.2.1–3).[68]

Scipio's family were among the very powerful in Rome. He was extremely well connected and had married the daughter of Aemilius Paullus, the consul who died at Cannae. The young Scipio was, by the reports in the sources, recognized as militarily talented, devout and politically astute. He was also extremely conscious of his public image and it is reported that he never went out into public life without first visiting the temple, meditating, sacrificing and, if one is cynical, making sure he was seen (Livy 26.19.5–9).[69] Polybius' close relationship with Scipio's family provides an insider's view. As Polybius was a client of the family in the second century, his history of the Hannibalic War is often seen as written from their perspective to counter earlier pro-Carthaginian histories that had been written in Greek.[70] Scipio, as described by Polybius, was a talented general and canny politician whose successes lay in his ability to command and inspire confidence in his soldiers. As for the claims of divine support, Polybius the rationalist explains these as providing a practical way of encouraging his followers to believe in him, a necessity of

Hellenistic leadership and one that Hannibal also encouraged.[71] There is no reason to doubt, however, that he was extremely devout and sought favour from the gods.

Livy's narrative of the Second Punic War was written to parallel the lives of Scipio and Hannibal, Rome's greatest general versus Rome's greatest enemy. The story sets out to balance the pure virtue of Scipio against the duplicity and faithlessness of Hannibal.[72] As a result, the focus of our evidence shifts over the course of Livy's narrative from Hannibal on to Scipio, the younger Roman general becoming the main protagonist in the later books of Livy's history of the Hannibalic War. It becomes increasingly difficult to view events from Hannibal's perspective as he was sidelined in the account of the last years of the war.

In 210 BCE Scipio was twenty-five years old, almost the exact age Hannibal had been when he came to lead the Carthaginian army in the Iberian peninsula eleven years earlier (Livy 26.18.7).[73] Scipio represented the new generation of Romans reared on fighting Hannibal, who was now in his thirties and worn down by years in the field. These young Roman commanders were educated and sophisticated in the ways of Hellenistic warfare. Their initiatives changed the paradigm in which the Romans fought and turned Hannibal's tactics back on to him. In 210 BCE Scipio left Rome with a fleet of thirty ships, all of them quinqueremes. His route took him from the mouth of the Tiber, around the coast of the Etruscan Sea, the Alps and 'the gulf of Gaul', then rounding the promontory of the Pyrenees. Scipio first put ashore at the Roman-friendly port of Emporium (Empurias), in origin 'a Greek city whose people also derive from Phocaea' (Livy 26.19.11) (Map 2).[74] An escort had accompanied him there from Massalia and the Roman allies gathered around him. A coalition of the enemies of Carthage found in Scipio a unifying figurehead for their fight.

Taking Hannibal as his teacher, Scipio planned his approach to Iberia audaciously from the start. He spent his first winter north of the Ebro river at Tarraco (modern Tarragona), collecting information, charming the allies, and understanding the lie of the land. From the outset his strategy differed from what the Romans had done in previous years. Scipio aimed to capture New Carthage and cut the Carthaginian armies off from supplies and reinforcements. This was an extremely bold move since New Carthage was a fortified stronghold with a deep port and good access to Africa. A long siege would be difficult to sustain; however, there was an obvious opportunity that Scipio's scouts had reported to him. The three Carthaginian armies in Iberia were dispersed into the hinterland fighting 'at least a ten day march' from the city, so New Carthage lay relatively unprotected (Polyb. 10.7.5).[75] A high level of confidence seems to have led the younger Barcid brothers and their colleague Hasdrubal Gisgo to relax their vigilance after their victory over the elder Scipios. Polybius notes that 'they imagined their position in Iberia had been secured beyond any possible doubt' and did not seem to have considered the possibility that the Romans would return in force (10.36.3). The Carthaginians, although their armies outnumbered the Romans, left a large part of the territory undefended. This was a massive and surprising miscalculation.[76]

Scipio recognized what we would call today the psychological impact of a quick, dramatic win. An attack on New Carthage would shock the enemy, divide their allies and shake their confidence to the core. The Carthaginian capital city held the treasury and the supplies of the army but the garrison in the city was only about a thousand men. Scipio understood that he could undermine the Carthaginians' support in Iberia by occupying the hub of Punic culture and wealth, threatening their hold on the whole territory (Polyb. 10.8.1–9).

The element of surprise, so long a feature of Hannibal's strategy, was put to use by Scipio early in the spring of 209.[77] He kept his carefully laid plans secret from everyone except Gaius Laelius, his trusted lieutenant, right-hand man and fleet commander.[78] This secrecy highlights Scipio's belief that his allies might turn out to be unreliable and be infiltrated by enemy spies, an understandable precaution considering the fate of his father and uncle. Laelius sailed to New Carthage 'while Scipio advanced with his army' (Polyb. 10.9.4–7). The Romans marched quickly, although Polybius' claim that it took only seven days to reach New Carthage from the Ebro would mean they covered the approximately 500 kilometres in a week – a feat that seems unlikely, if not impossible.[79]

Scipio arrived at New Carthage with an army of 25,000 men and pitched camp to the north while Laelius and the fleet sailed into the harbour, blockading the city from the sea.[80] The sudden and simultaneous appearance of a fleet and an army was timed to take the city by surprise. Scipio knew that, apart from the garrison who occupied the citadel, a large part of the population were artisans, merchants and sailors who could not be expected to defeat highly trained, battle-hardened Roman soldiers (Polyb.10.8.4–5). New Carthage must have had a certain sense of security about it for despite years of war no real threat had presented itself since its foundation twenty years earlier.

New Carthage was well fortified and situated on difficult terrain, including the high points of the two hills on which sat the citadel with the temple to Eshmun and the so-called Barcid palace.[81] The Carthaginian garrison commander sent out his forces to face the Romans to the north of the city – a tactic often employed to keep attackers away from the city walls to try to limit the positioning of scaling ladders.[82] These troops were pushed back towards the walls and then skirmished at the city gate with the Romans. The Carthaginians fought bravely but were eventually overwhelmed by the superior numbers of the Roman forces. There was little chance for the thousand men of the garrison and 2,000 citizens hastily recruited for the defence of the city.[83] At low tide, when the lagoon that surrounded the port to the west was passable on foot, Scipio ordered men to cross there and scale the city walls. The Romans found the defences deserted on the lagoon side and they were able to access the west section of the city walls 'without striking a blow' (Polyb. 10.14.1–15).[84]

New Carthage was taken in just one day. Once inside, Scipio 'let loose the majority of his troops against the inhabitants, according to Roman custom; their orders were to exterminate every form of life they encountered, sparing none, but not to start pillaging until the word was given' (Polyb. 10.15.4–5). The large population inside the city meant that the 'carnage was especially frightful'. The Carthaginian commander had remained in his citadel stronghold with a clear view of the slaughter. He surrendered the citadel and accepted that the city was lost. Once the looting and pillaging started it continued through the night, with Livy reporting that the Roman forces captured ten thousand male citizens and a huge volume of booty (26.47.1–2). New Carthage, the capital city of Punic Iberia, had fallen to the Romans.[85]

# CHAPTER 10

# OVER THE ALPS, AGAIN

To Carthage no more shall I send proud messages:
ended is all hope of mine, and ended
the fortunes of all my family,
since [my brother] Hasdrubal's destruction.
**(Horace, *Odes* 4.4)**

H OW HANNIBAL REACTED TO the news of the loss of New Carthage is
not recorded but his frustration with his brothers, who had left the
city undefended, must have been keenly felt. There had been no strategy
to preserve the city and secure it from attack. Their supplies, baggage and,
even more importantly, hostages who had been held at New Carthage were
now in Roman hands. These captives were made up of family members of
the Iberian leaders who served with the Carthaginian troops and were kept
as security in exchange for Iberian loyalty. The 'baggage' included the
wives, children and belongings of the soldiers fighting with the Carthaginians.
It is entirely possible that Hasdrubal and Mago (and even Hannibal)
had wives and families in New Carthage (although no mention is made in
the sources).

By taking New Carthage, Scipio acquired the treasury of the Carthaginians
amounting to 600 talents, as well as the relatives of key Iberian allies and the
families of the Carthaginian military. There were members of the government
from Carthage in the city as well, 'two of them being . . . of the council of
elders and fifteen members of the senate' (Polyb. 10.18.1–4). Scipio was now

in control of the war in Iberia and the Carthaginian commanders were placed firmly on the defensive. Hannibal's treatment of Roman allies after both Trasimeno and Cannae may well have influenced Scipio in the crucial period after the city had fallen. He restored the Iberian hostages to their families and thus immediately undermined the Carthaginian position with their allies. Winning the allegiance of the Iberians as well as triumphing on the battlefield were the keys to Roman success in Iberia. Scipio had again applied the lessons provided by his Carthaginian teacher (Livy 26. 49–50; Polyb. 10.16.1–20.7).

The loss of New Carthage unfolded just as the Romans were applying more pressure to Tarentum in Italy. Pro-Hannibalic forces in the city continued to hold out in the spring of 209 BCE but throughout that period the garrison of Roman soldiers (and pro-Roman Tarentines) had maintained their precarious position at the citadel. There had been moments when the Carthaginian/ Tarentine alliance looked capable of ousting the Roman soldiers. In 210 BCE, with supply lines cut and the garrison starving a fleet sent to provision them was sunk by Tarentine ships in a fierce engagement off the city (Livy 26.39.1– 19). Despite the continued pressure from the Carthaginian and Tarentine forces the besieged managed to cling on to the citadel. Once Syracuse and then Capua fell to Rome, Hannibal's forces were increasingly outnumbered by troops released from those theatres. Thus the net around Tarentum gradually tightened. By the time Fabius Maximus, again the consul for 209 BCE and in his last campaign of the war, took Manduria just to the east of Tarentum, he had succeeded in encircling the city (Livy 27.15.4).[1]

The superior Roman manpower eventually decided the fate of Tarentum. Two Roman armies were sent to distract Hannibal so that he was forced to relieve the siege of Caulonia, an allied city in Bruttium about 300 kilometres from Tarentum. Fabius Maximus then boldly 'established his camp right at the harbour entrance' of Tarentum (Livy 27.15.4–5). The ease of this manoeuvre illustrates just how ineffective the Carthaginian garrison was at this point. The Romans were now unopposed from outside the city. Carthaginian ships that had been stationed in the harbour had moved over to Corcyra (Corfu) in aid of Philip V whose Macedonians were attempting an attack on the Aetolian League. Without fear of reprisals from the sea, the way was clear for Fabius Maximus to take the city.

Tarentum eventually fell from within and the saga involved a romantic tale of star-crossed lovers. The Carthaginian garrison that held Tarentum at the time was partially manned by Bruttian soldiers. Their commander was 'deeply in love' with a Tarentine woman whose brother served with Fabius' Roman army. With the consent of Fabius Maximus the brother posed as a deserter and went into Tarentum where his sister introduced him to her lover, the garrison commander. The love-struck Bruttian was eventually persuaded by the siblings to betray the city to the Romans and a plot was hatched. Fabius Maximus' troops scaled the part of the city wall where the Bruttian and his unit were on watch. These men gave the Roman army access to the city. Fierce fighting broke out but the undermanned Tarentines could not match the Roman forces. Romance aside, this story of the betrayal of Tarentum reflects the reality of life for the population in southern Italy who were caught between the two opposing powers (Livy 27.15.9ff.).[2]

In the battle for the city both the Tarentine and Carthaginian commanders were killed, including Carthalo who was one of Hannibal's lieutenants. Livy describes how Carthalo had laid down his arms and been on his way to 'the consul [Fabius Maximus] to remind him of the ties of hospitality between their fathers' when soldiers struck him down (27.16.5). In this interesting aside Livy notes a close link between the Carthaginian commander and a Roman senatorial family. These connections between elite Carthaginian families and the Roman senatorial class have been largely buried under the tales of war but may have been more prevalent than we are led to believe.[3] Widespread slaughter followed the fall of Tarentum and the Romans sacked another famous city of the Greek south of Italy. The estimate of the loot taken includes thirty thousand slaves, massive amounts of silver and 3,080 pounds of gold, along with statues and paintings 'almost to rival the artwork of Syracuse' (Livy 27.16.7–8).[4]

When the news reached Hannibal that Tarentum was under attack he raced from Caulonia on a forced march. Livy recounts how he almost made it to the city and was only a few kilometres away when a messenger brought the report of Tarentum's fall (27.16.9–10). Now, with his options limited, Hannibal had to halt the march and turn back, retreating westward towards Metapontum. By the end of 209 BCE Hannibal's mystique had been greatly diminished. He had lost both Capua and Tarentum, his two most important allies in Italy, and his allied cities in Apulia and many in Lucania had been captured. The rebellion in Sicily lingered on but was all but over with the fall and brutal suppression of Agrigentum in 210 BCE.

The sack of Syracuse, the fall of rebel Capua and the destruction of the wealthy port city of Tarentum sealed an eventual Roman victory in Italy. The epic stories of these years involved a cast of great characters and their achievements. Feats of magnificent engineering skill, betrayals, assassination, espionage and plague all played a part. As the famous cities of Italy along with their wealth fell one by one, their stories became woven into the Roman legends of the war with Hannibal. The accumulation of wealth in Roman hands allowed them to further strengthen the manpower resources that eventually wore Hannibal down and isolated him. Hannibal brought a war to Italy that forced the Romans to realize their potential for power and conquest. The struggling Roman economy was rebooted by a reorganization of the coinage (*c.* 211 BCE). The new silver coinage, based on the denarius, was struck on a revived accumulation of precious metal and is symbolic of the renewal of the fortunes of the Roman state.[5]

Hannibal's choices in Italy after 209 BCE were now further diminished, yet he fought on. He was still undefeated in battle and continued to best his opponents when given the chance to draw them into combat. A number of victories are recorded but he found himself largely confined to the lands of the Bruttii and Greeks of western Magna Graecia for allies and support.[6] In Bruttium, which roughly corresponds to modern Calabria, there were a number of cities including Cosentia (Cosenza) from which Hannibal could operate. On the coast he still maintained the support of the port towns of Locri and Crotona. Despite his greatly reduced circumstances, Hannibal did not retreat to Carthage but continued to fight the war in Italy for another six years.

Did Hannibal have any realistic expectations, at this point, about his ability to threaten Rome's hegemony in Italy or was his continued presence in Italy part of a larger Carthaginian strategy? By remaining in Italy Hannibal ensured that at least some of the Roman forces were occupied there as long as there were regions still allied to him. He must have felt a deep sense of responsibility for his followers, allies and those cities that had chosen to remain with him. Hannibal had certainly not given up hope and there was still fight left in him. Perhaps his scope was narrower than it had been ten years earlier but he could still put pressure on the Romans. In this way he could make sure that not all of the Roman military might was brought down on his brothers in Iberia, or ultimately on the city of Carthage in North Africa.

In the Iberian peninsula, Hannibal's brothers were struggling. Livy's report, that they did not show undue concern about the loss of New Carthage, does not ring true. Their first instinct may have been to suppress the rumours of the fall of their capital city. Perhaps they believed they could win it back quickly and not disrupt their allies. Livy claims they 'made light of it but in their hearts knew full well what a weakening of their strength, in every respect, the loss of New Carthage represented for them' (26.51.1). Hasdrubal Barca had doggedly defended Carthaginian territory from the Romans for almost a decade and the fall of his capital must have come as a personal catastrophe for him and the army in Iberia. With news of the loss of New Carthage coming so closely on that of Syracuse and Capua and followed by the loss of Tarentum in the same summer, the Barcid family must have felt their fortune (*tyche*) and even divine patronage slipping away. The momentum lay squarely with the Romans and to change that Hannibal needed bold measures and quick success more than ever.

Our sources tell us nothing of Hasdrubal Barca's plans or Hannibal's thinking directly after the fall of New Carthage. In Iberia the Carthaginian allies were deserting to the Romans. Iberian claims of gross mistreatment at the hands of the Carthaginians allowed Scipio to take full advantage of this erosion of support. There was discord between the Carthaginian generals, with Hasdrubal Barca, his brother Mago and Hasdrubal Gisgo at odds over how to proceed. We can imagine that the three men blamed each other for squandering their advantages by allowing the reinvigorated Roman fighting force to shift the paradigm (Polyb. 10.37.2).

Early in the following year and at the start of the campaigning season (208 BCE) Hasdrubal Barca chose to engage Scipio in battle near the town of Baecula. Spanish archaeologists working near the town of Turruñuelos claim to have recently identified the site of this battle. The location, just south of the river Baetis, is in a region known as the High Guadalquivir, lying to the east of the Carthaginian strongholds of Castulo and Illurgia (Map 2).[7] The discovery of distinctive Numidian javelin tips, lead projectiles and Carthaginian coins of the correct type and date at the battlefield has led excavators to identify the site as Baecula.[8] Here Hasdrubal was in command of an excellent position when Scipio approached from the south, eager to engage the Carthaginians and 'try their strength' in open battle. Hasdrubal remained in position while Scipio assessed his choices. The sources emphasize that Hasdrubal's superior position made any engagement difficult for Scipio, who had to be careful not to get trapped by the arrival of the other Carthaginian armies (Polyb. 10.38.7–10). Confident in his and his army's abilities, Scipio drew up in formation and attacked Hasdrubal's superior numbers by putting his light troops first into battle, then using his heavy infantry to challenge the flanks.[9] Hasdrubal's troops were caught out of position and forced back. His advantageous situation was not enough and Hasdrubal pulled up when he saw his forces thrown into chaos by the Romans. He turned and retreated north across the river (Polyb. 10.39.1–9).[10]

Hasdrubal was able to get away with about two-thirds of his soldiers, as well as his treasury and elephants.[11] His goal was to cross the Pyrenees, pass over into Gaul and eventually on to Italy to meet up with Hannibal.[12] This was no spontaneous dash for the mountains: the Carthaginians must have planned the march beforehand. Polybius and Livy say nothing of a Carthaginian strategy but it only makes sense if it was a prearranged departure. This is emphasized by the fact that a new army was sent from Carthage to replace Hasdrubal under the general Hanno. Hasdrubal Barca did not risk his entire army in the battle but seems to have held back and retreated as soon as the tide was about to turn. His route took him across the river Baetis and north from there perhaps to the Atlantic coast and around the Pyrenees. Scipio let Hasdrubal and his army go, wary of a trap and the possibility of the other Carthaginian armies catching up with him from behind (Polyb. 10. 39.8–9). This cautious approach left Scipio open to criticism at Rome from Fabius Maximus ('the delayer', of all people). It was not a policy Scipio would repeat in later battles (Livy 28.42.14–15).

By the time Hasdrubal departed from the Iberian peninsula the situation in Italy from Hannibal's perspective was bleak. His ability to manoeuvre had been greatly reduced and only the region of Bruttium and the cities of southern Magna Graecia remained under Carthaginian control. The area in which he could operate had been severely eroded yet he still managed to elude Roman power and inflict the occasional defeat on the many different armies he faced. The advent of Hasdrubal supplied Hannibal with a glimmer of possibility. He must have hoped that the joined-up Carthaginian armies could inflict another setback on the Romans big enough to shift the momentum in Italy. This must have been the brothers' aspiration.[13]

Not everything in Italy had gone according to Roman interests and there was underlying turmoil and support for Hannibal's cause that may have sustained his ambitions. In 209 BCE, the stalwarts of the Roman coalition, the Latin allies, were extremely unhappy after years of pressure on their resources. Evidence for the strain on the relationship comes from reports that twelve out of the thirty Latin allies told the Roman consuls that they would no longer supply the men necessary to fill their quotas for recruitment. The Latin cities complained about their soldiers' length of service and the cost: 'a compatriot conscripted by the Romans was more lost to them than one captured by the Carthaginian' they claimed (Livy 27.9.1–6). There had also been trouble among the Etruscans and in Etruria the propraetor Varro (the surviving consul of Cannae) was sent to deal with uprisings and disturbances near Arretium (modern Arezzo).[14] Despite these internal problems the general feeling at Rome in the summer of 208 BCE was confidence that a final strike at Hannibal might end the war quickly.[15] The glory, reputation and honours won by Fabius

Maximus at Tarentum and Marcellus at Syracuse spurred on other commanders who were hoping to build up their own reputations.

Marcellus had once more been elected consul, for 208 BCE, and his colleague was Titus Quinctius Crispinus. Crispinus took his army and made for Bruttium, where he attacked the town of Locri. When Hannibal approached Locri with his army, Crispinus was forced to raise his siege (Livy 27.25.10–12). Marcellus had his legions at Venusia in Apulia and Crispinus moved north to confer. Hannibal now spent his time marching back and forth from the scene of one military crisis to another. The two Roman consuls planned to join forces to deliver a crushing defeat. Despite his forces being substantially outnumbered, often on the defensive and their movements restricted to an ever-shrinking territory, Hannibal was still dangerous. A multitude of Roman armies seemed to block every route and were constantly harassing his remaining allies. The consuls set up their camps close to each other in an area between Venusia and Bantia, on the border between Apulia and Lucania. Hannibal remained the consummate risk-taker and was still confident of his abilities to match any army in the field. He moved up from the south into the same area as the consuls, looking to engage them. The Roman commanders were also eager, lining up their soldiers 'almost daily' in their enthusiasm to do battle with Hannibal (27.25.13–14).

The target of the engagement was a hill between the main Roman and Carthaginian camps, where Hannibal had stationed some Numidian cavalry in ambush. The Roman consuls, with a small number of cavalry (two squadrons) and skirmishers (about thirty *velites*), moved to survey the hill on horseback. As they climbed the hill the Numidians shifted to block their return to camp. Fierce fighting broke out until Crispinus, struck by two javelins, turned his horse and fled, whilst Marcellus was run through the side with a broad spear (Plut. *Marc.* 29.8).[16] Roman confidence had been extremely high but the fact that the two experienced consuls failed to learn from all the previous encounters with Hannibal and blindly stumbled into a trap is both surprising and revealing. Polybius scathingly comments that Marcellus brought 'this misfortune on himself by behaving not so much like a general as like a simpleton' (10.32.7).

In the Roman camp they watched in horror as the skirmish ended before they could send out cover. To Hannibal it must have seemed almost too easy. The venerable Roman general Marcus Marcellus, many times consul and defender of Nola, taker of Syracuse and illustrious opponent of Hannibal, met his death on that hill in 208 BCE. He had an immense reputation among both the Romans and the Carthaginians, and was immortalized by Virgil:

They were struck with awe as father Anchises paused,
Then carried on: 'Look there, Marcellus marching toward us,
Decked in splendid plunder he tore from a chief he killed,
victorious, towering over all'.
(*Aeneid* 6.852–856[17])

At well over sixty at the time of his death, Marcellus came to his end rather
ignobly, plunging into a trap having failed to take proper precautions, and
putting his army at risk (Livy 27.26–28; Polybius 10.32.1–12). He was brave,
however, and had always been willing to fight Hannibal head on when others
dared not. Hannibal is said to have confessed that he 'feared Fabius as a
schoolmaster and Marcellus as an adversary' (Plutarch, *Marc.* 9.4). He held
his old rival in great esteem. Plutarch reports that when Hannibal 'was told of
Marcellus' death, [he] immediately rushed to the hill'. On that spot Hannibal
looked down upon the face of his long-time foe, 'his fierce and troublesome
enemy, and gave the order to have the body properly clad and adorned and
honourably burned' (Plutarch, *Marc.* 30.1).[18]

Before he cremated the consul, Hannibal had taken his consular ring, no
doubt thinking it might come in useful. His first move after Marcellus' death
was to try to take advantage of this victory and recapture the nearby city
of Salapia. His approach was a ruse: he tried to use the ring of the dead
consul to convince the guards of the city to open the gates. The townsfolk
wanted nothing to do with Hannibal and some of his men were trapped
and killed when the trick was discovered. If nothing else, the story illustrates
just how far Hannibal's status in Italy had fallen by the summer of 208 BCE.
Once he had been shown unable to protect his allies he was isolated and
unwelcome in the cities across the south.[19] Thus even though this was the first
time in Roman history that both consuls had been killed in battle (or as
a result of battle) there was little respite for Hannibal and his army. The
Romans did not miss a step and Crispinus, although he died a few days later,
lived long enough to appoint T. Manlius Torquatus dictator for the rest of that
year (Livy 27.33.7).

After his failure at Salapia Hannibal immediately left for the south to
relieve another siege of Locri, which had begun when Roman troops arrived
from Sicily. He had just killed one consul and fatally wounded the other but
the Romans still returned in full strength. Tracking Hannibal's whereabouts
every season reveals he was almost constantly on the move, against one or
another of the Roman armies that appeared as soon as yet another was
defeated. The analogy of the many-headed Roman Hydra had never been

more apt as they came back at him with more men no matter what success he had (Livy 27.28.1–17).

Through the winter of 208/207 BCE Hannibal was in Bruttium while his brother's passage through Gaul was creating quite a stir. Reports arrived at Rome claiming that Hasdrubal carried with him large quantities of gold to raise a new army. Word must have reached Hannibal that his brother had left Iberia and was spending the winter, after crossing the Pyrenees, in Gaul. In the early spring of 207 BCE Hasdrubal crossed the Alps with his army 'more quickly and easily' than his brother had just over a decade earlier (Livy 27.39.7; Polyb. 11.1.1).[20] It is possible that Hasdrubal crossed the mountains via the most southern of the Alpine passes, the main route that follows the Durance valley.[21] He moved quickly through to the Po valley and gathered recruits along the way, laying siege to the Roman colony of Piacenza en route. Both Hannibal and the Romans were caught out by the speed at which Hasdrubal crossed the mountains and had not 'anticipated that his journey would be anything like as easy and swift as it turned out to be' (Livy 27.39.13–14). Hannibal therefore left his winter quarters later than was ideal to rendezvous with his brother.

The city of Rome was thrown into a panic at the news that another Barcid brother had crossed the Alps and that his army was now in Italy. The potential for terror was great, 'now there were two Punic wars in the country, two mighty armies and practically two Hannibals' (Livy 27.44.5) but the situation a decade on was remarkably different. The reality of the threat posed by the Carthaginians had been severely diminished by 207 BCE and it is a testament to Hannibal's reputation that such dread was aroused by Hasdrubal's arrival (27.39.1). Livy claims that the citizens of Rome went into a frenzy of religious placation of the gods as prodigies and omens were recorded that heightened the alarm. With wolves mauling guards at Capua and a stream of blood flowing through a gateway in Minturnae, nine days of religious ceremonies and public prayer and sacrifice were employed to calm the 'public conscience' (27.37.1–4). Particularly vivid details of the birth of a child at Frusino who was the size of a four-year old and had no visible gender caused Etruscan soothsayers to be brought in. They ordered that the child be taken from Roman territory, placed alive in a box and thrown into the sea. The great defeats of the previous decade had left a superstitious Roman public haunted and the gods had to be ritually placated.

The consuls elect for 207 BCE, Gaius Claudius Nero and Marcus Livius (Salinator), divided Italy in two. Nero moved south against Hannibal and Salinator faced north and the newly arrived army of Hasdrubal. These were two experienced Roman commanders determined to keep the two brothers and their armies apart. The Romans faced the new Carthaginian threat with the huge numbers at their disposal in Italy. There were a total of twenty-three legions in action that year and fifteen of those were in Italy. This amounted to four times as many soldiers as Hannibal had faced in Italy when he arrived in 218 BCE.[22] In addition to the consular armies, there were armies in Etruria and in the region of modern Rimini (Ariminum, called the *Ager Gallicus*) ready to block any route that Hasdrubal might take over the Apennines (Livy 27.36.10–13, 40.1).[23]

Hannibal approached Grumentum to meet the consul Claudius Nero as he moved south. He had to be more cautious than ever as the Romans were now more confident in their approach and a more experienced set of military commanders was (usually) less likely to be surprised or outmanoeuvred.[24] Hannibal had to contend with the army of the new consul, two legions in Bruttium under Q. Fulvius Flaccus and two more near Tarentum and one in Capua.[25] In this period Hannibal's resources were at an all-time low and the greater number of Roman troops meant he could not rest in one place. He could not afford to be caught between two armies. Intense skirmishes took place at Grumentum and Venusia. Livy reports that Hannibal's army was deeply demoralized by the large number of casualties suffered by the Carthaginians troops (27.42.10–13).[26]

Hannibal turned south to Metapontum and then advanced his troops north to Canusium (Canosa). There he awaited word from his brother. The consul Claudius Nero set up his camp nearby, tracking Hannibal's movements. Hannibal's wayward route through Apulia and Lucania is puzzling, and reconstructing his movements and motivations difficult.[27] He may well have been so harried by Roman armies that he took evasive action or he may have needed to collect more troops because of the losses he had suffered in the skirmishes at Grumentum and Venusia (Livy 27.42.1–17).[28]

Meanwhile when Hasdrubal was in the Po valley laying siege to the town of Placentia he sent 'four Gallic horsemen and two Numidians' with a letter to his brother. The messengers crossed most of the length of Italy through enemy territory and reached Metapontum but found that Hannibal had already moved on. The messengers set out to follow him but were caught and handed over to the Roman praetor Quintus Claudius somewhere near Tarentum (Livy 27.43.1–4). The praetor pressured and questioned the messengers who, under the threat of torture, revealed their mission. Quintus Claudius sent the letter containing the details of the Carthaginian brothers' plan with the messengers directly to the consul's headquarters. The Romans now knew that Hannibal was meant to move north and meet Hasdrubal in Umbria.[29] Hasdrubal did not know that their plan had been uncovered and it is not clear that Hannibal was aware of the specifics at all. The Barcid brothers were seemingly in disarray. This illustrates the degree to which Hannibal's once superior intelligence network seems to have fallen apart and was no longer functioning.

It was now early midsummer and Hannibal waited in vain at Canusium for word from his brother.[30] Hasdrubal marched first east and then south along the Via Aemilia crossing the Po valley to the Adriatic coast (Livy 27.46.4). Reports placed the Carthaginian camp near the town of Sena (modern Senigallia) on the sea.[31] The consul Marcus Livius Salinator tracked Hasdrubal and camped nearby. The two sides prepared for battle. Meanwhile, Claudius Nero left his camp in Apulia in the utmost secrecy. Employing a subterfuge that Hannibal had used in the past he left some of his forces in place and stole away with the balance in the night. In a forced march he and seven thousand troops (including one thousand cavalry) surprised even his consular colleague with his swift appearance at his camp near Hasdrubal (Livy 27.43.8).[32] The younger Barcid general, waiting for his brother, may have been puzzled at the lack of contact. As the two sides drew up their lines Hasdrubal noticed some unfamiliar shields in the Roman forces opposite him. After extensive reconnaissance his scouts reported they had heard two trumpet calls at the Roman camp, indicating that both consuls were present. Hasdrubal came to the realization that he now faced both the consuls and their armies. It dawned on him that Claudius Nero had somehow linked up with his colleague, and that his brother Hannibal was nowhere in sight (Livy 27.47.1–5; Polyb. 11.1.2).[33]

Hasdrubal was in a quandary, 'tormented by how one of the consuls had slipped away from Hannibal' (Livy 27.47.5). He may have assumed that Hannibal had been defeated in a battle and that he had arrived too late. Outnumbered, he now faced the armies of two experienced generals in unfamiliar territory. Hasdrubal made a quick decision to leave his camp by night and head for the Via Flaminia, where he planned to cross the Apennines into Umbria. The route took Hasdrubal north from Sena in order to cross the Metaurus; he was probably heading for the most accessible route for moving his army, including elephants, across the Apennines. Hasdrubal's army may have numbered about 30,000 to 35,000 men, made up of Carthaginians, Numidians, Spanish and Celtic troops, cavalry, recruited foot soldiers and elephants.[34] As they tried to retreat by night, they were abandoned by their guides and wandered along the twisting banks of the river Metaurus.[35] These

nocturnal wanderings gave the Romans enough time to catch up. At the banks
of the Metaurus, as Hasdrubal was searching for a place to ford the river, he
was forced into battle.[36]

At the Metaurus Hasdrubal faced the Roman consuls whose numbers
could have been in the region of forty thousand. The Romans imposed a battle
as soon as they caught up with the Carthaginian army, not wanting to give
Hasdrubal a chance to compose himself. Hannibal's brother had no choice but
to fight even though he had been marching through the night and his soldiers
were unprepared for battle. As Polybius puts it, 'none of these things was
favourable to Hasdrubal, but as circumstances did not admit delay . . . he was
obliged to draw up his Iberians and Gauls' (11.1.2). Hasdrubal placed his ten
elephants in front of his line. He waited just behind them with his army
arrayed narrowly after him. His troops fell on the enemy, 'determined either to
conquer or die in this battle' (Polyb. 11.1.3). The two sides fought with equal
ferocity but eventually the younger Marcellus (son of the slain consul) was able
to circle around the Roman camp and attack the flanks of the Carthaginians.
At the Metaurus the outflanking manoeuvre, so often used successfully by
Hannibal, was turned against his brother by the younger generation of Roman
commanders. The elephants, trapped in between the two armies, flailed around
and as such they were 'of equal service to both sides'. Six of the elephants were
killed with their drivers and the other two captured. The young Marcellus cut
down the Iberian troops on the flanks and the fierce battle favoured the
Romans. Casualties were high, although the numbers are difficult to ascertain
with any certainty. Many of Hasdrubal's soldiers were killed on the field and
many captured (Livy 27.49.5–9; Polyb. 11.3.2–3). The Romans too suffered
high casualties but it was a devastating loss for the Carthaginians. So much so
that Livy would claim that they 'had been repaid for Cannae' (27.49.5).[37]

Polybius calls Hasdrubal a 'brave man', especially 'at this his last hour when
he fell in the thick of the fight', and the Augustan poet Ovid adds that he died
'by his own sword' (Polyb. 11.2.1; Ovid, *Fasti* 6.770).[38] Only his elder brother
rivalled him in excellence as a general but Hasdrubal never attained the
legendary status of Hannibal. The poet Horace, who wrote a poem that glorified the family of Claudius Nero, celebrated this defeat of Hasdrubal as one of
the great moments of Roman history (*Ode* 4.4). It was revenge for earlier
defeats and another turning point for Hannibal in Italy. In Rome news of the
victory was met with joyful celebrations in the streets and the temples filled
with offerings. The Senate 'decreed three days of public thanksgiving' as the
Romans began to believe that the gods were back on their side and again
'dared to carry on business as in peacetime' (Livy 27.51.8).

The Roman consul Claudius Nero had detached Hasdrubal Barca's head and kept it as a token and proof of his victory. It is not clear whether Hannibal even realized that Claudius Nero had left the vicinity (although it is hard to believe that this was so). When the consul returned to his camp near Canusium he ordered that the head of Hasdrubal be catapulted before the advance guards of the Carthaginian positions. In this way it was taken to Hannibal in his camp.[39] Claudius Nero released two of his African prisoners so that they could go to Hannibal and provide a first-hand account of what had happened. It was a dramatic gesture perhaps designed to force Hannibal to surrender. When he learned of his brother's death and the destruction of the army that had been coming to his aid Hannibal was shaken to the core. Livy claims prophetically that 'he now clearly saw the destiny of Carthage' (27.51.12).

A series of paintings by the eighteenth-century Venetian artist Tiepolo captures the image of the aftermath of the Metaurus. An ornately plumed Hannibal lurches back in horror at the site of the rotting head of the younger brother he had not seen since he left Iberia eleven years earlier (see Plate 7). This was the final blow to Hannibal's aspirations in Italy and was the last season of major campaigning between the two sides there.[40] After the Metaurus Hannibal struck camp and retired to Bruttium. He now carried out mainly defensive operations, fending off Roman armies rather than attacking any new positions. Livy notes that throughout the next year (206 BCE) 'there was no encounter with Hannibal. After the recent misfortune that had fallen both on his country and on him personally he did not initiate any hostilities and while he remained inactive the Romans did not provoke him' (Livy 28.12.1).

The battle for Italy was well and truly over with the death of Hasdrubal but the Carthaginians kept fighting and Hannibal himself had yet to be defeated. In Iberia the war dragged on and 'it was not only in Italy that the god of war smiled upon the Romans' (Silius Italicus 16.23). The Carthaginian command continued under Mago Barca. The youngest of the three brothers carried on fighting in Iberia along with Hasdrubal Gisgo, whom Livy notes was 'the greatest and most famous Carthaginian leader after the Barcids' (28.12.13). The Carthaginian generals lost more territory but an intense struggle between the Celtiberians, Romans, Numidians and Carthaginians continued. For Scipio it was a period of consolidation and victory. Politics as much as military prowess won the day as Scipio's assiduous courting of the Celtiberian chieftains and the Numidians over this period broke up the alliances that had been so essential to Carthaginian (especially Barcid) successes.

The decisive battle for the Iberian peninsula took place near Ilipa in the early spring of 206 BCE (Silpia in Livy 28.12–15; Polyb. 11.20–24), (see Map 2).[41] This town is situated just north of modern Seville on the banks of the strategic Baetis river. We have seen that control over the region, which was rich in resources, was sought by both Carthage and Rome. Hasdrubal Gisgo and Mago had held troop levies across the Baetis river valley and well into Lusitania (modern Portugal) and raised a large army.[42] The numbers of troops they managed to pull together may have been as many as 70,000 (Polyb. 11.20.2), although a lower number of 50,000 is also mentioned (Livy 28.12.13). The cavalry contingent was thought to be in the region of 4,000 strong.

The Roman sources describe Scipio as greatly outnumbered, his total force being 45,000. The Carthaginians had massed in this strategic location with the hope of tackling the Roman army once and for all. The news of Hasdrubal's death on the Metaurus must have reached them and perhaps they were willing to risk Iberia in a win or lose scenario. Scipio's role as the foil to Hannibal is nowhere clearer than in the narrative around the subsequent battle of Ilipa. Scipio carefully prepared his troops for the battle. His plan was to surprise the Carthaginians in their camp by catching them off guard. He made sure his own soldiers had breakfasted and were organized to attack and fight (Polyb. 22.11.4–8). This is the reverse of events of the battle of Trebia in 218 BCE, when Hannibal had drawn the Romans unprepared into a battle at which Scipio was present. By startling the Carthaginians with an early morning attack on their camp he was able to unsettle them. As Hasdrubal Gisgo hastily drew his army into a battle line Scipio outsmarted the much larger Carthaginian force with a series of very complicated manoeuvres.[43] These involved turning whole sections of his army at angles through various steps in order to outflank the Carthaginian army.[44] The battle was won by Scipio's tactical brilliance and ended in the destruction of the newly raised army of Hasdrubal Gisgo.[45] Hannibal's brother Mago was also supposedly present at the battle of Ilipa but we do not have a clear picture of his movements.

The survivors of the Carthaginian army retreated in disordered flight after Ilipa, harassed by the Roman cavalry. Livy claims that Hasdrubal Gisgo eventually 'abandoned his army and fled to Gades by night' (28.16.8).[46] He sent boats back for Mago who had continued to hold out with his army and with this help the Carthaginian forces dispersed to safety. Shortly thereafter Hasdrubal returned to Africa, crossing over from Iberia and stopping at Siga, the western capital of the Numidian king Syphax, trying to drum up continued support for the Carthaginian cause.[47]

In Iberia Scipio founded a new Roman city, a colony for his veterans on the Baetis river, called Italica.[48] The years of fighting, however, did not come to a close with Ilipa and the rest of the Iberian peninsula was 'mopped up' by the Romans but not without fierce local resistance (Polyb. 11.24.10–11; Livy 28.19.1–23.5).[49] Livy puts it succinctly when he notes that 'the time for reprisals seemed to have arrived' (28.19.7–8) and the Roman troops meted out revenge on those who had opposed or betrayed them over the previous years of war. The so-called 'treacherous towns' of Castulo and Ilurgia were attacked (Appian, *Ib.* 32).[50] At Illurgia, 'nobody considered taking captives alive . . . it was a massacre, of armed and unarmed alike, and of women as well as men, the invaders' ruthless fury descending even to the massacre of infants' (Livy 28.20.6–7). At Castulo, so closely linked to Hannibal through his wife, the city surrendered the Carthaginian auxiliaries in the town and thus managed to diminish the impact of the Roman retribution. The people of Astapa (near modern Osuna), long allies of the Carthaginians, no doubt having heard of the fate of Illurgia, chose mass suicide over capture by the Roman commander.[51] Further into the clean-up operations Scipio fell seriously ill and this became the catalyst for a mutiny, revealing just how important the personality of the individual commander was to the army in Iberia and how unstable the situation remained (Polyb. 11.25–33). Eventually 'all the Carthaginians were driven from the land of gold and departed from Spanish territory' (Silius Italicus 16.24–25).[52]

The legacy of Barcid rule in the Iberian peninsula lived on after the departure of the Carthaginian armies. Through the previous decades settlements had been established that were populated with Barcid veterans and there had been immigration from Carthaginian cities in Africa (Appian, *Ib.* 56).[53] This perhaps contributed to the continuing dissent, rebellion and upheaval in the Iberian peninsula up until the first century CE. The threat no longer came from Carthage itself and the Romans made sure they controlled the strategic centres for communication and mineral wealth. Gades was the last stronghold of the Carthaginians on the peninsula. It was the place where Hamilcar Barca had landed some thirty-three years previously: the Carthaginian adventure in Iberia had come full circle. Mago Barca had remained holed up at Gades with the remnants of the Carthaginian army while Hasdrubal Gisgo returned to Africa. Orders from Carthage directed Mago to abandon Iberia and return to Italy with his forces. As he sailed from Gades en route to Italy, Mago made a desperate attempt to attack New Carthage, perhaps holding some hope of reclaiming the old capital. When his attack on the city was repulsed, Mago and his fleet were forced back westwards and attempted to take refuge again in Gades. At this point, the long-time ally and the last pro-Carthaginian city in the Iberian peninsula refused him entry (Livy 28.37.10). Mago, with nowhere to turn, retreated to the island of Minorca before eventually sailing on to Genua (Genoa) in Liguria and capturing the city in c. 205 BCE.

Was it Mago's hope and perhaps Carthage's dream that he would be able to link up with Hannibal and again try to distract the Romans from the inevitable invasion of Africa?[54] Mago may also have been sent to Liguria to recruit much-needed soldiers for Carthage. Carthage faced a shortfall in allies able to supply troops, as the Iberians were now largely serving Rome. There were again two Barcid brothers in Italy, with Mago in the far north and Hannibal deep in the south. It is a matter of some debate to what extent this strategy was being directed from Carthage. Hannibal may again have hoped for greater success in Italy, with Mago's attack in Liguria part of an overall strategy to bring about a more generous peace, but it doesn't seem credible.[55] The political situation at Carthage and the politics of the Carthaginian state played out behind the scenes as the Barcid power base in Iberia fell to Rome and Hannibal's military successes faded from view. Hannibal's opponents in Carthage were in the ascendant and Carthage was now extremely vulnerable to a Roman attack. These two factors must have held the fate of Hannibal in the balance.

Hannibal may have continued to believe that reinforcements would arrive in the south of Italy, either from Carthage (as Livy suggests) or perhaps he believed they would come from the Macedonian king Philip V. This would make him less of a pragmatist than seems likely. It is more realistic to assume that maintaining a presence in Italy was now a policy designed to keep the Romans from invading Africa. Hannibal was determined to keep a foothold on the southern coast of Italy. Although his power was diminished, he was not yet defeated.[56] When the consuls of 206 'marched their troops into the territory of Cosentia [modern Cosenza] and plundered far and wide' they were ambushed in a narrow pass. Livy describes more 'of a brawl than a battle' but the Roman consuls retreated out of Bruttium and focused on consolidating the territory of Lucania.[57] 'Such were Hannibal's powers', the Romans still thought better of provoking him and no fewer than four legions were assigned to watch his movements in Bruttium (Livy 28.11.11–12.1).[58]

One of the most revealing aspects of Hannibal's remarkable leadership and personality was the loyalty of his army through this period in Italy. Despite being 'often short of money for pay and short of provisions as well', the army did not abandon him or rebel. Livy finds it 'amazing that there was no mutiny in his camp' and it is a testament to the loyalty the men owed their commander, and their belief in him (28.12.1–6).[59] The description of Hannibal's army is particularly evocative, 'not made up of his own countrymen, but a mixture scraped together from all nations . . . dissimilar in appearance and in dress, with different arms, religious rites and practices, and almost with different gods'. It was Hannibal who bound these men together into a force that remained true to its commander when 'all else was falling apart'.[60] Hannibal's personal commitment and loyalty to his troops may have been another reason that he did not leave Italy. He was fighting not for Carthage by this time but for his army and remaining allies.[61]

During these years of isolation and hardship, much of Hannibal's time and energy were devoted to maintaining and feeding his army in a devastated countryside. The rugged and mountainous region of Bruttium had inadequate arable land to sustain his army, and what there was had lain fallow whilst 'most of the young men had been swept away from agriculture by the war' (Livy 28.12.7). Hannibal spent a substantial part of 205 BCE in and around the beautiful city of Crotona. That summer, at the renowned sanctuary and temple of Juno Lacinia, he dedicated an altar to the goddess. The monument was inscribed in both Punic and Greek with the achievements that Hannibal considered worthy of recording. We can only wonder about the details of the text, whether it was truly written as a kind of *res gestae* (as Livy describes), but it must have been a telling statement of Hannibal's self-assessment. The bilingual inscription was also a testament to the 'huge ambition' of the man and how he wanted to be remembered (Polybius 3.33.56; Livy 28.46.16).[62]

Hannibal left other evidence of his time in Italy in the form of coinage minted to pay his soldiers. The vast majority of the Hannibalic coins issued in Italy are preserved in hoards found in Bruttium.[63] The coins, based on the Carthaginian shekel standard, preserve recognizable imagery of the Carthaginian type, with the head of a female goddess, in this case perhaps Tanit (or equally Juno) and the image of the horse, or a horse with palm tree. The coin evidence illustrates how Bruttium became almost a 'Carthaginian state' during these years.[64] It was the only place where Hannibal and his army of the last loyal soldiers still held sway.

The size of the army Hannibal commanded in these years of isolation is unknown. He had devoted soldiers in considerable enough numbers to keep the Romans on their guard.[65] Nonetheless, the Carthaginian war effort was waning and support for Hannibal's position in Italy dissipated. Philip V and the Macedonians made peace with the Roman-allied Aetolian League in Greece in 206 BCE.[66] This developed further into the Peace of Phoenice in

205 BCE between the Macedonian king and the Romans (Livy 29.12.1–16).[67] Clearly Hannibal could now expect no help from that quarter. He may have hoped that his continued presence in Italy would make it impossible for the Romans to concentrate their military strength on Carthage but it was to be events in Africa that would ultimately decide his fate. The narrative at the end of Livy's twenty-eighth book sees the mighty Hannibal stranded at the tip of the peninsula, clinging to Italy. Hannibal is helpless, Scipio is powerful and the tables have turned.[68]

# CHAPTER 11

# HANNIBAL RETURNS

When they considered the worth of Hannibal and the greatness of his acts, it offended them to think that they had been so base as to make humble suit unto Rome for peace, whilst they had such a brave champion alive to maintain their cause by war. (**Sir Walter Ralegh**)[1]

T HERE HAD BEEN A time when 'Italy trembled' at Hannibal as he brought 'thundering war to Rome' but increasingly he was a sideshow in a conflagration that had shifted its focus south to Sicily where preparations were being made to invade Africa (Justin 32.4). In the final years of the conflict Hannibal looked on as a spectator while the action relocated to Africa where Carthage and her most important allies, the Numidians, took centre stage. The Numidian cavalry that had fought with Hannibal to such devastating effect in his victories were the Carthaginian allies most frequently referred to by the Roman sources.[2] Their leaders were tied to the Barcid generals and other elite Carthaginian families through bonds of loyalty and marriage.[3] We have seen how the alliances of the Numidians shifted over the course of the war, with the Romans vying to entice allies away from Carthage. The approach taken by Scipio and the Romans in Africa was not dissimilar to that taken by Hannibal in Italy. Carthage, if isolated from her neighbours, would not have the resources to keep fighting.[4] The earlier invasions of Agathocles, that of Regulus in the First Punic War and the Mercenary War had proven how vulnerable the city was in the face of an African revolt.

The background to the final stages of the war in Africa is closely connected to the dynastic struggle and inter-kingdom rivalries between the key allies: the

Masaesylian king Syphax and Massylian king Masinissa. Through their alliance with the two competing superpowers the Numidian kings developed their own realms in this period. They used their positions as allies of Carthage and then Rome to gain advantage over each other.[5] It was after the battle of Ilipa in Iberia that Masinissa chose to enter into discussions with the Romans about abandoning his alliance with Carthage (Livy 28.16.11).[6] The reputation, personal prestige and victories of the Roman army under the younger Scipio may have influenced Masinissa into changing sides but practical considerations about his own role in politics at home must have driven his choice.[7] Masinissa met secretly with one of Scipio's deputies (and perhaps Scipio himself), agreed an alliance with Rome and encouraged the Romans to invade Africa. Carthage would not last long, Masinissa said flatteringly, if the Romans had Scipio as commander (Livy 28.35.11).[8] He then dashed off to Africa where his father's and uncle's deaths had left his Massylian kingdom in turmoil.[9]

The alliance between Masinissa and the Romans would be of fundamental importance to the outcome of the war. However, in 205 BCE the reality of Masinissa's situation was more complex. His father's kingdom was now ruled by a distant relative who had made overtures to Carthage and King Syphax.[10] At this point Scipio must have realized that Masinissa needed Rome as much as or more than he (and the Romans) needed Masinissa.

Things were going badly for Carthage on all fronts. Hannibal and the Carthaginians would have been aware that Scipio had sailed back to Rome from Iberia with ten ships in time for the consular elections for 205 BCE. It was no secret that Scipio's plan was to take the war to Africa as soon as he could (Livy 28.38.1). His arrival in Rome with a large fleet 'loaded down with captives, money, arms and all kinds of booty' created great excitement (Appian, *Ib.* 38). Scipio's complete victory in the Iberian peninsula put him in a natural position for political success. He was the man of the moment. Yet, as the head of an important family in Rome he also faced opposition from fellow senators who were perhaps wary of his achievements and the acclaim they brought. Nonetheless, he quite easily won the consulship for 205 BCE with P. Licinius Crassus as his colleague. Scipio viewed his plan for an invasion of Africa as a natural continuation of his success in Iberia. His colleagues in the Senate were not all in agreement and the proposed invasion faced strong opposition. A long debate took place with the venerable ex-consuls Fabius Maximus and Fulvius Flaccus, both veterans of the war with Hannibal, resisting Scipio's plans. The older generation argued that with Hannibal still in Bruttium the focus of the war should remain in Italy (Livy 28.40–45).[11] The broader context

of the disagreement was the long-term strategy of Roman military engagement, with the two sides embodied in the conservative Fabius Maximus and
the adventurous younger generation of Scipio. Eventually Scipio was given a
broad mandate and assumed the province of Sicily as his responsibility. He
was also 'given leave to cross to Africa' if he felt it was in Rome's interest (Livy
28.45.9).[12]

The wealth from the war in Iberia paid for public games and entertain-
ment in the city and the Romans sent two citizens to make a dedication to the
god Apollo at Delphi.[13] These men 'bore a gold crown weighing two hundred
pounds, and reproductions of the spoils made from one thousand pounds of
silver'. These gifts 'from the spoils of Hasdrubal' (Livy 28.45.12) give some
indication of the vast wealth that had been accumulated in Rome over the
previous few years as successive cities fell.[14] As the people of Rome became
accustomed to the flow of the wealth of conquest they were enthusiastic as
Scipio began to prepare for his next adventure. An invasion of Africa had been
the original Roman plan in 218 BCE even before hostilities had first broken
out. Only now, fourteen years later, would they proceed. Scipio was so popular
in Rome that, although he was not granted a troop levy by the Senate, he
received 7,000 volunteers eager to follow him into battle and further glory
(Livy 28.45.14–46.1).[15]

Throughout 205 BCE Scipio meticulously prepared for a massive invasion
of Africa, with supplies and troop training being key to his plans. He would
not, however, embark his forces until the following year.[16] Instead he sent his
lieutenant Laelius on a raiding expedition with sixty ships to reconnoitre the
coast of Africa, pillage and wreak havoc in the rich agricultural heartland of
Carthage.[17] For the Carthaginians, Laelius' arrival combined with the rumours
of an imminent invasion to spread fear through the city, 'first terror and panic
gripped their hearts, and then a gloomy foreboding' (Livy 29.3.9). It was the
turn of the people of Carthage to fear the coming invasion. Carthaginians in
Africa must have become used to Roman ships raiding the coastal regions over
the period of the war. Roman raiders had consistently taken captives and
pillaged widely across the countryside but a full-scale invasion was another
matter altogether.[18]

The Carthaginians sprang into action and even when they realized Laelius'
arrival was only a raid, not the dreaded invasion of Scipio, they began to
prepare for the inevitable. Envoys were dispatched to Hannibal and Mago in
Italy encouraging them to do as much as possible to divert Scipio's attention
from his planned invasion. Reinforcements and warships went out to Mago in
Liguria but it may have been too difficult to supply Hannibal in Bruttium,

with the consul and fleet now at Lilybaeum.[19] Mago was encouraged to move his armies farther south but the ten Roman legions that stood in between Mago and Hannibal were an insurmountable problem. The Carthaginians sent an embassy to Philip V asking for military aid and promising to pay 200 talents if he would invade Sicily or Italy. That same year the Romans had signed a peace treaty with Philip, which ensured that no help for Carthage would come from the Macedonians. In the city of Carthage the fortifications were repaired, supplies massed and more troops levied for the defence of Africa (Livy 29.4.1–3).[20]

Once aware of the imminent invasion, the Carthaginians worked to lure King Syphax back to their side in alliance. Syphax liked to view himself as a moderator between the two sides and had maintained relatively good relations with both Scipio and the Carthaginian leader Hasdrubal Gisgo. He was eventually persuaded to return to the Carthaginian fold through an alliance sealed by marriage to Sophonisba, the beautiful daughter of Hasdrubal Gisgo.[21] This marriage would ensure that the people of Carthage and the king 'would have the same friends and enemies'. Syphax, coaxed by his new young wife, was encouraged to send envoys informing Scipio of the official pact he now had with the Carthaginian people. Syphax told Scipio that he would be 'obliged to fight for the land of Africa' against any Roman invasion (Livy 29.23.1–5). Livy endows Sophonisba with a great deal of influence over her husband's decisions at this crucial time. It is difficult to know how much of this plays into the construction of a femme fatale and how much may actually be reflective of her personality. She is one of the few women whose name we know from this long tale of war and conquest that would have had such devastating consequences for so many women in Rome and Carthage.[22]

Meanwhile at Carthage they must have watched with some trepidation as Masinissa struggled to regain the kingdom of his father Gaia that had been usurped by a distant relative.[23] Once he had sealed his alliance with Scipio in Iberia he crossed to the kingdom of the Mauri (modern Morocco) and raised a small army (Livy 29.30.1). This force grew as Masinissa won over supporters and defeated the usurpers. In Livy's words, he began to 'nurture a kingdom that had only just begun to coalesce' (29.31.6). With Syphax now allied with Carthage and Masinissa now allied to Rome, the two kings were poised to fight the war in Africa by proxy for their more powerful allies. Urged on by Hasdrubal Gisgo, Syphax turned to attack the new king next door.[24] Containment of Masinissa would be of great strategic value to the Carthaginians, for without allies Scipio's upcoming invasion would be a much more challenging task. An initial encounter saw Masinissa defeated and he fled with 'a few horsemen' to a mountain called Bellus (perhaps near modern Tabarka) situated close to wealthy and fertile Carthaginian farmland.[25] There the Massyli of Masinissa plundered widely, looting and killing.

The Carthaginians pushed Syphax to finish off the young king. In a 'fierce battle' that, Livy claims rather vaguely, took place 'on some hills' between Cirta (Syphax's capital, modern Constantine) and Hippo (Hippo Regius, modern Annaba) the two kings drew up their armies. Syphax was eventually victorious but Masinissa again escaped with 'sixty cavalrymen' despite being pursued across the countryside by Syphax's son Vermina. Eluding capture in dramatic style, which included plunging, wounded and on horseback, into the Bagradas river, Masinissa reached the region of the Lesser Syrtis (about 320 kilometres south-east of the battle site), now a king in exile (Livy 29.30–33).

In the preparations for the invasion of Africa Hannibal was not forgotten by either side. The Romans directed four legions against him in Bruttium while Scipio made his plans in Sicily.[26] At some point after Laelius had returned to Sicily from his raiding party in Africa, Scipio decided that 'the recovery of the city of Locri' would be in his interests (Livy 29.6.1). Locri, held by the Carthaginians since 215 BCE, had been a mainstay of Hannibal's support. As the Romans closed in around Hannibal many in the city were having to take stock of their situation. For the population in and around Locri life must have been unbearable as the stalemate in Bruttium turned to lawlessness and raiding. Numidians, Bruttii and the Romans all 'took pleasure in looting and made raids on enemy farms' (29.6.1–9). Tradesmen from Locri who had been captured in a raid by soldiers allied to Rome plotted to betray one of the citadels in the city to their captors. These men were sent off to meet Scipio at Syracuse and presented the plan to him.

Roman forces from Rhegium were diverted along with the Locrian exiles to try to seize the town by stealth. The plan was partially successful and one of the two citadels in the city fell to the Roman forces by night. Carthaginian troops in Locri were commanded by Hamilcar, who immediately sent messengers to Hannibal warning him that they were under attack. Hannibal was nearby and as soon as he received the news made his way to the aid of the garrison. The Carthaginians now held one citadel in Locri and the Romans the other, with the population caught in the middle. As Hannibal approached Locri by land, Scipio, hearing that his forces were at risk, sailed over from Messana in Sicily with ten ships (Livy 29.7.1). Hannibal ordered his troops to attack the Roman forces in the town while he planned a surprise assault on the city. Scipio, at the same time as Hannibal's attack was under way, sailed into the harbour at Locri. The following day, when Hannibal was preparing to scale the walls, Scipio marched his forces out of the main gate of the town and 'took the Carthaginians by surprise'. Hannibal lost some two hundred men in the resulting skirmish.

Livy reports that when Hannibal realized that Scipio was present he ordered a retreat and sent word to his men remaining in the citadel that they should 'look out for themselves' (29.7. 8–10). Locri, one of the first cities to go over to Hannibal and the place that had remained most loyal throughout his time in Italy, had fallen. To what extent the events around Locri related to Hannibal's orders from Carthage to attempt to divert Scipio cannot be determined. He may have lured the Roman commander there as a distraction, and Livy criticizes Scipio for diverting his attention from Africa: 'this major scheme was put on hold by a lesser one' (29.6.1). Even though Hannibal lost Locri he did manage to get most of his men out alive. In that regard he could view the engagement as a success, as the town was of little use by this stage in the war, whilst the men held much more value.[27]

Thus the first round of the battle between the two most famous generals of their generation went to Scipio. The aftermath of Scipio's capture of Locri was marred by atrocities committed by his commander in charge, Pleminius. Livy claims Pleminius made life miserable for the Locrians and 'so outdid' the Carthaginians and 'inflicted unspeakable abuse' on the people in the city. Pleminius, according to Appian, even 'robbed the temple of Persephone' (*Hann.* 55) and the crimes and atrocities committed in this phase of the war remained a blight on Scipio's reputation. They also helped to ensure that upheaval in Bruttium rumbled on for many years after the war with Hannibal was over.[28]

After Locri fell to the Romans in 205 BCE and up until Hannibal left Italy in 203 BCE, the territory available to him shrank steadily to almost nothing.[29] Cosentia (Cosenza) and six other towns in Bruttium were 'detached' from Hannibal by the proconsul Crassus (in 204 BCE) and then Thurii was abandoned (Appian, *Hann.* 57). Polybius describes these last years in Italy for Hannibal as 'shut in there [on the Lacinian promontory] and almost besieged' (15.1.11–12). Hannibal was now powerless to do anything to divert Scipio's invasion.

At the start of the campaigning season of 204 BCE Scipio gathered his ships and men at Lilybaeum and launched his offensive. The Roman consul landed with his invasion force on African soil at the 'headland of the Beautiful One' known today as Cap Farina north of Utica (Livy 29.27–29; Polyb. 21.21) (Map 3). As soon as Scipio landed he was eagerly joined by Masinissa, who had made his way north, accompanied only by a few horsemen.[30] Masinissa, now a king without a kingdom, was even more eager to support the Roman invasion than he had been before.

In Carthaginian territory the arrival of Scipio had brought 'frantic dread' to the population of the cities and the farmlands nearby. There were crowds of men and columns of women and children clogging the roads, peasants driving their animals. The people of Carthage had not, Livy points out, seen a Roman army for over fifty years, hence 'the heightened excitement and panic'. The city gates were shut, men were posted on the walls and sentries and outposts readied for what they believed was an imminent attack. Carthage prepared for a war the population did not believe they could win. They did not have 'a strong enough commander or a strong enough army' to field against the Romans. They were, as Livy notes, only too keenly aware of Hasdrubal Gisgo's poor record against this very same Scipio in Iberia and now he had landed on their shores (Livy 29.28.1–8).

A young Carthaginian nobleman named Hanno was sent out to harass the Romans and reconnoitre their position. The Roman cavalry engaged in a skirmish and managed to kill large numbers of the Carthaginian cavalry squadron, including the commander (Livy 29.29.1). Carthage then summoned Hasdrubal Gisgo and Syphax 'to come to the support of Carthage and the whole of Africa'. There followed another disastrous cavalry encounter with yet another young Hanno which saw Carthage lose 2,000 horsemen including 200 Carthaginian nobles (Livy 29.34.1–6). These initial encounters did not bode well.[31]

In late summer Scipio moved to besiege the Carthaginian allied city of Utica while Hasdrubal Gisgo pulled together an army and Syphax gathered his forces. In the autumn of 204 BCE the Carthaginian army included 30,000 foot soldiers and 3,000 horsemen. When combined with Syphax's cavalry numbering about 10,000 and another 50,000 foot soldiers they substantially outnumbered the Romans (Livy 29.35.9–12; Polyb. 14.1.14).[32] The threat of such a large army moving against him forced Scipio to give up the siege of Utica and move off.[33] He wintered precariously on the sea, where he constructed a camp that allowed him to enclose his navy and army inside 'a single circumvallation' on a promontory in the delta of the Bagradas river (Livy 29.35.13–15). The defences built for the winter camp reveal just how insecure Scipio must have felt.

The unsolvable issue of actual troop numbers reflects the ambiguities in our sources and their narrative intent to exaggerate Scipio's achievements. Estimates for the number of troops Scipio took with him from Sicily range from a high of 35,000 to a low of 17,000 and arguments to support both

numbers exist. A reasonable quantity of troops for the invading force probably
lies somewhere in the middle of the two numbers, around 28,000 men in
total, close to 10,500 Roman troops and about 17,500 allied forces.[34] The
combined Carthaginian forces must have been more than Scipio's but it is
unlikely that they were as vastly superior as Livy claimed. If the numbers had
tilted so far in the Carthaginians' favour it is unlikely that Scipio would have
been able to quietly retreat to his camp for the winter without an attempt
being made to dislodge him.[35] It could be that Scipio's reputation and his
military celebrity, like those of Hannibal before him, made the Carthaginians
wary of launching an outright attack.

   March 203 BCE saw new consuls in Rome who had to contend with
Hannibal in Bruttium, his brother Mago Barca in Liguria and an uprising in
Etruria. There does not seem to have been a coherent strategy from Carthage
at this point. Carthage may have wished Hannibal to maintain a presence in
Italy but he was not able to have any impact on the Roman campaign in
Africa. Keeping Hannibal from returning to Carthage must have been part of
the Roman strategy, isolating him farther and farther until he was surrounded,
with little room to manoeuvre, clinging on to the edge of Italy. The spring
also brought a renewal of Scipio's command from Rome.[36] The winter in
Africa had seen Scipio trying to lure Syphax back into an alliance with Rome
but Syphax was more interested in a negotiated peace between the two sides.
A proposal for peace suggested by Syphax, surely with Carthage's approval,
would see Hannibal recalled from Italy and Scipio leave Africa. Scipio may
have considered this option but it is more likely he was bluffing, biding his
time and lulling the opposition into complacency. He was also unwilling,
it seems, to face the combined forces of Syphax and Hasdrubal Gisgo, and
could not entice Syphax over to Rome. The old king's young Carthaginian
wife, Sophonisba, kept him loyal to the cause and Livy includes plenty
of innuendo about the licentiousness of the barbarian and Syphax's innability
to control his libido. These Roman cultural stereotypes of the Numidian
serve to obscure the political implications behind Syphax's actions (e.g. Livy
30.3.4–5).

   Scipio hesitated, while pretending to engage with Syphax's peace plan. He
then conceived an opportunity to deliver a crushing blow to the Carthaginian
forces whilst not risking many of his own troops. It would be a classic example
of the use of ruses and stratagems that Hannibal would have been proud of.
'The Carthaginian winter quarters,' Livy tells us, 'had been built from materials indiscriminately brought together from the countryside, so the structures
were almost entirely of wood.' The Numidian camp nearby consisted mostly

of reed and thatch huts. Scipio diverted the attention of soldiers in camp by
moving out of his winter quarters towards Utica and then sent Laelius and
Masinissa along with 'some of his troops' and ordered them to attack the
camps by hurling firebrands into them. The Carthaginians and Numidians
were taken totally by surprise and both the camps burned to the ground.
Although Syphax and Hasdrubal escaped, many of their soldiers were
caught by the flames or struck down by the Roman soldiers as they tried
to flee the camps. Livy's estimate of 40,000 men 'slaughtered or consumed
by flames' again seems extremely high but there is no doubt that the
Carthaginians suffered a disastrous loss of life, elephants, weapons and
supplies (30.3–6).[37]

Scipio then pressed on with the siege of Utica while Hasdrubal and Syphax
scrambled to levy more troops and regroup their armies. Not long afterwards,
just days, according to Livy (but in any event probably late in the spring), the
Carthaginians were able to field another army against the Romans. Smaller
numbers this time, about 30,000 hastily recruited, poorly trained peasants
from the fields or anyone the Carthaginians could find to press into service.
The armies met at a place called the Great Plains, which is thought to be in
the valley of the Bagradas river, a five-day march from Utica. Scipio's army,
with Masinissa's cavalry playing a key role, drew up against the hastily gathered forces of Hasdrubal Gisgo and Syphax plus four thousand Celtiberians
recruited from Iberia. The Romans and allies easily won the day. Hasdrubal
and Syphax again retreated, defeated this time in battle rather than by fire.
After these two successive disasters the city of Carthage was in an uproar and
expected a direct attack within days. Inside the walls the people gathered
supplies and prepared for a protracted siege. Debate raged about what to do.
Some among the population must have talked of Hannibal and his forces in
Italy. The reality was that their most famous and successful commander was
not in any position to alleviate the suffering of the city, as he was essentially
trapped. Scipio moved to take Tunes (Tunis), just south of Carthage, from
where he could cut the city off from its heartland (Livy 30.9.7–12).

Carthage's only substantial ally in Africa was now defeated and after the
battle of the Great Plains, Masinissa and Laelius were sent to pursue Syphax
and to reclaim the land of the Massylians as Masinissa's kingdom. Ovid's *Fasti*
tell us that it was on 23 June that Masinissa captured Syphax, who had been
thrown by his horse in a cavalry engagement between the two kings (6.769).
The Masaesylian king was to be handed over to the Romans but first Masinissa
took him straight to the impregnable stronghold of Cirta. There Syphax was
paraded in chains before the walls of the city and, as Masinissa had wagered,

when the population saw their king bound and defeated they opened the gates to the conqueror (Livy 30.12.1–10).[38]

Masinissa took the city, Syphax's realm, and also took his wife, the Carthaginian Sophonisba. The daughter of Hasdrubal Gisgo had been instrumental in keeping Syphax loyal to Carthage in the year of Scipio's invasion. Now she flung herself on the mercy of Masinissa, begging him to take her life rather than see her paraded in chains in Rome.[39] Sophonisba was 'a woman of great beauty and in her prime' and Livy tells us that she moved the Numidian king's heart with her nobility and bravery (30.12.17). Masinissa then decided that, rather than hand her over to the Romans, he would marry Sophonisba himself. As she was the wife of the king he had just conquered, this would have been customary in the Numidian tradition. Needless to say it was not a custom that impressed Scipio. Masinissa had, by marrying Sophonisba, saved her from Roman captivity and removed her from Scipio's power.[40]

Once Masinissa was again in the company of Scipio, the Roman general insisted that he hand over his wife as a captive of war. Sophonisba, born of Carthaginian nobility and wife of a defeated king, would be a valuable commodity. In the legend as told, rather than deliver her to Scipio, Masinissa had a cup of poison secretly passed to his queen by a servant. She chose death over slavery and took the cup with the words 'I accept this wedding gift . . . it is not unwelcome, if my husband has found it impossible to give his wife a greater one'. With dramatic flourish she drank the poison and died. The story of Sophonisba as narrated by the Roman sources has echoed down the centuries. She was, by her beauty and persuasive power, able to 'make everyone subservient to her wishes' (Appian, *Lib.* 27). The romance and nobility of the Carthaginian queen in a story otherwise filled with battle-hardened men have been celebrated in poetry, plays, paintings and opera from Petrarch and Boccaccio through to Voltaire. Sophonisba's courage in the eyes of the Romans meant that Scipio was denied his trophy and Syphax was sent alone to Rome in chains to be presented as the great prize to the Senate (Livy 30.13.1–15.8).[41]

In the Senate at Carthage the leaders of the city could think of few options after the defeat at the Great Plains and now the capture of Syphax.[42] A period of fraught activity and negotiations took place as the final outcome seemed inescapable. Scipio intended to lay siege to Carthage, and to avoid this fate a delegation from the Carthaginian Senate formed of thirty 'leading elders' went to Scipio at his camp at Tunes to negotiate (Livy 30.16.2–5).[43] These leading men of Carthage came before the Roman general. Their approach was customary, which means they 'not only saluted the gods and did obeisance to the Earth, as is the custom with other men, but they debased themselves by falling prostrate on the ground and kissing the feet of the members of the council' (Polyb. 15.1.6–7).[44] With these gestures of flattery and obsequiousness, which the Romans found foreign, the Carthaginian elders asked for a pardon and also shifted the whole responsibility for the war on to Hannibal and his supporters (Livy 30.16.4).[45] The Barcids and their followers were distinctly out of favour at Carthage at this moment and Hannibal, still in Italy, could only watch impotently from afar as the negotiations continued.

Scipio was swayed by the Carthaginian council to offer peace terms. These were harsh and insisted that 'the Carthaginians were to hand back all prisoners of war, deserters and runaway slaves. They were to remove their armies from Italy and Gaul . . . to stay out of Iberia . . . to leave all the islands that lay between Italy and Africa, surrender all but twenty warships and hand over five hundred thousand measures of wheat and three hundred thousand of barley', and pay a significant financial indemnity (Livy 30.16.10–13).[46] The Carthaginian Senate was given three days to consider the terms. Crucially for our understanding of Hannibal, Livy insists that these negotiations were a subterfuge and that Carthage was only 'playing for time' to 'allow for Hannibal to cross from Italy'. The Senate at Carthage did not feel it should reject any terms at this point, no matter how harsh; effectively, it was stalling.

Then envoys from both sides went to Rome for the treaty to be ratified. The elders from the Senate at Carthage were granted an audience and appeared before the Roman Senate at the Temple of Bellona, where negotiations continued. At this critical moment in the story of Hannibal, of Rome, of Carthage and the run-up to the final battle of the war, our two main sources provide two versions of events and there is no way to reconcile the difference in the statements: one of them is wrong.[47] The issue lies in whether or not the terms dictated by Scipio were accepted and ratified by the Romans and Carthaginians. Livy, as we have seen, believed the Carthaginians' plea for peace was a stalling tactic and that the Romans knew they were only waiting for Hannibal and Mago to return with their armies to reopen hostilities. Livy calls the whole process a façade that was created to delay while Hannibal prepared for battle. Polybius, on the other hand, insists that the treaty was formally accepted by the Roman Senate and that there is no indication that the peace was not being seriously considered (Livy 30.23.8; Polyb. 15.1.3–4).

Following these negotiations Hannibal received envoys from the Senate at Carthage that commanded him to leave Italy and return home (Livy 30.9.19–20). In the north of Italy Mago was severely wounded in a battle with a Roman army 'in the land of the Insubrian Gauls' (north of Genoa) where he may have gone to recruit soldiers for his return to Africa. Mago was carried from the field of a fierce battle that saw many Roman losses. Livy claims that once their commander had fallen the Carthaginians 'ceded victory'. Mago was carried south towards the sea where a delegation from Carthage waited for him near Genoa. The youngest brother of Hannibal received his orders to return home to Carthage and was helped onboard a waiting ship. Mago's wounds were so severe that he died en route, before they had even passed Sardinia (Livy 30.19.1–6).[48]

Just how we interpret these events at the end of the war rests on whether we believe Livy's claims that the Carthaginians were stalling. Livy maintains that Carthage had not given up at all and that, by recalling Hannibal and Mago, was attempting to shore up numbers at home. In this case the peace negotiations were a subterfuge. The opposing view, from Polybius, implies that Carthage recalled Hannibal and Mago as part of the agreement with the Romans on a proposed peace. In accordance with the peace terms the Carthaginians had to remove their armies and commanders from Italy and Liguria. Rome, in the mind of Cassius Dio, would never have accepted peace with Carthage while Mago and Hannibal were still on Italian soil and thus the ratification of the treaty was delayed until they had departed (Cassius Dio 17.74).[49]

Hannibal prepared to leave Italy, where he had now spent fifteen years in arms. This amounted to almost one third of his life and longer than he had ever lived at Carthage. He was increasingly isolated in Bruttium and as reports of Scipio's victories in Africa spread, more of Hannibal's remaining allies 'revolted . . . and expelled their garrisons' (Appian, *Hann.* 57). Under these circumstances it is difficult to believe Livy's claim of his reluctance to depart: 'Hannibal listened to the words of the envoys [while] he was gnashing his teeth and groaning, and barely able to hold back his tears' (30.20.1). In truth, Hannibal had been trapped in a tiny patch of Bruttium for the last few years as Carthage lost battle after battle to Scipio.[50] Encircled as he was by Roman armies, it seems more probable that Hannibal was willing when ordered to return to Africa but certainly had regrets. A fleet was sent by Carthage. Hannibal had supplemented this by building his own transport and was ready when the Carthaginian envoys appeared to summon him home.[51] Given his precarious situation, Hannibal's return seems more likely to have been part of a negotiated deal, an evacuation, rather than a bold move by the Carthaginians to challenge Rome.[52]

'Such was the end of Hannibal's invasion of Italy' – and his tears may have been real enough to the people who had remained loyal all those years (Appian, *Hann.* 61). The Roman reprisals were not going to be kind to the Bruttii and Hannibal re-garrisoned the few towns that were still faithful with soldiers whom Livy calls 'unserviceable'. He also slaughtered his pack animals and horses (in the thousands), which would have been difficult to transport.[53] Livy claims that he brought with him 'the real strength of his army' but how many soldiers is difficult to estimate. He may, by supplementing the ships sent by Carthage, have surprised all sides by transporting a good proportion of his soldiers with him, estimated at between 12,000 and 20,000 men.[54] These men were those who had been loyal to their commander throughout his victories and losses, as well as those who had joined the cause in Italy. There are reports that some of the Italian soldiers were unwilling to go across to Africa and that Hannibal killed those who resisted in the temple of Juno Lacinia, where they had taken refuge. This would have been a significant act of sacrilege for a man who had bestowed spoils on the temple and who had also endowed it with an inscription of his life, and seems to have been an invention of later sources (Livy 30.20.6).[55]

Hannibal and his army did not sail directly back to Carthage when he departed from Bruttium. His destination was the Sahel region on the east coast of Carthaginian territory somewhere near Hadrumentum (modern Sousse) (Livy 30.25.11). Perhaps Hannibal wisely avoided the city because Scipio's fleet could cover the whole gulf from its port near Utica and it was safer to land his army to the south. More likely is that Hannibal landed his army in the region where his family had property. His chance of sustaining his troops with local support was much better than what would have awaited him at Carthage. Once he landed, the forces set up camp.

It is easy to read hostility towards Carthage in Hannibal's actions.[56] Hannibal may have avoided Carthage because he was functioning as a free agent, an independent commander with an army that he had recruited personally. He had become more a warlord than a general of the state. Certainly there is no indication that he was consulted about the Carthaginian peace plan or played any part in the ongoing negotiations. He had received no funding from Carthage for the upkeep of his army and his soldiers were loyal to their commander. There was also the possibility that Hannibal would be prosecuted by the state for his running of the war in Italy. All this must have played a part in his decisions. It seems certain that discussions between his camp and supporters at Carthage with the Carthaginian government would have been part of the wider diplomatic effort.[57] From Hannibal's perspective Carthage had been so unsupportive of his efforts in Italy that now he was recalled he might have been unwilling to follow their commands. There may be some truth in Livy's view that Hannibal 'had not been defeated by the Roman people, who have been so often slaughtered or routed, but by the Carthaginian Senate with its carping jealousy' (30.20.1–7).[58]

Hannibal spent the winter of 203/202 BCE in his family territory building up his forces and waiting to see who took the next step. Peace negotiations continued, with both sides in a kind of stasis. Some of Mago's army had made it back to Africa and may well have joined up with Hannibal's forces.[59] The winter passed, with the city of Carthage under a blockade – the Romans holding Tunes to the south and the fleet at Scipio's camp near Utica to the north. Early in the spring of 202 events at Carthage shifted the focus from peace again to war.[60] It was a period of great uncertainty and a truce of sorts was being upheld. What unfolded reflects the reality of war and peace in the ancient world, where the population of cities and generals in the field waited, sometimes for months, for the sailing season before receiving a response to negotiations.

Livy details how a fleet of transport ships carrying supplies from Sicily to the Roman army, 'two hundred freighters and thirty warships', was blown off course and 'scattered far and wide' (30.24.5–12). Many of the freighters were blown to the island of Aegimurus, at the mouth of the gulf north of Carthage, and others directly across the gulf from Carthage to Aquae Calidae (Korbous, see Map 1).[61] From inside Carthage, the population saw the Roman supply fleet being blown off course and 'people converged on the forum from all over the city'. The Senate at Carthage was convened. There was a great deal of excitement over the wrecked fleet and it was decided to fetch the Roman transport vessels and tow them back to the city. It was far from a unanimous decision but the Carthaginians had been living under a fairly comprehensive blockade for months now. They had also been supplying Scipio's troops with grain and barley as needed, thus hunger was rife in the city. So the sight of the Roman transports full of fresh supplies running aground across the bay may have proved too great a temptation and fifty warships were sent out to collect the remnants of the fleet.[62]

Scipio was reportedly furious at both the loss of his much-needed supplies and at the threat to his truce. His position in Rome may have been at the forefront of his reaction, for a failed peace would only weaken his proconsular role in Africa. The Carthaginians received three envoys who arrived by sea from Scipio's camp north of the city. The envoys were there to discuss the transport supplies and were given an audience by the Carthaginian Senate. They were then presented to the people of Carthage. Scipio's envoys spoke to the Carthaginians in 'insulting and overbearing' terms and told them that since the Romans had accepted the peace terms they had broken their word by attacking the supply ships. The population of Carthage were in no mood to listen and were so incensed by what the envoys had to say, and their tone, that they physically attacked them (Livy 30.24.5–25.8). However, Polybius (15.2.1) claims that the envoys left the city unharmed and were escorted by representatives of the Senate.

There was an emphatic rejection of any peace terms. The presence of Hannibal and his army remained in the background while the truce fell apart but must have been in the forefront of the minds of both sides as the events played out. The envoys departed Carthage in their quinquereme and once they crossed the mouth of the Bagradas river delta heading north back to Scipio's camp they were left by their escort ships. At that moment, from a Carthaginian fleet anchored near Utica, three triremes attacked the Roman envoys' ship and ran it aground before they could safely reach their camp.[63] The men on board the ship were killed but the envoys survived (Polyb. 15.2.12).[64]

The provocation by the Carthaginian fleet meant that the war now turned to bitterness as a resentful Scipio took his forces and pillaged town after town in the Carthaginian heartland. He sold the population into slavery and destroyed everything and everyone he came across. Either Scipio was trying to force a surrender or, more likely, provoke the Carthaginians into another battle. He must have had Hannibal in mind as he taunted the Carthaginians into coming out and fighting one more time. Through all these events, as far as we know, Hannibal remained on the coast at Hadrumentum with his army, perhaps wary of both Carthage and Scipio.[65]

Scipio was rampaging through the countryside when the Carthaginians sent messages to Hannibal 'imploring him not to delay' and to engage the enemy in battle. Hannibal does not seem to have been enthusiastic about confronting the Roman general given his army's distinct lack of cavalry (ruing the thousands of horses he had left behind in Italy) and his lack of substantial allies in Africa. He would have been under great pressure to respond to Scipio's provocations. By gathering together some of the fringe Numidian royalty, who had been part of the earlier battles with Masinissa, Hannibal added two thousand horse to his forces. His new ally was a king, hitherto unknown, called Tychaeus, who was related to Syphax (Polyb. 15.3.5–7).[66] Hannibal waited for a few days and then reluctantly shifted his camp from Hadrumentum to Zama, a few days' journey west of the coast.[67] He then sent out scouts to reconnoitre the Roman positions and troops. The scouts, three men, were caught and brought before Scipio, who treated them magnanimously, showed them around the camp and then sent them back to Hannibal.

Scipio was obviously feeling confident and wanted to be seen to be in control, unthreatened by having Hannibal and his army in the vicinity. The two strategists were perhaps trying to out-think each other. By releasing the captured scouts Scipio may have been playing mind games with Hannibal and, more importantly, Hannibal's allies. For Scipio was the known entitity in Africa among the Numidian allies and Hannibal was rather the unknown. Not only had Hannibal spent very little time in the countryside in which he was now operating, he had never fought an engagement there. Intrigued by Scipio's behaviour towards his scouts, Hannibal was overwhelmed by a 'strong desire' to meet Scipio in person and 'converse with him' (Polyb. 15.5.8). He sent a messenger to his Roman opposite, requesting a meeting where they could 'discuss the whole situation'. Scipio replied positively, saying that he would set a 'place and hour' for the rendezvous.

Scipio, whilst he had been pillaging and looting the cities around Carthage, had also 'constantly' sent messages to Masinissa 'begging' him to join the Romans as soon as possible.[68] For the previous few months Masinissa had been busy shoring up his ancestral kingdom and incorporating the newly conquered lands of the Masaesylians, with the help of ten cohorts of Roman cavalry and infantry (Polyb. 15.4.3–4). Finally Masinissa arrived at Scipio's camp with a force of 'six thousand foot and four thousand horse' (15.5.12–13). Only then, Polybius claims, did Scipio move his army towards Hannibal's position and when he reached a town called Naraggara he set up camp and sent a messenger. He informed Hannibal that he was now ready for a meeting.[69]

Hannibal received Scipio's messenger and then moved his army westward towards the Roman position, at a distance of not more than 30 stades (approx. 5 kilometres). He set up his camp on a hill, 'rather too far away from water' but otherwise 'convenient' for his needs (Polyb. 15.6.1–2). Scipio held the stronger position of the two. Hannibal's original plan may have been to intercept Scipio as he made his way south-west along the Bagradas valley. If Hannibal had been able to catch Scipio before he met up with Masinissa, or vice versa, he might have had a chance to divide and conquer. His reconnaissance mission, the captured scouts, would have reported to him that the Numidians were not, as yet, in the Roman camp.[70] The timing of the arrival of the crack troops – the Numidian cavalry and their fearsome leader Masinissa – is key to understanding Hannibal and Scipio's motives for this encounter. Polybius makes it very clear that it was only after Masinissa's arrival that Scipio felt comfortable agreeing to a meeting with Hannibal.[71]

The two sides then prepared for a battle that might resolve the situation for their respective cities. As Polybius notes, 'consequently not only all the inhabitants of Italy and Africa, but those of Iberia, Sicily and Sardinia likewise were held in suspense and distracted, awaiting the result' (15.3.4). Hannibal and Scipio held their much-anticipated meeting when both men felt their armies were in place. They rode out from their positions, accompanied by a few horsemen each. Eventually they left their 'escorts behind and met each other alone' and face to face the two greatest generals of their generation looked each other in the eye.

The meeting of the two men took place the day before the battle of Zama. Hannibal and Scipio each brought an interpreter to the meeting even though both were fluent Greek speakers and could easily have held discussions in a common language.[72] The symbolic intent of the interpreter was power. Scipio would have insisted on speaking Latin, the language of the Roman Republic.[73] Equally, Hannibal would have insisted on speaking Punic, leaving the translation to someone of lesser status. Neither man wanted to be the first to concede to the other but Hannibal spoke first and saluted Scipio from the position of the elder, wiser, more experienced man.

If we can believe the words as recorded, Hannibal lamented the wars fought between the two sides. He implored Scipio to let go of his pride and to negotiate a fair peace so that both Carthage and Rome could retain their dominions. 'Today you are just what I was at Trasimeno and at Cannae,' Hannibal said to Scipio (Livy 30.30.11). Carthage, Hannibal claimed, would give up all interests in Sicily, Iberia, Sardinia and all the islands between but he asked for an honourable peace. Scipio in turn refused. He blamed the Carthaginians for both wars and all the trouble that had been heaped on the people in their lands. He even claimed he had reluctantly invaded Africa and now that he, Scipio, held dominion over all the lands, was unlikely to accede to such a deal. Scipio demanded that the Carthaginians 'either put themselves and their country at Roman mercy or fight and conquer us' (Polyb. 15.6.4–15.8.14).[74]

At daybreak the following morning the two sides led out their armies. In the Roman sources we sense that Hannibal was far from eager for this battle. It was the autumn of 202 BCE, probably the month of October.[75] Hannibal may have had up to 40,000 troops under his command but the numbers, as always, are very difficult to ascertain, especially at Zama for which Livy does not even provide figures. Polybius only gives us the numbers of fatalities for Hannibal's army and does not include any totals for Scipio's forces. Estimates put the number of Scipio's troops at slightly less than Hannibal's, perhaps 38,000 soldiers. Hannibal may have had more infantry but was outnumbered in the all-important cavalry. There is little evidence that the Romans, once Masinissa had joined them, felt vulnerable. They were the superior fighting force and were not likely to have been significantly outnumbered.[76]

Hannibal drew his army up in three lines. In the first line were the remnants of Mago's army, the mercenaries who had made their way to Africa from Cisalpine Gaul. They included Ligurians, Celts and Balearic Islanders. Skirmishers were placed in front of this line along with eighty elephants. Significantly, elephants in any meaningful number had not played a part in Hannibal's armed tactics since his first major battle in Italy. The second line comprised Libyans and Carthaginians and the third line consisted of the troops that Hannibal had brought back from Italy with him. These were his loyal and most seasoned soldiers. The cavalry were placed on the wings with Numidians and Carthaginians on the left and right respectively (Polyb. 15.11.1–4). Hannibal's tactics were adapted to fit the Roman armies he had fought over the years, with his key infantry troops kept slightly back from the main line. His previous great victories had relied on superior cavalry whereas at Zama he was disadvantaged by inferior numbers and quality of horsemen.[77]

Scipio's troops were also drawn up in three lines but he placed his units of infantry directly behind one another, leaving spaces in between. The cavalry on the wings were commanded by Laelius on the left and Masinissa on the right. The formation, with gaps between his units, had been adapted to deal with the large number of elephants in Hannibal's army (Polyb. 15.9.6–10). Scipio's army was lined up to absorb the Carthaginian strengths and to take full advantage of his superior cavalry. When Scipio spoke to his troops he encouraged them: 'overcome your enemies for not only will you be unquestioned masters of Africa but you will gain for yourselves and your country the undisputed command and sovereignty of the rest of the world' (Polyb. 15.10.2).

Hannibal, more unusually, had each of the commanders of his different ethnic forces address their own troops. He wished them victory and said that they could 'rely on his own presence and that of the forces that he had brought back with him' to back them up. To his Carthaginian troops he had his commanders 'set before their eyes all the suffering that would befall their wives and children' should they fail. Then to his own loyal forces he recounted their great adventures in Italy, at Trasimeno and at Cannae. He bade them 'remember their comradeships of seventeen years' (Polyb. 15.10–11). Hannibal had never addressed sections of his army separately, to our knowledge, before this battle. Polybius is either making a rhetorical point about the disjointed nature of Hannibal's army or Hannibal did not consider the army he commanded at Zama to be his own.[78] Nonetheless, Hannibal understood how to instill confidence in his troops and although he must have known they were unlikely to win, his very presence could still inspire courage as the soldiers entered battle.[79]

After the armies had been lined up the commanders were ready. A few hours had passed and the Numidian cavalry skirmished on the flanks. There was eagerness to begin the fight. Hannibal first ordered his elephant drivers to charge. Some of the elephants were startled by the noise of trumpets and bugles, which caused them to turn back on their own side and Masinissa attacked at the same time. This left the Carthaginian left wing exposed. The elephants were largely ineffective. The gaps Scipio had left in his formation allowed them to pass right through his line without inflicting great damage. Laelius with the Roman cavalry attacked the Carthaginian horsemen and put them to flight. Then the two main bodies of troops clashed in a shower of noise: with 'war-cry and clashing their shields and their spears', the Romans fell on their foes, whose multilingual shouts added to the mayhem (Polyb. 15.12.9).

The battle was hand-to-hand combat with ferocious fighting. Hannibal's mercenaries at first got the better of the Romans. But the Roman troops continued to push and push, keeping their formation, holding their line. At this crucial point Polybius claims the Carthaginian troops behind the mercenaries did not come to the aid of the front line, which eventually collapsed and turned back under the Roman pressure. The mercenary troops then turned on the Carthaginian forces behind them and they began to fight among themselves and the Romans. It was carnage and the Roman troops cut through them. Hannibal commanded his core troops to hold the line and not allow the retreating fighters to join them. They were forced out to the flanks and the ground became soaked in blood and covered in 'slippery corpses . . . fallen in heaps'. Scipio regrouped and advanced over the dead towards Hannibal's crack troops: here 'they were nearly equal in numbers as well as in spirit and bravery'. This fierce fighting was relieved only when Masinissa and Laelius, who had returned from their pursuit of the opposing cavalry, fell on Hannibal's troops from behind, surrounded and cut them down. It was a rout and Polybius claims that 20,000 of Hannibal's army were killed and many more again were captured (Polyb. 15.13–14).

Hannibal and all that remained of his defeated army galloped back to Hadrumentum (Polyb. 15.15.3). Victory at Zama for Hannibal had never been very likely for he had fought with a vastly inferior army.[80] Scipio's superior force was trained in combat and had the power of momentum that successive victories bring. Hannibal was short of cavalry and allies, and although he had elephants and more infantry, he did not have a cohesive and unified force under his command. Indeed, his men were as destructive to each other as to the enemy. Scipio was a formidable military strategist and although Hannibal 'had shown incomparable skill' he would have needed more than just ability to pull off a victory at Zama.[81] For Scipio, success at Zama brought greater acclaim than any other deed in his career, for he was the first and only Roman to have defeated Hannibal in a large 'set piece' battle.[82]

CHAPTER 12

# HANNIBAL INTO EXILE

A fine sight it must have been,
Fit subject for caricature, the one-eyed commander
Perched on his monstrous beast! Alas, alas for glory,
What an end was here: the defeat, the ignominious
Flight into exile, everyone crowding to see
The once-mighty Hannibal turned humble hanger-on,
Sitting outside the door of a petty Eastern despot
**(Juvenal, *Satire* 10, 158–164)**

AFTER ZAMA, SCIPIO REMAINED the 'unconquered' and Hannibal, for the first time, was defeated.[1] Few of the ancient accounts of Zama find fault with Hannibal's command at the final clash and most praise both his bravery and ability. 'For there are times when Fortune counteracts the plans of valiant men, and again at times, as the proverb says, "A brave man meets another braver yet",', was Polybius' verdict (15.16.6). 'Scipio,' according to Livy, 'and all military experts, had to admit that Hannibal had deserved credit for his remarkably skilful deployment of the battle line that day' (30.35.5–6). So although no longer invincible, even in defeat Hannibal retained his status as a legendary military tactician and heroic leader.

Hannibal escaped the scene of the battle on horseback pursued by Masinissa as he galloped towards Hadrumentum with a few of his men.[2] Certainly wary of the fate that awaited a failed general at Carthage, Hannibal may have taken the opportunity to consolidate whatever support he had left.

From Hadrumentum he was summoned to Carthage and finally, for the first time in thirty-six years, at the age of forty-five, he set foot in the city where he was born.[3] He must have been as much of a curiosity to the people of Carthage as he had been to the Capuans fourteen years previously. In front of the Senate at Carthage Hannibal conceded defeat and advised the Carthaginians that their only hope now was to sue for peace. There were still some at Carthage who wanted to resist, but Hannibal forcefully opposed those he realized 'did not want peace but were incapable of war' (Livy 30.35–37).[4]

Scipio became the first Roman commander 'to be honoured with the name of the nation he defeated' and was known as Africanus after Zama (Livy 30.45.6). He dictated the peace terms, and the treaty to end the Second Punic War was ratified by 201 BCE. The conditions were, not surprisingly, punitive given the intensity and length of the war. In addition to the restoration of hostages and deserters, Carthage had to pay financial reparations to Rome in the form of 10,000 talents in instalments over fifty years.[5] On top of that Scipio chose one hundred hostages, young men between the ages of fourteen and thirty, to be taken to Rome as guarantors of the treaty. All of the war elephants at Carthage were surrendered and the entire Carthaginian fleet was burned in the bay off the city while the population looked on.[6] Their territory was restricted but left largely intact, although the Carthaginians were forbidden to wage war outside Africa, and within Africa they had to seek authorization from Rome to take military action against their neighbours (Polyb. 15.18.1–2; Livy 30.37.2).[7] It was a humiliating peace whose real beneficiary was Masinissa. He retained his ancestral kingdom and added that of his rival Syphax to his domains (Livy 30.44.12).[8] Masinissa had become the most powerful man in North Africa and a firm ally of the Romans.

Hannibal's whereabouts in the direct aftermath of the peace debate in the Carthaginian Senate remain unclear and for a period of almost five years he is virtually invisible. He was no longer a focus for the Roman sources that tell his story. Their attention moved on to other foes. His biographer Cornelius Nepos claims that Hannibal remained at the head of the Carthaginian army but Nepos' account of Hannibal's life includes some significant errors of fact, which make his version of events rather suspect (Hann. 7. 1–4).[9] Another story claims that Hannibal employed his troops in public works projects, planting olive trees in vast numbers in the period after Zama.[10] A surviving fragment of the later Roman historian Cassius Dio perhaps offers another glimpse into the aftermath of Hannibal's defeat. According to Dio, 'Hannibal was accused by his own people of having refused to capture Rome when he was able to do so and of having appropriated the plunder from Italy' (Cassius

Dio 17, frag. 86; Zonaras 14–15). Like the other Carthaginian generals before him, Hannibal may have stood trial at Carthage, prosecuted for his management of the war in Italy. The accusation that Hannibal could have captured Rome but chose not to remains a part of the long-standing debate on Hannibal's strategy. The idea that after Trasimeno or Cannae Hannibal could or should have attacked Rome was part of the popular narrative of the Second Punic War and the ancient historical debate.[11] The charges laid against Hannibal also included the appropriation of plunder, which suggests an on-going dispute between Hannibal and Carthage over financial support for the war. Hannibal, as far as we know, had received virtually no support in terms of supply and reinforcement from Carthage for the whole time he fought in Italy.[12] He would have retained any plunder for his own resources out of necessity, to supply and pay his troops. Dio goes on to note that Hannibal was not 'convicted' of these charges and mounted a successful defence of his actions. The great general still had many supporters at Carthage.[13]

It is worth considering whether Hannibal could have avoided the piecemeal war in southern Italy that played out after Cannae. Perhaps if he had managed to hold one of the three main cities he controlled, especially either port of Syracuse or Tarentum, there would have been a base from which to resupply and attack the Romans. The continued Roman dominance of the seas remained an intractable problem. Later, in exile looking back on his invasion, Hannibal remained convinced that his strategy had been the correct one. He encouraged the Seleucid king Antiochus III to invade Italy precisely because 'it would provide both supplies and troops to an external enemy, but that if nothing was attempted there and the Roman people were allowed to wage war outside of Italy with Italy's strength and forces, neither the king nor any nation was Rome's equal' (Livy 34.60.3).[14] If we are to believe Livy, even in defeat Hannibal still held that his strategy, although not successful, had been the only one worth attempting.

The fact that Hannibal was able to remain for so long in southern Italy is, in itself, an impressive statement of the talent of the man. The Roman forces in Italy vastly outnumbered the Carthaginian army. The unending replenishment of the manpower of the Roman legions illustrates what a formidable presence Hannibal was in Italy. Livy's narrative focuses on the heroic nature of the Roman fightback after Cannae but this detracts from the equally heroic Carthaginian war effort and the skill of Hannibal himself. His adaptability, force of personality and creativity in constantly threatening situations were extraordinary. That it took the Romans four years to dislodge Hannibal from Campania alone, when he was largely without reinforcements from

Carthage or Iberia, speaks highly of his strategic abilities even though he ultimately failed.[15]

At Carthage following the peace with Rome the atmosphere was fractious and divided, and many people blamed Hannibal for the woes of the city whilst Hannibal was embittered by his treatment there. He seems to have retired from the city and kept a low profile at this time. It is not until six years after Zama in *c.* 196 BCE that Hannibal reappears in the public sphere. Cassius Dio tells us that when his trial finished Hannibal was 'entrusted with the highest office in Carthage' and became one of the two *sufetes* in that year (Cassius Dio 17, frag. 86). This was Hannibal's first and only attempt at civilian administration at Carthage. It would have been an excellent use of his many skills, given that during the years in Italy he had kept his army together throughout the war. The appointment of Hannibal as *sufet* was a step too far, however, for the families that had opposed him and now had ascendancy in the Carthaginian Senate. Rivalry among the elite families of Carthage was as intense and ruthless as that in Rome. The resurrection of Hannibal as a political leader in Carthage created turmoil among the enemies of the Barcids. There were those at Carthage so hostile to any revival of Barcid power that they were willing to plot with the Romans to bring down their most famous citizen.[16]

Hannibal may well have applied the same rigour to government as he did to military matters (Cornelius Nepos, *Hann.* 7.5). He introduced reforms to the Carthaginian constitution that would weaken the power of the ruling elites.[17] He set about reorganizing the state finances to help pay the war indemnity to Rome. It has often been commented, with some surprise, that Carthage seems to have been unusually prosperous in the period just after the end of the war.[18] There are visible changes in town planning that indicate growth in the urban centre and new, elaborately constructed ports that date to this period. Thus despite its losses and the financial reparations paid to Rome, Carthage was a viable and thriving market in the decades after the war. Hannibal cannot take all the credit for this prosperity but it is possible that much-needed reforms introduced during his *sufetate* had a positive impact on the Carthaginian economy in the post-war years.

Equally important to Carthage's growing prosperity was the newly acquired prestige and developing identity of the Numidian kingdom of Masinissa. As Masinissa's enlarged realm developed, an increased demand for luxury goods and commodities traded through the Mediterranean aided the Carthaginian financial recovery.[19] Carthage was ideally placed to capitalize on growing Mediterranean commerce. The rapid growth in trade across the region in the second century saw the city prosper greatly. So although the Numidian kingdom of Masinissa would play an important part in bringing about the destruction of Carthage, in the short term its burgeoning wealth only added to Carthaginian prosperity. The Romans would have looked on with some alarm at the resilience of their recently defeated foes who appeared to be thriving. An offer from Carthage to pay off the entire indemnity in *c.* 191 BCE (forty years early) would have irked them even more (Livy 36.4.8).[20]

While acting as *sufet*, Hannibal accused some leading members of the Carthaginian Senate of embezzlement of public funds (Livy 33.46.3).[21] He must have been a divisive figure for the politicians in Carthage. Many would have resented his presence whilst others were intimately connected to the power system that sustained Hannibal. Livy comments that 'whatever popularity he won among the common people by this move was matched by the resentment he provoked in the majority of the leading citizens' (33.46.7). This suggests that Hannibal circumvented the hostility of some of his magisterial colleagues by appealing to the popular assembly. Once his year in office was finished, long-time enemies still active in the Carthaginian government conspired to get rid of Hannibal once and for all.

Concurrently, Rome was preparing for war in the eastern Mediterranean against the Seleucid king Antiochus III. Letters were sent to the Roman Senate claiming that Hannibal was conspiring against them and that he was in secret contact with the Seleucid monarch. On receipt of these accusations Scipio Africanus spoke on behalf of his old enemy in the Roman Senate but it was to no avail (Livy 33.47.4). The Senate at Rome sent an envoy to Carthage to ask that Hannibal be indicted on the charge of 'plotting war' with Antiochus. Hannibal was declared an enemy of the state at Carthage and was charged with breaking the treaty with Rome. He was outlawed in Carthage and his house destroyed by rival factions (Livy 33. 47–49; Cornelius Nepos, *Hann.* 7; Justin 31.1–2).

Hannibal had been undermined from within his own city and he had allowed his enemies to gain the upper hand. At that moment he faced a choice: stay and deal with prosecution in Rome or flee for his life. He chose to flee and left Carthaginian territory in 195 BCE. He travelled first (perhaps) to his home region near the city of Hadrumentum and then on to the sandy island of Kerkina, off the coast near the modern city of Sfax. On Kerkina, where merchants gathered to trade in the markets, he boarded a Phoenician trading vessel that carried him on to Tyre (Livy 33.48.3).

It is worth considering that Hannibal had been agitating against the Romans and as *sufet* would have had contact with many representatives from

across the Mediterranean. In this role he may well have listened to and encouraged those from the Hellenistic east who were hoping to put a halt to the
expansion of Roman power.[22] Nonetheless, there is the belief that the charges
against Hannibal were politically motivated and trumped up. Whatever
Hannibal's real intentions, it might have been naïve to assume that by entering
politics he would be allowed to escape the psychological impact of his years as
Rome's great enemy. His fellow Carthaginians and Roman enemies would not
allow his family to rise once again to a position of influence at Carthage.
Hannibal's political ideas had always been based on keeping Carthage beyond
the reach of Roman hegemony and retaining its existence as an autonomous
state.[23] These beliefs would have brought him into direct conflict with Rome's
increasing appetite for conquest.

On leaving Carthaginian territory Hannibal became a 'castaway of fortune'
and entered the murky world of Hellenistic politics (Plutarch, *Flam.* 20.2).
The journey took him from the sandy island of Kerkina on a Tyrian ship
heading east across the Mediterranean. The Barcid family traced their roots
back to the original colonists from Tyre and Hannibal arrived at the city, a
'son of Tyre' now in exile.[24] Tyre was part of the Seleucid kingdom at the time
and Hannibal's natural choice of refuge was with the king, Antiochus III.
Antiochus' power was increasing in the face of the Roman defeat of the
Macedonians. The second Romano-Macedonian war (200–197 BCE) had
ended in the defeat of Hannibal's old ally Philip at Cynoscephalae. Antiochus
had just come to peace terms with the Ptolemaic king in Egypt and he seemed
the strongest option to oppose the growing might of Rome.[25] The Romans
viewed Antiochus and the Seleucids as the biggest obstacle to their extension
of influence and control.

Hannibal was now in his early fifties. His fame had spread across the wider
Mediterranean and as Rome's power grew Hannibal seems to have been a
focal point for anti-Roman agitation. When he put himself in the service of
the Seleucid king he was welcomed and his reputation as Rome's great enemy
was celebrated. Conflict with the Romans was imminent and Antiochus may
have hoped that Hannibal held the secret of how to defeat Roman power.
What actual role Hannibal held at the court of Antiochus is nowhere clearly
defined. He is vaguely said to have provided the king with guidance and direction and in essence became a Hellenistic warlord at a foreign court. It was not
a position Hannibal was used to, and court life under Antiochus was full of
jealousies, intrigue, threats of usurpation and betrayals. This must have been
difficult for him to navigate as a military commander whose life had been
spent on the field of battle. Cicero describes a renowned Hannibal at Ephesus

where 'his name was held in great honour among all men' invited to hear a philosopher named Phormio pontificate 'upon the duties of a general and the whole military art'. Hannibal spoke rather frankly of what he thought of the philosopher 'in not very good Greek but with very good sense'. He commented wryly that 'he had seen many doting old men, but had never seen anyone deeper in his dotage than Phormio'. The impression of the world-weary commander with little time for the niceties of court life shines through Cicero's anecdote (*De oratore* 2.75–76).

The Romans were unnerved by Hannibal's links with Antiochus. We hear reports of how envoys from Rome and their allies the Attalid kings tried to undermine Hannibal's position with Antiochus. Scipio Africanus even visited the court and tried to drive a wedge between Hannibal and the king. There are suggestions that Antiochus was jealous of Hannibal's status and celebrity and disliked the fact that everyone had placed all their hopes in him (Cassius Dio frag. 19).[26] Hannibal responded to the accusations with the story of the sacred vow he had taken as a nine-year-old boy and the promise he made to his father – never to be an ally of Rome. The earliest version of the oath was (probably) written down by Polybius and was repeated so often that it has become an essential part of Hannibal's story. He might have felt slightly insulted at having to convince Antiochus of his loyalty and of his eternal enmity to the Romans (Polyb. 3.11; Livy 35.19). Such was the atmosphere of mistrust at the court that Rome's greatest enemy felt he had to prove to the king that his hostility towards the Romans was genuine.[27]

A few years after leaving Carthage (*c.* 193 BCE) Hannibal is rumoured to have returned to Africa, landing with five ships in the region of Cyrene. He may have been testing the ground to see if he could reach out to the Carthaginians. He must have met with representatives from Carthage there, perhaps drumming up support for Antiochus' upcoming battle against the Romans. Our report of this visit is fraught with difficulties and full of errors so it becomes problematic to accept the detail of the story as factual (Cornelius Nepos, *Hann.* 8.1–2).[28] However, it is not beyond the realm of possibility that Hannibal still had many supporters at Carthage who would be willing to continue to fight against Rome. Livy reports that Hannibal 'had every confidence that the Carthaginians also could be induced to rebel by his persuasion' (Livy 34.60.5). In Ephesus Hannibal had met a man from Tyre named Ariston. He trained him as an agent and sent him to Carthage loaded with gifts and 'a code of secret signs' to be used to make contact with the Barcid supporters (Livy 34.61.2–3). There is much of interest in Livy's tale of the agent Ariston who, with his secret handshakes, acted as a Barcid agitator at

Carthage. He held covert meetings with Hannibal's supporters but was quickly found out by his enemies as well. Ariston was called up in front of the Carthaginian Senate to explain his actions. Nothing further seems to have come of the attempts to increase support for another war at Carthage and Ariston escaped on a ship back to Tyre (Livy 34.61.14). We can see Hannibal here in his role of agitator against Roman power even though at Carthage, whilst he still had allies, his popular support seems to have waned.[29]

Antiochus never fully accepted Hannibal into his inner circle of advisors and the Carthaginian would play a peripheral role in the ensuing fight with Rome. Of the many councils of war held in the run-up to battle Hannibal was only invited to a few, and when he spoke the king and his advisors did not appreciate his counsel (Justin 31.5.1–9). At the battle of Magnesia in *c.* 190 BCE the Romans and their allies the Attalid kings defeated Antiochus. The ensuing peace treaty, signed at Apamea in 188 BCE, strictly limited the Seleucids' power and essentially stripped them of all their territorial possessions in Asia Minor. The specific terms agreed that 'they were to give up all possessions west of the Taurus mountains . . . and in addition Antiochus was to give up Hannibal the Carthaginian . . .' among others (Polyb. 21.17.3–7; Livy 37.45.3). Hannibal had not played a pivotal role in the battle and had commanded a small part of the fleet that was defeated by the Rhodian navy.[30] Now aged fifty-seven, Hannibal once again found himself on the losing side of a fight against Rome. Antiochus could no longer offer him a place of refuge and he was forced to depart from Seleucid territory.

After the Peace of Apamea the Roman-allied Attalid kings of Pergamon acquired temporary dominance among the Hellenistic kingdoms in the east. Hannibal's options narrowed further as Attalid influence expanded in the region. His trail becomes elusive in the five years after the battle of Magnesia. The stories of his travels are embellished by legends of tricks and stratagems performed on hapless locals and the great wealth which he carried with him. There is a rumour that he visited Gortyn in Crete before he took refuge in Armenia and then settled in Bithynia, an independent kingdom in Asia Minor whose king, Prusias, was at war with the Attalid king Eumenes II.[31] Hannibal continued to fight the anti-Roman cause for Prusias. One of his most impressive manoeuvres came while commanding the Bithynian fleet. Ships under Hannibal's command are reported to have catapulted ceramic pots filled with poisonous snakes on to the decks of the enemy vessels.[32] The soldiers on the Attalid ships at first laughed at the strategy, but as the vessels began to fill with the snakes laughter turned to panic and they conceded victory (Justin 32.4.6–8).

In the end, however, Prusias lost his war with Eumenes and a requirement of the subsequent peace treaty was again that Hannibal be handed over to the Romans. He remained their most wanted enemy. There are many versions of what followed. Most imply that Hannibal saw the end of his options and chose to commit suicide rather than fall into Roman hands, but none is certain. He was by then 'a frail old man' living in a house by the sea in the town of Libyssa (between Istanbul and Izmit in modern Turkey). We are told that Hannibal was living a quiet life in retirement. His Roman enemies were not content to let matters rest even though Hannibal now posed no real threat. By this time Hannibal's reputation alone was enough to rally opposition to Rome and the Romans would take no chances.[33]

The exact details of his death may rest with the contents of a ring he always wore. He reportedly carried poison with him so that he would never fall victim to a Roman plot to seize him. The Romans would have liked nothing more than to parade their great enemy through Rome in chains. In Livy's version Hannibal takes a cup of poison. Just before he drank he is reported to have said, 'Let us now put an end to the great anxiety of the Romans, who have thought it too long and hard a task to wait for the death of a hated old man' (Livy 39.51.9). Hannibal died aged sixty-five in the year 183/182 BCE, the year that saw the death of his nemesis, Scipio Africanus.[34]

Hannibal, the general and strategist whose brilliant military mind engineered some of the most devastating defeats ever inflicted on the armies of Rome, was perhaps surprised to meet his end quietly in old age. His implacable opposition to the growing power of Rome had made him the focus for resistance to its imperial ambitions for over forty years. He died as he had spent most of his life, as an outsider in a land far from Carthage. Yet he is inextricably linked to the fate of Carthage and is remembered as the most famous Carthaginian of them all. This is the ultimate paradox of Hannibal. The great adventures of his career and the stunning military victories put him in the league of elite Hellenistic commanders in an age of conquest. He was and has been universally considered one of the greatest military strategists of all time. Yet essential to his story is that just thirty-six years after his death, the city of Carthage was completely destroyed and burned to the ground by the Romans in a vengeful war. Hannibal had come very close to defeating Roman power but ultimately failed. His attempts to save Carthage from Rome's dominance may well have contributed to her ultimate destruction. Yet even in his failure the Romans both admired and feared Hannibal. As a result of this and 'his world renowned exploits', in death he has retained a kind of heroic notoriety far exceeding that of all his enemies (Diodorus Sic. 29.19).

# EPILOGUE
## HANNIBAL'S AFTERLIFE

M EMORIES OF WAR LINGER long after they are fought and memories of epic wars especially so.[1] There would not have been a family across the whole of the western Mediterranean at the beginning of the second century BCE that did not have a story, a memory or a familial death connected to the Hannibalic War. The war became the paradigm for subsequent great wars in Roman memory. Hannibal became the most renowned enemy of the Romans and outstanding general of his generation. We do not know how the Carthaginians remembered Hannibal or how Hannibal's position in the memory of the Punic people lived on in North Africa. We do know that members of the Carthaginian Senate who went to Rome to negotiate peace blamed the entire war on Hannibal and absolved themselves from any responsibility. The idea that Hannibal was driven by a hatred of the Romans passed on to him by his father and was the sole cause of the war seemed to be an explanation to which both sides were willing to subscribe.[2] Among his supporters at Carthage Hannibal may have been remembered as a hero who had challenged the Roman oppressor and as the greatest ever Carthaginian general. Few Carthaginian commanders had been able to inflict losses on the Romans in the previous decades of war; Hannibal and his brothers were among a very select group. With Carthaginian memories lost to us it is the memories of the conquerors that have been preserved for posterity. Hannibal's fame and skill were celebrated by his enemies, along with the paradox of his Carthaginian deceptions. These are the seeds from which Hannibal's heroic status grew and flourished across the ages.

Hannibal's legend was initially shaped in Iberia, where the destruction of Saguntum brought him face to face with the power of Rome. When he first appears in Livy he is a brave captain serving as an apprentice to his brother-in-law Hasdrubal. 'The older soldiers thought that a young Hamilcar had been brought back to them; they saw that same dynamism in his expression, the same forcefulness in his eyes, the same facial expression and features . . .' In Livy's picture Hannibal's appearance recalled his father and stirred the loyalty of his soldiers. Livy continues, 'there was no one whom Hasdrubal preferred to put in command when a gallant or enterprising feat was called for, while there was no other officer under whom the rank and file had more confidence and enterprise' (Livy 21.4.2–5). Hannibal's life had become legendary by the time Livy wrote and it is difficult to separate the reality of the man from the construction of his myth.

Aspects of Livy's description read like the quintessential Hellenistic leader. Hannibal's persona, as sketched by Livy, is not dissimilar to Plutarch's account of the general Pyrrhus: 'they compared his appearance and the speed and vigour of his movements to those of Alexander the Great, and felt that they saw in him an image and reflection of that hero's fire and impetuosity in the field' (*Pyrr.* 8). Hannibal, like Pyrrhus, was a youthful and heroic commander who could inspire his troops by his very presence. He reminded his men of the great generals who had come before. Hannibal was described like Pyrrhus, and Pyrrhus was compared to Alexander the Great.

Polybius lived closest to Hannibal's time and consulted some who had known him, including the one-time ally of the Carthaginians, Masinissa (9.25.4). From his researches he concludes that Hannibal was one of history's great men and calls him an 'extraordinary product of nature', capable of carrying out 'any project within the reach of human endeavour' (9.22.6; 11.19.1–7). Going even further he enthuses that 'no one can withhold admiration for Hannibal's generalship, courage, and power in the field' (11.19.1). Polybius portrayed Hannibal at the beginning of the war not only as a military genius but also as having all-round superior qualities as a man. The terms he used to discuss Hannibal were similar to those he employed when writing of the Greek scientist Archimedes during the Roman siege of Syracuse (8.5–7).[3] The loyalty to Hannibal among his troops was a product of his genius, his force of personality, and his practical approach to sharing out the spoils of the victories with all his soldiers. The inclusiveness Hannibal displayed towards his army was celebrated – all his soldiers had a place and were valued. He famously claimed, according to Ennius, that 'he who should strike the enemy, shall be a Carthaginian in my eyes, whoever he shall be. Wherever he hails from . . .'.[4] To join Hannibal's cause was enough and he maintained a strong sense of solidarity among his soldiers throughout his leadership. An incredible talent to manage people, to organize, negotiate and create loyalty augmented Hannibal's ability as a military strategist. He kept his army in service, in the field, highly functioning for the better part of sixteen years. He fed, clothed and supplied his men and, most importantly, kept them under his control and loyal in the most extreme circumstances.

Along with genius, however, came charges of cruelty and avarice, both flaws that Polybius was willing to concede might be a result of the 'force of circumstances' rather than the true nature of the man (9.24.1–3, 25–26). In fact the claims against Hannibal were fairly typical of those made by victors about the enemy: breaking of treaties, displacing inhabitants to other towns, confiscating property for plunder, impiety, cruelty.[5] The accusations of avarice made by Polybius should be seen in light of Hannibal's needs. His army and allies depended on him and to succeed he needed to secure a huge amount of wealth.[6] We are left, however, with the paradox of Hannibal's generosity to his troops and this alleged avarice, both of which play an important part in the construction of his afterlife.

Hannibal set out to change the paradigm of power in the western Mediterranean and succeeded, but not in the way that he intended. Instead of restricting Rome's power, it was the Romans who emerged as masters over the dominions of the Carthaginians by the end of the war.[7] The resulting transfer of power, the combination of the Carthaginian and Roman resources and skills, allowed the Romans to take on the divided eastern Mediterranean with the whole force of the west. The Punic Wars had honed the Romans' skills of warfare. Their navy was now unchallenged and their generals schooled by encounters with Hannibal. The newly allied troops from the Celtic and Iberian lands, combined with the cavalry capable of the best traditions of the Numidians, would help to create a military machine that conquered all in its path. The legacy of Hannibal was the creation of Rome as the only major power in the western Mediterranean and, subsequently, the only power in the whole Mediterranean.[8]

Thus the memory of Hannibal lies deep in the creation of Roman power. We have seen that the myth of Hannibal was born well before his death, its origins lying in ideas of Hellenistic heroic leadership and his own propaganda. This depiction lay in the heart of his supporters and his enemies, both in Carthage and in Rome. By linking his adventure to the labours of his patron god Melqart/Herakles in his propaganda, Hannibal ensured that the tales and legends of his divine patronage arrived in Italy well before he did in 218 BCE.[9]

The stories were propagated both to promote the cohesion of his army and to win over the population along his route. When Hannibal wrote his *res gestae* on a bronze plaque at the temple of Juno Lacinia near Crotona, he was attempting to place his deeds within the wider Hellenistic Mediterranean.[10]

Yet Hannibal's words were almost completely erased as the Romans went on to conquer the known world and build an empire without any serious challenge to their authority. The whole of the Mediterranean remained Roman territory for the next 500 years. The Hannibalic War was therefore a critical moment in the self-definition of the Romans both as a people and a power.[11] The Romans treated their wars with Carthage as worthy of epic from the very beginning. The First Punic War was glorified in the *Bellum Poenica* of the third-century Latin poet Naevius. Ennius' account of the Hannibalic War (second century) provided a contemporary view from the Roman perspective. The deeds of Rome in the war with Hannibal were lauded in epic poetry whose traditions can be traced back through the western Mediterranean to the Trojan War. The stories of the Punic Wars are connected with the myths and legends of the star-crossed lovers Dido and Aeneas, who are first linked together during this period of conflict between the two cities.[12] Thus the tales of Carthage and Rome were interwoven with the Greek traditions of famous deeds and heroic wars. These traditions combine through the surviving narrative history of the Hannibalic War.

As Rome went on to construct an empire, a key part of the process was the celebration of the heroes of its past. For Scipio Africanus to be considered a military genius it required that Hannibal be a worthy adversary, a foe equal to the conqueror. The Roman hero's success lay in his ability to adapt Roman troops to Hannibal's style. Hannibal's war taught a generation of Romans how to succeed against a Hellenistic army. Thus it is not just Scipio's reputation that was forged by his encounter with Hannibal but also that of the Roman generals Fabius Maximus, Marcellus and their sons.[13] So great was Rome during these decades of conquest that Hannibal had to be equally so. It is fascinating that over time it was the reputation and celebrity of Hannibal, even more than those of his Roman foes, that flourished in the Roman world and beyond.

In the city of Rome memorial and commemoration of the Hannibalic War would have dominated the ritual landscape for many decades. The victory monuments and temples vowed during the fighting became part of the city's architecture and memory. The list of structures set up in Rome over the period of the Punic Wars runs to hundreds of temples and altars dedicated by the victorious generals. These constitute the visible commemoration of the battles with Hannibal and were found throughout the centre of the city.[14] The spoils from the cities conquered during the war – Syracuse, Capua, Tarentum, and eventually Carthage – decorated Rome. For centuries afterwards the landscape of the city kept the memory of Hannibal alive. When Plutarch wrote '. . . near that of the great Apollo, brought from Carthage, opposite to the Circus Maximus' (*Flam.* 1) he reveals a snippet of the epic landscape that kept Hannibal and Carthage alive in the Roman mind.[15] Valerius Maximus adds to our knowledge of the Roman memorial landscape. He notes that the Apollo from Carthage stood in Rome without its cloak of gold or its hands. These had been chopped off during the looting of Carthage by soldiers who had committed sacrilege by doing so (1.1.18). The statue stood as a symbol in Rome of the sack of Carthage and the final destruction of the city's great enemy.

The defeats that Hannibal inflicted on the Roman armies were equally etched into the visual memory of the war. The spot where humans were sacrificed after the defeat at Cannae was still marked centuries later. The temples vowed by each senator during the war stood in the centre of the city. Moreover, a gold shield bearing the portrait of Hasdrubal Barca and weighing 137 pounds hung on the great temple of Jupiter Capitolinus at Rome.[16] The visual narrative of the Punic Wars became an integral part of the physical surroundings of the city of Rome.

The period of the Punic Wars was a time of great social change in the wider Mediterranean. As the Roman world expanded quickly and the Republic took on the entire Mediterranean and won, the records of these times reflected the conservative memory of those who created them. The upheaval and social change, political violence and civil wars that followed the conquests were ultimately blamed by some ancient commentators on the influence of foreign luxury, foreign gods and a loss of traditional Roman morality. Central to this period of social upheaval were the wars Rome fought with Carthage, but especially the Hannibalic War. In the mind of some Romans of the Late Republic – when there was no one left to conquer and Rome's generals had turned on each other in civil strife – historians could look back on the war with Hannibal with some nostalgia.

A contemporary theory held that fear of a mortal enemy was a restraining factor on the Roman state. This idea developed less than a century after the end of Hannibal's war when there was again fighting in Africa. At this time it was the Numidian king Jugurtha, a grandson of Masinissa, who challenged Roman hegemony.[17] This idea of the mortal enemy developed in the writing of Sallust, a historian of the Late Republic and the African wars of Jugurtha.

For Sallust the fall of Carthage in the second century BCE removed the fear of Carthage as embodied by Hannibal and the challenge he represented to the Roman state. Sallust believed that this fear had imposed a kind of political restraint on the state and that the Roman Republic needed the discipline of a great enemy for it to function at its best. Today we only have to look back to the fondness with which people remember the Cold War, or the social cohesion of the Second World War years, to understand this point of view.[18] Fear is an important factor in political unity within states, and this is perhaps only slightly less true today than it was for the Romans.

Through the chaotic years of the late Roman Republic this idea grew more powerful as the Romans turned on each other and civil war tore their society apart. The most enduring versions of the Carthaginian wars and Hannibal were developed in the period of the Late Republic and into the principate of Augustus. Rhetoric and poetry used the battles with Hannibal and Carthage as a backdrop to depict the true virtues of the Roman people. In these years Cicero, Livy and the poets Virgil, Horace, Ovid and Propertius wrote into orthodoxy the deeds of the Romans who fought Hannibal.[19]

The assessment of Hannibal's identity and legacy thus changed from the immediate aftermath of the war and the destruction of Carthage, through to the end of the Roman Republic. Representations of Hannibal varied according to the way the Romans remembered their own past.[20] Cicero, writing in the last years of the civil wars, both condemned Hannibal's Carthaginian treachery and also held him up, on occasion, as a model for Romans to live by.[21] For Livy (in the later first century BCE) Hannibal was the most dangerous enemy that Rome had ever faced and in his defeat Rome was at her best. At the time of Silius Italicus (first century CE) Hannibal could be seen 'merely as an Alexander impersonator' who squandered his talents but had orchestrated the greatest threat to Roman hegemony.[22] As Roman power grew, enemies of quality were harder to find, and the challenge that Hannibal had represented also grew. There were no more enemies like Hannibal to contend with. Pliny the Elder (first century CE) tells us that at least three statues of Hannibal could be found in the city of Rome in his time (*NH* 34.32). The commemoration of this illustrious enemy was essential to Rome's glorification of its own power and might.

The intended heroes of Silius Italicus' epic poem on the Punic Wars were the men of the Republic, whose virtues were held up as moral examples to the Romans of the Empire. These were the men who fought and defeated Hannibal. The tales of Roman glory and the moral example of the illustrious ancestors had an important part in the education of young Roman men in the

Empire. A fearful and great enemy was an idea in the political thinking of the ancient Romans and lent itself to traditional views of the rise and fall of states.[23] We are told that Scipio Aemilianus, grandson of Scipio Africanus, wept at the fall of Carthage in 146 BCE, because he saw in its demise the future of Rome itself (Appian, *Lib.* 132). Valerius Maximus, writing during the reign of the emperor Tiberius, evokes the memory of Roman glory as a linear progression towards the ultimate height, which is that of the imperial state.[24] In his description of the debate in the Senate at the end of the Hannibalic War, Valerius Maximus (7.2.3) also evokes the power of a great enemy. When the proconsul Metellus questions whether the peace will bring good or ill to the state, he implies that Hannibal's presence had kept the Romans alert and ready for anything.[25] The Romans of the Empire believed that the machine of the Roman Republic functioned at its best when facing an external threat. Hannibal's role in the formation of Roman greatness blurs real insights into his character. He became an enemy for all times.

Hannibal's story connects to many different Roman rhetorical and historical traditions. The satirist Juvenal succinctly reduced Hannibal's achievements to a few lines of poetry.

> Put Hannibal in the scales: how many pounds will that peerless
> General weigh today? A man for whom Africa
> Was too small a continent, though it stretched from the surf-beaten
> Ocean shores of Morocco east to the steamy Nile,
> To Ethiopian tribesmen – and new elephants' habitats
> Now Spain swells his empire, now he surmounts
> The Pyrenees. Nature throws in his path
> High Alpine passes, blizzards of snow: but he splits
> The very rocks asunder, moves mountains – with vinegar.
> Now Italy is his, yet still he forces on. (*Satires* **10.147–159**)

By the time Juvenal wrote his poetry the fear of Hannibal and of the threat he posed was two and a half centuries old. In two separate satires Juvenal mentions schoolboys having to debate whether or not Hannibal should have marched on Rome after Cannae. So deeply embedded was Hannibal in Roman culture that he became a rhetorical exercise for every child at school. His role was 'to entertain schoolboys, and provide matter for their speeches'.[26] Roman power had reigned supreme for centuries but the legend of Hannibal was still active. For Juvenal, Hannibal could be ridiculed without fear, the

potency had gone but the reputation remained, he was the 'one eye'd general
. . . who had troubled humanity'.

Scipio's legend equalled or surpassed that of Hannibal, as demonstrated
(or possibly imagined) by a famous scene at the court of Antiochus III at
Ephesus where the two old foes faced each other in the 190s BCE. The scene
was set in the gymnasium where Scipio, as Roman envoy at the court of the
Seleucid king, approached Hannibal. Scipio asked Hannibal whom he considered to be the greatest of generals. Hannibal's first answer was Alexander of
Macedon. 'To this Scipio agreed, since he also yielded the first place to
Alexander.' Then Scipio went on to ask Hannibal whom he placed second
to Alexander and Hannibal replied, 'Pyrrhus of Epirus' because he considered
boldness the first qualification of a general. Hannibal thought it would be
impossible to 'find two kings more enterprising than these'. Scipio was rather
piqued by this, but nevertheless he went on to ask Hannibal to whom he
would give the third place, 'expecting that at least the third would be assigned
to him'. Hannibal replied, however, 'to myself; for when I was a young man I
conquered Spain and crossed the Alps with an army, the first after Hercules.
I invaded Italy and struck terror into all of you, laid waste 400 of your towns,
and often put your city in extreme peril, all this time receiving neither money
nor reinforcements from Carthage.'

Scipio laughed at the answer and asked 'where would you place yourself,
Hannibal, if you had not been defeated by me? Hannibal, now perceiving his
jealousy, replied, "In that case I should have put myself before Alexander."
Thus Hannibal flattered Scipio in a delicate manner by suggesting that he had
conquered one who was the superior to Alexander' (Appian, *Syr.* 910). It is a
lovely story and reflects the view of later generations that Scipio and Hannibal
were among the most remarkable military commanders who had ever lived.
Livy describes them as 'the greatest generals not merely of their own day, but
of the whole of history down to his [Livy's] time' (30.30.1).

Appian's is not the only extant discussion on the eternal question of 'who
was the best' general of antiquity. The comic prose of Lucian of Samosata's
*Dialogues of the Dead* (380–398) presents the fantasy comparison between
Alexander the Great and Hannibal. The story is set before Minos, one of judges
of the dead in the Underworld, who is to announce the final verdict on each
man's claim to be the finest military commander in the world. The two men
bicker over who should go first. 'I should be heard before you, Libyan; I am
the better man,' claims Alexander. Their introduction before an impressed
Minos elicits the response, 'both famous [men] indeed'. There is room in the
competition for the glorification of the Roman soldiers of the mid-Republic

and denigration of the Persians through the words of Hannibal: 'My rivals were the ablest generals in the world, commanding the best soldiers in the world; I warred not with Medes or Assyrians, who fly before they are pursued, and yield the victory to him that dares take it.'[27] Scipio, as is fitting, makes an appearance and Hannibal ends up being judged the last of the three.[28]

By the time of Lucian, Rome's empire encompassed a vast world of diverse cultures and languages, from the Germanic and Celtic north to the Arabian peninsula and Sahara in the south. Throughout the Empire Hannibal's fame endured and it was perhaps his role in opposition to the prevailing power of Rome that sustained his celebrity. Hannibal was viewed as one of the renowned generals of antiquity but also remembered for his time in exile in the Hellenistic east where he became a rallying point for those who opposed Roman power.[29] In the late second century the Severan dynasty came to power and Septimius Severus (193–205 CE), an African with Punic roots from the city of Lepcis Magna (now in modern Libya) became emperor. It was in the reign of Severus, or more likely his son Caracalla, that the place of Hannibal's burial was commemorated with a new tomb. The site of the burial in Libyssa, the small city in Bithynia where Hannibal died, was well known and visited almost four centuries after his death but had apparently fallen into disrepair.[30] We are told that the Severan emperor built a white marble tomb dedicated to Hannibal, 'for he too was Libyan by race', according to a later Byzantine writer.[31]

This monument of the Severans, set up to commemorate a fellow African, reveals the complex attitude towards Rome's ultimate enemy in the imperial period. An important aspect of the myth of Hannibal was his evolution from the enemy into something more autonomous. We learn that Hannibal's tomb was a place of pilgrimage in the ancient world and that people came to his grave as to the graves of Alexander the Great and Achilles. Perhaps Rome's first African dynasty saw no conflict in honouring a famous Punic general. In fact, they may have been more interested in tapping into Hannibal's reputation as a brilliant military man. The shared cultural heritage may also have been seen as advantageous for the Severan dynasty. The Severans were outsiders and could not trace their family heritage back to legendary Roman ancestors but they could at least evoke the famed general of the Punic world. The Severan emperors, like Hannibal, used the image of Herakles in their propaganda.[32] Their interest in Hannibal may help to articulate his role for posterity as a symbol of the powerful outsider, an aspect of Hannibal's life that had existed probably since his death. The population of the second- and third-century Roman Empire were largely non-Roman in origin and they were ruled by a series of soldier emperors. Hannibal could be celebrated for his military prowess and opposition to Roman power. This celebrity endured and Hannibal's tomb stood visible until at least the eleventh century CE.[33]

The stories of the Romans of the Republic, as written chiefly by Livy, passed into the medieval and Renaissance imagination through the poems of Boccaccio and the poetry and biographies of Petrarch. Thus Hannibal's story became part of the mainstay of a classical education across Europe.[34] In the seventeenth century, as European powers began to develop into nation states, the story of the war between Rome and Hannibal captured the imagination and was used by writers and poets to express political views. It was a time when all education in Europe included the classics and Livy was read universally. For the educated of the early modern world, Hannibal and the Carthaginians became a recognizable moral tale.[35]

This is nowhere more apparent than in England in the early seventeenth century. When Sir Walter Ralegh was accused of taking part in a plot against James I (VI of Scotland) he was imprisoned in the Tower of London. The rule of the Stuart king James I was advertised as that of the 'New Caesar'. The Stuart king charged Ralegh, one of England's military heroes, with treason. While languishing in the Tower, Ralegh wrote a history of the world that included Hannibal. The character of Hannibal has always elicited admiration from military men through the ages because of his outstanding strategic victories. In addition to this, Ralegh was a staunch Protestant who believed that Catholic Spain was the greatest danger to England and in his history he presented the story of the Punic Wars and Hannibal from a Carthaginian point of view. With the Stuarts identifying themselves in the role of the Romans, Ralegh related his position to those much-slandered Carthaginians. His history focused on perceived Roman treacheries in the face of Hannibal's nobility.[36] Ralegh's history represents a continuous theme in the remembrance of Hannibal through the ages. Groups and individuals who find themselves in opposition to a larger, more imperial power often connect to Hannibal and the Carthaginians.

Another of Livy's tales that captivated European soldiery was how Hannibal and his army at Capua succumbed to an excess of luxury. This proved a popular cautionary tale. Livy's vivid digression recalls how the winter that Hannibal spent in luxurious Capua (216/215) had a disastrous effect: 'men whom the most intense misery had failed to break [were] now ruined by excessive comfort and unlimited pleasure – and the more thoroughly ruined because, thanks to their inexperience, they had immersed themselves all the more eagerly. Sleep, drink, dinner-parties, whores, baths and inactivity that, from habit, became sweeter every day – all this sapped their physical and moral strength' (Livy 23.18.10–13).[37]

The story of Capua resonated with many seventeenth-century Irish writers, who warned their soldiers not to engage in too much luxury, worried that the fate of Hannibal's army was waiting for them.[38] In a treatise on military discipline written in 1634 the Irish soldier Gerrat Barry referenced the story of Hannibal's winter stay at Capua as a warning of what can happen to a battle-hardened army if it is given too much time to rest. At Capua, Barry wrote, Hannibal and the soldiers became idle 'and forgetful of all military exercise, as though they never had managed arms. Which was the cause of the ruin and perdition of all his army . . .'[39] With Irish mercenaries fighting in contemporary European wars it may be that the luxuries of the sophisticated cities of Europe had turned some of the tough soldiers in their ranks. Livy claims that after their winter in Capua, many of Hannibal's men had formed relationships and would slip away from their duties, and 'the deserters' hiding-place was always Capua' (23.18.16). As Henry Burnell summed up in his tragicomedy *Landgartha*, 'this kingdome being more fatall unto them – than Capua was to Hannibal' (Act I).[40]

In early modern Europe Hannibal's deeds and great battles continued to be celebrated in tragedy and opera. It was not just among the educated that Hannibal's memory thrived. By the nineteenth century the poet Lord Byron wrote that 'every district of Italy has its hero. In the north some painter is the usual genius of the place . . . to the south we hear of Roman names. Near Thrasimene [Trasimeno] tradition is still faithful to the name of an enemy and Hannibal the Carthaginian is the only ancient name remembered on the banks of the Perugian Lake.'[41] This memory of Hannibal's victory had retained its part in the life and folklore of the Italian countryside.

The role embodied by Hannibal and the Carthaginians in the moral exempla of nineteenth- and early twentieth-century Europe continued and fluctuated depending on whose version of history was being told. In revolutionary France the Roman Republic played an important role yet in 1805 the painter David evoked Hannibal when painting Napoleon crossing the Alps. A glance through English newspapers from 1914–1918 reveals frequent allusions to Rome vs Carthage, with the Romans symbolizing England and the Carthaginians Germany or vice versa depending on which side was being expressed.[42] Rome versus Carthage was and is also an allegory for the fight of the colonized against the colonizer. 'I am Carthaginian, the earth is mine, not Britain's not Rome's,' states a character in Frank McGuinness' 1988 play *Carthaginians* (line 17).[43]

In the twentieth century a newly independent Turkey embraced Hannibal when Atatürk vowed to build a monument marking his supposed burial place, resurrecting the location of pilgrimage that the Severans had commemorated millennia earlier. A monument to Hannibal now stands on the grounds of the Tübitak Scientific and Technical Institute in Gebze in modern Turkey (see Plate 8).[44] The precise location of the original tomb of Hannibal is, however, uncertain. We only know that 'crossing the Bosphoros and passing by Chalcedon and Libyssa, where Hannibal the Carthaginian is buried' was noted by Ammianus Marcellinus in the fourth century CE (22.9). The name of Hannibal also resonated through post-colonial North Africa where he was considered a hero who fought Rome, embodied here by the European colonial powers. The former Libyan dictator Mu'ammar Gaddafi called his youngest son Hannibal and in post-Arab-Spring North Africa Hannibal's memory will certainly take on other meanings in the cultural patrimony.

Because of his military genius Hannibal is perhaps most often compared to Napoleon. His feats of brilliance and daring verged on insanity and his crossing of the Alps with elephants is remembered more than his origins and the culture that created him. The name of Hannibal has travelled through modern history as half superhero and half great enemy. Everyone recognizes his name but large parts of his real story are lost, enveloped by the memory created by Rome. The Hannibal who has passed down to our times is a chameleon who can be moulded to fit the guise of an enemy, a great fighter, a strategist, or an anti-hero. When Thomas Harris in *Silence of the Lambs* named his brilliant villain Hannibal, a man of superhuman intelligence who is able to outsmart his enemies, he surely had the great Carthaginian in mind. Even more incongruous perhaps is that today there are business management gurus who study and employ Hannibal's strategy.[45] Much more than his nemesis Scipio, it is Hannibal who continues to be celebrated up to this day in popular culture.[46]

Hannibal's vibrant afterlife derives, more than that of most historical figures, from a timeless appeal that mixes fact, a lost culture, Roman construction and an ambiguous persona that alters depending on who embraces his story.[47] When Arthur Miller called Al Capone 'the greatest Carthaginian of them all', the link from the New World in the twentieth century back to ancient Sicily and Hannibal is made in an instant.[48] This enduring interest in Hannibal is rooted in both our imagination and the few extraordinary details of his life that we know. He was a brilliant and daring general of the Hellenistic age who challenged and almost defeated Roman power, yet he remains an elusive and enigmatic Carthaginian.

# NOTES

## Introduction: No Ordinary Enemy

1. Numbers taken from Livy 22.49.15 are probably exaggerated but certainly reached into the tens of thousands. All dates in BCE unless otherwise stated.
2. All references to Livy throughout the book are from *Ab urbe condita* unless otherwise noted and translation used throughout is based on Yardley and Hoyos' 2006 edition.
3. The end of the Hannibalic War is often noted as a shift, Rome's power expanding rapidly from the second century BCE onward to encompass the whole of the Mediterranean.
4. 'And thus the Romans won the Carthaginian part of Africa, destroyed Carthage, and repopulated it again 102 years after its destruction' Appian, *Lib.* 136. Appian also mentions an earlier attempt at colonization by G. Sempronius Gracchus in *c.* 122 BCE. This colony, on the site of Carthage, never quite emerged due to Gracchus' assassination and the civil chaos in Rome that followed but there were settlers who took up their land grants and settled there. See also Plutarch, *C. Gracchus* 11, Livy, *Periochae.* 60; a *Lex Agraria* in 111 BCE gave possession of land to some colonists, see Bruns (ed.), 1909, vol. 1, 102–21.
5. Claire Stocks' recently published book on *The Roman Hannibal* looks specifically at the creation of Hannibal as a Roman hero/anti-hero in Silius Italicus and more broadly in Roman literature. There is a great deal of relevant and thoughtful detail on the means by which the Romans used Hannibal and constructed the enemy although it was published too late to fully incorporate all the arguments into this book.
6. All references to passages in Polybius used throughout the book refer to *The Histories* from the Loeb Classical Library text unless stated otherwise. For Polybius, Livy and the sources for the Punic Wars there is an enormous bibliography a selection consulted here includes, Walbank, vols 1–3; Champion, 2011; Eckstein, 2012, 2010 and 1989; see Levene, 2010; Jaeger, 2010 and 2006 and Feldherr, 2010, Gruen, 1978, Moore, 2010, Ridley, 2000 on Livy. Cornell (ed.), 2013 covers the fragmentary Roman historians such as Cato and Fabius Pictor; Mineo, 2011 the sources outside Polybius; Krings, 2005 on Sosylus in Polybius; there are sections in Hoyos, 2007, 2005 and 1998 that cover the relevant sources and details on the fragmentary pro-Carthaginian sources as well; Lancel, 1999, Lazenby, 1998, and Miles, 2010 provide clear overviews of the source material.
7. The negative portrayal in Livy's portrait of Hannibal may be based on Sallust's Cataline (*Bellum Cat.* 5.3–5) as has been frequently noted: see Rossi, 2004, 376 and note 40.

8. The ancient Phoenicians may have referred to themselves as *Kn'nm*. In English the term is Canaanites, familiar from the Hebrew Bible. Evidence from the later Roman Empire and for the use of the term Canaanite as a self-reference for Punic/Carthaginian people up until St Augustine's time see Aubet, 2001, 9–13. For the evidence of a much discussed *tessera hospitalis* found at Carthage with the name *Puinel* in Etruscan dating from the sixth–fifth centuries BCE and its possible implications on the term Punic see Palmer, 1997, 49 n. 95; Prag, 2006, 8; and Fentress, 2013, 162–164.

9. The term Punic is used for a range of linguistically linked cultures across the central/western Mediterranean. For a nuanced discussion see Prag, 2006 as well as Erskine, 2013; Gruen, 2011, 115–140 and Palmer, 1997, 48–50.

10. See Gruen, 2011, 115–140 on an assessment of the stereotype, Miles, 2010, 241–246 and 2011 on Hannibal and propaganda, Brizzi, 2006 on the legend. Barceló, 1994 looks at the Carthaginians in the Greek sources pre-Hannibal.

11. Here the terms Hannibalic War and Second Punic War are employed somewhat interchangeably and although other titles might be more appropriate, especially the 'Romano-Carthaginian Wars' (Toynbee, 1965, 1–2) or even 'Double Punic War' (Lancel, 1999, 1) they are less commonly employed. See more on the Punic label in Prag, 2006; and the Roman response to Carthage in Erskine, 2013; see Franko, 1994 on the use of *Poenus* and *Carthaginensis*. For the Phoenicians and the link to the colour purple see articles in Longo (ed.), 1998 especially Acquaro: 99–110. Bunnens, 1983, on the differentiation between Phoenician and Punic in the ancient sources; Krahmalkov, 2000, 11 on the Punic and Phoenicians names; see also Hoyos, 2010, 1.

12. This view was by no means universal and the destruction of Carthage did not have unanimous support at Rome – far from it. See Gruen, 2011, 130–131. For detailed discussions on the causes of the Second Punic War see Rich, 1996, and Hoyos, 1998 and a nuanced look at the development of the Punic stereotype can be found in Gruen, 2011, 115–140. For an overview and bibliographical references for the destruction of Carthage see Le Bohec, 2011.

13. For the historians of Hannibal's war see Walbank, vol. 1, 28–29 on the sources, Lazenby, 1998, 258–264 for a list and overview. See also Krings, 2005; Mineo, 2011; Schepens, 1989.

14. Walbank, vol. 1, 28–29 on Silenus and the other unknown pro-Carthaginian sources Polybius may have used. All references to Cornelius Nepos refer to his biographies of *Hamilcar* or *Hannibal* (books 22 and 23) included in his work *On Great Generals of Foreign Nations*.

15. The 'greatest enemy' is a much used label for Hannibal: see Lancel, 1995, 1, and the title of Hoyos, 2008, among many others. I have used Iberia and Iberian peninsula for what is commonly termed Spain here throughout except where Spain is preferred in some translations.

16. A comment taken from the editorial notes of Rachael Lonsdale, editor at Yale.

17. There is an enormous bibliography on the life of Hannibal and the Punic Wars and the following selection provides bibliographical references on the study of Hannibal over the past one hundred and fifty years: Walbank's commentary on Polybius provides essential bibliography for the key source on Hannibal; Toynbee, 1965, provides a detailed bibliography and looks at the impact on Italy and this has recently been discussed by Fronda, 2010. Brizzi, 1984 on the study of Hannibal; Seibert, 1993a and 1993b on the scholarship and the history; Barceló, 2004a; Hoyos, 2005 on the Barcid family; see Miles, 2010 for a current bibliography on Carthage; see Stocks, 2014 for the Roman sources and the creation of Hannibal.

18. The Phoenicians came roughly from what is known today as Lebanon – see Aubet, 2001, 13–17, who outlines the region with maps.

19. Discussion in Bonnet, 2005 looks at the representation of Carthage as 'the other' in both ancient and modern historiography.

## Chapter 1  Hannibal and Carthage

1. Translation here from John Dryden.

2. *Hnb'l* in the Punic language. Benz, 1972, 133–137 and 339, Krahmalkov, 2000, 270; for a comprehensive list of Carthaginian names and their meanings see Halff, 1963–4, Benz, 1972 and Krahlmakov, 2000.

3. I use the central Mediterranean as more accurate in a purely geographical rather than social/political sense. For a discussion on East and West in Hellenistic history, see Purcell, 2013.

4. For Phoenician colonization see variously in Aubet, 2001, Moscati (ed.), 2001, Lancel, 1995, Niemeyer, 1995, Lipinski, 2004, Neville, 2007.

5. For the development of Phoenicians as seafarers and explorers of the Mediterranean see Millard, 2000 and for the adoption of the alphabet by the Greeks in the *c.* ninth century, Millard, 1976. See Horden and Purcell, 2000, 134 on the redistributive networks and more generally on cabotage. The ancient author Diodorus Siculus tells us that 'the Phoenicians, who from ancient times on made voyages continually for purposes of trade, planted many colonies throughout Libya and not a few as well in the western parts of Europe' (5.20.1).

6. Demand for precious metals drove Phoenician exploration and subsequent political and population pressures on the Phoenician cities led to settlement there as well. See Aubet, 2001, 79 on Phoenician luxury goods for the Eastern market, Aubet-Semmeler, 2002, 79–112 on the economics of Phoenician colonization.

7. Gades is used here. Other passages (1 Kings 10: 23 – Tharshish; 2 Chronicles 9: 21 – Tarshish) refer to the faraway region whence gold, silver, ivory, apes and peacocks are brought. See Lipinski, 2004, 225–265 for a complete analysis of the different meanings behind Tarshish in sources. See also Bunnens, 1979 on the literary evidence and also López-Ruiz, 2009 for a recent exploration of the implications of the Tarshish-Tartessos interpretation.

8. See Aubet, 2001, 257–291, Aubet-Semmler, 2002 and Neville, 2007 on the economy of the Phoenician settlements in southern Spain.

9. The Latin author Velleius Paterculus claimed that Cadiz in Iberia was founded in 1110 BCE (1.2.3). Utica, a Phoenician colony just north of Carthage, was founded not long after Cadiz (Pliny, *NH* 19.63) and then exactly 287 years after Utica, Carthage was founded (Pseudo-Aristotle, *concerning reported wonders 134*). See Aubet, 2001, 194–211, 214–231, and Neville, 2007, 11, who points out that in the Iberian peninsula, so far, no archaeological evidence exists for settlement before the late ninth century BCE/early eighth century BCE.

10. A comprehensive discussion of Carthage's literary, mythological and actual foundation can be found in Lancel, 1995, 1–34; see also Aubet, 2001, 214–218. Evidence from the analysis of animal bone samples provided radiocarbon dates of *c.* 835–800 BCE, see Docter, et al., 2005. Bechtold and Docter, 2010 survey the amphorae evidence for the early centuries at Carthage. For the evidence for the rapid growth of Carthage in the early phases see Docter, 2003–3. See also Ameling, 2013 on the development of the city.

11. This version of the legend is found in Justin, *Epitome* 18.4–5, and discussed in Niemeyer, 2002, 44–45; Bonnet, 2011, 377. For a king list of Tyre see Aubet, 2001, 56. The Phoenician for Pygmalion and Mettenos is *Pumai* and *Mattan*. According to Justin, Elissa and her ships stopped at Kition on Cyprus and brought 80 virgins from the sanctuary of Astarte/Aphrodite with them in order that the men could have wives.

12. Lancel, 1995, 25. See Bonnet, 1989, 289–90; 2006, 370–371. This story may reflect legal traditions that can be found in the Hebrew Bible referring to acquisition of land as discussed by Lipinksi, 2004, 478–481. *Byrsa* in Greek etymology means 'hide'. For a full examination of the story and meaning of the word *Byrsa* see Lipinski, 2004, 477–492, Scheid and Svenbro, 1985.

13. See Bonnet, 2011, 377; used recently by George R.R. Martin, whose city Qarth in *The Game of Thrones* seems clearly based on legends of Carthage.

14. Earlier translations of the Carthaginian parts of the *Aeneid* in English begin with Chaucer's *The Legend of Good Women* in the late fourteenth century and run through Marlowe's *Dido, Queen of Carthage* of the late sixteenth. Virgil was extremely popular in the seventeenth century and Dryden's translation remains one of the classic texts. See the complete list of *Virgil in English* in Gransden (ed.), 1996.

15. For Marlowe's Dido, Elizabeth I of England, virginity and political power see Williams, 2006. Ben Jonson's Cary-Morison ode, published in 1640, equally noted 'prodigious Hannibal's' deeds in the public imagination (see more below in chapter 4). In 1761 Admiral Sir John Lindsay named his illegitimate daughter by an African slave Dido, which only confirms the impact of the legend on the public imagination, see King, 2004.

16. See also Aubet, 2001, 214–218.

17. The story of Aeneas and Dido may appear as early as the epic poem of Gn. Naevius, the *Bellum Poenicum*, about the first Punic War written at the end of the third century BCE. The version without Aeneas appears in Timaeus of Tauromenium frag. 23 and Justin, *Epitome* 18.4–6. See Gruen, 1990, 11–13, and also Erskine, 2001, 198–205 who discusses the Trojan links.

18. Niemeyer, 2002, 44–45.

19. The Punic world: 'the southern mainland and most of the islands of the western Mediterranean basin' with five specific regions including western Sicily, the southern Iberian peninsula, Ibiza, and the North African Mediterranean shore extending into the Atlantic. Following van Dommelen and Gomez Ballard, 2008, 3 who note the continued flourishing of Punic culture through to the first century BCE. Lancel, 1995, 49–93 on the birth of the city and Miles, 2010, 58–81 both provide excellent overview of this period.

20. The continuous pressure on Tyre from Assyrian and Babylonian forces (throughout the seventh and sixth centuries) must have had an impact. It has often been argued that the Babylonian capture of Tyre (in 575 BCE) was the rupture point for the colonial foundations but the intention of the capture was to participate in the Tyrian trade and profit from it, so may not have been as disruptive as originally thought, claims Neville, 2007, 163–164.

21. The stories of King Malchus and his expeditions to Sardinia, perhaps part legendary due to his name *mlk*, meaning just 'the king', correspond to this time in Carthaginian history. Malchus and his two sons are the first mention we have of a Carthaginian ruling family after Dido, see Justin, *Epitome*, 19.1.1, 18.7.19.

22. Ionian Greeks from Asia Minor being pushed out by the Persian expansion there were settling in the region. This is a very simplified account and the influence of the foundation of Massalia (Marseilles) is key to this battle.

23. See Krings, 1998, 93–160 on Alalia. The battle of Alalia, a Cadmean victory, is specifically referred to in Herodotus. Thucydides (1. 13, 6) mentions another battle between the Carthaginians and the Massalians (also a Phocaean foundation). These two battles may be conflated in the sources. See Rawlings, 2010, 253–257 on the Punic Thalassocracy.

24. For a detailed account of the treaties see Seratti, 2006.

25. Some scholars have traced the appearance of Carthage in Herodotus from the middle of the sixth century BCE to the beginning of the fifth century as reflecting the expansion of Carthaginian power and their replacement of the Tyrians in the western Mediterranean, as in Krings, 1998, 104–106 with a detailed bibliography.

26. This idea is clearly laid out in Eckstein, 2006, 160–180 and Rawlings, 2010, 258.

27. Herodotus (7.158 and 166), which link the battle of Himera to the Persian invasion of Greece, has long been seen as a conflation of events. See Prag, 2010, 55–57 on the dedication set up at Delphi to honour the victory. For two different opinions on Carthaginian imperialism see Whittaker, 1978 and Eckstein, 2006, 160–163. Krings, 1998, 261–326 provides a close analysis of the source material and scholarship. See also Prag, 2010, who looks at how the Greek tyrants used a perceived threat of Carthage to harness their own power and how this has fed into our negative portrayal of the Carthaginians; see also Ameling, 2011; Dench, 2005; Wilson, 2013; Zambon, 2006 and 2008.

28. Graphs in Parker, 1992 show a jump in Mediterranean shipwrecks in the third century BCE. The graph is reproduced with analysis in Horden and Purcell, 2000, 371.

29. Diodorus Siculus provides the most extensive detail of the battles between the Carthaginians and Greeks in Sicily over the fifth and fourth centuries, see 13.79.8–13.114; 14.40–14.96; 15.15–17; 15.15. 24; 16.66–83. See also Diodorus 20.8.4 for the irrigation and intensive agriculture practised by the Carthaginian elite.

30. The sailor's guide was called a *periplus* in Greek, see Lipinski, 2004, 433–434, who looks at the evidence from Pseudo-Scylax, fourth century BCE. The allied settlements to the west may have extended to Lixus and beyond on the Atlantic coast of Morocco. To the east, the legend of the *Ars Philenorum* (Altars of the Philaeni are referred to in Sallust, *Bellum Jugurthum*, 79) traditionally marked the boundary between Carthaginian and Greek allied territory along the coast (Map 2).

31. There may have been shared legal rights, cultural values, laws and magistracies based on similar systems. The identities of the various peoples that lived within the area of Carthaginian influence lie outside clear-cut ethnic distinctions. See Bonnet, 2011, 373 and also Quinn, 2011, 398, who discusses the 'openness of Carthaginian culture in the Hellenistic period'.

32. Hoyos, 2010, 39–42; and Eckstein, 2006, 160. For views on a Carthaginian empire see Whittaker, 1978 and also Lancel, 1995, 78–109 on the beginning of empire and expansion; more on Carthage's power in the time of Hannibal in Hoyos, 2005, with full bibliography. Serrati, 2006 analyses Carthaginian treaties and Eckstein, 2006 on *Mediterranean Anarchy* gives a broader picture; Miles, 2010, 58–159, outlines the development of Carthaginian power and includes an excellent bibliography.

33. Changes in the housing at Carthage to a more typical Levantine style in the seventh/sixth centuries BCE may indicate an influx of new peoples from cities in the east under pressure from the Assyrian/Babylonian expansions and then the Persian conquest of the region. For changes see Docter et al., 2007, 92–94. A further influx must have followed when Alexander sacked Tyre in 333 BCE.

34. 'They believed that Heracles (Melqart), who was worshipped in their mother city, was exceedingly angry with them, they sent a large sum of money and many of the most expensive offerings to Tyre.' The forenames of the Barcids and in fact most Carthaginians were 'theophoric'; Hannibal's brother and brother-in-law were both named Hasdrubal (*Zrb'l*), meaning 'Ba'al is my help'. Hamilcar is transcribed as *Bdmlqrt* in the Punic–Phoenician dialect of Carthage. Mago, another of the Barcid brothers, also written Magon, was *Mgn* in the Punic script, the meaning of which was derived from the root 'a gift' or 'to give'. Benz, 1972, 133–137 and 339; Krahmalkov, 2000, 270; for a list of Carthaginian names and their meanings see also Halff, 1963–4.

35. 'Sons of Tyre' noted in Miles, 2010, 61 from inscriptions at Carthage.

36. The *periplus* of Hanno provides the evidence for a Carthaginian expedition to the Niger delta on the west coast of Africa with 50 penteconters (a ship with 50 oars); see Lancel, 1995, 102–109 and recently González Ponce, 2010, who discusses the veracity of the document.

37. Tombs present a vivid picture of Carthaginian wealth, ritual and trade in the archaic period. Wealth in precious metals and their symbolism reveal a mix of influences that come together at Carthage. See Lancel, 1995, 215–228 on the burials.

38. See the discussion on the zones, unity and connectivity in the Mediterranean by Horden and Purcell, 2000, Bresson, 2005, esp. 95–104 for the Greeks, Phoenicians and Carthaginians, see also Millard, 2000, on the Phoenicians at sea, and Zimmerman Munn, 2003, on Corinth and Carthaginian trade in the Classical period, Fentress, 2013 on the Etruscans. See Palmer, 1997 on Rome and Carthage at peace, articles in Moscati (ed.), 2001 provide an excellent sample of the material culture of Carthage and the Western Phoenicians; and, more directly related to Hannibal's time, see Peters (ed.), 2004 for the material remains of Carthage from the third century.

39. See here Lancel, 1995, 111, recent work by Hoyos, 2010; Miles, 2010, and museum exhibitions and catalogues on the Phoenicians see Fontan and Le Meaux (eds), 2007, and for the Carthaginians and Hannibal see Peters (ed.), 2004; for many of the images see Moscati (ed.), 2001.

40. Cicero, *Leg. Agr.* 2.87. Cristofori, 2001, 6–11 traces the origins of this thinking back to Plato with the sea 'breeding in men's souls knavish and tricky ways' (Plato, *Leges* 4.705a); this notion is also found in Thucydides 6.34.2: 'they have an abundance of gold and silver, by which war and everything else is expedited'. See also Rawlings, 2010, 254–256;

Rich, 1993; and Eckstein, 2006, 164–167. Polybius reinforces the notion of Roman defensive imperialism, with Harris 1985, 163–210 providing the much discussed alternative view.

41. On the 'bellicose nature of Rome and Carthage' see Eckstein, 2006, 177–178. The agricultural importance of the rich and fertile lands of the Carthaginian heartland along the Bagradas river valley are often overlooked, also that one of the ancient world's foremost writers on agriculture, Mago, was a Carthaginian whose work survives in excerpts in Roman writers; e.g. Columella (3.12.5, 3.15.4, 5.5.4) records Mago's instructions on viticulture. The literary evidence for Carthaginian agriculture has recently been studied by Krings, 2008, who examines the ideological background to Roman claims of Carthaginian wealth.

42. Gruen (ed.), 2011, 125, argues for a grudging 'mutual respect' between 'fierce foes'. For the depiction of the Carthaginians in Greek sources see Barceló, 1994, and more recently the discussion in Prag, 2010 of the use of the Carthaginian threat by successive Greek despots in Sicily.

43. Translation used here from Leigh, 2004, 45–46. The *Poeni*, the Punic people, were so called because of their Phoenician heritage. The Phoenician label has uncertain origins from the Greek *phenix* – which can imply the colour 'purple/red' from the precious purple dye extracted in antiquity from murex shells by the Phoenicians. Or *phenix* could also mean 'palm' as in 'palm tree' in Ancient Greek, which is a symbol found frequently on Carthaginian coins and votive stelae. For a discussion of the significance of the palm tree see Prag, 2006, 26–28.

44. Gruen (ed.), 2011 on the identity of the Carthaginians provides a nuanced look at the positive and negative characterizations. Prag, 2006 on the idea of the Punics. The *Studia Phoenicia* series, published since 1983, is an excellent resource. Recent publications on the Carthaginians in English include Hoyos, 2010 and Miles, 2010. Further discussion of the identity of Carthage in Quinn, 2011 and Bonnet, 2011; and articles in Prag and Quinn (eds), 2013 on the Hellenistic West continue to provide more nuance and understanding. Lancel, 1995, although now out of date, can still provide an important overview.

45. Thought to have been written *c*. 190 BCE. A modern comparison might be trying to interpret the culture of 20th-century Germany from a British comedy, and the problems with this are fully acknowledged. See Palmer, 1997, 31–52 on Carthaginian cargoes at Rome, full of interesting detail derived from an analysis of Plautus. See also Lancel, 1995 405–406; Gruen (ed.), 2011, 126–129; Erskine, 2013, Franko, 1996 and Leigh, 2004, 24–56.

46. The term used is *puer cauponius*, with an innuendo of sexual exploitation.

47. Palmer, 1997, 34 note 15 suggests that such a garment may perhaps be viewed on the statue of a youth found at the site of Motya. For an image of the statue see Lancel, 1995 323–324, fig. 193 or Fentress, 2013 (note 48 below); see also Maes, 1989 on the clothing of Carthaginian men. The underwear comment from the fragmentary Polybius 12.26a.3–4 repeats the slur of Timoleon, who accuses the Carthaginians of 'holding their hands for the whole of their life idle inside their tunics, and above all wear undergarments under their tunics that they may not even when killed in battle be exposed to the view of their enemies'. This garment may be the kind of kilt or wrap that can be seen in Egyptian male dress, although opinions differ. See Maes, 1989, 19.

48. The wearing of earrings is illustrated on the sarcophagus of Larth Partunu found in Tarquinia from the fourth century that depicts an Etruscan aristocrat with a pierced ear, and his philo-Carthaginian attitude is confirmed by his adoption of Carthaginian dress. Recently see Fentress, 2013, 162.

49. Hanno's Punic is mistranslated into absurdities, so that African mice are imported to be used in the games (Plautus, *Poenulus* 1010–13) indicating a familiarity with wild animals from Africa as regular imports even by this date. See Lancel, 1995, 405–406; Erskine, 2013 for Roman responses to Carthage.

50. Again see Palmer, 1997, 37–44. Pigs are depicted on some ceremonial bronze razors at Carthage. Although Picard interprets them as wild boar, perhaps representing mythical events, one looks particularly pig-like. See Picard, C. 1967, plate 25, razor n. 30, plate 26, razor n. 31.

51. *Tyriosque bilingues*, other references in Gruen, 2011, 126–129.
52. Plautus' Punic may be mimicking slang or dialect, although there is some disagreement over the translation and meaning of the Punic used, see Palmer, 1997, 33–36.
53. As noted in Leigh, 2004, 24–56, which is a thoughtful discussion of Plautus and Hannibal.
54. Palmer, 1997 and also Lancel, 1995, 405–406; Franko, 1996, 425 and 429 for the translation used here.
55. See Gruen, 2011, 113–140.
56. Note the debate on Hanno's characterization as sympathetic or not in Franko, 1996 and Palmer, 1997, 30–35 on Hanno's *pietas*; Leigh, 2004 (as above, note 45); the ties of friendship and patronage between some Carthaginian and Roman families are discussed by Brizzi, 2009.
57. The image of the anchor and ship recounted in Rawlings, 2010, 255 and used by Picard and Picard, 1958, 168. Note the use of the plural 'harbours' in Cicero indicating more than one location for harbours. This would be useful in explaining why the current visible harbours seem to date from the late third/early second century BCE. In Cicero's time Carthage had yet to be officially rebuilt – his image must be of the Punic city.
58. For the sea walls and reconstruction, see Lancel, 1995 135–137, fig. 70 following excavations by the German Archaeological Institute, Rome.
59. Eshmun, in the role as 'son of justice' and civic god here, Lipinski, 2004, 488–492. For Eshmun as the 'Ba'al (Lord) of Sidon' see Clifford, 1990, 57. The Carthaginian god Eshmun was multifaceted and was sometimes identified with the Greek Apollo (see below note 60) and on the Byrsa hill with Asclepius, the role of lawgiver to the god who crowned the city discussed in Lipinski, 2004, 484–492. For the temple of Asclepius see Appian, *Libyca* 130, Strabo, *Geography* 17.3, 14, Livy 41.22 and 42.24. The famous temple of Bel at Palmyra may provide a good parallel for the style.
60. The Cape of Eshmun, north of Carthage, where Scipio landed his invasion force, was called the Promontory of the Beautiful One, or the Promontory of Apollo Polyb. 3.2.5, 23.1.4, 24.2.4). Livy (30.10.9) records the name as 'Rusucmona' (*rus usmun*, in Lipinski, 2004, 484).
61. See Lancel, 1995 156–172 for detailed plans of the Byrsa quarter housing.
62. Purely hypothetical assumption but there were more substantial homes down near the sea in the late Punic period, with peristyles, see Lancel, 1995, 153–154 but the presence of large Roman elite housing up on the hill of Juno makes the previous use at least a possibility. The Megara area, enclosed by the circuit walls and rich in agricultural land, may also have been where the elite houses were, and still are today. The archaic cemeteries present a problem for houses on the hills surrounding the Byrsa but recent excavations have shown that the Carthaginians moved their cemeteries at various times when the city needed to grow: see Docter, 2007 and 2002–3.
63. The details of the housing on the Byrsa come from Appian's description of the destruction of Carthage. A version of the god Reshep was worshipped in the agora and was equated with Apollo. A great statue from this temple wound up in Rome after the sack of Carthage ('the great Apollo from Carthage, opposite the Circus' see Plutarch, *Flam.* 1). See Miles, 2010, prologue, note 7 for the reference to the identification of the location.
64. The location of the pre-second-century ports is still debated, see discussion in Lancel, 1997, 172–192; also Hurst, 1994 and Hurst and Stager, 1978.
65. Hurst, 1994; Hurst and Stager, 1978 on the excavation of the harbour and date. The description of the impressive harbours of Carthage dates to the mid-second century, and archaeological evidence also places the earliest construction of the harbours we see at Carthage today to the period after the Hannibalic War. See Hoyos, 2010, 92. Recent detailed study in Blackman et al., 2013 on ship sheds discusses estimates of size, number and type of ships from the evidence for the great navies of the ancient world, including Carthage.
66. As described by Polybius in the second century BCE, Carthage 'is situated at the inmost point of a gulf into which it protrudes on a strip of land, almost entirely surrounded on one

side by the sea and on the other by a lake' (1.73.3–6). Like other Phoenician foundations (e.g. Cadiz and Motya) Carthage was located in a geographically perfect position for a port and had been placed for its strategic situation: see Hunt, 2009: 138.

67. Although Appian's description, taken from Polybius' account, may not be completely accurate to the mid-third century it does present an idea of Carthage just before its destruction. Hellenistic fortification walls, not dissimilar to those at New Carthage, incorporated the forces and supplies. These were known as 'casemates'.

68. The full extent of the working of government remains uncertain. The term 'commonwealth' is used by Bondi, 1995, 278; see also Sanders, 1988 on 'Punic politics and the shift in government from the fifth to the fourth century'; see Hoyos, 2010, 20–38 and Miles, 2010, 112–138. See Fariselli, 2006 on the political aspects of the Barcid family.

69. The 'people' here in Polybius most likely referred to the 'citizens assembly'.

70. This may be Polybius projecting the political shifts at Rome on to Carthage. Popular assembly called the *ham* (*'m*) in Punic.

71. For the assembly and its decision-making power see Aristotle, *Politics* 2.8.3: 'when the kings (*sufetes*) introduce business in the assembly, they do not merely let the people sit and listen to the decisions that have been taken by their rulers, but the people have the sovereign decision, and anybody who wishes may speak against the proposals introduced, a right that does not exist under the other constitutions.' In the same passage Aristotle mentions a 'board of five', not otherwise referred to, who 'controlled many important matters'. Hoyos, 2010, 31–32 provides a hypothesis.

72. The term *sufet* literally meant judge but the role had much broader implications than the English term implies. These magistracies, more like consular powers, lived on after the destruction of Punic Carthage and inscriptions attesting to *sufetes* are found in the first century BCE/CE to the east at Lepcis Magna, and in the west of North Africa at Volubilis which demonstrates the far-reaching influence of Punic culture in North Africa throughout antiquity. North Africa was never so Punic as it was after the fall of Carthage in 146 and the diaspora that must have followed its destruction: Lancel, 1995, 358.

73. Aristotle, *Politics* 2.8.2: 'the magistracy of the Hundred and Four corresponding to the *Ephors* (except one point of superiority the Ephors are drawn from any class, but the Carthaginians elect this magistracy by merit)'. Hoyos, 2010, 20–38 gives a concise overview of the government and state; see also 2005, 21–33, for the state at the time of Hamilcar. See Brizzi, 2009 on the political factions during Hannibal's time.

74. Rawlings, 2011, 257; Ameling, 1993, 155–180 on the aristocracy and Carthaginian warfare; for Carthage's change in outlook see Eckstein, 2006, 158–180.

75. The danger of projecting from Rome on to Carthage is acknowledged but can be useful in understanding the processes.

76. Eckstein, 2006, 158–168 discusses Carthaginian policy in the period between the sixth and third centuries BCE.

77. For *Rb mhnt*, equivalent to the Greek *strategos*, see Hoyos, 2010, 33–34. The ages of Hannibal's brothers are difficult to assess with certainty. Perhaps 2/3 years separated them; see the debate in Hoyos, 2005, 66 (note 15).

78. Hannibal was general first, then *sufet*; Scipio was also a proconsul before being consul; it was a time of extraordinary commands. For discussion of the known working of Carthage's government see Hoyos, 2010, 20–38; 2005, 21–33; Ameling, 1993, 83–117.

79. Hoyos, 2005, 29–33; 47–97 with detailed bibliography looks closely at the Barcid rule in Iberia.

80. Isokrates (fourth century BCE) comments that '. . . the Carthaginians and the Lacedaemonians, the best governed of all, are ruled by oligarchies at home, yet, in war, they are ruled by kings' (ref. from Isocrates, *Nikokles* 24 in *FGrH*) perhaps referring to the absolute power of a general in the field.

81. Eckstein, 1987, xii.

82. Hamilcar and Hannibal were prosecuted at the end of the First and the Second Punic Wars, respectively (according to Appian, *Iberica* 4 and Cassius Dio 17 (Zonaras, 14–15, frag. 86). The commander at Messana at the start of the First Punic War was crucified, according to

Polybius, as was a certain Hannibal in Sardinia after the battle of Mylae (Polybius 1.11.5, and 1.24.6).

83. It is notoriously difficult to estimate the populations of ancient cities. In 149 there were 'seventy myriads of men', according to Strabo (17.3.15) i.e. about 700,000. This seems a very high number when you consider that most population estimates from ancient writers would include only male citizens. The opinions are surveyed by Hoyos, 2005, 225–226. It was a large city, comparative in size and population to Syracuse certainly but perhaps not as large as contemporary Alexandria.

84. As noted in Krings, 2008, on the literary construction behind the descriptions of Carthaginian wealth and the fertility of the land and its use in the ancient sources as a topos.

85. The variety of housing, from elegant seafront to multi-family dwellings, is discussed in Lancel, 1995, 134–192.

86. There is some question as to whether these libraries existed. Legend contends that after the destruction of the city the Romans gave the libraries to the neighbouring Numidians, but no trace of them exists. See Lancel, 1995, 152, the only work preserved was said to be the treatise of Mago the agronomist, also discussed by Devillers and Krings, 1996 and more recently by Krings, 2008 who offers an up-to-date view of the state of Punic agriculture in the ancient sources.

87. The idea of a 'clash of cultures' has existed in the historiography of the Punic Wars for centuries (ie De Sanctis) with the Romans represented as embodying 'Western' values and the Carthaginians 'Eastern' or Semitic values – these views have long been dismissed for their colonial and anti-Semitic overtones. Both Rome and Carthage by the third century BCE were Hellenized, the importance of Greek cultural art, artefacts and ideas prevalent, but they were also fundamentally different in origins, language, religion and culture, aspects that became magnified once they were at war. To what degree the city was Hellenized is much debated but interesting discussions can be found in Bonnet, 2006, and articles in Prag and Quinn (eds), 2013.

88. For Tanit/Tinnit, 'face of Ba'al' see Lancel, 1995, 199–204, she is sometimes equated with Astarte. For Ba'al Hammon see Lancel, 1995, 194–199. See Lipinski, 1995 for a detailed study of the pantheon of Phoenician and Punic gods and goddesses and Clifford, 1990.

89. See Bonnet, 1986 for Melqart at Carthage; Miles, 2010, 96–111 on Melqart in the western Mediterranean. For full references see chapter 4, note 18.

90. Bonnet, 2011, outlines the function of the Tophet and its role in the multi-layered identity of the population at Carthage. The fascinating question of the site as the location of child sacrifice is well beyond the remit of this introduction. Bonnet's article, and that by Quinn, 2011 in the same volume, provide very up-to-date thinking and bibliography on the function of the site within the city, and beyond. The term *Tophet* is used here for convenience but the Carthaginians refer to a 'temple' or 'sanctuary' from inscriptions on the stelae found at the site.

91. Quinn, 2011, 389.

92. Dedicatory inscriptions often include reference to family links going back two or three generations, Quinn, 2011, 399. Where evidence of an inscription exists, some of these include the formulaic 'vowed . . . because he heard his voice'. See Xella (ed.), 2013 on the inscriptions.

93. Justin, 6.6–12 describes Dido's self-immolation. See Bonnet, 1986 on the Melqart ritual at Carthage. See also Miles, 2010, for the story of Hamilcar the leader at Himera in 480 BCE, which has aspects of ritual death by fire.

94. The debate has recently returned to the headlines, i.e. a *Daily Mail* headline (23 Jan. 2014) reads: 'Ancient Greek stories of ritual child sacrifice in Carthage are TRUE, study claims!' The analysis rests on the estimated age of the remains of the cremated infant. The two sides of the debate are discussed most recently in P. Smith et al., 2013; Schwarz et al., 2012; and Xella et al., 2013. For a detailed examination of the Tophet and the most recent thinking across the fields of study see articles in Xella (ed.), 2013, and, as above, Quinn, 2011 and Bonnet, 2011.

95. The evidence from Hannibal's treaty with Philip V (see below, chapter 8) places the legal language of Carthage firmly in the traditions of the Near East.

96. Bonnet, 2006, 373–376 discusses Demeter and Kore's introduction to the city as described by Diodorus Siculus 14, 77, 4–5, reminding us of the direct infusion of Hellenic concepts and ideas from Sicily into Carthage. She also points out that the cult was established to appease the gods after a Carthaginian general had sacked the sanctuary of Demeter and Kore in Sicily.

97. None more so than the sarcophagi covers found in Carthage that show a man and woman, whose features are styled in a Hellenic fashion and are thought to indicate growing Hellenization. The date of these sarcophagi is thought to be second century, and it is a difficult concept to prove, as argued by Bonnet, 2006. See Lancel, 1995, figs 194–196; the similar male image from Tarquinia is discussed recently by Fentress, 2013, 162–163.

98. The discussion in Malkin, 2011, 18–20 on the identity of the Syracusans makes for an interesting approach to the multi-layered identity of the Carthaginians. Quinn, 2011 and Bonnet, 2011 explore the cultural identity of the Carthaginians and Phoenician diaspora through the rituals associated with the Tophet. See also Palmer, 1997 on Rome and Carthage at Peace.

99. Slight adaptation of Arthur Miller, *A View from the Bridge* (1955), Act I, scene i.

### Chapter 2  The Great Man in the Hellenistic World: From Alexander to Hamilcar

1. With so much written about Hannibal, the secondary bibliography for the context of the Second Punic War is enormous. See the articles in Cornell et al., 1996, and more recently Eckstein, 2006, 79–117 on the interstate relations in the Hellenistic Age which provide detailed context for the Punic Wars in the wider Mediterranean; articles in Hoyos (ed.), 2011 on the Punic Wars provide excellent background to the topics covered here. See Miles, 2010 on Carthage and its rise and fall and Hannibal within that context. Barceló, 2004, 55–69 notes Hannibal's traumatic childhood in Carthage during these years. All dates in BCE unless otherwise stated.

2. This is a brief overview of a very complex period of history; for further reading in English see Gruen, 1986, Green, 1990, Shipley, 2000, and articles in Erskine, 2006. For the impact of Alexander on the way the Romans told their history see Spencer, 2002.

3. From the sixth/fifth centuries there had been growing connectivity between the big cities of the west/central Mediterranean and the struggles in the east (i.e. Syracuse and the Peloponnesian Wars and the knock-on wars between Carthage and Syracuse as described by Diodorus). See further discussion in Eckstein, 2006, 79–180 on the bellicose climate of the third century BCE. Krings, 1998 provides detailed context for the relationship between Carthage and the Greek world down to 480, and Barceló, 1994 looks at the Greek sources' perceptions of Carthage through this period.

4. *Mediterranean Anarchy* is the title of Eckstein, 2006.

5. He is Rhodinus in Frontinus, *Strat.* 1.2.3. See also Orosius 4.6.21; Arrian 7.15.4. Other great exploits and adventures, such as Xenophon and the ten thousand must also have had an impact. Is this Hamilcar related to Hannibal the Rhodian from the First Punic War? This is unknown but raises the possibility that Carthaginian surnames were passed on from generation to generation: see Polybius 1.44–47 for the exploits of Hannibal the Rhodian.

6. The boundary between the two powers (Hellenistic Egypt and Carthaginian allied territory) being the *Ars Philaeni* once the Ptolemies had established control over Cyrenaica: see Map 2.

7. Diodorus Sic. 17.17.1–2 on Alexander's spear-won land. The idea is captured brilliantly in an anonymous portrait of a Roman general as Hellenistic ruler: this well-known Roman bronze sculpture some identify as a Roman general, and others as a copy of a Hellenistic original of an unidentified Hellenistic king, can be seen in the National Roman Museum, Palazzo Massimo Terme, Rome, image reproduced in Zanker, 1998, 4, who notes that the un-diademed head is unlikely to represent a Hellenistic king. See Stewart, 1993, 158–190 for Alexander and the imagery associated with this concept and Eckstein 2006, 85, who outlines the right of conquest.

8. See Krings, 2008 for these descriptions as a kind of literary topos.

9. Diodorus Sic. 20.14.4–7 alleges that this dire situation led the Carthaginians to believe they had been abandoned by their gods, and a mass sacrifice of children ensued. The infamous description of the children being placed in the sloping arms of a bronze image of Cronos (Ba'al) and rolled into the fire has been embraced by many (including Gustave Flaubert in *Salammbô*), who imagined the rituals that took place at the Tophet. That Carthage turned to its gods in times of strife was certain; as with the Romans after Cannae, sacrifice may have been extreme but the numbers here seem outlandish and unlikely (see Chapter 7 below for the Roman reaction to the defeat at Cannae).

10. Ophellas, related to Ptolemy I of Egypt, was the governor of Cyrene, a client state that technically bordered Carthage. For Ptolemaic involvement in the Punic Wars, see Appian, *Sic.* 1: 'He [Ptolemy] was on terms of friendship with both Romans and Carthaginians'. Hölbl, 2001, provides a clear history of the Egyptian kingdom in this period. See Gruen, 1986, 675–678; also Adams, 2008, 98–99 on Ptolemy's supposed neutrality.

11. This abridged version of the eventful life of Agathocles is found in Diodorus book 20 and is full of difficulties. The rise of the Hellenistic hegemon in the central Mediterranean is discussed in Zambon, 2006 with reference to leaders in Syracuse from Agathocles to Hiero II; see Prag, 2010 on the Greek tyrants in Sicily and their use of the threat of Carthage. The events are closely linked to the battles of the Hellenistic monarchs and the pervasive influence of the Alexandrian model of power.

12. Zambon, 2006, 79–80 links Agathocles' campaign in Africa with the development of a Hellenistic style of kingship in Sicily. See articles in Prag and Quinn (eds), 2013 on the impact of the Hellenistic world on the western Mediterranean.

13. See Stewart, 1993, 266–269, and for a gold stater of Agathocles with the obverse head with the elephant scalp and Ammon's horn, ibid., fig. 87. The image is adopted from the Ptolemaic standards. See Dench, 2005, 301; also more generally on Italy and Sicily in the Hellenistic age. For an interesting case study of the coinage and the image of Herakles see Yarrow, 2013. For the term 'heroic leadership' see Keegan, 1987, 13.

14. For more on Hannibal's education see chapter 4. The influence of Agathocles as the first leader of the western Mediterranean to actively employ the image of Alexander on his coinage was important. The Barcid coinage used in Iberia may come from these models and perhaps we can see how the styles and imagery of leadership passed through the Greek tyrants and were adopted by Carthaginian leaders.

15. Witnessed by the growth in the number of shipwrecks found from the third century and these then increase enormously in the second century. See maps in Parker, 1992, and reproduced in Horden and Purcell, 2000, 368–371.

16. Casson, 1995, 137–140 for the 'naval arms race' in the Hellenistic period.

17. As described by Eckstein, 2006, 116. The epithet *Poliorcetes*, 'Besieger of Cities', was given to Demetrius I of Macedon (336–283 BCE), son of Antigonus I, one of the *Diadochoi* (Successors). Translation of Plutarch's *Demetrius* here by John Dryden.

18. There has been considerable debate on the workings of these ships. A very good discussion can be found in Casson, 1969; see also Casson 1995, chapter 6. Morrison (1995), 55, thoroughly discusses the various opinions offered by the ancient sources.

19. Diodorus Sic. 14.41.1 and 42.2 credit Dionysius the Sicilian tyrant with the invention of fives. For the development of these ships see Murray, 2012, 13–30 and appendices A and B; also for examples depicted on Macedonian coinage. For developments at Rome see Morrison, 1996, 270–271 and Steinby, 2007; and for Carthage see Medas, 2000 and Rawlings, 2010.

20. There may have been two different designs for fives: Morrison, 1996, 270. After much debate on how the quinquereme would have functioned, the generally accepted scenario was that it had two benches of oarsmen superimposed, one bench with two rowers per oar and the other with three rowers per oar; see also Morrison, 1996, 255–277. An excellent overview of the development of warships with up-to date bibliography in reference to the Roman navy can be found in Steinby, 2007, 23–29

21. Murray, 2012, 23–30 looks carefully at the development of the fives. See also Medas, 2000 on the Carthaginian navy; Steinby, 2007 on the Roman navy in the Republic; Rawlings,

2010, on the Carthaginian navy; Rankov, 1996 and 2011; Polybius' record of the First Punic War emphasizes the sea battles and probably exaggerates the numbers involved and, possibly, the types of ship. The results seem to be an aggrandizement of these battles for his rhetorical purposes.

22. It has been noted that the depiction of Carthaginian wealth and the issue of its sea trade are in some respects a topos in the ancient literature but there is no question that the essence of Carthage's power rested in its prowess at sea. For all aspects of the Carthaginian navy see Medas, 2000 and Rawlings 2010. Rawlings, ibid., 270–271 points out that the naval exploits and numbers of ships used in the third century mean that there would have been more than just citizens involved in the naval endeavours – mercenaries, allies, slaves may all have been drafted in to fill the ships needed to fight the wars.

23. Is this a grandson of the Hamilcar Rhodinus who had gone on a mission to Alexander? See above (note 5) on the surnames of Carthaginians. The comparison is made with Rhodes, whose elite owned and manned their own warships. The idea of the bonus culture derived from a comparable practice in Athens as noted by Rawlings, 2010, 269–271.

24. See Champion, 2009 for a recent biography of Pyrrhus, and Schettino, 2009 on the construction of the image of Pyrrhus as the archetypal Hellenistic king.

25. Livy 35.14.5–12 for Hannibal's knowledge of Pyrrhus, which may be imagined but it is implied that Hannibal was known to have studied Pyrrhus' battles with the Romans.

26. Crawford, 1992, 45; Plutarch's *Life of Pyrrhus*; see Dench, 2005 on the general context of Hellenistic Italy at the time of the Pyrrhic war.

27. Most previous engagements had been between Tarentum and other cities of Magna Graecia, i.e. Metapontum, Sybaris and Locri.

28. Gruen, 1986, 319 on the 'humbling of the Hellenistic invader'.

29. Lilybaeum was built after the city of Motya was destroyed in 397 BCE by the Syracusan tyrant Dionysus (Diodorus Sic. 14. 47–53). Also important was the city of Solunto (see Map 1).

30. On Pyrrhus in Sicily see Zambon, 2008, 97–175 and Schettino, 2009.

31. For the nature of Pyrrhus' kingship in Sicily see Zambon, 2008, 118–121 and 2006, 86.

32. Diodorus 22.8.10–13; Plutarch, *Pyrrh.* 22–24; Justin 18.2.11–12, 23.3.

33. The First Punic War would end up with a similar result but it took the Romans much longer to achieve than Pyrrhus. Were the Carthaginians better prepared the second time around, or the Romans less competent but with more staying power than Pyrrhus?

34. Diodorus Sic. 22.7.5 and Polybius 3.25 cover the terms; Justin, *Epitome* 18.2 claims that a general named Mago went to Rome to offer help to the Romans, but then continues on with Carthaginian double dealings and Mago's '*Punico ingenio*'. Not for the first time, Rome and Carthage had signed treaties: Serrati, 2006 charts the Roman and Carthaginian treaties from 509 to 226 BCE that are recorded in Polybius 3.21.9–3.26. Whether this treaty of 279/278 or the treaty mentioned by the historian Philinus barred the Romans from Sicily and Carthaginians from Italy, as Philinus claimed (Polyb. 3.26.1–6), is a matter for much scholarly debate – most recently in Eckstein, 2010, which provides an excellent survey of the past century of scholarly opinion on the matter (406–407, n. 3). See also Lazenby, 1996a, 32–34, Hoyos, 1984 and 1998, 9–16, Palmer, 1997, 15–17.

35. Polyb. 1.6.8: 'They succeeded, contrary to expectation, in overcoming the peoples of Italy except for the Celts, they laid siege to the city of Rhegium.'

36. See Serrati, 2006 on the treaties between Rome and Carthage, and Polybius 3.22–27 for a description of the treaties known to him. See also Palmer, 1997 for a fascinating study of *Rome and Carthage at Peace*; and the chapter by Ameling, 2011 on 'the Rise of Carthage to 264'. Again note the counter-argument in Eckstein, 2010 against the existence of the so-called 'treaty of Philinus'.

37. The role of Pyrrhus in the historiography of the First Punic War is discussed in Berrendonner, 2009, 249–266.

38. This is not a comprehensive discussion of the First Punic War; what follows is an overview of the key events. These wars were called the Punic Wars by the Romans of the third century, *Bella Punica*, from *Bellum Poenicum*, the title of a now fragmentary epic by the third-century Roman poet Naevius.

39. See Hoyos, 1998, 5–93 for a detailed study of the outbreak of the war. The treaties between Rome and Carthage and the existence of the 'Philinus' treaty are discussed most recently by Eckstein, 2010, who argues against the existence of the treaty and gives a full and up-to-date bibliography on the subject. For the opposite view see Steinby, 2007, 78–84. Serrati, 2006 has an overview of all the treaties, and see also Hoyos, 1984. Lazenby, 1996a provides an extensive history of the First Punic War; see also articles in Hoyos (ed.), 2011.

40. The most complete ancient account of the First Punic War is in Polybius 1.10–65. Polybius intended his audience to be impressed by the enormity of the war: 'we shall find that never before in the history of the world have two such immense forces been ranged against one another at sea' (1.63.8, trans. Ian Scott-Kilvert). Many scholars believe Polybius exaggerated the size of the battles, the numbers of ships and combatants to make this point, as noted below in relation to specific passages.

41. On whether we can believe Polybius' numbers see Hoyos, 1998, 7; Lazenby 1996a, 43–55.

42. In hindsight it may have seemed that way but Carthage was probably not quite as powerful an entity as Rome when they first clashed in the mid-260s BCE. Carthage had suffered serious defeat at the hands of Pyrrhus, and the wealth and prosperity of Carthage seem overstated in the Roman-friendly sources. Some disagreement exists between modern scholars on the relative power of the two entities: see Barceló, 2004b, 22, and 2004a. Lazenby 1996a, 11–30 assesses the populations of the two states (including allied peoples) as similar, and slightly greater on Carthage's side, but the access to manpower as greater on the Roman side by the nature of their alliances and territories. More is known of the Roman manpower resources in the middle Republic: see de Ligt, 2012 and Rosenstein, 2002, who provide extensive bibliography.

43. Oscan was one of the languages of Italy. It was spoken widely in the central Apennines and the south in the period up to the Roman conquests of Italy, after which Latin became the common tongue. The latest datable Oscan inscriptions come from c. first century BCE, for the non-Latin inscriptions of Italy see Crawford (ed.), 2011.

44. The exact chronology is unclear: the Romans took Tarentum in c. 272 and had set up colonies in Paestum and Cosa (c. 273). The Romans' seizure of Rhegium (Zonaras 8.6) from mercenaries there was the last step in their conquest of southern Italy, which had fallen quickly after Pyrrhus' departure in 276/275.

45. This could have happened as late as 265 but here I follow Zambon, 2008, 200, whose chronology seems to more clearly explain the inconsistencies in the sources. See also Hoyos, 1998, 33–46 for an outline of the chronological challenges presented; Lazenby, 1996a, 34–42 also presents the chronology in close detail.

46. It is possible that Polybius has condensed a series of events occurring over half a decade into a much shorter timeframe. For the discussions around an approximate chronology of the start of the war see Zambon, 2008, 200–207, and also Lazenby, 1996a, 36. The events are chronologically confused and Lazenby points out that Hiero's rule may have started as early as 270.

47. Again, Zambon's (2008, 200–207) reconstruction of the events seems most plausible and there is extensive treatment of the events and arguments in Hoyos, 1998, 33–115.

48. There is an excellent overview of the evidence for the beginning of the war in Lazenby, 2004, 229–230.

49. With or without the much-debated treaty of Philinus, the customary sphere of Carthaginian influence would seem to have been infringed upon in this case. If the Carthaginians had broken the treaty first by appearing at Tarentum (Zonaras 8.6) while it was under siege by the Romans perhaps they were the ones who had first stepped beyond the traditional sphere of influence. It is difficult to prove either way but as Eckstein, 2010, 406–407 argues, it has important ramifications for our understanding of Roman and Carthaginian imperialism.

50. The inconsistency lay in helping the Mamertines when they had just ousted their compatriot mercenaries from Rhegium.

51. The different views are outlined in most discussions of the First Punic War; see especially Hoyos, 1998, 1–115; Goldsworthy, 2003, 65–75; see also Harris, 1985, 63–64, 108, 113–114, 182–190; and Miles, 2010, 165–167, who takes a more pragmatic approach than Harris; see also Lazenby, 1996a, 31–42, and 2004, 229–230.

52. Goldsworthy, 2003, 70, who makes the point about each side having clear-cut spheres of influence according to their previous treaties; and Serrati, 2006, again for the details of the treaties. See also Lancel, 1995, 362–364. Eckstein, 2006, 165–66 defends Polybius here, denying the existence of the treaty.

53. Polybius 1.10.9–1.11.3, for the debate at Rome over whether to take this step and the implications.

54. The allies listed are the Tarentines, Locrians, Eleans and the people of Neapolis, newly conquered and perhaps not the most stable of allies. See also Walbank, vol. 1, 75 for a discussion of Roman adaptability as a popular Greek topos and the possibility of this being inaccurate or perhaps an understatement of Roman naval abilities at the start of the war. Steinby, 2007, 29–30 also questions Polybius' version of the Romans being naval novices.

55. Steinby, 2007, 77; and more broadly Steinby, 2007, 29–84 for an up-to-date assessment of Roman naval power at the start of the First Punic War; see also Murray, 2012; and the always useful Casson, 1995.

56. On the construction of the navy see also Dionysus of Halicarnassus 20.15; and Harris, 1985, 183–184 for the acquisition of the Sila Forest to provide wood for ships. Exactly how the fives functioned is still debated. They had either two or three banks of oars with five oarsmen on each side. There may have been two different designs for fives (see above n. 20) and further in Morrison, 1996, 255–277. An excellent overview of the development of warships with up-to-date bibliography in reference to the Roman navy can be found in Steinby, 2007, 23–29; see Frost, 1974 on the discovery of a Punic ship off Marsala and the evidence it provides for the mass production of ships.

57. This brief overview of the First Punic War touches on the key moments in the war down to Hannibal's birth. A full and detailed account can be found in Lazenby, 1996a, Goldsworthy, 2003, 65–133 and many other excellent histories. Particularly useful are the phases of the war laid out by Rankov, 2011, 149–166.

58. See Walbank, vol. 1, 67–68 for a plausible explanation of the events outlined in Polybius. The Roman army is well described by Fields, 2007; Potter, 2004.

59. This is undoubtedly the version of events taken from the pro-Roman writings of Fabius Pictor in Walbank's view, vol. 1, 67–69.

60. Following comments in Polybius 1.20.1–3.

61. Originally founded in c. 580 by the people of the city of Gela who were in turn Rhodian and Cretan in origin, according to Thucydides 6.4.4. For a summary of the early Greek settlement in Sicily see Holloway, 2000, 43–96. Agrigentum was held by Carthage from the first quarter of the third century.

62. The Romans, Polybius tells us, had just reduced their troop numbers from four legions to two and were relying on Syracusan forces as backup. For the Carthaginian army in the Punic Wars see Daly, 2002, 81–112 for Hannibal's time; see Rawlings, 2010 for the navy.

63. Chaniotis, 2005, 78–101 on professional soldiers and Hellenistic warfare; Hoyos, 2007, 6–12 on the make-up of the mercenaries at Carthage just after the First Punic War. Rome's citizen army was the exception rather than the rule. For an excellent analysis of the two fighting forces in the period of Hannibal see Daly, 2002, 48–112.

64. The mercenary element of the Carthaginian army may well have been overemphasized by pro-Roman sources for rhetorical purposes. See Daly, 2002, 81–84, which points out Polybius' prejudices and lack of knowledge in regard to the Carthaginian forces.

65. Polybius' information and detail on the siege of Agrigentum are likely to have come from the lost history of Philinus, who was himself from Agrigentum and considered a 'pro-Carthaginian' source, see Walbank, vol. 1, 70.

66. See Hoyos, 1998, 82–115 for a detailed explanation of the early stages of the war and the motivations of the main players. Hoyos, 2011, 131–147 (in Hoyos (ed.), 2011) provides a general overview of the arguments in 'The Outbreak of War'. Lazenby 1996a, 43–60 gives a detailed analysis of the early part of the war. Did the victory at Agrigentum shift the direction of Roman policy as Polybius claims or had conquest of Sicily always been the intention? Were the Romans only reacting to Carthaginian manoeuvres and Syracusan policies? With both sides fighting to advantage and the Romans' rolling successes over the previous

century of expansion, the appetite and economics of continuous warfare were integrated into their political and social systems to such a degree that there was perhaps never a conscious choice. Argued in Eckstein, 2006, 181–243 and the still valuable Harris, 1985, 182–190.

67. Polybius 1.22.1–11 is a detailed description of the innovation. See Steinby, 2007, 87–104 for the boarding-bridge as a naval innovation and for questions about whether Polybius' assessment that it was the *corvus* that gave the Romans the advantage. See also De Souza, 2007, 434–460 for an excellent technical explanation of the function of the *corvus* and more generally the tactics employed in naval battles. Rawlings, 2010, 279 observes that Carthaginian naval skills relied more on the ability to outmanoeuvre their opponents than on the boarding tactic. See Murray, 2012, 31–68 on frontal ramming and p. 225 on the *corvus/corax*.

68. The fleet was under the command of Hannibal, who had been commander at Agrigentum. Land and sea armies were commanded by the same individuals. Comparing Polybius' evidence for the battle of the Aegates Islands in 241 with the archaeological evidence recently uncovered, it is important to look sceptically at the numbers of ships and especially their size – were they mostly quinqueremes? See Tusa and Royal, 2012 and ongoing research at the battle site, which is providing unique information about naval warfare in the third-century western Mediterranean.

69. Lipinski, 2004, 444, has suggested that 60 ships was a standard designation of a fleet, merchant or military, based on its consistent appearance in sources that note the number of recorded ships. So the loss of 30 ships would equate to that of half a fleet.

70. Steinby, 2007, 92–93.

71. Rawlings, 2010 on the Carthaginian navy.

72. Walbank, vol. 1, 82–85 discusses these numbers in great detail and suggests revising down-wards for a range of well-argued reasons. He notes that Polybius' precise detail suggests that his source was an eyewitness to these events – possibly Philinus. For the numbers of ships, and the manpower needed to run them, oarsmen, marines, etc. see the estimates in Rawlings, 2010, 270.

73. Goldsworthy, 2003, 96–127 provides a clear and in-depth assessment of the war at sea, including the tactics and deployment at Ecnomus.

74. See Rawlings, 2010; de Souza, 2007, 434–441; also Steinby, 2007, 94–95.

75. Polybius claimed that the *corax/corvus* was the difference between the two sides and that 'all would . . . have been lost [for the Romans] if the Carthaginians had not been afraid of the ravens and simply hedged them in and held them close to the land' (1.28.11).

76. Diodorus Sic. 19.106.3 mentions this ritual in relation to an earlier defeat and here I am assuming that the practice continued. See Rawlings, 2010, 270 for the numbers of citizens in the Carthaginian fleet.

77. Valerius Maximus 6.6.2 and Cassius Dio 11, frag. 43.21a both claim that a Carthaginian leader named Hamilcar sent Hanno to the Romans with a peace proposal at this time.

78. They followed the same route and tactics that the Syracusan general Agathocles had used half a century previously. Diodorus Sic., 20.8.3–4. See Lazenby, 1996a, 97–110 for Regulus' invasion.

79. See Krings, 2008 on the landscape and a comparison between the accounts of Agathocles and Regulus. The later sources who provide these details may be constructing a landscape of prosperity linked to military intervention.

80. Perhaps implying they were not expecting much of a fight from Carthage.

81. The site was occupied from the sixth to the third centuries. Its destruction cannot be exactly dated to Regulus' invasion but is stated to have been roughly mid-third century by Fantar, 1987, 209. Some of this rests in the imagination after visiting the evocative site. It is briefly described in Lancel, 1995, 280–288. Miles, 2010, 78–81 notes the surprising number of bathtubs and proposes the idea of ritual bathing. Excavations at the site, found by accident, took place in the 1950s–1970s: see Fantar, 1987.

82. Agathocles had used the same tactics against Carthage, taking Tunes, as would the merce-nary forces in the war of 241–238. Scipio Aemilianus in the Third Punic War and the

seventh-century CE Arabic forces would employ the same tactics – it was understood that Carthage was vulnerable from the land.

83. We have no idea if he did or did not. His age suggests that he would have been active in military operations at this time and Hamilcar may have learned from the Spartan. We know Hannibal employed a Spartan historian (Sosylus, Cornelius Nepos, *Hann.* 13.3) as his teacher, so there was a Spartan connection. Appian, *Lib.* 4 claims that the Carthaginians had Xanthippus and his Spartan companions drowned on their way back to Greece, which might be part of a topos on Carthaginian cruelty. The drowning of Xanthippus is not mentioned by Polybius (1.36.2–4) but he does allude to resentment at Carthage towards the Spartan general and the acclaim his success brought him. The drowning of Xanthippus is repeated in Valerius Maximus 9.6. ext.1 and Zonaras 8.13.

84. See Lazenby, 1996a, 97–110, Goldsworthy, 2003, 84–92.

85. For the fate of Regulus see below, note 88.

86. Polybius' numbers (1.37.2) are that 80 out of 364 ships survived, other sources such as Diodorus Siculus tell us that 340 ships were lost (23.18.1), later compilers like Orosius (4.9.8) claim that only 80 of 300 ships were saved, and Eutropius again claims that just 80 survived, but out of a total of 464. Once again the numbers are unclear, but that the Romans suffered large losses at sea is not challenged. Some historians have suggested the idea that the *corvus*, so useful for boarding enemy vessels, made the Roman ships more unstable, and especially vulnerable to bad weather; see Goldsworthy, 2003, 115–116, whose view was originally discussed in Thiel, 1954, 274 n.1, and Steinby, 2007, 96 who argues against this view.

87. According to Thucydides 6.2.6, the Phoenicians settled at Motya, Panormus (Palermo), and Solonte in the *c.* eighth century BCE, although archaeological evidence at Palermo, so far, only dates back to the late seventh/early sixth century BCE from excavations at necropoleis there.

88. On Regulus see Lazenby, 1996a, 122, who notes that sending a prisoner of war to negotiate would not have been normal practice for the Carthaginians. Tipps, 2003 outlines the expedition and implications. On the failure of the Carthaginians to capitalize after 249 BCE see Lazenby, 1996a, 143 and Goldsworthy, 2003, 119–122. Walbank, vol. 1, 93–94 and Lancel, 1995, 369 are among those who object to Appian's account and note that if the torture had happened then Polybius would surely have mentioned it. See Horace, *Odes* 3.5; Appian, *Lib.* 4 and *Sic.* 2.1; for the career and sources for Regulus see Broughton, 1951, 209–210.

## Chapter 3  His Father's Son

1. Freud (1931, 194–196) saw Hannibal as the perfect antidote to the anti-Semitic sentiments of his classmates in school. Others before him also related to Hannibal, from Sir Walter Raleigh to Irish mercenaries: see more in chapter 12.

2. Freud, 1931, 195–196; see Reff, 1963 on Cézanne's poem and the 'dream of Hannibal'; Polybius (3.9.6) on the 'anger of Hamilcar' as the cause of the war, which was picked up on by Livy 21.1.5–2.2, Cornelius Nepos, *Ham.* 1.4, 4.2, Valerius Maximus 9.3.2: 'how passionate was Hamilcar's hate of the Roman people'. The son following the father's plans is likely a topos, i.e. Polybius in his discussion of the cause of war links Alexander's actions with the plans of Philip (3.6.1–14).

3. Cornelius Nepos, *Ham.* 1.1, calls Hamilcar a young man. Hoyos, 2005, 21 gives a rough age of 30, but also notes that Cicero at 40 referred to himself as 'young' so there is a fair bit of leeway here.

4. Roman elite families traced their lineages back to the founders of Rome and it would have been normal for them to assume the Carthaginian elites could do the same – and perhaps they did. Evidence for the grand estates of the Barcid clan comes from many years later when Hannibal was believed to have estates south of Carthage in the region of Thapsus and Hadrumentum (modern Sousse): Livy 33.48.1; for Hadrumentum see Pliny, *NH* 15.5.3. Earned epithet or family surname is difficult to know; for more on names see Lancel, 1999, 6–7; Miles, 2010, 193 translates it as a nickname meaning 'flash' – the nickname of the Hellenistic king Ptolemy 'Keraunos' has much the same meaning.

5. He is a somewhat elusive character, about whom we know very little, but what we do know of Hamilcar is best documented and explained in Hoyos, 2005, 21–22 and Lancel, 1999, 1–24, and Seibert, 1993a, 25–39 who provides a less than glowing account of his skills, which may well be overblown by Polybius or the sources he used.

6. Polybius 1.56.2 tells us that Hamilcar joined the war effort in Sicily in the eighteenth year of the war.

7. Lazenby, 1996a, 143–159 covers this part of the war in detail; see also Miles, 2010, 193–199; also Seibert, 1993b, 83–94, who questions the glowing account of Hamilcar's abilities.

8. See Hoyos, 2005, 7–20 on Hamilcar at the heights of Heirkte and Eryx. Heirkte is thought to be Monte Castellaccio north of Panormus, following Lazenby, 1996a, 147. At Eryx, the Phoenician–Punic deity Astarte had traditionally been syncretized with an Elymian deity worshipped there. The goddess was then syncretized with the Graeco-Roman versions of Aphrodite-Venus into Venus Erycina. This was a powerful and holy multicultural shrine that was significant for both sides. For the Carthaginians there is evidence for this version of Astarte (from Eryx) worshipped at Carthage, at Sicca Veneria and in Sardinia: see Bonnet, 1996, 115–120. Romans placed great significance on their Trojan origins and through the connection to Venus. See Erskine, 2001, 198–205 on the importance to Rome of its Trojan roots; and Myles, 2010, 274–276 on Venus Erycina and her temple at Rome.

9. Lazenby, 1996a, 111–122 for Carthage's defensive war in Sicily.

10. For the coinage of Carthage during the First Punic War see Visona, 1998; Alexandropoulos, 2000; and Crawford, 1985, 136 for the debased coinage.

11. Appian, *Sic.* 1 for the state of the Roman and Carthaginian economies. Appian asserts that the Ptolemies remained neutral in the war – perhaps watching to see who came out on top. See Gruen, 1986, 676 for Ptolemaic Egypt during the Punic Wars, and also Adams, 2008 on Ptolemaic neutrality. Rawlings, 2010, 265–272 notes that it would have been usual practice at Carthage, given the size of its citizen base, to recruit both from within and without the citizenry to man its fleets.

12. Tusa and Royal, 2012 for the recent discovery of the battle site and bronze rams from ships sunk there in 241.

13. Polybius does not mention that any Roman ships were lost, whilst Diodorus Siculus 24.11.2 provides different numbers, claiming 'Carthage lost 117 ships, 20 of them with all the men on board and that the Romans lost 80 ships, 30 of them completely, while 50 were partially destroyed'. Tusa and Royal, 2012 discuss the battle site and the evidence from the ships that were sunk.

14. 'the Carthaginians . . . already short of money, ships and men, sought an armistice from Lutatius (the Roman consul)' (Appian, *Sic.* 2.1).

15. The exact date for Sicily becoming a province is debatable, but from 241 the island was essentially under Roman control with Syracuse much like a client kingdom: see Serrati, 2000b, 109–111.

16. Lancel's (1999, 1) claim that the war and the subsequent invasion of Hannibal should be seen as one long 'double Punic War' was not the view in antiquity, although Hamilcar and Hannibal's intentions towards war with Rome were linked, there was a distinct period of 'peace' with declaration of war following the interval between 241 and 218. See Polybius 1.62–63 for the text of the treaty of Lutatius to end the war. Polybius continues to tell us that the treaty was amended by the people (people's assembly) in Rome in order to impose harsher conditions and a shorter reparations period. Superior Roman manpower and resource form a frequent topos in Polybius.

17. A point made by Seibert, 1993a, 11.

18. The Mercenary War, or *Truceless War*, as it is called by Polybius, 1.65.6; see Hoyos, 2007 and Loreto, 1995 for detailed studies of the events of these years.

19. Barceló, 2004a, 55–69 describes the 'traumatic childhood' of Hannibal. Polyb. 1.65–88 covers the events from 241 to 237 in North Africa in some detail (the Mercenary, or so-called 'Truceless', War). See also, more briefly, Appian, *Ib* 6.1.4; *Sic.* 1–2; and Diodorus Siculus, 25.2. Hoyos, 2007 provides a close look at the war and its context with an excellent

updated bibliography and Loreto, 1995 also devotes a volume to the political and military implications of the Mercenary War; see also Seibert, 1993a, 11–24 and 1993b, 95–107. Goldsworthy, 2003, 133–136 provides a brief overview of the main events.

20. Rawlings, 1996 on soldiers in the Second Punic War. Daly, 2002, 81–112 surveys the ethnic groups and their function in Hannibal's army, and see ibid., 107–108 for the Balearic slingers who Daly contends were mercenaries rather than allied soldiers. Diodorus Siculus 5.16 claims that Carthage founded its first colony on Ibiza in the seventh century so the relationship between the city and Balearic slingers may have been linked for many centuries as noted in Whittaker, 1978, 59. See Ameling, 1993, 212–215; Brizzi, 1995, 303–315; and Hoyos, 2007, 6–12; also Goldsworthy, 2003, 30–36 for the mercenary army of Carthage.

21. This may reflect Gisgo's thoughts and be derived from a pro-Carthaginian source, but also seems a bit like Polybian hindsight. Polybius was deeply hostile to mercenary armies.

22. As noted in chapter 1, Carthaginian civilian magistrates and military command did not seem to be as closely linked as in the Roman Republic.

23. Flaubert, *Salammbô*, 18.

24. For Carthaginian coinage see Jenkins and Lewis, 1963, and for the debased coinage at the end of the First Punic War see Carradice and La Niece, 1988, 48; also Acquaro et al., 1991. Crawford, 1985, 136 suggests that these were produced for the Libyans. An example is reproduced clearly in Hoyos, 2007, figs 7.3–7.4; ibid., 39 for the calculation of the worth of the coin.

25. Sicca is modern Le Kef, 170km south-west of Carthage, a Libyphoenician town under Carthaginian influence; however, it may not have been under its direct control: see Lancel, 1995, 257–259. Differing views on the status of Sicca are clearly outlined by Hoyos, 2007, 16–19. Sicca Veneria, as it was known, also housed an important version of the cult of Astarte/Venus from Eryx – which may also account for the destination of the soldiers.

26. Hamilcar's whereabouts during this period are unknown: see below, nn. 28, 29.

27. Polybius' account of the rebellion is pro-Carthaginian, which relates to his sources, or to the rhetorical point of barbarian versus civilization, in this particular case the Carthaginians. Polybius claims that the Carthaginians preferred ethnically mixed troops in their armies as it tended to minimize sedition (1.67.4). The command structure in the Carthaginian army of Hannibal is surveyed by Daly, 2002, 83, who notes that the highest-ranking officers were Carthaginian but the cohorts of different ethnicities had commanders as well. Could the 20,000 be the approximate number of soldiers that had been in Sicily as suggested by Hoyos, 2007, 25–29?

28. Hoyos, 2005, 35; 2007, 20–21 n. 11 argues that Appian confused the chronology of this prosecution. Appian places Hamilcar's prosecution after the Mercenary War (237) whereas Hoyos argues for the prosecution to have taken place directly after the loss of Sicily, which makes, to my mind, more sense. Seibert, 1993, 13–14 places the trial just after the outbreak of the rebellion. See Goldsworthy, 2003, 133–134 on Hamilcar's movements during this period.

29. Diodorus Siculus continues that 'the basic cause in this matter was the Carthaginians' severity in inflicting punishments'. Diodorus' discussion of military trials relates to events 70 years earlier than the Punic Wars, in the period of Agathocles (*c.* 310 BCE). Miles, 2010, 145–149 provides an interesting suggestion on this issue in connection to Agathocles, bringing up the possibility that a conflict between generals chosen by the people and the governing elite might lie behind some of this turmoil after peace had been achieved.

30. The furthest extension of direct Carthaginian control inland is recorded at Tebessa, in modern Algeria (Roman Theveste and in Greek Hecatompylus). See Lazenby, 1996a, 144 and Ameling, 2011, 48, from Polybius 1.73.1 and Appian, *Ib.* 4.

31. Walbank, vol. 1, 131 analyses the use of the term and the reasons Polybius invests so much energy in describing the events of these four years. Hoyos, 2007 uses the title for his study of the war and Loreto, 1995 refers to it as a Libyan insurrection.

32. This is much simplified: not all the Libyphoenician or Libyan population would have been favourable to the revolt and there existed a very intricate system of loyalties, intermarriage and cultural fusion between the Libyan and Carthaginian populations. See Hoyos, 2007, 83–84.

33. The number of troops is clearly exaggerated, according to Walbank, vol. 1, 139. Cornelius Nepos, *Ham*. 2.2 put the number at 100,000. Hoyos, 2007, 77–86 agrees on the inflation of the numbers contra Loreto, 1995, 97–89 and 119–121.

34. Polybius' sources for the Mercenary War are not known. This is discussed in Walbank, vol. 1, 130–131 and Hoyos, 2007, 261–274.

35. Brett and Fentress, 1996, 25; Fentress, 2006, 6–22 for an overview of the pre-Roman countryside in North Africa.

36. According to Hoyos, 2005, appendix 5, this Naravas could well have been related (perhaps an uncle) to the Numidian king Masinissa who would play such an important role in the fate of Hannibal and the Second Punic War. If Hamilcar indeed married his daughter to Naravas, then the connection between the Barcids and Masinissa would have been very close (for more on Masinissa and the family links to Hannibal see chapter 11, note 3). See Hoyos, 2007, 146–150 on Naravas. Interesting questions arise about how Carthage recruited its armies. Did Hamilcar personally recruit soldiers to fight for him or did Carthage raise the army and place Hamilcar in command? The issue of personal recruitment of an army would cause havoc in the Roman Republic in the last century of its existence and it is interesting to consider whether Carthage was facing some of the same issues.

37. It seems most likely that Naravas was married to Hamilcar's third daughter as the two elder were already married: this is Flaubert's eponymous heroine Salammbô. See Hoyos, 2005, 37–38 for the marriage. The kind of personal military leadership Hamilcar exercised would come to dominate the late Republican armies of Rome and was also key to the personal armies of Hellenistic commanders.

38. Exaggerated, according to Walbank, vol. 1, 143–144; discussed by Loreto, 1995, 156 and Hoyos, 2007, 150–151.

39. ΛΙΒΥΩΝ – the Greek script indicating there was a significant Greek presence among the soldiers, but there is also Punic text on most of the coins. For the coinage of the Libyans see recently Yarrow, 2013, 359–364; Zimmermann, 2001; Acquaro, 1989; and Carradice and La Niece, 1988. Crawford, 1985, 135 does not think that the possibility of these being struck at Carthage should be excluded, which would give a completely different meaning to the issues.

40. The chronology of the rebellion is not clearly laid out in Polybius. Walbank claims the Sardinian garrisons revolted after or at the same time as the second battle between Hamilcar and Spendius, although in the narrative it comes directly after the first. See Walbank, vol. 1, 144; Hoyos, 2007, 154–159. For Sardinia see van Dommelen, 1998 and van Dommelen and Gómez Bellard, 2008; Bernardini, 2004 on the Phoenician and Punic settlements.

41. Carthage was closely linked to Sardinia from the late sixth century. Polybius (3.22.3) lists two early treaties between Rome and Carthage that linked Sardinia and Libya together by defining the access allowed by Carthage to Rome. For the treaties see Serrati, 2006. For the extent of the Punic realm in Sardinia see discussion in van Dommelen, 1998.

42. Late in 238 or early in 237 is the accepted date for the end of the war. See Hoyos, 2007, 275–276 for an approximate outline of the major events discussed in this chapter.

43. The brutality of the Gauls who had marauded and pillaged their way through Italy and Greece in the previous centuries was a narrative construction in the Roman (and Greek) literary tradition, which may reflect Polybius' source here.

44. See Hoyos, 2007, 173–177 for Hamilcar's response and the rebels' attempts to deter their followers from going over to him.

45. Hanno lived to a ripe old age and was the standard-bearer of opposition to the Barcid family in the Carthaginian Senate according to Livy 21.3, 21.10, 23.12, 30.20, and Appian, *Lib*. 24.

46. Hanno's opposition to the Barcids is a theme in Livy's narrative of the Hannibalic War; see Fariselli, 2006 and Brizzi, 2009 on the political aims of the Barcids and the factionalism in politics at Carthage during the Punic Wars.

47. There were two areas Polybius may have been referring to: the most likely are cities along the eastern coast of modern Tunisia like Hadrumentum (Sousse) in what is referred to as the Sahel, or – further south along the Gulf of Gabes – ancient Tacape. *Emporia*, the Greek

word meaning 'commerce', came to be used to describe market centres and the cities that grew up around them. The term *Emporia* is also used (in Herodotus, for example) to refer to the cities further east along the coast of modern Libya called Oea, Lepcis Magna and Sabratha. These were Libyphoenician cities allied to Carthage and may have been supporting the Carthaginian war effort. Considering the loss of support from Sardinia, these cities would have been even more important to the Carthaginians. See differing interpretations in Walbank, vol. 1, 145, who presents the comparative source material for the region of the Gulf of Tacape (modern Gabes) and in Hoyos, 2005, 43–47. See also Lancel, 1995, 87, 291–302 on the origin of these cities and on the expansion of Carthage into Africa and the origins of these ties.

48. See Eutropius 2.27 and Valerius Maximus 5.1.1.
49. This refers to the landscape's similarity to a serrated ridge; the word is πριονα and is also used to describe the Sierra Nevada mountains in Iberia (see Walbank, vol. 1, 147).
50. Hoyos, 2007, 197–218 provides a full reconstruction of events.
51. In the area around Spendius' body he put to death another 30 high-ranking Carthaginians. Polybius makes the point that Hannibal is crucified 'alive' on Spendius' cross, differentiating between that and just crucifixion.
52. Polybius makes it three years and four months (1.88.7); Livy claims five years (21.2.1); and Diodorus Siculus (25.5.6) makes it out to be four years and four months. I use four years here as an average. See Walbank, vol. 1, 148–149 for the possible reasons for the discrepancy.
53. Eckstein, 2006, 168 claims the Romans changed tactics towards Carthage in 238/237, feeling that the peace had been 'too mild'.
54. The Romans occupied Sardinia in 238; it was made a province (along with Corsica) in 227: see van Dommelen, 1998, 25. See Polybius 3.27.7–9 for extended terms of the treaty.
55. Hoyos, 2007, 263–274 on Polybius' sources and Walbank, vol. 1, 130–150 for detailed assessment.
56. As he was writing in the second century BCE when Rome first established the province of Africa, we might view the narrative of the Mercenary War as a warning from Polybius to the Romans about the wider population of their new province and the governance of the landscape.
57. The modern term is Berbers, but the Greek and Roman sources refer to the North Africans as Libyans, Libyphoenicians and Numidians. According to Polybius, people called the Libyans inhabited the region extending along the fertile valley of the Bagradas river and reached south and west from Carthage into what is modern Algeria and the high plateau of the Atlas. The survival of the Libyphoenician culture across North Africa into the late antique period speaks of deeply rooted Punic influence and a layered and nuanced mixing of the populations. See Brett and Fentress, 1996, 24–25 for an overview of Punic and Berber North Africa.
58. A complex sequence of alliances, urban foundations and ethnic mixtures followed the consolidation of the hinterland by Carthage, see Ameling, 2011, 48–51; Lazenby, 1996a, 23 outlines the different cities coming under direct Carthaginian control during the third century; Lancel, 1995, 257–302 outlines the material evidence for the Carthaginian 'expansion' into Africa; whilst articles in van Dommelen and Gómez Ballard, 2008 trace the agricultural impact of Punic culture.
59. As Carthage pushed its power inland there was a parallel articulation of kingdoms among the people living just beyond the direct control of Carthage. Carthaginian territory expanded to its furthest point, Tebessa (Hekatompylos) according to Polybius 1.73.1 and Diodorus Siculus 24.10.2.
60. Previous centuries of Carthaginian battles in Sicily, variously allied with local Sicilians against Syracuse and Sicilian Greek tyrants, would have seemed quite straightforward in comparison with the danger posed by Rome and her new interest in Carthaginian territory.

## Chapter 4  Barcid Iberia from Gades to Saguntum

1. The Jupiter mentioned here is the Romanized version of the Carthaginian Ba'al Hammon. The region of modern Spain was known in antiquity as Iberia and also by the Latin

Hispania. I have used Iberia here in preference, especially when discussing the people who inhabited the regions beyond the Phoenician and Greek settlements on the coast before the Roman conquest. I use Spain when it is referring to the modern country and in some translations where the Latin Hispania is used.

2. As far as we know, Hannibal did not return to Carthage in the interim although there was the possibility of transport back and forth, and with frequent communication between Iberia and Carthage it is difficult to know for certain. Through the years in Iberia his brother-in-law Hasdrubal seems to have frequented Carthage. Livy's claim that Hannibal was sent from Carthage to Iberia in 221 after the death of Hasdrubal is considered to be erroneous as he contradicts himself (21.3.2, 4.2, and 30.37.9), as noted in Hoyos, 2006, 631, n. 3.

3. Evidence for the ritual practices in the Punic world is limited. For the cow's head on an altar as a ritual offering in Carthaginian practice see image in the Louvre: a white limestone stele from Carthage (AO 5081, Collection & Louvre Palace). The discussion in Ribichini, 2001 provides a clear introduction. Discussion of the evidence in Picard, C., 1975 and image reproduced clearly in Brouillet, 1994, 54 (catalogue no. 39).

4. Polybius used the Greek Zeus to refer to Ba'al Hammon here again.

5. Livy 21.1.4; Nepos, *Hann.* 2.4; Valerius Maximus 9.3; Appian, *Hann.* 3; Martial 9.43.9: 'by him [Herakles] the boy Hannibal took an oath at a Libyan altar'. For a complete list of references see Walbank, vol. 1, 314–315. See more in chapter 12 below.

6. See Walbank, vol. 1, 314 for the complete list of references to the oath in the ancient sources and Rich, 1996, 7 for an analysis of the origin of the story. Stocks, 2014, 87–88 and 90–91 look at how Silius Italicus weaves the oath of Hannibal, which he placed in the Temple of Dido at Carthage, with Virgil's curse of Dido and the influence of Hamilcar.

7. These ideas are explored by Gowing, 2005, 28–66, especially on the period of Tiberius' rule and more generally in terms of Carthage by Miles, 2010, 352–373. See more in chapter 12 below.

8. On the hatred of Hamilcar, see Polybius 3.9.6; on Hannibal's oath see Seibert, 1993a, 26–28; Lancel, 1999, 30 and 197.

9. For the Barcids in Iberia see Barceló, 1988, Goldsworthy, 2003, 136–138; Hoyos, 2005, 55–86 for Hamilcar and Hasdrubal; Lancel, 1999, 28–45; Seibert, 1993a, 25–51; Wagner, 1989 for background on the Phoenician and Punic ports in Spain; and before the Barcids see Arteaga, 2004. For a brief introduction to the Phoenicians, Greeks, Carthaginians and Romans in Spain in English see Collins, 1998, 8–14.

10. Hoyos, 1984, Lancel 1995, 34–35, Hoyos, 2005, but with even greater autonomy, it is thought.

11. This embassy is not mentioned in any other source but I agree here with Eckstein, 1984, 56–57 who supports the historicity of the episode. See Hoyos, 1998, 147–149 who outlines the reasons given to believe or disbelieve the authenticity and mentions the timing, 10 years after the end of the First Punic War.

12. The case for the autonomy of the Roman consuls in the field is made by Eckstein and he applies this to the Carthaginian generals as well (1987, 132–133) in 241 at the end of the First Punic War. At the end of the Hannibalic War, Livy (30.42.12) reports that the Carthaginian negotiators place the whole of the responsibility for the war on Hannibal's shoulders.

13. Seibert, 1993a, 105 discusses the relationship between representatives and generals, and Hoyos, 2007, 13–24 provides a clear discussion of the politicians and the generals at Carthage in this period. Most recently see Brizzi, 2009 on the divisions within the Carthaginian ruling elite and the range of scholarly opinions.

14. A large bibliography exists on the inter-war period and the causes of the Second Punic War. For a range of opinions see articles in Cornell et al.(eds), 1996 esp. Rich; see also Hoyos, 1998; Eckstein, 2006, 158–180 and 1984; and Erdkamp, 2009 on Polybius' narrative intent specifically. On the debate around the role of the Barcids and their degree of political autonomy in Iberia see Picard, G-C., 1983–84; Seibert, 1993b, 117–151; Hoyos, 2005, 47–54 and 1994, Miles, 2010, 218–234 for a selection of opinions.

15. Known in antiquity as Gadiera/Gades/Gadir. There are conflicting versions of the voyage – Polybius implies that the Carthaginian army marched across North Africa towards the west, while Diodorus Siculus claims the journey was made by sea. Polybius' account rings true, given the territorial gains made at the end of the Mercenary War, and in 237 a fleet capable of transporting the whole army may not have been available. Diodorus' account makes sense if the ships (and army) used were those that had been prepared for the expedition to Sardinia that never happened. See Polybius. 2.1.5–6; Diodorus Sic. 25.10.1; Cornelius Nepos, *Ham.* 3. Both views are clearly expressed in the modern scholarship, e.g. Hoyos, 2005, 55: 'it is very unlikely that Diodorus is wrong'; Lancel, 1999, 30 prefers to believe Polybius rather than Diodorus. Miles, 2010, 219 also takes Polybius' version as more accurate and makes an argument for the lack of ships.

16. There are coastal settlements of Phoenician origin extending from the Sado river (just south of Lisbon) to the Segura river (in the Alicante province of Spain). See Neville, 2007, 83–104 on Cadiz, and see above chapter 1 on the Phoenician settlements. Lowe, 2009, 8–53 charts the development of settlements along the coast from the first foundations to the Roman period.

17. A concentration of coinage in the Carthaginian style found at Gades may date to before 237 and may provide evidence of a strong commercial connection Visona, 1995, 179. Barceló, 1988 looks at the relationship between Iberia and Carthage from the first colony in the seventh century to the Barcids. Lancel, 1995, 35 notes that Polybius uses the term 'reconquest', indicating that there was a presumed link established before the Barcid conquests. The ceramic evidence for commercial traffic along the Baetis/Guadalquivir is surveyed by Ferrer Albelda et al., 2010. An overview of the current evidence for the relationship between the cities prior to the Barcids is available in Ferrer Albelda and Pliego Vásquez, 2011.

18. For Hannibal at Gades see chapter 5. For Melqart see Bonnet, 1986; and Rawlings, 2005, on Hannibal, Herakles and Melqart; Miles, 2010 and 2011 for Melqart and the Barcid family; Malkin, 2011, 119–141 on the dynamic duo who were heroes of the colonial west; Campus, 2005 on the links between Herakles, Hannibal and Alexander; Aubet 2001, 259–279 on Cadiz, location, foundation and function in the early first millennium BCE. Fear, 2005 charts the temple as a place of pilgrimage through antiquity. Mierse, 2000 looks at the temple in the Arabic sources.

19. Broader political motivations and close connections with the old Phoenician colonies seem possible but there is no existing evidence. The loss of Sardinia is given as the catalyst in Cassius Dio (see below page 66, and note 28). For Tarshish and Tartessos see chapter 1, p. 8 and note 7.

20. It was in this period of Carthaginian conquest in the 230s that the inland populations of Iberia were, for the first time, articulated historically. Thus no full picture of the landscape in the third century BCE exists, although recent archaeological research has done much to broaden our perspective on settlement and communications, in English see Neville, 2007; articles in Bierling, 2002 for the Phoenicians in Spain; see also Aubet, 2001, 257–346 for the colonies in the west and far west. See articles in Ferrer Albelda (ed.), 2010 for the Punic period and Morillo et al. (eds), 2003 for the early period of the Roman conquest.

21. See Hoyos, 2005, 55 for the number of soldiers in Hamilcar's army. Diodorus Siculus 25.12 for the army 10 years on; Lancel, 1995, 35 on the 'reconquest'.

22. Hamilcar probably had his younger sons with him, if not most of his family other than his daughters who were already married. See Zonaras 8.21 on learning the arts of war from his father. Hoyos, 2005, 54 and 66–67 notes the guidance Hannibal received from his father and how close they were. We do not know the age of the youngest son, Mago, but if he was born in *c.* 243 he was probably learning to ride etc. from the age of 6 or 7.

23. Cornelius Nepos, *Hann.* 13.3; Sosylus and Silenus both wrote histories, no longer extant, of Hannibal's campaigns.

24. In this period in the Iberian peninsula the geography of the peoples and leaders is vague at best and sometimes confused, especially by Livy. The leaders mentioned here were possibly leaders of the Tartessi and Turdetani who occupied the regions north and south of the Guadalquivir river. See Map 2.

25. See Miles, 2010: 222–225 here on the Hellenistic aspect of Carthaginian rule in Iberia; also Lancel, 1999, 34–43 and G-C. Picard, 1983–84 on Hannibal's Hellenistic-styled power, which he inherited from his brother-in-law and father.

26. Hoyos, 2005, 64 for the arguments for and against the location. Lancel, 1995, 36 calls it the 'White Headland', and the foundation is dated to either 235 or 231. Lack of evidence typifies the difficulty in piecing together Hamilcar's time in Iberia. Barceló, 2004a, 70–82 argues for a location inland. See Sala Sellés, 2010, who provides a clear overview of the changing ideas behind the identification of the Punic and Iberian sites in this part of Spain.

27. See Gruen, 1986, 359ff. on 'Rome, Macedon and Illyria' for the background on Rome and Illyria.

28. Eckstein, 1984, 56–57 makes a good argument for believing Cassius Dio's addition to the chronology contra Hoyos, 2005, 61; see also Rich, 1996, 19, who analyses the historicity of the claims – all provide analysis of the debate.

29. Miles, 2010, 222. This is one possible scenario in a very poorly documented sequence of events but it makes a plausible reconstruction.

30. A king of the Orissi, who are often identified with the Oretani mentioned by Strabo in his *Geography* (3.1.6, 3.3.2, 3.4.2): see Map 2.

31. Lancel, 1999, 37 takes Diodorus Siculus as the main source for Hamilcar's death; see also Hoyos, 2005, 71; and Barceló 2004a, 79–80. For the Vettones see Strabo 3.1.6, 3.3.1–3, 3.4.12, 3.4.16. Only Appian gives Hamilcar a relatively ungallant end when he has him fall for a ruse and die in the confusion of his troops.

32. The evidence for Hamilcar's age has been closely analysed by Hoyos, 2005, 239 n. 2. Hoyos discusses the fact that 'young' can mean a very wide range of ages in the ancient (and modern) world. Realistically, Hamilcar could have been as young as 45 or as old as 60 when he died, although early fifties seems about right.

33. These coins, minted on the Phoenician shekel standard, bearing the image of Melqart and reflecting the coinage of the wider Hellenistic world and of Phoenician cities, have been much discussed in terms of their significance and implications of Barcid power – Carthaginian Iberia in this period called a 'protectorate' in Miles, 2010, 222. For the coins see Jenkins, 1987 and Visona, 1998. The development of coinage at Carthage has always been linked to military pay but given the importance of image and the quality of the representation it is likely that these were carefully constructed, as noted by Miles, 2010, 220–222.

34. Hannibal's 'apprenticeship' is a term used in Seibert, 1993a, 40 for the period from 229/228 to 221 but the term can be extended to include the period before Hamilcar's death as well.

35. For Hasdrubal's tenure see Barceló, 2004a, 70–82, Hoyos, 2005, 73–86 and Lancel, 1999, 37–43. As discussed above (chapter 3, page 57), Appian's account claims the prosecution took place after the Mercenary War; however, this seems somewhat unlikely given Hamilcar's notable absence for the first few months of the war.

36. See the Barcid family tree above p. xiii. Hamilcar was as astute politically as he was militarily.

37. Livy emphasizes that the 'people' chose him, which is an allusion to the popular assembly, populist politics and loose morality that went together in Livy's experience. For more on the Roman attitudes towards sexual preferences see Williams, 1995.

38. See Hoyos, 2005, 74–75 for Hasdrubal's role and titles and their meaning. Hoyos notes that *hegemon* was also a title given to Alexander the Great by the League of Corinth. Diodorus claims that Hasdrubal's title was given 'by the whole of the Iberian people', which seems unlikely at this point and it more likely implies all Iberians under Carthaginian control. There is a sense of unification, however. See Picard, G.-C. 1983–84 on Hasdrubal's Hellenistic role and Miles, 2010, 222–224, who notes the Syracusan influence on the title. Hellenistic monarchs of the period were often polygamous and it is possible that Hasdrubal had more than one wife, although this was not a traditional Carthaginian custom: see Carney, 2000, 228–233 on Hellenistic royal polygamy.

39. Erdkamp, 2009 provides an interesting look at Polybius' motivations. The use of the popular assembly in political factionalism at Carthage is implied by the ancient authors but is also a reflection of what occurred in Rome in the late Republic and we should be wary of these parallels whilst accepting them as probable, as they are by no means certain.

40. The fact that Hasdrubal was already married to Hannibal's sister does raise an interesting question about polygamy, a Hellenistic practice among kings in the East. This is purely speculative.

41. Silius Italicus, *Punica* 3.97 and 4.775 is the only source to name a wife for Hannibal and he may have made up her name for poetic reasons. It is certain that intermarriage was used to seal the political base of Carthaginian power in Iberia and there is no reason to doubt that Hannibal was used as a tool in these alliances. Women, however, have little place in Hannibal's story.

42. Hasdrubal in Iberia: see Diodorus Siculus 25.11.1, 12; Appian, *Ib.* 6; Zonaras 8.19. For Castulo's location see Strabo's *Geography* 3.2.3, 3.2.10, 3.2.11, 3.3.2.

43. In Phoenician, Carthage meant 'New City', implying a New Tyre. A New Carthage thus means 'New New City'. Polybius refers to the places both as Carthage and as the New City, i.e. at 10.9.3 it is the siege of Carthage (Καρχηδονοσ), but in 3.15.3 Hannibal winters 'at the New City' *(Καινην πολιν)*. For the city and complete ancient references and description in Strabo see entry in the edition, *Geografía di Iberia*, with useful glossary, 347–350.

44. Polybius 10.9.8–10.10.13; see the description of New Carthage in Livy 26.43–48. There is an excellent topographical map in Ramallo Asensio, 2003, 327.

45. On the Punic casemate walls of New Carthage see Ramallo Asensio, 2003, 331–338 and for the points of interest from recent archaeological research see Keay, 2013, 311–312, who includes a bibliography of relevant archaeological reports and map. Twenty stades fits the size of the original walls relatively well.

46. This temple at New Carthage also became the temple of Asclepius in Roman times, mirroring the temple on the Byrsa hill at Carthage.

47. When the younger Scipio took the city in 209, he imprisoned no more than 'ten thousand' (Polyb. 10.17.6). When compared to the number of captives taken at the fall of Agrigentum in the First Punic War and Carthage itself in 146 (both about 50,000) the comparison would make it a rather small centre. Although the nice round numbers make them suspect, they are all we have to go on. The relative size is noted by Lazenby, 1998, 125.

48. See Miles, 2010, 218–226; G-C. Picard, 1983–84; Hoyos, 1994 and 2005, 73–86; Lancel, 1995, 40; Seibert, 1993a, 40–50. Hasdrubal's foundation was in line with Carthaginian practice and if he really fancied himself a Hellenistic monarch in waiting he would have been much more likely to name the city after himself – as Alexandria, Antioch or Seleucis – than New Carthage.

49. Disagreement among modern scholars is more about the degree of threat posed by the Gauls at this point than the motivation for signing a treaty; see, most recently, Eckstein, 2012; also arguments in Erdkamp, 2009; Lancel, 1995, 41–42; Hoyos, 1998, 150–173 and 2005, 81–83; Rich, 1996, 14–24; Eckstein, 1984. A full up-to-date bibliography on this much-debated topic can be found in Eckstein, 2012. The fact that we do not know the exact date of the treaty allows for a great range of potential reasons for its creation, depending on the situation at Rome from year to year.

50. See also Lancel, 1999, 42–43, who discusses the Greek cities of the region, Massalia Empurias, etc. and their potential influence on Roman diplomacy with the Carthaginians at this point.

51. See Barceló, 2004a, 22; and 'apprenticeship' is the term used in Seibert, 1993a, 40.

52. Hannibal may not have married until he came to power (see Hoyos, 2005, 74–75), but given that Hamilcar's daughters were used to seal alliances while he commanded it is also possible that the sons were too during Hasdrubal's rule: betrothed perhaps at first and then married at a later date. Silius Italicus in *Punica* 3. 97 refers to Imilce; this is a Punic name, however, not Greek as Silius appears to believe; Livy only mentions that she came from Castulo. The scene in Silius Italicus imagines representatives from Carthage led by Hanno, the opponent of the Barcids, deciding to take Hannibal's 'first born and only son' to sacrifice to the gods. For Hannibal, Silius Italicus and his son see Stocks, 2014, 96–102.

53. Walbank, vol. 1, 317–319 names the town as Salamanca (also called Helmantica).

54. Rawlings, 1996 outlines the Iberian, Gaulish, Numidian and Libyan troops in Hannibal's army.

55. For Hannibal and elephants see chapter 5, pp. 91–94 on the Rhône crossing.
56. The interior of the Iberian peninsula was no easy conquest and it would take the Romans until the late first century BCE to subdue it. This period of Hannibal's conquest has a resonance in some of the battles that Caesar and the later Romans fought in their conquest of Gaul and Britain in the 50s BCE and 40s CE. Iberians and Celtiberians (ethnically mixed Celts and the Iberians) who fought the Carthaginians and then the Romans were deeply divided and only came together sporadically to fight the superior armies of these more sophisticated military powers, even though this was their only hope of staving off conquest. Polybius' numbers here are certainly exaggerated. See Lancel, 1999 45–46, Walbank, vol. 1, 317–319; Hoyos, 2005, 90–92; and Seibert, 1993a, 51–62 on the 'young general'.
57. There is a large bibliography that reflects the interest and debate over the start of the Second Punic War. See Rich, 1996, 1, note 1 for a selective list of the important articles up to that date. Add to that discussion by Lazenby, 1998, 22–28; Hoyos, 1998, 174–195 and 2005, 87–102; Barceló, 2004a, 96–118 on Hannibal's command and the origins of the war; Sibert, 1993a, 51–74; Eckstein, 2012; Miles, 2010, 228–229; Beck, 2011.
58. Livy's passage on this embassy is chronologically flawed and placed during the siege at Saguntum but it must have occurred before the siege to have had any effect, see Lancel, 1995, 46–51; Rich, 1996; Hoyos, 1998, 196–218 and 2005, 92–93 where the important stature of the ambassadors is also noted.
59. They had previous ties to Iberia, it seems. For Baebius' post-war connections to New Carthage see Palmer, 1997, 132–139.
60. When this happened is a matter of some conjecture. It could have occurred just weeks before, according to Hoyos, 2005, 92–93, which might explain Hannibal's reaction, or up to a few years before if we follow Eckstein, 1984, 62–63. It is not specified by Polybius.
61. Eckstein, 1989 discusses this exact passage in detail and how it fits into Polybius' larger narrative.
62. Full discussion of the inconsistencies and problems with the chronology is given in Rich, 1996, 26–33; and in Seibert, 1993a, 63–74. Livy has the embassy come a year later, when Saguntum was already under attack, but this is usually considered inaccurate.
63. Polybius' account of these events is crucial, if we are to understand them at all, and Hannibal's emotional and angry response to the Romans was a critical error of judgement in his view. Anger, in Polybius' narrative, led to bad decisions, and the emotional response to a critical problem was the least valid one. So Hannibal behaved like a young man 'filled with a passion for war, and spurred on by his hatred of the Romans' (3.15.6).
64. If the relationship formed before c. 226 then the city would have been included in the Ebro treaty or previously, in the Peace of Lutatius, see Polybius (3.30.3). If the friendship was formed after the treaty was signed this implies that the Romans were reneging on the terms of the treaty by forming friendships with Saguntum, unless of course a third party like Marseilles formed the original friendship and then Rome, as an ally of Marseilles, became a friend of Saguntum.
65. Livy claims the Turdetani in 21.6.1 but this is most likely an error as the Turdetani were people from the region of Gades, and is one of many examples of Livy's confusion around the Saguntum issue. The accurate name may be the Torboletae: see Eckstein, 1984, n. 43 following Walbank, vol. 1, 323.
66. Following Rich, 1996, 25, who makes a good argument for this date; Eckstein, 1984 argues that the friendship between Rome and Saguntum may even have existed in the time of Hamilcar's premiership in Iberia c. 231.
67. Excellent discussions on the sources and the issue of *amicitia* can be found in Ridley, 2000 and Rich, 1996, Hoyos, 1998, 174–195; Seibert, 1993a, 63–74; and Eckstein, 1984, who argues for Rome's long-standing *amicitia* with Saguntum. Eckstein, 2006, 170–173 provides a good overview of the situation and points out that this was a natural event, two sides in dispute calling in larger allies.
68. See Rich, 1996, 28–33.
69. Appian, *Ib.* 43 reports some in the Senate arguing that 'they [Saguntum] were not allies according to the treaty . . .'. This reported inactivity also suggests a deeply confused

chronology in our sources and that there has been some 'fudging' to fit the narrative of blame. The gaps in our knowledge of the sequence of events make it difficult to understand the extent of Roman intentions towards the Iberian peninsula at this point, see Hoyos, 1998, 219–232.

70. Polybius briefly covers the siege at 3.17.1–11; Livy provides more detail 21.7.16 and Lancel, 1999, 49–50 believes Livy's source may have been Coelius Antipater. Silius Italicus tells the tale over two books, *Punica* 1–2, based on Livy (see below, note 73).

71. Maharbal will appear again as leader of the cavalry at Cannae.

72. 'To the immortall memorie, and friendship of that noble paire, Sir Lucius Cary and Sir H. Morison', *c.* 1640 (first published edition).

73. See Dominik, 2003 for the siege of Saguntum in the *Punica*, its parallels with the siege of Troy and with Plataea in the Peloponnesian War. As has been pointed out by Dominik, 2003, 472 the story of Saguntum takes up two whole books of the *Punica* – which seems an excessive treatment of an episode in terms of the whole story of Hannibal's war. Stocks, 2014, 103–114 for the depiction of Hannibal at Saguntum in Silius Italicus.

74. Ben Jonson dedicated this poem to his friends Morison (who died in 1629 at age 21) and Cary (who would be killed in the English Civil War after Jonson's death – 'the bravest of the cavaliers'). The poem opens with an infant born into the siege of Saguntum who chooses to return to the womb rather than live in the horror. Jonson and circle were Royalists (if not uncritical) in Stuart England and especially supporters of James I (VI of Scotland), who was an active patron of Jonson. James I as the 'New Caesar' provoked a distinctly different view of Hannibal from Sir Walter Ralegh's: see chapter 12 below, p. 236.

75. Following Rich, 1996, 30. A reasonable argument is that under the Roman system the preparations for a military campaign in that year would be put in place in March when the new consuls took up office. The Romans would have known that Saguntum was under siege by the summer of 219, but did not formally declare war until the following year and the new consuls were in place by March 218.

76. See Lancel, 1995, 49–50; Hoyos, 1998, 202–204; Rich 1996, 12–14 for the confusion over the dating. Livy claims an embassy arrived from Rome while the siege was ongoing (21.6.8) but Polybius makes no reference to this second embassy and the assumption is that Livy's embassy is actually Polybius' embassy at New Carthage from the autumn of 220.

77. Translation from Rich, 1996, 30–31, although Hoyos, 2005, 99 claims that this is probably not the same Q. Fabius Maximus who would campaign against Hannibal.

78. As soon as a ship could sail – March/April, contra Walbank, vol. 1, 333–334, who puts the embassy later, after Hannibal had crossed the Ebro (June?). Hoyos, 1998, 233–255 surveys the possibilities. See Wiedemann, 1986 on the formalities of declaring war in the Roman Republic. Rich, 1996 gives a detailed assessment of the sources and Ridley, 2000 looks at Livy's evidence.

79. See Brizzi, 2009, who examines the different factions in Carthage during the Punic Wars and the idea of an *amicitia* between the Fabii and the faction of Hanno at Carthage.

80. Hanno's speech is thought to be a Livian invention.

81. The details are preserved in Polybius' history and he provides a fascinating digression (3.22–29) that recounts the history of Roman and Carthaginian treaties going back to 509.

82. Harris, 1985, 205.

83. As noted by Miles, 2010, 231.

84. An interesting discussion on the Polybian view can be found in Eckstein, 1989.

85. This view is expressed by Walbank, vol. 1, 319. See also discussion in Ridley, 2000, 18–23, and Rich 1996, 14–18 on the Barcid intentions.

86. Blame for the Hannibalic War expressed here is largely based on the ideas presented in Eckstein, 2006. Also relevant is Eckstein's research (1987) on the individual Roman commanders and their decisions, especially on the 'ad hoc' diplomacy of a commander in the field.

87. The ongoing debate over the outbreak of the First World War in 1914 continues today, which only exemplifies the problem of apportioning blame in past wars and ideas of war

guilt. We cannot agree on 100-year–old wars, much less those that took place over two thousand years ago. Debate on the origins of the First World War can be found in publications such as M. McMillian, 2014, *The War to End All Peace*, M. Hastings, 2014, *Catastrophe*, and C. Clark, 2012, *The Sleepwalkers*. Politicians have entered the fray: 'Michael Gove blasts "Blackadder myths"about the First World War spread by television sit-coms and left-wing academics', 22:31, 2 January 2014 | Updated: 08:20, 3 January 2014, *Daily Mail* online. Or the rebuttal by Tristram Hunt in *The Observer*: 'Michael Gove, using history for politicking is tawdry', | Saturday 4 January 2014 21.05 GMT.

## Chapter 5  Legend: Hannibal into Italy

1. See Palmer, 1997, 31–52 on 'Carthaginian cargoes at Rome'.
2. Point made here by Woolmer, 2008 in regard to Greek merchant/spies and it can certainly be extended to include the Romano-Carthaginian connections.
3. *Speculatores* mentioned in i.e. Caesar, *BG* 1.47.6 and later in Ammianus Marcellinus 26.6.4–6. For an excellent overview of the methods of tactical intelligence in the Roman period see Austin and Rankov, 1995, 39–86.
4. Sheldon, 1986 provides a useful discussion of Carthaginian intelligence networks but perhaps underplays the Roman approach to the point of simplicity, the wily Carthaginian and solid, simple peasant Roman being too convenient an analogy. For spies embedded in the enemy's camp see Polyaenus, *Strategems* Excerpt 7.
5. See Rankov, 1996, 53 on 'The Second Punic War at Sea', which he admits was, to 'a certain extent, a sideshow'.
6. Polybius later refers to this as an 'inscription on the column at Lacinium' (3.56.4) and Livy mentions it in book 28.46.16
7. Again the chronology is confusing: if the Roman embassy returned from Carthage in April, the consuls were chosen in March and the preparations for war would have begun as soon as the consuls had been decided, before war had been officially declared.
8. The term *provincia* meant the region where a Roman consul could exercise complete authority for conquest as a general; it was his sphere of influence.
9. News of war probably reached Rome and New Carthage at a similar time, by April/May.
10. Lancel, 1999, 59–64. There are a number of excellent summaries of the two armies: see Goldsworthy, 2003, 25–62 and Daly, 2002, 81–112.
11. The best recent account of Hannibal's army can be found in Daly, 2002, 81–112, and see also Lazenby, 1998, 1–28 on Carthage and Roman forces.
12. As noted by Bagnall, 1990, 10–11. It is interestingly made explicit that military obligation was not part of Hannibal's agreements with the cities of Italy such as Capua and Tarentum; see further in chapters 8 and 9 below.
13. Or so claimed Polybius (3.35.8, 8.1.1–8, 15.14.6, 15.15.6–7, 18.28.9–10).
14. For the textbook description of a general in antiquity see Polyaenus, *Strategems* Excerpts 1–3 where Hannibal figures throughout as an exemplum.
15. For Alexander's self-restraint whilst still a boy, and his stern nature, see also Plutarch, *Alex.* 7.1.
16. See Hutchinson, 2000, 180–223 for an analysis of Xenophon's ideal commander; there is much of what we know of Hannibal in this. Hutchinson discusses how two of Xenophon's works, the *Kyropaideia* and *Hipparchicus* (Cavalry Commander) were written as if meant as leadership manuals for the ideal commander.
17. Due, 1993, 55 argues that Alexander was influenced by an ideal of command first set down in Xenophon's characterization of an ideal leader. There was a philosophy of leadership and command that influenced Alexander, Pyrrhus and perhaps Hannibal too.
18. The importance of cavalry to a commander in Xenophon studied by Hutchinson, 2000, 183–187 and 240–241.
19. Rawlings, 1996, 81–82, distinguishes between soldiers and warriors.
20. See Daly, 2002, 123–128 on command in Hannibal's army. For the supply of the army see Goldsworthy, 2003, 154–155.

21. See also Apollodorus 2.5.10; Herodotus 4.8; and Dionysius of Halicarnassus, *Roman Antiquities* 1.41 for the Herakles myth and his connection to the western Mediterranean. For what the Bay of Cadiz may have looked like in antiquity, see Aubet, 2001, 262–273, including maps.

22. See Bonnet, 1988, on Melqart, and the syncretism of the two traditions from early in the first millennium BCE; see also Seibert, 1993a, 75–76; Rawlings, 2005; Campus, 2005; Miles, 2010, 235–255. For Cadiz, the temple, its origin and worship see also Aubet, 2001, 259–291.

23. Referred to as a pilgrimage in both Seibert, 1993a, 75 and Lancel, 1999, 55; see also Huss, 1986 on the claims in Livy of Hannibal's impiety (223–238).

24. See Huss, 1986, on Hannibal's religion, and Livy 21.4 for Hannibal's impiety. The vows found on inscriptions from the Tophet at Carthage include the form 'because he heard his voice', Xella, et al., 2013, 1204. The prayer was also associated with the worship of Melqart from early in the first millennium: see Aubet, 2001, 50 for the Bar Haddad stele from Aleppo.

25. Although this chronology would make Hannibal a little late for the rebirth ritual it is possible he went to Gades first, then returned and made plans, etc. For the ritual of resurrection (*egersis*) of Melqart see Bonnet, 1988, 221–225, 1986, 214 and Aubet, 2001, 275–277. Miles, 2010, 33–34 describes the rite at Tyre. Silius Italicus' version takes the short mention of the visit by Hannibal to Gades and combines it with other literary and historical traditions as discussed in Gibson, 2005, 178. For Alexander at Tyre see Plutarch, *Alex.* 24–25

26. Roman sources pick up and develop this theme, see Gibson, 2005, 181. Plutarch, *Alex.* 27: 'Alexander made splendid offering to the gods and gave money to his priests'.

27. Seibert, 1993a, 76; Miles, 2010, 241–255; Rawlings, 2005, all discuss the role of Herakles and his legend in Hannibal's journey; see also Miles, 2011 for the way that Hannibal used the legend in his propaganda to subvert Roman claims to the hero.

28. Beacham, 2005, 152 uses the phrase 'myth management' in reference to Octavian, Antony and Sextus Pompey, but it can equally be applied here.

29. Rawlings, 2005, 169–170 discusses the soteriological aspects of Herakles' myth derived from Dionysius of Halicarnassus' version 1.41.1ff.

30. Miles, 2011, 268–269 and 2010, 235–255 on the subversion of the Roman claim; and Rawlings, 2005, on Hannibal and Herakles and the route to Italy.

31. Miles, 2011, 268 points out the battle for the patronage of the hero and provides the background to Roman claims to a 'Heraclean heritage', also noting that their tactic of 'evocatio' was being used against them.

32. This was the number of elephants with Hannibal when he reached the Rhône (we do not know for certain how many had left Iberia with him). See Polybius 3.35.1 for the troop numbers and Appian, *Hann.* 1.4 for the elephant numbers; for some scepticism about the elephants, see Lazenby, 1998, 33.

33. Late May departure, Seibert, 1993a, 96, Hoyos, 2005, 102. For a departure of 8 June see Lazenby, 1998, Appendix III (275–277), which includes a detailed diary of the march and distances covered, whose chronology of events is generally followed here although I would perhaps bring the events forward by a week or so.

34. Perhaps modern Pensicola, following Seibert, 1993a, 96.

35. For the dream: Cicero, *de div* 1.49, repeated also in Valerius Maximus 1.7.1, Silius Italicus, *Pun.* 3. 163–214, and Zonaras 8.22.9; see also Devilliers and Krings, 2006, 337, Miles, 2010, 250–255. Valerius Maximus, 1.7 *(de somnis)* records a long list of dreams of great generals in Antiquity from Cyrus to Croesus through Alexander to Hannibal to the Roman emperor Augustus.

36. For Silenus see Cornelius Nepos, *Hann.* 13.3.

37. Devilliers and Krings, 2006, 338–339 question the assumption that it does and also note that the dream seems ill placed in the narrative; better to have dreamt at Gades in the presence of the god, or in the Alps, or just before the first battle with the Romans. Miles, 2010, 252–255 comments on the Hannibalic propaganda in play.

38. Noted in Miles, 2010, 250–252; Rawlings, 2005, 170.
39. See Miles, 2010, 251 and Daly, 2002, 135 on aspects of Hellenistic leadership and divine sanction in Hannibal's army. See Hutchinson, 2000, 46–47 on the importance of dreams in Xenophon.
40. For Hannibal convincing 'his own men that those who died courageously in war returned to life after a short period' see Polyaenus, *Stratagems* 3.38.2.
41. Hoyos, 2005, 104–105.
42. The number of soldiers does not add up – if Hannibal started with 90,000 from New Carthage and twenty were either sent home or stationed with Hanno that leaves 20,000 missing soldiers. Either that number of men was lost in the battles after the Ebro ('with great loss' Polyb. 3.35.4) or the numbers were wrong from the outset, which seems most likely. See Seibert, 1993a, 97 n.122. Hoyos, 2005, 106–108 believes the original number is the problem and that 50,000 is the correct number for departure. Seibert, 1993a, 97 proposes the crossing of the Pyrenees in three columns, each taking a separate pass, and reconvening on the other side. However, he admits there is no real clue as to which of the passes over the Pyrenees were taken.
43. Hoyos, 2005, 103–104 contends that Hannibal delayed here in the region for a time, waiting to see how and what the Romans would do, giving himself the option to react.
44. See more in Sheldon, 1986.
45. Scullard, 1974, who claims that Carthage must have had a decade or two of training the elephants before they employed them.
46. The image of an elephant decorated Carthaginian coinage minted in Iberia during the rule of the Barcids and at Carthage they appear on votive stelae (Plate 5 above). Both the elephant with rider and elephant alone appear on these famous coins; other evidence from Hannibalic coinage minted in Italy also shows an elephant symbol, as noted most recently by Charles and Rhodan, 2007, 364.
47. Ibid.
48. The Indian elephant was probably not used by the Carthaginians, although the knowledge of training and adapting elephants for warfare originally came from India: see Scullard, 1974, 146–177. Ibid. on the first Carthaginian use of elephants in the early third century. Polybius (1.40.15) describes the Romans capturing 'then elephants and their Indian drivers' is explained by Charles and Rhodan, 2007, 364 (and others) as a generic term used for elephant handlers.
49. Charles and Rhodan, 2007, 366, Scullard, 1974, 174–177 for an Indian elephant and see also Rance, 2009 for an interesting interpretation of a fragment of Polybius. Livy 28.14.4 may imply turrets on the elephants but not necessarily Indian elephants.
50. Or perhaps our sources had less of an idea of the ability of elephants than Hannibal did. Scullard, 1974 158 provides a clear explanation for the elephants not swimming across. There is an interesting discussion of the elephant issue in Edwards, 2001.
51. Scullard, 1974 156, who thinks we should believe Polybius' account of the method of the elephant crossing and O'Bryhim, 1991, 121–14, who points out that herd instinct follows the female but shows that elephants are good swimmers and challenges the account in Polybius and Livy, arguing that time made it more likely that the elephants were driven into the river and swam/walked across, following a rejected account in Livy 21.28.
52. The easiest route would have been along the Durance (a tributary of the Rhône) but Hannibal may have judged this too close to the coast and the Roman army there.
53. A point made by Lancel, 1999, 69; Seibert, 1993a, 99–100, 105; Miles, 2010, 263; Lazenby, 1998, 51 among others.
54. Lazenby, 1998, 35–36 would put the crossing between Arles and Avignon; for the argument for north of the Durance see Lancel, 1999, 67–70 (including map that surveys various options), and see Seibert, 1993, 100–105. The 'Heraklean Way' along the Durance is discussed in Miles, 2010, 263, Lazenby, 1998, 37. The route outlined on Map 2 is a general overview rather than a specific choice of pass, as we just do not know.
55. See Hoyte, 1960.
56. BBC4's 2010 series, *On Hannibal's Trail* (broadcast July–August).

57. Follow the most recent dispute in Mahaney, 2013, rebutting Kuhle and Kuhle, 2012, who rebut Mahaney, 2010; see Mahaney, 2010, 157 for a map that shows three possible routes; see also Leveau and Mercalli, 2011 whose illustrated paper provides a detailed geography; Dalaine, 2011 with an overview map showing the many options and survey of the literature; Prevas, 1998; and Seibert, 1993b, 199–200, who provides a comprehensive list of relevant publications for the various options up to his time.

58. The complications and permutations derive from the name of the river, written as the Isère in the Loeb Classical Library Polybius text but in the original manuscript given as Skaras or Skoras, as variously in Livy. The arguments are lengthy, but well discussed in Walbank, 1985, and Lazenby, 1998, 37–38; also see Appendix 2 in J. Yardley's translation of Livy (Hoyos, 2006). Specific studies that deal with the Alps question are also numerous (see Hoyos, 2005, 227–228, who gives a good summary in an appendix and above, note 54). See also discussions in Seibert, 1993a, 106–113, 1993b, 195–200, and Lancel, 1999, 70–80. The Isère is considered one of the most likely routes but it is impossible to be sure.

59. See Lancel, 1999, 74–80; Hoyos, 2005, 110–111; Lazenby, 1998, 37–48. Livy becomes 'like a rambler whose compass has gone haywire' in Lancel, 1999, 74.

60. Walbank, vol. 1, 382–387 provides a detailed analysis and comparison of Livy and Polybius.

61. Seibert, 1993b, 197–200 surveys the options and suggests they were hostile and friendly members of the same large group. See Lazenby, 1998, Appendix 3 for a chronology of the march.

62. This interpretation was suggested by Michael Crawford in conversation, May 2012, and would indicate Fabius Pictor as the source. Walbank, vol. 1, 390 for a survey of options, and Mahaney, 2010, who believes the Col de Traversette would provide the view.

63. Hoyos, 2006, 634–635 n. 35; see also Walbank, vol. 1, 390, who claims the term is used more generally to signify the approach of the bad weather and that the actual date may have been a month earlier, in late September/early October.

64. All the options were over 2,000 metres: see Seibert, 1993b, 199–200.

65. For the use and history of vinegar see Mazza and Murooka, 2009, 19–21 on 'Vinegars through the Ages'; see also Hoyos, 2006, 635 n. 37, who cites Vitruvius 8.3.19, and see also Seibert, 1993a, 109–110 (and n. 173) on the methodology employed. Appian, *Hann.* 4, also mentions the vinegar and that the road through was called 'Hannibal's pass' in his day. Juvenal, *Satire* 10.54–155 celebrates the technology as well: 'Nature then bars his passage with the snowy Alps; whose rocks/he splits with vinegar and fire, bursting through the mountains'.

66. Lazenby, 1998, Appendix 3.

67. This is a low estimate but hard to dispute since Polybius claims the numbers were taken from Hannibal's inscription in Lacinium. Livy (21.38.1–5) gives a range of numbers that his sources provided which go much higher, to 80,000. Polybius 3.60.5, states that from the Rhône he had an army of 46,000 (38,000 infantry and 8,000 cavalry) with him. Daly, 2002, 29–31 notes (following others) that some forces that turn up at the battle of Trebia are missing from Polybius' total. Walbank, vol. 1, 366 (35.1) provides a good range of options and thinks the losses are an exaggeration.

68. A suicide mission, according to Seibert, 1993b, 200, and although it is likely that desertions made up a big part of the missing numbers, a large amount of casualties is a certainty.

69. The Gothic invasion in the early fifth century CE. Even more so, considering that when the Gauls sacked Rome some 172 years or so previously (390 BCE) they had been a marauding force rather than an invading army and Pyrrhus had acted on invitation from Tarentum.

70. Here from Miles, 2011 on Hannibal's active use of the idea of the Labours of Herakles in each of his obstacles and the mirror image that it left in our sources. Which of Polybius' sources is he referring to? His reference to the divine guide could refer to the dream, which Cicero records came from Coelius Antipater (Cicero, *de div.* 1.49). The whole list of possibilities can be found in Walbank, vol. 1, 381.

71. Livy 21.38.5 calls these people the Taurini, *semigalli* (half-Gauls).

72. Walbank, vol. 1, 395 calls the numbers 'scarcely credible'.

73. Plon and Dumaine (eds), vol. 29, 88f.

74. From Englund, *Napoleon, A Political Life*, 174.
75. Excerpts taken from Plon and Dumaine (eds), vol. 29, 88f. and vol. 32, 307.
76. Plon and Dumaine (eds), vol. 32, p. 307. The translation used here is by Marie-Luce Constant.
77. On a nineteenth-century engraving of an idealized triumphal arch: see for example at British Museum online collection (number 1875,0710.5866) for a seventeenth-century Flemish arch depicting the deeds of the heroes with Hannibal in the company of Achilles and Jason.

### Chapter 6  Hannibal the Conqueror: From the Trebia to Trasimeno

1. In *The Complete Works of Lord Byron*, Paris, 1831.
2. The Romans may have been better prepared than our sources allow; making the most of Hannibal's abilities at this point in the narrative plays into his superhuman reputation.
3. Referred to here as Sempronius Longus. See Lazenby, 1998, 54–55, and Seibert, 1993a, 121–126.
4. See Cornell, 1995, 369–402 for this complex process down to 264.
5. See Lomas, 2011 on the status of the Roman allies and allied citizens during the Second Punic War. On Hannibal's strategy see Miles, 2011, 262–263.
6. For the exact location see Lazenby, 1998, 52–53.
7. Miles, 2010, 256–276.
8. Walbank, vol.1, 375–377 explores the Roman troop numbers, as does Lazenby, 1998, 52; see also Seibert, 1993a, 114 for Publius Scipio's journey to the north of Italy.
9. For the exact location and various options see Walbank, vol. 1, 399. See also Daly, 2002, 12–14; Seibert, 1993a, 116–118; Goldsworthy, 2003, 169–173; Lazenby, 1998, 52–54.
10. Livy claims here that Publius Scipio was saved by his son (a tradition not mentioned in Polybius' version of the battle but noted later in Polybius' discussion of the young Scipio, 10.3.6–7); Coelius Antipater has a Ligurian slave saving the consul (Livy 21.46.9–10). Seibert, 1993a, 118.
11. Seibert, 1993a, 120; Lazenby, 1998, 55.
12. Lazenby, 1998, 53 on the superiority of the Carthaginian cavalry.
13. Ariminum had been a Latin colony since 268 BCE.
14. Livy 21.51.1–7; Polybius 3.68.12. Does it matter by which route the Roman army arrived in the north? Although Livy gives by far the more detailed account the tendency is to believe Polybius because it was already late October/early November when sea travel was dangerous. Livy's account is more convincing as a whole. Perhaps a part of the army risked the sea journey by hugging the coast to make it up to northern Italy more quickly or, more likely, these events took place earlier in the season. Lazenby 1998, 54–55 deals with the discontinuity and prefers Polybius' account, as does Hoyos, 2006, 636 (n. 51). Seibert, 1993a, 123, n. 247 analyses the issue. See Derow, 1976 on the problems with the Roman calendar in these years.
15. Since Polybius' patrons were the Scipio family and one of their distinguished ancestors was being discussed, it makes it difficult not to question the fact that all the blame is placed on Sempronius Longus in his narrative. Then again, Publius Scipio would have had the more realistic experience with Hannibal, while Sempronius Longus' Sicilian experiences would have made him all the more confident. But Walbank, vol. 1, 404 notes that portraying Sempronius as 'ambitious, full of false confidence and jealous of his colleague and successors' should be overlooked as part of the pro-Scipionic tradition.
16. See also Seibert, 1993a, 126–131; Lancel, 1999, 85–88; Lazenby, 1998, 56–59; Goldsworthy, 2000, 173–181 (plus clear map); Daly, 2002, 14–15.
17. See chapter 10 below, p. 193. Polybius 11.22.4–8. It is the reverse scenario and deals with the preparation of Scipio's men before the battle of Ilipa in Iberia; see also Livy 28.14.7.
18. Seibert, 1993a, 126–127; Lazenby, 1998, 56–57 for analysis of the differing numbers; see also Walbank, vol. 1, 404–408 with an analysis of the numbers.
19. Lazenby, 1998, 58. Textbook material for a Hellenistic general – aspects of which appear in the Xenophon (*Oecon.* 21.4–8 and *Mem.* 3.1.6) on military strategy and the instilling of loyalty in the men. See Hutchinson, 2000, 52–53.

20. The exact location of Hannibal's winter camp is nowhere made clear. Livy 21.59.10 claims he withdrew to Liguria for winter quarters. See Erskine, 1993 on Polybius' rhetorical use of the 'freedom agenda' of the Hellenistic generals from Alexander. There seems no reason not to believe that Hannibal's strategy was to win over the Italian allies but the rhetoric used here may be Polybius' creation.

21. As in Zonaras 8.24.8; for Punic bilingualism as a source of distrust, see chapter 1, pp. 16, 245n. 51. One thinks again of Hannibal's studies when reading about Xenophon's views on secrecy and deception; see further in Hutchinson, 2000, 67–73.

22. Poseidon among the Greek soldiers urging on the troops was a popular theme on vase painting, as in Homer, *Iliad* 13.42–59. Walbank, vol.1, 410 considers this a 'worthless anecdote'. See also Seibert, 1993a, 139–140.

23. Miles, 2010, 270–276 and 2011, 274–279 discusses the impact of Hannibal's propaganda and the Roman response in the period up to Trasimeno and Cannae.

24. For Livy's account of an earlier aborted departure over the Apennines and another battle with Sempronius see 21.58–59. This is largely rejected as fictitious but may reflect some advance scouting done by the Carthaginians, as suggested by Hoyos, 2006, 637. See also Seibert, 1993a, 140.

25. This allowed enough time for the Roman consuls to take up their offices and organize their troops and camps. The various calculations for the exact date rely on the date for the upcoming battle of Trasimeno, which Ovid places on 21 June (*Fasti*, 6. 767–8); see Walbank, vol.1, 413 for a May departure.

26. Seibert, 1993b, 218–219 and Walbank, vol.1, 413: 'the most probable pass is that via Bologna–Porretta–Pistoia'; see Hoyos, 2005, 114–115; Lazenby, 1998, 60–61; Seibert, 1993b, 218 points out that the swamp in Polybius is given no geographical reference and is the valley of the Arno in Livy. Goldsworthy, 2003 184 notes that 'Hannibal moved quickly and in an unexpected direction'.

27. Seibert, 1993b, 218; Lazenby, 1998, 60–61.

28. Seibert, 1993a, 148–150, and Cornelius Nepos, *Hann.* 4.3: 'he never afterwards had equally good use of his right eye', as opposed to Polybius 3.79.12: 'severe attack of ophthalmia, which finally led to the loss of one eye'.

29. The tradition of one-eyed generals in modern history includes Lord Nelson, the Russian Kutuzov, and Moshe Dayan. See Africa, 1970, for an article on 'the one-eyed man against Rome'.

30. The same Hiero II from the First Punic War, he lived close to 90 years.

31. Conflicting with Polybius 3.75.5: 'the consuls designate were busy mustering the allies and enrolling their own legions' suggests they raised new legions instead of taking on the existing ones. An amalgamation of the two seems possible.

32. There is some confusion about the location of the legions and the camps of the Romans: Livy (21.63.1) states that Flaminius sent written instructions to have the legions wintering in Placentia meet him at Ariminum, while Polybius (3.77.1–2) claims that he 'advanced through Etruria and encamped before Arretium while Servilius advanced as far as Ariminum'. Lazenby, 1998, 61 who refers to Appian, *Hann,* 8, says that Servilius had Publius Scipio's old legions, while Flaminius had Sempronius' (Livy. 21.63.1).

33. Here following Lazenby, 1998, 65; Hoyos, 2005, 115; and Daly, 2002, 32, who notes 'it is vital to bear in mind at all times that these figures are far from certain and by no means precise' in regard to Cannae and that the troop numbers for the Carthaginians are 'entirely without confirmation'. We cannot be sure of the numbers in any of these battles.

34. See Derow, 1976, 275, who places these events in May based on the degree to which the Roman calendar was out. There is some debate as to whether these events took place in May or June; here we use Ovid's date of 21 June for the battle, with the understanding that the calendar could have been out by a month.

35. As noted by Walbank, vol. 1, 414, Hannibal could not have had Cortona and Trasimeno on the left and right simultaneously but would have first passed Cortona on the left and then had Lake Trasimeno on the right.

36. Suggested by Lazenby, 1998, 65.

37. The exact location is still unclear, Lancel, 1999, 93 follows an earlier reconstruction by De Sanctis (1917, vol. 3, 2, 109–115) to the west of Passignano; while Lazenby, 1998, 63 and Walbank, vol.1, 415–418 follow other earlier reconstructions by Kromayer and Veith (1912, 150–193) that put the battle closer to Torricella, which seems the more likely. See Seibert, 1993a, 152–156 for the battle and Hoyos, 2006, 640 for a summary of current thinking on the location.

38. Again here suggested by Lazenby, 1998, 65.

39. For the sound of battle in the ancient world see Daly, 2002, 168–170.

40. This is suggested by Brizzi, 1984, 40–41 and mentioned by Lancel, 1999, 96.

41. Daly, 2002, 89–90 on the Libyan troops at Cannae; and Rawlings, 1996 on the 'warriors in a soldiers' war'.

42. Livy claims that he attacked Spoletum, a Roman colony (modern Spoleto) and then marched into the territory of the Picenum (22.9.1–3). There is a tendency to discredit this account in Livy.

43. Why Hannibal did not march on Rome at this point has been discussed in detail. See Lazenby, 1996b, who suggests that the possibility of winning over allies in the south was the main motivation; Lancel, 1999, 96–97 takes Polybius at face value, adding that to lay siege to Rome would tie his army up for months and that the mobility of his forces was a key part of Hannibal's plans. See also Hoyos, 2005, 118–121.

44. Hoyos, 2005, 213 suggests this was part of a combined operation with the intent to attack Rome but that Hannibal changed plans after Trasimeno.

45. Polybius places this event after Trasimeno. See Rankov, 1996, 49 on how the Roman control of the sea kept Hannibal isolated.

46. Roth, 1999, 62 provides some interesting observations on the amount of fodder needed to keep horses healthy, which emphasizes how much the supply chain would have dominated Hannibal's strategy.

47. See discussion in Walbank, vol.1, 414; Seibert, 1993b, 220–221; and more recently in Fronda, 2010, who surveys each city and region in southern Italy in detail. The ethnic make up of the Italian peninsula before the complete conquest of Italy by the Latin Roman people is clearly laid out in Lomas, 2004 and 2011.

48. Bonfante, 1990, 50: *hanipaluscle* in Etruscan means 'with the ones of Hannibal'.

49. See Seibert, 1993a, 158–164 on the Roman response.

50. Lazenby, 1998, 67–69 makes this point following comments in Livy (22.8.5, 22.31.9) that a dictator could be appointed without the consul coming to Rome, and the suggestion that Fabius Maximus engineered his own election. His opponents therefore ensured that his second in command was a political opponent. For the careers of both men see Broughton, 1951.

51. The Sibylline Books were sacred scrolls kept in the temple of Jupiter Optimus Maximus in Rome and used by the Romans as a kind of guidebook to the will of the gods. The decemvirs were the ten men charged with the consultation of the books and were drawn from the senatorial classes. On their role after 367 BCE as well as on the Sibylline Books and their uses see Orlin, 1997, 76–97.

52. A *lectisternium* was also to be held – where effigies of the gods were set out on banqueting couches in public and offerings were made to them. A divine feast was created.

53. For a recent discussion see Malkin, 2011, 119–141; also Bonnet, 1996, 115–120 and 1986, 215–216 where she notes the epigraphic evidence for the connection, Melqart as the husband of Astarte. See also chapter 3, pp. 45 and 245*n*. 8, above. The Eryx was originally sacred to an Elymian goddess who was early on syncretised with the Phoenician/Carthaginian Astarte.

54. See Miles, 2010, 274–275; see also Erskine, 2001, 198–205 on the Roman acquisition of a Trojan past and the connection to Sicily and Venus Erycina; also Palmer, 1997, 66–67. On the syncretism of the two goddesses Astarte and Aphrodite (and, by extension, Venus) see Bonnet and Pirenne-Delforge, 1999.

55. Noted by Miles, 2010, 275, who observes that Fabius' actions seem pragmatic in terms of public perception more than religious belief according to Plutarch, *Fab.* 4.1–5.

56. Erskine, 2001, 201 also points out that the great-grandfather of Fabius Maximus had vowed a temple to Jupiter Victor in 295 on the battlefield when victorious against the Samnites.

57. See discussion in Erskine, 2001, 200–201 on the way that the establishment of a temple drew the Romans into illustrious victories of the past. For a discussion on the politics and temple foundations in Rome during the Republic see Orlin, 1997 especially 97–113 on the Sibylline Books and the construction of new temples.

58. For the worship of Mens see Orlin, 1997, 102; in the context of Fabius Maximus see Miles, 2010, 435 n.66

59. Seibert, 1993a, 131–134; Lazenby, 1998, 125–127; and Goldsworthy, 2003, 246–249 for the period between autumn of 218 and 217 in Iberia.

60. Lazenby, 1998, 125.

61. Walbank, vol.1, 409 placed this near Tarraco, with a discussion of some of the other options nearby.

62. Appian's comments therefore – 'Gnaeus [Scipio] did nothing in Spain worthy of mention before his brother Publius [Scipio] returned there' – seem a little unfair. Appian, *Hisp.* 15.

63. Strategy is discussed in Edwell, 2011, 321–322.

64. Again following Walbank, vol.1, 410 from Polybius 6.37.11

65. The one extant fragment of Sosylus (176F1) may or may not refer to this battle at the mouth of the Ebro.

66. For the Balearic slingers see Daly, 2002, 107–108.

67. Gn. Scipio's further adventures described by Livy (22.20.4–10) are thought to be unhistorical by Lazenby, 1998, 127 and render the chronology of events too complicated to make any sense of.

68. See Polybius 3.95–96 and Livy 22.19–20, which are summarized by Briscoe, 1989, 57; Edwell, 2011, 321–322.

### Chapter 7  The Apogee: Cannae and the War in Italy

1. Livy claims the Capuans came but there were certainly others who joined them in making enquiries.

2. See also Livy 22.12.3–4. For Hannibal's strategy on marching south see Fronda, 2011, 256; and specifically, for heading to where he might best accrue allies, see Lazenby, 1998, 68–69. See also Seibert, 1993a, 167–170 for Rome's strategy under Fabius Maximus.

3. An observation frequently made – most recently for example in Hill, 2010, 87.

4. See Lazenby, 1998, 68; Seibert, 1993a, 167–170; Lancel, 1999, 99 on the new strategy and the scorched-earth policy. Goldsworthy, 2003, 192–194 comments on Fabius' great skill in keeping an army close to Hannibal but not engaging. See also Zimmermann, 2011, 284–286 on Roman strategy and aims in the period of 218–216 BCE.

5. On the exact status of the towns noted here in Polybius see Walbank, vol.1, 425–426.

6. See Livy 22.12–13 on Hannibal's marching through the countryside with a guide leading him to the wrong location, noted by Hoyos, 2006, 641 n. 13 as possibly made up to expose Hannibal's cruelty in crucifying the guide.

7. As Walbank, vol.1, 426 notes Polybius' exaggeration.

8. Lazenby, 1998, 69–70 notes that Fabius' troops would have been in a position to cover the 'via Appia and via Latina'.

9. Livy calls this a 'crafty scheme'. However, Hannibal seems to have been kept very well informed of events and feelings at Rome, which has led to the assumption that he had a complex network of spies in place. See Sheldon, 1986. His lack of knowledge of the countryside left him very dependent on informers, scouts and spies: see p. 265*nn.* 3 and 4.

10. Livy (22.13.2–3) makes the point that Hannibal's being encouraged into Campania by Roman allies from Capua who convinced him the area was ripe for rebellion is entirely possible, although some details seem inaccurate (see n. 6 above). There would have been many who flocked to join Hannibal and he would have been constantly negotiating with his guides and local experts about where and how to get to places and which cities might

remain loyal to Rome. Hannibal's dependence on local guides for his manoeuvres made him vulnerable.

11. See Walbank, vol.1, 427–428 for Hannibal's route into Campania. See also Seibert, 1993b, 224; Lazenby, 1998, 70–71; Goldsworthy, 2003, 194–195.

12. Lancel, 1999, 100.

13. Walbank, vol.1, 427–430 with a map showing two possible routes; see also Seibert, 1993b, 224–225; Lancel, 1999, 100; Lazenby, 1998, 70–71.

14. Hasdrubal is mentioned elsewhere in Polybius 3.66.6, 3.114.7, 3.116.6, and Livy 22.46.7.

15. This would be a remarkable coincidence, as mentioned by Hutchinson, 2000, 241.

16. See Seibert, 1993a, 170–171, Walbank, vol.1, 429, and also Plutarch, *Fab.* 6, 3–7, 2.

17. Livy contradicts himself later (22.23.9), claiming that Hannibal took the town and burned it, leaving a few buildings for grain stores. On *Geronium/Gerunium*, see Walbank, vol.1, 432; Seibert, 1993b, 225–226. It lay 200 stades (approx. 36km) from Luceria, according to Polybius (3.100.3).

18. On the timing of Fabius' visit to Rome (Polyb. 3.94.9; Livy 22.18.8) see also Walbank, vol.1, 430 and 433 and Lazenby, 1998, 71. It makes more sense for Fabius to have visited Rome from northern Campania than to have followed Hannibal back to Apulia and then set off for Rome, which is Polybius' version. See also Seibert 1993a, 173–175 on Fabius' trip to Rome. Although *paedagogus* does not have to be considered an insult, that was implied in the use here.

19. Livy's account in 22.24.1–14; see also Lazenby, 1998, 71–72; Lancel, 1999, 100; Daly, 2002, 16; Seibert, 1993a, 175–177; Goldsworthy, 2003, 195.

20. See also Livy 22.24.14 on the overblown report at Rome of Minucius' victory.

21. For Livy's account see 22.25.1–25.11; for the discussion of the identity of Metilius and the constitutional position of Minucius see Lazenby, 1998, 72; Seibert, 1993a, 174–175. They were in fact behaving as the two consuls would have done.

22. The Latin reads '*unus homo nobis cunctando restituit rem*'. Here taken from Cicero, *de off.* 1.84 but also in Livy 30.26.9; see Elliot, 2013, 165 and also Lancel, 1999, 101.

23. Briscoe, 1989, 51.

24. See Gruen, 1978, 62, and generally, for a detailed assessment of Livy's account of these elections and whether it is credible. These are elections that have been discussed a great deal by scholars in relation to their implications for the Roman system and how it changed during the period of the Punic Wars.

25. Debate on strategy and personal motivation was at the heart of the confusion, according to Gruen, 1978, 70; see also Lazenby, 1998, 73–74, who provides a clear assessment of the different appointments and factions at play.

26. See Miles, 2010, 276 for the 'damaging effect of Hannibal's propaganda on the Roman people'.

27. For the coinage that Hannibal minted in Italy see Alexandropoulos, 2000, 104–108 and Jenkins, 1987, and it must be said that the evidence points to the likelihood that the coins we have from Hannibal's time in Italy were minted in the region of Bruttium.

28. Perhaps giving rise to a recent book on success in management entitled *Hannibal and Me*, by Andreas Kluth, published in 2011.

29. Early June, according to Walbank, vol.1, 441, and for the debate on the state of the Roman calendar and whether the dates here should be brought forward see Derow, 1976. The exact date of these events does not impact on the overall story.

30. On the consular elections for 216 see Gruen, 1978, and for the lack of military experience among men elected consul in the mid-Republic see Rosenstein, 1993. Daly, 2002, 16–17 and Lazenby, 1998, 73–76 on the elections and the arrival of the consuls, plus further bibliography.

31. Varro reportedly served in one of the Illyrian wars, probably in *c.* 219, as noted in Rosenstein, 1993, 324 n. 34 following a reference in Servius, *Ad Aen.* 11.743.

32. On the location of Cannae see the map in Daly, 2002, 17 and extensive bibliography, also Goldsworthy, 2007, 78–79; Walbank, vol.1, 441. Seibert, 1993b, 227–228 provides a detailed bibliography of research on Cannae up to 1993.

33. So many have written about Cannae that all cannot be listed here. There are excellent recent studies such as Daly, 2002 that provide detailed assessment of the entire battle, background and implications along with wide bibliographical resources. Here I have mainly consulted Daly, 2002; Goldsworthy, 2007; Lazenby, 1998; Seibert, 1993a; Walbank, vol.1, 435–449; Briscoe, 1989; along with Lancel, 1999, plus the useful articles in Hoyos, (ed.), 2011. There are excellent maps in Daly, 2002 and Goldsworthy, 2007.

34. See Walbank, vol.1, 442.

35. Numbers provided here generally follow the assessment given in Daly, 2002, 29–32; for a complete breakdown of all the options see Walbank, vol.1, 439–441; Seibert, 1993b, 228–229; Lazenby, 1998, 75 and 81 for the Roman troop numbers and for the Carthaginian strength.

36. Again here see Daly, 2002, 25–29 for a detailed breakdown of the various arguments.

37. Daly, 2002, 29; Walbank, vol.1, 439–441; Seibert, 1993b, 227–232; Lazenby, 1998, 75–76.

38. Daly, 2002, 29–30.

39. The traditional date given for the battle of Cannae is 2 August, which I adopt here while acknowledging the possible issues with the calendar and that it could have taken place a month earlier: see Derow, 1976; Lazenby, 1998, 77; Daly, 2002, 17; Lancel, 1999, 105. Polybius 3.107.1 believed it took place earlier in the summer, within a month of Hannibal moving out of camp and occupying Cannae.

40. The prevailing summer wind from the south or south-west (called the Volturnus by Livy), would have raised the dust. Livy claims the wind caused problems for the Romans in the battle by getting in their eyes (22.43.10).

41. Following Polybius, although the question of command on the day of battle has been raised: see Daly, 2002, 120–123. Given the connection to Aemilius Paullus (Polybius' patron was Aemilius Paullus' grandson) Polybius may have been recording a rather skewed version of the command structure, one that has absolved Aemilius Paullus and condemned Varro.

42. This is probably what Polybius imagined he said rather than his actual words but as we do not know which source Polybius used here it is possible that Hannibal's words were to that effect. Polyaenus, *Stratagems* 6.38.2 discusses Hannibal's claim about the reincarnation of brave soldiers. The theology of the dying and rising god Melqart is interestingly linked to Hannibal's ideas presented here by Huss, 1986.

43. The various hypotheses for the exact locations are surveyed in Daly, 2002, 33–35, with a map that lays out the different views of the locations. See also Goldsworthy, 2007, 86–94. This account follows Polybius' narrative, discussed in Walbank, vol.1, and see also Lazenby, 1998, 77, who notes that 'Polybius' view is quite clearly stated and there is no good reason to doubt him'.

44. Arguments for this day being the day of battle, with Paullus in command, presented in Daly, 2002, 120–121.

45. See Daly, 2002, 36 for the suggestion that Paullus declined to fight the first time in order to deny Hannibal the 'psychological advantage' of picking the battlefield. See also Lazenby, 1998, 75–78 for the lead-up to the battle.

46. Arguments for Paullus in command presented in Daly, 2002, 120–121, who points out that Appian, *Hann.* 19 believed Paullus was in command on the day of battle.

47. Much debated; see Daly, 2002, 36–37 for the varying opinions on the Roman tactics. Maniples were 'the tactical sub-units of the Roman infantry'.

48. See Daly, 2002, 145–155 for 'commanders battle'.

49. This very simplified version of the battle follows Daly's synopsis, 2002, 38–41, which also provides excellent diagrams that mark out its various stages. For the battle strategy and plans for both sides see Lazenby, 1998, 78–86; Goldsworthy, 2007; Seibert, 1993a, 191–198; Lancel, 1999, 105–109.

50. Lazenby, 1998, 84 and Goldsworthy, 2007, 191.

51. Daly, 2002, 202 on Hannibal's losses and Goldsworthy, 2007, 193–195 (appendix 2).

52. As Daly, 2002 and Goldsworthy, 2007 focus specifically on Cannae; see also Lancel, 1999, 107.

53. Many modern scholars have questioned the veracity of this story and some argue that perhaps it was after Trasimeno, when the road to Rome was clear and the city much closer, that it was suggested. Hoyos, 2006, 646–647; see discussion in Lazenby, 1998, 85–86 and 1996b; Lancel, 1999, 109; Seibert, 1993a, 198–204.

54. See Hoyos, 2000 on this being spoken after Trasimeno, Hoyos, 2005, 119–120; Lazenby, 1996b, on 'Was Maharbal Right'; see also Goldsworthy, 2003, 216, and Siebert, 1993a, 198–204.

55. See Fronda, 2010, 34 n. 84 for a summary of the scholarship on Hannibal's strategy.

56. As set out by Goldsworthy, 2003, 156; see also Hoyos, 2005, 125. In 146 the Romans also destroyed Corinth.

57. Plutarch, *Fab.* 18.2: 'it is the honours they receive from the fortunate that give most pleasure to the gods'.

58. Livy 1.56 and 5.15–16 record the other instances when the Oracle at Delphi was consulted by the Romans.

59. Várhelyi, 2007, 278 n. 2 provides a comprehensive list of references. Eckstein, 1982 argues against the sacrifices being directly connected to the sacrilege of the Vestals.

60. As argued in Eckstein, 1982.

61. For the renewal of the war effort see Eckstein, 1982, 75. This practice is attested to in 228, and also in 114/113 BCE; see Várhelyi, 2007 for a recent approach to the issue.

62. The use of slaves in the armies of the ancient world became more frequent over the course of the late Republic but was rare in the Imperial period. Gracchus freed his slaves before the battle of the River Calor, two years after they had served (Livy 24.14.3–10).

63. Lancel, 1999, 111.

64. Livy writes that 'surely no other nation would not have been crushed by such an over-whelming disaster' (22.54.10). The Roman determination to fight on was what made Polybius believe that they were destined to rule the world. 'It was a lesson to their own men that they must either conquer or else die on the field' (Polyb. 6.58.11). Translation here from Eckstein, 1995, 66–67, who writes on this particular passage in Polybius and its role in defining Roman power.

65. Suggested by Hoyos, 2006, 649 nn. 10, 11.

66. Seibert, 1993a, 215–216.

67. The translation here notes that the manuscript is corrupt in places in this passage and neither the amount of silver nor who was sent to Iberia with Mago is clear: see Hoyos, 2006, 650 n. 23.13.

68. Some of these reinforcements did eventually arrive in Italy but part must have been redirected to Iberia where the battle against the Romans was running into trouble.

## Chapter 8 After Cannae

1. Goldsworthy, 2003, 30–36 points out how difficult it is to describe a 'typical' Carthaginian army as there probably wasn't one; see also Lancel, 1995, 361–362 on the two 'weak' points in the Carthaginian armour – its lack of a homogeneous territorial base and its mercenary army.

2. Daly, 2002, 156–202 for the battle in detail; Lazenby, 1998, 77–86.

3. There is discussion of Hannibal's strategy, well synthesized in Fronda, 2010, 34–52; see also Fronda, 2011. The freedom agenda is discussed above, p. 270*n.* 20.

4. The speech also accuses the Carthaginians of cannibalism, making them less than human. For Varro's speech and the propaganda of Rome vs Hannibal see Lazenby, 1998, 88, who also notes that Fabius in Livy 24.47.5 refers to 'foreigners and barbarians'.

5. The list in Livy 22.61 includes towns and regions that switched sides in the period from 216 to 212 rather than immediately after Cannae.

6. See Fronda, 2010, who analyses the specific circumstances of each city and its defection, and provides a thorough discussion of why some did and some did not go over to Hannibal.

7. It is worth considering how much this reflects Livy's own agenda and how much this was the reality of each situation or a reflection of the late Roman republican rivalries at Rome.

8. See Fronda, 2010, 32–33 and 64–65, note 45 for Compsa.
9. For Arpi and Apulia see Fronda, 2010, 53–99, who points out that neither Livy nor Polybius was concerned with the exact chronology, so any specific timing can only be assumed very generally, Livy for example lists all the defections from 216 to 212 rather than those in the immediate aftermath of Cannae.
10. Lazenby, 1998, 89.
11. A west coast port would remove the need to circumnavigate Sicily (where the Roman navy was based) to access supplies and communications with Carthage; a more direct route would then be available (Map 1). See Fronda, 2010, 130–146 for the Campanian cities that remained loyal; also Lazenby, 1998, 87–114.
12. For the Etruscan origins see Livy 4.37.1–2. The foundation of Greek colonies dates from the eighth century BCE onwards.
13. The term means 'citizenship without the vote': Crawford, 1992, 37; a detailed examination of Roman citizenship in Humbert, 1978. See Fronda, 2010, 117–119 for a discussion of the implications of the status in terms of the other allies.
14. See Humbert, 1978, 167–170, and 173 on the possibility that some Campanian knights had received full Roman citizenship in the fourth century. Also Fronda, 2010, 117 nn. 77–118, who points out that the other cities with *civitas sine suffragio* in the region did not change sides so it is unlikely that status itself was a mitigating factor. See Fronda, 2007 on the revolt and its implications.
15. As noted by Fronda, 2010, 124, the Capuans pursued their own agenda of conquest after their alliance with Hannibal.
16. See Fronda, 2007 for the background to Roman–Capuan relations.
17. On Capua in Livy's narrative of the war see Levene, 2010, 354–375, and Capua siding against the Romans in previous wars, Fronda, 2010, 126–130; for intermarriage see Hoyos, 2005, 122, and on the prisoner exchange, Lancel, 1999, 114–115; also Goldsworthy, 2003, 224; Seibert, 1993b, 216–220; Lazenby, 1998, 89–90.
18. Note a similar story about Nuceria in Cassius Dio (frag. 57.30), which may indicate some confusion about the details of this event, see Hoyos, 2006, 649 n. 7. They had public baths in Capua from the third century and it is always important to note that these cities in Campania considered themselves more 'civilized' than contemporary Rome.
19. Late September or early October 216.
20. It is entirely possible that this is an historically accurate depiction, Hannibal's *adventus*, as pointed out in Fronda, 2010, 105, note 26.
21. We know that there was another prominent opponent of the Carthaginians whose name was Decius Magius. He advocated murdering the Punic garrison in Capua and returning the city to its Roman allegiance. Livy tells us that Magius was rounded up by Hannibal, arrested, and sent to Carthage on a ship (without details of where he boarded the ship). The vessel was blown off course and Magius sought asylum with the Egyptian king Ptolemy IV.
22. See Fronda, 2010, 139–143 on the Nola, Neapolis, Cumae allegiance.
23. Again see Fronda, 2010, 100–147 for a detailed assessment of each city's position during the war.
24. Hannibal makes four attempts, between 216 and 214/213.
25. For the literary topos of luxury, Capua and Hannibal see below, Epilogue, pp. 236–237.
26. Lazenby, 1998, 92–93 points this out.
27. As noted by Miles, 2010, 286 and Fronda, 2010, 146–147.
28. As pointed out by Fronda, 2010, 50–52, 101, 146–147; and in 2007, 84 he states that the success at Capua led to Hannibal's failure in Campania.
29. As noted by many; for example see Goldsworthy, 2003, 224, Fronda, 2010, 41, Hoyos, 2005, 122–133, Lazenby, 1998, 87–88.
30. Fronda, 2007, 83, and this did not include their armies in Iberia, Sicily, Apulia, etc.
31. Manpower and the army after Cannae: see de Ligt, 2012, 72–77 on the Polybian numbers. Polybius estimated that the total manpower available to the Romans, including recruits from all their allies, just before the time of Hannibal was over 700,000 men: see Rosenstein,

2002, Lazenby, 1998, 90–124, Lancel, 1999, 127–30, Fronda, 2010 100–103. See also Rosenstein, 2002 on changes to land qualifications for recruitment.

32. For the standing army under Augustus see Eck, 2007, 114–122.

33. The figures may be greatly exaggerated but in the absence of any other estimates these are the best figures we have. De Ligt, 2012, 77 argues that there are 'no good grounds to dismiss the Polybian figures'. See also Fronda, 2010, 51. Lazenby, 1996b, 43–45 points out that for Hannibal to succeed it was essential he fight the war with 'Rome's resources'.

34. These elections are much discussed: see below, note 35 and Rosenstein, 1993.

35. A very useful list of consuls for each year of the war is available in Lazenby, 1998, 278–283 and an excellent discussion of the politics at Rome can be found in Briscoe, 1989, 67–74. Broughton, 1951 covers the career of each of the magistrates during the period discussed here. For the competition between the Roman elite see for example Rosenstein, 1993 and Gruen, 1978.

36. In Sardinia the commander described much the same situation.

37. Lazenby, 1998, 93–95 notes the debasement, following Zonaras (8.26.14), who puts it in the year 217; see also Lancel, 1999, 122, who puts the devaluation in 217. Crawford, 1974, vol.1, 30 and vol. 2, 604 notes that the Roman loss of control in Italy meant the commanders were making their own arrangements for pay, and that standardization from Rome disappears.

38. As described in Livy 24.11.9 and 24.18.1–15.

39. Crawford, 1985, 60–62.

40. As noted in Rawlings, 2005, 157–161 and 2011, 306.

41. On Hannibal rating Pyrrhus' strategic and military capabilities see Livy 35.14.5–12.

42. For manpower comparison see Goldsworthy, 2003, 225–227.

43. The following numbers are calculated by Erdkamp, 1998, 168–169.

44. According to Polybius he aspired 'to world domination'. See Walbank, 2002, 127–136 for a discussion on whether Philip was really as ambitious as that. Walbank notes, however, that Philip was descended from a family that tended to think along these lines. 'Make higher the walls of Olympos, Zeus/Philip can scale everything' is a line from Alcaeus of Messine's epigram that speaks of the ambition of the Antigonid king (*Anth. Pal.* 9.518, translation from Walbank, 2002, 128).

45. The view here is of Livy and Plutarch constructing a Hellenistic Hannibal but a contemporary impression of Hannibal in the Hellenistic court is much harder to glimpse. The subsequent alliance between Philip and Hannibal implies that the world was watching. A clear discussion on the Roman relationship with Greece during this period can be found in Errington, 1989; see also Gruen, 1986, 359–382.

46. Errington, 1989, 94–97.

47. To the Romans the narrow Straits of Otranto that separated Italy from Illyria needed close protection in an effort to control piracy in the Adriatic.

48. The real impact of the newly constructed Macedonian fleet was, in fact, negligible. When it was deployed in the Adriatic in 216, it quickly disappeared when challenged by Roman ships (Polyb. 5.110.8–11).

49. Polybius claimed to have read the document and provided a copy of it in his history (7.9), whilst the background to the drama comes solely from Livy.

50. Livy's version of the treaty claimed that Hannibal and Philip were intent on world domination and the destruction of Rome, but this is in clear opposition to the text preserved in Polybius (7.9).

51. Bickerman, 1952, 5; see also Barré, 1983, and Lancel, 1999, 117–118.

52. See Bickerman, 1944, and 1952.

53. This is further affirmation that he acted on behalf of the Carthaginian state in this war, rather than the post-war claims that Hannibal acted as a rogue general.

54. According to Bickermann, 1944.

55. Can we learn about Carthaginian statecraft from the terms of this treaty and from the gods invoked by it? The oath invokes the Greek versions of the Punic gods Ba'al Hammon, Tanit and Reshef. It continues: 'in the presence of the god of Carthage, of Heracles and of Iolaus;

in the presence of Ares, Triton and Poseidon;' – which may be a standard formula listing gods that the Carthaginians included in their treaties. Some scholars have argued that the deities called upon in the treaty were more personal to Hannibal, but others have pointed out that the Carthaginian state was the key player in this alliance and that the god-list reflected the official pantheon of Carthage. A detailed study can be found in Barré, 1983, who looks at the god-list in light of the tradition of Near Eastern treaties. See also Miles, 2010, 289–290; Lancel, 1999, 118.

56. For an overview see Rankov, 1996.

57. In 211 the Roman state reached an agreement with Philip's enemies in Greece, the Aetolian League, including the provision of 25 Roman quinqueremes, and the Aetolians were expected to immediately engage Philip in a land war; in that way the Romans could be sure he would not interfere in the Italian theatre. Philip was constrained by his lack of a reliable navy and called on the Carthaginians to support him, but Carthage could ill afford to divert any resources from its own interests in the war. In 209/208 the admiral Bomilcar took his fleet from Tarentum to Philip. The result for Carthage was the loss of the city. By 206 the Aetolians had made peace with Philip, against the provisions of their treaty with Rome and in the following year Philip and the Romans reached a treaty agreement. By that time the war against Carthage had turned strongly in the Romans' favour and they were less concerned with Philip's intervention. See Edwell, 2011, 324–326 for a summary of the main events; see also Errington, 1989, esp. 94–106.

58. Gruen, 1992, 94 calls it a 'major turning point' in the Hannabalic War.

59. Hiero was first tyrant, then king, or even 'client king'; his precise dates are unclear – he may have ruled from as early as 270, or 265, see Lazenby, 1996a, 36 on the reason for uncertainty; see also Walbank, vol. 1, 54–55 for a discussion of the sources and dates. For details of Hiero's hegemony and the nature of his kingship see also Zambon, 2006, 88–90.

60. Polybius 7.7.7 implies that Gelo ruled as co-regent with Hiero. For the spelling used here I prefer Gelo and Hiero as opposed to Gelon and Hieron – although both can be used.

61. The power struggle at Syracuse and its significance in the story of Hannibal reflect its long regional hegemony in the Greek west. What happened was of keen interest to a wide audience. Livy's account is derived from Polybius' detailed description, although we only have fragments of the Polybian version of events (7.2–7.8, 8.2–8.7). For other further influences on Livy's Syracuse and intertexuality see Jaeger, 2010.

62. Their mother was Carthaginian and their grandfather had been an exile from Syracuse (Livy 24.6.1–2; Polyb. 7.2.4); see Walbank, vol. 2, 32 for further thoughts on who these men might have been and whether or not they were Carthaginian citizens. Polybius tells us that their Syracusan grandfather had 'adopted Carthage as his country'.

63. In fact Livy omits the Carthaginians from his version (24.6.4), perhaps to lessen the insult to Rome, as suggested by Walbank, vol. 2, 33.

64. The formulation of an inter-state treaty as laid out here may reflect a different process from the treaty made with Philip V but the incomplete set of evidence prevents an accurate comparison.

65. Lazenby, 1998, 103–105 lays out some of the densely complicated events that led to the Roman siege of Syracuse. See Walbank, vol. 2, 2–3, 69 on the chronology in Polybius' account, and Eckstein, 1987, 136–144 on the role of Appius Claudius Pulcher in the events before Marcellus arrived late in 214.

66. Marcellus was in command of the legions and the navy, according to Walbank who claims that Polybius (8.3.1) is inaccurate in attributing the land forces to Appius Claudius and the fleet to Marcellus, see Walbank, vol. 2, 70.

67. See Walbank, vol. 2, 77–78, and Livy 24.27.5, 36.4.

68. Strabo 7.2.4 included *Epipolae* whilst Diodorus Siculus 26.19 calls Syracuse a *tetrapolis*, leaving out *Epipolae*.

69. 180 *stadia* in Strabo. For the length of the circuit walls of Syracuse, see Lawrence, 1946, 9; see also Seibert, 1993a, map 9a.

70. They functioned as a kind of boarding-bridge, which is described by Polybius in some detail in 8.4.3–11. Plutarch, *Marc.* 14.3 implied that the machine was used across eight ships together; see Walbank, vol. 2, 72.

71. Polybius 8.3.3, in similar words.
72. For the biography of Archimedes we rely on the Byzantine source Tzetzes, *Chil.* 2.35.105. See Chondros, 2007, 1–2 for a brief biographical sketch and more in Jaeger, 2008.
73. Tangible evidence for Archimedes' contribution to Syracusan defensive fortifications is elusive. The tyrant Dionysus originally built the walls in the fifth century. The assumption is that modernization work was done during Hiero's rule and Archimedes was a part of the planning of the defence of the city. The failure of the Roman siege means the walls must have been updated since they were built to withstand the very state-of-the-art siegecraft of the Roman army and navy: see Lawrence, 1946 and Chondros, 2007.
74. See Jaeger, 2008, 101–122 on the 'defence of Syracuse', see also Walbank, vol. 2, 69–78 on Polybius' account of the siege, Karlsson, 1989, 89 on Sicilian fortifications and Lawrence, 1946 on the design of the Euryalus fort.
75. A full account of the death and legend of Archimedes in Jaeger, 2008, and on the passages in Livy see Jaeger, 2006 and 2010.
76. Walbank, vol. 2, 77 takes Polybius to mean the eight months from the beginning of the siege in 213 to the spring of 212 when Appius Claudius left to take up the consulship in Rome. The city did not fall until the autumn of 212.
77. Livy 24.37.1.
78. Enna was the site of a sacred shrine to the goddess Persephone whose kidnap by Hades tradition located nearby.
79. Livy notes that Marcellus made sure his men had 'taken refreshments and rest in good time' for the night operation ahead; this is similar to Polybius' reports of Hannibal's concerns for his men in the lead-up to Trebia and Trasimeno (Livy 25.23.) and reflects the actions of the 'good' Hellenistic general.
80. See Jaeger, 2006 and 2010 on the influences of Cicero's Verrine speeches on Livy's stories of the Syracuse episode in the war – the intertextuality of Livy's Marcellus.
81. For weeping generals see Hoyos, 2006, 662–663, note 24.
82. Livy does not say if this included the 35 he originally left with, but the assumption is yes – so the Carthaginians supplied another 65 ships at short notice.
83. The plague of 211 was followed by food shortages in 210 at Rome, due to the impact of the fighting, especially in Sicily whose wheat crop was perhaps essential for feeding Rome even at this early date. The Romans appealed to the Egyptian king Ptolemy for corn supply, for the embassy: see Polybius 9.11a.1–4. See Walbank, vol.2, 137–138.
84. Marcellus' triumph is termed an 'ovation' by Livy (26.21), who describes the sumptuous victory parade and the debate around the celebration. For Polybius' disapproval see 9.10.

### Chapter 9  Hannibal's Dilemma, 212–209

1. Polybius 7.14b, 8.3a.3–7, 37, 9.10; Livy 24.21–39, 25.23–31.11, 26.21.1–13; see also Plutarch, *Marc.* 13–21. Lazenby, 1998, 119. Agrigentum falls in 210.
2. Welch, 2006, 112 and McDonnell, 2006, 71–72.
3. McDonnell, 2006, 78, see also Gruen, 1992, 94–108, who remarks on this 'literary trope' that appears again and again when Romans come into contact with the wealthy cities of the Hellenistic world. Wallace-Hadrill, 2008, 346 points out that Pliny believed that he was looking at 'successive waves in a continuous process' of growing wealth and luxury. For an excellent discussion see Wallace-Hadrill, 2008, 316–355, on 'Luxury and the consumer revolution' at Rome and the specific discussion on Hellenistic precedents for the impact of luxury on the fall of states, 338–345.
4. Jaeger, 2008, 77–100 on 'who killed Archimedes?' Plutarch provides three different versions in *Marcellus* 19.4–6, see Lazenby, 1998, 119.
5. Compare Fabius' sack of Tarentum below – it is an interesting motivation explored by McDonnell, 2006, 77–81; see also Eckstein, 1987, 169–171. Livy 26.21.1–5 on the deliberations in the Senate meeting at the temple of Bellona on Marcellus' return.
6. Fronda, 2010, 246–247 points out the many instances of the Romans taking advantage of Hannibal's absence to reconquer cities that had defected. Hannibal would have needed a

grand unifying alliance of all his strategic partners for his policy to work but he does not seem to have been able to create that.

7.  Livy's account does not drift far from Polybius'.

8.  For the source Polybius used for the Tarentum material thought by Walbank to be firmly pro-Hannibal see Walbank, vol. 2, 100–101. For the case of Tarentum and the region of south-east Magna Graecia during the war see Fronda, 2010, 188–233 and especially on the 'tenuous loyalty of Taras', 189–211 for the background.

9.  Venusia sat on the border between Samnium and Apulia, and was made a Latin colony in 291 BCE; Brundisium, originally Messapic, was a Latin colony from 246 BCE and was the most important port for embarkation to the East.

10. Fronda, 2010, 190 note 9, and 208–211 on the specific conditions that kept Taras loyal from 216 to 214.

11. See Fronda, 2010, 191; the Carthaginians in Iberia also kept hostages (or guests) of their allies at New Carthage to ensure their loyalty.

12. Also consider that Livy tells of Hannibal's appeal to the 'young men' not as a compliment; they would be considered rash, impetuous, unstable, and the wisdom rested with the elder men in Livian narrative.

13. The Tarentum link with the treaty with Philip V is discussed in Fronda, 2010, 211–212.

14. Casilinum typified Hannibal's problems in Campania. Taken in 215, a strategic location at the crossing of the river Volturnus on the Via Appia, the city was recaptured the following year by the Romans – who threw their resources at it.

15. The old city of Salapia had been abandoned by Pliny's time, destroyed in the social war in the first century BCE (Appian, *BC* 1.51). The population moved 6km from its original location and became a Roman *municipium* and colony.

16. Appian seems to be conflating the story of Salapia in Apulia and the luxury of Capua in Campania here – as it is recounted in a passage where the details of elite infighting in Salapia occur.

17. Lancel, 1999, 129.

18. Fronda, 2010, 213; see Lancel, 1999, 127–130 and Lazenby, 1998, 110 for issues about the dating; see also Appian, *Hann.* 32–33 for the story of the fall of the city.

19. See Fronda, 2010, 210, 214–217.

20. Hannibal's unwillingness to impose any burden on his allied cities was in the long run to his detriment, as noted in Fronda, 2010, 211–217.

21. Polybius (8.28.6) connects the tradition of intra-mural burial at Tarentum to its mother city Sparta, and to an ancient oracle. For Spartan intra-mural burial see Plutarch, *Lycurgus* 27.1. On the origins of the Spartan tradition see Malkin, 1994, 131–132 and Sourvinou-Inwood, 1995, 437.

22. See the discussion in Fronda, 2010, 221–228 for a detailed consideration of each case.

23. Appius Claudius Pulcher and Quintus Fulvius Flaccus were the consuls for 212.

24. If the total numbers of men lost by Hannibal in Livy were counted, his numbers would have diminished to nothing by this point. As noted, Livy's numbers are either greatly exaggerated or Hannibal had a steady flow of recruits and numerous allied forces into his army, which maintained his army in sustainable numbers.

25. People seem to be moving in and out of the city freely enough at this point.

26. Once again Livy provides different versions of the death and burial that reflect the different disposition of his sources; the event is also put at different locations in Lucania (25.16.23–17.3). See Lazenby, 1998, 113, who suggests the differing traditions may obscure a larger defeat for the Romans.

27. Fronda, 2010, 250–251.

28. As noted by Lazenby, 1998, 113–114.

29. Questions about the historicity of the first battle at Herdonea have been raised by some scholars and because of the similarity of the description of the second battle of Herdonea in 210, and the similarities between the names of the Romans involved, there may be some confusion (Livy 27.1.3–15). See Lazenby, 1998, 114; Lancel, 1999, 130; and Fronda, 2010, 258 n. 93, who provides an outline of the arguments for and against. Here

it is taken as historical, given the strategic location of Herdonea on the route between Beneventum and Brundisium: there could have been two battles here. Both of which Hannibal won.

30. Lazenby, 1998, 119; Goldsworthy, 2003, 265; Seibert, 1993a, 296–299.

31. Lazenby, 1998, 121–123, Goldsworthy, 2003, 234–235, Fronda, 2010, Lancel, 1999, 130–132.

32. The details of this event differ quite significantly between Livy and Polybius, and there is a completely different scenario in Appian, *Hann.* 38–42. See Seibert, 1993a, 304–311; Lazenby, 1998, 119–124. Salmon, 1957 details the differences in the versions presented.

33. Sources (above, note 32) disagree on the routes taken by Hannibal and Flaccus to Rome from Campania and the time it took to march there.

34. Livy mentions that Flaccus was granted consular imperium so as not to invalidate his own proconsular power by entering the city (26.9.10). The presence of Flaccus is questioned by Lazenby, 1998, 123.

35. Miles, 2010, 294–296.

36. Using deserters for espionage has been noted above, and the number of times this ruse was used by Livy suggests either a high desertion rate or a motif in Livy on the ease with which the Numidians were perceived to be turned. For the use of deserters see Austin and Rankov, 1995, 69–91.

37. For the events in Iberia see Lazenby, 1998. The best summary of the war in Iberia in English may still be Briscoe, 1989; the yearly analysis laid out by Seibert, 1993a, provides a clear picture of the available information and source material, and of the confusion around the events recorded in Livy.

38. If we believe that Hannibal's intention when he invaded Italy was to defeat Roman hegemony, not to conquer and rule, whereas the Spanish territories had been the lifeblood of the Carthaginian economy in these decades since 237. The way he treated the Italian allies certainly bears this out.

39. Part of Hannibal's grand strategy, perhaps, which, had it been successful, given the events of 216 and victory at Cannae, might have been enough to force a peace on Rome.

40. Livy says the revolt was among the Tartesii, long-time Carthaginian allies, but this has been rejected (originally by Scullard, 1930, 47), given Livy's questionable knowledge of Spanish geography, and it is thought more likely that the Turdetani had rebelled (as noted in Lazenby, 1998, 128; Lancel, 1999, 134). Seibert, 1993b, 220–223 n. 201 goes with the Tartessi, seeing Ascua as the main city (equated with Osqua).

41. Livy 23.13.7–8 also contains these exact same figures – and there seems to be a conflation of two sources; see notes in Hoyos, 2006, 650 n. 13 and 652 n. 32.

42. When envoys from leading tribes in Sardinia arrived in Carthage, giving the Carthaginians hope of the recovery of the island (Livy 23.32.11–12), another army was raised with the prospect of wresting Sardinia from Roman control, and this was a further diversion of resources from Hannibal. While the Sardinian theatre soon fizzled out with the loss of a Carthaginian fleet there, the result left Hannibal to fend for himself in Italy.

43. See Brett and Fentress, 1996, 25–27, on Syphax. The gifts were symbols of the power of a Roman magistrate. It is entirely possible that the Roman contact with Numidian kings began during the Mercenary War when Rome seems to have been supplying the enemies of Carthage (see above, chapter 3). Storm, 2001, 30–32 on the early encounters between Syphax and the Romans.

44. Lancel, 1999, 134; Lazenby, 1998, 129; Goldsworthy, 2003, 246–253.

45. See Briscoe, 1989, 57. Appian, *Ib.* 16 implies that Hasdrubal has been withdrawn to North Africa and it is only after Carthage has 'made peace with Syphax' that he returns. This is disputed. Appian, *Ib.* 3.15–17 for the elder Scipio brothers in Iberia.

46. Lazenby, 1998, 129 details the claims made by Livy over the period discussed here; see also Lancel, 1999, 134; and Seibert, 1993a, 266–267, 299 and 318–322 who chronicles the events by year.

47. Livy places the Roman success at Saguntum in 214, but since it fell in 219 to Hannibal, the date is thought to be 212: 'the fall of the important town of Castulo to the Romans in 214',

and then Saguntum, 'seven years in enemy hands', was taken back by the Scipio brothers (Livy 24.42.9). This reflects the confusion in Livy's Spanish narrative and the sources he used. See Hoyos, 2006, 658 n. 42; Lazenby, 1998, 129; Lancel, 1999, 134; Seibert, 1993a, 266–267.

48. By this time Carthage had made peace with Syphax in Africa, Appian, *Ib.* 15.

49. As suggested by Lazenby, 1998, 130–131, the argument that these events described took place in 211 is convincing, and that Livy compressed the events of two seasons into one.

50. Hoyos, 2006, 663 n. 32 points out that, according to Appian, the Romans may have been based at Castulo at some point in this campaign (*Ib.* 16), but this strongly pro-Carthaginian town was certainly considered hostile by Scipio when he mopped up after his victory in 206 so it is unlikely and again seems to reflect confusion with geographical references. Amtorgis is unknown otherwise, and its location is assumed to be in the upper Baetis region but that is not certain. Was Hasdrubal the son of the Gisgo who had been Hamilcar's lieutenant in Sicily in the First Punic War and was killed by the Mercenaries (see above, chapter 3, p. 55)?

51. Lazenby, 1998, 130 suggests that the Romans may not have known how outnumbered they were. This seems unlikely, given their tenure in Iberia and the dominance of the Roman navy.

52. For more on Masinissa see his biography by Storm, 2001; see also Brett and Fentress, 1996, 25–27; Walsh 1965, 150 outlines Masinissa's early career.

53. Appian, *Lib.* 10 also claims that Masinissa had been betrothed to Sophonisba before he went off to Iberia with Hasdrubal Gisgo, not an impossible scenario as the Carthaginian elite often employed marriage to form alliances – see more on Sophonisba in chapter 11 (pp. 201–207) below and in Storm, 2001, 30–34.

54. Livy gives the age of Masinissa as 17 but this does not accord with his age at death, as recorded by Polybius (36.16.11). Masinissa is thought to have been born *c.* 240, which would make him about 27, and he died in *c.* 149/148 aged around 90, having fathered a child at 86. For a note on Masinissa's age see Hoyos, 2006, 659 n. 49.

55. Walbank, vol. 2, 114–115 places the narrative fragment from Polybius (8.38) just before Hannibal's march on Rome.

56. The destruction of the Roman armies in Iberia and the deaths of the commanders in 211 compelled Rome to focus attention there. The troops that remained after the defeat probably numbered around 8,000 (with 1,000 cavalry) and were led by two surviving lieutenants. For the calculations see Lazenby, 1998, 131.

57. Following Lazenby, 1998, 133, see also Goldsworthy, 2003, 270. The debate between Fabius Maximus and Scipio in 205 BCE over the strategy for the final phases of the war – where the options were to stay and defeat Hannibal in Italy vs invasion of Africa – may reflect similar views in the Senate at this earlier period (Livy 28.40.1–45.9).

58. Scipio had been *curule aedile* in 213 (Livy 25.2.6–8); Walbank, vol. 2, 199–200 points out some of the errors of fact here. On Scipio's status and imperium, see discussion in Lazenby, 1998, 132–133; Seibert, 1993a, 327; on Scipio's career see Acimovic, 2007, 6–12 and Eckstein, 1987, 209–228, who provides an excellent summary of Scipio's time in Iberia. For the careers of the Scipio family see entries in Broughton, 1951.

59. Lazenby, 1998, 133 points out that Livy's story of young Scipio's appointment is hardly credible and the Romans 'just did not do things like that', and that the appointment was probably made by the *comitia centuriata*, perhaps on recommendation of the Senate.

60. For the Iberian soldiers in the Second Punic War, see Rawlings, 1996 and Daly, 2002, 95–101.

61. The risk is noted by Hoyos, 2013, 698.

62. Seibert, 1993a, 326–330 discusses the events in Rome in 210; see also Lazenby, 1998, 133.

63. Livy claims he is 18 at Ticinus, see Polybius 10.3.3–7 and Livy 21.46.7–10; others claim it was a slave who saved the elder Scipio.

64. Rossi, 2004, 363.

65. Traditionally the minimum age for a *curule aedile* was 27. The claim that Scipio had to get his mother's permission (his father was away in Iberia) to stand for the aedileship

(Polyb. 10.4.1–5), is discussed in Walbank, vol. 2, 199–200, means he would have been 21/22, which makes his mother's intervention unlikely.

66. *Paradise Lost*, 9.510, the reference comes from Ennius' poem on Scipio originally. For the reference to Alexander's mother and quasi-divine status see Spencer, 2002, 178–180.

67. Again see Spencer, 2002, 178–180 for a discussion of the 'Roman Alexander Complex'.

68. See Polybius 10.2.1–10.5.9 for the 'character of Scipio'. Walbank notes that Polybius' lament is useful for its proof that by his time, not long after the death of Scipio, the legends of Scipio's quasi-divinity existed (vol 2, 196–197).

69. The story is repeated in Valerius Maximus 1.2.2, and Aulus Gellius 6.1.

70. For example Sosylus and Silenus and the unknown Charaeus. Polybius' relationship with Scipio Aemilianus, who was the adopted son of one Publius Scipio, the son of Scipio Africanus, began in *c.* 168. Although technically a captive in Rome, he acted as mentor to Scipio Aemilianus and accompanied him during his tour of duty in Iberia, and in Africa, where he met Masinissa (*c.* 150/149). Scullard, 1970, 11–14 outlines the connection; and see Walbank, vol. 1, 1–6 on Polybius' life.

71. Scipio in Polybius 10.2.12.

72. See Rossi, 2004 on the construction of parallel lives in Livy. The reasons for the relatively noble portrayal of Hannibal in Livy, especially at the end of the war, have been explored by Moore, 2010.

73. Livy gives the year as 211 and his age as 24, but the year has to be 210: see Scullard, 1930, 36 note 1, and also Walbank, vol. 2, 14–15 and 191–192.

74. Modern Empurias in Catalonia.

75. Polybius and Livy provide slightly different accounts of the whereabouts of the Carthaginian armies. Polybius (10.7.5), who is the preferred source, claims that Mago was near Gades, Hasdrubal was in the Carpetani region, and that Hadrubal son of Gisgo was near the mouth of the river Tagus (in Lusitania, modern Atlantic coast of Portugal). Livy's account of the whereabouts (26.20.6) places Hasdrubal in the neighbourhood of Saguntum.

76. This makes little sense as reported – one wonders if the Carthaginian armies might not have been occupied elsewhere with a rebellion or a recall to Africa? After almost a decade of fighting the Romans the Barcid brothers must have known that they would not be deterred by a total defeat and that another army would return to avenge the deaths of their procon-suls – either a misjudgement of the enemy on a massive scale or something is missing from our sources here. The sequence of events and exact timing leave many questions unan-swered.

77. See Livy 27.7.5–6 where he questions his own dating of these events, which he puts in 210. The fall of New Carthage took place in 209 although some anomalies persist, like what Scipio and the Carthaginian generals did for the rest of the campaigning season, as is mentioned by Hoyos, 2006, 675 n. 27.7. See also Lazenby, 1998, 140.

78. Laelius was still alive when Polybius wrote his history and Polybius (10.3.2) consulted him as an eyewitness to these events, probably about 160 BCE: see Walbank, vol. 2, 198.

79. See Lazenby, 1998, 135; Hoyos, 2006, 672 (note on Livy 26.42); Polybius 10.9.7.

80. Scipio's forces totalled 28,000 plus 3,000 cavalry, according to Polybius 10.6.7, 10.9.6, but some must have been left to guard his supplies, etc. See also Livy 26.42.1–2.

81. The description of the city in Polybius is invaluable as it is our only eyewitness account of it (see also Polyb. 10.9.8–10.10.13).

82. Goldsworthy, 2003, 273–275.

83. Scipio only used Roman soldiers at this point – perhaps not trusting his allies, who had abandoned his father and uncle. He may have left the Spanish allies to guard their rear: see Polybius 10.6.1–10.17.16 on the account of the taking of the city and the sack. For an overview see Eckstein, 1987, 209–228 on Scipio in Iberia.

84. Livy 26.45.7–8 also mentions this draining of the water. On this curious phenomenon of an ebb tide see Seibert, 1993a, 355–356; Walbank, vol. 2, 192–193. Hoyos, 1992 exam-ines the issue in detail and suggests it was a natural phenomenon. He raises the question of why that side of the city was left as exposed as it was. It is a curious passage and still not fully explained.

85. One wonders whether the garrison could have held out – as the Roman garrison at Tarentum had, just to make it more difficult for Scipio – but the Carthaginians once again proved not quite as determined and their navy seems to have gone missing. Many unanswered questions persist in this account.

## Chapter 10  Over the Alps, Again

1. See Walbank, vol. 2, 189–191 on Polybius' Tarentum narrative. Again Livy's chronology for the fall of New Carthage is wrong: see Hoyos 2006, 664 n. 25.36 and 675 n. 27.7.
2. Goldsworthy, 2003, 235–236.
3. See Hoyos, 2006, 677 n. 16; explored in Brizzi, 2009 and for the background see Palmer, 1997, 115–130.
4. Fabius Maximus was commended for his 'strength of character' during the sack of Tarentum where he 'passed up booty' such as colossal statues of the gods. This swipe at Marcellus' behaviour in Syracuse was further magnified by the celebration at Rome of an official triumph by Fabius, granted by the Senate. Fabius Maximus is commended by Livy for his piety: 'the people of Tarentum were to be left their angry gods' (27.16.8). The triumph of Fabius Maximus vs ovation of Marcellus discussed in Eckstein, 1987, 169–171. See Lazenby, 1998, 191 for the first triumph celebrated for a victory in battle (as opposed to the taking of a city) granted to Claudius Nero and Salinator after the Metaurus.
5. Crawford, 1985, 60.
6. Livy is suspected of concealing Roman defeats in his narrative: Goldsworthy, 2003, 236.
7. For the excavations and survey see Bellón et al., 2009, 259, who argue that the location is Cerro de las Albahacas. Previous scholarship has placed the battle further west of Castulo, at modern Balien.
8. The archaeological material can help unravel the confused narrative in the literary sources, especially the geography, as Livy's text is muddled and contradictory for this key period in the battle for Iberia.
9. The same description of Scipio's superior troops vs Hasdrubal's greater numbers is the reverse situation of Hannibal's victories over the Romans. One does wonder about the literary construction of strategic victory rather than the true facts of the day. See chapter 11, p. 193, on Ilipa.
10. For the exact location and recent excavations at the site see Bellón et al., 2009. The intensive survey focused on 20 hectares of land to uncover an array of armour, clothing and coins from both sets of troops, as recently reported in *El Pais* (http://cultura.elpais.com/ cultura/2013/03/09/actualidad/1362850068_856601.html) consulted 30 March 2013.
11. Lazenby, 1998, 142.
12. His escape route, as noted in the excellent map by Bellón et al., 2009, 254.
13. Difficult to imagine what else the brothers believed might happen. Hannibal's victories at Trasimeno and Cannae had not forced a peace from Rome; it was always unlikely that any defeat in 208/207 would meet with a different reaction – but perhaps they were hopeful of a more favourable peace, and even now realized an invasion of Africa was likely.
14. Trouble in Etruria would continue for years afterwards.
15. Although favoured by some, this was not a policy agreed by the leading military commanders at the time.
16. Marcellus' son was also injured in the attack. Here again some information is missing: for both consuls and the son of the consul to be trapped is extraordinary, especially at this stage of the war. The imprudence of the consuls that allowed them to be caught like this is mentioned by Polybius 10.32.7, and followed by Livy 27.27.11. See Lazenby, 1998, 179, and for the complete career of Marcellus see Broughton, 1951, 289–290.
17. Translation of Virgil here by Fagels, 6.985ff.
18. See also Livy 27.28. 1–2.
19. Livy 27.28.1–13 on the ruse with the ring The question of whether or not a Roman garrison had been left in the town also arises, but it is difficult to assess as Livy contradicts

himself. See Fronda, 2010, 258–260, who notes the lack of credibility and assesses the evidence for a garrison.

20. Or possibly the intention of the line is 'more quickly than expected', as suggested by Lazenby, 1998, 182.

21. Although Livy claims that Hasdrubal took the same path as Hannibal (27.39.1–9 for Hasdrubal's crossing) it seems unlikely that he would have choosen a more difficult route than necessary.

22. Numbers calculated in Lazenby, 1998, 181.

23. Commanded by Terentius Varro and Porcius Licinus respectively, following Lazenby, 1998, 181–182.

24. Making Marcellus' and Crispinus' deaths the year before even more perplexing.

25. Command of the legions at Tarentum was with Q. Claudius Flamen, a praetor for 208, and at Capua another propraetor named C. Hostilius Tubulus (Livy 27.36.10–13), Lazenby, 1998, 181–182.

26. Livy may be overstating the losses: see Walbank, vol. 2, 267, Lazenby, 1998, 185.

27. Lazenby, 1998, 184–185 claims that Livy's account of Hannibal's movements 'makes little or no sense as it stands' and that he has mixed up the events of 208 with those of 207.

28. Hoyos, 2006, 680 views Hannibal's 'zigzagging' around the south of Italy as evidence of his loss of men and thus his need to muster more troops.

29. Etruria would have welcomed the Barcids, and Livy (28.10.4–5) mentions Romans investigating communities in Etruria that had been planning on going over to the Barcid brothers. Hannibal and Hasdrubal had coordinated this with locals, including people of Arretium (Arezzo). Rumours of an Etruscan rebellion are mentioned in Livy 27.21.6–8, 27.24.1–9, 28.10.4–5; see Fronda, 2010, 239 n. 17, 289–290. For the famous inscription found at Tarquinia of the 106-year-old Larth Felsnas, whose epitaph notes that 'he fought with Hannibal's people at Capua', see Pfiffig, 1967, 663.

30. The date taken from Ovid (*Fasti* 6.770) is 22 June but see Derow, 1976, 281, who would place it about a month earlier, with calculations to redress the imbalance in the calendar, on 19 May. See the wider arguments in Walbank, vol. 2, 270–271. Lazenby, 1998, 182–190 covers the whole period from the Alps to the Metaurus.

31. For the debate on the location of Hasdrubal at Sena and not further north at Fanum see Walbank, vol. 2, 267–269; Lazenby, 1998, 183–189; Goldsworthy, 2003, 238–243; Seibert, 1993a, 382–393.

32. Nero had sent messengers ahead but had moved quickly.

33. Polybius' account is incomplete; it picks up with Hasdrubal being displeased about something and launches into the battle: see Walbank, vol. 2, 267–274.

34. Estimates vary. Livy (27.49.6) gives the number at 56,000 and Appian (*Hann.* 52) concurs, but Walbank (vol. 2, 273) points out that this figure seems to be greatly inflated – especially given Hasdrubal's willingness to fight Livius and Porcius but hesitation about fighting the armies of the two consuls combined even though Claudius Nero's army was only some 7,000 selected troops.

35. Missing detail here about which river was forded by whom: if Hasdrubal was to reach the Metaurus, he and his army would have had to cross the river Misa or the Cesano before he got there (if his camp really was at Sena), as noted by Hoyos, 2006, 681.

36. Hasdrubal's movements are well reasoned by Lazenby, 1998, 183.

37. Livy's claim of 57,000 enemy dead cannot be trusted and is considered far too high; Polybius' claim of 10,000 Carthaginian and Celtic troops slain seems closer to the mark. The number of captured soldiers is also significant – they raised more than 300 talents in ransom, which has been estimated as the equivalent of close to 10,000 prisoners: see Walbank, vol. 2, 273–274 for the references to calculations.

38. Ovid, *Fasti* 6.770, 'Hasdrubal fell by his own sword' does not contradict the depiction in Polybius – the battle being lost, Hasdrubal, assuming his brother had also been defeated, did not see a way out other than victory; capture by the Romans was not an option for him. Polybius' digression supports the use of suicide as an honourable way out for a defeated general (11.2.1–11).

39. The time elapsed could not have been too long or the head would have rotted beyond recognition.
40. As Briscoe, 1989, 55 points out.
41. Appian, *Ib.* 25–27 is considered unreliable and irreconcilable with Polybius and Livy, as noted by Walbank, vol. 2, 296. The name of the place – Ilinga in Polybius, Silpia in Livy and Karbone in Appian – is confused but the location near Seville largely agreed upon. See Lazenby, 1998, 145; Lancel, 1999, 150; Goldsworthy, 2003, 279–284; Seibert, 1993a, 393–396.
42. Perhaps north to Gallicia as well, the region referred to by its Roman provincial name Hispania Ulterior in Livy 28.12.13.
43. Regarding the superior numbers of the Carthaginian forces, in Polybius (20.2) listed as 70,000, plus 4,000 cavalry and 32 elephants and in Livy (28.12.13) 50,000 plus 4,500 cavalry. Appian (*Ib.* 25) follows Polybius on foot soldiers but puts the number of cavalry at 5,000, Scipio's army was in the neighbourhood of 45,000 foot and 3,000 cavalry. The Carthaginians had a 'slight but not very substantial numerical advantage', according to Walbank, vol. 2, 297; whereas Lazenby, 1998, 145 is inclined to accept Polybius' numbers as an explanation for the complicated stratagem that Scipio employed.
44. The very specific details of the three manoeuvres are covered by Lazenby, 1998, 147–149 following Polybius 11.22.8–11.24.11; see also Walbank, vol. 2, 269–304 with diagrams. See also Goldsworthy, 2003, 280 for a clear plan.
45. Ilipa was 14 km north of Seville on the Guadalquivir river; see Walbank, vol. 2, 296–304 for the detailed breakdown of Scipio's complicated movements, and also Scullard, 1930, 135 for a diagram of the stages of the battle.
46. Hoyos, 2006, 685 n. 28.16 notes that this retreat could have taken weeks and that Livy has compressed the events to make it seem a few days.
47. Hasdrubal Gisgo went to Syphax's capital Siga for a rendezvous with the Numidian king and at the same time Scipio showed up in the harbour. One wonders if this was not a prearranged meeting, some kind of summit? Livy covers the meeting and the importance of Syphax in 28.17.10–16.
48. For Scipio's new foundations see Appian, *Ib.* 38, home of the future emperors Trajan and Hadrian.
49. Briscoe, 1989, 60; and Iberia would not be a fully settled province of Rome (the provinces of Hispania) until the period of Augustus, as Livy notes in 28.12.12.
50. Silius Italicus gives Hannibal a wife named Imilce from Castulo (see chapter 4). Livy's line from 28.19.16 where Scipio approaches the walls of Illurgia putting himself in danger mirrors Hannibal outside the walls of Saguntum (21.7.10) rushing the wall and receiving a spear in the thigh. Hannibal's injuries sent his men into retreat, whereas Scipio's caused them to rush the walls with greater determination.
51. L. Marcius Septimus. For location see Walbank, vol. 2, 305. Appian, *Ib.* 33, Livy 28.23.4, and Polybius 11.24.10–11.
52. Events summarized here cover the period between 207 and 205: see Livy 28.12.12–28.38.1 and Polybius 11.20–11.33, including detailed accounts of the battle of Ilipa and the mutiny of the Celtiberians under Andobales, Scipio's illness and the final battle in Iberia somewhere south of the Ebro.
53. Appian refers to these settlers as Blastophoenicians. See Lowe, 2009, 52 and the translation and commentary on Appian's Iberian books by Richardson, 2000, 151, who notes that Appian may be conflating the name originating from earlier settlement of Phoenicians with Hannibal.
54. Scipio's visit to Syphax (see above, *n.* 47) and subsequent alliance being enough of an indicator.
55. Were the Carthaginians trying to resupply their generals in Italy? The nature of the mission of the 80 Carthaginian freighters that were captured perplexed Livy himself, as his sources conflict: Coelius Antipater claimed they were aimed at resupplying Hannibal, whilst Valerius Antias claimed it was booty from the north where Mago was causing trouble. See Hoyos (2006, 691 n. 46), who believes Livy/Coelius. On Mago's last years and the

Carthaginian strategy in Italy see Seibert, 1993a, 418–419; Lazenby, 1998, 196; Lancel, 1999, 158. References from Livy here (28.11–12).

56. Following Lancel, 1999, 153–154.

57. The retributions exacted and settlements made by the Romans in the south of Italy were, as noted by Fronda (2010, 307), the final stages in their complete conquest of Italy. As each city and region was retaken, specific conditions would have reflected their role in supporting Hannibal as well as the local elites' relationship with Rome – although generally speaking the treatment of the communities was punitive and severe punishments were inflicted. See Fronda, 2010, 234–279, and 307–329 on 'Rome and the Italians'; see also Toynbee, 1965.

58. See Lazenby 1998, 195 on the legions in the field in 205; Seibert, 1993a, 413–423.

59. Here Livy echoes Polybius 11.19 on Hannibal's character: 'No one can withhold admiration for Hannibal's generalship, courage and power in the field . . .'

60. See also Polybius 11.19, and Lancel, 1999 151–157 on 'Hannibal at Cape Lacinium'.

61. The rise and fall of support from Carthage meant that for much of the period when Hannibal was in Italy he was fighting for himself. The loyalty of Hannibal's troops in Livy is interestingly balanced with a passage on rebellion among Scipio's troops.

62. Lancel, 1999, 157, Jaeger, 2006 and Brizzi, 1983. The narrative of Hannibal in Bruttium at the temple of Juno in Crotona is the perfect example of how Livy's epic has constructed our image of Hannibal. On the nature of the text and whether it served as a type of memoir of Hannibal's deeds, a true *res gestae*, there is much debate: see Meister, 1990 for an interesting discussion on Hellenistic autobiography.

63. These Carthaginian-style coins may be the identifiable ones and Hannibal could have minted coins in the Greek style as well, making them less distinguishable. See Robinson, 1964; Jenkins, 1987; Alexandropoulos, 2000, 104–108.

64. See Crawford, 1985, chapter 4 on the Second Punic War and 62–69 on the Hannibalic and allied coinage.

65. No numbers are provided in the sources other than those relating to the army he took with him back to Africa. Livy contends that it was still a 'large' force and the Roman reactions to Hannibal suggest it was considerable enough to keep them wary of full engagement.

66. Much to Roman chagrin, Livy insists.

67. Thus bringing to an end the First Macedonian War that had rumbled on in the background over the period from *c.* 212/211: see Gruen, 1986, 373–381 for the background. Livy (27.30.10) reported that during the diplomatic negotiations (in 208) leading up to the peace treaties the intention was to end the war 'so that neither the Romans nor Attalus would have reason to enter Greece'. The Mediterranean world was sensing Rome's growing power and the demise of the Carthaginian threat.

68. As noted by Jaeger, 2006, 390.

## Chapter 11 Hannibal Returns

1. *The History of the World* book 5, sect. 21, chapter 3.

2. Kunze, 2011, 397. Reflecting Polybius' interests in Masinissa and his connection with Scipio Aemilianus, no doubt.

3. Family ties include Naravas, a Numidian prince married to a daughter of Hamilcar in Polybius (1.78.1–9), and Masinissa's uncle, who was married to Hannibal's niece (daughter of his sister, in Livy 29.29), perhaps the daughter of Naravas and his sister. On the Barcid family and Numidian ties see Hoyos, 2005, 25–26 and Kunze, 2011, 399 n. 8.

4. Scipio makes this point in his speech to the Senate during the debate over the invasion of Africa in Livy (28.44.4–5; along with Livy's slander of 'faithlessness' etc.).

5. The discussion in Eckstein, 1987, 233ff. For a detailed study of Masinissa, see also Storm, 2001 (especially pp. 35–60 for the period discussed here) and an interesting discussion in Walsh, 1965. On the formation of the Numidian kingdoms see Camps, 1960 and Quinn, 2013 on their ideological development.

6. Masinissa travelled back and forth between Africa and Iberia in the following years, he was at Carthage in 210/209 with a unit of 5,000 cavalry and he returned to fight in Iberia in 208–207 (Livy 27.5.11). After Hasdrubal Barca lost the battle of Baecula and departed for Italy, Masinissa was given a force of 3,000 cavalry to roam the region attacking the enemy and assisting the allies (Livy 27.20) – although Lazenby raises some interesting questions about Livy's account of the aftermath (1998, 143).

7. Discussions were held between Silanus, Scipio's deputy, and Masinissa, after the Carthaginian general Hasdrubal son of Gisgo had abandoned his forces and fled to Gades (Livy 28.16.11–12). Masinissa's father Gaia had recently died and the struggle for succession was unfolding in Numidia. Masinissa's uncle had been married to Hannibal's niece (perhaps the daughter of his sister and Naravas, or the daughter of another sister). See Walsh, 1965, 150–151.

8. The sentiments of Masinissa may have been real, perhaps reported to Polybius personally and then picked up by Livy. Livy's depiction of Masinissa being almost 'dazed at merely meeting' Scipio sounds very much like flattery.

9. Livy's claim that Masinissa stayed with the Carthaginians until late in 206 and that – while he was with Mago Barca at Gades, just before Scipio left Iberia to return to Rome – the two men met face to face seems unlikely. The conflicting accounts of the meetings in Livy (28.16.11 and 28.35.1–13) are unlikely both to be correct and the suspicion that Livy has constructed the meeting with Scipio is a distinct possibility: see Walsh, 1965, 150; Lazenby, 1998, 151–156.

10. Masinissa's dynastic rivals and familial situation summarized by Livy 29.29.6–13.

11. For Scipio's election as consul for 205 see Scullard, 1930, 160–162, Lazenby, 1998, 193, Hoyos, 2005, 158–159. For the wider Roman view on events here, including the summoning of the Magna Mater from Asia Minor, see Gruen, 1990, 47–48, and Burton, 1996. For a breakdown of the rhetorical nature of both 'set-piece' speeches and the wider historiographical contexts see Laird, 2009, 204–208. Scipio was advocating a policy that would have been pursued by his father and uncle from Iberia if they had survived, according to Livy's estimation (24.48.1) and this debate was a long-standing one, going back to 218.

12. See also Livy 28.38.12; 28.38.40–45; Plutarch, *Fab.* 25; Appian, *Hann.* 55 and *Lib.* 7; Silius Italicus 16, 692–700. Scipio could never be certain that he would not be recalled to Rome and another commander given his army. Scipio's allies, with the backing of the popular assembly in Rome, continuously supported Scipio's command and would work to ensure that he was not recalled from Africa until the end of the war (Livy 30.27.2–4, 43.1–3). See Eckstein, 1987, 233ff. on Scipio's command from 205 and the prosecution of the war in Africa. See Briscoe, 1989, 73–74. Livy 30.27 describes the attempts in later years to take the control of the Africa campaign away from Scipio – but the popular assembly continued to vote to leave him in command.

13. The games had been vowed by Scipio during the mutiny the previous year: Livy 28.24–29, 28.45. On the mutiny of Scipio's troops and his illness see Polybius 11.25–30 and Walbank, vol. 2, 310–11; Lazenby, 1998, 152–153; also Goldsworthy, 2003, 269–285; Eckstein, 1987, 224–226.

14. Yardley's 2006 translation uses 'gifts from the spoils of Hannibal' (Livy, *Hannibal's War*, 511), but the Oxford and Loeb Latin texts state Hasdrubal so I have used that here.

15. Was a troop levy denied or deemed unnecessary as Sicily was already well manned? With the 7,000 volunteers there were at least four legions at Scipio's disposal, and the refusal of some of the Latin allies to fill their requirement of troops may have made a levy difficult, according to Lazenby, 1998, 195. Scipio funded the construction of the ships built for the transport himself, and with the support of the allies, according to Livy 28.45.13.

16. Goldsworthy provides an excellent account of the preparations needed for such an expedition – for example, building transport ships, training troops to the necessary standard for battle. Scipio's expedition was supplied from Sicily for the whole time he was in Africa (2003, 288–289).

17. Livy 29.3 claims Laelius landed at Hippo Regius (Annaba in Algeria), but Hoyos, 2006, 692 n. 3, points out that this must be a mistake: Hippo Regius was in Massyli territory and

hundreds of kilometres from Carthage, so it is more likely that he landed at Hippo Diarrhytus (Hippo Accra, modern Bizerte) situated about 60 km north-east of Carthage and an allied city. Lazenby, 1998, 197, in contrast, accepts Hippo Regius as the destination.

18. From 217 onwards there was raiding, pillaging, looting, including a massive raid that year by the consul Gnaeus Servilius Geminus with 120 ships, who attacked the islands off the coast of Tripolitania including Meninx (Djerba) and, further north, Kerkina. A raiding party had landed but was ambushed (Livy 22.1.6–9; 22.31.1–7). A gap in the records for the years between 214 and 211 may mean that the concentration of the fleet on Sicily gave some reprieve to the Carthaginian lands; see Lazenby, 1998, 196–197 for the complete references in Livy and also see Rankov, 1996. Carthage had equally been raiding, but less successfully, the Italian coast and the islands.

19. We have little information on Carthaginian efforts to supply the Barcid brothers in Italy. Mago had sent over half his ships to Africa to protect it from Scipio's invasion (Livy 28.46.10), and Carthage sent back to Mago 6,000 infantry, 800 cavalry and seven elephants in transports escorted by 27 warships. As Lazenby (1998, 196) points out, it is amazing that these reached Mago, given the overall poor success rate of the Carthaginian navy in the war; see also Rawlings, 2010. There is some confusion with a report in Livy (28.46.14) of 80 merchant ships captured off Sardinia in 205 – these may have been heading to Mago, although Livy's sources say they were meant for Hannibal.

20. See Hoyos, 2006, 693 n. 4.

21. Her name is Saphonbal, in Punic SPNB'L, which means 'Saphon is protected by Ba'al', Halff, 1963–64. For the god Ba'al Saphon attested to at Tyre, see Bordreuil, 1986, 84–86.

22. Appian (*Lib.* 10) claims that she had previously been engaged to Masinissa.

23. The inheritance pattern in Numidian kingdoms, horizontally through the male line, meant the kingdom fell to the oldest living brother, not son. Livy calls Masinissa's father Gala (24.48.13) but his name is recorded in inscriptions as Gaia: see Hoyos, 2006, n. 29.29, p. 696, and for the family connections see Hoyos, 2005, 153–154. The complicated scenario is clearly set out by Lazenby, 1998, 198 and Livy describes Masinissa's adventures before he met up with Scipio's invasion in 29.29–29.33. For Masinissa's visit to Laelius in 205 and encouragement to Scipio to invade see 29.4–29.5.

24. Masinissa and Syphax had encountered each other in battle before. In 213/212 Masinissa and a Carthaginian army battled (possibly led by Hasdrubal, Hannibal's brother, who had returned from Iberia) against Syphax (in a great battle, says Livy) which caused Syphax to flee westwards to the Mauri people. Masinissa pursued Syphax and 'without any assistance from the Carthaginians, he covered himself with fame' (Livy 24.49.4–6).

25. Hoyos, 2006, 697 n. 29.31.

26. See Fronda, 2010, 269–279 for a detailed assessment of the situation in Bruttium down to 203; see also Lazenby, 1998, 195–203, Goldsworthy, 2003, 289–290, Seibert, 1993a, 413–423 Lancel, 1999, 151–157 on the events surrounding Locri and the encounter between Scipio and Hannibal.

27. As noted by Lazenby, 1998, 199, who suggests we might view this as a success for Hannibal. The victory was Scipio's even if Hannibal had not intended to try to retake the town.

28. Livy reports legions stationed in Bruttium through the second century, and see Lazenby, 1998, 199–202 for the impact of Pleminius on Scipio's reputation; Livy details the aftermath and the political ramifications of the scandal in 29.8–9, 29.16, 17, 19.

29. Livy 29.38.1 and 30.19.10 lists the cities lost along with 'other unimportant cities'.

30. Eckstein, 1987, 240–241 argues that up until the last minute Scipio had been trying to persuade Syphax back into alliance, which would have spelled the end of Masinissa's hopes. However, Syphax remained loyal to Carthage and Masinissa's power benefited. Scipio, according to Livy (29.27), had meant to land at Kelibia on Cap Bon, where both Agathocles and Regulus had landed their invading armies, but the wind had sent the fleet west to Cap Farina. Livy's sources claim Masinissa either had 200 horsemen with him or 2,000 (29.29, 29.33.8) and Polybius 21.21 claims 60 horse.

31. Clearly demonstrates the repetitive nature of Carthaginian names. The Romans had some similar issues when the consuls for 204 were the seemingly unrelated Gnaeus Servilius and Gaius Servilius (Livy 30.1.1); see also Lancel, 1999, 165.

32. These enormous numbers are generally considered to be fantastical, but there is little else to go on.

33. Hoyos, 2006, 698 n. 29.35, Lancel, 1999, 158–169 for the invasion up to Hannibal's recall; Lazenby, 1998, 202–213; Goldsworthy, 2003, 286–298; Eckstein, 1987, 233–246 on Scipio's actions up until Zama; Seibert, 1993a, 429–442.

34. The numbers vary. Lazenby's (1998, 203) estimate and the breakdown of foot to cavalry are well reasoned and listed here but there are also numbers available in Goldsworthy, 2003, 287–88 for Scipio's troops and 292–293 for the Carthaginian and Syphax' numbers.

35. As noted in Goldsworthy, 2000, 292–293 and Hoyos, 2006, 698 n. 29.35. For location of Scipio's winter camp as the modern village of Galaat el-Andless see Lancel, 1999, 165.

36. Livy 30.1.1 names the consuls as Gn. Servilius and G. Servilius – not related. The Etruscans had been agitating for some years (back to 208 and Hasdrubal Barca's invasion of Italy).

37. For Scipio's ruse and the destruction of the camps see Goldsworthy, 2000, 293–294; Lazenby, 1998, 207–208; Siebert, 1993a, 437–442.

38. Cirta was the inland capital and stronghold of the Numidians; it had changed hands over the course of the Punic Wars and was now held by Syphax. See also Lancel, 1999, 168–169; Kitouni-Daho, 2003, 95–96.

39. A story in Appian (note 10 above) claims that Masinissa had been betrothed to Sophonisba as a young man in Carthage, but this is nowhere else repeated. It is much more likely that as Syphax' wife she went with the kingdom into the power of Masinissa and it would have been his choice to marry her.

40. Storm, 2001 35–45 on Masinissa's kingdom; Poirel, 2003, 154–159.

41. Ancient sources include Diodorus Siculus 27.7; Appian, *Lib.* 27–28; Cassius Dio (Zonaras 9.11). Polybius' only mention is of the daughter of Hasdrubal and wife of Syphax (14.7.6). She appears in Boccaccio *De mulieribus claris*, 1374; Petrarch, *Africa, c.* 1396; Voltaire, *Sophonisbe*, premiered in 1774, originally by Jean Mairet but revised by Voltaire. Poirel, 2003, 154–159 provides an excellent assessment with reproductions. European fascination with the tragedy of Sophonisba has inspired plays and poems in English, French, German, Spanish and Italian from the fourteenth century through to the present day.

42. For the run-up to Zama see Hoyos, 2005, 164–176, Lazenby, 1998, 213–221.

43. Polybius 15.1.6–8. An inner council of the Carthaginian Senate, Lancel, 1995, 116; Hoyos, 2010, 30–31. Eckstein, 1987, 246–255 on Scipio's motives and the 'ad hoc' diplomacy.

44. Polybius' narrative picks up again just after these negotiations took place.

45. Polybius omits this detail of blaming Hannibal but Livy includes it. Livy comments that the kowtowing 'derives from their country of origin' and Polybius calls it the custom of 'other men', reflecting the Phoenician origins of the Carthaginians and their cultural alterity.

46. Livy's sources conflict on the amounts asked for, either 5,000 talents or 5,000 pounds of silver, or double Scipio's men's pay (30.16). Hoyos (2006, 704 n.16) comments that 5,000 pounds of silver, worth only about 60 talents, seems unlikely and that Polybius 15.8 mentions 5,000 talents. Appian (*Lib.* 32) includes passages that granted Masinissa his own kingdom and Syphax' realm as well as a limit to Carthaginian territory – but this may be conflated with the settlement after Zama.

47. As Lazenby notes, 1998, 214.

48. Appian, *Lib.* 49 puts Mago still in northern Italy after Hannibal was defeated at Zama in 202; Cornelius Nepos seems to believe that he lived through to the 190s in *Hann.* 7.3–4.

49. Cassius Dio claims that no Carthaginian envoys would even be received by the Roman Senate until the Barcid brothers left Italy, and that terms were then discussed after the armies had departed.

50. Lazenby, 1998, 215 recounts the key events of the last two years as far as we can tell; Livy 29.36.4–9, 29.38.1.

51. Livy 30.20, Appian, *Hann.* 58–59. It seems unlikely that the Romans were content to sit back and watch as Hannibal and his army built a transport fleet when they were under

orders to keep him in Italy; the suggestion that much of the transport actually arrived from Carthage in Hoyos, 2005, 170–171 makes sense.

52. Hoyos, 2005, 166–170.

53. Appian asserts that Hannibal killed 4,000 horses and also pack animals and that he committed atrocities before he left, slaughtering some of his soldiers who were unwilling to cross over with him. This certainly would not be in keeping with his acknowledged care and duty to his soldiers and is generally dismissed as slander, but given that the situation was desperate, it may well have happened (Appian, *Hann.* 57–59, Diodorus Sic. 27.9). Livy 30.20.5–6 also mentioned his killing soldiers who would not accompany him.

54. Lancel, 1999, 171 provides the higher estimate whilst Lazenby, 1998, 215 estimates 12,000 by back-calculating from Hannibal's army at Zama.

55. Note especially that Livy (42.3) makes it clear that the temple of Juno at Crotona had not been 'violated' by Hannibal. His words are: the 'most venerable temple in the region, which neither Pyrrhus nor Hannibal had violated', which seems to contradict this statement. The looting of the region by Fulvius Flaccus in *c.* 173 is discussed by Miles, 2008, 76–82.

56. Despite Livy's hyperbole it does reveal underlying hostility between those in power at that time in Carthage and the Barcids. See Lancel, 1999, 171–172 and also Hoyos, 2005, 172, who calls him autonomous.

57. According to Cassius Dio he did face prosecution after the battle of Zama, on charges of which he was cleared: see chapter 12, pp. 220–221.

58. This may play into a Roman narrative more than the real situation and Livy may also be projecting the experiences of the Roman Senate's opposition to Scipio's success on to Hannibal.

59. Livy 28.37.9 and Polybius 15.11.1 mention Balearic and Ligurian soldiers. Mago had both with him and his army must have continued back to Carthage after Mago's death. Timing follows Hoyos, 2005, 170–171.

60. Hoyos points out that the following events could also have occurred in the autumn of 203, (2006, 707 n. 24). The chronology of events here is not entirely clear – Livy contradicts himself on when Hannibal arrived, and we only have the aftermath of these events preserved in Polybius, so it is difficult to construct a precise, step by step, outline. I follow the chronology set out by Lazenby, 1998, 215–216 here.

61. Equates to modern Korbous, across from Carthage where there are warm water springs (Aquae Calidae), and the island of Zembra (Aegimurus). It would be difficult to see the ships at Zembra as it lies to the north, but Korbous is clearly visible from Carthage across the bay of Tunis even with today's less clear air (Hoyos, 2006, 707 n. 24). Ships may have been heading for Scipio's camp, the Castra Cornelia near Utica, and to Tunes south of Carthage, which is why some ended up at Zembra and others at Korbous.

62. Lazenby, 1998, 216–217; Hoyos, 2005, 170–174; Goldsworthy, 2003 298–300.

63. A spontaneous attack or a pre-planned expedition? Livy 30.25.5–12 and Polybius 15.2.1–15 differ in their versions. For quadriremes and quinqueremes see Livy. Hannibal had returned to Italy before the envoys returned from Rome.

64. Appian, *Lib.* 34 claims some ambassadors were killed.

65. At Hadrumentum, but according to Livy (30.25.12) Hannibal had just landed at Leptiminus but had camped near Hadrumentum and then gone directly on to Zama, not a likely scenario and carefully explained in Hoyos, 2006, 709 n. 29.

66. Syphax' son Vermina was expected but showed up late for the battle and approached Carthage some time later (on the first day of the Saturnalia –17 Dec.), according to Livy, which would make it some months later if the battle was in October: see below, note 75. If the Roman calendar was indeed off by a month then about a month exists between the dates. Vermina and his army were routed but the prince escaped; the battle may have happened but details are sketchy, see Hoyos, 2005, 175 (Livy 30.36). Eckstein, 1987, considers Hannibal to have acquired a force equal to that of Masinissa's cavalry by the time of the battle.

67. Many different versions of the location exist: *apud Zamam* (Cornelius Nepos, *Hann.* 6.3) was where Hannibal's camp was, but the battle took place some distance from there. There

are a few towns in modern Tunisia that claim to be the location of this famous site, see Map 1 for the rough location. A survey of opinions on the location in Hoyos, 2005, 172–178; Lancel, 1999, 172–176; Seibert, 1993a, 446–447 and map 7 and 1993b, 311–318 for a summary of the bibliography and analysis of the location; Lazenby, 1998, map 20.

68. Laelius had returned to Scipio from Rome with news of some of his senatorial colleagues' ambitions to unseat him from his command of the forces in Africa, which cannot have improved Scipio's mood. His insistence on provoking a final battle may also have stemmed from criticism from Rome. Interesting to see the Romans upset with the Carthaginians for subterfuge and delay (although Scipio had used just those tactics to destroy the camps with fire in 203), and for refusing to give up when defeated, another noted Roman trait.

69. See Map 2. Again on the location of the battle, Polybius is clear that it occurred closer to a place called Margaron, as he calls it; Livy (30.29.9) refers to Naraggara. This may be near Sidi Youssef, or somewhere on the Sidi Youssef–El Kef road: see the various possibilities in Walbank, vol. 2, 447–448, Lazenby, 1998, 218. The map in Scullard, 1970, 144 gives a clear picture of the camps and the battle.

70. Lazenby, 1998, 218–219.

71. Lazenby, 1998, 218–221 for the positioning before the meeting of the two generals.

72. Polybius (15.6.3) claims they had an interpreter with them, and Livy (30.30.1) states they had one translator each.

73. Gruen, 1992, 237 discusses the cultural imperialism behind the use of Latin in a wider context and states that Scipio would never have held high-level discussions in Greek, and we can assume that Hannibal would have insisted on using Punic – the use of translators on both sides being clue to the status of the speaker (Cornelius Nepos, *Hann.* 13.3, Livy 29.19.11–13).

74. The speeches are probably made up; certainly Livy's evocative version is filled out with rhetorical flourish. Polybius' record possibly preserves the Roman memory of the conversation between the two men from the Cornelii. For the echoes of Sallust *Bellum Catiline* and Livy's versions of the speech see Rossi, 2004 and Feldherr, 2010.

75. The date is unknown but later sources link the battle to the appearance of a comet that is backdated to October 202: see Hoyos, 2006, 709 n. 29 and Walbank, vol. 2, 449–450, who provide full references.

76. These estimates in Lazenby, 1998, 220–221; see also Goldsworthy, 2003, 302–303; Walbank, vol. 2, 449–450.

77. Goldsworthy, 2003, 303–304 makes the argument that Hannibal intended to punch through the Roman centre.

78. The speeches are probably an invention of Polybius; at least Hannibal's speech and actions – as if he were distancing himself from the whole and unwilling to take responsibility for the fight. He knew he was going to lose.

79. The psychological impact and Hannibal's ability to inspire his troops are noted in Siebert, 1993a, 483.

80. Polybius 15.15.3–8 admits as much; he had an inferior army.

81. Bagnall, 1990, 290–291, whose book on the Punic Wars from the perspective of a field general asks if Hannibal was just stressed out by this point, no longer capable of his best performance, worn and tired from the years of battle and struggle to keep his army together in Italy. He could not muster the enthusiasm for the fight, nor did he perhaps believe in what he was fighting for. Lazenby, 1996b, 40 notes that 'the master had lost none of his cunning' and deployed his inferior forces to try to distract the enemy.

82. As noted by Eckstein, 1987, 255.

### Chapter 12  Hannibal into Exile

1. For Ennius' Scipio '*invicte*', a panegyric to the Roman hero of the Hannibalic War, see Gruen, 1990; also for a discussion of Ennius in the Roman political landscape.

2. Pursued by Masinissa, according to Appian, *Lib.* 47, whom Hannibal outmanoeuvred and left injured.

3. According to Walbank, vol. 2, 471, who estimates his birth year as mid-247, he was 45 in 202.

4. Polybius 15.19.3–9 records Hannibal's impassioned plea for Carthage to accept the Romans' 'lenient terms': see Walbank, vol. 2, 471. Interesting words, as the terms were only lenient when considered retrospectively after Carthage's destruction in the Third Punic War, which Polybius witnessed. Livy (30.37.7–8) records a man named Gisgo, perhaps a son of Hasdrubal Gisgo as being the senator who advocated continued resistance.

5. One talent was equivalent to roughly 26kg of silver (compare with the 2,000 talents demanded at the end of the First Punic War in 241); numbers from Lancel, 1999, 177. Hoyos, 2005, 180 points out that the yearly sum was less than the yearly amount of the First Punic War indemnity but was to be paid over a longer period – most likely the amount that was considered feasible on a yearly basis, although Carthage offered to pay off the entire amount in 191. The Romans did not wait long after the period of payment lapsed in c. 151 to provoke the Third Punic War, which began in 149, with the city destroyed in 146.

6. Five hundred ships, according to Livy (30.43.11) were burned, whilst they were left with ten triremes.

7. The exact meaning of Appian, who discusses the ceding of all territories and cities outside the 'Phoenician Trenches' (*Lib.* 54) discussed by Walbank, vol. 2, 466–467; also see Lancel, 1999, 178; Eckstein, 1987, 258–259; and Hoyos, 2005, 180 (among others). Livy and Polybius are clear that their territory remained 'intact'. This may be a term for what was considered traditional Carthaginian territorial hegemony or perhaps it is confused with the later '*fossa regia*' between the first Roman province in Africa and the Numidian territory. Eckstein sees no reason to doubt Appian or the claim that all the war elephants were to be surrendered.

8. Livy 30.37, 43–44 covers the terms of the peace. See Seibert, 1993a, 496–505 for the period directly after the war; see also Lancel, 1999, 176–180 on the peace; Hoyos, 2005, 179–181.

9. For example Nepos also claims that his brother Mago was at his side, although according to Livy Mago died in 203 en route from Liguria back to Africa (30.19.1–5). However, Appian, *Lib.* 49, 54 also claims that Mago stayed in Italy in 203, yet Cassius Dio (18) states it was a Carthaginian named Hamilcar who was left among the Insubrian Gauls.

10. Aurelius Victor, *De Caesaribus*, 37.2–3, using Hannibal as an exemplum, indicates that as head of the army he employed the soldiers in public infrastructure jobs. Hannibal's home region of the Sahel was later known for large-scale olive oil production (and still is) but this is hardly proof.

11. See Lazenby 1996b; Juvenal, *Satires* 7 and 10; Livy 22.51.2–4.

12. The one example mentioned in Livy, noted above, was in 215.

13. It is even possible that Hannibal was provided with some protection from prosecution by Scipio in the peace terms but the sources are confused and conflict in this matter and it is difficult to determine the exact course of events, as noted by Lancel, 1999, 181. The period is surveyed by Seibert, 1993a, 476–495, Miles, 2010, 317–319, Hoyos, 2005, 179–189, Lancel, 1999, 176–182.

14. See Fronda, 2010, 34 n. 84 for a good summary of the scholarship on Hannibal's strategy, and 231–233 for an interesting discussion of how Hannibal might have been able to turn things around from a base in Magna Graecia. See also Barceló, 2004a, 168–178 for this period when the war turns against Hannibal. Livy likes to view all foreign enemies of Rome as wanting to invade Italy for world domination, and this becomes a rhetorical trope in his concept of the enemy – based on Hannibal.

15. To our knowledge the only substantial reinforcements from Carthage had landed in 215 at the Bruttian port of Locri under the general Bomilcar (Livy 23.41.11); see Lancel, 1999, 113–116.

16. Livy (30.42.12) tells of Hasdrubal nicknamed 'the Kid' (*Haedus*) who had been one of the envoys to Rome in the peace negotiations and had 'always been a promoter of peace and opposed to the Barca faction', who shifted the responsibility of the war on to 'a few greedy men'. The blame was put squarely on the shoulders of Hamilcar and Hannibal from the

very beginning of the post-war period. There were surely other members of the Barcid clan whose names are not remembered in the historical record.

17. We can hear of echoes of these reforms in those going on in the Roman Republic.

18. See Lancel, 1999, 185; 1995, 404–409 on late Punic prosperity; Seibert, 1993a, Miles, 2010, 324–329; Hurst, 1983 and Hurst and Stager, 1978 on the ports specifically.

19. On aspects of the growth of Numidian royal power and their representations recently see Quinn, 2013, Kuttner, 2013; and Brett and Fentress, 1996, 24–32 for an overview.

20. Miles, 2010, 324–329 describes this phenomenon as the 'revenge of the losers'. Rome is bogged down in wars in the eastern Mediterranean; Carthage flourishes. 'The Romans would not take any [of the money] before it was due' according to Livy (36.4.8).

21. Financial irregularities, including the payment of the war indemnity to Rome in coin with a debased silver quantity, had been ongoing (Livy 32.2.1–2). Hoyos, 2005, 194–196 on reforms to the *sufetate*.

22. Hoyos, 2005, 189 notes this and points out that the accusations may be true. See Gunther, 1989 for a discussion of the period of exile and the argument for Hannibal's agitation against Rome.

23. Peters, 2004, 22–23.

24. See chapter 3, note 4. Miles, 2010, 60–62 on the Tyrian connection at Carthage.

25. The Romans would declare the 'freedom' of the Greeks in 194. For Antiochus' rising power see Ma, 2002, 82–89.

26. Antiochus 'found him burdensome in any case, since everybody ascribed every plan to him': Cassius Dio, *frag.* 19

27. Gunther, 1989 asks how big a role Hannibal played in focusing hostility towards Rome.

28. The area bordering Cyrenaica was no longer Carthaginian territory after the peace of 201 so it is difficult to give credibility to this passage. This is compounded by the fact that Cornelius Nepos places the long-dead Mago in frame, claiming that Hannibal sent him back to Italy.

29. Livy 34.61 covers the story, as does Justin 31.1–3. See also Gunther, 1989 and Hoyos, 2005, 204.

30. Livy 38.38.9–18; Appian, *Syr.* 22.108–109; Justin 31.6.6–10.

31. Hannibal may have visited Crete before Armenia, where he tricked the locals who were after his wealth, Cornelius Nepos, *Hann.* 9.1, Justin 32.4.3–5; see Hoyos, 2005, 205–206.

32. This seems a fantastic story from Frontinus, *Strat.* 4.7.10–11, but from the fourth century BCE catapults had been mounted on ships and used for siege warfare: see de Souza, 2007, 441–444.

33. Differing versions of Hannibal's death, in Libyssa on the coast of Bithynia, are recorded by Appian *Syr.* 11, who claims Hannibal was poisoned by Prusias on the orders of Flamininus; Justin 32.4 claims he took poison to avoid capture by Roman envoys, Juvenal, *Satire* 10, 166 'a little poisoned ring'; see also Plutarch, *Flam.* 20, Livy 39.51. For the location of Libyssa, more in the Epilogue, notes 30 and 31.

34. Repeated by Plutarch, *Flam.* 20, Livy's tale is an exemplum on the decline of Roman moral standards more than on the death of Hannibal. Hannibal died in the same year as the distinguished Achaean commander Philopoemen, as noted in Polybius 23.12–14, who compares the men; Diodorus Siculus 29.18ff.; Livy 39.50.10.

## Epilogue: Hannibal's Afterlife

1. Hannibal's legacy can be found in many different accounts, specified below. The large bibliography ranges from Toynbee, 1965 through to Garland's interesting discussion on his afterlife and unintended legacy (2010, 128–153). See also Lancel, 1999, 211–224, who looks at the heritage of Hannibal; Barceló, 2004a, 246–258 and many works by Hoyos, including 2008 and articles in Hoyos (ed.), 2011. The excellent exhibition catalogue, *Hannibal ab Portas* (Peters (ed.), 2004) provides a visual presentation of the time.

2. This strain of historiography, the hatred of Hamilcar and anger of Hannibal is discussed above, chapt. 4, p. 62 and p. 259*n*. 8.

3. As expressed here by Champion, 2011, 107 and in the sense of the genius of one man driving events. See also Polybius 3.48.2 for the claim to have spoken to eyewitnesses.
4. Cicero, *Pro Balbo* 50–51, quoting Ennius, *Annales* 234–235, cited in Elliott, 2013, 166.
5. Brizzi, 2011, 483–487 on the accusations made about Hannibal during the war.
6. Polybius says this in the context of 'the incorruptibility of the Romans' (18.35). The point he makes is that great Roman successes came when their generals showed no interest in avarice. This may fit a Polybian construction of the Roman versus the Greek rather than being an accurate depiction of Hannibal's flaws.
7. A point made by Fronda, 2010, 330.
8. Roman adaptability and willingness to learn and to take on what worked from their enemies has been shown to be a key to their success (from Polybius onwards). So many examples come from the Punic Wars, i.e. the Punic ships of the First Punic War, the cavalry and tactics of the brilliant Barcid generals, the Celtiberian tactics adopted by their horsemen. The Romans do not, however, exploit the cavalry in their future conquests to anything like the degree used in the Punic Wars. How Hannibal was remembered and shaped by Silius Italicus and Roman literature is the subject of Stocks, 2014.
9. Both Livy and Polybius make it clear that stories of his omnipotence preceded Hannibal, as discussed in Myles, 2010, 235–255, Rawlings, 2005; Silius Italicus describes the gods as 'awestruck' by his deeds.
10. Polybius had seen the monument but we don't know if Livy had seen it in person or had just learned of the monument from others. For Livy's sources on the monument see Jaeger, 2006, 393. Hannibal was attempting to create his legacy, and the inscription has been interpreted as euhemerist in form (Brizzi, 1983) or in the more straightforward Near Eastern tradition of recording achievements (Meister, 1990, 87); see also Miles 2008, 79–80.
11. Following the logic of Polybius here, but also more modern theories on the creation of an identity, and the creation of a literature which is just developing in the late third century. The wars with Carthage frame the period of the Romans learning to write their own story. See Gruen, 1990, 79–123 on Livius Andronicus, Naevius and Ennius, and Roman politics and the commentary and texts in Cornell (ed.), 2013, vols 1–3.
12. The earliest known reference may come in Naevius' *Bellum Poenicum* but it is fragmentary; also in Timeaus of Tauromenium, both third century BCE.
13. Among many others, e.g. Claudius Nero et al. at Metaurus.
14. See Pietilä-Castrén, 1987 for the complete list.
15. This Apollo was likely the Phoenician–Punic god Reshep (or perhaps Eshmun) brought to Rome after the sack of Carthage in 146 BCE: see Lipinski, 2004, 486–488; Miles, 2010, 3, n. 7 and ibid., 289.
16. The temple burned down in *c.* 83 BCE. Pliny, *NH* 35.14 and Livy 25.39.12–15; see Acquaro, 1999 on what the shield of Hasdrubal might have looked like.
17. Jugurtha was one of Masinissa's grandsons outside the line of succession. There were many; Masinissa is reported to have had around 50 children over his long life: see Camps, 1987 and 1960, as well as Storm, 2001. Sallust, *Bellum Jugurthinum*, is the main source for his life.
18. Kapust, 2011, 29–32.
19. Whilst true for many aspects of Roman Republican history it is especially so for Hannibal and Carthage. Cicero of course died before the principate of Augustus but was central to the orthodox version of these events. Augustan rhetoric was very careful about the representations of contemporary enemies: see for example Rose, 2005 on representations of the Parthians in Augustan Rome. For Carthage in the literature of the first century BCE see Syed, 2005, 150–151.
20. See Brizzi, 2011 and Gruen, 2011 on the representations of Hannibal and the Carthaginians in the post-war period.
21. Cicero's *Pro Balbo* 50–51, where he holds up a 'dignified Ennian Hannibal' as an exemplum, according to Elliott, 2013, 166.
22. See Rawlings, 2005, 172; and recently Stocks, 2014.

23. Jacobs, 2010 on the idea of 'the fearful enemy'.
24. Gowing, 2005, 49–66 on Valerius Maximus and Roman memory.
25. See Jacobs, 2010, 124, who traces this theme back to Sallust's work, and see also Kapust, 2011, 30–32 on fear of Carthage.
26. Juvenal evokes Hannibal as a rhetorical exercise in both Satire 10, 167 and Satire 7, 161, see Starks, 1999.
27. Lucian's dates, in the second century CE, when Rome's great enemy is the Parthian Empire in the east, make these jibes at the Medes and Assyrians especially fruitful. Hannibal comes across as even greater for the quality of his opponents.
28. This story from Lucian was so popular in the European Renaissance that a sixteenth-century gilt-bronze circular badge made in Germany is thought to show the scene. The heroic generals stand awaiting judgement before the god of the Underworld waiting for the decision on who is the best general (image visible at British Museum online collection number: 1915, 1216.130).
29. A forged letter from Hannibal to the Athenians written in the first century BCE on papyrus is a fascinating document. The letter writer reported in high prose full of poetic 'Pathos' the war deeds of Hannibal and it encourages Athenians to hold a competition on the warlike abilities of Hannibal and the Carthaginians. The letter gives the impression that it is a rhetorical and historical practice piece from an anti-Roman background. See Peters (ed.), 2004, 25, fig. 3 for an image and Brizzi, 1984, 87–102, who provides a close analysis of the document.
30. Was it Severus or Caracalla? Both would have had the opportunity to visit the tomb, but the personality of Caracalla seems to fit the act: the argument is surveyed in Moscovich, 1990, who notes that Caracalla had also worshipped at the tomb of Alexander, Achilles and Sulla. Herodian 4.8.5 claims Caracalla 'admired Sulla the Roman and Hannibal the Libyan most of all generals and set up statues and pictures of them'. See also Birley, 1999, 142, who argues for Severus, as does Miles, 2010, 372; and Barnes, 1967, 97, who claims Caracalla.
31. We only know of the Libyssa monument from a very late Byzantine source, Johannes Tzetzes, c. 1110–1180 CE and the reference is thought to have been taken from Cassius Dio (Tzetzes, *Chiliades* 1.798ff.; Zonaras 9.21).
32. Especially in the forum at Lepcis Magna; see Wilson, 2007 for a recent survey.
33. Moscovich, 1990, provides the full set of references.
34. See Livy along with Plutarch, Sallust and Polybius; and for the discovery and use of the classical authors in the Renaissance see Weiss, 1969.
35. In English Shakespeare and Marlowe, as well as the dramas about Sophonisba (see chapter 11) there was also *Scipio and Hannibal* by Thomas Nabbes, all of which engaged with the popular and educated views on the ancient world.
36. See Ralegh, *The History of the World*, vol. 6, bk 5, chapter 3.
37. The notion developed in the Roman tradition that this winter at Capua was what really lost Hannibal the war, and even Cicero claimed that 'Capua corrupted Hannibal himself' (Cicero, *de agr.* 1.7).
38. Rankin, 2005 notes that the most common reference, in this period, is to the time that Hannibal and his soldiers spent in Capua: 'Both at home and abroad, then, in the decade before war gripped the Three Kingdoms, Irish writers invoked, in their efforts to strengthen their moral and military resolve, the negative example of the North African leader of colonial resistance, Hannibal. . .' (2005: 151). The image of Hannibal as a resistance fighter against the imperial power is evoked here – and his losses at Capua used as a cautionary tale.
39. Barry, 1978 [1634], 39. I have slightly modernized the language of the original. Hannibal is called, 'one of the moste famouseste Captaines of the world'.
40. *Landgartha* was first performed in Dublin on St Patrick's Day in 1640; see Rankin (ed.), 2013.
41. Byron, 1831,121.
42. A poem published in 1914 called 'Gods of War' reads: We swim beneath the epic skies:/A Rome and Carthage war once more; A.E. 'Gods of War', *The Times* [London, England] 30 Sept. 1914: 9. The Times Digital Archive. Wed. 20 Aug. 2014. Another example comes

from an article called 'The New Rome and New Carthage' excerpted in *The Times* from the German newspaper, *Frankfurter Zeitung*, with Germany representing Rome and England Carthage. "Through German Eyes" Times [London, England] 17 Sept. 1914: 4. The Times Digital Archive. Wednesday 20 August 2014.

43. For a discussion of this play and the role of Carthage in modern Irish writing see Cullingford, 1996.

44. The Atatürk-inspired monument to Hannibal can be found in modern Gebze. Libyssa – between Istanbul and Izmit – has also been identified as a place farther along the coast at Tavsançil Deresi, see Strobel, 2006. The precise location is debated.

45. *Hannibal and Me* by Andreas Kluth, 2011.

46. In fiction, film, online games and even T-shirts. There is a variety of Hannibal T-shirts available online, including one that reads 'My dad crossed the alps with Hannibal and all I got was this lousy t-shirt'. See http://www.zazzle.co.uk/dad+crossed+the+alps+gifts

47. In many ways Hannibal's afterlife becomes like that of Cleopatra who has both fascinated and been reviled in popular culture from the Romans to the present.

48. 'I often think that behind that suspicious little nod of theirs lie three thousand years of distrust. A lawyer means the law and in Sicily, from where their fathers came, the law has not been a friendly idea since the Greeks were beaten. I am inclined to notice the ruins in things, perhaps because I was born in Italy. . . I only came here when I was twenty-five. In those days, Al Capone, the greatest Carthaginian of them all, was learning his trade on these pavements'. Arthur Miller, *A View from the Bridge*, 1955, Act I, scene i.

# BIBLIOGRAPHY

## Primary Sources

Ammianus Marcellinus, *The Later Roman Empire*, trans. W. Hamilton, Penguin, London, 1986.

Apollodorus, *The Library*, 2 vols, trans. Sir James George Frazer, Loeb Classical Library, Harvard, Cambridge MA, 1921.

Appian, *Roman History*, 4 vols (referenced in the text by section: vol. 1, *Sicelica, Iberica, Hannibalica, Libyca (Punica)*; vol. 2, *Illyrica, Syriaica;* vol. 3, *Bellum Civile*), trans. Horace White, Loeb Classical Library, Harvard, Cambridge MA, 1955–1964.

Appian, *Wars of the Romans in Iberia (Iberike)*, Intro., trans. and commentary J.S. Richardson, Aris and Phillips, Warminster, 2000.

Aristophanes, *Birds. Lysistrata. Women at Thesmophoria*, trans. J. Henderson, Loeb Classical Library, Harvard, Cambridge MA, 2000.

Aristotle, *Politics*, trans. H. Rackham, Loeb Classical Library, Harvard, Cambridge MA, 1959.

Arrian, *Anabasis*, vol. 2, trans. P.A. Brunt, Loeb Classical Library, Harvard, Cambridge MA, 1983.

Aulus Gellius, *Attic Nights*, vol. 2, trans. J.C. Rolfe, Loeb Classical Library, Harvard, Cambridge MA, 1927.

Aurelius Victor, *De Caesaribus* (Livres de Césars), Texte établi et traduit par P. Dufraigne, Budé edn, Paris, 1975.

Caesar, *The Gallic War (Bellum Gallicum)*, trans. H.J. Edwards, Loeb Classical Library, Harvard, Cambridge MA, 1917.

Cassius Dio, *Roman History*, trans. E. Cary, Loeb Classical Library, Harvard, Cambridge MA, 1914–1927.

Cicero, *De Divinatione (De div.)*, trans. W.A. Falconer, Loeb Classical Library, Harvard, Cambridge MA, 1959.

Cicero, *De Finibus (De fin.)*, trans. H. Rackham, Loeb Classical Library, Harvard, Cambridge MA, 1968.

Cicero, *De Lege Agrarian Contra Rullum (De agr.)*, trans. John Henry Freese, Loeb Classical Library, Harvard, Cambridge MA, 1945.

Cicero, *De Officiis (De off.)*, trans. Walter Miller, Loeb Classical Library, Harvard, Cambridge MA, 1951.

Cicero, *De Oratore*, vol. 1, trans. E.W. Sutton, Loeb Classical Library, Harvard, Cambridge MA, 1968.

Cicero, *Orationes*, vol. 6, trans. J.H. Freese, Loeb Classical Library, Harvard, Cambridge MA, 1930.

Cicero, *Pro Balbo*, trans. R. Gardner, Loeb Classical Library, Harvard, Cambridge MA, 1958.

Cicero, *Pro Sestio*, trans. R. Gardner, Loeb Classical Library, Harvard, Cambridge MA, 1958.

Cicero, *The Verrine Orations* (*Verr.*), trans. L.H.G. Greenwood, Loeb Classical Library, Harvard, Cambridge MA, 1948.

Cornelius Nepos, *On the Great Generals of Foreign Nations*, trans. J.C. Rolfe, Loeb Classical Library, Harvard, Cambridge MA, 2005 [1984].

Diodorus Siculus, *Library of History*, trans. F.R. Walton et al., vols 1–13, Loeb Classical Library, Harvard, Cambridge MA, 1956–1957.

Dionysius of Halicarnassus, *Roman Antiquities*, trans. E. Cary, Loeb Classical Library, Harvard, Cambridge MA, 1937–1950.

Ennius, *Annales*, fragments ed. E.M. Steuart, Cambridge, 1925.

*FGrH* = F. Jacoby et al. (eds), *Die Fragmente der griechischen Historiker*. Leiden/Berlin, 1923–58.

Frontinus, *Strategemata*, trans. C.E. Bennet, Loeb Classical Library, Harvard, Cambridge MA, 1925.

Herodian, *History*, vol. 1, trans. C.R. Whittaker, Loeb Classical Library, Harvard, Cambridge MA, 1969.

Herodotus, *The Histories*, trans. A.D. Godley, Loeb Classical Library, Harvard, Cambridge MA, 1946.

Herodotus, *The Histories*, trans. T. Holland. Introduction P. Cartledge, Penguin, London, 2013.

Hesiod, *Theogony. Works and Days. Testimonia*, trans. G.W. Most, Loeb Classical Library, Harvard, Cambridge MA, 2007.

Horace, *Odes and Epodes*, trans. C.E. Bennett, Loeb Classical Library, Harvard, Cambridge MA, 1914.

Justin, *Epitome of the Philippic History of Pompeius Trogus*, trans. J. Yardley, Atlanta, 1994.

Juvenal, *The Sixteen Satires*, trans. and intro. P. Green, Penguin, London, 1974.

Livy, *Ab urbe condita*, Oxford Classical Texts, vols 3–5, Books XXI–XXXV, 1950–1965.

Livy, *Hannibal's War* (Books 21–30 of *Ab urbe condita*), trans. John Yardley and Dexter Hoyos, Oxford World Classics, Oxford, 2006.

Livy, *Rome and the Mediterranean* (Books 31–45 of *Ab urbe condita*), trans. Henry Bettenson, Penguin Books, Harmondsworth, 1976.

Livy, *Summaries, Fragments and Obsequens* (*Periochae*), vol. 14, trans. A. Schlesinger, Loeb Classical Library, Harvard, Cambridge MA, 1959.

Lucian, *Dialogues of the Dead*, trans. M.D. MacLeod, Loeb Classical Library, Harvard, Cambridge MA, 1969.

Martial, *Epigrams*, ed. and trans. D. R. Shackleton Bailey, Loeb Classical Library, Harvard, Cambridge MA, 1993.

Cn. Naevius, *Bellum Poenicum*, ed. and trans. Enrico Flores, Liguori Editore, Naples, 2011.

Ovid, *Fasti*, trans. Sir J.G. Frazer, Loeb Classical Library, Harvard, Cambridge MA, 1989.

Plato, *Laws*, vols 1 and 2, trans. R. Bury, Loeb Classical Library, Harvard, Cambridge MA, 1926–1931.

Plautus, *Poenulus* [The Little Carthaginian], trans. P. Nixon, Loeb Classical Library, Harvard, Cambridge MA, 1951.

Pliny, *Natural History*, vols 1–10, trans. H. Rackham, W.H.S. Jones and D.E. Eichholz, Loeb Classical Library, Harvard, Cambridge MA, 1947–1962.

Plutarch, *Demetrius*, in *The Age of Alexander*, trans. Ian Scott-Kilvert and Tim Duff, Penguin, London, 1973–2012.

Plutarch, *Life of Alexander*, trans. Bernadotte Perrin, Loeb Classical Library, Harvard, Cambridge MA, 1949.

Plutarch, *Life of Fabius Maximus*, trans. Bernadotte Perrin, Loeb Classical Library, Harvard, Cambridge MA, 1951.

Plutarch, *Life of C. Gracchus*, trans. Bernadotte Perrin, Loeb Classical Library, Harvard, Cambridge MA, 1921.

Plutarch, *Life of Lycurgus*, trans. Bernadotte Perrin, Loeb Classical Library, Harvard, Cambridge MA, 1914.

Plutarch, *Life of Marcellus*, trans. Bernadotte Perrin, Loeb Classical Library, Harvard, Cambridge MA, 1955.

Plutarch, *Life of Pyrrhus*, trans. Bernadotte Perrin, Loeb Classical Library, Harvard, Cambridge MA, 1920.

Plutarch, *Life of Sertorius*, trans. Bernadotte Perrin, Loeb Classical Library, Harvard, Cambridge MA, 1919.

Plutarch, *Life of Titus Flamininus*, trans. Bernadotte Perrin, Loeb Classical Library, Harvard, Cambridge MA, 1921.

Polyaenus, *Stratagems of War*, vols 1 and 2, Books 1–8, ed. and trans. P. Krentz and E. Wheeler, Chicago, 1994.

Polybius, *The Histories*, vols 1–6, trans. W.R. Paton, Loeb Classical Library, Harvard, Cambridge MA, 1922.

Polybius, *The Rise of the Roman Empire*, trans. Ian Scott-Kilvert; Introduction F. Walbank, Penguin Classics, London, 1979.

Propertius, *Elegies*, trans. H.E. Butler, Loeb Classical Library, Harvard, Cambridge MA, 1967.

Sallust, *Bellum Catilinae* and *Bellum Jugurthum*, trans. J.C. Rolfe; rev. John Ramsey, Loeb Classical Library, Harvard, Cambridge MA, 2013.

Servius, *Commentary on Book Four of Virgil's Aeneid*, ed. and trans. C. McDonough, R. Prior and M. Stansbury, Wauconda, IL, 2004.

Silius Italicus, *Punica*, vols 1 and 2, trans. J.D. Duff, Loeb Classical Library, Harvard, Cambridge MA, 1949–1950.

Sosylus, *Sosylos (176)*, trans. D.W. Roller, in *Brill's New Jacoby*. Editor in Chief: Ian Worthington (University of Missouri). Brill, 2012. Brill Online. University of Edinburgh. 15 March 2012. <http://www.brillonline.nl/subscriber/entry?entry=bnj_a176>

Strabo, *Geography*, Book 3, trans. Horace Jones, Loeb Classical Library, Harvard, Cambridge MA, 1969.

Strabo [Estrabón], *Geografía di Iberia*, trans. J. Gómez Espelosín; commentary G. Cruz Andreotti, M. V. García Quintela and J. Gómez Espelosín, Alianza Editorial, Madrid, 2007.

Suetonius, *Lives of the Caesars*, vol. 1. (for *Tiberius*), trans. J.C. Rolf, Loeb Classical Library, Harvard, Cambridge MA, 1914.

Timeaus of Tauromenium, trans. C. Champion in *Brill's New Jacoby*. Ed. Ian Worthington. Brill Online, 2014. Ref. 15/4/2014 http://referenceworks.brillonline.com/entries/brill-s-new-jacoby/timaios–566-a566.

Tzetses, Johannes, *Chiliades*, ed. P.A.M. Leone, Instituto editoriale Cisalpino-La goliordica, Naples, 1968.

Valerius Maximus, *Memorable Doings and Sayings*, vols 1 and 2, ed. and trans. D. R. Shackleton Bailey, Loeb Classical Library, Harvard, Cambridge MA, 2000.

Velleius Paterculus, *History of Rome*, trans. F.W. Shipley, Loeb Classical Library, Harvard, Cambridge MA, 1924.

Virgil, *Aeneid*, trans. John Dryden, Sir John Lubbock's Hundred Books, London, 1891.

Virgil, *Aeneid*, trans. R. Fagles, Penguin, London, 2006.

Xenophon, *Cyropaedia: The Education of Cyrus*, trans. and annotated by W. Ambler, Cornell University Press, London, 2001.

Xenophon, *Hipparchus (Cavalry Commander)*, in *Xenophon: Scripta Minora*, vol. 7, trans. E. Marchant, Loeb Classical Library, Harvard, Cambridge MA, 1925.

Xenophon, *Memorabilia* and *Oeconomicus*, trans. E. Marchant, Loeb Classical Library, Harvard, Cambridge MA, 2013.

Zonaras, *Epitome of Histories*, sections referenced here taken from Cassius Dio, *Roman History*, trans. E. Cary, Loeb Classical Library, Harvard, Cambridge MA, 1914–1927.

### Secondary Sources

Acimovic, A., 2007, *Scipio Africanus*, iUniverse, New York.

Acquaro, E., 1983–84, 'Su i "ritratti barcidi" delle monete puniche', *Rivista Storica dell'Antichità*, vol. 13–14: 83–86.

Acquaro, E., 1989, 'Les Emissions du "soulèvement Libyen": types, ethnies et rôles politiques', in H. Devijver and E. Lipinski (eds), *Studia Phoenicia X: Punic Wars*, Orientalia Lovaniensia Analecta 33, Louvain, 137–144.

Acquaro, E., 1999, 'The Shield of Hasdrubal', in G. Pisano (ed.), *Phoenicians and Carthaginians in the Western Mediterranean*, Rome, 31–34.

Acquaro, E., Mandredi, L. and Tusa Cutroni, A., 1991, *Le monete Puniche in Italia*, Libreria dello Stato, Istituto poligrafico e Zecca dello Stato, Rome.

Adams, G., 2008, 'The Unbalanced Relationship between Ptolemy II and Pyrrhus of Epirus', in Paul McKechnie and Philippe Guillaume (eds), *Ptolemy II Philadelphus and his World*, Mnemosyne supplements, vol. 300, Brill, Leiden, 91–102.

Africa, T., 1970, 'The One-Eyed Man against Rome: An Exercise in Euhemerism', *Historia*, 19.5, 528–538.

Alexandropoulos, J., 2000, *Les Monnaies de l'Afrique antique, 400 av. J-C – 40 ap. J-C*, Presses universitaires du Mirail, Toulouse.

Alfaro Asins, C., 1994, *Sylloge Nummorum Graecorum Espana, Vol. I Hispania, Ciudades Fen-Punicas, part 1: Gadir y Ebusus*, Museo Arqueólogico Nacional, Ministerio de Cultural Madrid.

Ameling, W., 1993, *Karthago: Studien zu Militär, Staat und Gesellschaft*, C.H. Beck, Munich.

Ameling, W., 2011, 'The Rise of Carthage to 264', in D. Hoyos (ed.), *A Companion to the Punic Wars*, Blackwell, Oxford, 39–57.

Ameling, W., 2013, 'Carthage', in P. Bang and W. Scheidel (eds), *The Oxford Handbook of the State in the Ancient Near East and Mediterranean*, Oxford University Press, Oxford, 361–382.

Arteaga, O., 2004, 'Die phönizisch-punischen Häfen im Westen', in S. Peters (ed.), *Hannibal ad Portas: Macht und Reichtum Karthago*, Theiss, Stuttgart, 118–125.

Aubet, M.E., 2001, *The Phoenicians and the West*, 2nd edn, Cambridge University Press, Cambridge.

Aubet-Semmler, M.E., 2002, 'Notes on the Economy of the Phoenician settlements in Southern Spain' and 'Phoenician Trade in the West: Balance and Perspectives' in M. Bierling (ed.), *The Phoenicians in Spain: An Archaeological Review of the Eighth–Sixth Centuries BCE: A Collection of Articles translated from Spanish*, trans. and ed. Marilyn R. Bierling, Eisenbrauns, Winona Lake, IN, 79–112.

Austin, M., 2006, *The Hellenistic World from Alexander to the Roman Conquest*, 2nd edn, Cambridge University Press, Cambridge.

Austin, N. and Rankov, B., 1995, *Exploration: Military and Political Intelligence in the Roman World from the Second Punic War to the Battle of Adrianople*, Routledge, London.

Bagnall, N., 1990, *The Punic Wars: Rome, Carthage and the Struggle for the Mediterranean*, Pimlico, London.

Baldus, H.R., 2004, 'Karthagische Münzen', in S. Peters (ed.), *Hannibal ad Portas: Macht und Reichtum Karthago*, Theiss, Stuttgart, 294–313.

Balmuth, M., Gilman, A. and Prados-Torreira, L. (eds), 1997, *Encounters and Transformations: The Archaeology of Iberia in Transition*. Monographs in Mediterranean Archaeology 7, Sheffield.

Barceló, P., 1988, *Karthago und die Iberische Halbinsel vor den Barkiden*, R. Habelt, Bonn.

Barceló, P., 1994, 'The Perception of Carthage in Classical Greek Historiography', *Acta Classica* 37, 1–14.

Barceló, P., 2004a, *Hannibal: Stratege und Staatsmann*, Klett-Cotta, Stuttgart.

Barceló, P., 2004b, 'Ideologische Kriegsführung gegen Rom', in S. Peters (ed.), *Hannibal ad Portas: Macht und Reichtum Karthago*, Theiss, Stuttgart, 18–25.

Barnes, T.D., 1967, 'The Family and Career of Septimius Severus', *Historia* 16.1, 87–107.

Barré, Michael, 1983, *The God-List in the Treaty between Hannibal and Philip V of Macedonia: A Study in Light of the Ancient Near Eastern Treaty Tradition*, Johns Hopkins University Press, London.

Barry, Gerrat, 1978 [1634], 'A Discourse of Military Discipline' in D. M. Rogers (ed.), *English Recusant Literature 1558–1640*, vol. 389, Scolar Press, London.

Beacham, R., 2005, 'The Emperor as Impresario: Producing the Pageantry of Power', in Karl Galinsky (ed.), *The Cambridge Companion to the Age of Augustus*, Cambridge University Press, Cambridge, 151–174.

Bechtold, B. and Docter, R., 2010, 'Transport Amphora from Punic Carthage: An Overview', in *Motya and the Phoenician Ceramic Repertoire between the Levant and the West 9th–6th century BCE*, Proceedings of the International Conference held in Rome, 26 February 2010, Rome, 85–116.

Beck, H., 2011, 'The Reasons for the War', in D. Hoyos (ed.), *A Companion to the Punic Wars*, Blackwell, Oxford, 225–241.

Bellón, J., Cabeza, F., Ruiz A., Molinos M., et al., 2009, 'Baecula, An Archaeological Analysis of the Location of a Battle of the Second Punic War', *Gladius*, Appendix 13, 253–265.

Bénichou-Safar, H., 2004, *Le Tophet de Salammbô à Carthage: Essai de Reconstitution*, Collection de L'École Français de Rome, 342.

Bénichou-Safar, H., 2007, 'Les Rituel Funéraires des Puniques' in E. Fontan and H. Le Meaux (eds), *La Méditerranée des Phéniciens de Tyr à Carthage*, Somogy: Institut du monde arabe, Paris, 246–255.

Benz, F., 1972, *Personal Names in the Phoenician and Punic Inscriptions*, Biblical Institute Press, Rome.

Bernardini, P., 2004, 'Das phönizsche und punische Sardinien', in S. Peters (ed.), *Hannibal ad Portas: Macht und Reichtum Karthago*, Theiss, Stuttgart, 142–183.

Bernardini, P. and Zucca, R. (eds), 2005, *Il Mediterraneo di Herakles*, Carocci, Rome.

Berrendonner, C., 2009, 'Les Raisons du plus fort: La reconstruction par l'historiographie antique des liens entre la guerre de Pyrrhus et la première guerre punique', in *Pyrrhus en Occident, Pallas* 79, 249–266.

Bickerman, E., 1944, 'An Oath of Hannibal', *Transactions of the American Philological Association*, 87–102.

Bickerman, E., 1952, 'Hannibal's Covenant', *American Journal of Philology*, 71, 1–23.

Bierling, M. (ed.), 2002, *The Phoenicians in Spain: An Archaeological Review of the Eighth–Sixth Centuries BCE: A Collection of Articles translated from Spanish*, trans. and ed. Marilyn R. Bierling, Eisenbrauns, Winona Lake, IN.

Birley, A., 1999, *Septimius Severus: The African Emperor*, Routledge, London.

Blackman, D. et al., 2013, *Shipsheds of the Ancient Mediterranean*, Cambridge University Press, Cambridge.

Bondi, S., 1990, 'I Fenici in Erodoto', in O. Reverdin and B. Grange (eds), *Hérodote et les peuples non grecs*, Entretiens sur L'Antiquité Classique, 35, Geneva.

Bondi, S., 1995, 'Les institutions, l'organisation politique et administrative' in V. Krings (ed.), *La Civilization phénicienne et punique: manuel de recherche*, Brill, Leiden, 290–302.

Bonfante, L., 1990, *Etruscans*, British Museum Press, London.

Bonnet, C., 1986, 'Le Culte de Melqart à Carthage: Un cas de conservatism religieux', in C. Bonnet, E. Lipinski and P. Marchetti (eds), Studia Phoenicia IV Religio Phoenicia, Namur: Société des études classiques, Brussels, 209–222.

Bonnet, C., 1988, *Melqart. Cultes et myths de l'Héraclès tyrien en Méditerranée*, Studia Phoenicia VIII: Peeters, Presses universitaires de Namur, Louvain.

Bonnet, C., 1989, 'Les Connotations sacrée de la destruction de Carthage', in H. Devijer and E. Lipinski (eds), *Punic Wars, Studia Phoenicia* X, Orientalia Lovaniensia Analecta, 33, Louvain, 289–305.

Bonnet, C., 1996, *Astarté: Dossier documentaire et perspectives historiques*, Collezione di Studi Fenici, 37, Rome.

Bonnet, C. 2005, 'Carthage, "autre nation" dans l'historiographie ancienne et moderne', *Anabases*, 1, 139–160 (online at http://anabases.revues.org/1437 last accessed 13 January 2014).

Bonnet, C., 2006, 'Identité et altérité religieuses. À propos de l'hellénisation de Carthage', *Pallas*, 70, 365–379.

Bonnet, C., 2011, 'On Gods and Earth: The Tophet and the Construction of a New Identity in Punic Carthage', in E. Gruen (ed.), *Cultural Identity in the Ancient Mediterranean*, Getty Research Institute, Los Angeles, 373–387.

Bonnet, C. and Pirenne-Delforge, V., 1999, 'Deux déesses en interaction: Astarté et Aphrodite dans le monde égéen', in C. Bonnet and André Motte (eds), *Les Syncrétismes religieux dans le monde méditerranéen antique*, Institut Historique Belge de Rome, Rome, 249–273.

Bordreuil, P., 1986, 'Attestations inédites de Melqart, Baal Hamon et Baal Saphon à Tyr', *Studia Phoenicia, 4*, 77–86.

Bresson, A., 2005, 'Ecology and Beyond: The Mediterranean Paradigm', in W.V. Harris (ed.), *Rethinking the Mediterranean*, Oxford University Press, Oxford, 94–114.

Brett, M. and Fentress, E., 1996, *The Berbers*, Blackwell, Oxford and Cambridge MA.

Briquel, D., 2003, 'Hannibal sur les pas d'Héraklès: le voyage mythologique et son utilisation dans l'histoire', in H. Duchene (ed.), *Voyageurs et antiquité classique*, EUD, Dijon, 51–60.

Briscoe, 1989, 'The Punic Wars', in the *Cambridge Ancient History*, 2nd edn, vol. 8, Cambridge University Press, Cambridge, 44–79.

Brizzi, G., 1983, 'Ancora su Annibale e l'ellenismo. La fondazione di Artaxata e l'iscrizione di Era Lacinia', in *Atti del i Convegno internazionale di studi fenici e punici*, vol. 1, Rome CNR, 243–259.

Brizzi, G. 1984, *Studi di Storia Annibalica*, Fratelli Lega, Faenza.

Brizzi, G., 1995, 'L'armée et la guerre' in V. Krings (ed.), *La Civilisation phénicienne et punique: manuel de recherché*, Brill, Leiden, 303–315.

Brizzi, G., 2006, 'Hannibal, sa religiosité, sa legend: pour une mise au point du problème', in A. Vigourt, et al. (eds), *Pouvoir et religion dans le monde romain*, Presses de l'Université Paris-Sorbonne, Paris, 17–27.

Brizzi, G., 2009, 'Gli schieramenti politici a Cartagine nell'età delle guerre puniche', in G. Zecchini (ed.), *'Partiti' e fazioni nell'esperienza politica romana*, V&P, Milan, 49–74.

Brizzi, G., 2011, 'Carthage and Hannibal in Roman and Greek Memory', in D. Hoyos (ed.), *A Companion to the Punic Wars*, Blackwell, Oxford, 483–498.

Broughton, T.R.S., 1951, *The Magistrates of the Roman Republic*, vol. 1, American Philological Association publication 15.1, Atlanta, GA.

Brouillet, M., 1994, *From Hannibal to St Augustine: Ancient Art of North Africa from the Musée du Louvre*, Catalogue of the exhibition, Atlanta, GA.

Bruns, C.G. (ed.), 1909, *Fontes Iuris Romani Antiqui*, vol. 1, Tubingen.

Buckland, W.W., 1908, *The Roman Law of Slavery*, Cambridge.

Bunnens, G., 1979, *L'Expansion phénicienne en Méditerranée, Essai d'interprétation fondé sur une analyse des traditions littéraires*, Institut historique belge de Rome, Brussels and Rome.

Bunnens, G., 1983, 'La Distinction entre phéniciens et puniques chez les auteurs classiques', in *Atti del i Convegno internazionale di Studi Fenici e Punici*, vol. 1, Rome CNR, 233–238.

Burnell, H., 1641, *Landgartha*, Dublin.

Burton, P., 1996, 'The Summoning of the Magna Mater to Rome', *Historia*, 45. 1, 36–63.

Byron, 1831, *The Complete Works of Lord Byron including His Lordship's Suppressed Poems in one volume*, published by A. and W. Galignani, Paris.

Camps, G., 1960, 'Massinissa ou Les Débuts de l'histoire', *Libyca* 8.1, Bulletin du Service des Antiquités Archéologie-Epigraphie, Algiers, 1–320.

Camps, G., 1987, *Les Berberes: Mémoire et identité*, Errance, Paris.

Camps, G., 1992, *L'Afrique du Nord au feminin*, Perrin, Paris.

Campus, A., 2005, 'Herakles, Alessandro, Annibale', in P. Bernardini and R. Zucca (eds), 2005, *Il Mediterraneo di Herakles*, Carocci, Rome, 201–221.

Caratelli, G.P. (ed.), 1996, *The Western Greeks*, Thames and Hudson, London.

Carey, B. T., 2007, *Hannibal's Last Battle*, Pen & Sword, Barnsley.

Carney, E., 2000, *Women and Monarchy in Macedonia*, University of Oklahoma Press, Norman.

Carradice, I. and La Niece, S., 1988, 'The Libyan War and Coinage: A New Hoard and the Evidence of Metal Analysis', *Numismatic Chronicle*, 148, 33–52.

Casson, L., 1969, 'The Super-Galleys of the Hellenistic Age', *Mariner's Mirror*, 55.2, 185–193.

Casson, L., 1991 [1959], *The Ancient Mariners*, Princeton University Press, Princeton, NJ.

Casson, L., 1995, *Ships and Seamanship in the Ancient World*, Johns Hopkins University Press, Baltimore, MD.

Champion, C., 2000, 'Romans as *Barbaroi*: Three Polybian Speeches and the Politics of Cultural Indeterminacy,' *Classical Philology*, 95, 425–444.

Champion, J., 2009, *Pyrrhus of Epirus*, Pen & Sword Military, Barnsley.

Champion, C., 2011, 'Polybius and the Punic Wars', in D. Hoyos (ed.), *A Companion to the Punic Wars*, Blackwell, Oxford, 95–110.

Chaniotis, A., 2005, *War in the Hellenistic World*, Blackwell Oxford.

Charles, M. and Rhodan, P., 2007, '*Magister Elephantorum*: A Reappraisal of Hannibal's Use of Elephants', *Classical World*, 100.4, 363–389.

Chondros, T., 2007, 'Archimedes (287–212)', in M. Ceccarelli (ed.), *Distinguished Figures in Mechanism and Machine Science*, Springer, London, 1–30.

Clifford, R., 1990, 'Phoenician Religion', *Bulletin of the American School of Oriental Research*, 279 (Aug.), 55–64.

Collins, R., 1998, *Spain: An Oxford Archaeological Guide*, Oxford.

Cornell, T., 1995, *The Beginnings of Rome*, Routledge, London.

Cornell, T., (ed.) 2013, *The Fragments of Roman Historians*, vol. 2 (Texts), Oxford University Press, Oxford.

Cornell, T., Rankov, B. and Sabin, P. (eds), 1996, *The Second Punic War: A Reappraisal*, University of London, Institute of Classical Studies, London.

Crawford, M., 1974, *Roman Republican Coinage*, vols 1 and 2, Cambridge University Press, Cambridge.

Crawford, M., 1985, *Coinage and Money under the Roman Republic*, Methuen, London.

Crawford, M., 1992, *The Roman Republic*, 2nd edn, Fontana, London.

Crawford, M. (ed.), 2011, *Imagines Italicae: A Corpus of Italic Inscriptions*, 3 vols, Institute of Classical Studies, University of London, London.

Cristofori, A., 2001, 'The Maritime City in Graeco-Roman Perception. Carthage and Alexandria: Two Emblematic Examples', in L. François and A. Isaacs (eds), *The Sea in European History*, Edizioni PLUS, Pisa, 1–24.

Cullingford, E., 1996, 'British Romans and Irish Carthaginians: Anti-colonial metaphor in Heaney, Friel and McGuinness', *Paper of the Modern Language Association (PMLA)*, 111.2, 222–239.

D'Agostino, B. and Ridgway, D. (eds), 1994, 'ΑΠΟΙΚΙΑ: i più antichi insediamenti Greci in Occidente: funzione e modi dell'organizzazione politica *e sociale*.' Scritte in Onore di Giorgio Buchner, Instituto Universitario Orientale, Naples.

Dalaine, L., 2011, 'Par quel col Hannibal est-il passé? Une literature sans fin . . .' in J-P. Jospin and L. Dalaine (eds), *Hannibal et les Alpes: une traversée, un mythe*, Infolio Editions, Gallion, 126–137.

Daly, G., 2002, *Cannae: The Experience of Battle in the Second Punic War*, Routledge, London.

Davis, E., 1959, 'Hannibal's Roman Campaign of 211 BC', *Phoenix* 13.3: 113–120.

Dean, R., 1945, 'Nicholas Trevet's Commentary on Livy', reprinted from *Medievalia et Humanistica*, 3, 86–98.

De Ligt, L., 2007, 'Roman Manpower and Recruitment during the Middle Republic', in P. Erdkamp (ed.), *A Companion to the Roman Army*, Blackwell, Oxford, 114–131.

De Ligt, L., 2012, *Peasants, Citizens and Soldiers: Studies in the Demographic History of Roman Italy 225 BC–AD 100*, Cambridge University Press, Cambridge.

Dench, E., 2005, 'Beyond Greeks and Barbarians: Italy and Sicily in the Hellenistic Age', in A. Erskine ed., *A Companion to the Hellenistic World*, Blackwell, Oxford, 294–310.

Derow, P., 1976, 'The Roman Calendar, 218–191 BC', *Phoenix*, 30.3, 265–281.

De Sanctis, G., 1904–1967, *Storia dei Romani*, 4 vols, Nuova Italia, Turin.

De Souza, P., 2007, 'Naval Forces' and 'Naval Battles and Sieges', in P. Sabin, H. van Wees and M. Whitby (eds), *Cambridge History of Greek and Roman Warfare*, vol. 1, Cambridge University Press, Cambridge. 357–367 and 434–460.

De Souza, P., 2013, 'War at Sea', in *The Oxford Handbook of Warfare in the Classical World*, Oxford University Press, Oxford, 369–394.

Devijver, H. and Lipinski, E. (eds), 1989, *Studia Phoenicia X: Punic Wars*, Orientalia Lovaniensia Analecta 33, Louvain.

Devillers, O. and Krings, V., 1996, 'Autour de l'agronome Magon', in *L'Africa Romana* 11.1, Atti dell' XI convegno di studio Cartagine, 15–18 Dicembre, Carthage, 489–516.

Devillers, O. and Krings, V., 2006, 'Le Songe d'Hannibal. Quelques réflexions sur la tradition littéraire', *Pallas* 70, 337–346.

Dietler, M. and López-Ruiz, C. (eds), 2009, *Colonial Encounters in Ancient Iberia: Phoenician, Greek and Indigenous Relations*, University of Chicago Press, Chicago.

Docter, R., 2002–2003, 'The Topography of Archaic Carthage', *Talanta*, 34–5, 113–133.

Docter, R. et al., 2005, 'Radiocarbon Dates of Animal Bones in the Earliest Levels of Carthage', in G. Bartolin and F. Delpino (eds), *Oriente e Occidente: Metodi e Discipline a Contronto: Riflessioni sulla Cronologia dell'Età del Ferro in Italia. Atti dell Incontro di Studi, Roma, 30–31 Ottobre, 2003*, in *Mediterranea*, vol. 1, 2004 Pisa and Rome, 557–575.

Docter, R. et al., 2007, 'Punic Carthage: Two Decades of Archaeological Investigations', in José Luis López Castro (ed.), *Las ciudades fenicio-púnicas en el Mediterráneo occidental*, Centro de Estudios Fenicios y Púnicos, Almería, 85–104.

Dodge, T., 1994, [1891], *Hannibal*, Da Capo, Oxford Publicity Partnership Cambridge MA.

Dominik, William, 2003, 'Hannibal and the Gates: Programmatising Rome and *Romanitas* in Silius Italicus' *Punica* 1 and 2' in A. Boyle and W. Dominik (eds), *Flavian Rome: Culture, Image and Text*, Brill, Leiden, 469–498.

Dubuisson, M., 1983, 'L'Image du carthaginois dans la littérature latine', *Studia Phoenicia I–II (OLA 15)*, Louvain, 159–167.

Due, B., 1993, 'Alexander's Inspiration and Ideas', in J. Carlsen et al. (eds), *Alexander the Great: Reality and Myth*, Analecta Romana Instituti Danici, Suppl. 20, Rome, 53–60.

Eck, W., 2007, *The Age of Augustus*, 2nd edn, Blackwell, Oxford.

Eckstein, A., 1982, 'Human Sacrifice and Fear of Military Disaster in Republican Rome', *American Journal of Ancient History*, 7.1, 69–95.

Eckstein, A., 1984, 'Rome, Saguntum and the Ebro Treaty', *Emerita* 52.1, 51–68.

Eckstein, A., 1987, *Senate and General: Individual Decision Making and Roman Foreign Relations, 264–194*, University of California Press, Berkeley.

Eckstein, A., 1989, 'Hannibal at New Carthage: Polybius 3.15 and the Power of Irrationality', *Classical Philology* 84.1, 1–15.

Eckstein, A., 1995, *Moral Vision in the Histories of Polybius*, University of California Press, Berkeley.

Eckstein, A., 1997, '*Physis* and *Nomos*: Polybius, the Romans, and Cato the Elder', in P. Cartledge, P. Garnsey and E. Gruen (eds), *Hellenistic Constructs: Essays in Culture, History and Historiography*, University of California Press, Berkeley, 175–198.

Eckstein, A., 2006, *Mediterranean Anarchy, Interstate War and the Rise of Rome*, University of California Press, Berkeley.

Eckstein, A., 2010, 'Polybius, the "Treaty of Philinus" and Roman Accusations against Carthage', *Classical Quarterly* 60.2, 406–426.

Eckstein, A., 2012, 'Polybius, the Gallic Crisis, and the Ebro Treaty', *Classical Philology*, 107, 3, 206–229.

Edwards, C. (ed.), 1999, *Roman Presences: Peceptions of Rome in European Culture, 1789–1945*, Cambridge.

Edwards, J., 2001, 'The Irony of Hannibal's Elephants', *Latomus* 60, 900–905.

Edwell, P., 2011, 'War Abroad: Spain, Sicily, Macedon, Africa', in D. Hoyos, (ed.), *Companion to the Punic Wars*, Blackwell, Oxford, 320–338.

Elliott, J., 2013, *Ennius and the Architecture of the Annales*, Cambridge University Press, Cambridge.

Englund, S., 2005, *Napoleon, A Political Life*, Harvard University Press, Cambridge, MA.

Erdkamp, P., 1998, *Hunger and the Sword: Warfare and Food Supply in the Roman Republican Wars (264–30 BC)*, Gieben, Amsterdam.

Erdkamp, P., 2009, 'Polybius, the Ebro Treaty and the Gallic Invasion of 225 BCE', *Classical Philology* 104.4, 495–510.

Errington, R., 1989, 'Rome and Greece to 205 BC', in *Cambridge Ancient History* (2nd edn), vol. 8, Cambridge, 81–106.

Erskine, A., 1993, 'Hannibal and the Freedom of the Italians', *Hermes* 121, 58–62.

Erskine, A., 2001, *Troy between Greece and Rome*, Oxford University Press, Oxford.

Erskine, A., 2013, 'Encountering Carthage: Mid Republican Rome and Mediterranean Culture', in A. Gardner, E. Herring and K Lomas (eds), *Creating Ethnicities and Identities in the Roman World*, Institute of Classical Studies, School of Advanced Study, University of London, London, 113–129.

Erskine, A., 2006 (ed.), *A Companion to the Hellenistic World*, Blackwell, Oxford.

Fantar, M., 1987, *Kerkouane: Une cité punique au Cap-Bon*, Maison tunisienne de l'édition: Institut national d'archéologie et d'art, Tunis.

Fantar, M., 1993, *Carthage: Approche d'une civilisation*, vols 1 and 2, Alif: Éditions de la Méditerranée, Tunis.

Fantar, M., 2001, 'Propos sur les divinités féminines dans l'univers libyco-punique', in K. Geus and K. Zimmerman (eds), *Studia Phoenicia XVI: Punica, Libyca, Ptolemaica*, Louvain, 221–233.

Fariselli, A-C., 2006, 'Il progetto politico dei Barcidi', *Pallas* 70, 105–122.

Fear, A., 2005, 'A Journey to the End of the World', in J. Elsner and I. Rutherford (eds), *Pilgrimage in Greco-Roman and Early Christian Antiquity: Seeing the Gods*, Oxford, 319–331.

Feldherr, A., 2010, 'Hannibalic Laughter: Sallust's Archaeology and the End of Livy's Third Decade', in W. Polleichtner (ed.), *Livy and Intertextuality*, Bochumer Altertumswissenschaftliches Colloquium, Band 84, Wissenschaftlicher Verlag Trier, 203–232.

Feldherr, A. (ed.), 2009, *The Cambridge Companion to the Roman Historians*, Cambridge University Press, Cambridge.

Fentress, E., 2006, 'Romanizing the Berbers', *Past and Present* 190, 3–33.

Fentress, E., 2013, 'Strangers in the City: Elite Communication', in J. Prag and J.C. Quinn (eds), *The Hellenistic West: Rethinking the Ancient Mediterranean*, Cambridge University Press, Cambridge, 157–178.

Ferrer Albelda, E. (ed.), 2010, *Los Púnicos de Iberia: Proyectos, Revisiones, Síntesis*. Mainake 32, vols 1 and 2, Servicio de Publicaciones, Centro de Ediciones de la Diputación de Málaga, Malaga.

Ferrer Albelda, E. and Pliego Vásquez, R., 2011, 'Carthaginian Garrisons in Turdetania: The Monetary Evidence', in A. Dowler and E. Galvin (eds), *Money, Trade and Trade Routes in Pre-Islamic North Africa*, British Museum Research Publication no. 176, London, 33–41.

Ferrer Albelda, E., García Fernández, F. and Escacena Carrasco, J., 2010, 'El tráfico comercial de productos púnicos en el antiguo estuario del Guadalquivir', in Ferrer Albelda (ed.), 2010, vol. 1, 61–85. British Museum Research Publication no. 176, London, 33–41.

Fields, N., 2007, *The Roman Army of the Punic Wars, 264–146 BC*, Osprey, Oxford.

Fields, N., 2010, *Hannibal: Leadership, Strategy, Conflict*, Osprey, Oxford.

Flacelière, R., 1937, *Les Aitoliens à Delphes: contribution á l'histoire de la Grèce centrale au iii^e siècle*, E. de Boccard, Paris.

Flaubert, G., *Salammbô*, trans. A.J. Karilsheimer, Penguin, London, 1977.

Flower, H. (ed.), 2004, *The Cambridge Companion to the Roman Republic*, Cambridge University Press, Cambridge.

Fontan, E. and Le Meaux, H. (eds), 2007, *La Méditerranée des Phéniciens de Tyr à Carthage*, Somogy: Institut du Monde Arabe, Paris.

Fowler, D., 1996, 'Even Better than the Real Thing: A Tale of Two Cities', in Jaś Elsner (ed.), *Art and Text in Roman Culture*, Cambridge University Press, Cambridge, 57–74.

Franko, G., 1994, 'The Use of *Poenus* and *Carthaginiensis* in Early Latin Literature', *Classical Philology* 89.2, 153–158.

Franko, G., 1996, 'The Characterization of Hanno in Plautus' Poenulus', *American Journal of Philology*, 117.3, 425–452.

Freud, S., 1954 [1931], *Interpretation of Dreams*, trans. and ed., James Strachey, Allen & Unwin, London.

Fronda, M., 2007, 'Hegemony and Rivalry: The Revolt of Capua Revisited', *Phoenix* 61.1, 83–108.

Fronda, M., 2010 *Between Hannibal and Rome: Southern Italy during the Second Punic War*, Cambridge University Press, Cambridge.

Fronda, M., 2011, 'Hannibal: Tactics, Strategy, and Geostrategy', in D. Hoyos (ed.), *A Companion to the Punic Wars*, Blackwell, Oxford, 242–259.

Frost, H., 1974, 'The Punic Wreck in Sicily, Second Season of Excavation', *International Journal of Nautical Archaeology* 3.1, 35–54.

Gardiner, R. (ed.), 1995, *The Age of the Galley: Mediterranean Oared Vessels since Pre-Classical Times*, Conway Maritime Press, London.

Garland, R., 2010, *Hannibal*, Bristol Classical, London.

Geus, K. and Zimmermann, K. (eds), 2001, *Studia Phoenicia XVI: Punica – Libyca – Ptolemaica, Festschrift für Werner Huß, zum 65. Geburtstag dargebracht von Schülern, Freunden und Kollegen*, Orientalia Lovaniensia Analecta 104, Louvain.

Gibson, B., 2005, 'Hannibal at the Gates, Silius Italicus 3.1–60', in F. Cairns (ed.), *Papers of the Langford Latin Seminar*, 12, 177–195.

Goldsworthy, A., 2003 [2000], *The Fall of Carthage*, Cassell Military Paperback, London.

Goldsworthy, A., 2007 [2001], *Cannae*, Phoenix, London.

González Ponce, F., 2010, 'Veracidad Documental y Deuda Literaria en el *Periplo de Hanón*', 1–8, in Ferrer Albelda (ed.), *Los Púnicos de Iberia: Proyectos, Revisiones, Síntesis*. Mainake 32, vol. 2, 761–780.

Gowing, A., 2005, *Empire and Memory: The Representation of the Roman Republic in Imperial Culture*, Cambridge University Press, Cambridge.

Gransden, K. (ed.), 1996, *Virgil in English*, Penguin, London.

Green, P., 1990, *Alexander to Actium: The Historical Evolution of the Hellenistic Age*, University of California Press, Berkeley.

Gruen, E., 1978, 'The Consular Elections for 216 and the Veracity of Livy', *California Studies in Classical Antiquity*, 11, 61–74.

Gruen, E., 1986 [1984], *The Hellenistic World and the Coming of Rome*, University of California Press, Berkeley.

Gruen, E., 1990, *Studies in Greek Culture and Roman Policy*, University of California Press, Berkeley.

Gruen, E., 1992, *Culture and Identity in Republican Rome*, Cornell University Press, Ithaca, NY.

Gruen, E., 2011, 'Punica Fides' in *Rethinking the Other in Antiquity*, Princeton University Press, Princeton and Oxford, 115–140.

Gruen, E. (ed.), 2011, *Cultural Identity in the Ancient Mediterranean*, Getty Research Institute, Los Angeles.

Gunther, L.M., 1989, 'Hannibal im Exil: seine antirömische Agitation und die römische Gegnerwahrnehmung', in H. Devijver and E. Lipinski (eds), *Studia Phoenicia X: Punic Wars*, Orientalia Lovaniensia Analecta 33, Louvain, 241–250.

Halff, G., 1963–1964, 'L'Onomastique punique de Carthage', *Karthago* 12, 62–145.

Harris, W., 1985 [1979], *War and Imperialism in Republican Rome 327–70 BC*, Clarendon Press, Oxford.

Hill, C., 2010, 'Fighting Stories' in A. Wiest and M. Doidge (eds), *Triumph Revisited: Historians Battle for the Vietnam War*, Routledge, New York, 79–89.

Hölbl, G., 2001, *A History of the Ptolemaic Empire*, Routledge, London.

Hollis, M. and Smith, S., 2003 [1990], *Explaining and Understanding International Relations*, Clarendon Press, Oxford.

Holloway, R. R., 2000 [1991], *The Archaeology of Ancient Sicily*, Routledge, London and New York.

Horden P. and Purcell N., 2000, *The Corrupting Sea: A Study of Mediterranean History*, Blackwell, Oxford.

Hoyos, D., 1984, 'The Roman–Punic pact of 279 BC: its Problems and its Purpose', *Historia* 33, 402–439.

Hoyos, D., 1992, 'Sluice-Gates or Neptune at New Carthage, 209 BC?' *Historia: Zeitschrift für Alte Geschichte*, vol. 41.1, 124–128.

Hoyos, D., 1994, 'Barcid "Proconsuls" and Punic Politics 237–218 BC', *Rheinisches Museum für Philologie* 137, 246–274.

Hoyos, D., 1998, *Unplanned Wars: The Origins of the First and Second Punic Wars*, Walter de Gruyter, Berlin.

Hoyos, D., 2000, 'Maharbal's *bon mot*: authenticity and survival' *Classical Quarterly* 50, 610–614.

Hoyos, D., 2005 [2003], *Hannibal's Dynasty: Power and Politics in the Western Mediterranean 247–183BC*, Routledge, Oxford.

Hoyos, D., 2006, *Livy: Hannibal's War, books 21–30, Introduction, Notes etc.*, Oxford World Classics, Oxford University Press, Oxford.

Hoyos, D., 2007, *Truceless War: Carthage's Fight for Survival, 241–237 BC*, Brill, Leiden.

Hoyos, D., 2008, *Hannibal, Rome's Greatest Enemy*, Bristol Phoenix, Exeter.

Hoyos, D., 2010, *The Carthaginians*, Routledge, Abingdon.

Hoyos, D., 2013, 'The Second Punic War', in B. Campbell and L. Tritle (eds), *The Oxford Handbook of Warfare in the Classical World*, Oxford University Press, Oxford, 688–707.

Hoyos, D. (ed.), 2011, *A Companion to the Punic Wars*, Wiley-Blackwell, Malden MA.

Hoyte, J., 1960, *A Trunk Road for Hannibal: with an Elephant over the Alps*, Geoffrey Bles, London.

Humbert, M., 1978, *Municipium et Civitas sine Suffragio: L'organisation de la conquête jusqu'à la guerre sociale*, Collection de L'École Français de Rome, 36, Rome and Paris.

Hunt, P., 2009. 'The Locus of Carthage, Compounding Geographical Logic', *African Archaeological Review* 26, 137–154.

Hurst, H., 1983, 'The War Harbour at Carthage', in *Atti i Congresso Internazionale di Studi Fenici e Punici*, 603–610, vol. 2, Rome.

Hurst, H., 1994, *Excavations at Carthage, The British Mission, vol. 2.1: The Circular Harbour, North Side: The Site and Finds Other than Pottery*, Oxford University Press, Oxford.

Hurst, H. and Stager, L., 1978. 'A Metropolitan Landscape: The Late Punic Ports of Carthage', *World Archaeology* 9, 334–346.

Huss, W., 1986, 'Hannibal und die Religion', in C. Bonnet, E. Lipinski and P. Marchetti (eds), *Studia Phoenicia IV. Religio Phoenicia*, Brussels, 223–238.

Hutchinson, G., 2000, *Xenophon and the Art of Command*, Greenhill Books, London.

Jacobs, J., 2010, 'From Sallust to Silius Italicus: *Metus Hostilis* and the Fall of Rome in the *Punica*', in J. Miller and A. Woodman (eds), *Latin Historiography and Poetry in the Early Empire*, Brill, Leiden, 123–139.

Jaeger, M., 2006, 'Livy, Hannibal's Monument, and the Temple of Juno at Croton', *Transactions of the American Philological Association* 136.2, 389–414.

Jaeger, M., 2008, *Archimedes and the Roman Imagination*, University of Michigan Press, Ann Arbor.

Jaeger, M., 2010, 'Once More to Syracuse: Livy's Perspective on the Verrines', in W. Polleichtner (ed.), *Livy and Intertextuality*, Bochumer Altertumswissenschaftliches Colloquium, Band 84, Trier, 15–45.

Jenkins, G., 1987, 'Some Coins of Hannibal's Time', in *Studi per Laura Breglia*. Parte I Generalia – Numismatica Greca, *Bolletino Numismatica* 4, 215–234.

Jenkins, G. and Lewis, R., 1963, *Carthaginian Gold and Electrum Coins*, Royal Numismatic Society, London.

Jospin, J.P. and L. Dalaine (eds), 2011, *Hannibal et les Alpes: une traversée, un mythe*, Infolio Editions, Gallion.

Kapust, D., 2011, *Republicanism, Rhetoric, and Roman Political Thought: Sallust, Livy and Tacitus*, Cambridge University Press, Cambridge.

Karlsson, L., 1989, 'Some Notes of the Fortifications of Greek Sicily', *Opuscula Romana* 17, 77–89.

Keay, S., 2013, 'Were the Iberians Hellenised?' in J. Prag and J. C. Quinn (eds), *The Hellenistic West: Rethinking the Ancient Mediterranean*, Cambridge University Press, Cambridge, 300–319.

Keegan, J., 1987, *The Mask of Command*, Penguin, New York.

King, R., 2004, 'Belle, Dido Elizabeth (1761?–1804)', *Oxford Dictionary of National Biography*, Oxford University Press, 2004; online edn, Oct. 2007 [http://www.oxforddnb.com/view/article/73352, accessed 8 June 2014].

Kitouni-Daho, K., 2003, in G. Sennequier and C. Colonna (eds), *L'Algérie au temps des royaumes numides: Ve siècle avant J.-C – 1er siècle après J.-C.*, Somogy, Rouen, 95–96.

Krahmalkov, C., 2000, *Phoenician–Punic Dictionary, Studia Phoenicia XV*, Orientalia Lovaniensia Analecta, 90, Louvain.

Krings, V., 1995, *La Civilisation phénicienne et punique: manuel de recherché*, Brill, Leiden.

Krings, V., 1998, *Carthage et les Grecs, 580–480 av. J.C.*, Brill, Leiden.

Krings, V., 2005, 'La Critique de Sosylos chez Polybe III 20', in G. Schepens and J. Bollansée (eds), *The Shadow of Polybius: Intertextuality as a Research Tool in Greek Historiography*, Studia Hellenistica, 42, Louvain, 223–236.

Krings, V., 2008, 'Rereading Punic Agriculture, Representation, Analogy and Ideology in the Classical Sources', in P. van Dommelen and G. Gómez Bellard (eds), *Rural Landscapes of the Punic World: Studies in Mediterranean Archaeology* 11, Equinox, London, 22–43.

Krings, V. (ed.), 1995, *La Civilization phénicienne et punique: manuel de recherche*, Brill, Leiden.

Kromayer, J. and Veith, G., 1912, *Antike Schlachtfelder: in Italien und Afrika*, vol. 3, Weidmann, Berlin.

Kuhle, M. and Kuhle, S., 2012, 'Hannibal Gone Astray? A Critical Comment on W. C. Mahaney *et al.*', *Archaeometry* 54.3, 591–601.

Kunze, C., 2011, *Carthage and Numidia*, in D. Hoyos (ed.), *A Companion to the Punic Wars*, Wiley-Blackwell, Malden, MA, 395–411.

Kuttner, A., 2013, 'Representing Hellenistic Numidia, in Africa and at Rome', in J. Crawley Quinn and J. Prag (eds), *The Hellenistic West: Rethinking the Ancient Mediterranean*, Cambridge University Press, Cambridge, 216–272.

Lancel, S., 1995, *Carthage: A History*, trans. Antonia Nevill, Blackwell, Oxford.

Lancel, S., 1999 [1998], *Hannibal*, trans. Antonia Nevill, Blackwell, Oxford.

Lawrence, A.W., 1946, 'Archimedes and the Design of Euryalus Fort', *Journal of Hellenic Studies* 66, 99–107.

Lawrence, A.W., 1979, *Greek Aims in Fortifications*, Clarendon Press, Oxford.

Lazenby, J., 1996a, *The First Punic War*, UCL Press, London.

Lazenby, J., 1996b, 'Was Maharbal Right?' in Cornell et al. (eds), *The Second Punic War: A Reappraisal*, University of London, Institute of Classical Studies, London, 39–48.

Lazenby, J., 1998 (paperback edn of 1978), *Hannibal's War. A Military History of the Second Punic War*, University of Oklahoma, Norman.

Lazenby, J., 2004, 'Rome and Carthage', in H. Flower (ed.), *The Cambridge Companion to the Roman Republic*, Cambridge University Press, Cambridge, 225–241.

Le Bohec, Y., 2011, 'The "Third Punic War": The Siege of Carthage (149–146 BC), in D. Hoyos (ed.), *A Companion to the Punic Wars*, Wiley-Blackwell, Malden, MA, 430–445.

Leigh, M., 2004, *Comedy and the Rise of Rome*, Oxford University Press, Oxford.

Leveau, P. and Mercalli, L., 2011, 'Hannibal et les Alpes: l'identification du col franchi et son context environmental', in J-P. Jospin and L. Dalaine (eds), *Hannibal et les Alpes: une traversée, un mythe*, Infolio Editions, Gallion, 94–106.

Levene, D., 2010, *Livy on the Hannibalic War*, Oxford University Press, Oxford.

Lipinski, E., 1995, *Dieux et Déeses de l'Univers Phénicien et Punique*, Orientalia Lovaniensia Analecta 64, Peeters, Louvain.

Lipinski, E., 2004, *Itineraria Phoenicia*, Studia Phoenicia, 18, Orientalia Lovaniensia Analecta, 127, Peeters, Louvain.

Lo Cascio, E., 2001, 'Recruitment and the Size of the Roman Population from the Third to the First Century BCE', in W. Scheidel (ed.), *Debating Roman Demography*, Brill, Leiden, 111–137.

Lomas, K., 1993, *Rome and the Western Greeks 350 BC–AD 200*, Routledge, London.

Lomas, K., 2004, 'Italy during the Roman Republic: 338–31 B.C.', in H. Flower (ed.), *The Cambridge Companion to the Roman Republic*, Cambridge University Press, Cambridge, 199–224.

Lomas, K., 2011, 'Rome, Latins, and Italians in the Second Punic War', in D. Hoyos, (ed.), *A Companion to the Punic Wars*, Wiley-Blackwell, Malden, MA, 339–356.

Longo, O. (ed.), 1998, *La Porpora: realtà e immaginario di un colore simbolico*, Atti del convegno di Studio Venezia, 24–25 Ottobre 1996, Venice.

López-Ruiz, C., 2009, 'Tarshish and Tartessos Revisited: Textual Problems and Historical Implications', in M. Dietler and C. López-Ruiz (eds), 2009, *Colonial Encounters in Ancient Iberia: Phoenician, Greek and Indigenous Relations*, University of Chicago Press, Chicago, 255–280.

Loreto, L., 1995, *La grande insurrezione Libica contra Cartagine del 241–237 a.C.: una storia politica e militare*, Collection de l'École Français de Rome, 211, Rome.

Lowe, B., 2009, *Roman Iberia: Economy Society and Culture*, Duckworth, London.

Ma, J., 2002, *Antiochus III and the Cities of Western Asia Minor*, Oxford University Press, Oxford.

McDonnell, M., 2006, 'Rome Aesthetics and the Spoils of Syracuse', in K. Welch (ed.), *Representations of War in Ancient Rome*, Cambridge University Press, Cambridge, 68–90.

Mackinnon, M., 2007, 'Peopling the Mortuary Landscape of North Africa: An Overview of the Human Osteological Evidence', in L. Stirling and D. Stone (eds), *Mortuary Landscapes of North Africa*, University of Toronto Press, Toronto.

Maes, A., 1989, 'L'Habillement masculin à Carthage à l'époque des guerres puniques', in H. Devijver and E. Lipinski (eds), *Studia Phoenicia X: The Punic Wars*, Louvain, 15–24.

Mahaney, W., 2009, *Hannibal's Odyssey: Environmental Background to the Alpine Invasion of Italia*, Gorgias Press, Piscataway, NJ.

Mahaney, W., 2013, 'Comments on M. Kuhle and S. Kuhle (2012): "Hannibal Gone Astray? A Critical Comment on W. C. Mahaney *et al.*, The Traversette (Italia) Rockfall: Geomorphological Indicator of the Hannibalic Invasion Route" (*Archaeometry*, 52, 1 [2010] 156–72)', *Archaeometry*, 55.6, 1196–1204.

Mahaney, W. et al., 2010, 'The Traversette (Italia) Rockfall: Geomorphological Indicator of the Hannibalic Invasion Route', *Archaeometry* 52.1, 156–172.

Malkin, I., 2003 [1994], *Myth and Territory in the Spartan Mediterranean*, Cambridge University Press, Cambridge.

Malkin, I., 2011, *A Small Greek World*, Oxford University Press, Oxford.

Malkin, I. (ed.), 2005, *Mediterranean Paradigms and Classical Antiquity*, Routledge, London.

Markoe, G., 2000, *The Phoenicians*, The Folio Society, London.

Mazza, S., and Murooka, Y., 2009, 'Vinegars through the Ages', in L. Solieri and P. Giudici (eds), *Vinegars of the World*, Springer-Verlag, Milan, 17–39.

Medas, S., 2000, *La Marineria Cartaginese: le navi, gli uomini, la navagazione*, C. Delfino, Sassari.

Meister, K., 1990, 'Autobiographische Literatur und Memoiren (Hypomnemata) (*FGrHist*, 227–238)', in H. Verdin, G. Schepens and E. De Keyser (eds), *Purposes of History: Studies in Greek Historiography from the 4th to the 2nd centuries BC*, Studia Hellenistica 30, Louvain, 83–89.

Mierse, W., 2000, 'The Sanctuary of Hercules–Melkart at Gades and the Arabic Sources', in R. Ross Holloway (ed.), *Miscellanea Mediterranea*, Center for Old World Archaeology and Art, Brown University, Providence, R.I., 1–10.

Miles, M., 2008, *Art as Plunder*, Cambridge University Press, Cambridge.

Miles, R., 2010, *Carthage Must Be Destroyed*, Allen Lane, London.

Miles, R., 2011, 'Hannibal and Propaganda', in D. Hoyos (ed.), *A Companion to the Punic Wars*, Wiley-Blackwell, Malden MA, 260–279.

Millard, A., 1976, 'The Caananite Linear Alphabet and its Passage to the Greeks', *Kadmos* 15, 130–144.

Millard, A., 2000, 'The Phoenicians at Sea', in G. Oliver, R. Brock, T. Cornell and S. Hodkinson (eds), *The Sea in Antiquity*, BAR International Series 899, Oxford, 75–79.

Mineo, B., 2011, 'Principal Literary Sources for the Punic Wars (apart from Polybius)', in D. Hoyos (ed.), *A Companion to the Punic Wars*, Wiley-Blackwell, Malden MA, 111–127.

Moore, T. J., 2010, 'Livy's Hannibal and the Roman Tradition', in W. Polleichtner (ed.), *Livy and Intertextuality*, Bochumer Altertumswissenschaftliches Colloquium, Band 84, Trier, 135–167.

Morillo, A., Cadiou, F. and Hourcade, D. (eds), 2003, *Defensa y territorio en Hispania de Los Escipiones a Augusto*, Universidad de León: Casa de Velázquez, León.

Morrison, John, 1995, 'The Trireme', in R. Gardiner (ed.), *The Age of the Galley: Mediterranean Oared Vessels Since Pre-Classical Times*, Conway Maritime Press, London, 49–65.

Morrison, John, 1996, *Greek and Roman Oared Warships*, Oxbow, Oxford.

Moscati, S., 1988, 'Fenicio o punico o Cartaginese', *Rivista di Studi Fenici* 16, 3–13.

Moscati, S. (ed.), 2001 [1997], *The Phoenicians*, I.B. Tauris, London.

Moscovich, M.J., 1990, 'Septimius Severus and the Tomb of Hannibal', *Ancient History Bulletin* 4.5, 108–112.

Murray, W., 2012, *The Age of Titans: The Rise and Fall of the Great Hellenistic Navies*, Oxford University Press, Oxford.

Neville, A., 2007, *Mountains of Silver and Rivers of Gold, The Phoenicians in Iberia*, Oxbow, Oxford.

Niemeyer, H., 1995, 'Expansion et colonisation', in V. Krings (ed.), *La Civilization phénicienne et punique: manuel de recherche*, Brill, Leiden, 247–267.

Niemeyer, H., 2002, 'The Phoenician Settlement at Toscanos', in M. Bierling (ed.), *The Phoenicians in Spain, an Archaeological Review of the Eighth–Sixth Centuries BCE*, trans. and ed. Marilyn R. Bierling, Eisenbrauns, Winona Lake, IN, 31–48.

Niemeyer, H., Docter, R. et al., 1993, 'Die Grabung unter dem Decuman Maximus von Karthago. Vorbericht über die Kampagnen 1986–1991', *MDAIR (Mitteilungen des Deutschen Archäologischen Instituts, Römische Abteilung)* 100, 210–244.

Niemeyer, H., Docter, R., Schmidt, K. and Bechtold, B., 2007, *Karthago: Die Ergebnisse der Hamburger Grabung unter dem Decumanus Maximus*, Philipp von Zabern, Mainz.

O'Bryhim, S., 1991, 'Hannibal's Elephants and the Crossing of the Rhône', *Classical Quarterly*, New Series, 41.1, 121–125.

Orlin, E., 1997, *Temples, Religion and Politics in the Roman Republic*, Brill, Leiden and New York.

Palmer, R., 1997, *Rome and Carthage at Peace*, F. Steiner, Stuttgart.

Parker, A.J., 1992, *Ancient Shipwrecks of the Mediterranean and the Roman Provinces*, BAR International Series, 580.

Peters, S. (ed.), 2004, *Hannibal ad Portas: Macht und Reichtum Karthago*, Theiss, Stuggart.

Pfiffig, A.J., 1967, 'Eine Nennung Hannibals in einer Inschrift des 2. Jahrhunderts v. Ch. aus Tarquinia', *Studi Etruschi* 35, 659–663.

Picard, G-C., 1963–1964, 'Le Problème du portrait d' Hannibal', *Karthago* 12, 29–42.

Picard, C., 1967a, *Sacra Punica: Études sur les masques et rasoirs de Carthage*, *Karthago* 13, Paris.

Picard, C., 1967b, *Hannibal*, Hachette, Paris.

Picard, G-C., 1970, *Vie et mort à Carthage*, Hachette, Paris.

Picard, C., 1975, 'Les Représentations du sacrifice molk sur les ex-voto de Carthage', *Karthago*, 17, 67–138.

Picard, G-C., 1983, 'Est-il possible d'écrire une histoire de Carthage?', *Atti i Congresso Internazionale di Studi Fenici e Punici*, 279–83, vol. 1, Rome.

Picard, G-C., 1983–1984, 'Hannibal hégémon hellénistique', *Rivista Storica dell'Antichità*, 13–14, 75–81.

Picard, G-C., and Picard C., 1958, *La vie quotidienne à Carthage au temps d'Hannibal*, Hachette, Paris.

Pietilä-Castrén, Leena, 1987, *Magnificentia publica: The Victory Monuments of the Roman Generals in the Era of the Punic Wars*, Commentationes Humanarum Litterarum 84, Helsinki.

Pisano, G. (ed.), 1999, *Phoenicians and Carthaginians in the Western Mediterranean*, Studia Punica 12, Rome.

Plon, H. and Dumaine, J. (eds), 1870, *Correspondance de Napoléon Ier publiée par ordre de L'emperur Napoléon III*, Henri Plon, Paris.

Poirel, E., 2003, 'Sophonisbe, Reine de Numidie', in G. Sennequier and C. Colonna (eds), *L'Algérie au temps des royaumes numides: Ve siècle avant J.-C.–1er siècle après J.-C.*, Somogy, Rouen, 154–159.

Potter, D., 2004, 'The Roman Army and Navy', in H. Flower (ed.), *The Cambridge Companion to the Roman Republic*, Cambridge University Press, Cambridge, 66–88.

Prag, J., 2006, '*Peonus plane est* – But Who Were the "Punickes"?', *Papers of the British School at Rome*, 74, 1–37.

Prag, J., 2010, 'Tyrannizing Sicily: The Despots Who Cried "Carthage"!' in A. Turner et al. (eds), *Private and Public Lies: The Discourse of Despotism and Deceit in the Graeco-Roman World*, Brill, Leiden, 51–71.

Prag, J. and Quinn, J.C. (eds), 2013, *The Hellenistic West: Rethinking the Ancient Mediterranean*, Cambridge University Press, Cambridge.

Prevas, J., 1998, *Hannibal Crosses the Alps*, Spellmount, Staplehurst.

Purcell, N., 2013, 'On the Significance of East and West in Today's "Hellenistic" History: Reflections on Symmetrical Worlds, Reflecting through World Symmetries', in J. Prag and J.C. Quinn (eds), *The Hellenistic West: Rethinking the Ancient Mediterranean*, Cambridge University Press, Cambridge, 367–390.

Quinn, J.C., 2011, 'The Cultures of the Tophet: Identification and Identity in the Phoenician Diaspora', in E. Gruen (ed.), *Cultural Identity in the Ancient Mediterranean*, Getty Research Institute, Los Angeles, 388–413.

Quinn, J.C., 2013, 'Monumental Power: "Numidian Royal Architecture" in Context', in J. Crawley Quinn and J. Prag (eds), *The Hellenistic West: Rethinking the Ancient Mediterranean*, Cambridge University Press, Cambridge, 179–215.

Ralegh, Sir Walter, 1829, *The Works of Sir Walter Ralegh volume VI, The History of the World*, book V chapters 1–3, Oxford.

Ramallo Asensio, S., 2003, 'Carthago Nova. Arqueologiá y epigrafía de la muralla urbana', in A. Morillo, F. Cadiou and D. Hourcade (eds), *Defensa y territorio en Hispania de Los Escipiones a Augusto*, Universidad de León, Casa de Velázquez, León, 325–362.

Rance, P., 2009, 'Hannibal, Elephants and Turrets in Suda 438 (Polybius Fr. 162$^B$ – an unidentified fragment of Diodorus', *Classical Quarterly* 59.1, 91–111.

Rankin, D., 2005, *Between Spenser and Swift: English Writing in Seventeenth-Century Ireland*, Cambridge University Press, Cambridge.

Rankin, D. (ed.), 2013, *Landgartha: a tragi-comedy by Henry Burnell*, Four Courts Press, Ireland.

Rankov, B., 1996, 'The Second Punic War at Sea', in T. Cornell et al. (eds), *The Second Punic War: A Reappraisal*, University of London, Institute of Classical Studies, London, 49–57.

Rankov, B., 2011, 'A War of Phases: Strategies and Stalemates 264–241 BC', in D. Hoyos (ed.), *A Companion to the Punic Wars*, Wiley-Blackwell, Malden MA, 149–166.

Rawlings, L., 1996, 'Celts, Spaniards, and Samnites: Warriors in a Soldiers' War', in T. Cornell et al. (eds), *The Second Punic War: A Reappraisal*, University of London, Institute of Classical Studies, London, 81–95.

Rawlings, L., 2005, 'Hannibal and Hercules', in L. Rawlings and H. Bowden (eds), *Herakles and Hercules Exploring Graeco-Roman Divinity*, The Classical Press of Wales, Swansea, 153–184.

Rawlings, L., 2010, 'The Carthaginian Navy: Questions and Assumptions', in G. Fagan and M. Trundle (eds), *New Perspectives on Ancient Warfare*, Brill, Leiden and Boston, 253–287.

Rawlings, L., 2011, 'The War in Italy, 218–203', in D. Hoyos (ed.), *A Companion to the Punic Wars*, Wiley-Blackwell, Malden MA, 299–319.

Reff, T., 1963, 'Cézanne's Dream of Hannibal', *Art Bulletin* 45.2, 148–152.

Ribichini, S., 2001, 'Beliefs and Religious Life', in S. Moscati (ed.), *The Phoenicians*, I.B. Tauris, London and New York, 120–152.

Rich, J., 1993, 'Fear, Greed and Glory: The Causes of Roman War-making in the Republic', in J. Rich and G. Shipley (eds), *War and Society in the Roman World*, Routledge, London, 38–68.

Rich, J., 1996, 'The Origins of the Second Punic War', in T. Cornell, et al. (eds), *The Second Punic War: A Reappraisal*, University of London, Institute of Classical Studies, London, 1–37.

Richardson, J.S., 1975, 'The Triumph, the Praetors and the Senate in the Early Second Century BC', *Journal of Roman Studies* 65, 50–63.

Ridley, R., 2000, 'Livy and the Hannibalic War', in C. Bruun (ed.), *The Roman Middle Republic: Politics, Religion and Historiography c. 400–133BC*, Acta Instituti Romani Finlandiae vol. 23, Rome, 13–40.

Rives, J., 1995, 'Human Sacrifice among Pagans and Christians', *Journal of Roman Studies* 85: 65–85.

Robinson, E., 1956, 'Punic Coins of Spain and their Bearing on the Roman Republican Series', in *Essays in Roman Coinage presented to H. Mattingly*, Oxford University Press, London, 34–62.

Robinson, E., 1964, 'Carthaginian and Other South Italian Coinages of the Second Punic War', *Numismatic Chronicle* 37, 37–64.

Rose, C., 2005, 'The Parthians in Augustan Rome', *American Journal of Archaeology* 109.1, 21–75.

Rosenstein, N., 1993, 'Competition and Crisis in Mid-Republican Rome', *Phoenix* 47.4, 313–338.

Rosenstein, N., 2002, 'Marriage and Manpower in the Hannibalic War: "Assidui", "Proletarii" and Livy 24.18.7–8', *Historia* 51.2, 163–191.

Rossi, A., 2004, 'Parallel Lives: Hannibal and Scipio in Livy's Third Decade', *Transactions of the American Philological Association* 134, 359–381.

Roth, J., 1999, *The Logistics of the Roman Army at War 264 BC to AD 235*, Brill, Leiden.

Rundin, J.S., 2004, 'Pozo moro, Child Sacrifice and the Greek Legendary Tradition', *Journal of Biblical Literature* 123.3, 425–447.

Sabin, P., 1996, 'The Mechanics of Battle in the Second Punic War', in T. Cornell et al. (eds), *The Second Punic War: A Reappraisal*, University of London, Institute of Classical Studies, London, 59–79.

Sabin P., van Wees, H. and Whitby, M. (eds), 2007, *The Cambridge History of Greek and Roman Warfare*, 2 vols, Cambridge University Press, Cambridge.

Sala Sellés, F., 2010, 'Nuevas perspectivas sobre las relaciones púnicas con la costa ibérica del sureste peninsular', in *Los púnicos de Iberia: proyectos, revisions, síntesis*, Mainake vol. 32.2, 933–950.

Salmon, E.T., 1957, 'Hannibal's March on Rome', *Phoenix* 11.4, 153–163.

Sanders, L., 1988, 'Punic Politics in the Fifth Century BC', *Historia: Zeitschrift für Alte Geschichte* 37.1, 72–89.

Scheid, J. and Svenbro, J., 1985, 'Byrsa. La ruse d'Elissa et la foundation de Carthage', *Annales. Histoire, Sciences Sociales*, 40e Année, no. 2, 328–342.

Schepens, G., 1989, 'Polybius on the Punic Wars. The Problem of Objectivity in History', in H. Devijver and E. Lipinski (eds), *Studia Phoenicia X: Punic Wars*, Orientalia Lovaniensia Analecta 33, Louvain, 317–328.

Schettino, M., 2009, 'Pyrrhos en Italie: la construction de l'image du premier ennemi venu de l'Orient grec', *Pyrrhus en Occident, Pallas* 79, 173–184.

Schwartz, J. et al., 2012, 'Bones, Teeth and Estimation of Age of Perinates: Carthaginian Infant Sacrifice Revisited', *Antiquity* 86, 738–745.

Scullard, H.,1930, *Scipio Africanus in the Second Punic War*, Cambridge University Press, Cambridge.

Scullard, H., 1970, *Scipio Africanus: Soldier and Politician*, Thames and Hudson, London.

Scullard, H., 1974, *The Elephant in the Greek and Roman World*, Thames and Hudson, London.

Seibert, Jakob, 1989, 'Zur Logistic des Hannibal-Feldzuges: Nachschub über die Alpen?' in H. Devijver and E. Lipinski (eds), *Studia Phoenicia X: Punic Wars*, Orientalia Lovaniensia Analecta 33, Louvain, 213–221.

Seibert, Jakob, 1993a, *Hannibal*, Wissenschaftliche Buchgesellschaft, Darmstadt.

Seibert, Jakob, 1993b, *Forschungen zu Hannibal*, Wissenschaftliche Buchgesellschaft, Darmstadt.

Serrati, J., 2000a, 'Sicily from Pre-Greek Times to the Fourth Century', in C. Smith and J. Serrati, *Sicily from Aeneas to Augustus*, University of Edinburgh Press, Edinburgh, 9–14.

Serrati, J., 2000b, 'The Coming of the Romans: Sicily from the fourth to the first century BC' and 'Garrisons and Grain, Sicily between the Punic Wars', in C. Smith and J. Serrati, *Sicily from Aeneas to Augustus*, University of Edinburgh Press, Edinburgh, 109–133.

Serrati, J., 2006, 'Neptune's Altars: The Treaties between Rome and Carthage (509–226 BC)', *Classical Quarterly* 56.1, 113–134.

Sheldon, R., 1986, 'Hannibal's Spies', *International Journal of Intelligence and Counterintelligence* 1.3, 51–70.

Shipley, G., 2000, *The Greek World after Alexander*, Routledge, London.

Smith, C. and Serrati, J., 2000, *Sicily from Aeneas to Augustus*, University of Edinburgh Press, Edinburgh.

Smith, P. et al., 2013, 'Age Estimations Attest to Infant Sacrifice at the Carthage Tophet', *Antiquity* 87, 1197–1207.

Sourvinou-Inwood, C., 1995, '*Reading' Greek Death to the End of the Classical Period*, Clarendon Press, Oxford.

Spencer, D., 2002, *The Roman Alexander*, University of Exeter Press, Exeter.

Starks, J.H. (Jr.), 1999, 'Fides Aeneia: The Transference of Punic Stereotypes in the *Aeneid'*, *Classical Journal* 94.3, 255–283.

Steinby, C., 2007, *The Roman Republican Navy, from the Sixth Century to 167 BC*, Commentationes Humanarum Litterarum, 123, Helsinki.

Stewart, A., 1993, *Faces of Power: Alexander's Image and Hellenistic Politics*, University of California Press, Berkeley.

Stocks, C., 2014, *The Roman Hannibal: Remembering the Enemy in Silius Italicus' Punica*, University of Liverpool Press, Liverpool.

Storm, E., 2001, *Massinissa: Numidien im Aufbruch*, Steiner, Stuttgart.

Strobel, Karl, 2006, 'Libyssa', *Brill's New Pauly*, Antiquity volumes edited by: H. Cancik and H. Schneider. Brill Online, 2014. Reference. The University of Reading. 22 August 2014 <http://referenceworks.brillonline.com/entries/brill-s-new-pauly/libyssa-e704070>.

Syed, Y., 2005, *Vergil's 'Aeneid' and the Roman Self*, University of Michigan Press, Ann Arbor.

Sznycer, 1978, 'Carthage et la civilisation punique', in C. Nicolet (ed.), *Rome et la conquête du monde méditeranéen* vol. 2, Presses Universitaires de France, Paris, 545–593.

Thiel, J., 1954, *A History of Roman Sea-Power before the Second Punic War*, North-Holland, Amsterdam.

Tipping, B., 2007, '*Haec tum Roman fuit'*: Past, Present and Closure in Silius Italicus' Punica', in S. Heyworth, P. Fowler and S. Harrison (eds), *Classical Constructions: Papers in Memory of Don Fowler, Classicist and Epicurean*, Oxford University Press, Oxford, 221–241.

Tipping, B., 2010, *Exemplary Epic: Silius Italicus' Punica*, Oxford University Press, Oxford.

Tipps, G., 2003, 'The defeat of Regulus', *Classical World* 96.4, 375–385.

Toynbee, A.J., 1965, *Hannibal's Legacy: The Hannibalic War's Effect on Roman Life*, vols 1 and 2, Oxford University Press, Oxford.

Turfa, J.M., 1977, 'Evidence for Etruscan–Punic Relations', *American Journal of Archaeology* 81.3, 368–374.

Tusa, S. and Royal, J. 2012, 'The Landscape of the Naval Battle at the Egadi Islands (241 BC)', *Journal of Roman Archaeology* 25, 7–48.

van Dommelen, P. 1998, 'Punic Persistence: Colonialism and Cultural Identities in Roman Sardinia', in R. Laurence and J. Berry (eds), *Cultural Identity in the Roman Empire*, Routledge, London, 25–48.

van Dommelen, P. and Gómez Bellard, C., 2008, 'Defining the Punic World and its Rural Contexts', in P. van Dommelen and G. Gómez Bellard, *Rural Landscapes of the Punic World, Studies in Mediterranean Archaeology* 11, London, 1–21.

Várhelyi, Z., 2007, 'The Spectres of Roman Imperialism: The Live Burials of Gauls and Greeks at Rome', *Classical Antiquity* 26.2, 277–304.

Visona, P., 1995, 'La Numismatique *partim* occident' in V. Krings (ed.), *La Civilization phénici-enne et punique: manuel de recherche*, Brill, Leiden, 166–181.

Visona, P., 1998, 'Carthaginian Coinage in Perspective', *American Journal of Numismatics* 10, 1–27.

von Mohr, Deborah, 2006, *Das Bild Hannibals im 19. und 20. Jahrhundert: eine Analyse der deutschen Schulgeschichtsbücher und der historischen Jugendliteratur*, Tectum, Marburg.

Wagner, C.G., 1989, 'The Carthaginians in Ancient Spain: From Administrative Trade to Territorial Annexation', in H. Devijver and E. Lipinski (eds), *Studia Phoenicia X: Punic Wars*, Orientalia Lovaniensia Analecta 33, Louvain, 145–156.

Walbank, F.W. (1957, 1967, 1979), *A Historical Commentary on Polybius*, 3 vols, Clarendon Press, Oxford (cited as vol. 1, 2, or 3).

Walbank, F.W., 1985, 'Some Reflections on Hannibal's Pass' in *Selected Papers: Studies in Greek and Roman History and Historiography*, Cambridge University Press, Cambridge, 107–119.

Walbank, F.W., 2002, *Polybius, Rome and the Hellenistic World*, Cambridge University Press, Cambridge.

Wallace-Hadrill, A., 2008, *Rome's Cultural Revolution*, Cambridge University Press, Cambridge.

Walsh, P.G., 1965, 'Massinissa', *Journal of Roman Studies*, 55.1, 149–160.

Weiss, R., 1969, *The Renaissance Discovery of Classical Antiquity*, Blackwell, Oxford and New York.

Welch, K., 2006, '*Domi Militaeque*', in K. Welch (ed.), *Representations of War in Ancient Rome*, Cambridge University Press, Cambridge, 91–161.

Whittaker, C., 1978, 'Carthaginian Imperialism in the Fifth and Fourth Centuries', in P. Garnsey and C. Whittaker (eds), *Imperialism in the Ancient World*, Cambridge University Press, Cambridge, 59–90.

Wiedemann, T., 1986, 'The Fetiales: A Reconsideration', *Classical Quarterly*, New Series 36.2, 478–490.

Williams, C., 1995, 'Greek Love at Rome', *Classical Quarterly*, New Series 45.2, 517–539.

Williams, D., 2006, 'Dido Queen of England', *English Literary History*, 73.1, 31–59.

Wilson, R., 2013, 'Hellenistic Sicily, *c.*270–100 BC', in J. Prag and J.C. Quinn (eds), *The Hellenistic West*, Cambridge University Press, Cambridge, 79–119.

Wilson, S., 2007, 'Urban Development in the Severan Empire', in S. Swain, S. Harrison and J. Elsner (eds), *Severan Culture*, Cambridge University Press, Cambridge, 290–326.

Woolf, G., 2013, *Rome: An Empire's Story*, Oxford University Press, Oxford.

Woolmer, M., 2008. 'Tinker, Trader, Sailor Spy? The Role of the Mercantile Community in Greek Intelligence Gathering', in E. Bragg, L. Hau and E. Macaulay-Lewis (eds), *Beyond the Battlefields. New Perspectives on Warfare and Society in the Greco-Roman World*, Cambridge University Press, Cambridge, 67–83.

Worthington, Ian, 2008, *Philip II of Macedonia*, Yale University Press, New Haven and London.

Xella, P. (ed.), 2013, *The Tophet in the Phoenician Mediterranean*, Studi Epigraphici e Linguistici, vol. 30, Verona.

Xella, P. et al., 2013, 'Phoenician Bones of Contention', *Antiquity* 87, 1199–1207.

Yarrow, L., 2013, 'Heracles, Coinage, and the West: Three Hellenistic Case-Studies', in J. Prag and J. C. Quinn (eds), *The Hellenistic West*, Cambridge University Press, Cambridge, 348–366.

Zambon, Efrem, 2006, 'From Agathocles to Hieron II: the birth and development of *basileia* in Hellenistic Sicily' in S. Lewis (ed), *Ancient Tyranny*, University of Edinburgh Press, Edinburgh, 77–92.

Zambon, Efrem, 2008, *Tradition and Innovation: Sicily between Hellenism and Rome*, Franz Steiner Verlag, Stuttgart.

Zanker, P., 1988, *The Power of Images in the Age of Augustus*, trans. A. Shapiro, University of Michigan Press, Ann Arbor.

Zimmermann, K., 2011, 'Roman Strategy and Aims in the Second Punic War', in D. Hoyos (ed.), *A Companion to the Punic Wars*, Wiley-Blackwell, Malden MA, 280–298.

Zimmermann, L., 2001, 'Zur Münzprägung "der Libyer" während des Söldnerkrieges', in K. Geus and K. Zimmermann (eds), *Studia Phoenicia XVI: Punica – Libyca – Ptolemaica*, Orientalia Lovaniensia Analecta 104, Louvain, 235–252.

Zimmerman Munn, M.L., 2003, 'Corinthian Trade with the Punic West in the Classical Period', *Corinth, The Centenary: 1896–1996*, Corinth, vol. 20, 195–217.

# INDEX

Achradina, neighbourhood of Syracuse 156, 158

Acragas *see* Agrigentum

Actium, battle of (31 BCE) 24

Adranodorus, uncle and guardian of Syracusan king (*c.* 215–214 BCE) 153–155

Adriatic (Map 1, sea and coast) 29, 66, 104, 113, 114, 119, 150, 152, 162, 163, 190, 277*nn.* 47, 48

Adyn (possibly modern Uthina) 39

Aegates Islands (Map 1, modern Egadi) 47, 253*n.* 68

Aemilius Paullus, Lucius (Roman consul at Cannae) 78, 128, 130–131, 132, 176, 274*n.* 41

Aeneas 10, 99, 116, 230, 242*n.* 17

*Aeneid see* Virgil

Aeolian Islands (Map 1) 35, 47

*see also* Lipara

Aetolian League 181, 196, 278*n.* 57

Agathocles, Tyrant of Syracuse 26–27, 32, 101, 198, 249*nn.* 11–14, 253*nn.* 78, 79–82, 256*n.* 29, 289*n.* 30

assault on Utica 27–28

daughter Lanassa marries Pyrrhus 29

encourages revolt of the Libyan allies of Carthage 54

route of the invasion copied by Romans 37–39

*Ager Falernus,* in Campania 121

aggression, Roman perception of Carthaginian 14

Agrigentum (Acragas, Map 1, modern Agrigento) 37, 252*nn.* 61, 65, 66, 253*n.* 68, 262*n.* 47, 279*n.* 1

falls to the Romans (210 BCE) 182

Muttines operates out of 160

siege and fall of in First Punic war (261 BCE) 34–35

taken by Carthage in Second Punic War (213 BCE) 155, 157

Akra Leuka (possibly modern Alicante) 65, 66

Alalia (Aleria, Map 1), battle of (late sixth century BCE) 11, 242*n.* 23

alcohol, laws on use at Carthage 20

Alexander (III of Macedon, known as 'the Great') 5, 24, 25, 27, 86, 87, 99, 150, 176, 248*nn.* 2, 7, 249*n.* 14, 250*n.* 23, 254*n.* 2, 260*n.* 18, 261*n.* 38, 265*nn.* 15, 17, 266*nn.* 25, 26, 35, 270*n.* 20, 283*nn.* 66, 67, 296*n.* 30

siege of Tyre 25, 243*n.* 33

successors 25

in fictional competition with Hannibal 228, 232, 234, 235

Alexander of Epirus (uncle of Pyrrhus) 30

Alexandria 156, 247*n.* 83, 262*n.* 48

foundation of and potential rival to Carthage 25

allies and alliances 5, 27, 30, 47, 89, 174

Carthaginian 11, 12, 26, 33, 39, 52, 54, 58, 75, 83, 86, 92, 96, 103, 117, 118, 160, 167, 194, 195

Roman 33, 38, 45, 66, 70, 71, 75, 76, 78, 84, 100, 103, 117, 119, 121, 122, 128, 140, 143, 173, 177, 252*n*. 54, 269*n*. 5,
Roman allied casualties at Cannae 132
Hannibal's strategy towards 101–102, 104, 105, 107, 108, 110, 134, 141, 146–147, 149, 162, 164, 165, 169, 170, 181–182, 183, 187, 196, 270*n*. 20, 271*n*. 43, 272*n*. 2, 281*n*. 38
Allobroges, Celtic tribe in the Alps 95
Alps 71, 85, 86, 87, 89, 92, 94, 95–97, 98, 99, 100, 101, 104, 109, 171, 177, 188, 234, 237, 238, 266*n*. 37, 268*nn*. 58, 65, 285*n*. 30, 297*n*. 46
Col du Clapier 94, 95
Col de la Traversette 95
Pleiades 96
Ammianus Marcellinus 265*n*. 3
on the place of Hannibal's burial 238
Amtorgis, Iberian city on the upper Baetis river 172, 282*n*. 50
Andalucía 64
Andobales, Celiberian chieftain and Carthaginian ally (Indibilis in Livy) 117, 173, 286*n*. 52
Anio, river 168
Antigone, wife of Demetrius Poliorcetes 29
Antigonid, dynasty of Hellenistic monarchs 25, 277*n*. 44
Antigonus, 34, 110, 249*n*. 17
Antiochus III, king of the Seleucid kingdom 220, 222, 223, 224, 225, 234, 294*nn*. 25, 26
Apamea, peace of (188 BCE) 225
Aphrodite *see* Venus Erycina
Apollo 135, 200, 231, 245*n*. 60
equated to Reshep in the Carthaginian pantheon 17, 245*n*. 63, 295*n*. 15
Appius Claudius Pulcher (praetor in Sicily 214–213 BCE) 153, 155, 278*n*. 65
Roman consul in 212 BCE 280*n*. 23
Apulia (Map 1), region of southern Italy 1, 119, 122, 124, 128, 129, 136, 137, 139, 140, 141, 144, 146, 148, 161, 163, 166, 167, 182, 186, 189, 190, 273*n*. 18, 276*nn*. 9, 30, 280*nn*. 9, 16
Archimedes 156, 279*nn*. 72, 73, 75, 4
defence of Syracuse 156–157
death 161
legend 157, 161, 228
*Scorpians,* catapults designed by Archimedes 156

Ariminum (Map 1, modern Rimini) and the *Ager Gallicus* 104, 108, 109, 110, 189, 269*n*. 13, 270*n*. 32
Ariston of Tyre, agent of Hannibal at Carthage (after *c.* 196 BCE) 224–225
Arno river (in Etruria) 109, 110, 111, 270*n*. 26
Arpi (Map 1) 119, 276*n*. 9
first city in Apulia to join Hannibal after Cannae 141
retaken by the Romans in 213 BCE 163
Arretium (Map 1, modern Arezzo) 110, 185, 270*n*. 32, 285*n*. 29
Arrian, on Alexander's traits 86
Ars Philaeni (Map 2), eastern border of Carthaginian territory in North Africa 248*n*. 6
Artemis, festival celebrated at Syracuse 158
Astapa, allies of the Carthaginians in Iberia 194
Astarte 45, 116, 241*n*. 11, 247*n*. 88, 255*n*. 8, 256*n*. 25, 271*nn*. 53, 54
*see also* Venus Erycina
Asturians 82
Atatürk, Mustafa Kemal, monument to Hannibal at Gebze 237, 297*n*. 44
Athens and Athenian 13, 150, 158, 250*n*. 23, 296*n*. 29,
Atilius Regulus, Marcus (known as Regulus), consul in First Punic War (255 BCE)
command in First Punic War 37
invades Africa after Ecnomus 39–40, 101, 198, 253*nn*. 78, 79, 81, 289*n*. 30
defeated by Xanthippus and captured 40
sent to Rome by Carthage to negotiate a peace deal in *c.* 254 BCE 41
dies at Carthage 41, 254*nn*. 85, 88
wife accused of atrocities towards Punic prisoners of war 41–42
Atilius Regulus, Marcus, Roman magistrate (217/216 BCE) 127, 129, 132
Atlantic Ocean and coast of Africa 8, 12, 54, 63, 64, 185, 242*n*. 19, 243*n*. 30, 283*n*. 75
Attalid, Hellenistic rulers and kingdom in Asia Minor, allies of the Romans 224, 225
Aufidius, river 130, 141
Augustus, Rome's first Emperor 2, 11, 147, 232, 266*n*. 35, 277*n*. 32, 286*n*. 49, 295*n*. 19
Ausculum (Map 1), location of battle in southern Italy between Pyrrhus and Rome (279 BCE) 30

Autaritus, Gaulish leader of the Mercenary rebellion (241–238 BCE) 55, 57

Ba'al (Baal), chief god of the Carthaginian Pantheon 7, 21–22, 61, 243*n*. 34, 245*n*. 59, 247*n*. 88, 249*n*. 9, 258*n*. 1, 259*n*. 4, 277*n*. 55, 289*n*. 21
Ba'al Hammon *see* Ba'al
Ba'al Saphon 289 n.21
Baebius Tamphilus, Quintus 75, 263*n*. 59
Baecula (Map 2, modern Turruñuelos), battle of (208 BCE) 184, 288*n*. 6
Baetis river (Map 2, modern Guadalquivir) 8, 64, 70, 172, 184, 185, 193, 194, 260*n*. 17, 282*n*. 50
Bagradas river (maps 2 and 3, modern Medjerda) 202, 204, 206, 212, 213, 244*n*. 41, 258*n*. 57
Balaeric slingers *see* Balaeric Islands
Balearic Islands (Map 2) 8
  origin of renowned 'slingers' of the Carthaginians 49, 112, 215, 256*n*. 20, 272*n*. 66, 291*n*. 59
  reportedly first colony of Carthage was at Ebusus (Ibiza), *c.* 654 BCE 11
  surrender to Romans in 217 BCE 118
Bantius, Lucius, soldier from Nola favoured by Hannibal 141
Barca (surname or epithet), meaning 'Lightening' 44
Barmocar, representative from Carthaginian Senate sent to Philip V of Macedon (215 BCE) 152
Bellus (Map 2, near Thrabaka), mountain on north coast of North Africa 202
Beneventum (Map 1, modern Benevento) 165, 166, 281*n*. 29
Boccaccio, Renaissance poet 207, 236, 290*n*. 41
Boii, Gallic tribe of northern Italy 84, 102, 148,
Bomilcar, Carthaginian admiral at Syracuse and Tarentum (214–209 BCE) 158, 165, 278*n*. 57,
Bomilcar, Carthaginian commander who brought reinforcements to Italy (215 BCE) 149, 293*n*. 15
Bonaparte, Napoleon 76, 97–99, 120, 237, 238, 269*n*. 74
Bostar, Carthaginian commander at Capua (211 BCE) 169
Bostar, Carthaginian commander in the First Punic War against Regulus' invasion (255 BCE) 39

Bostar, Carthaginian envoy sent from Hannibal to Philip V (215 BCE) 151
Breakfast, illustrates Hannibal's concern for well-being of his soldiers 105–106
  Scipio shows same concern at Illipa 193
Brundisium (Map 1, modern Brindisi) 150, 162, 280*n*. 9, 281*n*. 29
Bruttium, Bruttii (Map 1, roughly equivalent to modern Calabria) 141, 144, 149, 150, 151, 165, 166
  raided by Hamilcar Barca in the First Punic War 45
  supported Hannibal quickly after Cannae 137, 140
  Bruttians served in Hannibal's army 146, 181–182
  last place of refuge for Hannibal as the Romans closed in 183, 185, 186, 188, 189, 192, 195, 196, 199, 200, 202–203, 205, 209, 289*n*. 28
  Carthaginian coin hoards found 273*n*. 27, 287*n*. 63
  Hannibal departs back to Carthage 210
Byblos, Phoenician city now in modern Lebanon 8
Byron, George Gordon, poet 100, 237, 269*n*. 1, 296*n*. 41
Byrsa Hill *see* Carthage

Cadiz (Map 2) *see* Gades
Caere, Etruscan city 127
Calavius, Pacuvius, leader of the pro-Hannibalic faction at Capua 142
  son tries to assassinate Hannibal 142
Callicula, valley of (in Campania) 122
Campania and Campanians 33, 52, 121–122, 124, 137, 139, 140–148, 158, 161–163, 165–168, 170, 220, 272*n*. 10, 273*nn*. 11, 18, 276*nn*. 11, 14, 18, 28, 280*nn*. 14, 16, 281*n*. 33
Campus Martius *see* Rome
Cannae (Map 1), battle of (216 BCE) 1, 2, 15, 113, 119, 128–137, 139–141, 142, 145, 147, 150, 152, 162, 163, 166, 167, 168, 171, 175, 176, 181, 185, 191, 214, 215, 220, 231, 233, 249*n*. 9, 264*n*. 71, 270*nn*. 23, 33, 271*n*. 41, 273*n*. 32, 274*nn*. 33, 39, 52, 275*n*. 5, 276*nn*. 9, 31, 281*n*. 39, 284*n*. 13
Canusium (Canusia, Map 1, modern Canosa) 128, 135, 189, 190, 192
Cap Bon (Map 2) 26, 37–39, 289*n*. 30
Cap Farina (Map 3) 203, 289*n*. 30
Capua (Map 1), largest city in

Campania 121, 143, 147, 188, 189, 219, 231, 276nn. 15, 18
goes over to Hannibal 137, 141–143, 265n. 12, 272n. 1, 276n. 28, 285n. 29
as allies of Rome 115, 272n. 10, 276n. 13, 272n. 10, 276nn. 16, 17, 21
hosts Hannibal to much acclaim 143–144
Vibius Virrius, pro-Hannibal Capuan senator 170
citizenship status 142, 143
blockade by Roman legions 160, 165–167, 168, 169
fall 170, 173, 174, 175, 181, 182, 184, 285n. 25
luxury as a corrupting force 145–146, 236–237, 276n. 25, 280n. 16, 296nn. 37, 38
Carpetani (Map 2), Iberian tribe 74, 77, 90, 283n. 75
Carthage (maps 1, 2, and 3), city 2, 7–23
Apollo from Carthage (Reshep) in Rome 17, 231, 245nn. 59, 63
army 34–35, 252nn. 62, 63, 64
as source of wild beasts 15, 16
Byrsa 2, 9, 17, 71, 241n. 12, 245nn. 59, 61, 62, 63, 262n. 46
destruction of 2, 3
government 18, 19, 56, 246nn. 68, 69, 70, 71, 72, 73, 74, 76, 77, 78
location, Map 3
navy 28–29, 249 nn. 21, 22
ports 13, 17–18, 20, 21, 23, 28, 221, 245nn. 64, 65, 294n. 18
Tophet 21, 22, 23, 247nn. 90, 94, 248n. 98, 249n. 9, 266n. 24
walls 17, 18, 38, 47, 53, 245nn. 58, 62, 246n. 67
war indemnity 59, 63, 66, 81, 208, 221, 222, 293n. 5, 294n. 21
Carthago Nova (Map 2, New Carthage)
foundation 70–72, 262nn. 43, 44, 45, 46, 47, 48
fall (209 BCE) 177–179, 180, 181, 183, 283nn. 77–84
Polybius visits 70, 283n. 78
Hannibal at see Hannibal, Barca, at New Carthage
Carthalo, garrison commander at Tarentum (209 BCE) 182
Carthalo, Hannibal's lieutenant sent to Rome after Cannae (216 BCE) 135, 136
Casilinum, city in Campania 144
taken by Hannibal in 216/215 BCE 145

captured by the Romans 167, 280n. 14
Cassius Dio, Roman History
on Pyrrhus 31
on treaty between Rome and Carthage before the First Punic War 33
on Hamilcar and the Roman Embassy 63, 66, 261n. 28
on Hannibal's acting first 82
on the end of the Second Punic War 209, 290n. 49
on Hannibal after Zama 219, 221, 224, 246n. 82, 291n. 57, 294n. 26, 296n. 31
Castulo (Map 2), Iberian city 70, 73, 77, 173, 184, 194, 262nn. 42, 52, 281n. 47, 282n. 50, 284n. 7, 286n. 50
Caulonia, city in Magna Graecia 181, 182
Celtiberians, people of the Iberian peninsula of Celtic origins 69, 87, 173, 192, 206, 263n. 56, 286n. 52
Celts, also referred to as Gauls 34, 49, 51, 85, 86, 87, 89, 90, 91, 102, 103, 106, 107, 108, 109, 123, 250n. 35
at Cannae 131
high casualty numbers 112, 133, 215
Centenius, Gaius, Roman propraetor (217 BCE) 113
Ceres see Demeter
Cézanne, Impressionist painter, on Hamilcar and Hannibal 43, 254n. 2
Charaeus, no longer extant source of Polybius 283n. 70
Cicero 2, 4, 14, 17, 85, 89, 157, 161, 223, 224, 232, 243n. 40, 245n. 57, 254n. 3, 266n. 35, 268n. 70, 273n. 22, 279n. 80, 295nn. 4, 19, 21, 296n. 37
circumcision, Phoenician tradition of 17
Cirta (modern Constantine), Numidian capital held by Syphax in period of Hannibalic war 202, 206, 290n. 38
Cisalpine Gaul 84
Cissa 117
Clastidium (modern Casteggio), in northern Italy 104
Claudia, sister of Publius Claudius Pulcher, consul defeated off Drepanum by Carthaginians in First Punic War (249 BCE) 46
Claudius Nero, Gaius, commander sent to reinforce Iberia after death of elder Scipio brothers (211 BCE); consul (207 BCE) 174, 188, 189, 190, 191, 192, 284n. 4, 285n. 34, 295n. 13

Claudius Pulcher, Appius, commander in
    Sicily (215 BCE) 153, 155, 278n. 65,
    280n. 23
Claudius Pulcher, Publius, consul defeated
    by Carthaginians off Drepanum (249
    BCE) 46
Cleopatra, last of the Hellenistic
    monarchs 24, 297n. 47
Clupea (Map 2, modern Kelibia) 38, 39, 40
Coelius Antipater, source, now lost, for the
    period of the Punic Wars 89, 264n. 70,
    268n. 70, 269n. 10, 286n. 55
coins, coinage
    Carthaginian 46, 50, 184, 244n. 43,
        249nn. 13, 14, 255n. 10, 260n. 17,
        267n. 46, 294n. 21
    Hannibalic (Barcid) 128, 196, 261n. 33,
        273n. 27, 287nn. 63, 64
    Mercenary 54, 55, 256n. 24, 257n. 39
    Roman 141, 149, 183
Cold War nostalgia 232
Colonia Iulia Concordia Karthago, Roman
    colony at the site of Carthage 2
    Gracchan colony of 122 BCE 239n. 4
comitia centuriata, assembly of Roman
    citizens 115, 282n. 59
Compsa (Map 1), strategic city on border of
    Campania/Apulia 141, 276n. 8
conscription, Carthaginian 51
Constantine see Cirta
Constantine, fourth century CE Roman
    emperor, dream before battle of Milvian
    Bridge 89
Corcyra (modern Corfu) 181
Corinth and Corinthian 13, 243n. 38,
    261n. 38, 275n. 56
Cornelius Lentulus, Lucius, Roman
    senator 79
Cornelius Nepos
    biographer of Hamilcar and Hannibal 44,
        64, 67, 240n. 14, 257n. 33
    erroneous claims 219, 290n. 48, 294n. 28
Cornelius Scipio Aemilianus, Publius,
    adopted grandson of Scipio Africanus,
    destroys Carthage in 146 BCE 233,
    253n. 82, 283n. 70, 287n. 2
Cornelius Scipio Africanus, Publius, referred
    to here as Scipio 176–177, 198–217,
    219, 226, 230, 283n. 71
    at Locri with Hannibal 202–203, 289nn.
        26, 27, 28
    at Tarraco (modern Tarragona) 177
    Baecula, battle of (208 BCE) 184–185,
        284n. 9
    Great Plains, battle of (203 BCE) 206–207

burning of the camps (203
    BCE) 205–206, 290n. 37
consul (205 BCE) 199–200, 288n. 11
curule aedile 175, 282nn. 58, 65
defends Hannibal in Rome 22,
    293n. 13
legend and divine parentage 176, 283n.
    68, 292n. 1
fights at Cannae 175
founds Roman colony at Italica 194,
    286n. 48
Iberians and Celtiberians 192, 282n. 50,
    283n. 83, 286n. 50
Ilipa, battle of (206 BCE) 193, 269n. 17,
    286n. 45
in John Milton's Paradise Lost 176, 283n.
    66
invasion of Africa, courts the Numdian
    kings (204–203 BCE) 198–200,
    201–202, 203–204, 245n. 60, 282n.
    57, 286n. 47, 286n. 54, 287n. 4,
    288nn. 7, 8, 9, 16, 289n. 30, 290n. 33,
    34, 35
kept in charge of army in Africa through
    allies in the Senate at Rome 205, 288n.
    12, 292n. 68
mutiny of troops in Spain 194, 286n. 52,
    287n. 61, 288n. 13
negotiations with Carthage 207–209,
    219, 290n. 43, 45, 46, 291n. 61
oath to defend the Republic 175
proconsular imperium in Spain (210
    BCE) 175, 177, 246n. 78, 282n. 59
saves his father at Ticinus (218 BCE) 103,
    269n. 10, 282n. 63
at New Carthage (209 BCE) 178–181,
    262n. 47, 283n. 77
troop numbers 204–205, 283n. 80,
    286n. 43, 288n. 15
with Hannibal at Ephesus 224, 234
Zama, battle of (202 BCE) 214–217, 218,
    292nn. 73, 74
Cornelius Scipio, Gnaeus 94, 110, 117,
    118, 171, 272nn. 62, 67, 281n. 45
death 173–174
Cornelius Scipio, Publius (the elder) 84, 90,
    91, 92, 93, 102–105, 110, 118, 171,
    269nn. 8, 15, 270n. 32, 281n. 45
death 173–174
Corsica 11, 83, 258n. 54
Cortona (Map 1) 111, 270n. 35
corvus (corax), Roman adaptation to naval
    tactics in the First Punic War 36, 37,
    40, 253nn. 67, 75, 254n. 86
Cosa, Etruscan port of 114, 251n. 44

Cosentia (Map 1 modern Cosenza) 183, 195, 203

Cretans, unit sent to Rome from Hiero II of Syracuse after Trasimeno 110

Crispinus, Titus Quinctius Roman consul (208 BCE) 186, 187, 285n. 24

Crotona (Map 1) city in Bruttium 183, 196, 230, 287n. 62, 291n. 55

crucifixion, as punishment for failed Carthaginian generals 20, 32, 55, 246n. 82, 258n. 51

twenty-five slaves crucified in Rome (217 BCE) 127

Cumae (Map 1), city on the coast of Campania 121, 144, 147, 276n. 22

curule chair, gift to important client kings (i.e. Syphax and Ptolemy of Egypt) 172

Cynoscephalae, final battle between Philip V of Macedon and Romans (197 BCE) 223

Cyrus, Persian king 89, 266n. 35

David, painter of the French revolution 237

Delphi, oracle of Apollo at 135, 200, 242n. 27, 275n. 58

Demeter (Roman Ceres), goddess of grain and fertility, brought to Carthage from Sicily 22, 248n. 96

worship at Rome cancelled after Cannae 135

Demetrius of Pharos (Illyrian king) 78, 150, 151

Demetrius Poliorcetes, Hellenistic king 27, 29, 34, 249n. 17

Helepolis, Hellenistic siege engine 27

deserters

Roman 52, 53, 114, 122, 126, 128, 158, 182, 208, 219

Carthaginian 83, 170, 237, 281n. 36

dictator and dictatorship 115

Dido, Queen of Carthage, also known as Elissa (Greek) and Elishat (Phoenician) 8–11, 13, 22, 44, 242n. 21, 247n. 93, 259n. 6

and Aeneas 9–10, 230, 241n. 14, 242nn. 15, 17

Dionysius of Halicarnassus 266nn. 21, 29

Dionysius of Syracuse 249n. 19

Djebel es Serra (referred to as The Saw) 58

Drepanum (Map 1, modern Trapani), Carthaginian allied city on the west coast of Sicily 30, 40, 45, 46, 47, Plate 2

Durance river (Map 2) 94, 188, 267nn. 52, 54

earrings, as worn by Carthaginian men 15, 16

Ebro river (Map 2) 74, 75, 81, 88, 89, 90, 117, 118, 171, 177, 178, 264n. 78, 267n. 42, 272n. 65, 286n. 52

treaty of 71, 72, 75, 263n. 64

Ebusus (Ibiza), first Carthaginian colony founded seventh century BCE 11, 118

Ecnomus, battle of see under First Punic War

elephants 15, 16, 18, 29, 40, 53, 54, 56, 69, 137, 172, 184, 190, 191, 206, 219, 249n. 13, 267n. 48, 286n. 43, 289n. 19, 293n. 7

in Hannibal's army 74, 84, 88, 103, 106, 107, 109, 149, 215, 216, 266n. 32, 267n. 47, 267nn. 49, 50, 51; crossing the Alps 93–94, 96, 97, 98, 238; crossing the Rhône 91, 92–93, 263n. 55

Elishat see Dido

Elissa see Dido

Elymians, Carthaginian allies in Sicily 12, 255n. 8, 271n. 53

Emporia, cities on the coast of North Africa 56, 257n. 47

Emporium (Empurias, Map 2, modern Ampurias), Greek/Massalian colony on the coast of Iberia 117, 177

Ennius, author of second century BCE Latin epic poetry on Roman history 127, 228, 230, 283n 66, 292n. 1, 295nn. 4, 11

Epicydes, envoy of Hannibal sent to king of Syracuse (215 BCE) 153, 155, 158

Epipolae, neighbourhood in Syracuse 156, 158, 278n. 68

Epirus (Map 1), Adriatic kingdom of Hellenistic king, Pyrrhus 29, 30, 234

equites (knights) 137, 141, 143

Erytheia (Map 2) equated with Gades by ancient authors 87

Eryx (Map 1, modern Erice) 30, 45, 47, 49, 116, 255n. 8, 256n. 25, 271n. 53, Plate 2

Eshmun, Carthaginian deity 245n. 60, 295n. 15

Temple at Carthage 17, 245n. 59

Temple at New Carthage 71, 178

meeting place of the Senate 17

Etruria and Etruscans 140, 142, 177, 188, 276n. 12,

traditional allies of the Carthaginians, 11, 12, 14, 240n. 8, 244n. 48, 271n. 48; and see Alalia

Lar Felsnas, Etruscan who 'fought with Hannibal's men' 115

Etruria and Etruscans (*cont.*)
  unsettled allies of the Romans in Hannibalic
    War 185, 285*n*. 29, 290*n*. 36
Eumenes II, Attalid king (ruled 197–159
    BCE) 226
Ezekiel, Book of 8

Fabius Maximus (*Cunctator*), Quintus 57,
    79, 126, 127, 147, 168, 185, 200, 230,
    264*n*. 77, 272*nn*. 58, 2
  dictator (217 BCE) 115, 117, 120–125,
    271*n*. 50
  consul (in 233 BCE, 228 BCE, 215 BCE,
    214 BCE, 209 BCE) 148
  tricked by Hannibal in Campania near
    Calles 122
  vows a temple to Venus Erycina 116,
    272*n*. 56
  takes Tarentum 181–182, 284*n*. 4
  debate in Senate over Scipio's
    command 199, 282*n*. 57
Fabius Maximus, Quintus (son of
    *Cunctator*) 163
Fabius Pictor, Quintus, author of an
    annalistic history of the period of the
    Punic Wars in Greek 69, 96, 239*n*. 6,
    252*n*. 59, 268*n*. 62
  sent to Delphi after Cannae (216
    BCE) 135
Faesulae (modern Fiesole) 110
First Punic War (264–241 BCE) 16, 20, 28,
    31–48
  start 31–33; and *see* Mamertines and
    Pyrrhus
  phases 34
  siege of Agrigentum 34–35
  Mylae (Map 1), battle of (260
    BCE) 35–36
  Ecnomus (Map 1), battle of (256
    BCE) 37, 38, 253*n*. 73
  invasion of Regulus 37, 39, 40; legend of
    Regulus *see* Atilius Regulus
  Xanthippus 40, 48, 254*n*. 83
  Hamilcar commands in Sicily (247
    BCE) 42–48
  Carthaginian loss (241 BCE) 46–48
  peace after 47; *and see* Lutatius
Flaminius Nepos, Gaius, Roman consul (217
    BCE) 108, 110–113, 115, 117, 127,
    270*n*. 32
Flaubert, Gustave nineteenth-century French
    author of *Salammbô* 50, 249*n*. 9,
    256*n*. 23, 257*n*. 37
Freud, Sigmund, on Hannibal and
    Hamilcar 43, 254*nn*. 1, 2

Fulvius Flaccus, Gnaeus, brother of consul for
    212 BCE and praetor in that year 167
Fulvius Flaccus, Quintus, Roman consul
    (212 BCE) 166, 168, 169, 189, 199,
    280*n*. 23, 281*n*. 33, 291*n*. 55

Gaddafi, Mu'ammar 238
Gades (also Cadiz/Gadiera/Gadir, Map 2) 8,
    63, 64, 87, 193, 194, 195, 241*nn*. 7, 9,
    246*n*. 66, 260*nn*. 15, 16, 17, 18, 263*n*.
    65, 266*nn*. 21, 22, 25, 37, 283*n*. 75,
    288*nn*. 7, 9
Gaetulians, Numidian tribe south of
    Carthaginian territory 86
Gaius Livius, Roman commander at
    Tarentum 164
Gauls 66, 71, 83, 84, 87, 135, 136, 148,
    191, 208, 257*n*. 43, 262*n*. 49, 268*nn*.
    69, 71, 293*n*. 9
  *see also* Celts
Gelo, son and co-regent of Hiero, Syracusan
    king († 215 BCE) 153, 278*n*. 60
Genua (maps 1 and 2, modern Genoa) 195,
    208, 209
Geronium 124, 125, 273*n*. 17
*gerousia*, Aristotle's terms for the Senate of
    Carthage 19
Geryon, cattle of 87
Gisgo, Carthaginian envoy sent from
    Hannibal to Philip V (215 BCE) 151
Gisgo, Carthaginian general of the First
    Punic War and Mercenary War 49, 50,
    52, 55, 56, 256*n*. 21,
Gortyn, in Crete 225
Grumentum (Map 1) 189
Guadalimar, river in Iberia 70
Guadelete, river in Iberia 63

Hadrumentum (Map 2, modern Sousse) 14,
    210, 212, 216, 218, 219, 222, 254*n*. 4,
    257*n*. 47, 291*n*. 65
Hamilcar Barca, Hannibal's father 13, 69,
    72, 77, 171, 228, 240*n*. 14, 243*n*. 34,
    246*nn*. 73, 82, 254*n*. 3, 255*nn*. 5, 6, 7,
    8, 16, 259*n*. 6, 261*nn*. 32, 34, 35, 36,
    262*n*. 52, 287*n*. 3
  hostility to Rome 61–62, 81, 254*n*. 2,
    259*n*. 8, 293*n*. 16, 294*n*. 2
  in the First Punic War 40, 42–48, 51, 52,
    53, 116, 254*n*. 83, 282*n*. 50
  in the Mercenary War 53–60, 256*nn*. 26,
    28, 257*nn*. 36, 37, 40, 44
  in Iberia 62–67, 194, 259*n*. 9, 260*nn*.
    21, 22, 261*n*. 26, 263*n*. 66
  lion cubs 62

meeting with Roman embassy (231 BCE) 66
death 66–68, 261*n.* 31
Hamilcar Rhodanus, Carthaginian envoy to Alexander the Great 25, 248*n.* 5
Hamilcar, Carthaginian commander at Himera (480 BCE) 12, 247*n.* 93
Hamilcar, commander of Carthaginian troops at Locri (205 BCE) 202
Hammamet 58
Hannibal 'the Rhodian', commander of a fleet in the First Punic War (250 BCE) 29, 248*n.* 5
Hannibal Barca
  Alps crossing 4, 85, 86–89, 95–99, 266*n.* 37, 268*nn.* 58, 65, 285*n.* 30, 297*n.* 46
  army 85–86, 267*n.* 39, 279*n.* 79
  at Cannae 128–134, 270*n.* 33, 271*n.* 41, 274*n.* 33; *see also* Cannae
  at Capua 121, 137, 142–144, 145–147, 165–168, 276*nn.* 21, 25, 296*nn.* 37, 38; *see also* Capua
  at Locri 202–203, 289*nn.* 26, 27; *see also* Locri
  at New Carthage 73, 74, 76, 83, 85, 88, 90, 263*n.* 60, 267*n.* 42; *see also* New Carthage
  at Saguntum 74–80, 83, 87, 263*nn.* 58, 62, 64–67, 69, 264*nn.* 73, 74, 75; *see also* Saguntum
  at Tarentum 152, 162, 163–166, 181–182; *see also* Tarentum
  at the gates of Rome in 211 BCE 167–169, 281*nn.* 32–34
  birth 42
  childhood, at Carthage and in Iberia 31, 48, 65, 67, 86, 248*n.* 1, 255*n.* 19
  dream 88–89, 254*n.* 2, 266*nn.* 35, 37, 267*n.* 39
  escape from Campania in 217 BCE using oxen 123–124, 273*n.* 15
  exile and death at Libyssa 195–183/182 BCE 218–225, 226, 235, 238, 294*n.* 33, 296*n.* 31, 297*n.* 44
  eye infection (one-eyed) 109–110, 218, 270*nn.* 28, 29
  genius 228
  Hasdrubal's head 192
  in Bruttium 192, 195–196, 202, 203, 209, 287*nn.* 63, 64
  in disguise 107–108, 270*nn.* 20–22
  leadership philosophy 25, 27, 65, 82, 85–86, 107, 117, 195, 229, 249*nn.* 13–14, 265*nn.* 16–18, 267*n.* 39
  myth management 87–88, 176, 266*n.* 28

oath of enmity against Rome 61–62, 175, 224, 259*nn.* 5, 6, 8
  pilgrimage to Gades 87, 260*n.* 18, 266*nn.* 23–25
  post-war at Carthage, prosecution, *sufetate* 221–222, 293*nn.* 13–15, 294*nn.* 21, 22
  relationship with courtesan at Salapia 163, 280*nn.* 15, 16
  *res gestae* at Temple of Juno Lacinia 84, 150, 196, 210, 230, 287*n.* 62, 289*n.* 26
  Rhône crossing 90–93, 94, 267*nn.* 48–51
  speaks Greek 48, 65, 214, 224, 292*n.* 73
  strategy 88, 102, 112–113, 139–140, 146, 147, 149, 183, 220, 238, 269*nn.* 5, 19, 270*n.* 20, 271*n.* 46, 272*n.* 2, 275*nn.* 55, 3, 281*n.* 39, 293*n.* 14
  Ticinus, battle of *see* Ticinus river
  Trasimeno, battle of *see* Trasimeno
  Trebia, battle of *see* Trebia
  Zama, battle of *see* Zama
Hannibal, general in the Mercenary War crucified by Libyan leader Mathos 58, 258*n.* 51
Hanno, called 'the Great' enemy of the Barcids 51, 53, 56, 58, 63, 79, 137, 257*nn.* 45, 46, 262*n.* 52, 264*n.* 79, 
Hanno, Carthaginian commander at Agrigentum (*c.* 262 BCE) 35
Hanno, Carthaginian commander at Capua (211 BCE) 169
Hanno, Carthaginian navigator, fourth century BCE 13, 243*n.* 36
Hanno, character in Plautus 15, 16, 23, 244*n.* 49, 245*n.* 56
Hanno, commander crucified during the Mercenary War in Sardinia (*c.* 241–237 BCE) 55
Hanno, commander left in the region north of the Ebro river in Iberia (218 BCE) 90, 117, 267*n.* 42
Hanno, commander sent to Iberia to replace Hasdrubal Barca (208 BCE) 185
Hanno, son of Bomilcar the *sufet*, Hannibal's cavalry commander (and nephew?) xiii, 91, 132, 146, 165, 166
Hannos (204 BCE), two young cavalry commanders sent to harass Scipio 204
Harris, Thomas, author of *Silence of the Lambs* 238
Hasdrubal Barca, Hannibal's younger brother 65, 67, 243*n.* 34
  command in Iberia 83, 117, 118, 171, 178, 183–184, 283*n.* 75, 289*n.* 24

Hasdrubal Barca (*cont.*)
 losses and revolt of Iberian allies (217–216
  BCE) 171–172, 180
 defeats the elder Scipio brothers (211
  BCE) 172–174
 defeated by Scipio at Baecula (208
  BCE) 184, 200, 284n. 9
 crosses the Alps 185, 188, 285n. 21
 battle of Metaurus and death and head
  delivered to Hannibal (207 BCE) 180,
  189–191, 192, 285nn. 29, 31, 33, 34,
  35, 36, 38
 shield of, in Rome 231, 295n. 16
Hasdrubal, called *Haedus* (the kid) 293n. 16
Hasdrubal, Carthaginian commander in the
 First Punic War against Regulus'
 invasion 39
Hasdrubal, Hamilcar's son in law, *Trierarch*,
 chief naval officer and Hannibal's
 uncle 66, 67, 69, 257n. 37, 262nn. 40,
 52
 defends Hamilcar in Carthage 68, 259nn.
  2, 9
 commands in Iberia (*c.* 229/228 BCE) 68,
  69, 77, 228, 261nn. 25, 35, 38, 262n.
  42
 Ebro treaty 72
 founder of New Carthage 70, 71, 262n.
  48
 assassination (*c.* 221 BCE) 72, 73
Hasdrubal, Hannibal's 'officer in charge of
 services' (217/216 BCE) 123, 125, 132,
 273n. 14
Hasdrubal, son of Gisgo, father of
 Sophonisba 204, 282n. 50, 293n. 4,
 290n. 41
 command in Iberia 172, 173, 178, 184,
  192, 283n. 75
 defeated at Ilipa (206 BCE) 192, 284n. 9,
  288n. 7
 relationship with Syphax 194, 201, 204,
  286n. 47, 281n. 45, 286n. 47
 marriage of his daughter 201, 205, 282n.
  53
 defeated at the Great Plains (203
  BCE) 204–206
Heirkte (Heircte), strategic area in Sicily near
 Panormus (Palermo) taken by Hamilcar
 in the First Punic War (247–245
 BCE) 45, 255n. 8
Helice, city in Iberia 67
Hellenistic kingdoms and rulers 5, 22, 23,
 24–27, 29, 35, 65, 89, 134, 150, 152,
 177, 223–225, 248nn. 1, 7, 249nn. 11,
 12, 250n. 24, 252n. 63, 254n. 4, 257n.

37, 261nn. 25, 33, 38, 262n. 40, 269n.
 19, 279n. 3
 arms race 27, 156, 249n. 16,
Henna, modern Enna, in Sicily 158
Heraclea (Map 1) in Magna Graecia 30,
 165
Heraclea Minoa (Map 1) in Sicily 37, 155
Herakles, Hercules, Heraklean Way 8, 21,
 63, 64, 67, 86–88, 89, 94, 102, 108,
 109, 116, 229, 235, 249n. 13, 259n. 5,
 260n. 18, 266n. 21, 266nn. 27, 29, 30,
 31, 268n. 70
Herdonea, battles of (212 and 210
 BCE) 167, 280–281n. 29
Hermandica (Helmantica, Map 2, modern
 Salamanca) 74, 262n. 53
Hesiod 87
*hexireme*, decked war ship known as a
 six 28, 37
Hiero II, King of Syracuse (ruled *c.* 271–215
 BCE) 32, 34, 47, 57, 110, 149, 152,
 153, 155, 156, 249n. 11, 251n. 46,
 270n. 30, 278nn. 59, 60, 279n. 73
Hieronymus, grandson of Hiero of Syracuse
 (ruled 215–214 BCE) 153–155
Himera (Map 1), river in Sicily 154
Himera, battle of *c.* 480 BCE 12, 242n. 27,
 247n. 93
Himilco, Carthaginian commander sent to
 Iberia (216 BCE) 171
Himilco, Carthaginian commander, captures
 Agrigentum (215/214 BCE), dies at
 Syracuse (212 BCE) 155, 157, 159
Hippo Acra (also known as Hippo
 Diarrhytus, maps 1 and 3, modern
 Bizerte) 26, 53, 56, 289n. 17
Hippo Regius (modern Annaba) 202,
 288–289n. 17
Hippocrates, envoy of Hannibal sent to
 Syracuse (215 BCE) 153, 155, 159
Horace, Roman poet (first century BCE) 41,
 ·180, 191, 232, 254n. 88

Iberia and the Iberian Peninsula (Map 2,
 modern Spain and Portugal 4, 44,
 61–81, 82, 83, 84, 86, 90, 94, 97, 100,
 110, 117–118, 169, 170–175,
 177–179, 180–181, 183–185,
 192–195, 200, 204, 208, 213, 214,
 240n. 15, 241n. 9, 260n. 17, 263nn.
 56, 59, 281nn. 37, 45, 282nn. 51, 56,
 58
 *see also under* Hamilcar Barca, in Iberia;
  Hannibal Barca, childhood; Hasdrubal
  Barca, command in Iberia; Cornelius

Scipio Africanus, Iberians and Celtiberians

Iberians 34, 49, 51, 60, 89, 131–132 (at Cannae), 175, 184, 188, 191, 206, 260*nn*. 20, 24, 262*n*. 54, 282*n*. 60, 283*n*. 83, 284*n*. 8, 286*nn*. 49, 53

*Iliad* 108, 270*n*. 22

Ilipa (Map 2), sometimes Silpia as in Livy 28.12 (206 BCE) 193, 194, 199, 269*n*. 17, 284*n*. 9, 286*nn*. 41, 45, 52

Illurgia (Map 2), Iberian stronghold 184, 194, 286*n*. 50

Illyria and Illyrians (Map 1) 66, 78, 128, 150, 151, 152, 261*n*. 27, 273*n*. 31, 277*n*. 47

Imilce, named as Hannibal's wife, from Castulo 70, 73, 77, 262*nn*. 41, 52, 286*n*. 50

indemnity, paid by Carthage to Rome 59, 66, 81, 208, 221, 222, 293*n*. 5, 294*n*. 21

Indibilis *see* Andobales

Indortes, Iberian leader who resisted Hamilcar Barca 65

Insubres, tribe allied to Hannibal in northern Italy 98, 101

Irish 237, 254*n*. 1, 296*n*. 38, 297*n*. 43

Isère river 95, 268*n*. 58

Italica, Roman colony near modern Seville founded (206 BCE) by Scipio after Illipa 194

Italy and the Italian allies 45, 112, 114, 141, 270*n*. 20, 281*n*. 38

James I (of England, VI of Scotland) 236, 264*n*. 74

Jason and the Argonauts 99, 269*n*. 77

Jonson, Ben 78, 242*n*. 15, 264*n*. 74

Jugurtha, Numidian king 231, 243*n*. 30, 295*n*. 17

Julius Caesar, Gaius 2, 263*n*. 56, 265*n*. 3

Junius Pera, Marcus, dictator in 216 BCE after Cannae 136

Juno Lacinia, temple of and the Lacinian promontory 150, 196, 210, 230

Jupiter 61, 82, 88, 116, 231, 258*n*. 1, 271*n*. 51, 272*n*. 56
*see also* Ba'al

Juvenal, Roman satirist 134, 218, 233, 268*n*. 65, 293*n*. 11, 294*n*. 33, 296*n*. 26

*Karchedonias*, Greek for the Carthaginian 15

Kerkina (Map 2 ) island off modern Sfax 222, 223, 289*n*. 18

Kerkouane (Map 1) 39

Kutuzov, General Mikhail Illarionovich 120, 270*n*. 29

Laelius, Gaius, Scipio's trusted lieutenant 178, 200, 202, 206, 215, 216, 283*n*. 78, 288*n*. 17, 289*n*. 23, 292*n*. 68

Lake Avernus, Hannibal receives Tarentine enovys (214 BCE) 162

Lampedusa, ceded by Carthage in the First Punic War 47

Lanassa, daughter of Agathocles, wife of Pyrrhus 29, 30

Latins, allies of the Romans 162, 185, 269*n*. 13, 271*n*. 47, 280*n*. 9, 288*n*. 15

Lebanon, modern name for Phoenician homeland 8, 240*n*. 18

Leontinoi (Map 1) 30, 155

Lepcis Magna 12, 235, 246*n*. 72, 257–258*n*. 47, 296*n*. 32

Lesser Syrtis 202

Levant 6, 8, 11, 13, 243

Levanzo (Aegates islands, Map 1), location of the final sea battle of the First Punic War (March of 241 BCE) 47

Libyans 9, 10, 11, 26, 39, 49, 50, 51, 52–55, 57–60, 83, 86, 215, 234, 235, 238, 256*nn*. 24, 31, 32, 257*n*. 39, 258*n*. 57, 259*n*. 5, 262*n*. 54, 271*n*. 41, 296*n*. 30
infantry in Hannibal's army armed with weapons from Trasimeno 113, 132

Libyphoenician 50, 52, 53, 83, 86, 160, 256*nn*. 25, 32, 258*nn*. 47, 57

Libyssa *see* Hannibal Barca, exile and death at Libyssa

Licinius Crassus, Publius, consul (205 BCE) 199

Liguria and Ligurians, mercenary soldiers used by Carthage and Hannibal 34, 49, 50, 51, 83, 85, 89, 90, 103, 195, 200, 205, 209, 215, 269*n*. 10, 270*n*. 20, 291*n*. 59, 293*n*. 9

Lilybaeum (Map 1, modern Marsala) 29, 30, 37, 40, 47, 49, 52, 101, 155, 201, 203, 250*n*. 29

Lipara (Map 1, modern Lipari) 32, 35, 36
*see also* Aeolian Islands

Livy, as author of *Ab urbe condita* 239*nn*. 2, 6
on Hannibal's character 1, 3, 62, 68–69, 80, 85–86, 177, 196, 220, 228, 239*n*. 7, 277*n*. 45, 283*n*. 72, 287*nn*. 59, 61, 62

on Capua 142–144, 145–146, 276n. 17
confused chronology and numbers in
    Iberia 78, 172, 174, 260n. 24, 263nn.
    58, 62, 281n. 40, 282n. 47, 283nn. 73,
    77, 284nn. 1, 6, 8, 286n. 46
on the period before Zama vs
    Polybius 209, 290n. 46, 292n. 74
as the source for later historians and
    Medieval and Renaissance writers 78,
    80–81, 232, 236, 296n. 34
Locri (in Bruttium, Map 1) 45, 250n. 27,
    252n. 54, 293n. 15
    pro Hannibalic city 150, 183, 186, 187
    first meeting of Hannibal and
        Scipio 202–203, 289n. 26
Lucania and Lucanians 89, 101, 137, 141,
    146, 163, 166, 182, 186, 189, 195,
    280n. 26
Luceria (Map 1) 119, 124
Lucian of Samosata, author of second
    century CE comic prose Dialogues of the
    Dead 234–235, 296nn. 27, 28
Lusitania 49, 50, 193, 283n. 75
Lutatius, peace of to end the First Punic War
    (241 BCE) 47, 52, 59, 255nn. 14, 16,
    263n. 64

Macedon and Macedonians 24, 25, 27, 29,
    78, 150–151, 152, 162, 163, 181, 195,
    196, 197, 201, 223, 234, 249nn. 17,
    19, 261n. 27, 277n. 48, 287n. 67
Magilus, Celtic chieftain, ally of
    Hannibal 92
Magna Graecia 30, 161, 162, 164, 165,
    183, 185, 250n. 27, 280n. 8, 293n. 14
Magnesia, battle of (190 BCE) 225
Mago Barca, Hannibal's youngest
    brother 65, 67, 243n. 34, 260n. 22
    travels with Hannibal to Italy 86, 106,
        109, 132, 144
    sent to Carthage with rings from the dead
        equites at Cannae 136–138, 140
    diverted to Spain and campaigns
        there 171–172, 173, 180, 184, 192,
        275n. 67, 283n. 75
    defeated with Hasdrubal Gisgo at
        Illipa 193
    at Gades 194–195, 288n. 9
    at Genua (modern Genoa) and among the
        Ligurians 195, 200–201, 205, 211,
        215, 286n. 55, 289n. 19
    death 208–209, 290n. 48, 291n. 59,
        293n. 9, 294n. 28
Mago, 'the Samnite', commander in
    Hannibal's army 166

Mago, agronomist and author of a famous
    Carthaginian treatise 21, 244n. 41,
    247n. 86
Mago, Carthaginian envoy sent from
    Hannibal to Philip V 151, 152
Mago, Carthaginian general who offers
    alliance to Rome during Pyrrhus'
    invasion 250n. 34
Maharbal, son of Himilco, Hannibal's
    lieutenant 77, 113, 132, 134, 264n.
    71, 275n. 54
Mamertines, mercenaries named the 'men of
    Mamers' after Oscan god of war 32,
    33, 251n. 50
Manduria, town east of Tarentum 181
Manlius Torquatus, Titus, Roman dictator
    (208 BCE) 187
Manlius Vulso, Lucius, sent to control
    the Boii Gauls (218 BCE) 39, 84,
    102
Marcellus, Marcus Claudius, consul 141,
    186, 230, 279n. 80
    defends Nola (216 BCE) 144–145
    elected consul but disallowed 148
    goes to Sicily in 214 BCE and takes
        Syracuse (212 BCE) 155–159, 161,
        163, 167, 278nn. 65, 66, 279nn. 79,
        84, 4, 5, 284n. 4
    as consul (208 BCE) dies fighting
        Hannibal 186, 285n. 24
    poem by Horace 187
Marcellus, Marcus Claudius, son of
    consul 191, 284n. 16
Masaesyli, Numidian realm of Syphax 54,
    172, 199, 206, 213
Masinissa, prince then king of the
    Massyli 173, 199, 201, 202, 203, 206,
    207, 212, 213, 214, 215, 216, 218,
    219, 221, 222, 228, 231, 257n. 36,
    282nn. 52, 53, 54, 283n. 70, 287nn. 2,
    3, 5, 288nn. 6–10, 289nn. 22–24, 30,
    290nn. 39, 40, 46, 291n. 66, 292n. 2,
    295n. 17
Massalia, Massalians (modern Marseille) 11,
    66, 71, 76, 90, 91, 92, 117, 118, 177,
    242nn. 22, 23, 262n. 50
Massyli, Numidian realm of Masinissa 54,
    199, 202, 206, 288n. 17
Mathos, Libyan leader of mercenary
    rebellion 52, 53, 55, 56, 58, 59
Mauri, Numidian kingdom 54, 201, 289n.
    24
McGuinness, Frank 237
Melqart, important god at Carthage and
    Tyre 9, 67, 102, 109, 116

ritual of resurrection, *egersis* 247*n*. 93, 266*nn*. 24, 25

temple at Gades and syncretised to Herakles 21, 63, 64, 87, 247*n*. 89, 260*n*. 18, 266*n*. 22, 271*n*. 53

Hannibal's pilgrimage and patronage 21, 87, 88, 229, 261*n*. 33, 274*n*. 42

tribute paid by Carthage to temple at Tyre 13, 243*n*. 34

tied to the foundation of Carthage 13, 22

Mens, Roman cult of 116–117, 272*n*. 58

mercenary soldiers 26, 32, 34, 50, 51, 59, 85, 216, 252*n*. 64, 256*n*. 21, 275*n*. 1

Mercenary War (241–238 BCE) 52–60, 63, 81, 137, 198, 255*n*. 18, 256*nn*. 19, 28, 257*n*. 34, 258*n*. 56, 260*n*. 15, 261*n*. 35, 281*n*. 43

Messana (Map 1, modern Messina) 32, 33, 35, 202, 246*n*. 82

Metapontum (Map 1) 165, 182, 189, 250*n*. 27

Metaurus (Map 1), battle of (207 BCE) 190, 191, 192, 193, 284*n*. 4, 285*nn*. 30, 35, 295*n*. 13

Metellus, Quintus Caecilius, debate about end of Hannibalic War 233

Metilius, Marcus, Tribune in Rome (217 BCE) 125

Miller, Arthur, Carthaginians and Sicilians in *A View From the Bridge* 238, 248*n*. 99, 297*n*. 48

Minucius Rufus, Marcus, *magister equitum* and the co-dictator in Rome (217 BCE) 115, 121, 122, 124, 125, 126, 132, 273*nn*. 20, 21

Monte Tifata, location of Hannibal's camp near Capua 146, 167

Moors 86

Morgantina 157

Motya (Mozia, Map 1) 244*n*. 47, 246*n*. 66, 250*n*. 29, 254*n*. 87

Muttines, Hannibal's Libyphoenician commander at Agrigentum (212–210 BCE) 160

Mylae (Map 1, modern Milazzo), battle of (260 BCE) 35, 36, 37, 247*n*. 82

Myrcan, Carthaginian senator sent to Philip V of Macedon (215 BCE) 152

Naevius, Gnaeus, author Latin epic *Bellum Poenicum*, third century BCE 230, 242*n*. 17, 250*n*. 38, 295*nn*. 11, 12

Naravas, prince of the Massyli, son-in-law of Hamilcar Barca xiii, 54, 68, 257*nn*. 36, 37, 287*n*. 3, 288*n*. 7

Neapolis (Map 1, modern Naples/Napoli) 121, 141, 252*n*. 54,

Neapolis, neighbourhood of Syracuse 156, 158

New Carthage (Carthago Nova, Map 2, modern Cartagena) 70–71, 73, 118, 194, 262*nn*. 43, 44, 45, 46, 48, 263*n*. 59,

founded and constructed by Hasdrubal *c.* 229–225 BCE 70, 246*n*. 67

Hannibal at 221–218 BCE 73–74, 76, 83, 85, 88, 90, 97, 264*n*. 76, 265*n*. 9, 267*n*. 42,

taken by Scipio in 209 BCE 177–179, 180, 181, 183, 184, 280*n*. 11, 283*n*. 77, 284*n*. 1

Nola (Map 1) 141, 144, 145, 147, 148, 158, 162, 186, 276*n*. 22

Nuceria 121, 145, 276*n*. 18

Numidia and Numidians

as allies of Carthage 49, 54, 60, 68, 83, 86, 140, 168, 170, 172, 174, 184, 186, 190, 193, 202, 205–206, 215–216, 229, 257*n*. 36, 262*n*. 54, 281*n*. 36, 287*nn*. 3, 5

as allies of Rome 39, 192, 199, 206, 213, 293*n*. 7

cavalry 86, 92, 103, 104, 105, 113, 131, 137, 164, 189

in rebellion during the Mercenary War 50, 281*n*. 43

kingdoms 60, 68, 172, 173, 198–199, 212, 221–222, 231, 247*n*. 86, 258*n*. 57, 288*n*. 7, 289*n*. 23, 290*n*. 30, 294*n*. 19; *see also* Masaesyli, Massyli and Mauri

*see also* Masinissa; Syphax

Octavian *see* Augustus

Olcades, Iberian people, capital Althaea 73

omens and prodigies 61, 62, 108, 111, 127, 135, 188

Onussa 88

Ophellas, Ptolemaic allied king of Cyrene in the late fourth century BCE 26

Orissi (also Oretani), Iberian tribe 69, 70, 77, 261*n*. 30

Ortygia, neighbourhood of Syracuse 156, 158

Oscan, language 32, 121, 142, 144, 251*n*. 43

Ostia, port of 114

ostrich egg vessels 13

Otacilius Crassus, Titus, Roman commander Sicily (216–215 BCE) 149

Ovid, poet of Augustan Rome 191, 206, 232, 270nn. 25, 34, 285nn. 30, 38

paedagogus 124, 273n. 18
Panormus (Map 1, modern Palermo) 30, 40, 41, 45, 254n. 87, 255n. 8
Pantelleria 47
Periplus 243nn. 30, 36
Persephone 22, 203, 279n. 78
Persians, as compared to Roman soldiers 234
Petrarch 207, 236, 290n. 41
phalarica, specialized Saguntine weapon, as describes by Livy 77
Philemenus, Tarantine, ally of Hannibal 164
Philinus of Agrigentum, author of a lost history of the First Punic War 250n. 34, 36, 251nn. 39, 49, 252nn. 52, 65, 253n. 72
Philip V of Macedon 78, 150, 181, 195, 196, 201, 247n. 95, 278n. 64, 280n. 13
Phocaeans 11
Phoenice, peace of (205 BCE) 196
Phoenicia and Phoenicians 6–10, 11, 12, 14, 15, 16, 17, 21, 28, 40, 45, 63, 64, 85, 87, 151, 222, 240nn. 8, 11, 18, 241nn. 4–6, 8, 9, 11, 243n. 34, 243nn. 38, 39, 244n. 43, 246n. 66, 247n. 88, 248n. 98, 254n. 87, 255n. 8, 257n. 40, 259nn. 1, 9, 260nn. 16, 19, 20, 261n. 33, 262n. 43, 271n. 53, 286n. 53, 290n. 45, 293n. 7, 295n. 15
Phormio, philosopher at Antiochus III's court 224
Picenum (modern Le Marche) 108, 113, 114, 271n. 42
Pillars of Herakles 8, 63
  see also Melqart
Pisa (ancient Pisae) 102
Placentia (Map 1, modern Piacenza) 103, 104, 106, 189, 270n. 32
Plato 20, 243n. 40
Plautus, Poenulus 15–16, 244nn. 45, 49, 245n. 53
Pleiades 96
Pleminius, Quintus, legate and commander in Bruttium, accused of atrocities in and around Locri (205–204 BCE) 203, 289n. 28
Pliny (the Elder), author of Natural Histories 1, 21, 28, 163, 232, 278n. 3, 280n. 15
Plutarch, author of the Parallel Lives 27, 124, 126, 148, 157, 187, 228, 231, 277n. 45, 279n. 4, 296n. 34

Po, valley and river 96, 101
Polyaenus, author of Stratagems 265nn. 4, 14, 267n. 40, 274n. 42
Polybius, author of The Histories 2–3, 239n. 6
  criticism of the Roman seizure of Sardinia in c.238 BCE 59, 81, 257n. 54
  on Hannibal's character 109, 139, 218, 228–229, 263n. 63, 279n. 79, 287n. 59, 295n. 6
  on New Carthage 70–71, 262n. 43
  on the causes of the Hannibalic War 72, 75–76, 79, 80–81, 254n. 2, 259n. 8
  on the government at Carthage 19, 56, 246nn. 69, 70, 261n. 39
  on the Mercenary War 52–53, 59–60, 255n. 18, 256nn. 21, 27
  on the treaties between Carthage and Rome 31, 208–209, 250n. 36, 252n. 52, 255n. 16, 257n. 41, 263n. 64, 264n. 81
  relationship with the family of Scipio Africanus 105, 130–131, 176, 269n. 15, 274n. 41, 283n. 70, 287n. 2
  sources 4, 32, 78, 84, 96, 98, 135, 240n. 14, 252n. 65, 252n. 72, 257n. 34, 283n. 78, 292n. 74
Poseidon, in disguise among the Greek soldiers at Troy 108, 270n. 22, 278n. 55
Postumius Albinus, Lucius, consul elect (215 BCE) 148
propaganda 15
  Hannibalic or Barcid 44, 109, 116, 229, 235, 240n. 10, 266nn. 27, 37, 270n. 23, 273n. 26
  Roman 3, 16, 140, 275n. 4
Propertius 119, 232
Prusias, king of Bithynia in Asia Minor 225–226, 294n. 33
Ptolemaic Egypt and kings 25, 26, 29, 34, 46, 172, 223, 248n. 6, 249nn. 10, 13, 254n. 4, 255n. 11, 279n. 83
Punic 7–23
  culture and world 6, 11, 13, 17, 20, 21, 26, 39, 41, 49, 52, 61, 64, 178, 227, 235, 240n. 9, 242nn. 19, 23, 246n. 72, 247nn. 86, 88, 255n. 8, 258nn. 57, 58, 259n. 3, 277n. 55
  language 7, 13, 16, 19, 151, 196, 214, 240n. 8, 241n. 2, 243n. 34, 244n. 49, 245n. 52, 257n. 39, 262n. 52, 270n. 21, 289n. 21, 292n. 73
  stereotype 3, 4, 15–16, 79, 107, 240nn. 11, 12, 244nn. 43, 44, 250n. 34

Pyrenees 86, 90, 91, 98, 177, 184, 185, 188, 233, 267*n.* 42,
Pyrrhus 29–31, 32, 33, 36, 99, 140, 154, 162, 228, 250*nn.* 24, 30, 31, 37, 251*n.* 44
   admired by Hannibal 29, 86, 149, 234, 250*n.* 25, 265*n.* 17, 277*n.* 41
   compares Rome to the Lernaean Hydra 149

Qart Hadasht, name for Carthage in Phoenician/Punic language 9, 241*n.* 13
*quadrireme,* decked warships invented by the Carthaginians, known as a four 28, 83, 291*n.* 63
*quinquereme,* decked warship used by Carthage and Rome, known as a five 28, 33, 36, 83, 84, 177, 212, 249*n.* 20, 253*n.* 68, 278*n.* 57, 291*n.* 63
Quintus Claudius, Roman praetor (208 BCE) and propraetor (207 BCE) 189

Ralegh, Sir Walter 198, 236, 264*n.* 74, 296*n.* 36
*Rb mhnt,* term for a general at Carthage 246*n.* 77
Regulus *see* Atilius Regulus, Marcus, consul in First Punic War
Reshep 17, 245*n.* 63, 295*n.* 15
Rhegium (Map 1, modern Reggio Calabria) 32, 151, 165, 169, 202, 250*n.* 35, 251*nn.* 44, 50
Rhodes, navy 225, 250*n.* 23,
Rhône river (Map 2) 11, 66, 90, 91, 92, 93, 94, 95, 97, 102, 117, 263*n.* 55, 266*n.* 32, 268*n.* 67
Roman calendar, problems with 269*n.* 14, 270*n.* 34, 273*n.* 29, 274*n.* 39, 285*n.* 30, 291*n.* 66
Rome
   army and manpower 136, 147, 149, 161, 181, 183, 220, 251*n.* 42 (comparing Rome and Carthage), 255*n.* 16, 276*n.* 31, 277*n.* 42
   Campus Martius 127
   election of magistrates 108, 115, 127, 148, 174, 175, 199, 271*n.* 50, 273*nn.* 24, 30, 277*nn.* 34, 35, 288*n.* 11
   human sacrifice after Cannae 135–136, 275*nn.* 59, 60, 61
   imperialism 32, 33, 74–76, 243*n.* 40, 251*nn.* 49, 50
   memory of the Punic Wars in the city 230–231, 233, 237

navy 33–34, 36, 136, 152, 204, 229, 249*nn.* 20, 21, 252*nn.* 54–56, 282*n.* 51
Porta Collina and Temple of Hercules (Herakles) 168
Tarentine and southern Italian hostages thrown from the Tarpeian Rock 163
Temple of Jupiter Capitolinus 231
walls of 168–169

Sabines 127
Saguntum (Map 2), falls to Romans (212 BCE) 281*n.* 47
   *and see under* Hannibal Barca, at Saguntum
*Salammbô see* Flaubert
Salapia (Map 1), in Apulia 163, 187, 280*nn.* 15, 16
Salinator, Marcus Livius, Roman consul at the Metaurus (207 BCE) 188, 190, 284*n.* 4
Sallust, Roman author on the fear of an enemy 231, 232, 239*n.* 7, 292*n.* 74, 295*n.* 17, 296*nn.* 25, 34
*sambukas,* floating siege engine used by Marcellus at Syracuse 156
Samnites and Samnium (Map 1) 29, 89, 101, 116, 121, 124, 137, 139, 140, 141, 142, 272*n.* 56, 280*n.* 9
Sardinia (maps 1 and 2) 8, 14, 15, 36, 55, 59–60, 63, 66, 81, 83, 91, 110, 117, 152, 209, 213, 214, 242*n.* 21, 246*n.* 82, 255*n.* 8, 257*nn.* 40, 41, 47, 258*n.* 54, 260*nn.* 15, 19, 277*n.* 36, 281*n.* 42, 289*n.* 19
Scipio *see* Cornelius Scipio Africanus
Seleucid kings and kingdom 25, 220, 222, 223, 225, 234
   *see also* Antiochus III
Sempronius Gracchus, Tiberius 136, 148
   given an army of recruited slaves after Cannae 148
   dies in an ambush in Lucania (212 BCE) 166–167, 275*n.* 62
Sempronius Longus, Tiberius, Roman consul for (218 BCE) 84, 100, 104, 105
   at Trebia 106, 108
Sena (modern Senigallia), near the Metaurus on the Adriatic 190, 285*nn.* 31, 35
Senate, at Capua 142, 144, 170
Senate, at Carthage known as '*drm* 17, 19, 20, 39, 40, 51, 69, 72, 137, 140, 211, 212, 219, 257*n.* 45, 290*n.* 43
   blame Hannibal entirely for the war 227
   debate over declaration of war 79–80

Livy's claim that the senate at Carthage defeated Hannibal 210

members come to Scipio after the battle of the Great Plains 207–208

members with Hannibal in Italy 152

senators taken by Scipio at New Carthage 180

Senate, at Rome 34, 35, 41, 71, 74, 75, 84, 115, 118, 124, 127, 129, 132, 135, 136, 161, 168, 175, 191, 207, 225, 233, 279*n*. 5, 282*nn*. 57, 59, 284*n*. 4, 290*n*. 49

debate over declaration of war 78–80, 263*n*. 69

debate over Scipio's planned invasion of Africa in 205 BCE 199–200, 287*n*. 4

Septimius Severus, Severan dynasty, Caracalla 235, 238, 296*n*. 30

Sertorius 110

Servilius Geminus, Gnaeus, Roman consular colleague of Flaminius (217 BCE) 108, 110, 111, 113, 115, 127, 129, 132, 270*n*. 32, 289*n*. 18

shekel, Carthaginian coin standard 55, 67, 196, 261*n*. 33

Sibylline Books 109, 115, 135, 271*n*. 51, 272*n*. 57

Sicca Veneria (Sicca, Map 1) 50, 51, 255*n*. 8, 256*n*. 25

Sidon, Phoenician city on coast of modern Lebanon 8, 245*n*. 59

Silenus of Kale Acte (in Sicily), author of a lost history 4, 89, 96, 240*n*. 14, 260*n*. 23, 266*n*. 36, 283*n*. 70

Silius Italicus, author of the *Punica* 2, 44, 77, 82, 232, 239*n*. 5, 259*n*. 6, 262*nn*. 41, 52, 264*nn*. 70, 73, 266*n*. 25, 295*nn*. 8, 9

Siwa, oracle and Alexander 87

slaves 15, 20, 39, 46, 57, 125, 128, 182, 208, 250*n*. 22

conscription into the army in Rome after Cannae 136, 149, 166, 275*n*. 62

Sophonisba, daughter of Hasdrubal Gisgo 290*n*. 41

wife of Syphax 201, 205

wife of Masinissa 207, 282*n*. 53, 290*n*. 39

drinks poison 207

life celebrated by Voltaire, Boccaccio, Petrarch 207, 290*n*. 41, 296*n*. 35

Sosylus, Hannibal's Spartan tutor and author of a now lost history 4, 65, 78, 96, 239*n*. 6, 254*n*. 83, 260*n*. 23, 272*n*. 75, 283*n*. 70

Spain *see* Iberia and the Iberian Peninsula

Sparta/Spartans 4, 30, 40, 48, 65, 161, 254*n*. 83, 280*n*. 21

*speculatores* 83, 265*n*. 3

*see also* spy/spies/espionage

Spendius, Campanian leader of mercenary rebellion (241–238 BCE) 52, 55, 56, 57, 58, 257*n*. 40, 258*n*. 51

spoils of war/loot 35, 77, 83, 87, 114, 133, 159, 160, 161, 179, 182, 200, 202, 210, 213, 228, 231, 288*n*. 14, 289*n*. 18, 291*n*. 55

spy/spies/espionage 74, 83, 126, 153, 178, 265*nn*. 2, 4, 272*n*. 9

stater, gold coin 50–51, 249*n*. 13

Strabo, ancient geographer 155, 247*n*. 83, 261*nn*. 30, 31, 262*nn*. 42, 43, 278*nn*. 68, 69

Straits of Messina *see* Messana

Successors (*Diadochoi*), Hellenistic kings who followed Alexander the Great 25, 27, 249*n*. 17

Suetonius 46

*Sufet/Sufetes*, chief magistrates of Carthage 19, 80, 91, 221, 222, 246*nn*. 71, 72, 78, 294*n*. 21

Syphax, king of the Masaesyli 172, 173, 193, 199, 201, 202, 204–207, 212, 219, 281*nn*. 43, 45, 282*n*. 48, 286*nn*. 47, 54, 289*nn*. 24, 30, 290*nn*. 34, 38, 39, 41, 46, 291*n*. 66

Syracuse (maps 1 and 2) 24, 26–27, 30, 32, 57, 110, 173, 181, 184, 186, 202, 220, 228, 231, 247*n*. 83, 248*n*. 3, 249*n*. 11, 255*n*. 15, 258*n*. 60

battle for and fall of (215–212 BCE) 152–159, 160–161, 167, 175, 182, 278*nn*. 61, 62, 65, 68, 69, 279*nn*. 74, 80, 284*n*. 4

in the First Punic War 33–34, 40, 48

plague at (212 BCE) 159, 279*n*. 83

*see also* Agathocles; Hiero II; Hieronymus; Marcellus, Marcus Claudius, consul

Tagus river 74, 283*n*. 75

talent, measure of silver 17, 46, 47, 59, 137, 172, 180, 201, 219, 285*n*. 37, 290*n*. 46, 293*n*. 5

Tanit (or Tinnit), Carthaginian goddess 21, 22, 196, 247*n*. 88, 277*n*. 55

Tarentum (also Taras, Map 1, modern Taranto) 29, 30, 33, 110, 152, 184, 189, 250*n*. 27, 251*nn*. 44, 49, 280*nn*. 8, 13, 285*n*. 25

ally of Pyrrhus 29, 268*n*. 69

hostages held in Rome executed 162
intramural cemetery and Teminid
    gate 164, 280*n*. 21
taken by Hannibal 163, 164, 165, 220,
    265*n*. 12, 278*n*. 57
taken by Fabius Maximus 181–182, 186,
    284*n*. 85
sack of the city 182, 231, 279*n*. 5,
    284*nn*. 1, 4
Tartessos and Tarshish (Map 2) 8, 64, 241*n*.
    7, 260*n*. 19
Taurini (and modern Turin) 101
Terentius Varro, Gaius, surviving consul
    (216 BCE) after Cannae 128, 130, 131,
    132, 135, 140, 142, 185, 273*n*. 31,
    274*n*. 41, 275*n*. 4, 285*n*. 23
Thrabaka (Map 1, modern Tabarka) 202
Thraso, pro-Roman Syracusan
    nobleman 153
thunderbolt, epithet for the Barcid and
    Scipio brothers 44, 171
Thurii (Map 1) 164, 165, 203
Tian Dan, Chinese commander (*c*. third
    century BCE) 123, 273*n*. 15
Tiberius, Roman Emperor (14–37 CE) 46,
    62, 233, 259*n*. 7
Ticinus river (Map 1), battle of (218
    BCE) 102, 175, 282*n*. 63
Tiepolo, Giambattista, eighteenth-century
    Venetian artist 192, Plate 7
Toga praetexta, worn by youths and certain
    magistrates 136, 172
Toledo 67
Tophet *see* Carthage
Trasimeno (Trasimene, Map 1), battle of
    (217 BCE) 111–113, 115, 116, 117,
    119, 132, 141, 142, 150, 181, 214,
    215, 220, 237, 270*nn*. 23, 25, 35,
    271*nn*. 44, 45, 275*nn*. 53, 54, 279*n*.
    79, 284*n*. 13
treaties, between Rome and Carthage, 12,
    31, 33, 39, 47, 52, 57, 208, 209, 219,
    255*n*. 16, 258*n*. 54
    Hannibal and Philip V 151–152, 201,
    247*n*. 95, 277*nn*. 50, 55, 280*n*. 13
    Ebro 71, 72, 75, 262*n*. 49, 263*n*. 64
    of Philinus *see under* Philinus of
    Agrigentum
    Carthage and Syracuse 154, 278*n*. 64
Trebia (Map 1), battle of (218
    BCE) 104–107, 108, 110, 132, 193,
    268*n*. 67, 279*n*. 79
Trebius, Statius from Compsa 141
*tributum*, tax paid by Roman citizens 149
*trireme*, decked warship, known as a

three 28, 33, 36, 83, 153, 212, 293*n*. 6
troop numbers, estimates and exaggerations
    of the ancient authors 37, 40, 84, 90,
    106, 110, 111, 112, 129, 133, 137,
    145, 189, 191, 193, 204–205, 214,
    239*n*. 1, 249–250*n*. 21, 251*nn*. 40, 41,
    253*nn*. 68, 72, 257*n*. 33, 262*n*. 47,
    263*n*. 46, 267*n*. 42, 268*nn*. 67, 72,
    270*n*. 33, 280*n*. 24, 286*n*. 43, 290*n*. 32
Troy, Trojan and Trojan War 10, 108, 116,
    230, 242*n*. 17, 255*n*. 8, 264*n*. 73,
    271*n*. 54
Truceless War 52, 255*nn*. 18, 19
    *see also* Mercenary War
Tunes (maps 2 and 3, modern Tunis) 39,
    40, 51, 53, 58, 206, 207, 211, 253*n*.
    82, 291*n*. 61
Turdetani, Iberian people who occupied
    regions of Tartessos 171, 260*n*. 24,
    263*n*. 65
Tycha, neighbourhood of Syracuse 156, 158
Tychaeus, relation of the Masaesylian king
    Syphax 212
Tyre, Phoenician city (in modern
    Lebanon) 7, 8, 9, 11, 13, 16, 23, 25,
    44, 64, 222, 223, 224, 225, 241*n*. 11,
    242*n*. 20, 243*nn*. 33, 34, 35, 262*n*. 43,
    266*n*. 25, 289*n*. 21

Utica (maps 2 and 3), Phoenician colony
    north of Carthage 9, 11, 26, 27, 53,
    56, 57, 203, 204, 206, 210, 211, 212,
    241*n*. 9, 291*n*. 61

Vaccaei, Iberian tribe 74
Val di Chiana (in modern Tuscany), 111
Valencia 64
Valerius Flaccus, Publius, Roman consul and
    commander in Second Punic War 75,
    151
Valerius Maximus Messalla, consul at Rome
    and commander in the First Punic War
    (263 BCE) 34
Valerius Maximus, Roman author 3, 15, 62,
    231, 233, 296*n*. 24
Varro *see* Terentius Varro
Velleius Paterculus, Roman author 8,
    241*n*. 9
Venus Erycina (from Eryx) 116, 117, 255*n*.
    8, 256*n*. 25, 271*n*. 54
    Venus *Obsequens* 116
Venusia (Map 1, modern Venosa) 132, 140,
    142, 162, 186, 189, 280*n*. 9
Vermina, son of king Syphax of the
    Masaesyli 202, 291*n*. 66

Vestal virgins  135, 275*n.* 59
Vettones, Iberian tribe  67, 261*n.* 31
via Aemilia  190
via Appia  162, 272*n.* 8, 280*n.* 14
via Flaminia  190
Virgil, *Aeneid*  7, 10, 187, 241*n.* 14
Volcae, tribe in Gaul  94

Xanthippus, Spartan commander hired by
    Carthage in First Punic War  40, 48,
    254*n.* 83

Xenophanes, envoy from Philip V of
    Macedon (215 BCE)  150, 151
Xenophon  86, 248*n.* 5, 265*nn.* 16, 17, 18,
    267*n.* 39, 269*n.* 19, 270*n.* 21

Zaghouan  58
Zama (Map 2), battle of (202 BCE)  212,
    214–216, 217, 218, 219, 221, 290*nn.*
    33, 42, 46, 48, 291*nn.* 54, 57, 65, 67
Zoippus, guardian and uncle of Syracusan
    king (*c.* 215 BCE)  153